YALE UNIVERSITY PRESS
PELICAN HISTORY OF ART

FOUNDING EDITOR: NIKOLAUS PEVSNER

W. STEVENSON SMITH

THE ART AND ARCHITECTURE OF ANCIENT EGYPT

REVISED WITH ADDITIONS BY WILLIAM KELLY SIMPSON

W. Stevenson Smith

The Art and Architecture of Ancient Egypt

Revised with additions by William Kelly Simpson

Yale University Press New Haven and London

First published 1958 by Penguin Books Ltd
Third edition, revised by William Kelly Simpson, first published
by Yale University Press, 1998

10 9 8 7 6 5 4 3

Copyright © W. Stevenson Smith, 1958, 1965
New material copyright © William Kelly Simpson, 1981, 1998

Set in Monophoto Ehrhardt, and printed in China through
World Print Ltd

Designed by Kate Gallimore

Library of Congress Cataloging-in-Publication Data

Smith, William Stevenson.
    The art and architecture of ancient Egypt / W. Stevenson
Smith, – Rev. with additions / by William Kelly Simpson.
        p.   cm. – (Yale University Press Pelican history of art)
    Includes bibliographical references and index.
    ISBN 0-300-07715-7 (cloth: alk. paper). – ISBN 0-300-
07747-5 (pbk.: alk. paper)
    1. Art. Egyptian.   2. Architecture–Egypt.   3. Egypt–
Antiquities.   I. Simpson. William Kelly.
II. Title.   III. Series.
N5350. S5   1998
709'.32–dc21   98-24893
                                                         CIP

Illustration on pp. 2–3: Mourning men. Relief from the tomb of
Nesi-pa-ka-shuty at Thebes. Dynasty XXXVI. *Brooklyn Museum*
(fig. 404)

Contents

Acknowledgements to Previous Editions

The author would like to express his grateful thanks to colleagues and heads of institutions for their generous response to his requests for information and photographs and permission to reproduce illustrations. Their courtesy has been acknowledged in the list of illustrations, as well as in the notes in a few special cases. The friendly co-operation of the officials of the Cairo Museum and the Egyptian Department of Antiquities has been of inestimable assistance over a period of many years. A Fulbright award, which made it possible to spend most of the year 1951 in Egypt, provided an invaluable opportunity to re-examine familiar things and to see much that was new and important. The author owes a particular debt to his own institution, the Museum of Fine Arts in Boston, and to the Metropolitan Museum of Art in New York for the privilege of drawing upon the records of the expeditions which they long maintained in the field. However, so much help and encouragement has been freely offered from all sides that it would be virtually impossible to list each individual source. Many of the ideas expressed here have evolved in the process of lecturing on Egyptian art in the Fine Arts Department of Harvard University since 1948. Special thanks are due to Miss Suzanne Chapman, Miss Mary B. Cairns, and Mr Nicholas Millet for their assistance in preparing the illustrations and text for the press and to the publishers for their willingness to have text figures especially drawn by Mr John Walkey.   W.S.S.

To revise the work of a great scholar after his death is a hazardous undertaking, particularly when he was one's friend and mentor over a considerable number of years. The major changes in this edition consist of additions and revisions to the notes, additions to the illustrations, and the alteration of the text to take these additions into account. In only one major area have I ventured to alter Smith's basic exposition, and this is in his treatment of the Kerma burials and assemblage. Smith followed Reisner's interpretation of the great tumuli as burials of Egyptian governors of a Sudanese trading outpost. The consensus today is that the Kerma culture represents an indigenous Sudanese kingship contemporary with the Hyksos and Dynasty XVII. The Egyptian statues and other objects of the Middle Kingdom were therefore obtained by trade or as booty from raids to the north, and Kerma's floruit is dated in the Second Intermediate Period, not the Middle Kingdom.

In preparing this edition I wish to acknowledge the considerable assistance of Mr Whitney M. Davis. He has contributed sections and references on rock art, the theoretical considerations of Egyptian art, Aegean relations, and many other subjects, and has been responsible for many revisions and additions to the notes and illustrations. Acknowledgement of permission for illustrations has been made in the list of illustrations, but I should like to thank in particular the curatorial staff of the Brooklyn Museum, the Robert Lowie Museum at Berkeley, and my colleagues at the Museum of Fine Arts, Boston. Mme Christiane Desroches-Noblecourt of the Louvre and Dr Dietrich Wildung of the Staatliche Sammlung Ägyptischer Kunst in Munich have graciously permitted us to illustrate new acquistions in the collections in their charge. M. J. Lauffray of the Franco-Egyptian Center at Karnak has also kindly provided photographs which have as yet not been published.   W.K.S.

Preface

Since Smith's *Art and Architecture* was revised in 1981, mainly along bibliographical lines in the notes, the activity and productivity on the art and architectural history of Ancient Egypt have been impressive. Many changes have taken place in outlook. Well into the twentieth century the Egyptologist was a generalist with several areas of specialization. He (and rarely she) might produce excellent research on history, philology, grammar, archaeology, and papyrology, as well as art and architecture. Today research tends to be restricted to fewer and fewer aspects. Art and architecture have lagged behind historical, literary and philological studies, yet several scholars after the Second World War distinguished themselves in the field of art history and paved the way for a new generation with their students. Two in particular were Bernard V. Bothmer of the Brooklyn Museum and the Institute of Fine Arts of New York University and Hans Wolfgang Müller of Munich. Today there are many outstanding interpreters of Egyptian art and I am embarrassed to single out a few at the risk of slighting others. In the United States several of Bothmer's students have contributed to various periods of sculpture, painting and relief, especially Robert Bianchi, Edna Russmann, Richard Fazzini and James Romano of Brooklyn, Biri Fay and Marianne Eaton-Kraus now of Berlin, and Rita Freed of Boston. At Emory University in Atlanta Gay Robins continues her valuable research, particularly in the area of proportions. At the Metropolitan Museum of Art in New York Dorothea Arnold has organized major exhibitions and written on the Middle Kingdom and the Amarna period. Elsewhere active scholarship is exemplified by the late Cyril Aldred, as well as Nadine Cherpion, Maya Müller, Karol Mysliwiec, Sylvia Schoske, Hourig Sourouzian, Claude Vandersleyen, and Dietrich Wildung. Architecture was given an important impetus by the work of the late Herbert Ricke of the Swiss Institute for Architectural Studies in Cairo, ably followed by the work of Horst Jaritz, as well as Dieter Arnold of the Metropolitan Museum, the pre-eminent scholar in the field, represented by many of the bibliographical entries below. In terms of theoretical analysis of the phenomena of ancient Egyptian art, the works of Jan Assmann, John Baines, and Roland Tefnin should be singled out.

The past decades have seen an unprecedented increase in the level of activity in excavation and the copying of monuments by the Egyptian Antiquities Organization, the Egyptian universities, and the many foreign missions, frequently in association with an Egyptian team. Only a few can be singled out: the work of the Museum of Fine Arts, Boston, with associated institutions, at the sites of Giza, Saqqara, Bersheh and Gebel Barkal in the Sudan, the joint British and Dutch project at Saqqara, the Egypt Exploration Society expeditions at Saqqara and Amarna, the British Museum project at Hermopolis, the copying and publication of significant Fifth Dynasty tombs along the Unas causeway at Saqqara by Egyptian Archaeologists and the German Archaeological Institute, along with the excavations at the pyramids of Snefru (Rainer Stadelmann) and Amenemhet III (Dieter Arnold) at Dahshur. The outstanding work of the Czech Republic Archaeological Mission at the Fifth Dynasty site of Abusir has been directed by Miroslav Verner. The Middle Kingdom pyramid sites of Sesostris I at Lisht and Sesostris III at Dahshur have been re-excavated by Dieter Arnold for the Metropolitan Museum. Work at the early cemeteries at Abydos has been carried out by the German Archaeological Institute under the direction of Werner Kaiser and Günter Dreyer, while the Pennsylvania–Yale Expedition there under the general direction of David B. O'Connor and myself has concentrated on several areas, in particular: the Ramesside 'Portal' Temple, the cenotaph area, the townsite (Matthew Adams), the Sesostris III temple area (Josef Wegner), the Ahmose installations (Stephen Harvey), the overall survey of buildings and tombs (Janet Richards), and the Thutmose III temple (Mary Ann Pouls).

The activity in the Theban area has been extraordinary, especially in the copying of the tomb chapels on the west bank by a series of scholars, mainly from the German Archaeological Institute, as well as the Dynasty II tombs and the Mentuhotep complex at Deir el Bahri by members of the same institute. The work of the Polish Mission at the Hatshepsut temple is at the publication stage. Several major late period tombs (Ibi, Ankh-Hor) have been excavated, copied, and published by Austrian and German teams. At the mortuary temple of Merneptah extraordinary reused blocks of Amenhotep III have been found (Horst Jaritz of the Swiss Institute). Individual private tombs have been studied and published by a variety of scholars, many from Germany as well as Betsy Bryan and Daniel Polz from America (see blibliography).

The outstanding excavation and reconstruction of the temples on the island of Elephantine by Werner Kaiser, Günter Dreyer, Horst Jaritz and others will result in a multi-volume series of reports. The publications by Labib Habachi and Detlef Franke of the Middle Kingdom sanctuary of Heqaib on the island, with its magnificent photographs of the statuary, is a lasting achievement. For these and many other projects, see the annual report on archaeological activity in Egypt and the Sudan edited for many years in the journal *Orientalia* by Jean Leclant and his associates.

Major museums have embarked on ambitious programmes of publishing their collections in well illustrated monographs. Both the British Museum and the Louvre have been particularly productive in this area. The loose-leaf project with the title *Corpus Antiquitatum Aegyptiacarum* (CAA) has been used by other museums to record objects in detail, with photographs, drawings, translations, comparative material and bibliography: the Kunsthistorisches Museum in Vienna (11 vols to date) the Pelizaeus Museum Hildesheim (8 vols, including the important statuary and reliefs from Junker's work at Giza); the Museum of Fine Arts, Boston (3 vols, one on canopics and two on stelae); the Kestner Museum, Hanover (3 vols); and the Czech Republic (all museums, 1 vol. to date on sarcophagi). Other volumes seek to include the entire Egyptian collections of smaller museums or countries: Oslo, the Ethnographic Museum; Bremen, the Übersee Museum; the Museen der Rhein Mainz Region (2 vols); and Cuba, all collections. The quality of scholarship is high and the results laudable, but the ideal of publishing in this format all of the categories of all of the museums and collections is daunting and can never be achieved. In general the volumes/fascicles of these projects have not been included in our bibliographical references.

In reviews and otherwise, critics have noted that Smith's coverage of the earlier periods is quite disproportionate and that the later periods are not well covered. No attempt was made to alter this in the revised edition of 1981 and the original limited bibliography reflects the emphasis on the earlier periods. The additions to the bibliography in the present edition may be useful. In many cases extensive bibliographies are included in some of the entries cited and individual articles therein are not included here for that reason. I apologize for not including items which have escaped my attention. Similarly, items of minimal interest may not have merited inclusion. In a few cases the items have been annotated to give the reader some idea of the contents. When an article or report encompasses more than one period, the reference is made under the earlier period: for example an article covering the Old and Middle Kingdoms will be listed under the first. In several cases, bibliography before the 1981 revised edition (in the footnotes of that edition) is included. When a volume is published in more than one language, the English version is generally cited. I wish to acknowledge with gratitude the aid of Dr Donald Spanel. As this chapter was about to be completed, he read the text and made many valuable additions, particularly in the areas of the later periods and Egyptomania.

Chronological Table

PREHISTORIC

Before 4000 B.C.:
  Badarian
Predynastic: 4000–3200 B.C.
  Amratian (Nagadah I)
  Early Gerzean (Nagadah II)
  Late Gerzean (Nagadah III)

EARLY DYNASTIC

Dynasty I: 3200–2980 B.C.
  Narmer } Menes
  Aha
  Zer
  Zet (Wadji)
  Den (Wedymu)
  Az-ib
  Semerkhet
  Qay-a
Dynasty II: 2980–2780 B.C.
  Ra-neb
  Hetep-sekhemuwy
  Ny-neter
  Peribsen
  Sened
  Khasekhem
  Khasekhemuwy

OLD KINGDOM

Dynasty III: 2780–2680 B.C.
  Neterkhet (Zoser)
  Sekhem-khet
  Sa-nekht
  Kha-ba
  Neb-ka
  Huni
Dynasty IV: 2680–2565 B.C.
  Sneferu
  Cheops (Khufu)
  Radedef
  Chephren (Khafra)
  Mycerinus
  Shepseskaf
Dynasty V: 2565–2420 B.C.
  Weserkaf
  Sahura
  Neferirkara
  Shepseskara
  Neferefra
  Ne-user-ra
  Men-kau-hor
  Isesy (Zedkara)
  Unas

Dynasty VI: 2420–2258 B.C.
  Tety
  Weserkara
  Pepy I
  Mernera
  Pepy II

FIRST INTERMEDIATE PERIOD

Dynasty VII: Interregnum
Dynasty VIII (Memphite): 2258–2232 B.C.
Dynasty IX (Heracleopolitan): 2232–2140 B.C.
  Khety I (Mer-ib-ra)
  13 kings of Turin Papyrus
Dynasty X (Heracleopolitan): 2140–2052 B.C.
  Neferkara
  Khety (Wah-ka-ra)
  Merikara
  1 king of Turin Papyrus

MIDDLE KINGDOM

Dynasty XI: 2134–1991 B.C.
  Mentuhotep I (Tepy-aa)
  Intef I (Seher-tawy)
  Intef II (Wah-ankh)
  Intef III (Nekht-neb-tep-nefer)
  Mentubotep II (Se-ankh-ib-tawy; Neb-hepet-ra)
  Mentuhotep III (Se-ankh-ka-ra)
  Mentuhotep IV (Neb-tawy-ra)
Dynasty XII: 1991–1786 B.C.
  Amenemhat I
  Sesostris I
  Amenemhat II
  Sesostris II
  Sesostris III
  Amenemhat III
  Amenemhat IV
  Queen Sebek-neferu-ra

SECOND INTERMEDIATE PERIOD

Dynasties XIII–XIV: 1786–1680 B.C.
  About 30 kings partly contemporaneous
Dynasties XV–XVI: 1720–1570 B.C.
  Hyksos in north; local rulers in Thebes
Dynasty XVII: 1600–1570 B.C.
  Sekenenra
  Kamose

NEW KINGDOM

Dynasty XVIII: 1570–1314 B.C.
  Ahmose I
  Amenhotep I
  Tuthmosis I

Tuthmosis II
Hatshepsut
Tuthmosis III
Amenhotep II
Tuthmosis IV
Amenhotep III
Akhenaten
Semenkhkara(?)
Tut-ankh-amon
Ay
Horemheb
Dynasty XIX: 1314–1197 B.C.
  Ramesses I
  Sety I
  Ramesses II
  Merenptah
  Amenmesses
  Sety II
  Siptah (Merenptah)
  Tausert
Dynasty XX: 1197–1085 B.C.
  Sety-nekht
  Ramesses III
  Ramesses IV–Ramesses XI

THIRD INTERMEDIATE PERIOD

Dynasty XXI (Tanis and Thebes): 1085–950 B.C.
  Smendes
  Herihor (Thebes)
  Psusennes I
  Paynozem (Thebes)
  Amen-em-ipet
  Sa-amon
  Psusennes II
Dynasty XXII (Bubastite): 950–730 B.C.
  Sheshonq I
  Osorkon I
  Takelot I
  Osorkon II
  Sheshonq II
  Takelot II
  Sheshonq III and 2 kings contemporaneous with Dynasty XXIII
Dynasty XXIII: 817(?)–730 B.C.
  6 kings contemporaneous with end of Dynasty XXII

Dynasty XXIV: 730–715 B.C.
  Tef-nekht
  Bocchoris (Bakenrenef)
Dynasty XXV (Kushite): 730–656 B.C.
  Piankhy (Piye)
  Shabako
  Shebitku
  Taharqa
  Tanwetamani
Assyrian invasion:
  Esarhaddon captures Memphis: 671 B.C.
  Ashurbanipal sacks Thebes: 663 B.C.

SAITE PERIOD

Dynasty XXVI (Saite): 664–525 B.C.
  Psamtik I
  Necho
  Psamtik II
  Apries
  Amasis
  Psamtik III
Persian invasion under Cambyses: 525 B.C.

LATE PERIOD

Dynasty XXVII: First Persian Domination: 525–404 B.C.
  Cambyses
  Darius I
  Xerxes
  Artaxerxes
  Darius II
Dynasties XXVIII–XXIX: 404–378 B.C.
  6 kings maintain independence against Persia
Dynasty XXX: 378–341 B.C.
  Nectanebo I
  Teos
  Nectanebo II
Dynasty XXXI: Second Persian Domination: 341–332 B.C.
Conquest of Alexander: 332 B.C.

PTOLEMAIC PERIOD: 332–30 B.C.

Roman occupation of Egypt: 30 B.C.

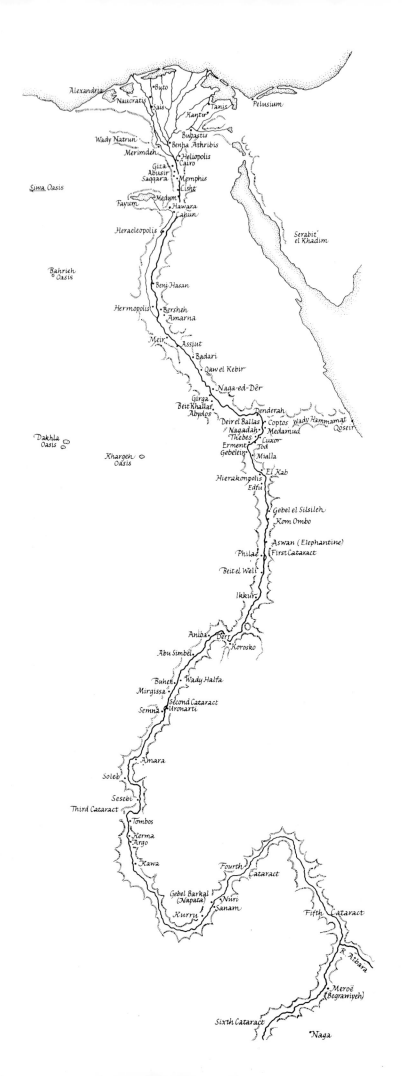

Alexandria
Buto
Naucratis
Sais
Tanis
Pelusium
Kantir
Bubastis
Benha Athribis
Wady Natrun
Heliopolis
Merimdeh
Cairo
Giza
Abusir
Saqqara
Memphis
Siwa Oasis
Lisht
Medum
Fayum
Hawara
Lahun
Heracleopolis
Bahrieh Oasis
Serabit el Khadim
Beni Hasan
Hermopolis
Bersheh
Amarna
Meir
Assjut
Badari
Qaw el Kebir
Naga-ed-Dêr
Girga
Beit Khallaf
Abydos
Denderah
Dakhla Oasis
Deir el Ballas
Coptos Wady Hammamat
Nagadah
Medamud
Qoseir
Thebes
Luxor
Erment
Tod
Gebelein
Mialla
Khargeh Oasis
El Kab
Hierakonpolis
Edfu
Gebel el Silsileh
Kom Ombo
Aswan (Elephantine)
Philae
First Cataract
Beit el Weli
Ikkur
Aniba Derr
Koroско
Abu Simbel
Buhen Wady Halfa
Mirgissa
Second Cataract
Semna
Uronarti
Amara
Soleb
Sesebi
Third Cataract
Tombos
Kerma
Argo
Kawa
Fourth Cataract
Gebel Barkal (Napata)
Nuri
Sanam
Kurru
Fifth Cataract
R. Atbara
Meroë (Begrawiyeh)
Sixth Cataract
Naga

CHAPTER I

Introduction

Ancient Egypt was protected by formidable desert barriers and confined to a narrow river valley. It was less subject to outside influences than the other great early civilization in Mesopotamia, and its culture presents, as one of its salient characteristics, a long, virtually unbroken continuity. In an almost rainless country the regular rise of the Nile every year provided the striking example of a renewal of life with each annual flood and gave the Egyptian a cheerful assurance of the permanence of established things, suggesting the acceptance that life would somehow continue after death in the same way. The peculiarly Egyptian concern with the continuity of life after death in a form similar to that which had been experienced upon earth provided an element in the development of the arts which was not present to such an extent in other countries. Thus, while architecture, painting, and sculpture ordinarily appeared in the service of the cult of a god or to glorify the wealth and power of a ruler, in Egypt we find emphasis laid upon providing a lasting dwelling-place for the dead, the re-creation of life magically in pictures to serve him, and lastly the provision of a substitute in stone for his perishable body.

This striving of the literal-minded and keenly observant Egyptian towards the re-creation of life for the dead man would seem to be intimately connected with the naturalistic elements in Egyptian art, and is primarily responsible for the impulse to produce portraiture which is a feature of the best of Egyptian sculpture. This worked against the formalizing tendencies which, particularly in Mesopotamia, led more towards the stylization of forms and the employment of geometric shapes. Its naturalistic elements lend a familiar quality to Egyptian art which never seems a wholly oriental creation, although it displays the same approach to representation which is common to all other ancient peoples before Greek times. All pre-Greek peoples give us a kind of diagram of a thing as man knew it to be, not as it appears to the eye under transitory circumstances. In spite of this attitude towards visual impressions, the Egyptian had an instinct to imitate closely what he saw about him.[1] His natural disposition towards balance and proportion, combined with a long-maintained tradition of orderly craftsmanship, strikes a sympathetic note for the Westerner.[2]

The availability of working materials is an influential factor which must be taken into consideration. The abundance of good stone was an advantage the Egyptian had over his contemporaries in southern Mesopotamia, who had to import their stone. The shape and small size of the slabs and boulders available to the Sumerian conditioned the rounded forms and somewhat uneven quality of his sculpture. The Egyptian early learned to cut blocks for building-stone, and the sculptor had a plentiful supply of rectangular blocks from the quarry for his work. This may well be a practical reason for his predisposition towards cubical form in contrast to the rounded, conical shapes preferred by the Mesopotamian. It certainly allowed for the largeness of scale which is another outstanding feature of Egyptian work both in sculpture and architecture.

One is always conscious that the Egyptian has hewed his forms from the stone block and not modelled them from softer materials, as in Crete, where the only large-scale work that has survived is in plaster relief which assumes a plastic form in contrast to the stone-cutter's technique. This has a modelled projection from the surface which is opposed to the Egyptian tendency to maintain a flat plane in reliefs. In contrast to the timeless, static permanence of Egyptian statues, the instinct of the Cretan, who excelled in the fashioning of delicate small figures of ivory, metal, and faience, was to catch an impression of movement and lively action. The Cretan might be said to see things with a painter's eye. The modelling of his reliefs produces the same impressionistic results as does his painting.

The Mesopotamian, on the other hand, tends away from natural forms in his sculpture and towards formal patterns. There is nothing in Egypt like the way in which the surfaces of the human face of one of the great Assyrian bulls are enlivened by unrealistic but superbly decorative undercuttings and contrasts in planes. It is as though the craftsman's preoccupation with seal engraving impelled him to approach larger works with the formal equipment developed in that craft as well as in textile-making and metalwork. Metal seems to have been a particularly congenial medium, and it is probably no accident that one of the Mesopotamian's finest early creations in sculpture is the magnificent Akkadian bronze head from Nineveh.[3]

The marvellous facility with which huge stones were handled became one of the outstanding characteristics of Egyptian architecture. Enduring stone forms were chiefly reserved for the building of temples and tombs, while secular architecture continued to employ sun-dried bricks and wood. This lighter construction has largely disappeared with the destruction of the cities in the Nile valley and the gradual accumulation of silt from the river's annual flood. More has survived of the domestic architecture of the New Kingdom than of other periods, particularly in the palace of Amenhotep III and at el Amarna. Considerable space will be devoted to this material, much of which is not well known, since it helps to balance the impression gained from the overwhelming mass of evidence which is derived from tombs. The excellent preservation of so much which represents the peculiarly Egyptian emphasis upon tomb architecture might have produced a distorted picture if it were not for the beliefs which caused so many personal possessions to be buried in the tombs and so much of the daily life to be represented on the walls of the tomb chapel. A great deal is reflected of what must once have existed in the cities and on the country estates. In the stone buildings, as well as in the pictures, there is evident a particularly happy facility for the adaptation of plant-forms to conventionalized design, especially in the shapes of columnar support. The palaces of the New Kingdom have also preserved something of a purely decorative use of naturalistically represented plant and animal life in ceiling- and floor-paintings, as well as on minor wall-spaces. Something of this sort must have occurred earlier in house decoration.

The covering of wall-surfaces with scenes representing the ruler's relationship with the gods of the temple or the glorification of his acts on earth seems to have been common to all ancient peoples. However, the Egyptian's impulse to re-create life for the dead man, which caused him to make statues for the tomb, also suggested that he cover the walls of the chapel with representations of life on earth. A desire for permanence early led to the use of low relief carvings on the stone-lined walls of a tomb chapel or temple. Like the statues, these were painted to complete their life-like aspect. In praising the beauty of these carvings there has been a tendency to overlook the fine quality of the painted detail or the work in paint alone which sometimes takes the place of these reliefs. The usual Egyptian practice, which combined the skills of the sculptor and the painter in creating one unified whole in painted relief, has to a certain extent obscured the Egyptian's very real contribution purely as a painter. In early times he was rivalled in this respect only by the Cretan. Egypt has provided us with an amazingly preserved series of examples in the field of wall-painting which range over the whole long period of Egyptian history. The finest examples of Cretan work are limited to a fairly short range of time at the beginning of the Egyptian New Kingdom, while accidents of preservation have confined our knowledge of the painting of Western Asia to a few examples widely separated in time. Thus Egypt provides by far the largest body of evidence for the development of early painting. Moreover, we shall see that the Egyptian, with his naturalistic approach and meticulous interest in recording the details of what he saw about him, developed an extraordinary dexterity of brushwork and a manipulation of a wide range of colour which is hard to match in ancient times. This is most evident in the breaking up of flat surfaces of colour by fine brush-strokes of different hues to suggest the fur of an animal or the feathering of a bird [249, 284, 307]. The success achieved in indicating texture is immediately clear if one examines a rare example of such an attempt outside Egypt in the bull's head from the wall-paintings of the palace of Mari in northern Syria[4] or another head of a bull from the Cretan palace of Knossos.[5] In these the detail is indicated summarily by rather coarse dark lines. The emphasis on the thick outlines of the Mesopotamian example is even more apparent in the paintings of the Early Assyrian palace[6] of Tukulti-Ninurta, where the strongly marked bordering of the different parts of the composition has been compared to the isolation of the various elements in the design of an oriental carpet. In contrast to this tendency to reduce forms to a decorative pattern, the Egyptian was interested in the outward look of living and inanimate things, and consequently endeavoured to perfect his skill in indicating their surface details. He never loses, however, his sense of the clarity of their form or the use that can be made of line for this purpose. The Cretan, on the other hand, seems impatient with such detailed rendering of an animal or a plant form. He presents us with a creature instinct with life and movement, but his lively, instantaneous, impressionistic treatment will not bear too close analysis as to the accuracy of its details.

Thus, within certain limits of his conventions, the Egyptian approaches his subject with careful, painstaking attention to detail. He has a matter-of-fact rather than an imaginative attitude to the world about him, and when he deals with supernatural things manages with a kind of cheerful assurance to give them a familiar, everyday look. Even the most remarkable monsters are rather dryly conceived, and one of his most surprising achievements was the convincing naturalness with which were combined human and animal parts in composite form for the representation of his gods. The Egyptian mind did not run riot in imagining such strange and frightening spirits as appear on the seal designs of Mesopotamia or Crete. Instead there is an almost complacent acceptance of the orderliness and continuity of existence in a mild climate which was spared a good many of the more frightening caprices of nature.[7] There is no expression of that anxiety with which the Mesopotamian regarded the harshness of nature, nor did the Egyptian's surroundings provide him with the broken mountain crags and seascapes that stirred the imagination of the inhabitants of the Aegean.

The rationalized approach to visual impressions developed by the Greeks was foreign to earlier peoples. The Greeks first contrived a consistent way of drawing figures so that their different parts were related to one another in the manner in which they appear to the eye. They then began to experiment with the placing of these figures against a background in which the lines correspond to a series of receding planes which appear natural to the observer. They ended by developing a system of aerial perspective. The absence of a desire on the part of the Egyptian to suggest depth and volume in his painting and reliefs is only one aspect of an attitude towards representation which prevailed throughout the ancient world. It tends to generalization according to the characteristics of the people who use it, whether this takes the form of avoiding movement, as in Egypt, or crystallizes a typical aspect of lively action, as in Crete.

Specific historical events, if represented at all, are treated as the symbolical memorial of a victory or some other action of the ruler. Often when a battle is actually represented it is given a form which might be considered an enlarged hieroglyph signifying the idea. This is perfectly illustrated by the complementary use of early word-signs and figure representation on the Narmer palette at the beginning of Dynasty I, but the intimate connexion between writing and drawing continues throughout all Egyptian monuments. The beautifully made hieroglyphs are small drawings in themselves and form an integral part of larger compositions, while the wall-scenes are really an extension of the written signs.[8] Inscriptions are also a necessary part of the statues. They provided the essential identity of the owner by giving his titles and name, although the portrayal of his outward appearance is usually generalized without individual characteristics, except in certain outstanding works that we shall see appear throughout Egyptian history at periods of remarkable creative effort. Similarly, the subject-matter of the wall-scenes is restricted to typical aspects of Egyptian life which ordinarily lack the narrative element in the sense that they seldom refer to specific happenings. Backgrounds are summarized, with a few trees, a vineyard, the selected parts of a building, or the upright stems of a papyrus thicket to suggest the setting of a scene. At first there is little attempt to deal with the spatial relationship between these simple stage-props and the men and animals which they accompany. Emotion or individual feeling, and the dramatic relationship between the figures which this might engender, had little place, although we may find certain typified exceptions such as the mourners at a funeral or the dying forms of animals.

However, within this general framework we shall find a constant enlivening of the whole by freshly observed detail and an increasing interest in the treatment of landscape and architectural backgrounds with experiments in the more complicated grouping of figures and their relationships in space. This reached its most advanced stage in the huge compositions of the Ramesside temple reliefs, where topographical and even historical elements, which had first made their appearance in the Eighteenth Dynasty, are handled in a fashion paralleled only by the later Assyrian reliefs. The royal sculpture of the Twelfth Dynasty also shows a first attempt to portray something of man's inner feeling in the sombre, careworn faces of Sesostris III and Amenemhat III.[9] At the same time the painter brought an advanced technique and a more subtle colour sense to the treatment of textures which had already interested the artists of the Old Kingdom. This was to be carried to a most sophisticated stage in the very extensive work of the Eighteenth-Dynasty painters.

Of course it is the significant changes which appear against the background of the long continuity of Egyptian civilization that quicken our interest. One of the fascinations of the study of Egyptian art is in learning to distinguish the variations in a style which is easily recognizable as belonging to that country over a vast length of time from the fourth millennium down to 332 B.C., when the conquest of Alexander the Great brought Dynastic Egypt to an end. Initially one may have the impression of an endless repetition of forms, but closer examination reveals definite characteristics of the Old, Middle, and New Kingdoms. Then we begin to realize the special qualities of the formative stages which led up to these great periods of achievement. First came that brilliant Early Dynastic Period in Dynasties I–II, when civilization was developing out of the primitive conditions of Predynastic times towards a culmination in the Old Kingdom. This so-called Pyramid Age of Dynasties III–VI began about 2780 B.C. and lasted for some five hundred years. The freshness of a new beginning appears again about 2100 B.C. in Dynasty XI, and shortly after 1600 B.C. in early Dynasty XVIII, when the Middle and New Kingdoms respectively emerged from the darkness of those times of political disintegration known as the First and Second Intermediate Periods. Once again, towards the end of the eighth century B.C. and after a long period of decline, we find new life poured into the old forms. This renewal was stimulated by the invasion of the Kushite kings of the Sudan (which the Greeks called Ethiopia and the Romans Nubia). It strikes us as a more conscious, archaizing effort, lacking in the spontaneity of earlier national revivals.

The development in the Early Dynastic Period had accompanied the growing strength of the royal house, which reached the height of its power in Dynasty IV. The later Old Kingdom in Dynasties V and VI witnessed the levelling off of this power, the growth of a provincial nobility, and finally the collapse of the monarchy at the end of the long reign of Pepy

II. A feudal age followed in the First Intermediate Period. The disastrous breakdown of the arts and crafts is tangible evidence of a profound social upheaval which is reflected in the later literature of the Middle Kingdom. It was to be the task of the Middle Kingdom rulers to restore order and re-establish the prestige of the royal house. This they succeeded in doing, but with a sense of their vulnerability which had hitherto not been expressed. Their task was accomplished in a changed atmosphere which had brought about a new recognition of the ruler's responsibilities to his subjects. Regional differences lingered on in the art of the Middle Kingdom. It thus presents a greater diversity than had the uniform style which earlier emanated from the court at Memphis. The kings of Dynasty XII drew deliberately upon the vestiges of the old culture which had survived somehow in the north. However, a fusion with the new Upper Egyptian elements was not completed before the unity of the country again broke down in Dynasty XIII, to be followed by the invasion of a Western Asiatic people called the Hyksos. The results of this occupation were chiefly felt in Lower Egypt.

In spite of the general impoverishment of the country, a more considerable degree of continuity was maintained at Thebes during the Second Intermediate Period than was evident in the time after the collapse of the Old Kingdom. Thus, after the liberation of the country from the Hyksos, the art of the early New Kingdom, while presenting all the freshness of a new start, appears in many ways as the end of a development which was already well advanced in the Middle Kingdom. The first half of the Eighteenth Dynasty brought to a close the simpler phase of a civilization which was now to be profoundly affected by the complexities of Egypt's new position in control of a wide empire.

The Middle Kingdom had considerably widened Egypt's contacts abroad, with the occupation of Nubia into the region of the Second Cataract, and the establishment of a considerable sphere of influence in Palestine and Syria. However, when Ahmose drove the Hyksos out of the Delta and pursued them into Palestine, he involved Egypt in a new policy of foreign conquest which was most completely realized through the Asiatic campaigns of Tuthmosis III.[10] This was accompanied by the subjugation and Egyptianization of a large part of the Sudan. The effects of the new wealth and power make themselves strongly felt at the close of the wars of Tuthmosis III. Force of arms had given way to international diplomacy by the time of Amenhotep III, when the luxury and splendour of the court reached a very high level. The spoils of war and foreign tribute dedicated to Amon had also vastly increased the power of his priesthood. To this came a remarkable reaction in the religious revolution of Akhenaten, who turned from Amon and the old gods to the worship of the Sun Disk, the Aten, as the supreme being.

The idea of a universal god that had created the world and all living things goes back to the ancient doctrine of Heliopolis. It applied also to Amon in his assimilation with the sun god Ra. The new creed, however, freed the Aten from association with other gods and replaced the anthropomorphic form of the sun god with the solar disk. This approached closely to monotheism and evidently originated in the personal beliefs of Akhenaten. The short-lived movement was bound up with the character of this extraordinary individual and forms a unique interlude in Egyptian history and artistic expression. Its new features took little hold upon the thought of the people, and rapidly disappeared under the restoration of the Amon priesthood at the end of Dynasty XVIII. Horemheb and the first Ramesside kings set out to eradicate all memory of Akhenaten and his ephemeral successors and to return to the forms which had prevailed before the heresy.

The relaxation of strong measures in the reign of Amenhotep III had invited turbulent conditions in the small city-states under Egyptian suzerainty in Palestine and Syria. The ominous unrest was aggravated by the intervention of the Hittites. Revolts multiplied as a result of the further neglect of foreign affairs in the Amarna Period. Horemheb was occupied with reorganization at home, and it was not until the energetic campaigns of Sety I that Egyptian prestige was restored abroad. Ramesses II was forced to admit Hittite dominance in the plains of northern Syria, but the equivocal battle of Kadesh at least achieved a half-century of peace, in which Egyptian control was accepted over a considerable part of her former possessions. In the latter half of the thirteenth century B.C. Merenptah drove off the first of the attacks which were part of that great mass movement which overwhelmed the Hittites about 1200 B.C. and, sweeping down through Palestine and Syria, brought the 'Sea Peoples' to the shores of the Nile Delta. Ramesses III was successful in meeting the full impact of this dangerous thrust, but the former empire had now been reduced to the position of defending the borders of Lower Egypt. In the following centuries Egypt's prestige depended chiefly on the persistence abroad of the recollection of her long-maintained strength. This had become largely an illusion, and the sporadic attempts that were made to reassert control in the north met with no lasting success and usually brought calamity upon those who had sought for help.

The long stretch of nearly eight centuries which followed Dynasty XX has been variously divided. For the first four hundred years, during Dynasties XXI and XXII, the New Kingdom forms of Ramesside times were maintained under conditions of all-too-evident decline. Then, about 730 B.C., the Kushite invasion from the south brought about a revival which continued under the Saite kings, after the interruption of the short Assyrian occupation. However, Egypt was no longer able to ward off foreign aggression, and the Assyrians were followed a century later by the Persians. Native rulers were able to shake off Persian rule for some sixty years until it was resumed a short time before the Macedonian conquest. Throughout all this the Egyptian held fast to his old traditions, proving himself peculiarly resistant even to the impact of the new Hellenic spirit. Dynasties XXI through the Kushite Dynasty XXV are considered as the Third Intermediate Period and followed by the not entirely successful Saite Dynasty XXVI. The dynasties from XXVII to XXX are regarded as the Late Period.

In looking back over the tremendous span of Egyptian civilization, it should be remembered that from the beginning of historic times the king was always referred to as a god. He was sometimes simply termed the Good God. As Horus he was considered the earthly embodiment of an ancient deity of the sky whose worship was pre-eminent at the time of the establishment of united rule over the two lands of Upper and Lower Egypt in Dynasty I. As Son of Ra the king represented the direct descent of royalty from the creator sun god. Finally in his assimilation with Osiris he would continue to reign over the realm of the dead for he was repeating the cycle of the god who was thought to be an ancient king who had passed through death to resurrection. Such a drastic simplification of the Egyptian conception of divine kingship presents ideas which were developed in succeeding periods, but which had been accepted by the end of Dynasty V when the earliest preserved body of religious literature, known as the Pyramid Texts, appears first on the walls of the burial-chambers of King Unas. These potent spells were compiled in order to assist in the king's translation from his earthly body into the world of the gods, and imply the recognition of his human qualities which must undergo transformation after death.

The manifold nature of Egyptian religious beliefs defies summary treatment. We are accustomed to the attempt to resolve opposing views, but we must expect instead a many-sided approach to a phenomenon, with the result that unrelated explanations are accepted side by side. Formidable difficulties are presented by the accumulation of beliefs over the centuries through an additive process which was reluctant to replace one idea wholly with another or to discard the old. There is both continuity and extraordinary fluidity in this. Two gods may be assimilated with one another without losing their separate entities. Likewise there may be various manifestations of the same god, as in the case of Horus, who as avenger of his father Osiris, or the infant son of Isis, is quite a different being from the sky god whose wings span the heavens and whose eyes are the sun and the moon.

We find a mixture of popular beliefs and the attempts of learned men to explain the emergence out of chaos of that order which was personified by the goddess Maat, who stood for justice, truth, and right. From the beginning the Egyptian felt that he was surrounded not only by friendly but also by hostile spirits which had to be propitiated. He also sensed the more remote and impersonal quality of the great forces of nature whose personifications were revered as well as the gods of each locality. The local deities had at first appeared in the shape of animals, or more rarely were represented by a plant or inanimate object. Later, when they assumed human form, the animal head was frequently retained, or else the original animal, plant, or object was borne as a symbol on the head. The goddess Nekhbet wore a vulture headdress, and Hathor was shown with the horns of a cow, although she might still manifest herself in the form of that animal. There were a number of different Hathors, although these were generally associated with the idea of a mother goddess. Her worship was accompanied by dancing and sistra-playing, and she came to be thought of as the goddess of love and joy. As Mistress of the Sycamore she was identified with a tree-spirit in an old sanctuary near the Giza pyramids and became the patroness of the royal family of Dynasty IV. In similar guise she is later found dispensing food and cool drink to the dead. Through an interchange of functions with the sky goddess Nut and the Goddess of the West she was associated with the western mountain at Thebes, where she received the sun at its setting.

In historic times the term 'city god' describes what must have been an early conception of a local deity who presided over a community. Generally he formed the head of a family triad, such as we have in the case of Ptah of Memphis with his consort the lioness Sekhmet and their son Nefertem, whose symbol was a lotus flower. As one of the primitive villages assumed leadership over neighbouring communities, its local god acquired supremacy in that district. Later political fluctuations might replace the god of such a district by another, or they might bring about his rise to national importance. In this process one god might take on the attributes of his predecessor or, if his worship spread throughout the country, he might assume the qualities of one of the great cosmic deities. In the latter case he was still associated with a particular place, of which he was considered the lord and in which lay his principal sanctuary. Something of this process can be learned from the sacred emblems on the standards of the Nomes or provinces which evidently reflect the independent districts of prehistoric times. Thus in Hermopolis the ibis-headed Thoth, the god of wisdom, had long supplanted Wenut, but her symbol, the hare, continued to be used on the standard of this Fifteenth Nome of Upper Egypt. Neith, on the other hand, always remained mistress of Sais, the capital of the Fifth Nome of Lower Egypt, whose standard bore her arms, a shield and crossed arrows.

The assimilation of one divine being with another is easier to understand if we can grasp something of the Egyptian's conception of a vital force which was present to a varying degree in all things animate and even inanimate. When, in the creation according to the doctrine of Heliopolis, the sun, Atum-Ra, brought into being Shu (air) and Tefnut (moisture), he spread his arms about them and his Ka entered into them. Here is suggested the transmission of a life-force which remained in continuous operation from the beginning of the world. It was thus that divine nature was imparted to the king, although its full potentialities could not be realized until after death. Lesser mortals were able to share some part of this force.

The Ka was one of three emanations of the spirit. It was related to, but separate from, the Akh and the Ba. These had all originally belonged only to the gods. They approximate to what we think of as the soul and were all associated with the personality of the individual. One could only become an Akh, a transfigured spirit, after death. Its place was in the heavens remote from the body. The Ba, on the other hand, was an animated aspect of the soul which could move back and forth from the dead body. From the Eighteenth Dynasty onwards it is pictured as human-headed bird, drinking cool water from a pool, perched in the branches of a tree, or fluttering down to join the body in the tomb chamber. The Ka is best viewed as a person's vital force which accompanied him both in life and in death. Certain of its qualities were intensified in the person of the king and they were fully possessed only by supreme beings. The Ka had a separate existence and in one sense can be thought of as a double or as a protective genius. It was closely associated with the tomb statue and with nourishment. Through it the dead man was able to avail himself of the food and drink that he had contracted with his funerary priest to present on stipulated occasions at the false-door of his tomb chapel, and which could be supplemented by the offerings pictured on the walls of this chapel.

Until well along in the Old Kingdom the prayers for the dead in these chapels were addressed solely to the jackal god Anubis. When his place was taken by Osiris, Anubis still continued to care for the dead as an embalmer god. Among the gods of nature, Osiris appears as the source of the ever-recurring inundation and the resurgence of plant life. In this sense he was temporarily overpowered by Seth, who represented drought, the sterility of waste places, and the violence of storms. Osiris was subject to perpetual renewal in the reappearance of growing things. Seth, as a spirit of nature, continued to be revered as one of the great gods, however much he may have been abhorred in connexion with the cult of Osiris. He was one of the company of the nine gods of Heliopolis, and acted as a defender of Ra against the never-ending attempts of the serpent Apophis to swallow up the sun. Seth had his particular periods of ascendancy. It was natural for the Hyksos to set him up as a national god against the royal Horus, but he was again favoured in the Nineteenth Dynasty, whose rulers originated in the eastern Delta, where the Hyksos had maintained their capital at Avaris.

The hope of resurrection through Osiris was maintained through the popular belief in him as a deified king who was slain by this brother Seth and revived by his wife Isis that he might continue as the ruler and judge of the world of the dead. Horus, the son of Osiris and Isis, vanquished his uncle Seth in the struggle for the earthly kingdom of Osiris. Here the two gods symbolize Upper and Lower Egypt, Seth the south and Horus the north. In the Pyramid Texts, at the end of Dynasty V, allusions to the Osiris legend are mingled with solar beliefs in the immense body of religious lore which had been assembled by the theologians of Heliopolis. According to their explanation of the origin of the world, the self-created Atum-Ra (the sun), emerging from the primeval ocean Nun, produced the divine pair Shu (air) and Tefnut (moisture). These were the parents of Geb (earth) and Nut (sky). Their children were the four gods, Osiris and his wife Isis, Seth and his wife Nephthys. This system of the nine gods which formed the Ennead of Heliopolis persisted in the face of other doctrines, such as that of Hermopolis, in which eight rather shadowy gods (including Amon, 'The Hidden One') produced out of the formless watery waste an egg from which the sun emerged. According to the Memphite Theology all things originated as thought in the heart of Ptah and issued through the commands of his tongue. At Elephantine it was believed that mankind was shaped by the ram god Khnum on his potter's wheel.

Other great gods were henceforth assimilated with Ra. Amon became the state god as Amon-Ra, and Horus, in one of his many forms, appeared as Ra-Horakhte (Ra-Horus-of-the-Horizon). The Aten of the Amarna revolution represented the creative force of the sun, freed from the association of other gods. In spite of the persisting force of the cult of Ra, the realm of the dead came more and more to be considered an underworld through the ever-widening popularity of Osiris. This was entered from the west, where the chief cemeteries lay on the edge of the desert, and contrasts strongly with the heavenly regions where the transfigured dead had been thought of as the stars and where solar beliefs placed the king with Ra in the 'Field of Reeds' and the 'Field of Offerings'. Through the nether regions passed the sun-bark of Ra during the night hours, but it still could be believed that the sun entered the body of the sky goddess Nut, to be born again each morning. Nut was represented in the form of a woman with her outstretched body supported by Shu, the god of the air, to form an arc above the earth, which was personified by the male form of Geb.

In the First Intermediate Period, portions of the Pyramid Texts that had been intended only for the use of the king were employed by private persons. This was one of the symptoms of the loss of prestige which the monarchy had suffered after the collapse of the Old Kingdom. Gradually there developed a new body of religious literature, known as the Coffin Texts, which in the Middle Kingdom formed a transition to the more familiar New Kingdom Book of the Dead. The Egyptian title of this later collection of material was 'The Going Forth by Day', and related to it were other works such as the Book of Amduat ('That which is in the Underworld') and the Book of Gates. Even from the titles of these it is evident that the bright celestial afterworld of earlier thought had been adapted to a gloomy underworld in which there was a vastly increased dependence upon magical spells and amuletic charms.[11]

PART ONE

The Prehistoric and Early Dynastic Periods

CHAPTER 2

Predynastic Egypt 4000–3200 B.C.

Art appears in the Nile Valley as early as the seventh millennium B.C. The earliest productions are the rock-drawings executed on the cliffs bordering the Nile in Upper Egypt and Nubia. The most ancient of these consist principally of geometric designs such as concentric circles or half-circles and net-patterns, or abstract figurations, the exact meaning of which is obscure.[1] Representational themes appear later. There are many hundreds of drawings of the animals pursued by the earliest hunters and of weapons and traps [1]. Although the publication of these drawings is quite complete, their chronology is still problematic.[2] Drawings of cattle and boats can be definitely associated with the developed neolithic cultures of Upper Egypt and Nubia, and with the Egyptian Predynastic, Nubian C-Group, and later historic cultures.

At some time around 4000 B.C. the early settlers in the Nile Valley were beginning to emerge from the neolithic culture of the villages of Upper Egypt and those of Merimdeh on the western edge of the Delta and on the shore of the lake in the Fayum. The last-named district is a sort of oasis reached through a narrow opening in the escarpment of the western desert a little south of Cairo. These primitive village communities lay on higher ground out of reach of the Nile flood. The people of these communities must have made a start at the long task of controlling the flood-waters by dykes and canals. It was a labour which could be undertaken only by joint effort and was a contributory factor towards the co-operation of several communities which came to accept the leadership of one of the villages and the pre-eminence of its local god. These districts are represented in later times by the different provinces or Nomes, each with its chief city. Gradually coalitions of the various districts were formed, and this resulted in the two kingdoms of Upper and Lower Egypt, late in Predynastic times, and the uniting of the whole country at the beginning of the historical period about 3200 B.C.[3]

The succeeding phases of the prehistoric age are better known from the many cemeteries which have been excavated. They fall into two well-defined groups: the earlier Amratian of Upper Egypt, and the Gerzean. The characteristic products of this second group have been found in the neighbourhood of the entrance to the Fayum, and therefore in northern Egypt. Scholars also use the terms Nagadah I for Amratian and Nagadah II for Gerzean. The conditions of the Delta, an alluvial plain which fans out between the branches of the river a little north of Cairo, have so far made it impossible to recover much tangible evidence concerning its early inhabitants. The largest quantity of Gerzean material has actually been found in Upper Egypt, where it succeeds the Amratian. These periods have long been termed Early and Middle Predynastic, to which was added a Late Predynastic Period (called Semainian, like Amratian and Gerzean, after a site where its remains first appeared). It has been pointed out that this last phase has such ill-defined characteristics that it would be preferable to drop the term, considering that certain Gerzean features continued down into the time of transition

into the historical period.[4] While the same types of pottery and other grave equipment continued into the Late Gerzean Period, many of the characteristics of the much more sophisticated culture of Dynasty I are also apparent in an advanced stage of development. This transition period, which might have lasted from fifty to two hundred years, represents part, if not all, of the time to which later tradition assigned lists of the prehistoric kings of the two kingdoms of Upper and Lower Egypt. The sculptured objects which were deposited in the ancient shrine of the southern capital at Hierakonpolis commemorate the victories of the south over the north in the struggle which finally resulted in the subjugation of the Delta which had been ruled from Buto. If we remember that there is no intervening stage between this transitional period and Gerzean, we can continue to call it Late Predynastic[5] or Protodynastic, which is a somewhat better term than Dynasty O, which has also been applied to it.

The Predynastic Period was a time in which man was beginning to learn the use of copper for tools and weapons and was slowly working out of a Stone Age culture. In the designs on pottery and the figures modelled in mud and fashioned from bone and ivory we can see the beginnings of Egyptian art. The craftsman was also learning how to work stone in the form of vessels as well as palettes for mixing the green paint, made from powdered malachite, which was smeared around the eyes. The skill thus gained was to form a basis for the Egyptian's extraordinary mastery of stone. Along with the fine blacktopped red pottery which had begun to appear in Badarian times, the Amratian potter produced a red polished ware which was decorated in cream-coloured paint. This light on dark painting is the peculiar characteristic of this time [4], in contrast to the designs in red line on buff-coloured vessels introduced by the Gerzean craftsmen [2, 3].

1. Rock-drawings from Sayala. Historic period (Nubian C-Group?)

2. Paintings on pottery. Amratian and Gerzean periods

Geometric patterns predominate in Amratian design, but the painter also begins to experiment with the drawings of plants, animals, and men. These decorated vessels really represent the beginning of painting in Egypt. They are wholly Egyptian in character and have little in common with the decorated wares which flourished in prehistoric Western Asia. The essential characteristics of a familiar animal are seized in the figures of the hippopotamus repeated around the centre of a bowl [4]. The same beast was also vigorously, if very simply, modelled in clay [5].[6]

By Gerzean times such figures were already being fashioned from stone, as in the case of the remarkable slate jackal [6] found at El Ahaiwah,[7] one of the early cemeteries which lie

3. Decorated ware with boats with standards. Gerzean period. *New Haven, Yale Art Gallery*

4. Pottery bowl with hippopotamuses from Mesaeed. Predynastic, Amratian period. *Boston, Museum of Fine Arts*

5. Pottery hippopotamus. Predynastic or Middle Kingdom(?). *Boston, Museum of Fine Arts*

6. Slate jackal from El Ahaiwah. Predynastic. *Berkeley, Museum of Anthropology, University of California*

along the eastern bank of the river in the Girga district. El Ahaiwah lies several miles downstream from Mesaeed, where the hippopotamus bowl was found, and Naga-ed-Dêr, which was to continue down into the Middle Kingdom as one of the burying grounds of the Thinite Nome. Thinis was the home of the family which founded Dynasty I. Its much more famous cemetery was Abydos, further south on the western edge of the valley. The legs and neck of the figure are not as long as in later representations of the standing animal. Nevertheless this would appear to be one of the jackal gods related to Anubis as protector of the dead, even though it is not recumbent like them. Such a jackal god was worshipped in the archaic temple of the Abydos cemetery.

The slate jackal [6] is flat, like the Predynastic palettes which were sometimes given the shape of animals, birds, or fish. It was evidently not intended for such a purpose, since it lacks a suitable space for the grinding of the eye-paint and is unusually large, being over a foot long. Although it could not stand, it was carved on both sides and would appear to be one of the earliest images of a deity in animal form.

Towards the end of the Predynastic Period the sculptors were daring to carve large figures of gods out of limestone. Three badly battered standing figures of the fertility god Min were found in the early strata of his temple at Coptos. They were about 13 feet (4m) high and are more remarkable for their size than for skill in handling the human figure. The body is in the form of a long cylinder and the stone is worked as little as possible. Only a portion of one bearded head was recovered, with its surface badly damaged. The drawings of shells and animals which are roughly cut on the strip which hangs down from the girdle show a better delineation of form than do the few summary details of the figures themselves. They are closely related to the small Protodynastic reliefs in stone and ivory and suggest an approximate date for the Min statues.[8] We know that ivory and stone figures of men and women were placed as votive offerings in the archaic temples at Hierakonpolis and Abydos. In this connexion it should be remembered that much of the earliest sculpture has been recovered from temples and was not made for the tomb.

The curious dwarfs [7] are the most primitive-looking of the ivories which have been assigned to Late Gerzean. They are thought to come from graves at either Nagadah or Semaineh.[9] These odd little creatures, which are only about 2 inches high, have a liveliness lacking in earlier figures, but vary considerably in treatment. The crawling or standing dwarf holding a child begins to suggest something of the greater naturalism in the forms of the body to be found in another group of ivories. These were deposited as offerings, with a variety of other carved objects of stone and faience, in the early shrine at Hierakonpolis. The little naked man in Philadelphia [8] is a fine example of this advance in representing the human figure. It is one of the smaller pieces, being about 4 inches (10cm) high. Although most of the surface detail has disappeared with the disintegration of the ivory, it is clear that the body has emerged from the rigid forms of the larger stone pieces.

The Hierakonpolis ivories present a considerable variety in pose, costume, and headdress. Like the larger pieces of sculpture and the carved palettes and mace-heads, they must have been deposited over a considerable length of time from Late

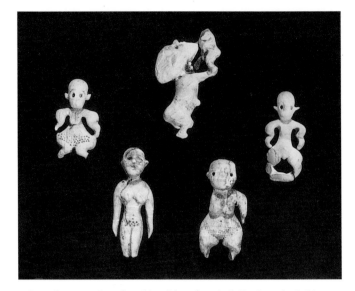

7. Ivory figures perhaps from Nagadah or Semaineh. Predynastic. *Baltimore, Walters Art Gallery*

Gerzean into the Early Dynastic Period. The ceremonial palettes and mace-heads, as well as the carvings with processions of birds and animals like those on the handles of the big flint knives, disappear early in Dynasty I.[10] However, it is not easy to distinguish an early group among the statuettes, since there is too general a resemblance to the small carvings of stone,

8. Ivory figure from Hierakonpolis. Late Predynastic-Dynasty I. *Philadelphia, University Museum*

faience, and ivory objects found in the Abydos temple deposit, which seems to have belonged largely to Dynasties I and II, and to ivory carvings found in the First Dynasty tombs at Helwan.[11] The execution of statues in stone was plainly not equal in quality to that of the small statuettes in ivory and the carvings in relief and, since there are no royal pieces which can be dated certainly to Dynasty I or the early part of Dynasty II, it is not yet possible to establish with any confidence a sequence in the order of the few pieces of large sculpture that have survived.

A recognizable archaic style was being established which would be developed in Dynasties I and II, reaching its culmination early in Dynasty III. In painting, we find a monumental treatment given to designs like those drawn in red line on the Gerzean buff-coloured vessels. They are enlarged on the plastered walls of a brick-lined chamber dug in soft crumbly marl. It lay on the edge of what must have been a part of the prehistoric town of Hierakonpolis, which flourished chiefly in Amratian times.[12] The structure had no entrance and contained a series of objects resembling the usual tomb equipment. It belongs to the Late Gerzean Period, and makes one of the earliest uses of brick construction. In the painting on one of the walls [9], the boats which are like those on the pottery [2] would appear to belong to a funeral scene. Two wailing women are placed above the uppermost boat with its figure seated under a light shelter. Animals are scattered about between the vessels with the same disregard for composition shown by the vase-painters. Below, on the left, a man strikes three prisoners with a mace in the first appearance of a motif which was to be adopted throughout Egyptian history as a symbol for the pharaoh dominating over his enemies. Beyond, on the right, another man grapples with two lions, as does the figure on the Gebel el Arak knife-handle. Animals are caught in a trap and pairs of armed men fight with each other. The drawing of the figures shows little improvement on that of the vase-paintings. These scarcely alter from the Amratian light-on-dark example with the hunter leading his dogs, through the Gerzean red-line drawings to the detail of a decorated vessel from the First Dynasty level of the Abydos temple with a ram and birds on a tree [2].[13] The Hierakonpolis painting does show an advance over the linear one-colour treatment of the vases in that the red of the flesh, the white of the skirts, and the black and white of the animals and boats are filled in with solid colour inside the red outlines. Green,

probably made from powdered malachite, seems to have been laid over a white underpainting on the hulls of some of the boats.[14]

The reliefs on a series of stone palettes and mace-heads not only display much more accomplished drawing than the paintings, but also show a progression towards orderly arrangement from the wild confusion of the animals on the Oxford palette from the Hierakonpolis temple,[15] which, in type at least, seems the earliest. The figures of the dead on the battle-field attacked by the lion [10] are similarly disposed in a loose fashion as they must have been on the Louvre fragment [11], but on the mace-head of the Scorpion King [12]

10. Carved palette from Hierakonpolis. Predynastic. *Oxford, Ashmolean Museum, and London, British Museum*

11. Fragment of slate palette. Predynastic. *Paris, Louvre*

9. Hierakonpolis, tomb, wall-painting (detail), watercolour copy. Late Gerzean

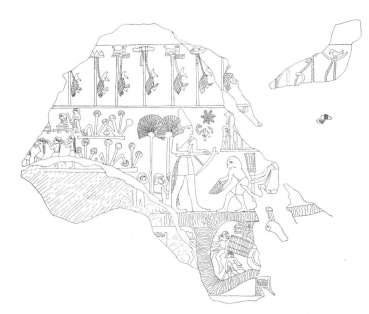

12. Scorpion King on a mace-head. *Oxford, Ashmolean Museum*

13. and 14. Narmer palette (verso and recto). Dynasty I. *Cairo Museum*

and the palette of Narmer [13, 14] the figures are placed on base lines which begin to establish the familiar Egyptian form of composition in superimposed registers [15].[16] The vigorous modelling is particularly evident where the craftsman has also made an attempt to relate his figures to one another [11]. The hoof of the bull presses into the flesh of the man prostrate between his forelegs.

These small monuments represent historical steps in the war between Upper Egypt and the Delta. The lion and the bull are different manifestations of the king's power as expressed in his titulary in historical times. In this case they certainly refer to the ruler of the south. The standards with the emblems of the gods of the southern confederation of states [11] have human arms and hands with which they pull upon a rope that evidently encircles the enemy. We are finally given the name of one of the last of the prehistoric rulers of the south, the Scorpion King [12]. On his mace-head he is evidently presiding at the opening of a new canal, holding a hoe, while a bowing official stretches out a basket for the earth. Fan-bearers and another official attend the king. A device later used for suggesting landscape appears here in the way that the irregular band of water sets off small areas in which are depicted men labouring, huts of woven reeds, a

15. Libya palette. Early Dynasty I. *Cairo Museum*

palm tree in an enclosure, and the prow of a boat. Men carrying standards are placed in a small sub-register above the chief figures. In the top register of this composition, which was ingeniously adapted to the surfaces of the pear-shaped stone mace-head, is another series of standards with images of gods [cf. 10, 11]. From the posts hang down the limp bodies of crested birds which later represent the common people, often in the sense of rebels. Here there must be another reference to a triumph over the men of the Delta for clumps of papyrus accompany the festive group of dancers and figures in carrying-chairs.

The meaning is made more plain on the Narmer palette, which clearly symbolizes a subjugation of the Delta. Not only have we reached a more developed stage in writing, but, as on the mace-head of the Scorpion King, most of the features of the later Egyptian style are established. The large size of the principal figure now dominates the rest of the composition

16. Abydos, tomb of Merneith
and Saqqara, tomb attributed to
Merneith. Dynasty I.
Reconstructions

and the conventions for drawing the human figure are reaching their standardized form.[17] On one side [13] the king, accompanied by an official carrying his sandals, brandishes his mace above a captive. Over Narmer's head, between two cow-horned heads of a Hathor(?) goddess, his name is set in a frame representing the façade and enclosure of the royal palace. The new hieroglyphic writing is also used for labels over the other figures, but the idea of the whole scene is expressed in an elaborate pictograph which still belongs to the picture-writing stage of the language. This shows a Horus falcon perched upon a clump of papyrus. In its human hand the bird holds tethered by a cord the bearded head which forms the end of the sign for land out of which the plants grow. Thus is expressed the domination over the northern land by the state-god of the south whose embodiment upon earth is the Horus Narmer. The king here wears the tall white crown of the south, but on the other side of the palette he has assumed the red crown of the north, when he goes out with his officials and standard bearers to inspect the slain on the field of battle [14].[18]

There had evolved, then, in the Protodynastic or Late Gerzean phase of the Predynastic Period the political development which made possible the brilliant civilization of Early Dynastic times, as well as two of its most important adjuncts, the use of writing and brick architecture. While little construction has survived except for such brickwork as the lining of the painted chamber at Hierakonpolis, the frame of the Horus name of Narmer provides evidence that the Protodynastic palaces were built of brick. The enclosure wall, with its projecting niched towers flanking the palace gate, is more elaborately represented in the Horus names of the later kings of Dynasty I, but its essentials appear here. The projecting bastions can be seen on the town enclosures which are shown as though in plan in the pictographs of the Protodynastic palettes, or in the sign over the fallen man at the bottom of the Narmer palette [13].[19]

The actual construction has survived in the recessed panelling on the faces of the large brick tombs of Dynasty I [16B].

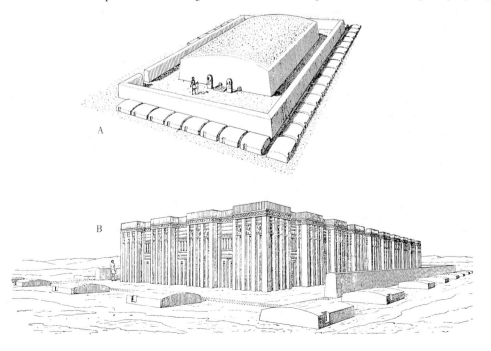

18. Impression of a cylinder seal from Naga-ed-Dêr. Predynastic. *Berkeley, Museum of Anthropology, University of California*

17. Confronted animals, including a Middle Kingdom example at Meir with a man standing on long-necked monsters

Evidence of relations between Egypt and Mesopotamia still remains tenuous and relies chiefly on resemblances between Mesopotamian examples[25] and such motives as the man dominating a pair of lions and the long-necked animals which appear in Egypt [17]. However, the synchronization of

19. Painted Syrian jar from Abusir. Dynasty I. *Leipzig, Ägyptologisches Institut*

It appears again in Dynasty II in the great brick enclosures at Abydos and on the buildings inside them,[20] which must repeat fairly closely the type of the fortified royal residence. The system of doors flanked by projecting panels with niches continues in the chapels of the archaic cemetery at Saqqara. The Third-Dynasty chapel of Hesyra, there, had preserved traces of the attachment of the wooden planks which covered the recesses and supported the brickwork above.[21] The gateways with niched flanking towers were copied in stone on the enclosure walls of the step pyramids of Zoser and Sekhemkhet at Saqqara in Dynasty III, which are thought to imitate the city wall of Memphis, traditionally founded at the beginning of Dynasty I.

The resemblance between this niched construction in brickwork and that used in the Protoliterate Period in Mesopotamia has been frequently stressed.[22] In both countries an exuberance in architectural detail was echoed in the modelling of the reliefs on relatively small objects. This was later refined into a traditional style. Brick buildings replaced structures of reeds and matting stretched over a light framework and with an arching roof such as appears in simple fashion in the hut at the bottom of the Scorpion mace-head [12]. The use of brick had evidently reached an advanced stage in Mesopotamia at an earlier time than in Egypt, and a stimulus from the former country upon the ideas of the latter has been claimed. Nevertheless, the possibility of a parallel and independent development in Egypt should be given serious consideration. In spite of superficial resemblances, there seem to be many differences in structural detail between the recessed panelling of Mesopotamian buildings, which have to be studied largely from plans, and the Egyptian examples, which are better known in elevation, being preserved to a greater height. The upper portion of the wall structure can be seen in later examples which continue the type and in representations on false-doors and sarcophagi.[23] The small representations on early Mesopotamian cylinder seals again show structural details unlike those in the First-Dynasty Egyptian drawings of the Horus-frame.[24]

the Late Gerzean period with the Protoliterate in Mesopotamia has been convincingly demonstrated through the discovery in Egypt of four cylinder seals of Jemdet-Nasr type, one of which with a fish and lattice design [18] was found in a Gerzean grave at Naga-ed-Dêr.[26] There is no doubt that the Protoliterate Period in Mesopotamia was one of expanding influence abroad. Nor was Egypt isolated within her borders. Her contacts seem to have been, as in later times, through the Delta with the Libyan tribes which bordered it on the west and with the peoples of Western Asia to the north-east across the upper end of the Sinai peninsula. These connexions with the Mediterranean littoral had begun in Early Gerzean times, but there was an increase in the importation of pottery from Palestine and Syria in Dynasty I. Most distinctive are the painted vessels which were long ago recognized as foreign in the First Dynasty royal cemetery at Abydos. Later they were found in tombs of Dynasty I at Saqqara and in the neighbouring archaic cemetery at Abusir [19]. More recently a few sherds with these characteristic designs in brown or red paint on a white slip have appeared at Kinnereth in Palestine and Tell-el-Judeideh on the edge of the Antioch plain in northern Syria.[27] The original source of this pottery has still not been determined. Curiously enough, little foreign pottery has as yet been recovered from Dynasties II and III. It begins to appear again with the Syrian oil-jars of combed ware in the Fourth Dynasty tombs at Giza.[28]

CHAPTER 3

Dynasties I–II 3200–2780 B.C.[1]

The kings of the First Dynasty not only achieved the military control of the whole country but developed a system of administration to govern it. This task, which depended upon the perfection of an irrigation system and the building and care of an elaborate network of dykes and canals necessary to make full use of the agricultural possibilities inherent in the annual inundation of the Nile, was facilitated by the use of the newly invented writing.[2] At the same time that monumental architecture in brick was reaching the height of a development begun in Protodynastic times, the quarrymen had gained a considerable mastery of the cutting of large blocks of stone. This was evidently developed in the north, where throughout Egyptian history there was to be exploitation of the fine white limestone in the quarries of the eastern cliffs across the river from Memphis. In the early cemetery there at Helwan, large worked slabs of stone were used to line the burial chambers of some of the stairway tombs of the second half of Dynasty I.[3] There is as yet less evidence for the use of worked stone in the much larger brick tombs which were being constructed on the western edge of the valley at Saqqara from the time of Aha, the second king of Dynasty I. However, at Saqqara large pits were for the first time excavated in the rock to contain the burial apartments. One of these in the reign of Zer, the third king of Dynasty I, had the central compartments lined with rough stone and roofed with stone slabs.[4] These were not yet entered by a stairway, but this arrangement was introduced by the time of the fifth king, Den, in the impressive substructure of another panelled brick tomb. The pit for the large central apartment was cut deep in the rock, and three side chambers were hollowed out of the rock. Large portcullis stones are preserved which blocked the door to one of these side rooms as well as the stairway, while two rectangular blocks may have formed part of the architraves to support the roof.[5]

Contemporaneously, granite slabs were being worked for the flooring of the burial chamber in the structure which Den built in the old Thinite cemetery at Abydos. The ability to shape hard stone into vessels had reached such a point that the craftsman could turn out pieces like the curious schist bowl from the small tomb of Sabu at Saqqara [20] of the time of Az-ib, Den's successor.[6] The vase-maker has played with the hard stone as though it were clay, turning in three lipped pieces towards the central container and leaving the thin rim unsupported. This skill was to make possible the carving of raised reliefs in granite by the time of Khasekhemuwy, the last king of Dynasty II,[7] in whose reign the Fifth-Dynasty annals of the Palermo stone record the erection of a temple of stone. The technical competence displayed in the working of hard stone under Khasekhemuwy is hardly suggested by the few surviving examples of limestone reliefs, with the exception of the round-topped stela of King Zet (now called Wadji) from Abydos.[8] This and the fact that such large decorated blocks of granite were being used as adjuncts to brick architecture make us realize that there is still much to be

learned about both architecture and sculpture in early dynastic times. This work of Khasekhemuwy did not long precede the Step Pyramid at Saqqara, which, at the beginning of Dynasty III, is the first great building in stone that has survived. Khasekhemuwy's burial chamber at Abydos was lined and floored with limestone, but the superstructure must have been of brick like those over the complicated suites of underground chambers that were being excavated in Dynasty II at Saqqara. Perhaps other intermediate steps in the use of worked stone in architecture may turn up in future excavations, as well as the examples of royal sculpture which are so badly needed to understand its development. The limited amount of material so far recovered leaves the impression that the execution of statues and reliefs lagged behind the immense facility and inventiveness displayed in the minor arts. This is perhaps due to the survival of only a limited number of works, most of which were executed for private persons. Such officials were probably dependent upon the less able craftsmen of the king's workshops. These must have served as training-schools, but they undoubtedly laid claim upon the services of the most skilled men for royal commissions.

A few years ago no one imagined that so much amazingly rich material would be recovered from the cemeteries at Saqqara and Helwan, although the brilliant civilization of Dynasty I had long been known from the more fragmentary remains at Abydos which were being supplemented from other early sites such as Abu Roash. It is as yet too soon to attempt to assess the full significance of what has been found, since new problems have been created which are far from being solved. The succession of the kings of Dynasty I was

20. Schist bowl from Saqqara. Dynasty I. *Cairo Museum*

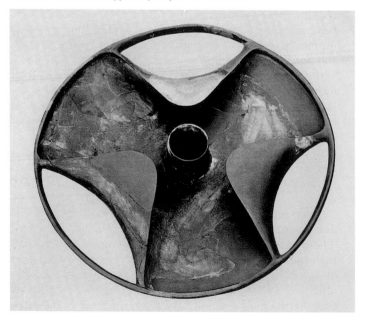

first determined from the cemetery at Abydos, where the tombs of all the kings of Dynasty I from Narmer to Qay-a, and those of two kings of Dynasty II, Peribsen and Khasekhemuwy, were identified by Petrie.[9] The tombs of at least two early kings of Dynasty II have been found at Saqqara south of the Step Pyramid enclosure.[10] At Abydos, Peribsen and Khasekhemuwy built the two great brick enclosures which have already been mentioned. These were near the cultivated land behind the temple of Khentiamentiu, and at a considerable distance from the royal cemetery, which lay on the mound of Umm el Gaab far out in the bay which the cliffs form behind Abydos. These high enclosures, with their panelled outer walls and partially cleared buildings inside, have been called forts, but they are more likely to have been imitations of the residence of the king. Perhaps they served to house him with his retinue when he came to visit the cemetery, as did the palaces connected with the funerary temples in the New Kingdom. They may also have been intended for the king's use in afterlife, as were the structures erected around the Step Pyramid at Saqqara. If one of their functions was that of a place of reception for royal visits, they were not unlike the valley temples which gave access to the pyramid precincts in the Old Kingdom.[11] East of these two structures were large rectangles of graves of the time of Zer, Zet, and Queen Merneith. Inside Merneith's rectangle there were traces of a mud brick wall, and considerable portions of a niched wall without any graves around it lay behind the Merneith complex. Since the Coptic Deir north of these is built inside an old enclosure like those of Dynasty II, the possibility should be seriously considered that a similar structure stood here in the First Dynasty.[12]

Khentiamentiu, 'Foremost of the Westerners', was very important in the first two dynasties. It was to be a long time before this old jackal god of the dead was assimilated to Osiris, when the latter's cult was brought from Busiris in the eastern Delta. Khentiamentiu's name alone was maintained in the inscriptions of this temple throughout the Old Kingdom, although the Pyramid Texts begin to associate Osiris with him and with Abydos. In the Fifth Dynasty the funerary formulae in the Memphite private tombs also recognize this connexion. Later in the Old Kingdom, Abydos became a place of pilgrimage which increased in popularity during the First Intermediate Period. Men built cenotaphs and set up stelae that they might be associated in death with Osiris, even though they were actually buried in their own districts. As an ancient king who suffered death at the hands of Seth but was revived by the devoted efforts of his wife Isis and son Horus, Osiris became the symbol of resurrection and the ruler of the living dead. Perhaps as early as the Middle Kingdom the tomb of Osiris was associated with the old mound of Umm el Gaab, where in late times it was certainly located in the tomb of the First-Dynasty king, Zer.[13]

It has long been thought that the sanctity of Abydos was due originally to the burial there of the kings of Dynasty I. The discovery at Saqqara of richly equipped tombs larger than those at Abydos and containing jar sealings and other objects marked with the names of the same kings and their officials obviously poses a problem. It has been suggested that the rulers of the united country, after the founding of

Memphis, chose to be buried near their new residence, erecting cenotaphs for themselves at Abydos that they might be associated with their ancestors, the Protodynastic rulers of Thinis. The concept of a cenotaph, literally 'empty grave', in the sense of a memorial structure for a person buried elsewhere is not unattested in Egyptian archaeology. There are proponents of two schools of thought on the question of the site of the real tombs of the rulers of Dynasty I and the latter half of Dynasty II. Is this Abydos or Saqqara? The excavation at the Saqqara North Cemetery of Dynasties I and II revealed much larger structures than those at Abydos and many more 'sacrificial' burials of dependants around the main burial. Saqqara too is well attested as a royal burial site for the first kings of Dynasty II, the rulers of Dynasty III (Zoser and Sekhem-khet), and several kings of Dynasties V and VI. Hence it seemed natural to regard the impressive Saqqara cemetery as the burial ground of kings rather than of important governors of the north. Kemp has tried to show, however, that the Abydos tombs must be considered along with the huge funerary palaces there, the so-called forts. When the area of the tomb of a specific reign is considered along with the corresponding palace and the number of subsidiary burials with both tomb and palace, the Abydos installation is seen to be much larger than the Saqqara tombs. Also there are several tombs of roughly equivalent size for the same reign at Saqqara, a circumstance which seems implausible for a royal cemetery. Lastly, the stela of Merka on the east side of a tomb of the end of Dynasty I at Saqqara seems to Kemp appropriately placed for that of the tomb's owner rather than that of an official of the king [21].[14] Four graves found by Petrie at Abydos near those of Narmer and Aha seem to have belonged to some of the kings which the Ptolemaic historian Manetho placed at Thinis in the dim past before Dynasties I and II, which he also called Thinite.[15] It is not clear when the capital of the south was moved to Thinis, the site of which has not been certainly identified, although it is thought to have been in the neighbourhood of the modern town of Girga. The monuments of the Scorpion King and Narmer were still dedicated at Hierakonpolis, as were those of Khasekhem and Khasekhemuwy at the end of Dynasty II. Thinis would have been geographically better placed for the administration of Upper Egypt and for operations against the north, just as Memphis later was strategically suited to control the Delta.

It may be that Aha, after constructing the tomb near that of Narmer at Abydos, later built the much larger tomb at Saqqara which contained so many jar sealings with his name.[16] An even bigger panelled tomb like the Saqqara one was built at Nagadah in Upper Egypt, perhaps for his queen, Neith-hetep. A similar large tomb, a little south of Giza, is thought to be that of a queen of the fourth king of Dynasty I, Zet (now called Wadji). In addition to Aha, impressive tombs at Saqqara contained the names of Kings Zer (two), Zet, Den (four), Azib, and Qay-a (two), as well as the Queens Merneith and Her-neith [23]. Thus all the kings known from Abydos are represented at Saqqara except the first king, Narmer, and the seventh, Semerkhet.[17] It will be observed that several kings are represented by more than one large tomb. Some of these were attributed to the officials whose names appear in them, but names of the same officials of Den occur in several

21. Saqqara, stela of Merka. Dynasty I

tombs as well as in Dynasty I tombs at Abu Roash and at Abydos.[18] The Saqqara tombs lack the pairs of round-topped stelae with a royal name which marked the Abydos graves,[19] but perhaps the greatest difficulty in identifying certain of them as the burial-places of kings is that none show that marked distinction in external appearance which is so characteristic of later tombs of rulers. All of them and others at Abu Roash and Helwan, which cannot have belonged to kings, have the same long, flat-topped rectangular superstructures (mastabas) with exterior niching [16B].

The superstructures have been destroyed in the royal cemetery at Abydos, but they must have had a distinctive form of their own; for the shape of the pits cut in the gravel and their close proximity rule out the possibility that they can have been covered by the known type of long panelled

mastaba. The form of the Old Kingdom sarcophagus, with its panelled sides and vaulted lid, has been used to support a theory that the panelled mastabas were derived from the tombs of the prehistoric kings of Buto, which copied a brick palace with a vaulted roof and were surrounded by a niched enclosing wall.[20] This involves the unlikely assumption that some kind of brick vaulting had been invented in the Delta in Protodynastic times. Actually the first corbel vaults have been found in Upper Egypt in Dynasty II, although they may have been used by Qay-a at Abydos at the end of Dynasty I. The arch and barrel vault have not been found before Dynasty III. The vaulted lids of the earliest wooden coffins probably imitated the arched framework roofing light reed structures such as the little hut on the Scorpion mace-head [12]. The mats lashed to posts and the paired papyrus flowers which appear on the niched walls of the 'Palace Façade' panelling are also surviving elements of such light structures which would certainly be at home in the Delta, with its swamps available to supply the materials. However, such constructions of matting have been assigned a southern origin, and the contrast has been drawn between the nomads of the south, with their tent-like dwellings and grave mounds, and the settled inhabitants of the north, who built in brick and copied their houses for their tombs.[21] This does not seem to allow sufficiently for the possibilities of development in the villages and towns of the agricultural communities, which must long have outnumbered any nomad elements up and down the Nile Valley. Nor does it take into account the variety of living conditions in different parts of the Delta, with its swamps and its fringe of desert land inhabited by nomad tribes.[22] In view of the uniform culture displayed by what has survived from Predynastic Egypt, considerable caution should be employed in the interpretation of architectural forms according to their derivation from Upper or Lower Egypt.[23]

The stepped brick construction which Reisner proposed to restore over the Abydos tomb has been considered too heavy to be supported by the wooden roofing laid on the brick lining and cross walls of the pits cut in the gravel.[24] In place of this has been suggested a low brick structure filled with gravel and surrounded by a wall which enclosed an open offering place in which were set up the two round-topped stone stelae bearing the king's Horus name [16A].[25]

At Saqqara a stepped rectangular brick structure was built over the burial-pit of a large tomb (No. 3038) of the time of Az-ib, the sixth king of Dynasty I [22]. The steps were laid on banks of sand and gravel piled against a heavy vertical wall constructed around the edge of the pit. They were only on three sides, leaving the principal eastern face a flat wall through which opened two stairways that gave access to the upper and lower storeys of the pit. A system of terracing was next added around this stepped structure, and finally the whole was covered over by the sand and gravel filling of a niched brick 'Palace-Façade Mastaba' of the usual type.[26] The first stepped stage of the superstructure of this tomb was only about 7 feet high (2.30 m.), and it resembles a monument represented on stone vase fragments and pottery marks bearing the name of Az-ib. This served as a base for a rectangular construction, but whether this was meant for a stela or mass of brickwork cannot be determined from the simple drawings. It has been calculated that the panelled mastabas at

22. Saqqara, superstructure of Tomb 3038. Dynasty I, reign of Az-ib

23. Saqqara, tomb of Her-neith. Dynasty I. Axonometric projection

Saqqara stood to a height of a little over 17 feet (5.24 m).[27] The apartments in the substructures of a number of these tombs show alterations, and it is beginning to look as though some initial protection was provided over the roofing of the chambers in the pit, that the original scheme was sometimes altered in the lifetime of the owner, and that perhaps some or all of the work on the final panelled mastaba and the upper storage compartments in its filling was executed after the funeral. At this time would have been built the subsidiary graves with their little plastered mounds, which are laid out in a row around the main tomb, for certain of the artisans and personal attendants of the owner. As at Abydos, these persons are thought to have been put to death to accompany their master into the other world, but this view has been contested. If it existed,[28] such a custom disappeared before the end of Dynasty I.

The most recent tomb discovered at Saqqara has been assigned to a Queen Her-neith who was apparently buried in the reign of Den.[29] This had a stairway inside the pit, and not, like other tombs of this time, in a sloping passage descending from the east. Over the pit was built a sloping-sided, rectangular mound covered with brickwork [23]. It is not clear whether the two superimposed large chambers of the substructure could have been entered after this covering was in place, as would have been possible through the use of the roofed staircase which ran under the stepped structure of the later Tomb 3038. Again, this first covering of the pit was

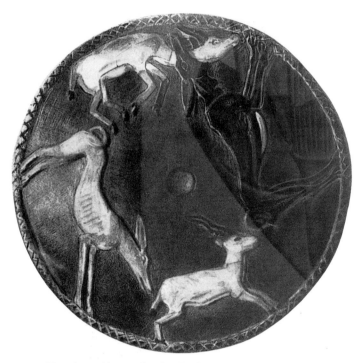

24. Hounds attacking gazelles. Steatite disk from Saqqara. Dynasty I. *Cairo Museum*

25. Two faces of an inlaid wooden panel from Abydos. Dynasty I. *Oxford, Ashmolean Museum*

enclosed in a niched mastaba, and storage compartments were built over it in the filling. It seems to be a simple form of the pit-covering developed in Tomb 3038, and both of these should be considered in relation to the kinds of superstructures built over the tombs at Abydos which may have shown similar stages of development. The stepped form of Tomb 3038 should also be remembered in connexion with the Step Pyramid of Zoser in Dynasty III, for which it is at present the only even remotely similar antecedent. At the Step Pyramid the niched outer face of the mastaba has become a separate wall enclosing the whole precinct, reverting to a closer imitation of its original use as the enclosure of the royal residence.

The problems connected with the identification of the burial-places of the kings of Dynasty I are of vital importance historically, and new evidence continues to appear from Saqqara. However, for the study of Egyptian art, the discoveries of recent years are perhaps even more valuable in supplementing the fragmentary Abydos material to present a picture of the brilliant civilization of Dynasty I. The perfection of craftsmanship evinced by the furniture, jewellery, and stone vessels is astonishing. It is in these objects of daily use in the palaces of the king and his great officials that we can best judge the accomplishment of the royal craftsmen. Such an object as the round plaque [24] anticipates on a small scale the style of the early Old Kingdom. One of the hounds attacking their prey is carved in relief from the black steatite of the disk. The other dog and the two gazelles are of pink-stained alabaster let into the surface. The whole piece is only a little over 3 inches (7.6 cm) in diameter. It was the most elaborately decorated of a series of such disks which may have been used for playing a game.[30] The broken pieces of beds, chairs, stools, and chests which were found both at Saqqara and Abydos[31] suggest the establishment at this early date of forms and decoration known from the furniture of Queen Hetep-heres

at the beginning of Dynasty IV [83]. The wooden panel found in the earliest excavations at Abydos[32] is a fine example of the use of bound-reed-mat patterns which were extensively used for furniture and architectural details. The panel may be from the back of a chair like that of Hetep-heres [87]. The place for the royal name has been left blank in the Horus frame set between protective emblems in the centre of the border on one face [25]. The other side was inlaid with a geometrical design of thin triangles of faience, the combination of silicates, usually quartz, and binding agents which had been invented in Predynastic times.[33] Fine carpentry equal to that of the cabinet-maker was also lavished on the wooden lining of tomb chambers. These give a hint of the appearance of the palace interiors in which the furniture was used before being placed in the tomb. Sometimes coloured mats were stuck on the mud-plastered walls, and in one case brick pilasters were faced with wood on which had been fastened long vertical strips of gold imitating bound reeds.[34]

In the tomb of King Zer at Abydos four bracelets were found still in place on the linen-wrapped arm which was all that remained of a body which was thought to be Zer's queen.[35] The Horus frames in the lowest bracelet [26] are of alternating gold and turquoise pieces. Lapis lazuli and turquoise beads are used with the gold in the other bracelets, one

26. Jewellery from the tomb of Zer at Abydos. Dynasty I. *Cairo Museum*

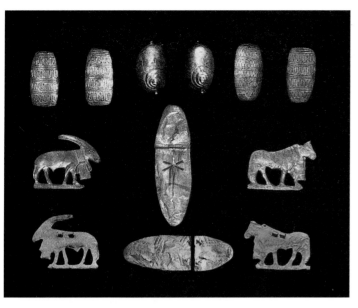

27. Gold jewellery from Naga-ed-Dêr. Dynasty I. *Cairo Museum*

29. and 30. Seated limestone figure, front and back views. Dynasty I–II. *Cairo Museum*

of which has a larger gold rosette. It was not only members of the royal family who could possess such valuable ornaments for in a First-Dynasty grave of the cemetery of Naga-ed-Dêr in the Abydos–Thinite district was found a body wearing a plain circlet of gold on its head and necklaces of stone and gold beads, as well as remarkable gold amulets.[36] There were twenty-four beads in the form of shells, of which two appear in the illustration [27]. There were also ten big barrel beads with bands of an odd wavy design. The front and back of several amulets are shown. The largest is a kind of capsule in the form of a beetle on which a design of the crossed arrows and shields of the Delta goddess Neith of Sais, on a standard, was cut out of the gold sheet and filled with blue paste. The head was removable, and the legs of the insect are marked on the underside of the body. The capsule had no means of attachment, and perhaps did not form a part of a necklace, as did the antelope and the bull. These two animals were likewise of thin gold which was pressed over a filling of pink cement. In front, the forms of the animals are vigorously modelled, while the back is a plain gold sheet. The antelope wears a collar from which hangs an emblem in the form of a girdle tie, while a Hathor head is attached to the band round the bull's neck.

28. Schist dish imitating basketry from Saqqara. Dynasty II. *Cairo Museum*

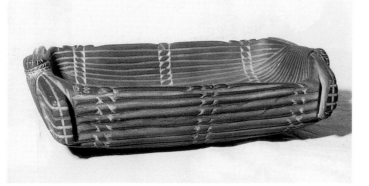

Parts of two large wooden statues from Abydos in Oxford and the base and feet of two other standing figures found at Saqqara[37] suggest that royal workmanship of Dynasty I may have been more advanced, at least in a softer material, than the few stone pieces which have survived would indicate, although expert treatment of harder materials is attested for this period by such pieces as a schist presentation vase or tray worked to simulate basketry [28]. The upper part of a small seated limestone figure in Cairo [29, 30] has part

31. Saqqara, niche-stone. Dynasty II

of its crisply carved surfaces well preserved. Its source is unknown, and the complicated headdress is not unlike that in some of the Hierakonpolis ivories which anticipates a wig with two heavy curls worn by queens in the Middle Kingdom. There is a certain resemblance to the royal headcloth, as in one of the two battered seated figures from Hierakonpolis which are thought to represent a protodynastic king and his queen.[38] There is again a similarity to a less expertly worked small seated male limestone figure in Berlin,[39] but the modelling of the eye, forehead, and cheek is finer. Stylistically, the Cairo piece is as close as sculpture in the round can be to the relief of a princess on a limestone niche-stone found by Professor Emery at Saqqara in one of the subsidiary tombs of Dynasty II [31].[40] There is the same fumbling disproportion in the parts of the figure and a

concentration of minute detail on certain areas, while others are left plain. It is impossible to be certain from the headdress whether a royal personage or a woman is represented by the statuette. The one braid hanging over the shoulder suggests the sidelock of a young prince, but both the statuette and the princess on the niche-stone wear the same kind of robe covering only one shoulder which is found in the case of both men and women in other reliefs.

There is a sharper edge to the outlines in the carving of a second niche-stone from a Dynasty II tomb at Saqqara [32]. Here the painted surface was remarkably well preserved to give a unique impression of a completed early relief. The restricted colour scheme, in which red, yellow, and black predominate, seems to accord well with the archaic character of the piece. However, there are a few touches of green and

32. Saqqara, painted niche-stone. Dynasty II

33. Khasekhem. Seated limestone statue from Hierakonpolis. Dynasty II. *Oxford, Ashmolean Museum*

Dynasty I. One at Helwan was even earlier, since it lay on the floor of one of the stairway pits of the second half of Dynasty I.[43]

We can no longer assign a rock carving at Sinai[44] to Dynasty I, since the name long read Semerkhet is now recognized to be that of Sekhem-khet, who followed Zoser in constructing a step pyramid at Saqqara in Dynasty III. Except for the badly damaged granite raised reliefs of Khasekhemuwy from Hierakonpolis and El Kab, which, like the statues of Khasekhem to be discussed presently, show a great advance in skill, the only other temple reliefs of royal workmanship which have survived betray the same rather faltering draughtsmanship and cutting as do the private pieces we have just been considering.[45]

Towards the end of Dynasty II, two similar seated statues of King Khasekhem show that the royal sculptor was overcoming the problems of representing the human figure. He has also acquired an equal facility whether working in hard or soft stone for the statue in Oxford is cut from limestone [33], while that in Cairo [34] is worked in slate.[46] In the shaping of

34. Khasekhem. Seated slate statue from Hierakonpolis. Dynasty II. *Cairo Museum*

blue – colours which were still used sparingly even in the early part of Dynasty IV. Green appeared in the Hierakonpolis painting in Late Gerzean times, but blue was unknown before the reign of Cheops in Dynasty IV[41] until recently, when it was found in the mat patterns on First-Dynasty tombs at Saqqara.[42] In the painted relief the man wears a black-spotted panther skin with red shoulder-ties and is seated before a stone table consisting of a bowl containing half-loaves of bread set on a cylindrical stand. The man's titles are written in front of his face, and food offerings are placed round the table and in the compartment list on the right, which is headed by various kinds of linen. There are here all the elements of what was to be the traditional table scene of the Fourth-Dynasty Giza slab-stelae [78] and the tablet over the Old Kingdom false-door. At Saqqara such stones were set into the brick niche of the exterior chapel of a mastaba which had a plain face without the panelling of

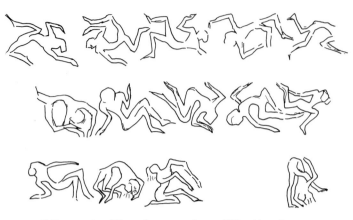

35. Fallen enemies of Egypt from statue-bases of Khasekhem from Hierakonpolis. Dynasty II

the hands and feet, and particularly in the modelling of the face, these statues show a great advance over anything known from an earlier time, while the general proportions of the figure are better balanced. The area of the eye and its upper lid has received a new plastic treatment, and there is an air of crisp, youthful tautness emphasized by the line of the robe which rises sharply around the neck of the Cairo figure. The king wears the tall white crown of Upper Egypt from which the ear still projects clumsily, although better formed than in the earlier limestone fragment [29]. Both statues were set up in the old shrine at Hierakonpolis and evidently commemorate some insurrection in the north, for on their bases are incised freely drawn figures of remarkably limp and contorted slain enemies [35], with a clump of papyrus springing from the head of one of them and numerals indicating the number of the dead. In these statues we find the sculptor working at his best in the archaic style which is more fully illustrated by a variety of works in Dynasty III.

PART TWO

The Old Kingdom

CHAPTER 4

Dynasty III 2780–2680 B.C.

The well-known statue of King Zoser in Cairo [36] was found still in place in the closed statue-chamber (*serdab*) beside his temple on the north side of the Step Pyramid at Saqqara.[1] It faced two round holes in the wall, as though looking out, so that the purifying smoke of incense offered there could penetrate to it, but also that the spirit might move freely to and from this embodiment in stone. The king is wrapped in the long robe associated with the Sed Jubilee. He wears the royal headcloth over a heavy wig and a long divine beard. He is seated on a throne, like that of Khasekhem, with the wooden frame imitated at the side in raised relief. The youthful suppleness and wiry strength of Khasekhem have given way to a heavier majesty. The wrenching out of the inlaid eyes and damage to the nose have not entirely deprived the full face, with its prominent mouth, of a character which appears also in reliefs representing Zoser [37]. Although the statue is in general treated in simple masses, the detailed carving of the strands of hair in the wig is a feature which we noticed in the Cairo statuette and reliefs of Dynasty II [29–30, 31]. In other fragments of statues from the Step Pyramid complex, which include portions of a colossal figure of the king, this is even more evident. The basically simple form is decorated with an intricate series of flat patterns to represent the strands of hair in elaborate wigs, the beadwork of belts and aprons, or the woven stuff of a girdle.[2] The same intricate detail is applied to the reliefs, which, although very low in carving, are boldly simple in composition, with a few large figures and big hieroglyphs. In architecture, also, we find elaborate details carved in relief on the face of the structure. It is this essentially archaic conflict between the desire to ornament the surfaces and at the same time to work with simple masses which lends a family resemblance to the monuments which range from Dynasty II to the reign of Sneferu at the beginning of Dynasty IV. Here also is the origin of two kinds of relief, one relatively high and the other very low, which we find side by side in the finest Giza work in Dynasty IV. As Dynasty III progressed, the bolder treatment, gradually employing relief of greater height, gained favour until the heavier style prevailed in the reign of Sneferu. This tendency towards solidity increases also in the statues and architecture. Eventually at Giza in Dynasty IV the excessive surface detail was refined and brought into better balance with the basic form.

It is the architecture of the reign of Zoser, at the beginning of Dynasty III, which, more than anything else, presents us with a picture of a young civilization approaching maturity. The builders, like the vase-makers of Dynasty I, were unable to resist the temptation to exploit their new-found technical skill. An abundance of vitality and invention led them to attempt things which were later wisely discarded, but the results which they achieved seem as surprising and fresh to us now as they must have to their admiring contemporaries. In the group of buildings which were erected round Zoser's funerary monument at Saqqara [38] were imitated a whole range of structures which had hitherto been built of light materials. They are precious in giving an indication of the appearance of large-scale early architecture that is otherwise known to us only from small drawings. They probably present many details of construction which continued to be used in domestic and public buildings that went on being made of brick, wood, and light materials after the introduction of stone for temples and tombs. We must remember, however, that while this was a temple intended for the funerary cult of Zoser, it was also apparently a simulacrum of edifices connected with the royal residence for Zoser's use in the other world. It is in large part a representation conceived in the same schematic fashion in which the Egyptian made up the pictures which he drew. Frequently only a façade with its sculptured details is set against a rubble core, with little or no indication of the original distribution of the rooms in the interior. These were dummy buildings which could no longer be used for the purpose originally intended for them, nor are

36. Zoser. Limestone statue from Saqqara. Dynasty III. *Cairo Museum*

37. Saqqara, South Tomb of Zoser complex, head of Zoser on false-door panel. Dynasty III

change to a high stepped construction introduced a new method in which successive layers of masonry were added round a central core with the courses tilted so that the pressure was exerted inwards. The technique can be seen clearly in the layer pyramid of Zawiyet el Aryan, a later example of Dynasty III, probably built by King Kha-ba, where a hole was broken into the masonry.[4] The same type of construction is to be found at the end of the Dynasty in the Medum pyramid. It was evidently the daring new idea of a high structure rising like a gigantic staircase to the heavens, conceived by Imhotep, the architect of the Step Pyramid, which led to this exploration of the possibilities of attaining stability in building with stone. In the course of this vast enterprise, Imhotep adapted to new purposes methods which had been developed in brick-work and laid a basis for the future handling of stone masonry on a large scale. The whole group of buildings long continued to arouse admiration, and Imhotep was revered in later times as a wise man and demi-god who had been Zoser's minister, architect, and physician. It is only comparatively recently that his name has been recovered in connexion with his work, on a statue base of Zoser discovered in the excavation of the columned processional hall which gave access to the Step Pyramid precinct.[5]

The structures around the pyramid remain unique and continue to arouse lively speculation. Although a similar method of construction was used later in the layer pyramid at Zawiyet el Aryan and at Medum [58], nothing resembling the complicated nature of the subsidiary buildings designed for Zoser was attempted at either site. It would appear that the Zawiyet el Aryan project was not completely finished, while at Medum, at the end of the Dynasty, the temple has been treated in a severely simple fashion which introduces the style of Dynasty IV. We shall see that it is probable that this was built by Sneferu when he completed the eight-staged structure left unfinished by Huni, the last king of Dynasty III. It is most likely that the steps were filled in and the whole cased to form a true pyramid while Sneferu was engaged in finishing the second of the two pyramids which he erected at Dahshur. Excavations have uncovered a new enclosure with a panelled wall like that of Zoser. This employed larger masonry blocks, following a tendency which was appearing in the latest work of the Zoser complex. It lies to the south-west of the latter and belonged to a previously unidentified King Sekhem-khet,

the forms newly introduced. They were simply transposed into stone from earlier models, as in a theatrical set.

The structure which towered above the panelled enclosure wall was a new form, and one which can be traced through several experimental stages from the square, flat-topped stone mastaba which was first planned to the final stepped pyramid in six stages measuring 413 feet by 344 feet (126 × 105 m) at the base, and standing 200 feet (61 m) high.[3] While in the mastaba small blocks were laid in horizontal courses, the

38 and 39. Saqqara, Step Pyramid Zoser complex. Dynasty III. Model with detail

evidently a follower of Zoser and probably his immediate successor. A rock carving executed for him at the Wady Maghara in the Sinai Peninsula has long been known, but the name had been read as that of the First Dynasty King Semerkhet.[6]

The underground galleries of the Sekhem-khet Pyramid are like those of the Layer Pyramid at Zawiyet el Aryan, south of Giza, which is probably to be attributed to Kha-ba, who perhaps succeeded Sekhem-khet.[7] Work on the new step pyramid was abandoned before the structure had risen very high, although the burial apartments contained a closed (but mysteriously empty) alabaster sarcophagus and funerary equipment. There is another great stone enclosure which must be taken into account. Its outline has long been recognizable on the surface to the west of the monuments of Zoser and Sekhem-khet.[8] Certainly no tomb structure of any height has survived inside it. At Zawiyet el Aryan there is a great rock-cut pit farther out in the desert from the Layer Pyramid which represents another unfinished tomb that is possibly to be assigned to Neb-ka, the last king but one of the Dynasty.[9] The impression is left at present that none of the other kings of Dynasty III were able to complete the great projects which they initiated in attempting to rival Zoser and his architect, Imhotep. Even at the Step Pyramid there had been no attempt to construct individual buildings in the whole of the area bounded by the outer wall, which is 589 yards long by 300 yards wide (544 m. by 277 m.). A large part of the space is occupied by masses of rubble filling which presented a facing of fine white limestone towards the accessible courts and which had a very limited number of rooms and passages constructed in their interiors.

In the reconstructed model of the Step Pyramid precinct [38], one is looking across the group of buildings from the south-east corner of the enclosing wall, where the only real gateway opened into the entrance hall. The visitor passed through this processional hall to a large court south of the pyramid in which two stones marked the course of the ritual race performed by the king in connexion with the Sed Festival. This court was faced on three sides by a panelled wall, above which rose the lightly vaulted covering of the rubble filling over the store-room galleries which occupied the whole western side of the precinct. A similar construction marked the secondary tomb which was placed behind the southern enclosure wall. An offering-place for this tomb projected out into the court in the south-west corner, with a frieze of raised cobra heads along the top of its panelled wall [39]. Just inside the gateway to the entrance hall, a passage led off to the north giving access to a second court, which was lined on the east and west sides by dummy shrines for the gods of Upper and Lower Egypt. At the south end was a platform for the double throne [39] used in connexion with the king's jubilee of the renewal of kingship, and the court was evidently planned for the celebration of such a Sed Festival which was to be repeated eternally in the afterworld. A passage led off at the south-west corner to a pavilion which repeated the details of a small royal dwelling and which probably served as a place for the ritual robing of the king during the ceremonies of the Heb-Sed.

To the north of the Heb-Sed court can be seen two buildings [38], each in a separate court, which represent Upper and

40. Saqqara, North Building of Zoser complex, courtyard, papyrus columns. Dynasty III

Lower Egypt, perhaps as two places of administration for the dual monarchy. The North Building is marked not only by its position but also by the use of papyrus columns [40] on the adjoining east wall of its court. The façade of the South Building is slightly different in detail, corresponding to representations of the type of archaic sanctuary employed in the south [41, 42]. The column on the adjoining wall of its court may originally have had as a capital the plant of Upper Egypt, a flowering sedge. This part of the building was reached through a doorway at the north-east corner of the southern court, and not through the Heb-Sed court, which seems to have formed an enclosed separate block. One passed on to enter another court in front of the *serdab* chamber, and into the structure built against the north face of the pyramid which served as the temple for the funerary cult of the king.[10]

The funerary temple lay above the passage which led down to the burial-chamber, which was constructed of granite slabs at the bottom of a great rock-cut pit over which the pyramid was constructed. The rectangular interior of this chamber was not much larger than was necessary to take the body of the king. It was closed by a curious large granite stopper which was let down through a round hole in the roofing slabs. A series of galleries opened out of the stairway passage to the pit. One of these was lined with limestone set with green-blue faience tiles imitating the reed-matting walls of shrines and framing three false-doors containing reliefs representing

41. Saqqara, south Building of Zoser complex. Dynasty III. Actual façade

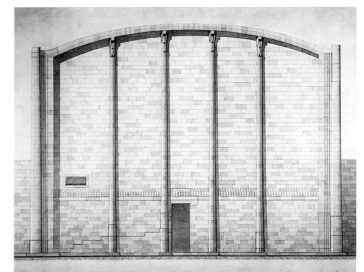

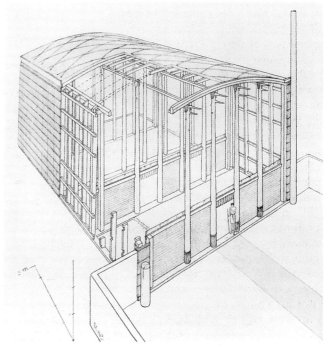

42. Saqqara, South Building of Zoser complex. Dynasty III. Reconstruction and prototype

43. Saqqara, South Tomb of Zoser complex, subterranean área, false-door. Dynasty III

Zoser. Another series of galleries belonged to the original mastaba construction. These were intended for the burial of members of the royal family, and were entered from a row of pits along the east face of the mastaba, later covered by the additions to the superstructure. A granite chamber, like that under the pyramid but smaller, was built at the bottom of a pit in the tomb inside the southern enclosure wall. This was reached by a long stairway passage and perhaps served for the burial of the canopic packages containing the entrails of the king, which later in the Old Kingdom were placed in a chest near the sarcophagus. More likely, however, the chamber served as the burial of the King's double or ka, represented by a statue. This granite chamber was again accompanied by rock-cut galleries lined with blue tiles [43], in imitation of archaic shrines like those in the Step Pyramid, and with similar reliefs of the king [37][11] set in false-doors.

One of the most striking aspects of Imhotep's work at the Step Pyramid is the use of plant-forms. These were evidently imitations in stone of long-used architectural elements. Some were to be eliminated in later construction, but two of the most effective types of Egyptian columnar support are already represented here: the papyrus and the channelled column. Perhaps there is a first step towards a third type, if the bundles of stems used in the columns of the entrance hall are not reeds, as was at first thought, but palm branches with a stylized representation of their leaves at the top. The later

44. Saqqara, entrance hall of Zoser group. Dynasty III. Reconstruction

The front of the original structure copied in the South Building [41, 42] was apparently open, except that between the columns ran a low screen wall made of plant-stalks with their tops tied in a fashion that has been stylized into the *kheker* pattern. This became a popular border for the top of a wall. In the original prototype structure the other three walls and the roof were probably made of matting lashed to a framework [42B]. The outline of this is clearly marked on the façade, with the curved front roofing-piece supported by the four columns. Part of the matting of the side-walls has been brought round the corner to form the panels at each end of the façade. Probably the rounded posts at the corners represent the tall poles in front of the Upper Egyptian sanctuary.[14]

The fine low reliefs at the back of the limestone false-doors in the underground galleries of the Step Pyramid precinct [37] have reached a high degree of technical accomplishment equalled only by the wooden panels from the contemporary brick mastaba of Hesy-ra at Saqqara. Zoser's reliefs associate the king with the shrines of the gods of Upper and Lower Egypt and seem to repeat the same idea expressed by the dummy chapels constructed around the Heb-Sed court.[15] No need seems to have been felt for representation in relief above ground in the temple itself, probably because the buildings were already simulated in more naturalistic fashion, while the king, perhaps his family, and probably the gods themselves were present in the form of statues, judging from the fragments of such sculpture which have been found. Such a

45. Saqqara, Zoser group, column capital. Dynasty III

palm column, although having a plain shaft, still retains a binding at the top where the leaves spread to form a capital. These bundle columns in the entrance hall [44] are very tall and slender. They are engaged at the end of short masonry walls evidently introduced to lend them support.[12] In the reconstruction of the entrance hall [44] can be seen the wooden roofing logs copied in stone, as were the wooden architraves and the double doors, carved as though flung open against the wall at the entrance gateway. The engaged papyrus columns [40] are probably also copied from a wooden form. Their shafts have the characteristic triangular section of the plant stem. The channelled columns would also seem to represent a wooden form intermediary between some use of reeds plastered with mud and the stone copy. The capitals of the tall, slender version of these fluted columns, used on the façades of the North and South Buildings and the shrines in the Heb-Sed court, have pendant leaf-like projections at the top [45]. The round holes beneath the bosses of these 'capitals' may have served for the attachment of a bracket to support a cult image, as in the early standards of gods, or, in the South Building, for the curved projecting elements which appear in representations of the Upper Egyptian sanctuary.[13] The fluted columns are employed again in the pavilion adjoining the Heb-Sed court, where they are still very tall, and in the funerary temple, where a shorter, sturdier form more nearly resembling the later type appears. These lack any ornamentation at the point where they support the impost block and are provided with round bases like the later examples.

46. Bearded deity from Saqqara (?). Dynasties III–IV(?). *Brooklyn Museum*

47 and 48. Wooden panels of Hesy-ra (details) from Saqqara. Dynasty III. *Cairo Museum*

statue is illustrated here [46], which, although it is not definitely associated with the Zoser complex, could very well have been used in this context.

The figures in the panels of the Step Pyramid are assuming the proportions with which we are familiar in the Old Kingdom. They have little of the pronounced slenderness to be found in the reliefs of the Third-Dynasty officials Hesy-ra [47, 48], Kha-baw-sokar [49, 50], and Akhet-aa. The hieroglyphs are large and boldly drawn, again with little suggestion of the thin, elongated shapes in the private reliefs. The relief is very low, with slight but telling modulations of

49 and 50. Offering niche of Kha-baw-sokar, with detail, from Saqqara. Dynasty III. *Cairo Museum*

the surface to suggest the bony structure and muscles [37]. There is no sharp accentuation of the cheek and collar-bones nor the marking of a deep furrow beside the mouth, as in other work of the period. Something of the heaviness of the seated statue of Zoser is suggested by the shape of the lips and nostril and the very slight modelling of the cheek. There is a family likeness to the head of Sa-nekht in his rock carving from the Wady Maghara in Cairo,[16] and a hint of the full faces of the royal family in Dynasty IV. Unfortunately all the rock carvings at the Wady Maghara in the Sinai Peninsula, whether of this period or later, are rather roughly worked and have the same heavy quality that we find in those of Sa-nekht, Neterkhet, and Sekhem-khet there, so that they are not as instructive from the point of view of style as one could wish.

When the royal sculptor was working in a limited space, as on the front of the statue base of Zoser,[17] his draughtsmanship becomes less expert and he produces tight, cramped, narrow hieroglyphs into which he attempts to crowd too much detail in the titles and name of Imhotep. The same is true of the drawing of the figures and hieroglyphs executed on a very small scale on the fragmentary reliefs of a small shrine discovered at Heliopolis and now in Turin. On one fragment, three royal ladies are so drawn beside the legs of a seated figure of Zoser.[18] One of them wears a full wig and a dress with shoulder-peaks resembling the costume of three queens related to Cheops in Dynasty IV at Giza.[19] The piece illustrated [51] represents the god Geb, with intricate archaic detail in the drawing of the wig, beard, and necklace, as well as the excessively slender hieroglyphs to be found in the

51. The god Geb. Relief fragment from the Zoser shrine at Heliopolis. Dynasty III. *Turin, Museo Egizio*

52. Saqqara, tomb of Hesy-ra. Dynasty III. Plan

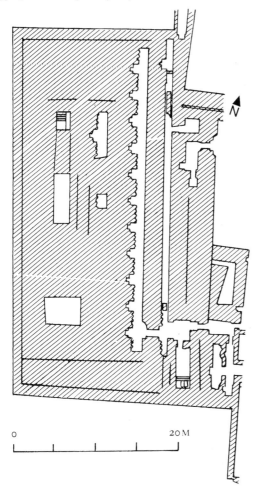

reliefs of Hesy-ra [47, 48], Khabaw-sokar [49, 50], and Akhet-aa. In fact the style is closer here to the earlier Gebelein temple reliefs (see Note 45, Chapter 3) than it is to the panels in the galleries of the group of the Step Pyramid. Since Geb appears with Shu and Seth in a row of seated gods which can be partly reconstructed,[20] it is possible that this is a representation of the nine gods, the Ennead of Heliopolis. Imhotep is called High Priest of Heliopolis on the base of the Zoser statue, and the cult of the sun god Ra, which was to be such a force in Dynasty V and in later Egyptian religious life, would appear to be established at Heliopolis in the form that is reflected by the spells of the Pyramid Texts.

The tomb of Hesy-ra at Saqqara is the private monument that best reflects the exuberant virtuosity displayed by the buildings of the Step Pyramid.[21] It is dated to the reign of Zoser by a jar-sealing with his name found in the burial-chamber. The long corridor chapel [52] had an elaborate 'Palace Façade' panelling forming the west wall along the face of the brick mastaba. This was brightly painted with variegated mat patterns, while the famous carved wooden panels were set in the backs of the doors of the deep niches. There is a close parallel between the way these are used and the Zoser limestone panels set in the false-doors of the simulated shrines with their matting walls imitated by blue tiles. The wooden reliefs of Hesy-ra show similarly accomplished carving and, like the Zoser reliefs, the establishment of the traditional Egyptian convention for drawing the human figure, a diagram of which is presented here [53]. The modelling is more sharply accentuated and the figures and hieroglyphs unusually slender. We should remember, however, in examining these panels in the Cairo Museum that the delicacy of their carving must originally have been somewhat obscured by the blaze of rather barbaric colour which surrounded them in the patterns of the painted hangings which seemed to be lashed to the intricately receding and projecting panelling. The same naturalistic impulse which caused the builder to imitate structures in stone at the Step Pyramid, or to cover a wall with blue tiles simulating matting, led the painter of the Hesy-ra tomb to draw carefully the grain of the wood on the doors at the back of the minor niches. He exerted the same painstaking care in representing the wooden furniture and other objects among the equipment painted as though set out under a mat shelter on poles along the eastern wall of the corridor. He took an equal interest in portraying the mottled surfaces of the various stone vessels, and, in a fragment of painting in the outer corridor, for the first time attempted to suggest by brush-strokes the hair on the legs of cattle. Here, where a crocodile lay in wait for the beasts fording a swamp, is the earliest appearance of one of those scenes from life which have added so much to our pleasure in examining Egyptian funerary reliefs and paintings.

The trend was now to be away from the use of painted brick panelling and towards the development of a cruciform chapel with stone-lined walls carved with reliefs like that in Firth's brick mastaba 3078 [66].[22] This was probably not built before the reign of Sneferu, judging by the bold, heavy reliefs. However, there are some transitional examples where stone elements are let into the brickwork. In the chapel of Akhetaa, which is earlier and probably of the reign of Huni, only the door-jambs and the lining of the niche have survived, and

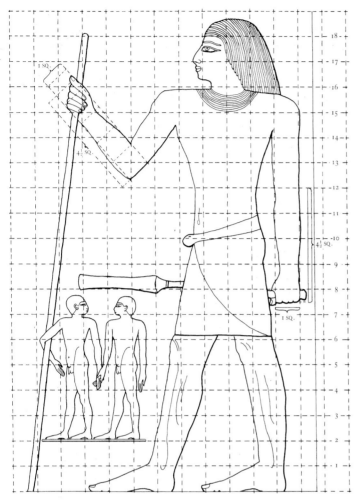

53. The Egyptian canon of eighteen fists from hair line to ground line

these were perhaps the only stone portions of a brick cruciform chapel.[23] The mastaba of Kha-baw-sokar had a long panelled corridor [54] like that of Hesy-ra, but from this opened a pair of cruciform chapels with panelling on the back wall. The deep central recess of each of these walls was lined with stone and carved with reliefs of the owner and his wife Hathor-nefer-hetep, and there still remained a stone lintel and drum over the entrance to each chapel.[24] This tomb could be as early as the middle of Dynasty III from its transitional form and the style of the reliefs on the two stone niches now in the Cairo Museum [49, 50].

54. Saqqara, chapel of Kha-baw-sokar. Dynasty III. Plan

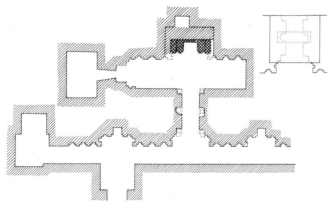

55. Redyzet. Head of seated statue. Dynasty III. *Turin, Museo Egizio*

56. Ankh-wa (Bezmes). Dynasty III. *London, British Museum*

57. Sepa (*centre and right*) and Neset. Dynasty III. *Paris, Louvre*

A half-dozen or so seated hard stone statuettes of private persons can be attributed to Dynasty III. They are characterized by a certain clumsy heaviness, and by the bent-wood supports carved in relief on the sides of the seat.[25] The latest of these – the small granite figure of Methen in Berlin – came from the statue chamber of his stone-lined cruciform chapel in a brick mastaba at Saqqara which is dated to the reign of the first king of Dynasty IV, Sneferu. The lower part of another statuette, belonging to Akhet-aa, also must have come from his tomb at Saqqara, which we have seen was probably constructed towards the end of Dynasty III. None of the others can be connected with known tombs, with the exception of two of the finest, the seated figures of Nezem-

ankh in Leiden and Paris. Nezem-ankh is probably to be identified with the man whose cylinder seal impression was found in a tomb at Beit Khallaf which also contained a sealing of Neterkhet (Zoser). This would certainly imply that these statues were made in the early part of Dynasty III, and suggests that the Beit Khallaf brick mastaba may have belonged to Nezemankh.[26] It may well be that the other two outstanding pieces of this group – the seated Princess Redyzet in Turin [55] and the metal-worker Ankh-wa (Bezmes) [56] in the British Museum – were also made fairly early in Dynasty III. Again we cannot be certain, but it is likely that the three near-life-size standing limestone figures of Sepa and his wife Neset in the Louvre [57] were made in the second half of

Dynasty III. The modelling is broadly treated in all these pieces, but the faces are excellently worked, in contrast to the summary execution of the hands and feet. The polished surfaces of the face of the Princess Redyzet [55] are contrasted with the rougher texture of the wig, and the eyes and eyebrows are carefully indicated. This is the largest of the seated figures, being nearly 3 feet (83 cm.) high, and is the masterpiece of the group. The princess must have been able to command the services of a good royal sculptor, and her face has something of the quality of that of the seated statue of Zoser. The sculptor, however, found the same difficulty in shaping the hieroglyphs in the hard, dark stone as did the makers of the other statuettes. Nor are the inscriptions of the limestone figures of Sepa and Neset better formed.

There were two identical large figures of Sepa and a slightly smaller one of his wife, Neset [57]. The wigs are unusually full and heavy, and there are traces of a stripe of green paint around the eyes, as in a few of the reliefs. The collarbones are strongly marked, as in the reliefs of Hesy-ra, but the most interesting archaic feature is the treatment of the staff and baton or wand held by the husband. These were carried by all men of position in the Old Kingdom, and are frequently represented in reliefs and in wooden statues, where they were cut from a separate piece without fear of breakage. Here they are held close to the body so that they can be carved in relief. This was evidently felt to be a clumsy compromise, and never appears again. Later statues have their hands hanging closed at their sides around two round objects which may stand symbolically for the staff and wand.[27]

The seated red granite figure of Ankh-wa [56] presents an unusual type, in that he holds an adze over his shoulder as a sign of his calling – apparently that of a metalworker, from the title inscribed on the lap of the figure. It is significant that most of the people whom we know in this period – Ankh-wa, Kha-baw-sokar, Hesy-ra, and Akhet-aa – hold titles which indicate that they were active, practical men connected with the crafts or with public works. Nezem-ankh, like Imhotep, bears hereditary titles of the old nobility, but none of these men is a prince. One gains the impression that in Dynasty III the process of centralization had not yet been completed, which resulted in Dynasty IV in the concentration of high offices within the circle of the king's family. Under Sneferu and Cheops the administration of public works was in the hands of the vizier, who was a close relative of the monarch. It may have been easier to rise in a profession through the king's favour in Dynasty III, when able men were particularly needed for the great building projects which were in an experimental stage of development.

CHAPTER 5

Dynasty IV 2680–2565 B.C.

The peculiar stepped structure at Medum now rises in three stages, although the lowest is hidden by the mounds of debris that have accumulated around its base [58, 59]. Originally it was constructed in eight steps, which were later filled in and cased as a true pyramid. Until recently this had all been considered the work of Sneferu. It now appears that he only finished a monument left incomplete by his predecessor Huni at the end of Dynasty III, giving it a form which had been established by the North Stone Pyramid at Dahshur, the first to be constructed throughout as a true pyramid. The South Pyramid at Dahshur, the so-called Bent Pyramid [60], had its angle changed to one which was less steeply inclined when the structure had reached a height not quite half that of the present one. It seems to be a transitional form between the stepped structure at Medum and the North Pyramid. Quarry-marks with the name of Sneferu on both pyramids at Dahshur make it clear that they were built by him. His two pyramids are mentioned in inscriptions which include a decree of Pepy I found among scanty vestiges of a valley temple on the edge of the cultivation in front of the northern pyramid.[1] If Sneferu completed Huni's monument at Medum, it would account for the mention of Sneferu in the later graffiti inscribed on the walls of the small stone temple built against its eastern face after the casing for the pyramid was in place. The dates roughly painted by the quarrymen or builders on the masonry of this casing and that of the North Stone Pyramid at Dahshur suggest that both monuments were being completed in the last years of the reign of Sneferu. Dahshur is near Saqqara; Medum further south.

We therefore have to take into consideration the possibility that the temple at Medum is a slightly later development in stone of the simple brick enclosure built as an offering-place in front of the Bent Pyramid at Dahshur.[2] In this stood a pair of large, free-standing, round-topped stelae inscribed with the king's name, and in front of them an altar covered by two low side walls and a roofing of stone. Later alterations to the brick court leave its original form uncertain [61, 62]. The rest of the space inside the enclosure wall around the pyramid has not yet been completely excavated. Another pair of inscribed round-topped stelae was set up in front of the small pyramid which lies to the south of the large one. They indicate that this was intended as a secondary tomb, a 'satellite' pyramid for his ka. Two similar stelae, also inscribed with Sneferu's name, stand outside the enclosure wall opposite the entrance to the lower temple [63], which is connected with the pyramid enclosure by an unroofed stone causeway with round-topped side walls. This temple is built of stone and, unlike the later valley temples, is not on the edge of the cultivation, but lies some distance up a sandy depression in the desert escarpment. It is not, therefore, strictly speaking a valley temple. It faces south and is entered by a long corridor which leads to a court [63, 64]. At the back of the court, two rows of large square pillars stand in front of a series of six niches which contained statues of the king flanked by reliefs. These figures of Sneferu are not free-standing but carved in one piece with the wall of the niche.[3] The sides of the pillars are decorated with figures of the king in association with various gods. The carving throughout is in the bold high relief which had been known from private work of this time in the two stone-cased niches of the brick mastaba of Prince Iy-nefer [65], east of the Bent Pyramid, in the deep stone-cased niches and cruciform chapels of Nefermaat and Rahotep at Medum, and the stone cruciform chapels of Methen and Tomb 3078 [66] at Saqqara. The superb effect produced by these big figures with their heavily rounded surfaces can best be visualized from the fragment with the lioness goddess (Sekhmet or Bastet) breathing life into the nostrils of the king [67]. The walls of the entrance corridor were lined with processions of female personifications of the king's estates bearing food offerings. Each group is headed by the Nome or province in which these properties lay [60, 68]. This is the first appearance of such figures, which served both as a record of the actual properties assigned for the maintenance of the funerary services at the tomb, and as a magical substitute which made this produce from the different parts of the country available to the king in his life after death. These fragmentary reliefs of Sneferu are the earliest decoration to survive from a funerary temple, and their importance will be realized if it is remembered that until recently it was not admitted that such reliefs had been in existence before the Fifth Dynasty.[4]

A few scattered tombs of members of the family of Sneferu have been partially cleared along the edge of the desert plateau, where the Twelfth-Dynasty kings Amenemhat II, Sesostris III, and Amenemhat III later built their brick pyramids. Farther to the west, overlooking the lower temple of the Bent Pyramid from the high-lying ground north of the valley which runs back between that pyramid and the northern one of Sneferu, can be seen three rows of mastabas.[5] These have never been examined, but evidently anticipate the regularly laid out family cemetery of Cheops at Giza with its streets and cross-streets. Something similar seems to have been attempted west of the Medum Pyramid, where only the substructures of the tombs have survived.[6] These tombs may never have been completed, and it was perhaps not until the reign of Sneferu that members of Huni's family and court, such as Nefermaat and Rahotep, were buried in the big brick mastabas which lie to the north of the pyramid.

The burial-chambers in the pyramids at Medum and Dahshur were covered by stone corbel vaults and reached by a long sloping passage opening in the north face of the pyramid. In each case the chamber was at a higher level than the passage or antechamber, evidently with the intention of confusing plunderers. At Medum and in the North Pyramid at Dahshur the interior rooms were constructed in, the masonry of the pyramid at ground level or a little above.

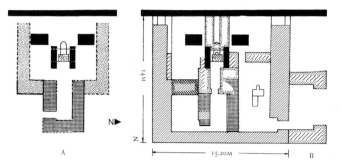

58. (*left*). Medum, causeway and pyramid. Dynasty III–IV

59. (*above*). Medum, view from pyramid over temple and causeway. Dynasty III–IV

60. (*below*). Dahshur, Lower Temple and Bent Pyramid. Dynasty IV

61. (*right, top*). Dahshur, offering-place before the Bent Pyramid. Dynasty IV. Plans. (A) Suggested original form; (B) with later additions

62. (*right, middle*). Dahshur, offering-place before the Bent Pyramid. Dynasty IV. Reconstruction

63 and 64. (*right, bottom*). Dahshur, Lower Temple of the Bent Pyramid. Dynasty IV. Reconstruction and plan

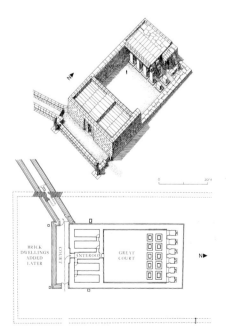

65. Offering niche of Iy-nefer from Dahshur. Dynasty IV. *Cairo Museum*

67. Dahshur, Lower Temple of the Bent Pyramid, Sneferu and goddess. Dynasty IV

However, there was a more complicated arrangement of apartments at the Bent Pyramid, where the lower chamber and its anteroom were built in a rock-cut pit with the floor of the main room lying at a level near the ceiling of its corbelled antechamber. This square lower chamber was covered by a high roof with corbelling on all four sides which is one of the most impressive architectural achievements of the Old Kingdom [69, 70]. It is rivalled only by the long ascending gallery in the Cheops Pyramid at Giza [92]. A similar corbel was attempted in an upper chamber of the pyramid, but this collapsed through some structural fault, leaving a ragged natural vault formed by the pressure of the masonry of the pyramid. The upper chamber was reached by a second sloping passage running down from the western face of the pyramid at a point about two-thirds of the way up before the

66. Saqqara, chapel of Tomb 3078. Dynasty III–IV

68. Dahshur, Lower Temple of the Bent Pyramid, personified estates. Dynasty IV

69. Dahshur, Bent Pyramid, corbel vaulting in lower chamber. Dynasty IV

70. Dahshur, Bent Pyramid, isometric view of interior passages, and portcullis. Dynasty IV

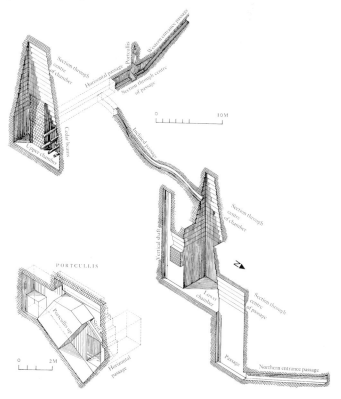

angle of inclination was changed. A horizontal east–west corridor led to the floor of the chamber at the level of the rock surface and a rough passage was cut northwards to open into the corbelling high up in the ceiling of the lower chamber [70].[7] The upper chamber was partly filled by a blocking of masonry set in and around a heavy framework of cedar logs. Beside and above this were packed rougher stones. Perhaps this was with the intention of strengthening the broken ceiling. The accident to the roofing evidently occurred during the course of construction and may have prompted the change in the angle of the pyramid, although this was undertaken at a point many feet above the chamber. The removal of the masonry in the upper chamber revealed no trace of a burial within the framework of posts and cross-timbering. These were remarkably well preserved, and would seem to be some of the coniferous wood which the Palermo Stone tells us that Sneferu brought by ship from Syria.

One suspects that Sneferu was buried in the later North Pyramid, where it seems to have been considered a safer expedient to adopt a more gradual slope, like that of the upper part of the Bent Pyramid, and a simpler disposition of the burial-chamber and its anterooms.

The small Medum temple[8] is a simple structure of two parallel rooms which open into an open court at the base of the pyramid in which were set up two uninscribed round-topped stelae [59]. An unroofed causeway flanked by masonry walls led up from a valley temple on the edge of the cultivation. The nearness to the surface of subsoil water has so far made excavation here impossible [58]. This building, which formed an entrance to the enclosed area of the pyramid, may not have been completed, and other structures may have been planned inside the walled upper precinct. The walls of the little offering temple had not been entirely smoothed, and the absence of inscriptions on the round-topped stelae is probably also due to the work being left uncompleted here. This may be the reason for the complete absence of the reliefs and paintings which are to be found in the offering-places of two of the brick mastabas in the adjoining cemetery.

A wide range of subject-matter is represented in the chapels of the large brick mastabas of Nefermaat and Rahotep at Medum. Two stone-lined niches served as the offering-places for the separate burials of Nefermaat and his wife, Atet [71]. They are deeper than those of Iy-nefer at Dahshur, with a very high passage leading to a false-door at the back. When the tomb was later enlarged, they were converted into cruciform chapels by a painted corridor leading through the brickwork of the addition to a room in front of the wide stone façade of each niche. A third addition to the mastaba blocked this corridor and another niche was added in the thickness of the brickwork [72]. Something similar to these curious alterations occurred also in the Rahotep mastaba, where additions blocked the entrance to Rahotep's stone-lined cruciform chapel and his wife's subsidiary deep niche. The chapel was used as a statue-chamber. In it were found the celebrated seated figures of Rahotep and Nofret [80].[9] In these chapels the tablet of the false-door now shows the owner seated at a table of bread, as on the early niche-stones [31, 32], and much space is devoted to the provision of food-offerings, including the personified estates which we have seen in Sneferu's temple. However, there is also a varied treatment of agricul-

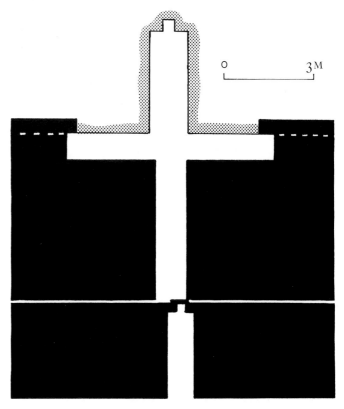

72. Medum, chapel of Atet. Dynasty IV

tural pursuits, hunting in the desert and swamp, boat-building, and even pictures of the children of the family playing with their pet animals [73]. Traces of such scenes from life had appeared already in the paintings of the outer corridor of Hesy-ra's chapel in Dynasty III, but they are infrequently preserved in Dynasty IV.

The larger expanses of wall in the early corridor chapels and in the long passages of Nefermaat and Rahotep were better suited for such scenes than were the more restricted wall-spaces of the cruciform chapel and the later L-shaped offering-room at Giza. This seems to be one reason why the

71. Medum, mastaba of Nefermaat and Atet. Dynasty IV

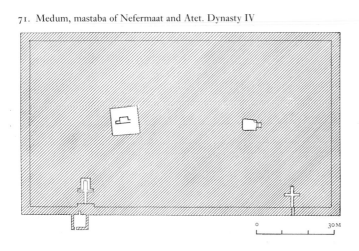

73. Medum, chapel of Atet, Atet's children with pets. Dynasty IV

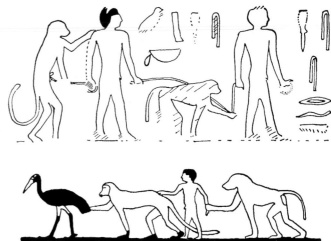

subject-matter in the decoration of these rooms is generally restricted to the essential requirements of the funerary cult and to the presentation of food and equipment in the presence of the owner and his family. At Medum, small groups of figures engaged in various activities appear to have been abstracted from larger scenes and adapted to the restricted area of the panels on the façade of the stone niches of the Nefermaat tomb or the narrow wall-surfaces of the cruciform chapel of Rahotep. It is particularly in the reliefs on the walls of the passage to Rahotep's chapel[10] and in the swamp scene which can be reconstructed[11] from the fragments of painting broken from the mud-plastered wall of Atet's brick corridor that we can form an idea of a large composition of the time with big, widely spaced figures placed in superimposed registers [77]. The famous panel of the geese in the Cairo Museum forms a sub-register to the group of Atet's sons who are shutting a trap for water-birds set out in the marshes. The artist has chosen an attractive way of bringing unity to the whole wall by the use of the flowering plants which grow between the feet of the geese and along the side of the pond. The boys have twisted these into wreaths for their heads, as have the men sowing and ploughing in the register below.

There seems no good reason why such scenes should have developed in a king's funerary temple, although one would expect the royal sculptors to implement the spread of new ideas. Such scenes from life do appear as an unexpected rarity in the pyramid temple of Weserkaf [121–2, 124] at the beginning of Dynasty V. One is tempted to associate their appearance there with the increasing influence of the cult of the sun god Ra. A short time afterwards the decoration of a room in the Sun Temple of King Ne-user-ra at Abu Gurob shows the spirits of the three seasons offering the fruits of the year's activities. These curious representations are found at the foot of the platform for an obelisk built of stone which reproduced in the royal necropolis the Ben-ben stone of the sanctuary of Ra at Heliopolis. Long before the Weserkaf reliefs were known it was suspected that the pursuits in field, swamp, and desert depicted in the private tombs might reflect these 'Seasons' scenes.[12] Such a picturing of human, animal, and plant life might well have originated as an expression of man's dependence upon the vital force of the sun in an earlier sanctuary of Ra. The Heliopolitan theological system appears to have been undergoing a particularly rich period of development in the reign of Zoser, when Hesy-ra's fragmentary painting gives us the first preserved example of such a representation.[13] The purpose of such scenes in the private tombs, as has generally been explained, was to aid the dead in the continuance of life as on earth, but they need not have originated for funerary purposes. Another possible source from which they could have been drawn has recently been suggested. If the brick palaces of the early dynastic kings were decorated with wall-paintings, this would account for the development of the technical skill displayed by the painting in Atet's corridor, but not entirely for the subject-matter of the tomb walls at Medum. The character of some of this material implies that it might have been taken from paintings in the houses of the people of the court who had imitated the royal custom.[14]

While the chapel of Rahotep and the niche of his wife Nofret are carved in bold relief in the style which we have seen in the Sneferu temple [67, 68] and the stone-lined niches of Iy-nefer at Dahshur [65], the craftsman attempted a new experiment in the Nefermaat tomb. He hollowed out the space within the outlines of his figures, somewhat in the fashion that the later sunk relief was worked. Ridges of stone were left to separate different parts of the figure and rough bosses to help hold in place the different-coloured pastes with which the depressions were filled. This difficult technique achieved a remarkable effect of varied colouring and detail, but was evidently not considered successful. It was used again only once, in the inscriptions on the base of the seated statue of Nefermaat's son Hemiunu [103] at Giza, but otherwise abandoned. The same technical skill was employed in the fine paintings in Atet's brick corridor. These appear at their best in the beautifully drawn hindquarters of the gazelle from the hunting scene and the hieroglyphs and marvellously painted geese of the swamp scene on the opposite wall [74–7].[15] In their beauty of line, harmonious combination of a wide colour range, and in the meticulous care with which the details are added, these paintings have seldom been surpassed in ancient times. The stippling and the rippled marks of the feathering were supplemented by fine brush-strokes to indicate the texture and gradations of colour in the plumage. They are applied also to the coats of the animals. Against the light grey background the pinkish desert ground was dotted with red, black, white, and green specks to indicate pebbles and tiny plants. Various shades of red, brown, and orange, a blue-grey, and an olive-green appear with the usual yellow, black, and white. A bright blue does not occur on any of the painted fragments, and it is missing from the Giza slab-stelae, three of which have preserved their painted surfaces [78, 79]. We have seen that it had appeared already in the mat patterns of Dynasty I and seems to be recorded from the painted reliefs of Rahotep. It certainly is to be found on the reliefs of one of the queen's pyramids and in the fragmentary chapel reliefs of the family of Cheops in the Eastern Cemetery at Giza. To be noted are the brush-strokes of grey-blue overlapping red on the wing of the vulture hieroglyph, the wash of yellow on the upper part of the body of the quail chick [76], and the blobs of red to suggest the flowers of the plants, under the feet of the geese. The bold simplicity with which the large figures and hieroglyphs have been composed is in keeping with the reliefs and sculpture of the period, as well as the patterns on the furniture of Sneferu's wife, Queen Hetep-heres [83–8]. In spite of the carefully executed detail, all traces of archaic fussiness have been eliminated.

The classic style of the Old Kingdom is equally apparent in the seated limestone statues of Rahotep and Nofret in the Cairo Museum [80], where the sculptor has perfected his idea of the completely painted tomb statue. The unusual preservation of the painted surfaces and the liveliness lent to the features by the inlaid crystal eyes make them one of his most appealing productions. It is easy to believe the astonishment and terror felt by the workman who first gazed on these faces by the light of a candle, after removing the last stone in the blocking of the passage to Rahotep's chamber.[16] The statues are unquestionably the first preserved work of the school of sculpture which produced the limestone Giza 'reserve' heads

74–7. Medum, chapel of Atet, paintings in the outer corridor, with restoration drawing. Dynasty IV. *Oxford, Ashmolean Museum, and Cairo Museum*

[105, 106] and the seated statue of Prince Hemiunu [103]. However, they belong to the reign of Sneferu rather than to that of Cheops. One of the reserve heads was found at Dahshur in a tomb belonging to a member of Sneferu's court,[17] and it now seems probable that the people buried at Medum are of Sneferu's generation and were related to Huni, the last king of Dynasty III.

The forms have been simplified, with a concentration upon the convincing portraiture of the heads. The large feet and thick ankles are a feature which was never too adequately handled by the Fourth-Dynasty sculptor, like the rather clumsily protruding ears. The skin of Rahotep is painted yellow-brown with less of a reddish cast than is conventionally employed, while that of the wife is the usual light yellow.

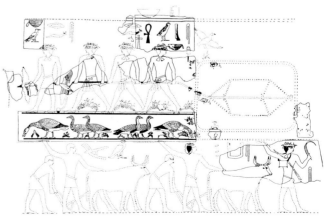

78 and 79. Slab-stela of Wepemnofret from Giza, with detail. Dynasty IV. *Berkeley, Museum of Anthropology, University of California*

80. Rahotep and Nofret from Medum. Dynasty IV. *Cairo Museum*

The figures are effectively framed by the white surface of the high backs of the seats, with their rectangles of black inscription giving the titles and names of the pair. The bright colours of Nofret's necklace are repeated in the flower designs on her head-band. These are made up of rosettes and a voluted form [90D], which appears to be a stylized adaptation of the sedge-like flower in the wreaths worn by Atet's sons [88B]. It is combined with a pair of buds in the rosettes on the Hetep-heres furniture [89C].

81. Granite head of a king. Dynasty III–IV. *Brooklyn Museum*

82. Cheops. Ivory statuette from Abydos. Dynasty IV. *Cairo Museum*

A sixteen-petalled rosette of yet another form is found with Min-emblems, and an overlapping feather pattern, like those in the Hetep-heres furniture designs, on the bracelet of one of the fragments of the statues of Sneferu carved in the shrines at the back of the court of his Valley Temple. It is not easy to judge the style of these pieces in their present condition. They were large[18] and excellently worked in the limestone. The faces of the two heads that have survived are less full and seem more conventionally treated than an impressive red granite head of a king, also wearing the white crown of Upper Egypt, in the Brooklyn Museum [81].[19] It is well over life-size ($21\frac{1}{4}$ inches, 54 cm) and bears a family resemblance to the head of the tiny ivory seated statuette of Cheops [82], which even on its small scale produces something of the same forceful impression. The little Cheops figure is the only comparable royal piece from Early Dynasty IV, since nothing but a few small fragments of this king's statues and statuettes were recovered at Giza. In the granite head the treatment of the eyes, showing the fold of skin of the upper eyelid, is like later royal work, as in the Louvre head of the Dynasty IV Radedef [114]. The facial type resembles that of Sneferu's rock-carving from the Wady Maghara in Sinai (now in Cairo), as well as other members of the royal family of Dynasty IV. One would like to assign the head to Sneferu, but unfortunately there is little to support this in the Dahshur pieces and we must remember that the heavy facial type was beginning to appear with Sa-nekht and Zoser. At any rate this is one of the rare masterpieces of the royal sculptor at the end of Dynasty III or the beginning of Dynasty IV.

Before turning to the great cemetery which Cheops laid out at Giza and where the equipment of his mother, Hetep-heres, was buried in about the fifteenth year of this second reign of the Dynasty, we must take some account of this remarkable furniture. Some of the pieces from her palace, like the bed-canopy [83] and its curtain-box, were presented to her by her husband, Sneferu. She is called Mother of the King of Upper and Lower Egypt on the carrying-chair [84], the gold-covered box containing her silver bracelets, and the elaborately inlaid lid of a chest [88], which must have been made for her by Cheops after his father's death. These pieces present the same clean-lined simplicity and large-scale design as the architecture, sculpture, and painting of Dynasty IV, combined with a richness of ornament inherited from Dynasty III. Hetep-heres was evidently the daughter of the shadowy King Huni and by her marriage to Sneferu became the ancestress of the royal family of Dynasty IV and one of the greatest ladies of the Old Kingdom. She lived at a time when her husband and son had achieved a measure of absolute power seldom to be equalled and still physically evident in the great masses of the pyramids at Dahshur and Giza.

Due to George A. Reisner's expert handling of the archaeological problems, it is now possible to visualize the original appearance of this bewildering deposit in which much of the woodwork had decayed to the consistency of cigar-ash between layers of gold furniture casings and inlaid designs.[20] The gold-cased parts of the dismantled bed canopy and the inlaid box for its curtains had been placed on top of the alabaster sarcophagus [83, 84]. Two arm-chairs stood near the entrance from the shaft. Beside the coffin was a chest having an inlaid lid and filled with various objects, including

83. Furniture of Hetep-heres from Giza. Dynasty IV. *Cairo Museum*

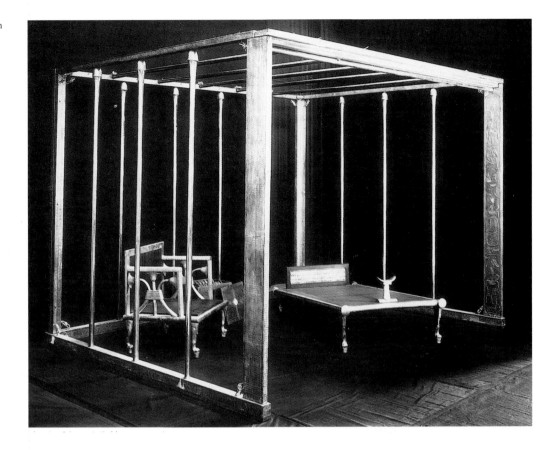

a box containing silver bracelets. Beside this a carrying-chair, with heavy gold palm capitals forming the pole ends, rested on a bed which lay upside down. Against these leaned a cylindrical leather holder for walking-sticks, while the debris

of a reed basket lay on the floor. Most of these pieces could be reconstructed on new wooden frames, as in the case of the arm-chair with the open-work papyrus design on the arms, the gold-covered bracelet box, and the bed which had an

84. Back of Hetep-heres carrying-chair from Giza. Dynasty IV. *Cairo Museum*

85. Giza, reconstruction of original position of furniture in the tomb of Hetep-heres

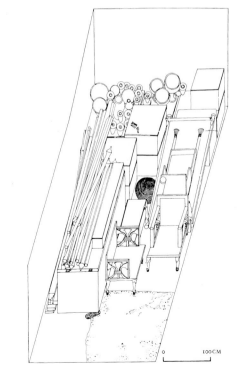

86. Detail of the gold casing of Hetep-heres bed canopy from Giza. Dynasty IV. *Cairo Museum*

inlaid foot-board and a silver covered head-rest. These all appear under the bed canopy [83]. The canopy is an actual example of one of the light tent structures with characteristic poles such as are frequently pictured and had evidently continued in use since early times. Often these were hung with mats, but here light curtains probably ensured privacy and protection against insects. Mat panels run down the backs of the door-frame and mat patterns are tooled in the gold covering of the corner posts and floor- and roof-beams, as they are frequently used on the frames of the other pieces of furniture and as covering for the sides of the boxes. The inner faces of the door-frames have the titulary of Sneferu in large hieroglyphs wonderfully worked in the gold [86]. The architrave is formed of an L-shaped piece of wood with a slender horizontal pole below, typical of the scheme of the heavier 'drum' and architrave set over Old Kingdom doors and suggesting that this 'drum' frequently imitates the first log of the roofing and not always the rolled-up mat copied in tiles over the Zoser niches [43]. One of the mat-patterned gold frames can be seen on the back of the carrying-chair [84], where exquisitely worked hieroglyphs of solid gold were set into ebony strips to form the name and titles of the queen.

The designs of the coloured faience inlays [87–9] employ elements of feather pattern obviously drawn from the wings of the Horus falcons which are perched on palm columns under the arms of the second arm-chair. The feather patterns alternate with flower rosettes to frame the crossed arrows and shields of the standards of the goddess Neith of Sais on the two faces of the chair-back. On the inner face these standards were of coloured inlays set in a gold sheet, but on the other side they were of plaster covered with gold leaf and set in a

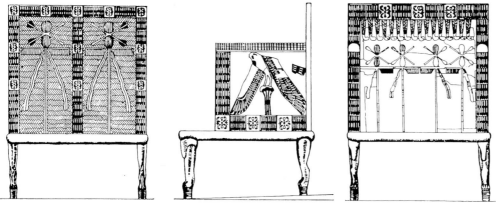

87. Restoration of Hetep-heres carrying-chair from Giza. Dynasty IV

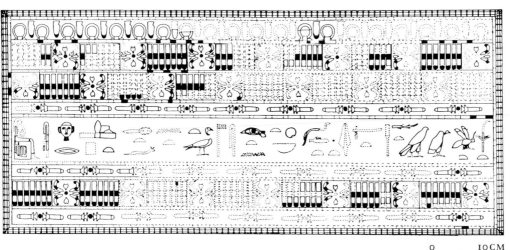

88. Restored lid of Hetep-heres chest from Giza. Dynasty IV. *Cairo Museum*

0   10 CM

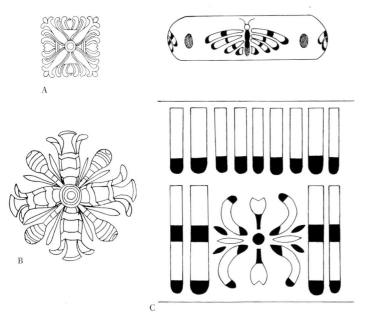

89. Old Kingdom decorative patterns. (A) Sahura rosette, Abusir; (B) G 2416 rosette, Giza; (C) Hetep-heres bracelet and footboard of bed, Giza

mat design of criss-cross blue faience inlays. The brilliant effect of this incrustation was repeated on the lid of the chest. The inlays were set in silver sheeting and included, in addition to the feather pattern and rosettes, a band at the top of protective *šn*-rings alternating with the distinctive marking under the 'Horus-eye' which appears on the falcons of the arm-chair. In view of this use of elements taken from the falcon, it is possible that the emblem repeated in the borders framing the inscription on this lid, and again on one of the walking-sticks, does not stand as usual for Min, the fertility god of Coptos, but for Letopolis, as used in the epithet of the Horus of Letopolis, Khenty-khem.[21]

The butterfly design [89C] of turquoise, lapis-lazuli, and carnelian inlays set in the silver bracelets does not seem to have been used again. The flower rosette, however, was to be considerably enriched in the Old Kingdom and provided a basis for the voluted plant ornaments that appear in new forms in the Middle Kingdom. The sedge-like flower in these rosettes appears in its most natural-looking form growing beside the pond in Atet's painting at Medum [90A], but similar plants are to be found in the hunting scene of the pyramid temple of Sahura in Dynasty V [90E]. The form was stylized into the symbol for Upper Egypt, but still retains a close resemblance to the growing plants in the hieroglyph on the Giza slab-stela of Wepemnofret [90C, 78]. Once, when this Southern Plant is joined to the papyrus of Lower Egypt on the side of the throne of a Chephren statue, it is given a base with a voluted form [90F] like that which later appears at the top of the stem and which has often been called a lily. This must have been one of the sources of the so-called palmette which begins to appear in the Middle Kingdom and is elaborated in the Eighteenth Dynasty. The palm actually replaces the Southern Plant on another of the thrones of Chephren

statues, and there is thus an early association of two plants with curving side elements [90G]. Volutes which turn inward towards a bud, as in the Hetep-heres design [89C], are to be found in the more complicated flower rosettes of the Fifth Dynasty. Here they are the side-pieces of bound papyrus elements which have a form like the *Atef*-crown associated with Osiris. They are painted green with blue bands on the disks from a head-band of a Dynasty V burial from Giza (G 2416 D III) [89B] and are found again in the rosettes on the base of a shrine in the Sahura reliefs [89A].[22] It is only a short step from the pairs of volutes opposite one another in these rosettes to the figure-8 design which appears in the Middle Kingdom among the spiral patterns [206].

The gold ends of the poles of Hetep-heres's carrying-chair have the form of the palm capital known from the large granite columns in the court of the Abusir pyramid temple of Sahura, the second king of Dynasty V. It would seem that such columns, at least of wood, were being used early in Dynasty IV. There were bases for round wooden columns in the outer brick chapel of Prince Ankh-haf in the Eastern Cemetery at Giza.[23] Part of a granite column inscribed with the king's name was found in the pyramid temple of Radedef, the son and successor of Cheops, at Abu Roash north Giza. This certainly suggests that hard stone columns, like those of Sahura, were already being employed in Dynasty IV.[24] There was also evidence for two polygonal limestone columns in a room of the exterior chapel of one of the sons of Cheops at Giza (G 7310–20). These were not fluted, as in the Zoser Temple, but again would indicate that other forms of support were being used in Dynasty IV in addition to the rectangular pillars and piers which alone appear in the royal temples at Giza.

These examples should be taken into consideration so that we do not over-stress the unrelieved plainness of Fourth-Dynasty architecture, which can be judged now only from the funerary monuments. Among these the Chephren Valley Temple produces a lasting impression because of the unusually fine preservation of its granite walls and pillars [97, 98].[25]

90. Plant forms. (A) and (B) Atet painting, Medum; (C) Wepemnofret hieroglyph, Giza; (D) Nofret crown, Medum; (E) Sahura hunting scene, Abusir; (F) and (G) Chephren statues

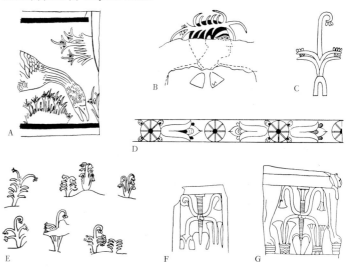

91. Giza, Pyramid of Mycerinus with Queen's Pyramid (left), looking west.
Dynasty IV

The very little which has survived in the Old Kingdom of buildings of a non-funerary nature and the abbreviated tomb-pictures of light structures tell us little more than that houses, public buildings, and even temples continued to be constructed of brick and wood with some stone fittings such as door-frames and pillars.[26] Certainly the chief characteristic of the Giza monuments was the employment of large simple masses as in the smooth, cased surfaces of the pyramids themselves [91] or the large flat-topped rectangular stone mastabas which Cheops laid out in regular rows in the family cemeteries which he planned on the west and east of his Great Pyramid [96]. This was the largest of all pyramids, although the slightly smaller one of his son Chephren stands on higher ground and appears equally immense. The First Pyramid is at present 450 feet high (137 m), but must have risen some 30 feet (9 m) more when complete with its fine limestone casing and capping stone. The granite burial-chamber with its plain hard-stone sarcophagus lies at an unusual height, above the so-called 'Queen's Chamber', which has a pointed roof of massive limestone slabs. The high corbelled ascending gallery [92] connects the two levels of these chambers, which were constructed in the stonework of the pyramid and belong to different stages in the enlargement of a structure planned originally with a burial-chamber cut deep in the rock at the foot of a long passage descending from the north face of the pyramid.[27] The unadorned simplicity of these interior apartments of the Cheops Pyramid is echoed in the plain surfaces of the granite casing of the massive limestone core walls and the granite pillars of the Chephren Valley Temple [98]. The skill shown in the handling of huge blocks of stone and the accuracy with which they are joined command as much respect as the huge scale of the construction and are characteristic of all Fourth-Dynasty work at Giza.

Contrary to former belief, it has become apparent in recent years that the walls of the royal temples at Giza did not all present unrelieved surfaces of plain granite, like the interior of the Valley Temple of Chephren. The clearance of the badly destroyed Cheops Temple at the base of the eastern face of his pyramid has made it possible to reconstruct its plan and general appearance [93, 94].[28] It consisted largely of a great basalt-paved court with limestone walls. This was surrounded by a roofed portico, supported by granite pillars, which was evidently introduced to protect the wall decorations. Fragments of these limestone reliefs show the superlatively fine, low carving to be found only in royal work of Dynasty IV and early Dynasty V, as in the chapel of the middle pyramid of the three belonging to Cheops' queens (G 1b; [93]),[29] the Giza slab-stelae [78], and a few chapels of important people, such as the Vizier Hemiunu and Prince Ankh-haf. This beautifully worked low relief is found again on a quantity of Old Kingdom blocks which were re-used in the Twelfth-Dynasty pyramid of Amenemhat I at Lisht.[30]

92. Giza, Great Pyramid, gallery. Dynasty IV

93. Giza, area east of the Cheops
Pyramid. Dynasty IV. Plan

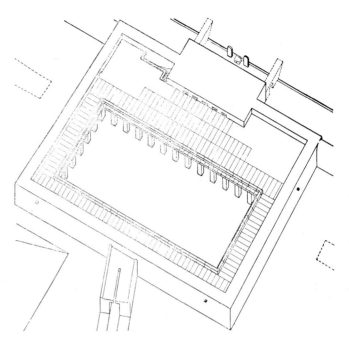

94. Giza, Cheops Temple. Dynasty IV. Reconstruction

Some of these, like the personification of one of the royal estates [95], bear the name of Cheops and may actually have come from this court in his temple at Giza.

The back of the court had three rows of granite pillars, diminishing in number to form a kind of porch leading to a chamber which may have contained a series of statue niches such as are found in the Chephren Temple [99] and later in the Old Kingdom. Few traces of the construction remain here, but, as in the temples of Chephren and Mycerinus, a corridor led from a corner of the court to the open space inside the round-topped wall which enclosed the pyramid. It would appear that there was not yet a roofed sanctuary

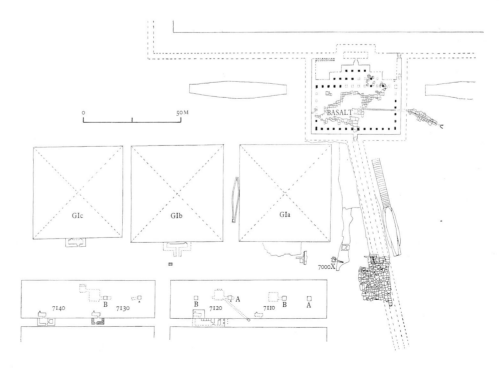

95. Personified estate. Cheops relief from Lisht. Dynasty IV. *New York, Metropolitan Museum of Art*

with the exception of the colonnaded court of Sahura, which was again walled off from a surrounding corridor. Chephren's court, unlike that of Cheops, which was approached directly by an entrance from the causeway corridor, had a system of entrance halls resembling the plan of his Valley Temple [99]. This was simplified to a single deep hall in the pyramid temple of his successor, Mycerinus. This temple of the Third Pyramid was under construction at the time of the king's death, and his successor, Shepseskaf, finished some parts of it in mud brick and also constructed the valley temple of the same material. The pyramid temple was planned with only one large statue niche behind a portico like that of Cheops at the back of the court. This may have been intended for the colossal seated alabaster figure of Mycerinus now in Boston. Somewhat in the same way a huge seated granite statue of Weserkaf, the first king of Dynasty V, was placed against one wall of his court, although in this case the colonnade was omitted on this side and the statue was not in a shrine.

Cheops constructed small pyramids for his three queens to the south-east of his pyramid temple. The tomb furniture of his mother, Queen Hetep-heres I, had been buried in a secret shaft without any superstructure and hidden under the pavement of the street between the northern queen's pyramid and the great twin-mastaba of the Crown Prince Kawab and his wife, Hetep-heres II. These structures appear in illustration 91 and the general plan of Giza [96], which show also the great cuttings in the rock for the king's three funerary barks and a smaller one south of his chief queen's pyramid. Another boat-grave has been discovered beside the second (middle) queen's pyramid since these plans were made, as have other rock-cut emplacements for funerary ships around

containing an inscribed stela in the form of a false-door such as is found in the offering-room of the private chapels of this time and in the royal temples of Dynasty V. This door provided a magical means of access for the owner to and from the tomb and the place at which he received the regular offerings of the funerary priests. This important part of the funerary ritual seems to have been performed for the king in the open space at the foot of the pyramid, perhaps before two round-topped stelae like those at Medum and Dahshur (as restored by Ricke [94]).[31]

In the court of the pyramid temple of Chephren the pillars were replaced by wide granite piers, or walls, between which there were regularly spaced openings to a corridor which ran all round the court. The openings were flanked by vertical lines of inscription giving the king's titulary, like those framing the entrances on the façade of Chephren's Valley Temple. The big hieroglyphs provide one of the earliest examples of the use of sunk relief. Instead of the large standing statues which were first restored upon the evidence of the emplacements for their bases, it is now thought that seated figures of Chephren were placed against the piers between the openings leading from the court. It has also been suggested that the outer walls of the corridor were decorated with limestone reliefs above a granite dado.[32] The later Old Kingdom temples reverted to a type of court with pillars or columns,

96. Giza, general plan

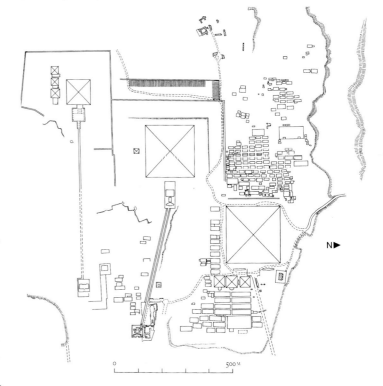

N▶

0   500 M

97 and 98. Giza, Chephren Valley Temple, exterior with Sphinx and interior. Dynasty IV

the Chephren pyramid temple, and south of the Cheops Pyramid. In the last case the remarkably preserved wooden parts of the actual vessel were found sealed in by the intact roofing-blocks.[33] The Giza pyramids were approached, as at Dahshur and Medum, by long causeways from their valley temples lying at the edge of the cultivation [96]. The valley temple of Cheops is buried under the present village, while the plan of the granite-faced Chephren temple [97–9] differs from the one which Shepseskaf built in mud brick to complete the Mycerinus group. The Mycerinus temple continued to be used into the Sixth Dynasty. In Dynasty V it was connected with the group of buildings which were constructed in front of the great mass of rock which Queen Khent-kaw-s turned into a sarcophagus-shaped tomb like that which Shepseskaf had built at South Saqqara towards the end of Dynasty IV [100].

Queen Khent-kaw-s formed the connexion between Dynasties IV and V. She seems to have been a daughter of Mycerinus who married Weserkaf and became the mother of both the second and third kings of Dynasty V, Sahura and Neferirkara. A block of houses belonging to her funerary priests is all that has survived of the straggling town which, since the time of Cheops, had gradually extended southwards along the foot of the desert plateau during the construction

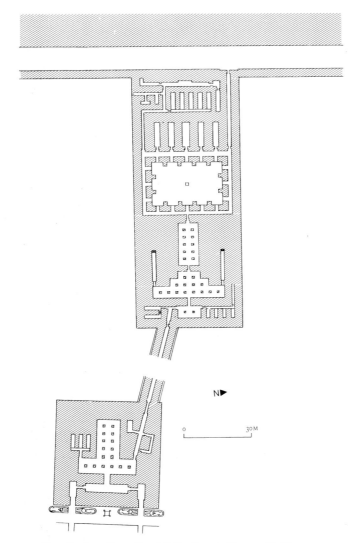

99. Giza, Chephren Pyramid and Valley Temple. Dynasty IV. Plan

of the successive pyramids. It contained the mortuary work-shops as well as the dwellings of the officials in charge of the building operations and the administration of the cemetery and its funerary services. These various buildings grew up in the neighbourhood of each successive valley temple, which originally consisted of a landing-place reached over the waters of the inundation or by canal when the flood had abated. Here the barges brought the fine limestone from the Tura quarries across the river, and granite from Aswan at the First Cataract, to be dragged up the causeway to the plateau. Later, when the covered causeway corridor and the valley temple had been completed, there was a system of

100. Saqqara, funerary monument of Shepseskaf. Dynasty IV. Reconstruction

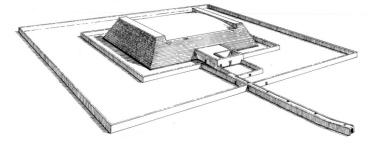

terraces and ramps in front of them, such as is partly preserved at the Chephren Valley Temple[34] and in examples of Dynasties V and VI. These would have facilitated approach to the temple by boat.

None of the successors of Cheops evidently commanded the means to lay out such a large, regularly planned cemetery as is to be found around his pyramid. It appears in the view [91] which looks south-westwards across the Great Pyramid of Cheops, the Second Pyramid of Chephren, and the Third Pyramid of Mycerinus (see also the general plan of Giza [96]). To the west of his pyramid Cheops constructed the cores of sixty-four stone mastabas for the older members of his family and court, including that of the vizier Hemiunu (G 4000), who, as Overseer of All the King's Works, must have been in charge of much of this construction as well as that of the pyramid. East of the pyramid were built eight enormous twin-mastabas for the king's favourite children, in front of the small pyramids of his three queens. This Eastern Cemetery was later increased by the very large tomb of Prince Ankh-haf (G 7150) and several others, while some of the cores in the Western Cemetery were completed in later reigns. The family of Chephren and Mycerinus were mostly buried in less expensive rock-cut tombs in the old quarry faces around the Second and Third Pyramids. As the reign of Cheops progressed, the simpler tombs in the Western Cemetery, which were planned with an exterior brick chapel around a tablet or slab-stela [78] set in the stepped face of the mastaba, were reconstructed with stone offering-rooms. These imitated the interior L-shaped chapel, constructed inside the core of the mastaba, which was first used in the large tombs of the princes east of the Great Pyramid. These chapels also had exterior stone rooms in the street. The brick offering-rooms in the Western Cemetery were covered with barrel-vaults, which had come into use in Dynasty III along with the round arch.[35] Brick-vaulted chapels continued to be used in the less expensive tombs at Giza in Dynasties V and VI, and there is at least one example of a small brick dome, in the chapel of the dwarf Seneb, where the transition from the square plan to the round vault is made by a few bricks plastered with mud in a very simple, small version of the later pendentive.[36]

In a number of cases the stone additions to the mastabas in the Western Cemetery, as well as work on the tombs of the princes east of the Great Pyramid, were left unfinished at the end of the twenty-three-year reign of Cheops and the acces-sion to the throne of Radedef, his son by a secondary queen. Radedef went several miles to the north of Giza to build his own pyramid at Abu Roash, and there are hints of family strife which troubled the rest of the Dynasty.[37] Radedef's succession seems to have been due to the death of the Crown Prince Ka-wab, whose wife, Hetep-heres II, became a queen of Radedef. This grand-daughter of the first Hetep-heres survived both her husbands as well as her daughter by Ka-wab, Queen Meresankh III. She married this daughter to Chephren, and at the end of the Dynasty prepared for her a splendidly decorated rock-cut tomb [101, 102]. From the pictures of the family and the inscriptions in this tomb we can gain some notion of this remarkable woman's career and of the struggle for power between the children of the queens of Cheops.[38]

101. Giza, chapel of Meresankh III.
Dynasty IV

102. Giza, chapel of Meresankh III:
Ka-wab, Meresankh and
Hetep-heres II, and personified
estates. Dynasty IV

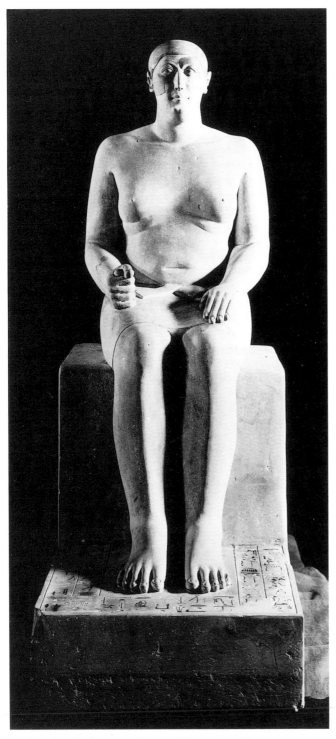

103. Hemiunu. Seated statue from Giza. Dynasty IV *Hildesheim, Pelizaeus Museum*

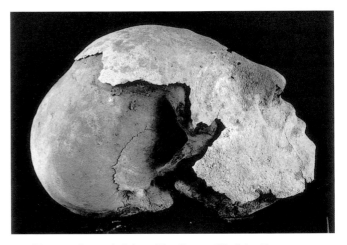

104. Plaster mask on a skull from Giza. Dynasty IV. *Cairo Museum*

plastic and detailed modelling. The two types of modelling are found side by side in the reign of Chephren and in the statues from the Mycerinus temple. Characteristic examples of the earlier school are the statues of Rahotep and Nofret from Medum and, in the reign of Cheops, the seated figure of his vizier, Hemiunu, found in one of the largest of the mastabas of the Western Cemetery at Giza and now in Hildesheim [103]. The inlaid eyes were wrenched out in antiquity, and this portion of the face has been somewhat restored. The aquiline nose and the shape of the mouth and strongly marked chin are repeated in a relief portrait from his chapel.[39] The folds of flesh on the torso also present in striking fashion the personal characteristics of the man, while the modelling of the hands and finger-nails is amazingly life-like, even though this effect is obtained by the simplest means with broadly rendered planes. This imperious-looking man appears fully capable of handling the problems of administration and construction for which he was responsible.

An equally effective portrayal of individual characteristics, with the same rigorous elimination of minor details, is to be found in the white limestone heads from Giza. These are peculiar in that they did not form part of a statue, but were complete in themselves. Instead of being placed in the chapel or in a closed statue chamber, as were other Old Kingdom statues, they were deposited in the burial-chamber. The intention seems to have been to provide a more permanent substitute in case of damage to the head of the mummy, which was wrapped in linen to simulate the form of the dead person. Evidently the idea of the 'reserve head' was connected with this attempt to give the wrapped body a natural outward appearance. This was carried to the extent of painting the linen and imitating the dress, with the addition of such ornaments as head-bands. The desire to strengthen the fragile wrappings led to the use of a coating of plaster which has survived on some of the burials of Dynasties V and VI, where the faces were carefully modelled over the linen covering of the head [104].[40] These plaster coverings evidently formed a basis for the cartonnage anthropoid cases which were developed in the First Intermediate Period.

One of the most fascinating of the limestone heads, which evokes a definite personality in spite of its broken nose, is that of the Princess Merytyetes [105]. The head of Prince

It has been thought possible to recognize the characteristics of two schools of sculpture in the round in Dynasty IV, which developed in the royal workshops connected with the cemeteries at Medum, Dahshur, and Giza. Both schools strive for naturalistic effect with equal technical competence, but the work of the earlier of the two presents a more severe appearance with a simplified rendering of the surfaces. The later group of sculptors began, at least as early as the reign of Radedef, to produce in certain of their pieces a softer, more

105. Merytyetes. Reserve head from Giza. Dynasty IV. *Cairo Museum*

106. Sneferu-seneb. Reserve head from Giza. Dynasty IV. *Cairo Museum*

Sneferu-seneb [106] presents a leaner, bonier type of face than those of Hemiunu and Merytyetes. These heads, like the slab-stelae, probably represent the special favour of the king and are found particularly in the early tombs of the western field, although they continue sporadically into Dynasty V. Their style is closely reflected in the large figures in the reliefs of the chapel of Prince Khufu-khaf [107, 108]. Here there is not so much a question of suggesting the individuality of the owner, which was more difficult to do in relief, given the conventions employed for drawing a head in profile, but rather of portraying the Old Kingdom ideal of the good-looking young man or woman. Khufu-khaf is indeed shown as a portly man of an advanced age on the façade of the chapel, as is Prince Ka-wab in the tomb of his daughter, Queen Meresankh III [102]. In rare instances the relief sculptor noted individual peculiarities, as in the face of Hemiunu mentioned above or the remarkable head of a man called Itwesh (or Semenkhu-Ptah) at the end of Dynasty V [132].[41] The Khufu-khaf reliefs are still in place in the only chapel which has survived nearly intact from the end of the reign of Cheops in one of the large tombs in the Eastern Cemetery (G 7140 [93] in front of the southernmost of the three queen's pyramids, and south of the twin-mastaba of Prince Kawab, G 7110–7120).[42]

While the Khufu-khaf figures represent the relatively high relief which was a refinement of the bold style of the reign of Sneferu, the slab-stelae of the older members of the family and court in the Western Cheops Cemetery are carved in the very low relief employed in the royal temples and in a few

badly preserved chapels like those of Hemiunu and Ankh-haf. The slab-stelae of the Princess Nefert-yabet in the Louvre, Prince Iwnw in Hildesheim, and Wepemnofret at Berkeley, California, still preserve some of their colour.[43] Like the Atet paintings and the painted reliefs in the rock-cut chapel of Meresankh III at the end of the Dynasty, the Wepemnofret tablet [78] is an example of the finest skill of the Old Kingdom painter whose ability has been scarcely appreciated, since the loss of so much of the best coloured work through weathering has left us only fragmentary examples or the coarser products of the workshops. The precise detail of the fine cutting of the reliefs is supplemented in paint, as in the hairs on the brow of the lioness, while flat colour is broken by the mottling on the back of the frog [79] or the grey markings on one of the birds and the fish.[44]

The finest creations of the first school of sculpture are to be found among the hard stone royal statues of Chephren and Mycerinus. One of the seated diorite statues which stood against the granite walls of the Valley Temple of Chephren is justly famous [109]. Like the standing slate statues of Mycerinus and his queen from the Valley Temple of the Third Pyramid [110], it displays the ideal of god-like majesty. In the Chephren statue the falcon spreads its protecting wings around the royal headcloth. This expresses the same idea of the identity of the king with Horus which appears in the falcon perched on the top of the frame of the royal Horus Name. It is more literally stated in the Dynasty VI alabaster statuette of Pepy I [141], where the back of the king's throne is carved to represent such a *serekh* with the 'Palace Façade'

107. Giza, Khufu-khaf and wife. Dynasty IV

108. Giza, Khufu-khaf. Dynasty IV

109. Chephren. Seated statue from Giza. Dynasty IV. *Cairo Museum*

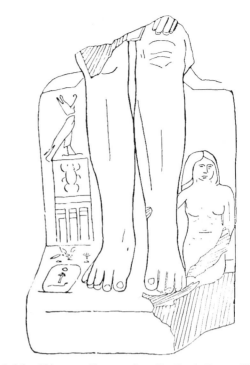

111. Radedef and his queen. Fragment from Abu Roash. Dynasty IV

110. Mycerinus and his queen. Standing statue from Giza. Dynasty IV. *Boston, Museum of Fine Arts*

The standing slate pair of Mycerinus and his queen in Boston [110] was not completely finished when the king died, and only the heads and part of the upper part of the bodies have received their final polish. The inscriptions on the base were left uncut, but traces of colour exist to show that the greenish slate was completely painted before being placed in the Valley Temple at the order of Shepseskaf. There is something infinitely appealing about the confident way in which this pair faces eternity, the wife placing her arm about her husband's waist. This royal example was to set the type for a large number of private statues of man and wife. Similarly a fragment from Abu Roash with Radedef's queen seated at his feet [111] introduced a form which was to prove popular, with a number of variations, in Dynasties V and VI. Both of these are examples of the new tendency to bring figures together into a well co-ordinated group, whereas, earlier, the statues of Rahotep and Nofret and those of Sepa and Neset had been made in separate pieces. The triads of Mycerinus are justly famous for the superb sculptural achievement they embody [112].

The contrast between the modelling of the two schools of Giza sculpture can best be felt by comparing one of the 'reserve heads' [106] with another piece of unusual form, the red-painted limestone bust of Prince Ankh-haf in Boston [113]. This lay on the floor of a room in the exterior brick chapel of the largest tomb in the Eastern Cemetery (G 7510). It gave the impression of having fallen forward from a low bench built against the wall, rather than that it had been dragged out of the empty statue-chamber of the stone interior chapel.[45] Ankh-haf may have been a half-brother of Cheops who became vizier under Chephren, in whose reign his tomb was built. More than a hint of the softer modelling which appears in the red bust is to be found earlier in the red quartzite head of Radedef in the Louvre [114], where a similar treatment is given to the area of the cheeks and mouth.

below the king's name, as in the Zet stela of Dynasty I, and the falcon standing free above. The falcon is thus placed rigidly at right angles to the seated king, in contrast to the Chephren statue, where the forms flow freely into one another. This would suggest that formalizing tendencies were gaining ground in the late Old Kingdom over the naturalistic impulses of the Fourth Dynasty.

112. Triad of Mycerinus with the goddess Hathor and the personification of a Nome, from Giza. Dynasty IV. *Cairo Museum*

This was the most complete piece of the badly smashed statuary in the brick temple of Radedef's terribly ruined and probably uncompleted pyramid at Abu Roash.

The sculptor of the Ankh-haf bust has observed the bony structure of the head under the skin and has modelled the brows, the pouches under the eyes, and the fold of the upper eyelid in a manner quite different from that of the 'reserve heads', which show none of this interest in detail. An even softer modelling of the flesh of the full face is to be found in the life-size alabaster head of Mycerinus from his valley temple in Cairo [115]. This closely resembles the carving of the larger head of the big seated figure in Boston which, as we have seen, was perhaps designed for the deep niche at the back of the court of the pyramid temple of Mycerinus.[46] The bony structure of the knees of this statue is worked out with the same interest in the minor planes and presents the same decided contrast to the simplified modelling of the Hemiunu statue.

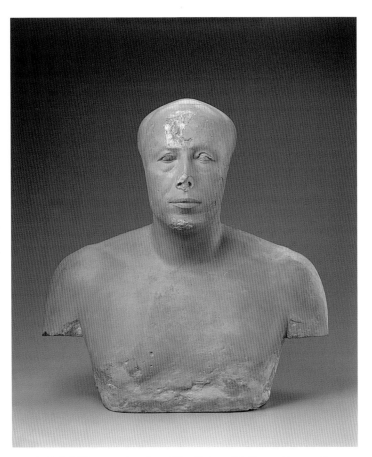

113. Ankh-haf. Limestone bust from Giza. Dynasty IV. *Boston, Museum of Fine Arts*

We have seen that the scenes in the interior chapels of the Dynasty IV mastabas at Giza were generally restricted to the presentation of offerings and the funerary meal, but there was evidently a representation of carpentry in Hemiunu's long corridor chapel (G 4000), and fishing and bird-trapping appeared in the interior chapel of Akhet-hetep and the Princess Merytyetes (G 7650), which is probably of the reign of Chephren. There were fragments of such swamp scenes from the exterior chapel of the Crown Prince Ka-wab (G 7110–7120) and those of Queen Meresankh II and Hor-baf (G 7410–7420).[47] However, these scenes were given a more developed treatment in the rock-cut tombs of the Chephren family. In the chapel of Queen Meresankh III they are preserved in a most attractive form, with the paint well preserved on the plaster-coated, rather roughly carved, coarse nummulitic limestone walls. The three rooms provided space for rock-cut statues as well as numerous relief figures of the queen, her family and household. This combination of statues and painted reliefs produces a brilliant effect in the large outermost room [101], where one can see between the pillars, standing against the wall of the northern room, the long row of figures of the queen and of her mother, Hetep-heres II, who prepared this tomb.[48] The openings originally could be closed by wooden doors.

There were also craft-work scenes on the walls, including pictures of furniture like that found in the tomb of Hetep-heres I. The steward, Khemetnu, had a little rock-cut statue of his own and appears in the reliefs administering the queen's estate and her funerary endowment. The estates

114. Radedef. Quartzite head from Abu Roash. Dynasty IV. *Paris, Louvre*

115. Mycerinus. Alabaster head from Giza. Dynasty IV. *Cairo Museum*

which provided the substance for this endowment are personified in the line of men and women bearing food offerings along the top of the east wall [102]. They were all properties of Cheops except one which the queen had inherited from her step-father, King Radedef. On this wall stands the portly figure of her father, Prince Ka-wab, and, behind him, Meresankh and Hetep-heres II are shown in a little skiff pulling papyrus flowers from a thicket which has been destroyed by rain-water that ran into the room from the slit window above. Partly hidden by the debris which had drifted in are other pictures of activities in the marshes and the fields. These are still given an abbreviated treatment such as we found at Medum, and are not yet spread out over the wall, as in the later Old Kingdom cycles which follow the agricultural work from the sowing of the grain to the storage of the harvest.

CHAPTER 6

Dynasty V 2565–2420 B.C.

If Weserkaf was the son of Radedef's daughter Nefer-hetep-s and married Khent-kaw-s, a descendant of the main line of kings, there would have been combined in this first reign of Dynasty V the two conflicting strains in the royal family of Dynasty IV.[1] Certainly Khent-kaw-s formed the connexion between Dynasties IV and V, as had Queen Ny-maat-hap, the mother of Zoser, at the end of Dynasty II, and Hetep-heres I, the mother of Cheops, at the beginning of Dynasty IV, although the factors governing these changes in dynasty are still far from clear. It is likely that Khent-kaw-s was the mother of both Sahura and Neferirkara, who succeeded Weserkaf in that order. Some hint of this in folk tradition is to be found in the legend of the Westcar Papyrus, which makes the first three kings of Dynasty V the offspring of the sun god Ra and the wife of a priest of one of his sanctuaries.[2] This story picturesquely stresses the dominant position of the priesthood of Heliopolis and the cult of Ra in Dynasty V, which is evident from the records of temple building and endowments and the introduction of Sun Temples into the Western Necropolis. The first of these was built by Weserkaf near Abusir, a little north of Saqqara.[3]

It is evident in many ways that the royal house had been weakened through family strife, the expenditure of the resources of the country upon tremendous building projects, and the breaking up of the king's lands by the assignment of estates for funerary purposes to an ever-widening circle of dependants. The viziership was no longer held by a close relative of the king. In fact, the great official posts were seldom occupied by princes in Dynasty V. The tight personal control of the state by the king must have been considerably relaxed. A few rock-cut tombs began to appear in the provinces, built by men who preferred to be buried in their own districts rather than near the court. While negligible in number they provide a first hint of the dangerous decentralization which was to take place in Dynasty VI, leading to the independence of the various provincial districts, particularly in Upper Egypt, at the end of the Old Kingdom and in the First Intermediate Period. The royal pyramids were planned on a smaller scale and were less solidly built. However, work on the great buildings at Giza had trained such a large body of able craftsmen that the decoration of the temples of these monuments of Dynasty V was carried out in a fashion hitherto unequalled.

Accidents of preservation have blurred our impression of the use of sculpture in the royal temples. The life-size greywacke head in Cairo [116] and the huge granite head of Weserkaf from his pyramid temple[4] testify that the taste for the colossal, which was spectacularly displayed in the Giza sphinx of Chephren, continued into the early part of Dynasty V. However, the large scale of the preceding period diminishes in sculpture, as in architecture, and the few other royal statues which have survived are smaller and less fine in quality. Some use was still made of statue groups like those from the valley temple of Mycerinus[5] in which the king was

accompanied by the personifications of the Nomes or provinces of the country. Only one Fifth-Dynasty example is at present known, with a seated figure of King Sahura and the Nome of Coptos.[6] It lacks the protective figure of the goddess Hathor who appears in the Mycerinus triads. Apart from the royal statues necessary for the ritual of the deified king in his mortuary temples, there is evidence for a wider use of sculpture in the beautifully executed animals employed as waterspouts or as some kind of architectural support and in the kneeling figures of bound captives.[7] More clearly recognizable as cult images are two seldom-mentioned Fourth-Dynasty examples of animal sculpture, the recumbent slate jackal representing the God of the Dead, Anubis, from the Mycerinus Valley Temple, in Boston,[8] and the forepart of a basalt ram inscribed with the name of Cheops, in Berlin.[9] The latter is not necessarily from a funerary temple, but, since the name of Cheops is sometimes hyphenated with the ram god Khnum (Khnum-Khufu), the protective powers of that god may have been particularly associated with the temples of the Great Pyramid, as were those of Hathor and Bastet with the valley temple of Chephren, or a special form of Hathor as Mistress of the Sycamore Tree with the valley temple of

116. Weserkaf. Greywacke had from Abusir. Dynasty V. *Cairo Museum*

Mycerinus. A cult of Sekhmet was in later times carried out in the pyramid temple of Sahura at Abusir and may have had its origin in the Old Kingdom.[10] Unfortunately the other statues of gods in the Old Kingdom have disappeared with their temples. That they were sometimes made of precious metal is shown by the mention of an electrum statue of Ihy, the son of Hathor, in the annals of Neferirkara on the Palermo Stone.[11]

In the same way that high administrative posts were now opened to a wider range of aspirants and no longer confined to the members of the king's immediate family, many more people were able to command the services of good craftsmen to build fine tombs and supply them with wall reliefs and statues. In the first years of the Fifth Dynasty the tradition of the large portrait statue was maintained and has left us such masterpieces as the Louvre Scribe, the over-life-size limestone statues of Ranofer,[12] and the wooden standing figure of Ka-aper [117]. When first found, this vivid likeness of a fat, ageing man was dubbed the Sheikh el Beled because of his resemblance to the familiar figure of the headman of a modern village. The statues come from the simple, old-fashioned chapels in the brick mastabas built on the flat ground to the west of the early Fourth-Dynasty tombs which continued the archaic cemetery at Saqqara.[13] Similar fine large pieces of sculpture were executed at Giza for people who had strong family connexions with the old cemetery. It had become a secondary site after the kings, beginning with Shepseskaf, had returned to the Saqqara region for the construction of their funerary monuments. As the Old Kingdom advanced, the stone statues of most private persons became smaller, although an occasional big stone figure, like that of Ti,[14] occurs and life-size statues were still carved of wood. A surprisingly high level of skill was maintained considering the quantity of the output of the ordinary workshops. There was also an increased variety of statue types which parallels the expansion of the subject-matter in the wall reliefs. At first the representations of daily life were crowded into the offering-room at Saqqara, which kept its old cruciform shape with only slight modification or else conservatively held to a corridor form. The same pull of tradition led to the retention of the L-shaped chapel at Giza with its simple offering scenes. It was hardly before the reign of Ne-user-ra in the middle of the Dynasty that the number of interior rooms began to increase, providing much more space for wall reliefs. By the end of the Dynasty these rooms and courts filled a large part of the superstructure of the large tombs.

We have seen that the grouping of man and wife in a single statue had been established in Dynasty IV [110, 111], but now the children are sometimes added to the group and the poses are varied in a number of ways. A few small single limestone figures of servants preparing food had been placed in the tomb of Meresankh III at the end of Dynasty IV. These became popular in Dynasty V. They portray a wider range of activities, and several figures are grouped together on the same base. Groups of servant figures baking and brewing or manning small boats were also made of wood, but these have almost completely disappeared through decay and the depredations of the white ant. They formed the basis for the elaborate wooden models of the Middle Kingdom. The form of the frequently occurring statues of scribes had been introduced in

117. Ka-aper ('Sheikh el Beled'). Upper part of standing wooden figure from Saqqara. Dynasty V. *Cairo Museum*

the hard stone figures of Kawab, the eldest son of Cheops.[15] The sons of Radedef and Mycerinus had also been shown in this characteristic attitude, squatting on the ground with crossed legs and holding a pen poised above the papyrus roll on the lap. This was not the menial pose of a servant waiting to take his master's dictation, but represented a highly respected accomplishment which originally had been limited to a few. A fine painted example has been found in the far western part of the Giza cemetery [118] which is fit to stand beside the finest sculpture of the early part of the Fifth Dynasty.[16] It is about 18 inches high (45.7 cm), only slightly smaller than the Louvre Scribe, but instead of the bony face and the rolls of fat on the torso of that exceptional piece, it presents a more generalized impression of alert youth.

Weserkaf, the first king of Dynasty V, erected his pyramid at the north-east corner of the old enclosure of Zoser's Step Pyramid at Saqqara. On the east of the pyramid stood only a small chapel for the food offerings supplied to the dead king. Further clearance has shown[17] that this offering place was inside the enclosure wall and not straddling it as has been assumed in an earlier reconstruction [119],[18] and was reached by a corridor in the temple area walled off on the south side of the pyramid which included a small subsidiary pyramid with its own court [120]. Except for its entrance system, the temple resembles that of Cheops and, as in Dynasty IV, was intended for the cult connected with the statues of the

118. Giza, painted scribe. Dynasty V

119 and 120. (*right*). Saqqara, Weserkaf Temple. Dynasty V.
Reconstruction and plan

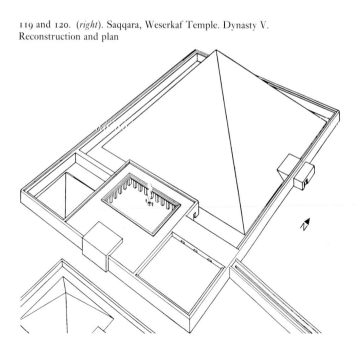

deified king. The statue shrines have been destroyed but were orientated away from the pyramid, south of the great court with its covered colonnade on three sides. On the south side of the court a wall closed off the pillared hall which had replaced the open porch of the Cheops and Mycerinus temples. Against this wall, facing the court, probably stood the huge granite statue of Weserkaf, of which only the head has survived. It has been suggested that the influence of the worship of Ra is responsible for the peculiar position of the temple on the south of the pyramid in order that the shadow of the pyramid should not fall upon the court, where it is possible that there may have been an altar to the Sun God, as restored [119].

There is a hint of the influence of the cult of Ra in the unusual subject-matter of some of the badly shattered but extraordinarily fine reliefs that covered the walls under the porticos on three sides of the court. The spearing of fish and the hunting of birds with a throwing-stick in a papyrus marsh, from which come the beautifully drawn birds [121], are not surprising in a royal temple. Like the hunting of game in the desert, they were sports in which the king took part and appear in the reliefs of Sahura in the next reign at Abusir. A ritual significance was attached to the harpooning of the hippopotamus which may have appeared here as it did in the Dynasty VI temple of Pepy II and on a Dynasty I seal impression.[19] On the other hand, the orchard scene which has been reconstructed [122][20] would belong more suitably to the life of a private person. A net has been thrown over one of the trees to catch the small birds busily picking at the round orange-coloured fruit. Other birds hover in the air above the trees as in a scene which must have been copied from this in the tomb of Nefer-her-n-ptah [123] or in two other bird-trapping scenes which resemble this composition even more closely.[21] Although these adaptations belong to the finest tradition of

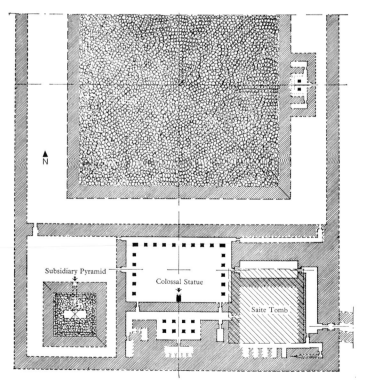

Subsidiary Pyramid

Colossal Statue

Saite Tomb

121. Birds in a papyrus marsh.
Relief from the Weserkaf Temple at
Saqqara. Dynasty V. *Cairo Museum*

122. Saqqara, Weserkaf Pyramid Temple, orchard scene. Dynasty V

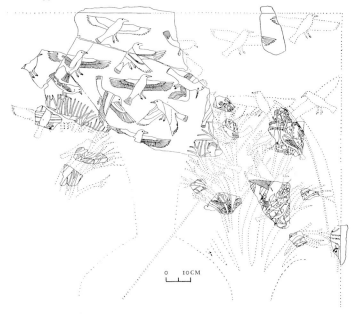

Fifth-Dynasty craftsmanship, they cannot match the royal sculptor's beautiful spacing of his intricate shapes or the firm clarity of the carving which is like that of the birds over the papyrus marsh [121]. There is a lively new spirit here which is amazingly expressed in the rhythmic movement of the men paddling a boat [124]. Nothing quite like the progressive action expressed here is known to have been repeated again.

In discussing the possible origin of the scenes from life, attention was called to the room with the personifications of the three seasons of the year in the Sun Temple which Ne-user-ra built at Abu Gurob, a little north of Abusir. Behind the big figures of the spirits of the seasons were grouped various appropriate activities such as hunting, fishing, and agricultural pursuits. Stiff rows of plants and animals were added to form a composition which baffles description, particularly in its incomplete state, and combines in a peculiar way formal and naturalistic elements.[22] It may well be that before the representation of the 'Seasons' had become fixed in this distinctive manner, which was repeated in later examples as on the walls of the causeway corridor of

123. Saqqara, chapel of Nefer-her-n-ptah, orchard with bird-catchers.
Dynasty V

Unas, there had been an earlier large-scale expression of the different elements of the idea. This would have been appropriate decoration in the great sanctuary of Ra at Heliopolis and might account for the use of some of the unusual material in the reliefs of Weserkaf and Sahura.

124. Saqqara, Weserkaf Temple, boating scene. Dynasty V

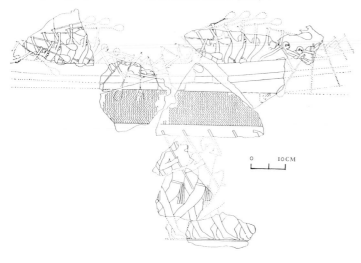

0   10 CM

Sahura began a new pyramid field at Abusir, north of the old archaic cemetery at Saqqara and not far from the place where Weserkaf had erected the first of the sun temples on the edge of the western desert. Neferirkara and Ne-user-ra also built their pyramids at Abusir, while the latter went farther north to find a site for his sanctuary of Ra at Abu Gurob [126, 127]. The other sun temples of Dynasty V have not been found, although the names of at least six are known, nor is the identification of two or three of the king's pyramids certain. The next to last king of the Dynasty, Zedkara Isesy, returned to the region south of Saqqara, where three of the Sixth-Dynasty kings followed him in building their pyramids. The last king of Dynasty V, Unas, selected a place near the south-west corner of the Zoser precinct, and the first king of Dynasty VI, Tety, built his tomb to the north of Weserkaf's. The temples of all these monuments were approached by a causeway from a rather small valley temple with porticos and terraced landing stages. The pyramid temple of Sahura [125] introduced a long covered east-west offering room with a false-door stela in the west wall at the base of the pyramid. This was copied in the private chapels a little later. On the side walls the king was represented seated at his funerary meal accompanied by pictures and lists of food and offering-bearers. This sanctuary was surrounded by

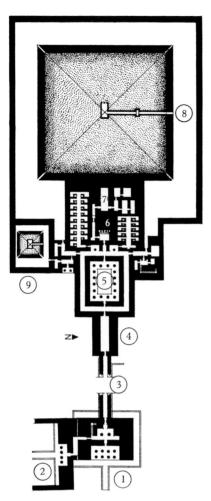

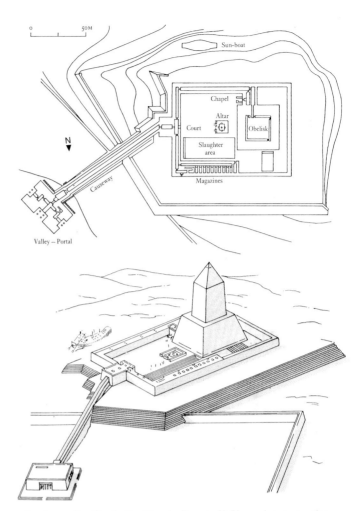

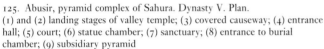

125. Abusir, pyramid complex of Sahura. Dynasty V. Plan.
(1) and (2) landing stages of valley temple; (3) covered causeway; (4) entrance hall; (5) court; (6) statue chamber; (7) sanctuary; (8) entrance to burial chamber; (9) subsidiary pyramid

126 and 127. Abu Gurob, Sun Temple. Dynasty V. Plan and reconstruction

store-rooms and entered through two intervening halls from the room with the statue shrines. A cross corridor separated the statue-chamber from the court of the temple. The block of rooms around the sanctuary formed, from now on, the inner temple which, with the small ritual pyramid, lay inside the enclosing wall of the pyramid. The outer part of the temple consisted of the court and deep hall which formed an entrance from the top of the causeway corridor. This plan was followed with only minor variations throughout the rest of the Old Kingdom and was imitated again by the kings of the Twelfth Dynasty when they established their capital again in the north. The court of the Sahura temple was surrounded by a portico of granite palm columns, as was that of Unas at the end of the Dynasty. The granite columns of the court of Ne-user-ra imitated a bound cluster of papyrus stems with the closed buds forming the capital. A lighter wooden lotus column was used by Neferirkara in the brick-and-timber construction of the court of his temple, where only the sanctuary was built of stone. The stems in this type of bundle column are rounded and do not have the pointed triangular section of the papyrus, although the half-opened buds of the lotus are not always easy to distinguish from those of the papyrus. A somewhat heavier limestone version of the lotus

column appears for the first time in the chapel of the son-in-law of Ne-user-ra, Ptah-shepses, at Abusir.[23]

In the Sun Temple of Ne-user-ra at Abu Gurob, the central element was a squat masonry obelisk set on a high sloping-sided base [126]. The platform round the obelisk was reached by an interior ramp. Only the core-work of the base is preserved, with part of this ramp, and the structure has been restored on the basis of the hieroglyphic determinatives of the names of the Ra sanctuaries of Fifth-Dynasty kings [127]. The temple enclosure consists largely of a plain court with an altar for offerings, open to the sun, and an area on the north for the slaughter of sacrificial animals and for store-rooms. Approach is from a small portico with a covered causeway like the valley temples of the pyramids. There is a deep entrance hall opening into a covered corridor which runs round the east and south sides of the enclosure turning in to reach the foot of the ramp leading up in the base of the obelisk. It is in the reliefs on the walls of the last short section of this corridor that the 'Seasons' are portrayed. On the east of this is a small chapel which contained the most complete early representations of temple foundation ceremonies and the celebration of the jubilee of the renewal of kingship, the Heb-Sed.[24]

The Ne-user-ra reliefs begin to show a carelessness in the carving not apparent in those of Weserkaf and Sahura, which maintained the high standard of the finest low reliefs of Dynasty IV. The new methods of cutting partly resulted from experiments which had been made with the poor nummulitic limestone of the rock-cut tombs of Giza, where fine detail could be obtained only by working with a coating of plaster laid over the walls. It was discovered that the effect of low relief, where the whole background had been removed to a slight depth, could be achieved by cutting away only a small area of the stone in immediate proximity to the figures and blending this smoothly with the background. In hasty workmanship this amounted to little more than an incision around the figures, and in all cases the background was left with an uneven surface. When the wall had been painted these labour-saving devices were scarcely noticeable, but they continued both in royal and private work even after a bolder type of carving with higher relief had appeared towards the end of Dynasty V. The beauty of the draughtsmanship and the liveliness with which the life of the times is conveyed by the vast quantity of wall reliefs of the later Old Kingdom make this slight falling off of technical skill in the work of Dynasty V a matter of minor importance.

The Sahura temple gives us our best idea of the great cycle of scenes from the public life of the king which were placed on the walls of the court and the corridor which ran round it. The fine quality of the workmanship, which closely resembles that of the more fragmentary Weserkaf reliefs, is apparent in the detail from the big hunting scene. The king, accompanied by his attendants, dominates the wall. The arrows from his bow strike the game that has been driven by beaters into a stockade indicated by vertical bands of netting. The animals are rather stiffly placed in long horizontal registers which rise one above the other in front of the king.[25] A natural touch is given by the undulating strip of desert ground, interspersed with little plants, on which the animals stand, but the base-line of each register is straight. This is the typical building up of a large wall composition which we have seen already in the Medum swamp scene [77] and in the rock-tomb of Meresankh III [102], but the king is taking part in the action and not simply viewing what occurs in the subsidiary registers. In spite of the horizontal divisions, these registers manage to suggest the wide expanse of desert ground in which the hunt was taking place. Later, in the Middle and New Kingdoms [190, 248], an occasional gifted artist succeeded in giving a better sense of the terrain and unifying the whole by eliminating the straight base-lines.

Sahura devoted much space on the walls of the court to representations of the ceremonial sacrifice of foreign captives and the recording of booty by the goddess of writing, Seshat.[26] This chiefly consisted of the herds of cattle, sheep, goats, and donkeys obtained from raids on the Libyan tribes of the western desert. The tall-necked jars with handles and the bears from the mountains of Syria, which are all that has survived from the Asiatic booty, were more probably obtained as barter or propitiatory gifts than as actual plunder or tribute. We know that expeditions for the much-prized pine wood had been made by sea to the Syrian port of Byblos since at least the end of Dynasty II. Such a trading venture is pictured in the sea-going Egyptian vessels filled with bearded Asiatics accompanied by men with the title of 'Interpreter' which appear on the east wall of the cross corridor at the back of the court. There is little to suggest extensive campaigns to the north-east in the Old Kingdom. One is recounted by Weni in the reign of Pepy I in Dynasty VI,[27] but an occasional show of force against the Bedouin tribes would probably have been sufficient to keep the way open to the mines of the Sinai Peninsula. The exploration of the Red Sea coast had certainly commenced, and the far-off land of Punt was known. This incense country lay between the Upper Nile and on the east coast of Africa near the mouth of the straits of the Bab el Mandeb in the region of modern Somaliland. There is a brief mention of a voyage made there in the reign of Isesy in the second half of Dynasty V.[28] We hear little about Nubia, but the lucrative caravan trade through the cataract region, which in Dynasty VI we find in the control of the Nomarchs of the old southern border town of Elephantine (modern Aswan), must have been carried on for quite a considerable time.

At the end of the Fifth Dynasty, a block with fighting men from the causeway corridor of Unas is the first known attempt to represent a battle scene. Later, two Sixth-Dynasty chapels show Egyptians attacking fortresses of their Libyan and Asiatic neighbours.[29] This more explicit statement of what had hitherto been recorded in very generalized fashion is paralleled by the biographical inscriptions which in Dynasty V give us more information about a man's career. Something in the nature of historical documentation is indicated in Sahura's reliefs, where the names of the family of the vanquished Libyan chieftain are inscribed over their heads. Admittedly these were repeated verbatim in a copy of the scene in the temple of Pepy II towards the end of Dynasty VI and in other temples. Nevertheless, there is a similar sense of factual record in the freight-boats which bring the granite palm columns from Aswan for the temple of Unas among the remarkably varied scenes in his causeway corridor.[30] The most startling of these is the portrayal of the starving victims of famine [128].[31] These grotesquely emaciated people form a grim contrast to the men bartering produce in a market-place and the long lines of personified estates bearing food offerings for the king on other parts of the walls of the causeway. They also show how indifferent the craftsman could be to the final cutting and surface finish of a remarkably conceived piece of draughtsmanship. One need only compare this relief with the

128. Saqqara, Unas causeway, famine scene. Dynasty V

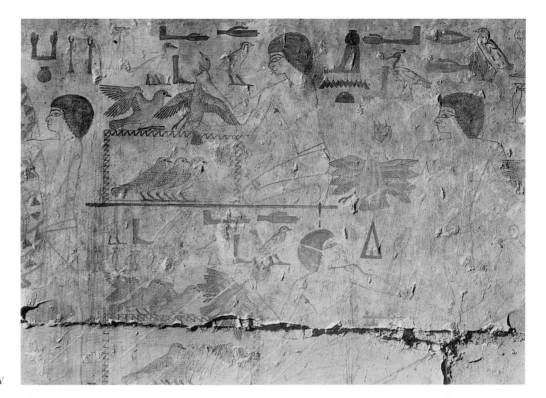

129 and 130. Saqqara, chapel of Nefer-her-n-ptah, bird-catching scene, with detail of bird. Dynasty V

Sahura reliefs to appreciate the variations in quality that can be found in royal work of Dynasty V.

Consistently fine work in low relief is carried out through the many rooms of the interior chapel in the well-known tomb of Ti at Saqqara in the middle of Dynasty V.[32] Decoration of comparable quality appears in a number of simpler chapels which still employ the single interior offering-room. Details from one of these have been selected for illustration because of the superb preliminary drawings which still remain on the wall beside the uncompleted carving. The chapel belonged to a man named Nefer-her-n-ptah and was constructed in a quarry beside the causeway of the Unas Pyramid. We have seen that the scene in relief with the capture of song-birds in an orchard [123] represents an unusual subject of which only fragments were preserved in the temple of Weserkaf [122]. Other small birds were being caught in the ordinary clap-net used for water-fowl, and in illustration 129 these are being placed in boxes for transport. To the left and below this group of figures are men picking figs. All this part of the wall is drawn in black over a preliminary red sketch with a marvellous sureness of touch.[33] Although all this detail would be lost to the chisel of the sculptor and replaced by the final painting of the completed reliefs, the draughtsman has stippled the upper part of the bodies of the birds with little black dots [130]. Since these lie over a red wash, and in other places the wider red brushstrokes of the preliminary sketch appear under the thin black final outline, there is obtained an extraordinary effect of texture and even of the rounding of the bodies. The appearance of a drawing in line and wash is partly due to the usual practice of correcting in black the outlines first sketched in red. At the same time, though, this is an experiment with brushwork which we shall see repeated in the painting of the Middle and New Kingdoms (cf. illustration 286, at the Malkata Palace).

Towards the end of Dynasty V, particularly in the big tombs of the family and courtiers of Unas which lie near his temple along the southern wall of the Step Pyramid enclosure, there is a change to a bolder style of relief. A hint of this had appeared in the preceding reign of Isesy in the offering-room of Ptah-hotep.[34] It is to be seen at its best in the fine group of Mereruka and his two sons in the best-preserved of the big tombs around the pyramid of King Tety early in Dynasty VI [131].[35] The style was refined in the royal reliefs, but these are insufficiently preserved to present an adequate impression of their appearance until we reach the last great monument of the Old Kingdom, the funerary temple of Pepy II. The bold treatment in high relief combined with a striking observation of the individuality of the owner are to be found in the head of Itwesh (Semenekhu-ptah) in Brooklyn from a Saqqara chapel of the end of Dynasty V [132]. Low relief was not entirely abandoned, especially in the case of the

131. Saqqara, chapel of Mereruka, Mereruka and his sons. Dynasty VI

132. Itwesh, Relief head from Saqqara. Dynasty V. *Brooklyn Museum*

subsidiary registers of a wall composition, although these are broadly treated on a larger scale. Several chapels cut in the rock or built free-standing south of the Step Pyramid at Saqqara were virtually sealed from access when the causeway of King Unas was constructed; they thus antedate the end of his reign. The most interesting of these chapels was built for two wealthy officials who held the court titles of king's manicurist. Their relationship was obviously a professional one as well as one of friendship, and it is quite possible that they were brothers and even twins and hence the popular designation of the chapel as the tomb of the Two Brothers. The decoration is carried out with a strict sense of symmetry to give almost equal prominence to the two men, each of them shown in parallel scenes. Nyankhkhnum was perhaps the elder brother or at least reached a higher rank at court; possibly he survived his brother Khnumhotep and thus was in charge of the decoration. Although both men are shown in parallel scenes with their respective wives and children, the two men dominate this double tomb chapel with its rich and varied repertory of scenes. In several places the two men are shown in a close embrace [133], a scene otherwise reserved for representations of a king with a deity or a husband and wife.

The *serdab* of Mitri, in one of the large tombs at the southeast corner of the enclosure of the Step Pyramid, had by a happy accident preserved its wooden statues intact [134]. There were eleven of them, and several were nearly life-size. They present a variety of types, including standing figures of the man and his wife and two in the pose of a scribe.[36] One

133. Nyankhkhnum and Khnumhotep. Relief from Saqqara. Dynasty V

134. Saqqara, *serdab* of Mitri, wooden statues. Dynasty V

135. The dwarf Seneb and his family. Statue group from Giza. Dynasty IV–VI. *Cairo Museum*

136. Uncircumcised youth. Wooden statuette. Dynasty V. *Berkeley, University of California, Lowie Museum of Anthropology*

statue, presumably of the owner, shows him naked, as do other Old Kingdom statues like the fine wooden figure in Boston of Senezem-ib Mehy, the vizier of Unas, from his Giza tomb.[37] There was also a curious smaller figure of a hunchback which is not visible in the photograph of the statue chamber.[38] As in the emaciated figures of the Unas reliefs, we have again a matter-of-fact recording of bodily defects. This is to be found also in statuettes of dwarfs who, like Mitri's hunchback, were generally minor members of the household, although the dwarf Seneb, whose statue group is illustrated here [135], was the owner of a fine mastaba at Giza.[39] Eleven wooden statues is a respectable number, even if it is not comparable to the large quantity of stone statues placed in the Giza *serdabs* of the early part of Dynasty V.[40] It makes us realize how much wooden sculpture of the highest quality must have disappeared. The isolated instances which are preserved are highly instructive. The statue of a boy now in the Lowie Museum of Anthropology [136], for example, must rank as a masterwork of naturalism. Unlike so many Egyptian treatments of children, this figure truly appears youthful. Only too frequently, however, the Giza *serdabs* were

137. Methethy. Painted wooden statue from Saqqara. Dynasties V–VI. *Kansas City, William Rockhill Nelson Gallery of Art*

138. Methethy. Wooden statue. Dynasties V–VI. *Brooklyn Museum*

empty. Sometimes a few bits of painted plaster in the sand-filling, or the crumbling plaster coating of the feet and base, is all that remains to show that these had contained wooden figures long since eaten by termites.

Several fine pieces have survived from another group of wooden statues which, like most of the chapels decorated in bold high relief, belong to the turn from Dynasty V to Dynasty VI. Their owner, Methethy, records on his stela that he was honoured by Unas. Of the preserved wooden statues of this official, one in Kansas City [137] and one in Brooklyn [138] are exceptional.[41] The wood has been covered with plaster and painted, while the eyes are inlaid with a disk of dark stone set in alabaster in the simple manner used after the early part of Dynasty V. They lack the translucence imparted by the rock-crystal covering of the iris and pupil in the statues of Rahotep and Nofret [80] and the Sheikh el Beled [117]. The striking impression produced by the bright colouring

and alert expression is not that of the earlier Old Kingdom. There is still a life-like quality, but at the same time an element of stylization not unlike that of the painted limestone sculpture of the Middle Kingdom [176, 177]. From about the middle of Dynasty V a change towards simplified, rather schematic modelling can also be detected in some of the limestone statues. This, one suspects, is part of a general trend towards formalism which increases as the Old Kingdom advances and is not primarily a matter of declining craftsmanship.[42] The change is apparent only in exceptional pieces of the Fifth Dynasty, while in Dynasty VI so much of the private sculpture continues along traditional lines that it is difficult to distinguish from earlier work. This can be seen even in the Methethy group, where the Boston statuette retains the naturalistic modelling established in Dynasty IV and has little in common with the other figures except for the name and titles inscribed on the base.

CHAPTER 7

Dynasty VI 2420–2258 B.C.

From our examination of the stylistic changes that were taking place towards the end of Dynasty V it was apparent that the monuments of the time of Tety, the first king of Dynasty VI, form a group with those of the reign of Unas. There are no apparent signs of political repercussion from the change of dynasty. At least two of the owners of the magnificently decorated tombs in the neighbourhood of the Tety Pyramid continued in service from the preceding reign. The biographical inscription of the vizier Kagemni states that he had held office under Unas, while that king represented Neferseshem-ptah among the courtiers on the walls of his causeway corridor. The reliefs of the chapel of Mereruka are finer in quality but continue in the same style as those executed in the last years of the reign of Unas. As in the tombs of the family of that king, the rooms fill nearly the whole of the mastaba superstructure. The kings of Dynasty VI continued the custom initiated by Unas of inscribing on the walls of the burial apartments the long columns of religious utterances, ancient ritual, and spells known as the Pyramid Texts. These drew upon both solar beliefs and those concerning Osiris to ensure the well-being of the king after death. Although these royal burial-chambers have been cleared and the texts copied, the temples of the pyramids of Pepy I and Mernera have only recently been excavated. The pyramid temple of Tety was badly damaged but followed the plan of the Unas temple and was substantially like that of Pepy II [139].[1] At the pyramid of this last king at South Saqqara it was possible to reconstruct the system of ramps and terraces which were built at the valley temple [140]. These seem to have been anticipated in the Unas Valley Temple.

The pyramid group of Pepy II was thoroughly investigated by Gustave Jéquier[2] and the fragmentary decorations of this last great monument of the Old Kingdom painstakingly reconstituted. These show that certain of the cycles of scenes from the public life of the king were continued. In fact the Libyan booty was copied from Sahura and Ne-user-ra, even to the names of the family of the conquered chief. Much space is devoted to religious ceremonies and to the association of the king with the gods, while the sanctuary retains the representations of the funerary meal. The carving shows a refinement of the bold style which came in at the end of the previous dynasty, and in a few places exceptionally fine painted detail was preserved. One would never suspect from the beauty of this work that the end of the reign, which was one of the longest in history, would see a disastrous decline of the arts and the political collapse of the Old Kingdom.

There is a drastic reduction of the naturalistic elements that had appeared in the temples from the time of Weserkaf to that of Unas. One finds nothing like the varied depictions of the life of the country such as had still lined the walls of the causeway corridor of Unas. The spearing of the hippopotamus in the entrance hall is pictured as a ceremonial rite. This may have been the traditional method of presenting such a subject,[3] since we can only suspect the occurrence of such a scene earlier from fragments of Sneferu and Weserkaf, although it appears on a First-Dynasty seal impression. The hunting of game in the desert, however, is reduced to a similar formula. Pepy II strikes an antelope with a mace, as though sacrificing the animal instead of hunting it in a more natural setting.[4] The registers of game in the Sahura temple have been reduced to a single line of very small animals and plants set against a strip of desert ground at the base of the wall. It is as though a hieroglyph conveying the idea of game in the desert had been substituted for the whole scene.

Since so little is left of the earlier royal reliefs of the Sixth Dynasty, we cannot follow the steps which led to such a modification of the subject-matter depicted in the pyramid temple and can only point to this as another example of the formalizing tendencies of the period. Attention has been called to this in comparing the protecting falcon of the Chephren statue [109] with the small alabaster figure of Pepy I in Heb-Sed dress with the falcon standing above his Horus-name on the back of the throne [141]. This is one of three remarkable statuettes in the Brooklyn Museum.[5] These include a kneeling slate figure of Pepy I holding forward two offering jars which, both in style and as a statue type, is a wholly unexpected work for so early a time. The third piece shows the queen of Pepy I holding her son Pepy II on her lap [142]. The figure of the king is small, but appears as a fully grown man with the royal head-cloth. He is placed rigidly at right angles to his mother in the same way that the falcon stands behind the head of Pepy I in the other statuette. Pepy II must have been very young when he came to the throne at the death of his elder brother, Mernera. Tradition, as handed down by the Ptolemaic historian Manetho, made him six years old at his accession and credited him with an age of a round hundred years. A little naked alabaster figure of the king squatting on the ground was found in his funerary temple.[6] It may represent the child-king as the youthful Horus, and is in keeping with the spirit of the Brooklyn statuettes.

The large copper statue of Pepy I in Cairo was accompanied by a smaller royal figure which stood beside it on the same base [143, 144]. These are the earliest metal statues which have survived, although one of Khasekhemuwy is already mentioned on the Palermo Stone at the end of Dynasty II.[7] The inscription on the base mentions the first Heb-Sed of the king, and the smaller figure is possibly assumed to be his son and successor, Mernera. This group may commemorate a co-regency of the two kings. The corroded state of the metal which obscured the modelling has now been ameliorated by conservation (1997). The long narrow inlaid eyes of Pepy I suggest the same stylizing tendencies as appear in some of the wooden statues and in the slender forms of the alabaster statuettes, but the face of the smaller figure is more rounded and has a prominent fleshy nose. The metal was beaten into shape and attached by copper nails to a wooden core.[8]

The copper group of Pepy I and his son was buried with the slate figure of Kha-sekhem and an archaic pottery lion in the floor of one of the side chambers of the sanctuary at Hierakonpolis.[9] In the central shrine was found the wonderful gold falcon's head in the Cairo Museum. This originally formed part of the copper image of the Horus of Nekhen, the old national god of Upper Egypt who presided over this temple. The copper parts have never been reconstituted along the lines of the reconstruction suggested for the figure with its stand [145], but on the base in front of the falcon image were the marks of the feet of a small figure, surely that of the king who dedicated it and stood under its protection.[10] The creation in metal of such a complicated cult object seems in keeping with the daring craftsmanship of the group of Pepy I, and it was reasonable to assume that both are of the same date. However, it now seems definite that part of the work properly belongs to the New Kingdom. The splendid working of the gold head speaks for the magnificence of the statues of deities which once stood in the temples and of which so little material evidence has survived.

Pepy I made a political marriage which secured the allegiance of a powerful provincial family at Abydos. This stresses the importance which Upper Egypt was assuming in the political picture, as do the number of decorated rock-cut tombs in the neighbourhood of the different Nome capitals. The kings of Dynasty VI had come to depend particularly upon the Nomarchs of Elephantine at the old southern border of the First Cataract. These men not only took charge of much of the quarrying and transport of the Aswan granite for the royal monuments, but they organized the lucrative

141. Pepy I. Alabaster statuette (back). Dynasty VI. *Brooklyn Museum*

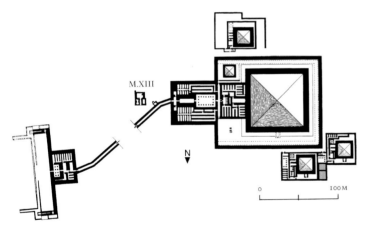

139. Saqqara, pyramid complex of Pepy II. Dynasty VI. Plan

140. Saqqara, valley temple of Pepy II. Dynasty VI. Reconstruction

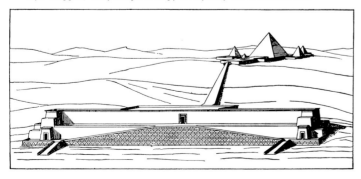

caravan trade which was pushing farther south into the Sudan. Although it is doubtful whether the men of the Old Kingdom can have penetrated so far, fragments of stone vessels with the names of Pepy I, Mernera, and Pepy II were found in the lower level of the Middle Kingdom buildings at Kerma in the Province of Dongola. These would certainly seem to form a parallel to the fragments of similar vessels with the names of Old Kingdom kings which are part of the evidence for trade with the Syrian port of Byblos. Some of the Nomarchs of Elephantine mention taking part in the sea trade with the Syrian coast as well as voyages down the Red Sea to

142. Pepy II and his mother. Alabaster statuette. Dynasty VI. *Brooklyn Museum*

Punt. The Punt expeditions set off from a place near modern Qoseir on the Red Sea coast. This embarking point lay at the end of the old desert track from Coptos through the Wady Hammamat, which also served the important stone quarries in this part of the eastern desert. Mernera's state visit to receive the Nubian chieftains at Aswan is a sign of the government's interest in the expeditions to the south which were partly carried out by river-boat and partly by donkey caravan over routes in the western desert. In the reign of Pepy II we hear of skirmishes with the southern tribes and trouble also on the Red Sea coast. Peaceful relations seem to have been maintained with Syria, but in the reign of Mernera a series of military expeditions was organized by Weni the Elder which were probably chiefly concerned with protecting access to the Sinai mines. The last of these, however, involved the transport of troops by sea to some point which must have been in Palestine. Mercenaries from the Nubian tribes were employed in this venture.[11]

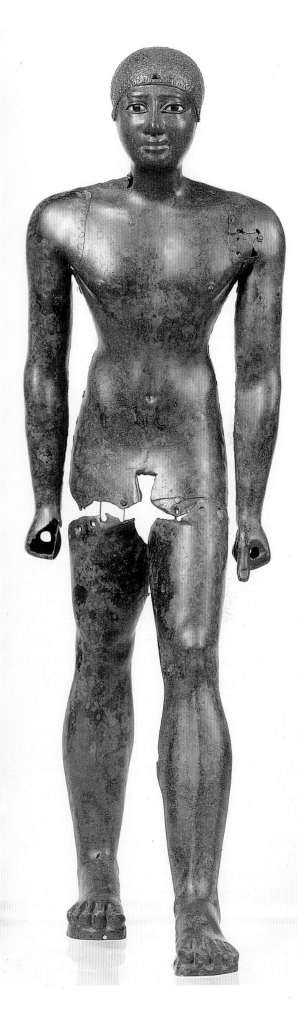

143. Pepy I. Head of copper statue from Hierakonpolis. Dynasty VI. *Cairo Museum*

144. (*right*). Mernera(?). Copper statue from Hierakonpolis. Dynasty VI. *Cairo Museum*

Mernera attempted to curb the powerful provincial families by making Weni the Elder, the trusted official of his father, governor of Upper Egypt with special powers over all the twenty-two Nomes. In a similar move to prevent hereditary rule from taking firm hold in a province, he sent a man named Qar from court to be nomarch at Edfu. Mernera could rely on the support of the Thinite Nome through his mother's brother, Zau. After Mernera's death Zau was vizier during the minority of Pepy II. Of the old Memphite families who still kept important positions at court there was one in which the title of Overseer of All the King's Works had been held since the time of Isesy's favourite, Senezem–ib–Yenty. His son had been the vizier of Unas and their descendants continued to be buried in the group of family monuments at Giza near the northwest corner of the Great Pyramid into the time of Pepy II. In the reign of Pepy I, Nekhebu left a biographical inscription mentioning royal constructions like those undertaken by his grandfather, Yenty. Under his second name, Mer-ptah-ankh-mery-ra, we find him at the Hammamet quarries with a son who inherited his office. This son, Impy, appears among the courtiers in the temple of Pepy II and was also buried at Giza.[12]

Thus the Old Kingdom retained a prosperous appearance until the end, although we can see that the rise of the

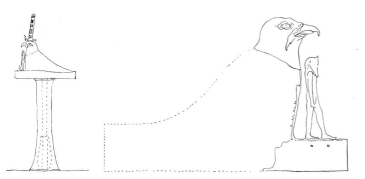

145. Falcon from Hierakonpolis. Gold. Dynasty XVIII. Reconstruction. *Cairo Museum*

provincial nobility in Upper Egypt coincided with the gradual impoverishment of the royal house.[13] The constructions undertaken at royal expense and the innumerable temple and funerary endowments exempt from taxation were exhausting the king's resources. The place which foreign trade had assumed in the economy of the state can be seen from the lamentations of Ipu-wer. Among the calamities which he lists as occurring with the breakdown of law and order at the end of the Old Kingdom is the fact that men no longer sailed to Byblos.[14] Pine and oil for embalming were no longer available, and in the absence of commodities from abroad the arrival of the oasis-people with reed mats and

birds seemed important. These contacts with foreign lands had produced no visible effect upon Egyptian arts and crafts. Only a few Syrian pottery vessels, mainly two-handled oil-jars of combed ware, can be pointed to as actual imports. Most of these were found at Giza, and they continue from the reign of Cheops to the time of Pepy II.[15] Presumably Egypt's neighbours had little to contribute apart from the raw materials of their lands, chiefly minerals and timber. With the collapse of the Memphite government we hear of incursions of Asiatics into the Delta. There is little to suggest that these people brought with them anything to contribute to the superior civilization of the Nile Valley. On the other hand, Egypt must have influenced the developing cultures of Palestine and Syria.[16] Mesopotamia during the Old Kingdom seems to have been separated from Egypt by too many barriers for any exchange of influences to have made themselves felt. It is now questioned whether the long claimed Egyptian influence upon Crete can have existed before the end of the Old Kingdom.[17] Byblos certainly seems to have been a connecting link between the two countries. It should be remembered that Keftiu, which was probably the Egyptian name for Crete, is first mentioned in the same passage of Ipu-wer's lamentations which refers to the absence of shipping to Byblos. The extensive sea-trade of the later Old Kingdom would have been more favourable for the establishment of contact with Crete than the confusion and poverty prevalent during the First Intermediate Period.

PART THREE

The Growth of the Middle Kingdom and its Collapse

CHAPTER 8

The First Intermediate Period: Dynasties VII–X 2258–2052 B.C.

We do not know exactly what political event was the immediate cause of the collapse of the Old Kingdom. The diminished power of the royal family is painfully evident at the close of Dynasty VI. A brief period of confusion, evidently a sort of interregnum known as Dynasty VII, was followed by the weak kings of Dynasty VIII who made some attempt to carry on Memphite traditions. We can see from decrees set up in the temple at Coptos, how dependent the throne was upon the support of a powerful provincial family there.[1] The rise of the governors of Heracleopolis, which lay south of Memphis near the entrance to the Fayum, really brought the Memphite royal house to an end. The rulers of Heracleopolis of Dynasties IX and X drove the Asiatics out and restored order in the Delta. They had no more than nominal control in the south even in the middle provinces of Egypt. Our best glimpse of events in this exceedingly dark time is in the period after Intef I had established Dynasty XI in Thebes, around 2130 B.C. At this time the Theban territory extended as far as the Thinite Nome. Fighting began around Abydos, which the princes of Assiut attempted to hold for Heracleopolis in the struggle which was to result in the conquest of the north by Neb-hepet-ra Mentuhotep and the uniting of the country about 2050 B.C. The early part of Dynasty XI at Thebes thus ran parallel with Dynasty X during this period of the rise of Theban power, against which Assiut formed a bulwark in Middle Egypt for the suzerain power of Heracleopolis. We know very little about conditions in the Delta, but in Upper Egypt each Nomarch attempted to maintain the independence of his district which had been gained at the end of the Old Kingdom, and it was to be the problem of the Middle Kingdom kings to break the power of this provincial nobility.

We need not attempt here to follow the decline of the Memphite style in Lower Egypt, where some traces of the small monuments which continued to be built at Saqqara into Heracleopolitan times have survived. The many-chambered mastabas at Saqqara are now in part replaced by small false-doors with side panels; the repertory of scenes is selectively abbreviated to the essentials.[2] The decoration of the burial chamber with the scenes usually placed in the superstructure, a practice not uncommon earlier, becomes prevalent.[3] In Upper Egypt the decoration of the rock-cut tombs is more interesting as containing elements of a new style. There is something here, as in the few small pieces of sculpture in the round, which cannot be dismissed as merely the result of the poor craftsmanship everywhere evident. Until well into the Sixth Dynasty the tombs in Upper Egypt had simply imitated in a provincial fashion the work done at court. The quality of the workmanship varies considerably from place to place, with an increasing use of paint alone where the local rock in which the chapels were cut did not encourage carving in relief.[4] In Dynasty VI, one extreme is represented by the roughly cut reliefs of the Nomarchs of Elephantine at Aswan, which are scarcely to be distinguished in style from work of

the First Intermediate Period. At Meir, on the other hand, Saqqara models were followed closely, particularly from such tombs as that of Mereruka.[5] Even there, the chapel of Pepy-ankh-herib begins to show a clumsier cutting of the reliefs, crowded composition, and coarse detail in the painting.[6] The pinkish-grey of the donkeys contrasts oddly with the other simple masses of bright colour and with the blue-grey background. The wall decoration at other places such as Deir el Gebrawi has a rough vigour, an elongation of the proportions of the figures, and a change in the colour scheme which show a divergence from the old Memphite style. It is just these qualities which were accentuated by the technical deficiencies of the craftsmen in the First Intermediate Period.

While the continuous use of the cemeteries from Dynasty VI into Dynasty XI can be determined at Denderah[7] or in the Naga-ed-Dêr district of the Thinite Nome,[8] the meagreness of inscriptional evidence has placed formidable obstacles in the way of arranging the material from these sites in chronological order. Even in the Hare Nome, where there is assistance from the rock inscriptions in the alabaster quarries of Hat-nub, it has not been possible to fill in the gap between the Old Kingdom Nomarchs whose tombs are at Sheikh Said and the men buried at Deir el Bersheh in Dynasties X–XII. There are resemblances between work executed at the end of Dynasty VI and that of a painter working for a member of the court at Thebes in the reign of Neb-hepet-ra Mentuhotep in Dynasty XI [149].[9] At Naga-ed-Dêr there is reason to believe that three of the painted chapels which have survived in very bad condition, and possibly the few rock tombs which have some carvings on the walls, were made at the end of Dynasty VI or shortly afterwards. The stelae set in the rough walls as the only decoration of poorer chapels appear to belong to a later time during Dynasties IX and X. An elaborate example is that of a Thinite official, where the paint is well preserved on the sunk relief [146].[10] The drawing and modelling of the men and animals are schematic, and the old naturalism has given way to patterns of harsh colour on the cattle and in the spotted panther skin of the owner's ceremonial dress and the cross-hatching of the wings of the birds among the food offerings piled above the offering-stand.

Three tombs in the south have extraordinary paintings and bear a close resemblance to one another. Those of Ankhtifi at Mialla[11] on the east bank of the Nile south of Luxor and Ity at Gebelein,[12] across the river a little farther north, are probably to be dated to the beginning of Dynasty X before the establishment of Dynasty XI at Thebes. Set-ka, the owner of a tomb at Aswan,[13] was a priest of the temple of Pepy II and could hardly have lived into Heracleopolitan times after Dynasty VIII. On the east wall of the chapel appear black-skinned bowmen, as at Mialla and Gebelein [147].[14] What they are attacking has disappeared with the fall of the plaster on the right. One figure kneels, and three of the standing men are placed at different levels above the base-line. One man bends his knee as he raises his bow to shoot. This lively

146. Offering scene. Painted limestone stela from Naga-ed-Dèr. First Intermediate Period. *Philadelphia, University Museum*

irregularity of placing and attitude is echoed by the change in ground colour from one register to another and the odd hues employed. The bowmen are set against a white background, but this changes to mud-colour for the cattle above. In the top two registers, which show the game stalked by a huntsman on the left, the pink gazelles are backed by the more usual blue-grey ground colour, but the wild asses are silhouetted against a dark blue strip which makes their warm grey look lavender. The cattle have the peculiar mottling to be found at Gebelein [148] and Mialla, and the strange pendant strips below their throats (wrinkles of fat or slaver?) are repeated in Ankhtifi's chapel.[15]

The same bizarre colouring is found at Mialla in the chapel of Ankhtifi and can be detected to a lesser extent on the badly worn walls of Sebekhotep's tomb there. Wild asses as well as gazelles were painted pink, a colour that was combined unpleasantly with yellow and deep red on the spotted cattle. The warm grey of the domesticated donkeys once takes on a purplish hue in Ankhtifi's paintings, where these strange shades clash in a colour scheme dominated by red and green

with subordinate notes of yellow, black, and white. Similar harsh combinations of bright pigments appear in the chapel of Ity at Gebelein, as well as at Naga-ed-Dèr and on the crudely painted coffins of the time. The strident dissonances are hardly pleasing, but the painters of Upper Egypt, in breaking away from the conventions of the Old Kingdom, laid a basis for new combinations of colour and the softer nuances of a more varied palette in the Middle Kingdom. The disturbed conditions and general impoverishment of the country cut one district off from another and reduced to a minimum the influence of traditions which may have lingered in the north, where the old royal monuments remained to provide examples for a renewal of the Memphite style in Dynasty XII. The craftsmen were left free to experiment in their clumsy fashion with lively gestures and the addition of scenic accessories in their new groupings of figures. The same change was taking place in the wooden model scenes in which the servant statuettes were now grouped.[16] These began late in Dynasty VI, were elaborated in Heracleopolitan times, and continued into the Middle Kingdom, where we find the finest examples in

147. Stela of a Nubian mercenary from Gebelein. First Intermediate Period. *Boston, Museum of Fine Arts*

the tomb of Meket-ra at Thebes towards the start of Dynasty XII [158, 159]. In these, as in the wall-paintings, the troubled state of the land is reflected by the appearance of armed men.

The big room in the chapel of Ankhtifi at Mialla had been cut out of the rock with thirty unevenly spaced, clumsy columns, some of which were round and some polygonal. In its rough irregularity it resembled the tombs of the earlier

Nomarchs at Aswan. Ity's chapel at Gebelein was a simpler brick construction with a mud-plastered barrel vault. It was conceived as though the action on the walls were taking place under a canopy supported by the light wooden columns which are painted at the corners of the room. The mourners and wailing women on the end wall [148] adjoin a representation of the wooden coffin set out under a small canopy, round

148. Mourners and cattle. Wall painting from the chapel of Ity at Gebelein. First Intermediate Period. *Turin, Museo Egizio*

the corner on the side wall.[17] The markings on the typical cattle in the register below show the preference of the period for reducing the shapes to a series of patterns, an unrealistic formal approach which was inherited by the Middle Kingdom both in design and colouring as well as in the sculpture in the round. This was never completely eradicated as the Twelfth Dynasty turned to more naturalistic forms.

One of the best preserved and most characteristic examples of the style of the First Intermediate Period is the agricultural scene of the tomb of Djar at Thebes [149]. This chapel must have been decorated by an old-fashioned country painter, for its owner lived at a time when much more sophisticated work was being executed for other members of the court of Neb-hepet-ra Mentuhotep in Dynasty XI.[18] The angularity of the men ploughing with a yoke of oxen, as well as the animals themselves, is paralleled by the roughly cut and brightly painted little figures in some of the wooden models. The legs of the pair of oxen have been inextricably confused in the drawing. The row of pack-donkeys above, loaded with bags of grain, is like those in the Gebelein and Mialla tombs. They proceed docilely and do not roll on their backs or kick up their heels like two in the tomb of Ankhtifi, or a wild ass in the chapel of Set-ka at Aswan, or the donkey in a later painting at Beni Hasan.[19]

While the style of Dynasty VIII to early Dynasty X was still continuing side by side with the highly developed products of the royal school at Thebes in Dynasty XI, signs of improved prosperity and orderly craftsmanship were being displayed in Middle Egypt in the few reliefs and paintings which have survived in the Tenth-Dynasty tombs of the Nomarchs of Assiut and in the only one of the shattered rock-chapels of this time which still produces some impression of its sunk relief decorations at Deir el Bersheh.[20] These follow the style of Upper Egypt, but no longer show the eccentric forms and peculiar hieroglyphs in their inscriptions that appear at other sites in the south. The resemblance is to good Middle Kingdom work, rather than to the stelae mentioning the name of the pyramid of the Dynasty X king, Merikara, recovered at Saqqara near the Tety Pyramid, where the cutting of the inscriptions could be mistaken for conventional work of Dynasty VI. The latter suggest that, if everything belonging to Dynasties IX and X has not been completely destroyed at Heracleopolis and in the Delta, it might be possible by future excavation to trace some continuity of Memphite traditions in the north, where they had certainly continued through Dynasty VIII.[21]

At Assiut sculpture in the round was beginning to emerge from the stick-like forms of the earlier wooden statues. The

149. Thebes, chapel of Djar, agricultural scene. Dynasty XI

150. Wepwawet-em-hat. Wooden statue from Assiut. First Intermediate Period. *Boston, Museum of Fine Arts*

same vigorous spirit which has characterized all work of the First Intermediate Period is to be found in the large wooden figure of a man named Wepwawet-em-hat [150] from that site.[22] Its chief characteristic is a rude strength. The staring eyes and sharply edged planes of the face, as well as the very long fingers of the hands, are typical of the time. The modelling of the body, however, shows a renewed technical skill which corresponds to the improvement in quality of the painting and relief in the tombs of the two Nomarchs, Tef-ib and Khety II. The statue was probably made in that period of Assiut's prosperity under the last Heracleopolitan kings, before it was overwhelmed by Neb-hepet-ra Mentuhotep.

Thus around 2130 B.C. there were signs of a revival, with King Neferkara and his two strong successors, Wah-ka-ra Khety and Merikara, ruling in the north and Seher-tawy Intef I declaring himself king in Thebes. It was the house of the latter which was to triumph. Heracleopolis fell to Neb-hepet-ra Mentuhotep about 2052 B.C., and it is with the uniting of the country under Thebes that the Middle Kingdom was really established. In the next chapter we shall have to go back earlier to trace some of the remarkable developments that were taking place at Thebes in the early part of Dynasty XI. In spite of its new strength, Thebes never really set its stamp upon the country, as had Memphis in the old days. This was partly due to the regional differences which had become established in the chaotic times after the fall of the Old Kingdom, and partly because Memphite traditions showed a tenacity to survive even after the shockingly low level to which its culture had descended. Old monuments remained to inspire the new craftsmen of Dynasty XII. The earlier complacent sense of stability had been rudely shaken, and Egypt never regained that simple confidence in an enduring continuity. The shock of the collapse of a stable world is reflected in the so-called pessimistic literature which pictures the social upheaval at the end of Dynasty VI. The cynical distrust of his fellows expressed in the instructions of one of the great Middle Kingdom kings is quite different from the cheerful maxims which advise a man how best to make his way in a predictable world that have come down from the wise men of the Old Kingdom.

CHAPTER 9

Dynasty XI 2134–1991 B.C.

The varied nature of the art of the Middle Kingdom typifies a new age of experiment and invention that grew out of the turbulence of the First Intermediate Period. It returned in strength to the forms of the Old Kingdom, but never recaptured the unity of the Memphite style. It anticipated the sophistication of the New Kingdom and began to look abroad, but without acquiring the international flavour of Dynasty XVIII. Its forms were a little stiff, changing from one locality to another and here and there retaining the provincial mannerisms that are everywhere evident in its earlier phases. Nonetheless there was the power to achieve a meticulous delicacy of craftsmanship as well as a disturbingly brutal strength. At their best the craftsmen showed not only great sensitivity to line, colour, and modelling, but also an intuition of character of which the seemingly happier world of the Old Kingdom had appeared scarcely conscious. While evident in the literature of the early reigns of Dynasty XII which reflects the pessimism of the hard times that extended from the end of Dynasty VI well into the first half of Dynasty XI, this interest in man's feelings towards his environment does not appear to have found expression in sculpture until later in Dynasty XII in the extraordinary heads of Kings Sesostris III and Amenemhat III. These portraits are exceptional in Egyptian art, which at all times showed a reluctance to portray inner feeling. In other ways the Middle Kingdom seems not to have lasted sufficiently long to resolve all its contradictions. This was in one sense a virtue, since much of the initial freshness and vigour was retained until the end of Dynasty XII. Viewed in a broad perspective the early New Kingdom seems to continue a development that was under way in Dynasty XII and was taken up again after the break of the Second Intermediate Period. However, if we examine each period in detail, it will be seen that Dynasty XI and early Dynasty XVIII were times of a renewal of Egyptian civilization, both having much in common with the brilliant Early Dynastic Period that preceded the Old Kingdom.

The rule of the first kings of Dynasty XI did not extend farther north than Abydos in Upper Egypt, and the Middle Kingdom was not really founded until the Two Lands were united by Neb-hepet-ra Mentuhotep[1] after the subjugation of Lower Egypt about 2052 B.C. This king is certainly the outstanding personality of the early Middle Kingdom. We know him as the builder of a highly original structure, his funerary monument at Deir el Bahari on the western bank at Thebes [151, 152],[2] which inspired the terraced temple that Queen Hatshepsut built beside it in the Eighteenth Dynasty. It consisted of a square element, perhaps a pyramid, in the midst of a columned hall fronted by porticoes and approached by a ramp. The outer wall of the hall or ambulatory around the central element was in turn surrounded by a pillared portico. The appearance of the building, as one approached it from the east, was thus one of terraced porticoes with rectangular

supports and with the central element rising above the roof of the upper one. The first excavators and all early reconstructions render the central element as a pyramid set upon a high platform [151], but in his recent work Dieter Arnold argues against this pyramidal structure in favour of a flat-topped altar-like element [152]. The columns of the ambulatory were octagonal, and such columns were used again round a court at the back and in the deep columned hall behind it. The tomb of the king lay in the rock under this hall and was reached by a sloping passage from the court. Another underground chamber had been cut at the end of a long, sloping passage. The mouth of this passage was in the vast courtyard in front of the temple, which was planted with trees and reached by a causeway from the edge of the cultivation. In the chamber was found a seated sandstone figure six feet high [153]. It was painted, and represented the king in Heb-Sed dress wearing the red crown of the north and with black flesh. Standing and seated sandstone statues, in similar dress and with the body treated in the same rude massive fashion, lined the way across the courtyard leading to the temple.

In a very simple way the tombs of Mentuhotep's predecessors seem to have set a precedent for his funerary monument. At the edge of the cultivation, north of the great amphitheatre in the cliffs of Deir el Bahari, Intef I and two of his successors had excavated large rectangular courts in the gravel and soft stone of the lower slopes. In the side walls opened doorways to the tombs of the king's followers, and at the back was a series of entrances which served his own burial-place. Thus the impression gained was that of a long court opening into the hillside and surrounded by colonnades. The principal tomb was marked further by a pyramid. That of Intef II is mentioned in the Abbott Papyrus, and traces of these structures still remained in the nineteenth century. It is not certain, though, whether the pyramid stood in the court at the back or was built above the king's burial chamber.[3]

The idea of a terraced structure may also have been derived partly from a house type which had a stairway leading from a court with a portico to a columned porch on the second storey. This is reflected in the so-called 'soul-houses' which are of pottery and served as trays for food offerings at the tomb.[4] Their form is very suggestive of the arrangement of the terraced courts with porticoes and rock-cut chambers at the back in the Twelfth-Dynasty tombs of the nobles at Qaw el Kebir [186]. These later structures with their causeways and valley temples obviously return in other ways to Old Kingdom forms. The grandness of Mentuhotep's plan, which went through a number of alterations during the course of his long reign, may also have been influenced by what he and his craftsmen saw in the north. There is a new breadth in the treatment of the reliefs which decorated the walls of the ambulatory round the base of the pyramid, while the subject of the king as a sphinx or a griffin trampling on his enemies[5] was certainly derived from an Old Kingdom pyramid temple.

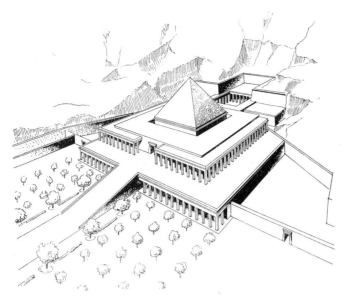

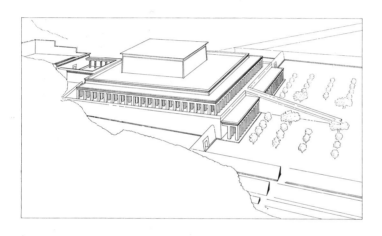

151 and 152. Deir el Bahari, temple of Mentuhotep. Dynasty XI. Earlier and later reconstructions

The court of the tomb of Wah-ankh Intef II had some sort of chapel in which was set a stela still found intact by the men investigating the tomb robberies in Dynasty XX as recounted by the Abbott Papyrus. The lower part of this stone was found by Mariette and is now in Cairo. The detail [154] shows the leg of the king and four of his five dogs with their names written beside them. Clearly the sculptor has made an enormous advance over the crude carvings of his predecessors. This type of bold relief with heavily rounded surfaces and broadly treated modelling continued into the reign of Mentuhotep, when the royal sculptors employed it in a small shrine at Denderah[6] and in a monument at Gebelein.[7] It is to be found on the shrines for the ladies of Mentuhotep's household, which were set in a row at the back of the temple as part of the first construction undertaken at Deir el Bahari. They were later incorporated into the wall between the ambulatory and the court. Reliefs of similar style appear in the chapel of the chief queen of Mentuhotep, Neferu, which was another early work of the reign. These were carved in the masonry lining of a rock-cut chamber which lay above the painted burial crypt. A procession of ladies holding hands from one of the walls can be partly pieced together from the smashed fragments.[8] The figures are very tall and slim, being dispro-

portionately long from feet to waist. At least one other frieze of women appeared in the corridor of this chapel, and they occur again in the Middle Kingdom, as in the long line of ladies of Djehuty-hetep's family in Dynasty XII at Bersheh [197]. The corridor which led to the offering chamber was decorated with sunk reliefs that present a somewhat different appearance but closely resemble those in the chapel of the chancellor Khety.[9] One of these shows an acacia tree under which stand two large water-jars [155].[10] The fine interweaving pattern of the bare branches and the diamond-shaped seed-pods has something of that mannered quality which appears so clearly on the sunk reliefs of the coffins of the ladies buried under the shrines at the back of the Mentuhotep temple. The acacia tree in flower with its feathery leaves and little yellow balls is to be found in the Twelfth-Dynasty paintings of Khnum-hotep at Beni Hasan [200].

153. Neb-hepet-ra Mentuhotep. Seated sandstone statue from Deir el Bahari. Dynasty XI. *Cairo Museum*

the First Intermediate Period, and have a mannered quality that we have not found before.

The sculptors who must have worked at a later time in the reign of Mentuhotep gave breadth to this style in the fine hard limestone reliefs which decorated the ambulatory around the pyramid and the lower porticoes of the Deir el Bahari temple. Unfortunately these scenes, which showed Nile craft, a desert hunt, activities in the swamp lands, and a lively representation of a battle, have been broken into such small fragments that the compositions cannot be restored and their position on the walls is uncertain. They differ in style from the sandstone sunk reliefs of the court at the back of the temple and the more tightly drawn figures in raised relief on the limestone screen walls of the altar in the pillared hall behind. They show broad masses of fairly low relief with wide sweeping lines and less recourse to minor detail.[13] This style is reflected in the paintings and painted reliefs of the tomb of one of Mentuhotep's viziers, Dagi.[14] Here there is a marked drawing upon Old Kingdom sources for the subject-matter, although one finds also the typical Middle Kingdom representation of spinning and weaving that is familiar from the wooden model of Meket-ra in Dynasty XII and the paintings at Beni Hasan, Deir el Bersheh, and Aswan in Dynasty XII. The large scale of the figures and the blue hieroglyphs of the inscriptions give the paintings a different appearance from their Old Kingdom models. The chapel had a portico of heavy piers cut in the bedrock of the northern slope of the Qurneh hill. It faced the

154. Stela of Wah-ankh Intef II (detail) from Thebes. Dynasty XI. *Cairo Museum*

Considerable variations in style and workmanship exist in the decorations of the stone sarcophagi from the Deir el Bahari temple. The sunk relief carvings on the outside of the coffins of Kawit and Aashayt[11] resemble those in the chapels of Queen Neferu [156] and Khety, but both Kemsit's sarcophagus and the paintings on the wall of her chamber betray in their drawing and colouring considerable traces of the earlier style of the First Intermediate Period.[12] The hairdressing scene carved in sunk relief on the lady Kawit's coffin [157] shows, as in the bold raised reliefs, a concentration of rather fussy detail on certain parts, such as the wigs and jewellery, while other parts are left with plain flat surfaces. The harshly treated faces are a heritage from earlier times, as are the elongated slender limbs. Nostrils and lips are accentuated, while the long, narrow eye turns down at the tear-duct. The balanced pattern of the serving girl's fingers as she braids the curls held up by a pin, and the similar exaggeration of the hand with which the lady holds a milk-bowl to her lips, show how much of the spirit of the preceding period in Upper Egypt has entered here. It is the taut, nervous energy of the lines which gives life to this work in which a naturalistic approach is still denied. Whereas the bolder raised carvings remind us of the stage in development reached at the time of Sneferu [67, 68], these sunk reliefs are reminiscent of earlier archaic work, such as the Heliopolis reliefs of Zoser [51]. They betray, however, the change which has taken place in

155. Acacia tree and water jars. Sunk relief of Neferu from Deir el Bahari. Dynasty XI. *New York, Metropolitan Museum of Art*

156. Sunshade bearer. Relief of Neferu from Deir el Bahari. Dynasty XI. *Yale University Art Gallery*

tombs of other members of the court which lay high up in the northern cliffs. Thus Mentuhotep was surrounded by his courtiers in the Deir el Bahari valley, as in the old Intef cemetery the little chambers of the followers of the king had been grouped round the courtyard of his tomb. On the floor of the valley, known as the Asasif, Djar had built a porticoed tomb, resembling that of Dagi, but nothing could better illustrate the variations of workmanship and style occurring in this reign than the difference between the large-scaled, carefully drawn paintings of the vizier and the old-fashioned crude work executed by Djar's craftsmen [149].

These craftsmen had become more articulate than their predecessors in the Old Kingdom, if we can judge from the remarkable inscription of a certain sculptor, Iritisen, who belonged to the reign of Neb-hepet-ra Mentuhotep.[15] He states the facility which he had acquired in his craft in which his son had also become proficient. He lays special emphasis upon his knowledge of how to represent the pose of different kinds of figures, including the captive and the hippopotamus hunter. Clearly, like other master craftsmen, he was concerned with precious materials such as silver and gold, ebony and ivory.

In the following reign of Se-ankh-kara Mentuhotep a refinement in the cutting of low relief appears which reminds one of a similar development that had occurred in Dynasty IV in the reign of Cheops. This is apparent from blocks that have been recovered from a monument which the king erected at Tod,[16] south of Luxor. Another example of these fine limestone reliefs came from Erment across the river and is now in the Brooklyn Museum.[17] Se-ankh-kara began to lay out a funerary monument along the lines of that of his predecessor. He had only reached the stage of grading a platform in a bay in the cliffs south of Deir el Bahari when he died.[18] Facing this site, in the back of the Qurneh hill, Meket-ra later completed a rock-cut tomb which was once decorated with limestone reliefs that rivalled in quality those of the earlier king. They are now reduced to small fragments.[19] The paint was

freshly preserved and shows the subtle new colour scheme that had developed out of the strident colouring of the First Intermediate Period which, as we have seen, still existed on Kemsit's coffin in the preceding reign. Soft brown and tannish shades appear with orange, lemon-yellow, grey-blue, and accents of black and white. There is a delicacy and precision both in the cutting and the painted detail which had been evident already in the few relief fragments that have survived from Dagi's tomb.

A small statue chamber escaped the pillage of the rest of Meket-ra's tomb, and in this was found intact the series of wooden models which give us such a lively impression of Middle Kingdom life.[20] Since the little scenes are worked out in the round, they are helpful in enabling us to understand the action which is taking place in the great cycles of

157. Hair-dressing scene. Coffin of Kawit (detail) from Deir el Bahari. Dynasty XI. *Cairo Museum*

158. Meket-ra model of cattle inspection from Thebes. Dynasty XI. *Cairo Museum*

159. Portico of wooden model of house of Meket-ra from Thebes. Dynasty XI. *New York, Metropolitan Museum of Art*

Twelfth-Dynasty paintings at Beni Hasan and Deir el Bersheh, where the conventions of the ancient artist sometimes make interpretation difficult. Although the agricultural labours are curtailed to the representation of the granaries being filled, the other models present a full picture of the life on a great estate in Dynasty XII, as well as providing all sorts of river craft, including those used for fowling and fishing. Perhaps the most appealing of all, and certainly the most elaborate, is that with the spotted cattle being driven before a columned shelter where Meket-ra and his scribes take count of the herds [158]. This pavilion gives a valuable hint of the appearance of domestic architecture, as do the two models of Meket-ra's house and garden and the butcher's shop with its upper terrace for drying meat. The gaily striped papyrus columns support a flat roof from which project two water-spouts like those on Meket-ra's house [159], where the rain

that falls so infrequently in Thebes could run off into the pool under the trees in the enclosed garden. Columns such as these were cut out of the rock in an Eleventh-Dynasty tomb at Beni Hasan, where wooden construction is clearly imitated [166].[21] The Beni Hasan columns have clusters of lotus buds instead of papyrus. The plant-forms are difficult to distinguish in the capitals of these two very similar types of columns, but even on the small scale of the models of the Meket-ra house the craftsman has rounded the stems of the lotus and given the papyrus its characteristic triangular section and sheathing round the base.[22]

CHAPTER 10

Dynasty XII 1991–1786 B.C.

The vizier of the last king of Dynasty XI was a certain Amenemhat whom we know from an inscription at the quarries in the Wady Hammamat. It is probable that this was the man who seized the throne and, as Amenemhat I, founded the powerful Twelfth Dynasty. One of the important measures adopted by this king was the establishment of his capital in the north at Ith-tawe, not far south of Memphis, and it was at Lisht nearby that he built his tomb. In thus attempting to control more securely the northern part of his kingdom, Amenemhat brought the court within range of old Memphite influences which still survived in the form of ancient monuments, and the effect is strongly evident in the art of the Twelfth Dynasty. Except for funerary structures, the great architectural projects of the Middle Kingdom have disappeared under the rebuilding of the pharaohs of the New Kingdom. This is particularly evident in the temple of Karnak at Luxor and at Medamud, Tod, and Erment in the Theban district,[1] as well as in the temple precincts of the Delta cities. Some of these earlier temples seem to have vied in grandiose scale with those of the Empire, as is suggested by the obelisk of Sesostris I, which is all that remains standing of his temple at Heliopolis, or the huge architectural members of granite usurped in a hall or court at Bubastis by Ramesses II. Only the very general outlines of this building have been recovered, and it is impossible to visualize how the parts were related to one another even in Ramesside times. However, columns corresponding to two sizes of architrave blocks bearing the names of Sesostris III were found, and all seem to have belonged to the same Middle Kingdom structure.[2] There were four very large papyrus-bundle columns and four smaller palm columns like those used in the Old Kingdom temples of Sahura and Unas. With these were found four large Hathor-head capitals and four smaller ones. The architraves evidently rested directly on the Hathor heads without the intervening naos-shaped block which appears later. From the size and shape of the under part of the large capitals it appears that they surmounted square pillars.[3]

At Karnak it has been possible to reconstruct a small Heb-Sed pavilion of Sesostris I [160–62]. Almost all of its limestone blocks were recovered from the Third Pylon of Amenhotep III, where they had been used in the foundations.[4] It stood on a raised base and was approached by ramps on two sides. Low balustrades connected the outer pillars and, inside, four pillars surrounded the throne for the Jubilee ceremonies. Later in the Middle Kingdom this throne was replaced by a stone stand, which suggests that the building was converted into a way station for the bark of Amon such as are known from the New Kingdom. The pillars were decorated with reliefs of the finest workmanship, showing a development of the style of the monuments of Se-ankh-kara in the Theban district [160, 162].

Only one other structure of the Middle Kingdom still remains standing in nearly complete condition. This is a small chapel with three statue shrines built by Amenemhat III at Medinet Madi on the southern edge of the Fayum,[5] the region which he developed by irrigation works into one of the most fertile parts of the country. The name of Amenemhat III was still associated with the Fayum and its lake in Greek and Roman times, and the funerary temple beside his brick pyramid at Hawara continued to be visited; it was known as the Labyrinth because of its complicated plan. Unfortunately, little remained of this when it was excavated towards the end of the last century,[6] nor was there much left of Amenemhat's colossal seated quartzite figures at Biahmu mentioned by Herodotus.

The pyramid of Amenemhat I was more solidly constructed than those of his successors, with a core of small stones and a limestone casting. Among these stones were inscribed blocks from royal monuments of the Old Kingdom. The reliefs on these stones have preserved the names of Cheops, Chephren, Unas, and Pepy. A granite block with the name of Chephren is thought to have formed part of one of the architraves in the court of his pyramid temple at Giza,[7] and it seems that all these blocks were taken from funerary monuments at Giza and Saqqara. The older buildings were studied while they were being plundered for their stone, and the result of this is that the Old Kingdom fragments are not easy to distinguish from the broken pieces of the decorated walls in the badly destroyed temple of Amenemhat. This interest in the old forms is also evident in the following reign, where the better-preserved plan and decorations of the temple of Sesostris I at Lisht are clearly derived from that of Pepy II at South Saqqara. The pyramid is constructed in a new way, with rough retaining walls radiating from the centre and cross walls forming compartments which were filled with rubble and sand. The whole was then cased with stone. A similar method was used by the successors of Sesostris I. Amenemhat II still employed a rubble filling in the pyramid which he constructed at Dahshur east of the North Stone Pyramid of Sneferu, while Sesostris II used brick in his funerary monument at Lahun near the entrance to the Fayum. Sesostris III built a brick pyramid north of that of Amenemhat II at Dahshur, while his successor, Amenemhat III, constructed two brick pyramids, one at Dahshur, east of the old Bent Pyramid of Sneferu, and another, in which he was probably buried, at Hawara in the north-eastern corner of the Fayum. These were all intended to be cased with stone, and much labour and ingenuity were expended upon the burial-chambers, for which enormous blocks of the hardest stone were frequently used.[8] Little has survived of the temples of these pyramids, and they have not all been as completely cleared as that of Sesostris I at Lisht, which is the only one in which the plan and decoration of a Middle Kingdom pyramid temple can be studied [163]. We shall return to it later in examining the royal reliefs and statues of the period.

In 1890 Sir Flinders Petrie completed the excavation of a walled town beside the valley temple of Sesostris II at Lahun. Nothing like this has since been found from such an early

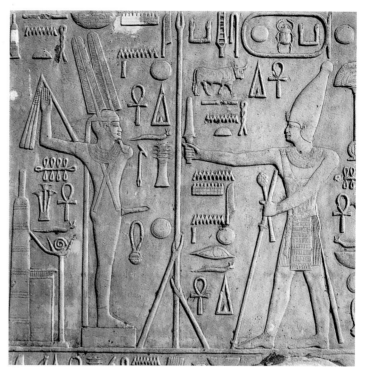

160–62. Karnak, pavilion of Sesostris I. Dynasty XII. Reconstruction (*top, left*), detail (*left*) and further detail (*above*)

period. The buildings inside the forts of the Second Cataract were naturally intended for a different purpose and were occupied again in the New Kingdom. Thus the site which Petrie called Kahun provides us with our most valuable evidence for the domestic architecture of the Middle Kingdom.[9] The town was built to house the officials and workmen concerned with the construction of the Lahun pyramid and the maintenance of its funerary services. The location would have been convenient also in connexion with the extensive works that were carried on in the Fayum throughout the later Middle Kingdom, and the town continued to be inhabited into Dynasty XIII. It was built on the low ground beneath the edge of the desert escarpment, but a projecting spur of rock inside the north wall was revetted with brick and utilized as a platform for a building which thus dominated the town at a higher level [164]. What was left of this badly denuded

163. Lisht, pyramid temple of Sesostris I. Dynasty XII. Plan

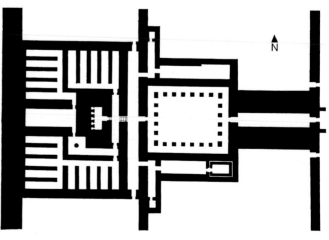

164. Kahun town. Dynasty XII. Plan

structure resembled the other large houses, and it was probably intended as a residence for the king when he came to inspect the work, and perhaps also to house the governor of the pyramid town. It was surrounded by a thick wall which separated it both from the enclosure containing the blocks of small workmen's dwellings and from the large houses of officials which lined the street leading from the eastern gate to an open square in front of this residence. A brick staircase led straight up to the platform from the gate that opened on to the square, and a pair of smaller service stairs were set at right angles to one another on the left of the gate. Two other similar stairways are known, one leading up to the garrison's quarters in the thick masonry base of the fort at Kerma, and a more impressive example in the early New Kingdom South Palace at Deir el Ballas [275, 277].

A few small dwellings had encroached upon the southern side of the street with the big houses of officials, but most of this area of the town seems to have been occupied by store-rooms, while some of the blocks of buildings with units that look like small houses may have been used for administrative offices. The workmen's village proper was walled off on the west. The large houses of the officials on the north side of the street were laid out on the same plan with numerous rooms and courts grouped in four well-defined parts. The three houses south of the street have the space somewhat differently arranged, but are similarly divided. In the northern houses [164] the door from the street opened on a cross corridor with a porter's room facing the entrance. The service quarters opened from the left end of this corridor, with a court in which food could be prepared and store-rooms. To the right of the porter's lodge two parallel corridors ran the length of the house. That on the right served a series of rooms and courts that may have accommodated guests as well as the transaction of business. The wider, main corridor led to a court where the house backed up to the town wall. It had a portico with a single row of columns along its south side. From this opened two separate suites of living quarters which thus faced northwards away from the entrance to the house and ensured extra privacy for the owner and his family.

The master's quarters occupied the central block of the house, and to the west of these lay the women's apartments, isolated from the rest of the house with only one entrance under the portico of the northern court. The wife had a living-room, bedroom, and bath on the south side of a columned court, and on the north of the court were three smaller rooms for her serving-women. The bedroom had an alcove for the bed, as in Eighteenth-Dynasty houses. The master's bedroom was a larger room of this sort which opened on the left (west) of the central hall with four columns. With its narrow reception hall running the width of the block and the rooms grouped round the central columned hall, the master's suite bears a resemblance to the Eighteenth-Dynasty houses at Tell el Amarna. It is to be noted, however, that these later houses do not have an isolated set of apartments for the women of the family.

The columns were generally of wood on round stone bases. The lower part of an octagonal wooden column was actually found.[10] Some use of stone supports was made, however. Part of a fluted column, like those at Beni Hasan [165], was found, and there was also one example of a ribbed shaft which

165. Beni Hasan, chapel of Amenemhat, looking out from shrine. Dynasty XII

166. Beni Hasan, Tomb 18. Dynasty XI

represented one of the types with a cluster of bound plants such as we have seen in the Meket-ra models and at Beni Hasan. In fact the southern façade of the north court, with its two doors opening into the reception hall under a columned portico, must have resembled the house model of Meket-ra [159] or the pavilion in which he viewed the counting of his cattle [158]. The tombs at Beni Hasan obviously imitated the interiors of such houses as these [166].

The space occupied by these big town houses would probably not have been available in a crowded city, but was possible here, where the whole was planned for a special purpose and all laid out at once at the king's orders. These buildings are probably much more like what one would have found on a great country estate. Naturally one could not expect anything approaching such luxurious arrangements in the crowded quarters of the garrison in the Middle Kingdom forts erected in the region of the Second Cataract south of Wady Halfa. These forts protected communications in this difficult region and controlled the trade with the Sudan that passed along the river. Amenemhat I and Sesostris I had undertaken the subjugation of Nubia, which was thoroughly completed by Sesostris III. The forts were placed at strategic intervals in the rocky country of the lesser rapids between the big fortified town of Buhen, just above the Second Cataract proper, and Semna, some 50 miles southwards.[11] There were two forts at Semna, one on each bank of the river, and we know from a stela of Sesostris III that this point formed the southern boundary of Egyptian occupation.

The fortress at Mirgissa (also called Matuka) had an outer wall where it was more approachable, on the land side. Inside stands the main inner fort with its great corner tower and regularly spaced buttresses. A glacis with a low outer wall and

ditch inside it was used at Semna West. Although such a system is thought to have been introduced in Western Asia with the advent of chariotry, which did not appear in Egypt until Hyksos times, it was certainly earlier in these cataract forts. The base of the high walls of these forts frequently has a pronounced batter. This is represented on a besieged Egyptian fortress with crenellated walls in the Dynasty XI tomb of Khety at Beni Hasan,[12] and can be seen on the plan of the fort on Uronarti Island [167] on the north side, where there was flat open ground. This sloping-faced extra thickness strengthens the lower part of the wall and buttresses on the south-east wing or bastion that ran sharply down to the river [168]. The view in this illustration gives a good idea of the wild rocky country along the river as well as the way in which the builders adapted their structures to the uneven terrain.

Uronarti Island lies near Semna, considerably upstream from Mirgissa. In the plan [167] part of the long eastern bastion and covered stairway to the river has been omitted. The ground fell away sharply to the river (at the bottom of the plan). Greater protection with big towers was given to the northern side, where the ground was flatter and approach easier. There is a gate at each end of the fort, and inside each one is a large administrative building provided with storerooms. A third building of this sort stands on the south side of the main street which bisects the interior of the fort. Another street runs all round the building inside the walls. In between the large buildings were repeated small units of rooms, in blocks separated by only two cross streets. These seem to have been houses for the men of the garrison and their families. The space was very constrained, and there is no open square, although the larger buildings have courts. One

167. (*right*). Uronarti fortress, plan.
Dynasty XII

168. (*below*). Uronarti fortress,
south-east wing. Dynasty XII

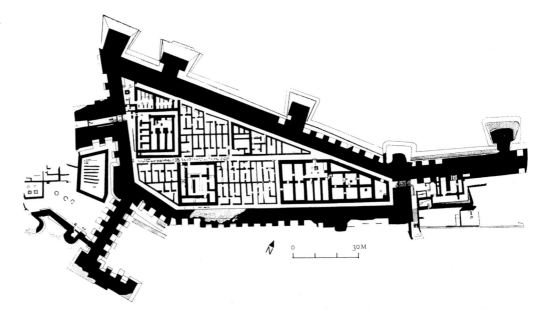

of these buildings probably housed the commandant, perhaps
with living quarters in an upper storey. Only two staircases
remain in the large building inside the west gate, but there
must have been access to the flat roofs, to the upper storey of

some of the buildings, and to the top of the walls. Although
Uronarti, like most of the other forts, was occupied in the
Eighteenth Dynasty, there is little sign of alteration to
the walls of the buildings, which seem to have maintained

169. Buhen, west gate. Dynasty XII. Reconstruction

their plan from the Middle Kingdom. A large residence or palace and a temple were added outside the walls in the New Kingdom.

Perhaps the best idea of these fortresses is obtained from the work of Emery and the Egypt Exploration Society at Buhen and particularly from his drawings of the reconstructions of the walls [169]. Many of the features anticipate the castle architecture of the Middle Ages in Europe: the crenellated walls, the moats, and the parapets with slots for the archers. Some of these features are again represented in the forts depicted in the battle reliefs of Sety I of Dynasty XIX at Karnak (see Chapter 19).

We must return to the court in the north from this grim frontier land, where the garrisons and their families dragged out a dull existence. It will be necessary to come back to the south again in considering the minor arts of the Middle Kingdom and to examine one of the finest of the statues of Dynasty XII which was made for a great lady of Assiut. At Lisht we have seen that the plan of the pyramid of Sesostris I [163] is very much like that of Pepy II at the end of Dynasty VI. The scheme of decoration seems also to have followed fairly closely that of a temple of the later Old Kingdom. The procession of offering-bearers [170] is modelled upon those in the sanctuary of Pepy II, but when the figures are compared with the earlier ones, it will be seen that there is a change in the proportions. The men are bulkier, and accessories and hieroglyphs are larger in scale. Moreover, there is a variation in workmanship and style between the reliefs in different

parts of this temple. Some of the work is on a smaller scale and not executed in such bold relief, while the sunk reliefs present an individuality of their own. They have more the character of the sunk relief from the Coptos temple in University College, London, which shows Sesostris I executing a ritual dance before the god Min.[13] The Lisht reliefs differ from those of the Heb-Sed pavilion of this king at Karnak, where, with the loss of the colour on the white limestone, the precise cutting of the excessively fine detail produces a colder impression. So little has survived of the decoration of the funerary temples of the other kings of Dynasty XII that it is impossible to trace any sort of development in royal relief sculpture in the north or to make comparisons with what has been recovered in fragmentary condition from Upper Egypt.

The causeway corridor of the Lisht temple had reliefs on its walls and was lined at regular intervals with Osiride statues of the king which were continued into the entrance hall. Ten large seated figures of Sesostris I[14] must have been placed in the temple court against the rectangular supports of the surrounding colonnade. Removed from the severe architectural setting for which they were planned, the repetition of so many identical figures becomes monotonous as they stand close together in the Cairo Museum. In spite of changes in proportion and modelling, there is clearly an attempt to recapture the form of Old Kingdom statues as they were intended to be used in such a pyramid temple. While displaying remarkable technical dexterity, they have lost the serene majesty of the

170. Offering-bearers. Relief from the temple of Sesostris I at Lisht. Dynasty XII. *New York, Metropolitan Museum of Art*

171. Sesostris I. Wooden statuettes from Lisht. Dynasty XII. *Cairo Museum and New York, Metropolitan Museum of Art*

earlier works and something of their strength. Two wooden statuettes of Sesostris I from Lisht are attractive examples of this milder approach towards the representation of the human figure [171]. They are two of the most beautifully executed works of the Middle Kingdom. There is none of the brutal vigour which appears in later royal sculpture, but the heads have an individuality which suggests the portraiture of the reigns of Sesostris III and Amenemhat III. This is less evident in the Cairo statuette wearing the tall white crown, but the head of the New York figure with the red crown of Lower Egypt portrays the features of the king as they appear in certain of the heads on the temple walls and in the Coptos relief mentioned above. There is a family likeness to his father Amenemhat I, some of the characteristics of which appear in a relief in that king's funerary temple. The portraiture of the later reigns was clearly anticipated at the beginning of the Dynasty.[15]

The softer modelling of the forms in wood continued and the idealized naturalism of the old Memphite tradition is still evident in a nearly life-size naked figure made in the north in Dynasty XIII [172]. It was found perfectly preserved in a wooden shrine accompanying the burial of King Hor. His tomb lay inside the enclosure of the pyramid of Amenemhat III at Dahshur.[16] The two raised arms on the head of this figure, with its divine beard, signify that this is the 'Ka' of the king, his vital force and one of the emanations of his spiritual being.[17]

A very fine private statue of the reign of Sesostris I belongs to the same stylistic group as his seated statues from Lisht. It has, however, a more warmly human quality. This is the seated grey granite figure of the Lady Sennuwy, the wife of Prince Hepzefa of Assiut [173, 174]. It was found at Kerma far to the south in the Sudan. The finely cut face and elegant

slender lines of the body make this perhaps the most appealing of the large works of the Middle Kingdom. It is of a quality comparable to the best royal workmanship and suggests that Memphite influence had penetrated into the workshops in Assiut. Part of a large statue of Hepzefa was found with that of his wife, and statues of other private persons, as well as royal ones, were found at Kerma.[18]

Sennuwy's statue has none of that heaviness which appears in other work of the period, such as the large, highly polished seated dark stone figure of Queen Nefret, the wife of Sesostris II, which was found at Tanis [175]. This heaviness is emphasized by the big lappet wig, and there is something of that harsh vigour which appears in the later royal portrait sculpture. In much of the private sculpture there is a tendency to stylize the forms of the body. Seated figures are wrapped in cloaks with little indication of the form beneath. Men are commonly shown in a squatting position with the knees drawn up so that the body, covered by a long garment, assumes a block-like form which provides flat surfaces to be covered with inscriptions. All the life seems to be concentrated in the face framed by a bulky wig. The process begun here was to turn such statues of a later period into something

172. Hor. Ka-statue. Dynasty XIII. *Cairo Museum*

The tombs of Wah-ka I and Ibu were probably successively built in the reigns of Amenemhat II and Sesostris III, while the last of the three Nomarchs, Wah-ka II, lived in the time of Amenemhat III.[21] From his tomb comes a fragment of a large standing figure of dark stone [178] which might be mistaken for work that was done in the Late Period from Dynasty XXV onwards. The deeply indented medial line of the abdomen is found, however, in hard stone royal statues of Dynasty XII. The contrast between the treatment of the highly polished surfaces of the statue of Wah-ka II and that of the limestone sculpture from Qaw is only another instance of the varied nature of the art of the Middle Kingdom.

Private statuary develops on several levels. In the Old Kingdom almost all of the statuary derives from the mastaba tomb chapels and the enclosed 'closets' called serdabs, which occasionally included a large series of limestone or wood statues. In Dynasty XII the context of the statues when known has generally shifted to the temples and to the cenotaphs, such as those at Abydos, where the statues represent the individual as a spectator, so to speak, of the temple rites and the great annual processions. These vary in size from the

173 and 174. Sennuwy. Seated granite statue from Kerma, with detail of head. Dynasty XII. *Boston, Museum of Fine Arts*

175. Nefret. Seated statue from Tanis. Dynasty XII. *Cairo Museum*

more like a cult object than the representation of a living person. This unrealistic approach is found in the remarkable pieces of brightly painted limestone sculpture in Turin from the terraced tombs of the Nomarchs Wah-ka I and Ibu at Qaw el Kebir. The surfaces are crisply cut, with the eyebrows and rim of the eye painted blue. The hair, with its regularly incised wavy lines, is black and the skin a light red. The lively impression produced by these fragments of over-life-size statues is apparent in the face of Wah-ka I. The piece with the left eye and hair has been fitted to a portion of the lower part of the face [176].[19] The head of Ibu [177] is better preserved, but lacks something of the strange superhuman intensity which the freshly preserved paint lends to Wah-ka's face.

Another badly damaged piece of limestone sculpture indicates that work in this style was being produced earlier at Thebes. This is the large seated statue of Senet, the wife of a vizier of Sesostris I, Intefiker. It has been put together from many small pieces and still stands in the dark shrine at the back of Tomb No. 60 at Thebes.[20] Such rarely preserved painted limestone sculpture of Dynasty XII has much in common with that of Queen Hatshepsut at Deir el Bahari in Dynasty XVIII [226, 227]. This is partly due to the similar colouring and crisp carving of the limestone. However, Hatshepsut's statues represented her as Osiris, and the craftsmen who executed the statues of Wah-ka I were evidently striving to endow the tomb statue of a private man with an other-worldliness like that which the royal sculptors had earlier imparted to the seated figure of King Mentuhotep [153].

176. Wah-ka I. Fragmentary head from Qaw. Dynasty XII. *Turin, Museo Egizio*

178. Wah-ka II. Fragment of statue from Qaw. Dynasty XII. *Turin, Museo Egizio*

177. Ibu. Head from Qaw. Dynasty XII. *Turin, Museo Egizio*

large squatting scribal statues of Mentuhotep, an official of Sesostris I and Amenemhet II, from the temple of Karnak (three in the Louvre, three in Cairo, and two in the Luxor Museum) to occasionally very small statuettes in stone, ivory, and wood. A statuette in Baltimore illustrates the high level of achievement of a sculptor working in ivory, with care devoted to the details of the pleating of the long frontal tab of the skirt and the articulation of the hands, even down to the meticulous treatment of the fingernails [179].

A private collection of bronze statuary of the time of Amenemhat III–IV continues the history of this medium from the time of the large statues of Pepy I from Hierakonpolis. The find included three royal statues, of which one with a separate headcloth is a bust from the waist about three-quarters life size. There were also four or five statuettes of stewards wearing the long fringed wrap-around skirt extending to the nipples, as exemplified by a statuette from this find in Munich [180]. The text on the base of another of these statues provided the name, titles, and filiation of Senebsuemai, an official known from Abydene stelae. Details of the technique of casting these statues must await their eventual publication. Use is made of gold/silver inlays for the eyeframes and other elements. Inlaid gold is also liberally used in the representation of the eyes, scales, and other markings of the extraordinary crocodile, said to be from the same find, in Munich [181]. Although it has been suggested that the crocodile belongs to a much later period, our knowledge of Middle Kingdom animal sculpture iconography is too scanty for us to reject the Middle Kingdom attribution at this point.

179. Official. Ivory statuette. Dynasty XII(?) *Baltimore, Walters Art Gallery*

180. Steward. Bronze statuette. Dynasty XII. *Munich*

181. Crocodile. Bronze with gold inlays. Dynasty XII(?) *Munich, Staatliche Sammlung Ägyptischer Kunst*

182. Sesostris III. Head from Medamud. Dynasty XII. *Cairo Museum*

183. Amenemhat III. Head of seated figure from Hawara. Dynasty XII. *Cairo Museum*

Undeniably the greatest creations of the sculptors of this period are the portrait statues of the two great kings Sesostris III and Amenemhat III. They express in the most striking fashion the rude vigour, brutal strength, and determination which had made possible the rise of this powerful family. Their vitality and harsh realism represent a Theban element in the art of the Middle Kingdom. However, the faces of the standing figures which Sesostris III placed in the old temple of Mentuhotep at Deir el Bahari have developed a wise maturity and an expression of feeling unique in Egyptian sculpture, even though it is held in control and remains subject to long-maintained conventions. The dominating quality of such heads is that of an intelligent consciousness of a ruler's responsibilities and an awareness of the bitterness which this can bring [182]. It is no coincidence that this represents the same feeling as was formulated in a famous literary work, the admonitions of Amenemhat I to his son, which warns him to guard against subordinates, to avoid making intimates, and, if he sleeps, to guard his own heart, for a man has no adherents in the day of adversity.[22] A brooding seriousness appears even in the face of the young Amenemhat III [183] in a seated limestone statue from his Hawara pyramid temple which has more of the idealized character of the earlier seated figures of Sesostris I. Although there is here none of the hardness or the signs of weary age to be found in other heads of Amenemhat III, it is immediately apparent that this man lived in a different time from that which produced the serene confidence of the people of the Old Kingdom.

Of course not all portrait-sculpture of this period is necessarily grim. A wonderful portrait of a young princess now in the Brooklyn Museum [184] is a case in point. Although her expression is controlled, it is nevertheless almost light and laughing. As is true of all of the finest sculptural work in this era, certain details, especially the planes of the living flesh, are extremely naturalistic. The sculptor also indulges an interest in formal patterning, seen here, for example, in the clean ordered lines of the princess's hair and the schematic elaboration of her eyebrows and eyelids. It is this concern for the

184. Princess. Dynasty XII. *Brooklyn Museum*

185. Official. Statue from Heka-ib chapel, Elephantine. Dynasty XII

abstract and idealizing generalization of specific individual features which marks even the most naturalistic Egyptian portrait-sculpture, and reminds us that it is usually difficult and possibly even incorrect to speak of an artistic genre of portraiture, as we understand the term today, in ancient Egypt.

In recent years it has become apparent that the remarkable portraits of kings were also reflected in the statues made for their followers. A group of seated figures has been found set up in small brick shrines around the court of a sanctuary on the island of Elephantine. It was dedicated by these Middle Kingdom notables to a man of the late Old Kingdom, a certain Hekaib, who had become a sort of local saint. His tomb has also been found among those of the other caravan leaders of Dynasty VI high up in the western cliff. Here the Middle Kingdom Nomarchs also cut their tombs and decorated them with paintings that are now badly damaged. They looked out over a landscape new to anyone coming from Egypt, with the dark granite rocks and the green vegetation of the islands in the river contrasting with the yellow sand of the desert which closes in here at the First Cataract. This southern border town was a remote place, however important it had

always been for the quarrying of its granite and for the organization of the trade into the south. Its chief men had evidently been satisfied with poor sculptors to decorate their tombs in the Sixth Dynasty, and the hands of provincial craftsmen are strongly evident both in the paintings of the Nomarchs' tombs,[23] which resemble most in style those of Beni Hasan, and in the statues of the Heka-ib chapel. The latter vary considerably in quality but are well represented by that of Sa-renput [185].[24] The hard, brutal quality of the royal faces and their vigorous modelling have been reduced to a few simple planes. Nevertheless, these statues represent the realistic strain in Middle Kingdom art in an unusually interesting manner.

Aswan typifies the individual character maintained by the little courts of the provincial nobility in Middle Egypt from Qaw el Kebir in the Xth Nome, south of Assiut, to Beni Hasan in the XVIth Nome, north of Hermopolis. This was the region that had played such a part in the wars between Thebes and Heracleopolis, and the considerable measure of independence which was allowed the local families until well into the reign of Sesostris III is reflected in the decoration of the impressive tombs which were constructed in the neighbourhood of the Nome capitals at Qaw, Assiut, Meir, Deir el Bersheh, and Beni Hasan. These contribute to the variety of styles prevalent in the Middle Kingdom. Some of these men remained wealthy and powerful. Wah-ka II constructed the most pretentious of the tombs at Qaw. Structurally it resembled that of the others, but it was planned on a larger scale. It lay to the right of those of Wah-ka I and Ibu which are shown in the reconstructed drawing [186]. The huge rock-cut hall on the upper terrace and one of the rooms flanking the shrines behind it had paintings of a delicacy matched only by the fine low reliefs of Ibu. The dancers and tumblers [187] give some notion of the unusual character of the badly damaged scenes which are only partially published.[25] The refinement and subtlety of the colour and brushwork are paralleled at Meir in the chapel of Ukh-hotep III [191, 192] and at Bersheh in that of Djehuty-hetep [198] and on the coffin of Djehuty-nekht [193–5]. The last is not dated, but is closely related in style to Djehuty-hetep's paintings, which, like those of Ukh-hotep III, are of the reign of Sesostris III.

Work of comparable quality from an earlier time must once have existed in the great tomb of Hepzefa at Assiut in the reign of Sesostris I, in which were inscribed a remarkable series of contracts with his funerary priests for the maintenance of the offerings there. Part of an orchard scene with beautifully drawn goats, an acacia tree, and boys picking figs can still be made out on the blackened walls. The decoration of the ceiling of this hall introduced a new series of patterns of a type which appears later at Meir and Qaw and again on faience vessels from Kerma, although in this latter case the colour scheme is entirely different [206].[26] Even in its present sad state this great tomb speaks for the existence of a school of fine craftsmen established at Assiut in the early years of Dynasty XII which would explain the exceptional quality of the statue of Hepzefa's wife, Sennuwy. There had been a tradition of fine craftsmanship at Assiut in Dynasty X, and in the next Nome to the north the nobles of Cusae were able to command the services of exceptionally able artists for the work on their tombs at Meir.

186. Qaw, tombs of Wah-ka I and Ibu. Dynasty XII. Reconstruction

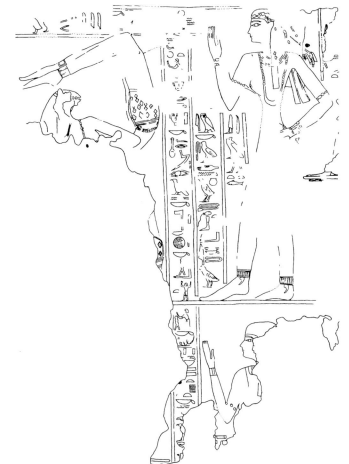

187. Qaw, tomb of Wah-ka II, dancers and tumblers. Dynasty XII

At Meir the tombs do not occupy the commanding position in which we find them at other sites in Middle Egypt. Their doorways open unobtrusively in the face of the featureless low slopes of the desert edge. The lack of architectural impressiveness is fully compensated by the fine workmanship inside. The craftsmen of the early reigns of the Twelfth Dynasty depicted the old repertoire of agricultural, hunting, and marsh scenes in low reliefs which carry on the naturalistic tradition of the Old Kingdom.[27] This work is a parallel to the accomplished adaptation of the Memphite style in the pyramid temples at Lisht. The quality of the relief varies, but the draughtsmanship remains at a very high level. The Meir artist handles an unusual pose smoothly, as in the old man carrying papyrus in the tomb of Ukh-hotep I, whereas Khnum-hotep's painter at Beni Hasan in a later reign folds back the shoulders awkwardly [188]. The stiff horizontal registers disappear in the hunting scene of Senbi's tomb, where the animals are placed upon undulating lines and show a new liveliness of action [189]. The hare springs forward with its hind legs raised [190].

In the latest of the Meir tombs, that of Ukh-hotep III of the reign of Sesostris III,[28] a new style has been developed which retains little to remind one of the Old Kingdom. The work is no longer in relief, but painted, and indeed executed by one of the finest painters of the Middle Kingdom. The big room has an offering-niche at the back [191]. A low stone bench ran

round the walls, but only the upper edge of this shows, since the sand had not been cleared away to floor level. A black-and-white false-door pattern formed a base for the paintings. Later cuttings have marred the walls, and the surfaces are badly scratched, but the colour retains its fresh pure tone. The back wall was covered with two big swamp scenes on each side of the offering-niche. Ukh-hotep spears fish on the left and hunts birds with a throwing-stick on the right. A detail of the fishing scene [192] gives some impression of the

188. Beni Hasan, tomb of Khnum-hotep, man with antelopes; Meir, tomb of Ukh-hotep I, peasant carrying papyrus. Dynasty XII

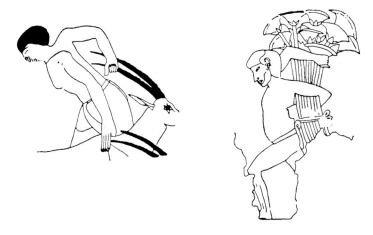

care lavished on the plants, water-birds, fish, and crocodile under the light craft, although the subtler nuances of colour are lacking. Ukh-hotep stands in the boat with his legs spread wide apart, and with one of the ladies of his family seated in a red dress beneath him. Another girl stands in front. Most unusual is the transparent skirt which the man wears over his short kilt. It is painted grey against the background. Where it covers the legs they are a deep red, while below the skirt they are stippled a light red. Similar transparent cloaks are shown on the women on this wall, and stippling and fine brush-strokes are used to indicate the texture of the plants, birds,

189 and 190. Meir, tomb of Senbi, hunting scene (details). Dynasty XII

191 and 192. Meir, chapel of Ukh-hotep III (*below*), with detail of swamp scene (*above*). Dynasty XII

193 and 194. Offering scene and offerings. Painted coffin of Djehuty-nekht
from Bersheh. Dynasty XII. *Boston, Museum of Fine Arts*

and fish. The same sophisticated brushwork appears on a
cloaked figure on the north wall. A transparent grey skirt
hangs down beneath the lower edge of the cloak, and the legs
and feet are stippled a lighter red below the hem of this skirt.
The cross stripes of the cloak are also stippled to produce a
change in colour from white along the lower part of each
band, through light green to a deeper green at the top.

Something like this shading with pigments appears again
on the outer coffin of Djehutynekht from Bersheh, where
there is a skilful suggestion of smoke from the coals of an
incense brazier held up by an attendant before the seated
figure of the owner [193]. The opalescent effect of a dove's
plumage is also imitated by the delicate grey and black strokes
that are applied with white over a pinkish underpainting
[194]. Sparing use is made of conventional outlines, the body-
colour being allowed to tell against the soft brown tone of the
cedar-wood which forms the background. This is particularly
evident in the green plants and vegetables in the pile of offerings which occupies the space to the right of the seated
Nomarch. When outlines are used, they are very fine, and the
most minute detail is lavished on the hieroglyphs and the

matting patterns of the 'palace façade' false-door on the left of
the offering scene [195]. The eyes above the door were
repeated on the outside of the coffin and again with the false-
door on an inner coffin of more ordinary workmanship which
fitted inside the painted one. The mummy lying on its side
faced these doors and eyes, and was thus given a magical
means of quitting or re-entering its burial-place.

These coffins, together with a pair for the Nomarch's wife,
were found with a set of wooden funerary models in the
burial-chamber of a collapsed rock tomb at Deir el Bersheh.
They are now in Boston.[29] It has been suggested, however,
that these coffins and the model procession should be
assigned to Dynasty XI. Djehuty-nekht is a different man
from the Governor of the Hare Nome with the same name
who was the owner of Tomb No. 1 at Bersheh. The decorations of this tomb of the reign of Sesostris I still have many of
the clumsy provincial characteristics of the preceding
period,[30] while the coffin paintings are like those of the tomb
of Djehuty-hetep, which, in the time of Sesostris III, is the
only one at Bersheh which represents the developed style of
Dynasty XII. Characteristically it is the last great tomb at that

195. False-door. Painted coffin of Djehuty-nekht from Bersheh. Dynasty XII. *Boston, Museum of Fine Arts*

site.[31] The chapel has only partially escaped the widespread damage done by quarrying and earthquake shock to the line of rock-cut tombs high up the cliff at the mouth of a desolate ravine [196]. These formed the cemetery of the chief men of Hermopolis in the Middle Kingdom. Djehuty-hetep's tomb is famous for the representation of a colossal statue being dragged from the alabaster quarries at Hat-nub. It was intended for a shrine which the Nomarch had established, perhaps in connexion with the temple in the town of Hermopolis.

There was once a portico with two palm columns painted to look like red granite, but this was destroyed and the east wall of the main chamber badly shattered by the subsidence of the rock. This rock-cut hall had a shrine in the middle of the back wall but no columns, as at Meir in the chapel of Ukh-hotep III [191]. There were reliefs on the walls of the portico, but in the hall only part of the lowest register and the large figures were cut in relief. The carving is very low and flat with little modelling and when painted is hardly to be distinguished from the rest of the walls, where the work was executed only in paint. This can be seen in the case of the ladies

of the Nomarch's family [197] standing in a long line in front of Djehuty-hetep, who is inspecting the various activities on his estate. In addition to the work in the fields, the vineyard, and the vegetable garden, the people of the household are cooking, making pots, and weaving. All this on the east wall, as well as the opposite wall with the transport of the colossus, the Nile vessels, and the fishing, bird-catching, and cattle-raising scenes, is painted in a manner closely resembling that on the inner faces of the great cedar-wood coffin of Djehuty-nekht. There is the same sureness of delicate line, meticulous detail, and variety of clear, pure colour. One suspects that the same master painter, or at least men trained under him, had a hand in both pieces of work. This painting is rivalled in quality only by that in the chapels of Ukh-hotep III at Meir and Wah-ka II at Qaw, although at the latter site the reliefs of Ibu are finer than those at Bersheh.

The same character is attractively represented by a fragment from the east wall with a slender man unloading a sheaf of grain from the back of a pink donkey to place it on the pile for the threshing-floor [198]. Exceedingly fine lines are used for the minute drawing of the heads of grain and for the delicate markings on the donkey. The man's hair has a rippled outline over his forehead, and the slender arms are arranged in a pattern, as are the tapering fingers with their

196. Deir el Bersheh cemetery. Dynasty XII

197 and 198. Daughters of Djehuty-hetep and the unloading of grain.
Paintings from the chapel of Djehuty-hetep at Bersheh. Dynasty XII. *Cairo Museum*

carefully indicated nails. The decorative elegance of the design, like the soft reds and browns, which in this period verge on lilac and rose at one extreme and deep crimson and chocolate colour at the other, shows a refinement of the Theban style, as it emerged from the First Intermediate Period in Dynasty XI. The slim ladies with their lotus crowns, curled wigs, and pectorals [197] recall those on the Kawit coffin [157] and the reliefs of Queen Neferu [156], as

do other figures in Ukh-hotep's chapel at Meir, in the tombs of Ibu and Wah-ka II at Qaw, and on the Bersheh coffin. There is nothing to suggest the Old Kingdom influence which had appeared farther south at Meir in the earlier part of Dynasty XII. Nor was this apparent at any time in the work of the Beni Hasan tombs in the next Nome to the north, which was even nearer to Memphis. The development at Beni Hasan breaks off in the reign of Sesostris II with the tomb of Khnumhotep, which still betrays many signs of the provincial clumsiness of the Dynasty XI tombs at that site. This is even more apparent in the paintings of the other well-preserved Dynasty XII tomb of Amenemhat, which is of the reign of Sesostris I. Evidently the time element has much to do with the fact that the style of the Beni Hasan tombs is much closer to that at Aswan, where there are no more painted tombs after the reign of Amenemhat II, and Thebes, where the one well-preserved tomb of Senet and her husband, Intef-iker, was painted in the reign of Sesostris I.[32] Whatever the regional peculiarities, there was a development in the latest tombs of a few provincial sites which had close affinities with the Theban style of Dynasty XI, and was based on Upper Egyptian work of the First Intermediate Period. The early-Twelfth-Dynasty tombs at Meir form an exception, with their strong signs of Memphite influence; this may have some connexion with the neighbouring workshops at Assiut, which in early Dynasty XII seem to have been well in advance of other provincial centres. Although the remains of the decorations of Hepzefa's chapel show no signs of Old Kingdom influence, the statue of his wife Sennuwy is an outstanding example of the continuance of Memphite forms in sculpture in the round.

The princes of the Oryx Nome chose a beautiful site for their tombs at Beni Hasan looking out over a wide sweep of the cultivated valley at a bend in the river which runs in close at the foot of the rocky slope. These tombs have long been famous for their well-preserved rock-cut architectural detail and for their lively rendering of Middle Kingdom life.[33] We have referred already to the hall with lotus columns in the unfinished Tomb 18 [166]. For the first time in the portico and hall of the two Twelfth-Dynasty tombs of Amenemhat [165] and Khnum-hotep we can appreciate the beautiful use which could be made of the fluted or channelled polygonal column. It goes back to the Zoser temple at Saqqara, where, in the temple north of the pyramid, the excessively slender forms used elsewhere in that group of buildings [41, 42] were reduced to sturdier proportions more like these at Beni Hasan. Fluted columns had been employed in the badly damaged terraced tombs at Qaw, and one was recovered from a house at Kahun, but the few examples of polygonal columns that have been found between Dynasty III and Dynasty XII had plain surfaces like the sandstone examples in the Mentuhotep temple at Deir el Bahari. The channelled columns at Beni Hasan, later employed so effectively in Dynasty XVIII, are copied, like other architectural elements, from wooden forms, and they had probably long continued in use in domestic and civil architecture. The tomb of Amenemhat [165] shows particularly well the geometric patterns on the ceilings which evidently imitate mats attached to the roofing-poles in houses to keep bits of the mud filling of the roof from falling into the room.

199 and 200. Beni Hasan, chapel of Khnum-hotep, fig-picking and bird-trapping scenes. Dynasty XII

The paintings at Beni Hasan are covered with a greyish natural film which obscures both their outlines and colour, unless they can be very closely examined. Since they run up to a considerable height on the walls, they are difficult to study and produce a disappointing effect upon the visitor.[34] The liveliness and rough vigour of Khnum-hotep's paintings are well illustrated by the men gathering figs from a tree in which apes are busily eating the fruit [199]. The details are drawn on a large scale, and the figures have bulky proportions. The boorish profile of the man on the left and the shoulders folded over to approximate an attitude seen in profile are typical of the Beni Hasan draughtsman. A larger

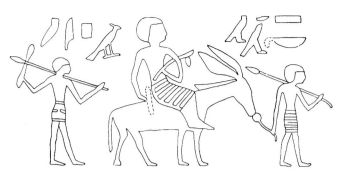

202. Serabit el Khadim, temple, Retenu chief riding a donkey. Dynasty XII

201. Foreign woman and child. Wooden statuette from Beni Hasan. Dynasty XII. *Edinburgh, Royal Scottish Museum*

panel placed over the entrance to the shrine at the back of the chapel [200] is flanked on the walls below by scenes of spearing fish and hunting birds in the marshes. Khnum-hotep sits behind a mat screen and pulls a cord to shut a bird trap. On each side of the water fowl in the pond below is an acacia tree in flower. The birds perched on the branches and fluttering beside the feathery green leaves and little yellow balls of the tree are carefully observed as to their species. They are a little stiff and have been described as resembling stuffed specimens, but they remain one of the most charming pieces of observation on the part of an ancient painter and a fine instance of the naturalistic impulse that remains constantly near the surface in all Egyptian work.[35] On one wall appears a caravan of Asiatic Bedouin traders in bright-coloured garments and with two children in a pannier on the back of a loaded donkey.[36] This group is echoed in an unusual little wooden figure of a foreign woman carrying a baby on her back in a fold of her robe [201], found in a tomb at Beni Hasan. Khnum-hotep's picture of the Bedouin caravan reminds us of the fact that, although the Egyptians are seldom represented as riding animals,[37] even after the introduction of the horse in the Second Intermediate Period, they recognized this as a custom of the people of Palestine and Syria. The Middle Kingdom stelae from the temple at Serabit el Khadim in Sinai show several of the friendly chiefs of Retenu on donkey back [202].[38]

CHAPTER 11

The Minor Arts and Foreign Relations of the Middle Kingdom

If we turn to the minor arts it is clear that the jewellers of the Twelfth Dynasty had reached a level of technical skill never exceeded at any other period of Egyptian history. Typical of the period are the magnificent necklaces with their big beads of amethyst and carnelian and the marvellously neat precision with which semi-precious stones are inlaid into cloisons of gold. The finest pieces of jewellery come from the tombs of ladies of the royal family at Dahshur and Lahun and are exhibited in Cairo and in the Metropolitan Museum in New York.[1] Two ivory-inlaid caskets which contained part of the Lahun treasure have been ingeniously reconstructed in New York.[2] The contemporaneous jewels of Princess Sat-Hathor and Queen Mereret were buried under the floor of the lower gallery of the princesses near the Pyramid of Sesostris III at Dahshur in similar wooden boxes encrusted with gold. Perhaps the loveliest of all these pieces belonged to a lady of a generation earlier, the daughter of Amenemhat II, Princess Khnumet, who with another princess named Ita was buried beside their father's Dahshur pyramid. This is a crown of interlacing strands of gold wire dotted with star-shaped flowers and at regular intervals studded with larger crosses formed of four open papyrus flowers set round a central disk [203]. The airy lightness of the gold work must have allowed the tiny carnelian and turquoise inlays which formed the flowers to appear as though scattered through the hair of the wearer. This is a more sophisticated version of the simple circlet of twisted wire with strings of gold rosettes pendant upon the hair worn later in Dynasty XIII, by a lady named Senebtisi, buried at Lisht.[3] Ordinarily the effect must have been somewhat heavier, as in the lotus-flower bands and the necklaces with their big pectorals[4] worn by the ladies of the family of the Nomarch of Bersheh, Djehuty-hetep, in the relief from his tomb [197], or the boldly modelled falcon heads from the ends of Khnumet's broad collar [204]. A second crown from Khnumet's tomb has lyre-shaped elements that seem to be derived from the volutes of the plant of Southern Egypt and the slender curling paired plant forms in the rosette of the crown of Sat-hathor-yunet [205],[5] a design that goes back at least to early Dynasty IV in the inlays of Queen Hetep-heres.

Both these crowns[6] had rather clumsy erections at the back which mar the effect of the beautifully designed head-bands. That of Khnumet was in the form of a slender gold tube from which projected thin gold leaves. Sat-hathor-yunet had two plumes cut from heavier sheet gold, while similar streamers hung down at the sides and back with small gold tubes strung on the plaits of hair in between. A detail of the front of the gold band gives an idea of the way in which the inlays were set in the regularly spaced flower rosettes and the cobra head which rears up above the forehead [205]. The rosettes are generally described as being evolved from lotus flowers, but, as so frequently in Egyptian ornament, they are composed of various plant forms derived from Old Kingdom designs which included bound papyrus elements (as in the Atef crown), the sedge which seems to have formed the basis for the Southern Plant, and buds which are hard to identify but may be lotus (see illustration 89).[7] It is only a short step from the volutes which frame the buds on the Lahun crown to the figure-8 plant-spiral which we shall see is used in wall and ceiling paintings in the Twelfth Dynasty [206] in designs which formed a basis for an even more elaborate development in the Eighteenth Dynasty.[8]

The lotus sometimes appears as one of the component parts of the Old Kingdom rosettes which as a whole may have been thought of as representing an open flower of this sort. Certainly the lotus was much used, as in the dainty bracelet clasps of Khnumet and Sat-Hathor [203], where the flowers hang down round protective symbols as though caught in the tiny gold bows which must have seemed to tie the ends of the bead bracelet.[9] Lotus flowers also appear as part of the design of one of the pectorals in the same illustration. Tiny lotus flowers connect the lyre-shaped volutes with simple rosettes on the second crown of Khnumet. The same lightness, delicacy, and precision of workmanship appears in other fascinating ornaments belonging to Princess Khnumet, such as the necklace [204] with its pendants of openwork stars and scalloped circles of granulated gold work, a technique also applied to a butterfly pendant from her tomb. The central element of the necklace has a recumbent bull or cow painted on a round plaque set in a gold frame and covered with a disk of rock crystal. This much discussed plaque is evidently not formed of inlaid stones or glass mosaic but presents an early example of miniature painting.[10]

The jewellery of the later group of princesses, Sat-hathor-yunet at Lahun and Sat-hathor and Mereret at Dahshur, is characterized by the girdles formed of gold cowrie shells or lion heads and by the five wonderful pectorals presented to them by the kings Sesostris II and III and Amenemhat III. Sat-hathor-yunet had two almost identical breast pieces with Horus falcons framing the name of her father Sesostris II on one and that of Amenemhat III on the other.[11] Sat-hathor received a similar pectoral from Sesostris II which appears at the top [204]. Here, instead of a triangular shape formed by the outline of the falcons, the composition has been placed inside a rectangular frame with a cornice like a small shrine. This treatment was to be followed in pectorals of a later period and is repeated in the Twelfth Dynasty by the two of Mereret which bear the names of Sesostris III and Amenemhat III.[12] That of Sesostris III is shown below [204], where the king takes the form of paired griffins trampling on his foreign enemies, although Amenemhat in human guise dominates Asiatics on the second piece. Both versions of the king's omnipotence over the foreigner are drawn from large wall compositions of the Old Kingdom. The chased gold back-frame repeats the design worked out in a harmonious combination of coloured inlays of semi-precious stones on the front. The exquisite workmanship and the deft arrangement of these symbols of royalty represent the Middle Kingdom

203. Crown of Khnumet from Dahshur. Dynasty XII. *Cairo Museum*

designer at his best. The griffins frame the name of the king, which is surmounted by the spreading wings of the protecting vulture goddess Nekhbet. The cornice rests on open lotus flowers and from their light stems a second flower bends down over the tail of the griffin. The amusing suggestion has been made that it may be from a misunderstanding of a design of this sort that a tail ending in a lotus flower has been given to a little female griffin[13] which is shown at Beni Hasan accompanying the Eleventh-Dynasty Nomarch Khety. Whatever inspired this bit of dry humour, which is of course earlier than our royal pectoral, it is typical of the Egyptian to come to grips with a fabulous monster by giving it a dog collar with a protective spike and naming it among the household pets, while at the same time employing the male form of the same beast as a symbol of royalty.

Precious objects like those from Dahshur and Lahun were sent as gifts by Amenemhat III and IV to the princes of Byblos far up the Syrian coast, where they were buried with these local rulers.[14] The gold-bound obsidian casket found there reminds one of the inlaid jewel boxes from Lahun. It is even richer in material and obviously of the best Egyptian workmanship, as is an obsidian ointment jar decorated with

gold which is a mate to those in the tombs of the princesses. The Byblos mirror is of a well known type, simpler than the Lahun piece, since it lacks the Hathor head which has been incorporated into the papyrus column of the handle. The Syrian craftsman at Byblos copied Egyptian jewellery as well as executing remarkable pieces of local type such as the scimitars, where hieroglyphic inscriptions are fashioned in different precious metals on a blackened ground. This is the earliest example yet known of the use of the niello technique. In spite of their renowned skill as metalworkers, the Byblos craftsmen lacked the Egyptians' exquisite neatness in the handling of inlaid stones. This is apparent in a pectoral which

204. Jewellery of Khnumet, Sat-hathor, and Mereret from Dahshur. Dynasty XII. *Cairo Museum*

205. Crown of Sat-hathor-yunet from Lahun. Dynasty XII. *Cairo Museum*

206. Decorative patterns. (A) and (B) Assiut, tomb of Hepzefa, ceiling; (C) Meir, tomb; (D) Lisht grey ware sherds; (E) Kahun painted sherd; (F) Kerma faience jar lid fragments; (G) Skirt of Keftiu

at first glance resembles those we have been examining from Dahshur and Lahun. As in an ornate oval pendant, with the name of the local ruler in a cartouche, there is a misunderstanding of the details being copied and a coarsening of the design.[15] Here in our first encounter with what was to be a long series of Syrian products incorporating Egyptian material, it is clear that methods of representation had been taken over from the old civilization in the Nile Valley by a people who were using them for purposes of their own without proper assimilation. A certain fantasy, alien to the Egyptian spirit, combined with an indifference to the original meaning of the design, lends an odd touch, even when there was an evident attempt to copy the original.

These Egyptian and Egyptianizing objects at Byblos are the clearest example of the strong influence which was being exerted upon the arts in the north, but they form only part of the evidence. In the Twelfth Dynasty there was an exchange of ideas, evident chiefly in a widespread give and take of decorative patterns and in the minor arts, which resulted from trade relations in the eastern Mediterranean of a more complex nature than anything known earlier. The firm rule re-established by Amenemhat I and his successors was accompanied by a foreign policy which produced stable conditions favourable to the sea trade between the Aegean, the Syrian ports, and Egypt. The borders of Egypt had been secured by the rulers of Dynasty XI, but they had not been able to go further than making the desert routes safe to the quarries and to the Red Sea at the point where expeditions had in the Old Kingdom set sail for Punt. The Sinai mines were evidently not worked again until the Twelfth Dynasty. Amenemhat, in re-establishing the very profitable old state-controlled caravan trade with the south, began the complete subjugation of Nubia as far as the region of the Second Cataract.

There is little or no record of a similar attempt to assert military control in Palestine and Syria, but it should be remembered that if it were not for the account of a rather obscure man on a stela at Abydos, we should have no inkling of a military expedition of Sesostris III which may have reached far into Palestine.[16] There was excavated at Megiddo a statuette of Djehuty-hetep, the governor of the Hare Nome, whose tomb at Bersheh we have seen to be one of the finest of the Twelfth Dynasty. Since he lived in the reign of Sesostris III, it is certainly relevant to speculate whether he may not have held a post at Megiddo. The mention of cattle of Retenu in his tomb has been doubted,[17] but should perhaps be considered as tribute exacted from Palestine, especially since cattle of the Aamu (Asiatics) are represented along with foreign herdsmen in a Meir tomb of the reign of Amenemhat II.[18] There is also the case of the vizier Sesostris-ankh, whose statuette was found at Ugarit, along with two small sphinxes of Amenemhat III and the statuette of a princess who may be the same as the daughter of Amenemhat II, Khnumet, whose jewels we have been examining at Dahshur.[19] Certainly Ita, who was buried with her sister at Dahshur, is represented by a small female sphinx at the inland town of Qatna in Syria. The royal statuettes can be explained as official presents to the cities in which they were found, but it appears that persons less exalted than the vizier Sesostris-ankh and the Nomarch Djehuty-hetep travelled widely, since their small statuettes are found in Palestine and Syria, at the Cretan palace of Knossos, at Adana in Cilicia, and even in central Anatolia.[20] There seems no reason why the statue of a private man should have been exported, and it is likely that in most of these cases the small piece was carried along with the person it represented to serve as a tomb statue, should he have the misfortune to die abroad.

Although we still do not understand the historical implications very well, it is clear that we have entered into a new period of interchange which was to continue through the Second Intermediate Period and take on a truly international character in Dynasty XVIII, although this was to be largely limited to the minor arts as far as Egypt was concerned. Recent discussion has centred upon the Aegean and Asiatic complexities of this situation,[21] but Egypt's part in the interchange should also be considered in relation to the objects found at Kerma and the part which Egyptian craftsmen may have played in the Sudan.

The Egyptianizing objects appeared at Byblos in the same tombs with spouted silver vases with fluted bodies and handles, as well as part of a bowl decorated with a design of running spirals. A closely related group of silver bowls and cups was presented a little earlier in Dynasty XII by Amenemhat II to the temple of Tod near Luxor. They were sealed up in four bronze chests with a silver lion, Mesopotamian cylinder seals, and other precious objects of foreign manufacture, including gold ingots and a quantity of lapis lazuli. Some of the silver vessels anticipate a type of bowl that was to have a long history in Egypt and Syria from the New Kingdom onward. These have plain fluted sides, but there are others with torsional fluting. Both types of fluting are imitated in Cretan pottery of the Middle Minoan Kamares ware, and one Tod cup had a handle which anticipates those of the famous Vaphio cups from mainland Greece.[22] Painted

207. Gold fish pendant from Harageh. Dynasty XII. *Edinburgh, Royal Scottish Museum*

208. Decorated faience vessel fragments from Kerma. Dynasty XIII. *Boston, Museum of Fine Arts*

Kamares ware has been found at two sites in Egypt associated with the Lahun Pyramid of Sesostris II: Kahun and Harageh. One nearly complete vessel was buried in a Dynasty XII tomb at Abydos. Examples of the ware have also been found in Syria at Ras Shamra, the ancient port of Ugarit, and at Byblos.[23]

The decoration of the thin Middle Minoan Kamares ware is unusual not only for the beauty of its polychrome patterns, but in that it essentially gains its effect by employing light designs against a dark background. The appearance of the ware in Egypt has aroused long discussion since its first discovery because of its importance for the dating of the period in Crete called Middle Minoan II. It has been established that the sherds found at Harageh belong to the first phase of this period, while those at Kahun represent the second, with the Abydos vase possibly belonging to a transitional stage between the two. The relevant material has recently been examined again in connexion with the relative chronologies of Egypt, the Aegean, and western Asia.[24] The Harageh sherds were found with a stone inscribed with the name of Sesostris II in rubbish-heaps deposited near a Dynasty XII cemetery and over an earlier cemetery. The site lies on the western side of an outcrop of rock several miles long which rises in the middle of the cultivation between the desert and the river. The cemetery and rubbish-heaps faced the Pyramid of Sesostris II and the town beside its valley temple which Petrie named Kahun, across about 3 miles of cultivation. The Dynasty XII graves which range from the reigns of Sesostris II to Amenemhat III were unusually rich and belonged to some of the wealthier people concerned with the building and administration of the Lahun pyramid. They probably lived in the big houses that adjoined the workmen's quarter of the Kahun town, but may have had country estates here. It was thought that the foreign pottery, with other typically Dynasty XII material, might have been carried up to the cemetery in the clearance of one of these estates. From the grave of a child came the delightful gold amulet in the form of a fish [207], which is as beautifully fashioned as anything from the tombs of the princesses, although four others which accompanied it were less well made. Other graves contained fragments of an inlaid silver pectoral with the name of Sesostris II, like one found at Rikkeh but not as exquisitely worked as those belonging to members of the royal family, an inlaid silver hornet fashioned in the round on a circular clasp, and gold cylinders with granulated work and inlays.[25]

The town of Kahun continued to be inhabited to a certain extent in Dynasty XIII and its dump-heaps still used, as is shown by the types of Cypriot and Syrian pottery found there with the Minoan sherds. The possible range of the two forms of Middle Minoan ware in Egypt seems, therefore, to be from about 1885 B.C. in the reign of Sesostris II to some time in Dynasty XIII, but probably not later than 1750 B.C. The appearance of this Cretan ware in Egypt is important for Aegean chronology, but it should be remembered that it was developed from an earlier imitation of metal forms and a use of light on dark decoration in Middle Minoan I vessels which had established a character of their own earlier than anything of a similar nature is known from either Syria or Egypt.

Patterns that should be considered in connexion with the Cretan pottery appear in the paintings on the ceiling of the great hall of the tomb of Hepzefa at Assiut, which was completed in the reign of Sesostris I. They also appear on the faience vessels at Kerma. Some of these designs are executed in a light on dark technique. One of them on two fragments of a faience lid [206F] has an interlocking net pattern with palmettes which is very like that on the Kamares sherd published from Ras Shamra.[26] The resemblance between the spirals and dotted flowers of the Kerma faience [208] and a fragment of a Kahun painted pottery vessel [206E] is also striking.[27]

There can be no question of the similar general character of the designs used on the Kerma faiences and those of the ceiling paintings of certain Middle Kingdom tombs. The ceiling of Hepzefa's Assiut tomb has patterns in blue on a black ground, producing the light on dark effect of certain of the faience fragments [208], where a light green-blue is used against a dark blue. Hepzefa's paintings are now so blackened with dirt and so high from the floor that the designs copied by Wilkinson [206B][28] can no longer be seen clearly, and it is only possible to be certain of the simpler spirals and interlocking rectilinear scrolls [206A]. The last is a pattern of much the same character as that on the two fragments of a Kerma cup [208]. Although it can be seen no longer, the figure-8 plant-spiral seems, from Wilkinson's drawing, to have existed already at Assiut, as it certainly did framing a doorway in a Meir tomb of the time of Amenemhat II [206C] and on the ceiling of the tomb of Wah-ka II[29] at Qaw el Kebir of the reign of Amenemhat III. The plant in these spirals is evidently a very simple palmette developed from the voluted forms of the Old Kingdom [89, 90]. The figure-8 spiral turns up again on the skirt of a Cretan envoy in early Dynasty XVIII [206G] and on the ceiling of the Theban Twenty-sixth-Dynasty Tomb of Pedamenopet.[30]

There is an extraordinary diversity in the patterns used in the hundred rectangles into which the ceiling of the huge rock-cut hall of the tomb of Wah-ka II is divided. They contain interlocking scrolls like that of Hepzefa [206A–B], as well as overlapping squares similar to the superimposed patterns on a piece of Kerma faience [208, upper right]. They are combined with rosettes, quatrefoils, circles and dots, and palmettes in addition to the plant-spirals. These new patterns replace the old geometric designs based on matting which still appear with quatrefoils and stars in the majority of the Middle Kingdom rock-cut tombs [165]. On the ceiling of the tomb of Djehuty-hetep at Bersheh the yellow quatrefoils on a blue ground have been freed from the squares which ordinarily enclose them, and in the Kerma chapel K XI they have been developed into a six-lobed shape which is cut out of blue faience and inlaid in stone.[31]

It would seem reasonable to suggest that one of the sources for these new designs was textiles which, like decorated pottery and faience vessels, are easily portable. Geometric patterns were certainly derived from coloured matwork, which was probably fastened to the roofing to keep the crumbled bits of the mud packing from falling down into the room. Later it appears that these mats, lashed to the roofing poles, were plastered over to provide a smooth surface for painting. The exposed roofing timbers generally limited the painted surface to small compartments, and this is certainly the origin of the multitude of rectangles with different designs in the Qaw ceiling just described. An early Egyptian example of a large figured textile is the sail of the state ship of Sahura represented in his reliefs at Abusir in Dynasty V. The rosettes on this are similar to the lotus rosettes at Qaw.[32] Certainly the plant elements in the Middle Kingdom designs did not come from abroad. For the Aegean source of the use of complicated spiral designs a good case has been presented. Basically it is the interweaving character of some of the new designs, which connect all parts of the surface in a continuous all-over pattern, that suggests the Aegean. The same is true of the torsional whirls and continuous spirals of the Tod and Byblos vessels. It is perhaps more important to recognize that this is a period of widespread interchange than to attempt to trace the exact source of each detail, even if this were possible. It is well to remember, though, in considering this interchange, that the Egyptians had long shown themselves particularly facile in the use of plant ornament and that they were in a dominant position in the Twelfth Dynasty.

The Middle Kingdom craftsmen are well known for their delightful glazed figures of the hippopotamus and other animals, but products like those from Kerma are uncommon in Egypt itself. The vessels and larger works such as the big inlays of walking lions from the funerary chapel Kerma II (the upper Defufa) are thoroughly Egyptian and have nothing of a local Sudanese character. The same is true of the somewhat similar figures made of glazed quartz.[33] Broken vessels found in similar quantity at Deir el Bahari and in Sinai are appar-

ently all of the New Kingdom.[34] A complete bowl with flying birds like those of illustration 208 was excavated in a grave at Qaw dated to the Second Intermediate Period.[35] Reisner found that the faience vessels increased in number in the great tumuli at Kerma which were built later. They continue through the Second Intermediate Period, but all form a remarkably homogeneous group in which it would be difficult to make distinctions between earlier and later pieces. In fact, it is now suggested that the typically Middle Kingdom faiences, hippopotami, animals, and vessels are much more likely to belong to Dynasty XIII and the Second Intermediate Period.

The same is true of the Syro-Palestinian pottery vessels with incised designs filled in with white pigment which are widely distributed in Egypt and Nubia. Ordinarily the ware is dark, but reddish fabrics occur. Best known are the little handled jugs, long called Tell el Yahudiyeh ware from the site in the Delta which was thought to be a Hyksos encampment. But in addition to their characteristic dot-filled triangles and geometric patterns, these jugs bear other designs which are related to those on the Kerma faiences and the ceilings of Middle Kingdom tombs. There are also a few other vessels of different shapes. In the rooms at the foot of the stairway to the 'fort' at Kerma was found a remarkable jar [209, 210] and part of the shoulder and a fragment of a base of one (or more probably two) of the characteristic little jugs,[36] several of which were found in the tombs. The shoulder fragment has a voluted plant which begins to suggest the Minoan lily, such as appears on three little jugs joined together which, with a vase in the shape of a bird, belonged to a mayor of Thebes named Yuy at the end of the Second Intermediate Period.[37] Part of another bird vase and a pottery fish were found at Lisht with jugs of dark ware. These were mostly decorated with the usual incised geometric patterns, but a few shoulder fragments had interesting designs such as the voluted plant, the twisted rope guilloche, running spirals, and a band of pot-hooks above the arm of a man [206D]. There was even a motif which resembles the whorl-shell pattern of Middle Minoan pottery [206D].[38] This material from Lisht apparently occurred in a context which makes it uncertain whether some of it belonged to the Dynasty XII graves there or was intrusive from the Dynasty XIII village which grew up around the pyramid of Amenemhat I. The most remarkable piece from this area was a vase with birds and dolphins painted in red on a pinkish-buff ground with the outlines and details incised and filled with white. A Middle Minoan source has been convincingly deduced for the dolphins, again suggesting the late Second Intermediate connexions of some of these designs.[39] The most elaborately decorated of the small jugs was found at the town of Kahun, where, as at Lisht and Kerma, there was evidently a possibility of the continuance of material from the Twelfth Dynasty into at least Dynasty XIII. It was of dark ware and had goats paired on each side of a vine and a palm.[40] Similar jugs in both red and dark ware are known, from a private tomb at Byblos and another at Sinet el Fil, in Syria, with plant and spiral designs as well as the more common geometric decorations.[41]

The Kerma vase [209] seems to belong to these others for which a Syro-Palestinian source is certain. Like them it does not resemble the coarser Nubian black pottery with its white

209 and 210. Incised grey ware vessel from Kerma, with detail. Dynasty XIII(?). *Boston, Museum of Fine Arts*

there, it provides evidence for the interchange between Egypt, Syria, and the Aegean.

The skilled craftsmen at Kerma came in contact with new materials and local manufactures. They assimilated these, and in turn influenced the local crafts. The result was a peculiar style, predominantly Egyptian but much modified by African elements. We have referred to the faience industry. However, one of the products peculiar to Kerma was a black-topped red pottery of unusual thinness and polish which was made in a number of new and interesting shapes.[43] There were also coarser vessels with incised decoration imitating basketwork which belong to a well-known tradition in Nubian pottery. In the compartments of the great tumulus were found a few red pottery vessels with a white slip on which decorations were painted in several colours. Painted pottery is rare in Egypt and is virtually unknown between Predynastic times, when the design was in one colour, and Dynasty XVIII, when polychrome decoration appeared. The incised pottery of the C-group people of Nubia at the time of the Middle Kingdom also employed several bright colours in its basketwork patterns, in addition to white filling in the incisions of the dark surface.[44] The painted vessels at Kerma have geometric designs similarly imitating basketwork, but one pot includes plant designs and another has a figure of a man between two lions [211].[45] The clumsy lotus flowers between dotted triangles and the way in which the two awkward beasts are painted are vaguely reminiscent of Syro-Palestinian design, but this evidently results from a similar attempt by a local craftsman to adapt himself to Egyptian methods of drawing. Elements derived from Nubian basketwork are used interchangeably on all these vessels which employ the same colour scheme. Yellow, red, and black are used on the white slip, while a little green appears in the lotus flowers. They may all be the products of one pot-painter who derived his ideas of figure subjects from wall-paintings earlier than the ones in the Kerma chapels II and XI. These were badly preserved, and the figures of animals in chapel XI suggest that their loss has not deprived us of a great work of art.[46] However, both chapels appear to have been repainted during alterations undertaken in the

211. Painted pottery from Kerma. Second Intermediate Period. *Boston, Museum of Fine Arts*

filled designs imitating basketwork. The body of the vase is covered with bands of running spirals, except on one side, where a flower rosette is flanked by lotus-flowers [210]. Under the rosette is incised a name, the hieroglyphs reminding one of the crudely formed signs on Hyksos scarabs. Traces of red and yellow pigment survive in the incisions, in addition to the usual white. It may be that we have here one of the latest examples[42] of this imported incised ware, like the triple jug of Yuy at Thebes. Thus in the Hyksos Period there returned to Egypt plant ornament which had been modified according to Syrian taste. Mingled with these plant-forms are elements which suggest designs on Middle Minoan painted pottery which we have seen had reached both Syria and Egypt in Dynasty XII. It has generally been thought that some of the dark incised ware also came to Egypt as early as that time. The examples which we have been discussing seem to cover a long range of time. Although there is still no clear evidence from the Egyptian side as to when it first began to be used

212. Ivory inlays from Kerma. Second Intermediate Period. *Boston, Museum of Fine Arts*

213. Mica cap ornaments from Kerma as remounted. Second Intermediate Period. *Boston, Museum of Fine Arts*

Second Intermediate Period. Unfortunately the partial answer which might have been supplied by the decoration of the burial-chambers of the great tumulus (K III) was also destroyed. Only a winged sun-disk and traces of coloured bands remained on the walls.[47]

The footboards of the beds on which the burials were made in the Kerma tumuli were decorated with remarkable ivory inlays in which the African element is pronounced,[48] as it is in the mica ornaments which were sewn on caps. These curious mica ornaments are not found in the other tumuli and apparently were not much used after late Dynasty XIII. Similarly the finest examples of the thin black-topped red vessels were early, as was the glazing of stone, although the faience industry apparently decreased its output, judging from the number of fragments found before the last two tombs (K III, K IV).[49] The skill in drawing the local animals of these fascinating designs was certainly Egyptian, as is the hippopotamus goddess Thueris among the ivories [212], but there are many curious un-Egyptian features. The bodies of the vultures are seen in profile instead of in front view, as in Egypt, and the

simplification of the foliage of the tree between the paired goats is unusual, as are the superimposed plant forms and the pose of the running gazelle. Particularly striking is the combination of paired animals, or parts of animals, back to back.

Nothing with quite such a fantastic twist had appeared in Egypt since Predynastic times. The griffin-like bird-heads of the mica inlays have this same quality, as do a number of other designs such as the double-headed vultures [213]. The 'griffin' heads were probably placed above one another in pairs according to a frequent principle of local design, rather than being placed under trees, as would at first appear. These birds and animals were sewn around the cap to form a wide band. On top of the head [213], in this case above double-headed vultures, was a centrepiece made up of two openwork plaques with three-petalled flowers at the sides and small triangles inserted between. Sometimes there was a circular disk in the centre, and once a many-petalled 'star'.[50] In one Kerma burial the skull was encased in a badly preserved silver cap with cut-out patterns.[51]

CHAPTER 12

The Second Intermediate Period: Dynasties XIII–XVII 1786–1570 B.C.

The burials in the large tumuli at Kerma were interpreted by their discoverer, Reisner, as being those of a succession of Egyptian governors of that fortified trading-post during a period of some two hundred years from Hepzefa's death in the reign of Amenemhat II to the end of Dynasty XIII. Strong objections have been voiced against this view,[1] although the analysis of the contents of the Kerma graves has produced one of the few sequences of related material that provides some continuity in this difficult period which is so hard to understand in Egypt itself. The main point which has been difficult to accept is that upper-class Egyptians should have adopted the barbarous local burial customs. The chief figure in each of the great tumuli was buried on a bed, usually a wooden one with its footboard decorated with rows of ivory inlays but, in the case of the burial with the statue of Hepzefa and his wife, one made of quartz. Ordinarily there was no coffin.[2] The ruler was accompanied by his household and many retainers who, perhaps drugged by the wine of the funeral feast, were covered alive by the filling in of the central sacrificial corridor when the mound was heaped up over the brick compartments of the substructure on the day of the funeral. At Kerma the burials were those of the inhabitants of a large town that lay in the immediate neighbourhood of the palace. It is unfortunate that denudation has removed the buildings of this town, leaving only broken pottery and other widespread evidence of occupation on the surface. Close by the palace a few remnants of walls remained, protected from erosion, as well as some of the raw materials and partially worked objects for the industries. There is evidence that the cataract fortresses were maintained into Dynasty XIII, and the mud-seal impressions with the names of Hyksos kings seem to indicate that Kerma was in operation late in the Second Intermediate Period.[3] In Dynasty XVII, at the beginning of the war of liberation against the Hyksos, we know that the kings of Thebes recognized the existence of an independent ruler of Kush as well as the Hyksos in the northern part of Egypt.

Fragmentary royal statues were found at Kerma. In addition to those of kings of Dynasty XII, there was part of a statue base with the name of Sekhem-ra-khutawy, the first king of Dynasty XIII. There was also a fine wooden statuette of a king whose name has been lost with the destruction of its base.[4] A piece of an offering basin of alabaster seems to have borne the name of one of the last kings of Dynasty XIII, Didumes, who was ruling when the Hyksos seized Lower Egypt. These statues may have been sent to Kerma officially by the kings whom they represent and may parallel the royal statues found in Syria at a period when Egyptian prestige was being maintained there. Obviously, the extraordinary material found at Kerma presents problems which cannot be entirely understood, but there is no doubt of the remarkable imprint which Egyptian crafts exerted upon a more primitive culture. The great tumuli were the burials of the kings of Kush, grown prosperous through trade, and the

Egyptian statues may have been acquired through this trade or taken as plunder from the northern forts.

In Egypt the kings of Dynasty XIII maintained the style and good craftsmanship of the Twelfth Dynasty in what smaller works were undertaken in the Theban district. There is remarkably little difference in style between a royal relief cut at the beginning of Dynasty XIII and one carved towards the end of the Second Intermediate Period.[5] Similarly, large royal statues found at Karnak and Tanis were executed in a manner that continues the traditions of the time of Sesostris III and Amenemhat III.[6] It appears also that the Lower Egyptian residence of the Twelfth Dynasty was maintained at Ith-tawe in Dynasty XIII, while four small pyramids of kings of Dynasty XIII are known on the edge of the western desert south of Memphis at Dahshur and Mazguneh.[7] Some influence was maintained in Syria, since a lapis cylinder seal couples the names of one of these kings, Sehetep-ib-ra, and that of Yakin-ilum of Byblos, and the son of this prince of Byblos, Yantin, is shown with a text citing a successor of Sehetep-ib-ra, King Kasekhem-ra Neferhotep, on a relief at that Syrian port. We shall see, though, that the international correspondence maintained with the Syrian towns which was discovered in the palace of Mari on the upper Euphrates ignores Egypt at the beginning of the eighteenth century B.C.

This is not then the complete collapse that was once thought to have occurred, nor did material culture reach the low ebb of the First Intermediate Period. On the other hand the long list of rulers to be divided between Dynasties XIII and XIV does indicate a state of political weakness with frequent reversals of power and a rival Dynasty which perhaps maintained itself in the western Delta after the arrival of the Hyksos. A general impoverishment is indicated not only by the absence of large public works and the small size of the few royal tombs known, but by the disappearance of decorated tombs of officials throughout the country. The two or three rock tombs known at El Kab and across the river at Hierakonpolis are as poor in execution as any of those carved and painted after the collapse of the Old Kingdom.[8] They do not have the same interest for us that the earlier poor tombs provided, since they seem to lack the clumsy flashes of originality which really led to something new in Dynasty XI through a shift from the style of the Memphite school to that of Upper Egypt. The art of the New Kingdom developed fairly directly out of the Theban style of Dynasty XII, which had been kept alive in the royal workshops throughout Dynasty XIII. Probably to be assigned to Dynasty XIII is the standing statue of the vizier Sobkemsaf, now in Vienna [214], which successfully captures the stately corpulence of the mature official.

The darkness which lies over the Second Intermediate Period results from the meagreness of historical record, and this is further aggravated by the Hyksos invasion. It was hardly a period of illiteracy, since some of our most important evidence for earlier literary documents, particularly those of a scientific nature, comes from copies which were made at this time. The Egyptians were naturally reluctant to dwell upon their subjugation, and the foreigners have left little to tell of their domination except for scarabs in a garbled Egyptian style and writing, which are found widely spread in Egypt, the Sudan, Palestine, and Syria. A few objects bear the names of these kings, as do statues usurped by them and found at Tanis. The origin of this people has not yet been determined satisfactorily. They were referred to as 'Rulers of Foreign Lands' or as Aamu, the usual term for nomad barbarians. Earthwork defences in Palestine and the Egyptian Delta have been associated with them as well as the Tell el Yahudiyeh ware which was certainly used in their time.[9] The advent of the Hyksos into Egypt seems at first to have resembled the earlier infiltration of nomadic people across the eastern border of the Delta which occurred after the collapse of the Old Kingdom. It is difficult to determine at exactly what time such foreigners had become established in Palestine. The first half of the eighteenth century B.C. was a time of prosperity for the Syrian coastal cities, and farther north there flourished

214. Sobkemsaf. Dynasty XIII. *Vienna, Kunsthistorisches Museum*

states such as Yamkhad, which included Aleppo and Alalakh, or on the Upper Euphrates, Mari, which was brought to an end by the conquest of Hammurabi. Palaces were constructed at Mari and Alalakh (Tell el Atchana) with wall-paintings which suggest an interchange long evident in the minor arts.[10] The seventeenth century was to see the growth of the great palaces in Crete and a brilliant development in painting which owes not a little to Egypt. The contacts which made this possible now have the support of written evidence which had remained so meagre before 1800 B.C. The cuneiform tablets known as the Mari letters, although they do not mention Egypt, show that the king of Mari was in communication with the cities of Ugarit and Byblos on the Syrian coast via the king of Yamkhad at Aleppo. Not only was he receiving copper from Cyprus (Alasya), textiles from Byblos, and other products from Crete (Kaptaru), but his new palace was so talked of that the King of Ugarit expressed a wish to see what it was like.[11]

A well stratified site is currently being excavated at Tell el Debaa in the eastern Delta in the neighbourhood of the original Avaris at Qantir. The Austrian excavators have in fact located a settlement corresponding in part to the Palestinian Middle Bronze II/b, c (Albright's terminology) or II/i–v (Kenyon's terminology), with quantities of Tell el Yahudiyeh ware, a Palestinian-type temple with tripartite sanctuary (Level F), burials of warriors with weapons and accompanying donkeys (Level E), and preceded stratigraphically by a destruction layer of ash. To all intents and purposes, the site suggests a settlement which is the archaeological equivalent to the historical concept of the Hyksos.[12]

The seventeenth century presents a confused picture in western Asia which excavation has not yet succeeded in clearing up. The situation much resembles that in Egypt. Contrasted with this is the rise of the flourishing Middle Minoan III civilization of Crete. The often-quoted appearance of the name of the Hyksos King Khian on a jar lid at the Cretan palace of Knossos and on a small, roughly made grey granite lion which had been built into the wall of a house in Baghdad[13] certainly suggested continued contacts of a far-reaching nature. Egypt may have been at a low ebb both politically and artistically, but the presence of Asiatic rulers could imply that the communications testified by the Mari letters had not ceased and that Syria still retained the cultural advantages gained in the preceding period. Even if we discount the extensive Hyksos empire that was once imagined, we could expect that a fairly unified control may have been maintained over northern Egypt, Palestine, and part of Syria. That trade must have continued under the Hyksos domination is evident from the interplay of influences appearing in Dynasty XVII and at the beginning of the New Kingdom before the full effect of Egypt's new foreign wars could be felt. The rich Asiatic booty brought back from these wars seems hardly consistent with a long preceding period of depression in Palestine and Syria. Even Kamose in one of the first attacks on the Hyksos strongholds in northern Egypt at the beginning of the war of liberation in Dynasty XVIII recounts a surprising treasure seized from the vessels of the enemy.[14]

At the height of the Hyksos power in the middle of the seventeenth century, Khian and one of his successors left inscriptions at Gebelein, a little south of Luxor, which makes it appear that for a brief time they controlled the Theban district.[15] In Dynasty XVII their power extended only as far as the region of Hermopolis in Middle Egypt, and Upper Egypt seems to have escaped during most of the period except for the probable payment of tribute. The Hyksos capital was at Avaris (Qantir) in the eastern Delta. The situation was in fact somewhat reminiscent of the position of Heracleopolis versus Thebes in Dynasties IX and X of the First Intermediate Period. As in those earlier times there again appears some written account of affairs when the Theban princes began to push northward. In a folk-tale we glimpse a council meeting in which King Sekenenra considers the complaint of the Hyksos King Apophis in the Delta that his sleep is troubled by the bellowing of the hippopotamus in the southern city of Thebes. The terrible head wounds of the mummy of this pharaoh have suggested that he died in an unsuccessful action against the hated enemy.[16] His son and successor Kamose records considerable progress against the Hyksos on two Karnak stelae. The second of these was discovered in 1954. It continues the narrative from the first and in an interesting passage tells of the interception of a letter from the Hyksos King to the King of Kush. The messenger was travelling by a desert route through the western oases. This confirms the establishment of contact between the Delta and the Sudan and by means other than traffic along the Nile Valley. It presents fascinating implications in connexion with objects at Kerma which we have been examining.

A ship's captain in his tomb at the southern town of El Kab laconically supplies a few details to carry the story to completion in the reign of Ahmose, the first king of Dynasty XVIII, with the capture of the Delta capital Avaris and the pursuit of the enemy into Palestine, where their stronghold of Sharuhen was taken.[17] In this war of liberation the Thebans displayed the same hardy spirit and intelligence as had their ancestors in Dynasty XI. They had now learned to use the new arms which had been introduced into Egypt by their oppressors. Infinitely more important than the new body-armour and weapons brought from Asia were the horse and chariot which supplied a mobility and speed of action hitherto unknown. No wheeled vehicle is represented until the Second Intermediate Period. It appears in the form of a rather clumsy carriage for a sacred bark in a Thirteenth-Dynasty tomb at El Kab and, somewhat later, in a model of a similar four-wheeled carrier for a small gold boat [215] among the funerary equipment of Queen Ah-hotep, the mother of Kamose and Ahmose, who was buried by the latter early in Dynasty XVIII.[18] Although both the horse and the chariot are mentioned in the accounts of the war with the Hyksos, representations of them only begin to appear in the early Eighteenth Dynasty and are not very frequent even at the time of Hatshepsut.[19]

In the warlike atmosphere of the end of the Second Intermediate Period it is not surprising that some of Queen Ah-hotep's most handsome burial equipment should have consisted of weapons [216, 217]. They display the same heavy magnificence that appears in the jewellery of the queen.[20] This is excellently exemplified by the massive quality of the inlaid gold bracelet with sphinxes flanking a cartouche of her son King Ahmose [218]. The design is apparently developed

from an earlier armlet with lions that belonged to the queen's elder son, Kamose. Spacers with recumbent cats, on the other hand, ornamented the bracelet of a queen who lived some years before in the Second Intermediate Period. However, these cats were lighter elements in beadwork bands, as were the couchant lions at Lahun, which apparently suggested such a use of animals in jewellery.[21] There is no question but that the lightness of touch of the Twelfth-Dynasty jewellery has disappeared. The altered character is particularly evident, in spite of the technical dexterity, in the inlaying of Ahhotep's pectoral and two other bracelets, as well as the magnificent weapons. It should be remembered that the axe and dagger [216, 217], the armlet [218], and other pieces of jewellery were presented to the queen in the first reign of Dynasty XVIII by her son Ahmose and show the improved craftsmanship of the more prosperous times after 1570 B.C. Kamose had also contributed a portion of his mother's burial equipment, and her coffin may have been provided by her husband Sekenenra before his untimely death. As in the case of Ahhotep's mother Queen Teti-sheri, who also lived on into the first years of Dynasty XVIII and whose statuettes might have been made for her tomb when she was an old lady, it seems better to consider the jewellery, weapons, and sculpture here, since they reflect the spirit of transition to a new period as do the few other statues which have survived from the beginning of Dynasty XVIII.

The richly encrusted ceremonial dagger and axe [216, 217] represent a culminating point in the interplay of foreign influences which we have been observing since the Middle Kingdom. They also anticipate a new period of truly international contact which followed Egypt's foreign wars. The people whom the men of the Nile Valley were beginning to meet in daily contact soon would be depicted as arriving in Egypt either as prisoners of war or as members of foreign embassies. It was not long before Cretans were shown with the Syrians and other people of western Asia in the paintings of the reigns of Hatshepsut and Tuthmosis III. On the axe-blade, below a figure of the king dominating a foreigner, lies a crested griffin of a form familiar from Minoan representations. The gold figures are set in a background formed of lapis lazuli inlays, the surface of which has disintegrated to a dark colour. The workmanship appears thoroughly Egyptian, the slenderness of the king and his victim being characteristic of this time and the details of anatomy and accoutrement carefully executed, considering the small scale.[22] The winged griffin, without a crest, is known from early times in Egypt and appears on the kind of Middle Kingdom pectoral which

215–18. Ah-hotep's gold model boat, dagger, axehead, and bracelet. Dynasty XVIII. *Cairo Museum*

was being imitated at Byblos in Dynasty XII. At the time of Hammurabi the paintings of the Mari palace show winged sphinxes beside an artificial tree with papyrus flowers which suggest a Syrian re-working of Egyptian material. Nearly two centuries later the crested griffin appears on the Ahmose axe at about the same time that it occurs with a female sphinx on the robes of women in a Knossos painting. It seems that these new forms were an oriental blending of Aegean and Egyptian elements which took place in such a coastal city as Byblos or Ugarit.[23]

The exchange of minor decorative elements is illustrated even more vividly by the dagger of Ahmose which was found with Ah-hotep's burial [216]. Not only does the blade exhibit an Aegean freedom of movement in the lion pursuing a calf in a rocky landscape treated in the Cretan manner, but the design is executed in a niello technique which is best known from famous examples at Mycenae. The animals and the row of grasshoppers towards which they leap, as well as the palmettes on the other side of the blade, are formed of gold wire let into a dark ground which is thought to be metallic sulphide.[24] Such a technique was already being employed at Byblos during Dynasty XII. The handsome weapon, with its

bull's head forming a transition to an inlaid handle terminating in gold-covered heads of women on the pommel, seems to have been made by an Egyptian craftsman like the other objects from Ah-hotep's burial. At the same time that these men were adapting a Minoan mode of representation, their contemporaries in the Aegean had developed an even more elaborate 'painting in metals' with which to depict cats hunting birds among papyrus plants, from an Egyptian source, but thoroughly Minoan in spirit.[25]

We have been examining the decorative arts of Dynasties XII–XVII more closely than will be possible with the overwhelming increase in the quantity of material under the Egyptian empire. Through this a glimpse has been obtained of certain basic elements which were to be used with considerable variation in later times. It should be emphasized that, while the designer continued to be intrigued by exotic new forms, he employed them as minor elements. The major arts remain outwardly unaffected, although a less easily definable change resulted from the mere existence of an empire with its attendant wealth and ostentation. The full effect of this is not apparent until after the reign of Tuthmosis III. It perhaps should not surprise us that the pull of old tradition in a long-established civilization should exert such force, but the vast length of time in which a consistent style was maintained is peculiarly Egyptian.

Reminiscent of the early Middle Kingdom are two seated limestone statuettes.[26] Both are more tentative in feeling out a new style. That of a nameless official, who probably lived in Dynasty XVII, suggests an experiment in the direction of the lighter, more graceful proportions of the New Kingdom. In this case daring undercutting has resulted in excessive thinness of limb as well as neck. On the other hand, the figure of Prince Ahmose, an elder brother of the king of that name and grandson of Teti-sheri, is more compactly conceived, like the painted limestone seated Amenhotep I in Turin,[27] no risks being taken with disengaged parts.

Thus on the eve of the New Kingdom forces appear which anticipate the elegance of the international age at hand. Yet prior to this final stage of the Second Intermediate Period the provincial and somewhat maladroit art of the south is still in evidence, as attested by stelae such as one in Cairo of a bowman and his wife [219]. The lifelessness and stiffness of the drawing can be unfavourably compared to the example from the First Intermediate Period [147].

219. Mentu-hotep and wife. Stela. Second Intermediate Period. *Cairo Museum*

PART FOUR

The New Kingdom

CHAPTER 13

The Early Eighteenth Dynasty: Ahmose–Tuthmosis III 1570–1450 B.C.

The art of the first half of Dynasty XVIII could be viewed as a final development of the classic Egyptian style which had grown up in the Middle Kingdom. Essentially the drive and inspiration came from Thebes, but there is completed here the fusion with basic elements of the Memphite school of the Old Kingdom which had begun in Dynasty XII, when Amenemhat I moved the court to the north. In architecture, sculpture, and painting a new breadth is given to already established forms, but with a restraint and simplicity which seem happily suited to the Egyptian spirit. There is a wonderful feeling of controlled vitality, of taut nervous energy, expressed in a perfected craft. This continues until the end of the reign of Tuthmosis III, when we begin to sense a change, as more complicated currents enter the mainstream of Egyptian civilization.

The great work of the period is the temple of Queen Hatshepsut erected in an original scheme of terraces rising against the towering cliffs of Deir el Bahari in Western Thebes. Although we can see how the design originated in earlier buildings, particularly in the Dynasty XI temple of Mentuhotep beside which it was built,[1] there is a broader conception here and a graciousness of line which make the earlier work seem tight and cramped by comparison. We have seen that the Normachs of Qaw in the Twelfth Dynasty had already used a system of terraces with structures partly built and partly cut in the rock [186]. One is tempted to seek a prototype of more recent date in the temple which Ahmose planned at Abydos at the beginning of Dynasty XVIII in connexion with his cenotaph there. Unfortunately all that remains is the foundations for a long terrace against the foot of the cliffs, and there appears to have been no resemblance between this and the scanty traces of a simple building of Amenhotep I which Hatshepsut replaced by her own funerary temple at Deir el Bahari. Moreover there is evidence that she at first only started on a project which adhered more closely to the plan of the Mentuhotep temple. This soon was replaced by the grander scheme we now know. Ahmose at Abydos seems to have been influenced by the courtyard on a platform which Sesostris III had constructed nearby at the foot of the desert escarpment. These two structures[2] bear a relation to one another similar to that of the Middle and New Kingdom temples at Deir el Bahari. It is the replacing of a squarish plan by elongated terraces that makes one suspect some connexion between the building of Ahmose and Hatshepsut's completed temple.

Evidently no search for origins can explain the satisfying results which have been obtained in Hatshepsut's temple. There is a rare understanding of the possibilities of the site which is lacking in the earlier buildings. The impression is one of thoroughly planned unity in which skilful use is made of rectangular supports and polygonal channelled columns, statuary and painted relief decoration. The building remains a unique conception, in a way that recalls the Step Pyramid group of Zoser at Saqqara. Like this famous old building of

Dynasty III and the Luxor temple of Amenhotep III, it suggests the imprint of a single mind. The form of the last-named building was to be repeated throughout later times and has a close contemporary rival in the less-known Soleb temple far to the south in the Sudan. While the name of Amenhotep son of Hapu cannot be directly connected by written statement with the Luxor temple and is more closely associated with the Nubian temple of Soleb, there seems little doubt that as the favourite Overseer of All the King's Works under Amenhotep III, his must have been the guiding hand in all the great buildings of this reign. Imhotep's name has come down to us associated with the Step Pyramid of Zoser, and Hatshepsut's favourite, Senmut, was the real architect of Deir el Bahari. Throughout the temple he caused to be carved a small kneeling figure of himself praying to Amon behind the folding doors of chapels and small statue niches when they were opened in the services of the cult. All but a few of these in the dark recesses of the Hathor Chapel were obliterated by the agents of Tuthmosis III, when he was intent on wiping out all traces of the name of his predecessor and her favourite minister. Ironically, the flanking side walls of the Ptolemaic chapel cut in the rock behind the central sanctuary on the upper terrace represent the deified Imhotep and Amenhotep son of Hapu followed by minor deities.[3] Senmut's name had evidently been forgotten, and the architectural achievements of these other wise men were probably not uppermost in the thoughts of the makers of this chapel. Nevertheless the three great builders remain pictorially enshrined in the building.

Something of the remarkable character of Senmut can be detected in the preliminary drawing of his head [220] which has survived on the wall of the tomb which he had the temerity to tunnel through the rock beneath the lower courtyard of the temple. Its decoration had reached the stage of a first draft of the designs when he fell from power. Unlike the very thorough wrecking of the earlier painted tomb which he had laid out on the Qurna hill overlooking Deir el Bahari, this one was simply filled up, leaving the unfinished designs looking as fresh as when the artists interrupted their work. The head and shoulders of Senmut are drawn in with the sure skill and brevity of the period, with the aid of a few squared guiding-lines. The profile has the imperious outline of the Tuthmosid family. A slight fullness of the throat, with two strokes of the brush suggesting folds, the sparingly executed lines around the eyes, and a reversed curve from the eye past nose and mouth indicate in masterful fashion the sagging plump features of the ageing man of affairs.

There are other sketches of Senmut which are similar to the one just cited, but what is more extraordinary is the large number of statues preserved for this exceptional official. Many of them have been intentionally damaged while others are virtually intact. In these statues a didactic, almost propagandistic programme is expressed. Several show him with his ward, the princess Nefru-re, in his arms, emphasizing not so much the affection of a parent for an offspring as the

220. Deir el Bahari, tomb of Senmut under the temple, portrait of Senmut.
Dynasty XVIII

political basis for Senmut's power. The ways in which the
sculptor managed this unusual challenge, the juxtaposition of
the steward and his ward, were various. In the statue in the
Field Museum in Chicago Senmut stands and holds the child

at right angles almost as a sort of property or emblem of
office. The same right angle, almost abstract relation, is maintained in the seated statue in Cairo (CCG 42116) in which the
large hands seem to suggest a feeling of love and warmth
which is belied by the stiff, almost effigy-like rigidity of the
child [221]. In the Berlin cube (block) statue the head of the
princess emerges through the steward's enveloping cloak, a
similar frontal arrangement of both figures as in the seated
statue of the steward and ward in the British Museum. The
same propagandistic tendency is seen to another end in the
statue of Senmut in Brooklyn [222]. Here the kneeling
steward holds before him an elaborately and artificially coiled
uraeus (cobra) wearing the sun disk with horns on its head
and supported by a pair of arms functioning as the hieroglyph
ka. This curious emblem is a rebus for the three signs Maat-
ka-re, the prenomen of Hatshepsut. The statue essentially
proclaims that Senmut offers to the deity the symbols of the
name of his sovereign and patroness. The folds of the serpent
echo his own folds of flesh on the torso; the features of the
steward's face show the familiar aquiline nose known from
ostraca and sketches. Not since the Old Kingdom have so
many statues of a private official been attested, and the latter
mainly in groups from a single tomb. Although eight statues

221. Senmut and Princess Nefru-re. Black granite statue from Karnak.
Dynasty XVIII. *Cairo Museum*

222. Senmut. Dynasty XVIII. *Brooklyn Museum*

of Mentuhotep, vizier under Sesostris I and Amenemhat II in Dynasty XII, were found at Karnak, the widespread promulgation of Senmut's statues must have been exceptional even for his day. Not until the reign of Amenhotep III did a courtier, Amenhotep son of Hapu, achieve a similar distinction.

Other master-builders of the early Eighteenth Dynasty are known. There was Inene, whose tomb-paintings, as we shall see, form one of the most interesting examples of the transition from the style of the Middle to the New Kingdom. He tells us how he carried out the work on the tomb of Tuthmosis I, 'no one seeing, no one hearing'. He mentions the construction of two pylons (and presumably the hall between them) at Karnak for that king and the erection of his obelisks. The vizier Hapu-seneb was in charge of work in Western Thebes and at Karnak in the reign of Hatshepsut, but it was Senmut who successed in creating the new architectural style of the first half of Dynasty XVIII in a building which is at the same time unique.[4]

None of the other buildings of the period produces such a coherent impression. This is partly due to poor preservation and partly to the alterations inspired by bitter family feeling in the course of the Tuthmosid succession to the throne.[5] These alterations have spoiled the design of Hatshepsut's Nubian temple at Buhen with its outer colonnade of channelled columns, and to a lesser degree have changed the character of her chapel at Medinet Habu. Although well preserved in the form completed by Tuthmosis III, this building can only be seen dwarfed by additions of Dynasty XXV and the Ptolemaic Period inside the enclosure wall of the great temple of Ramesses III [357]. It stood on a platform with an enclosed block of rooms preceded by a shrine which was open at both ends and surrounded by an ambulatory with square pillars connected by a low balustrade. As in other structures of the period at Karnak intended as way stations for the bark of the god on his processional visits to other temples, this outer colonnade was developed from the Middle Kingdom example of Sesostris I [161], where there are four inner pillars, instead of a walled shrine, and a ramp leading up both at front and back. This was apparently designed as a pavilion for the king's Heb-Sed ceremony. With the addition of two papyrus-bundle columns at each end of the inner shrine and a continuance all round of the colonnade, the early Dynasty XVIII form becomes that of the destroyed peripteral chapel of Amenhotep III on the island of Elephantine which is reflected by a painting in a Nineteenth-Dynasty tomb at Thebes [369, 370].[6]

We shall see in discussing the domestic architecture of Dynasty XVIII that the plans of two little-known palaces at Deir el Ballas may go back to the very beginning of Dynasty XVIII. Indeed the crowding of large halls with closely spaced wooden columns [275, 276] shows little advance over the Middle Kingdom examples imitated in the Beni Hasan tombs [166], and is in keeping with the rather cramped area of the hall which Tuthmosis I laid out between his two pylons at Karnak. This problem of interior space was never too satisfactorily solved by the Egyptians. Everyone who has visited the great Hypostyle Hall of the Nineteenth Dynasty at Karnak has felt the constraint of its crowded supports in spite of the wider central aisle and the great height of the ceiling.

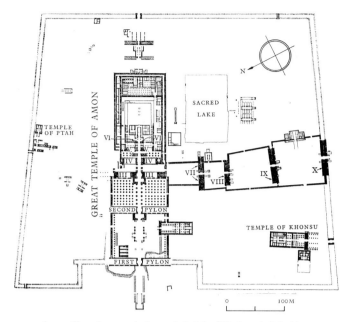

223 and 224. Karnak, general plan and obelisk of Tuthmosis I, looking west. Dynasty XVIII

The overwhelming sense of immensity is in this case largely conveyed by the masses of masonry, not by the areas they enclose, much as it was by the pyramid-builders of the Old Kingdom. It was the open temple court with its surrounding colonnades which seems to us the happiest conception of the early architects, and perhaps it is this element which gives such pleasure at Deir el Bahari and in the Luxor temple, where it is accidentally heightened by the loss of the outer wall so that one looks through the beautiful columns of Amenhotep III towards the Nile and the valley and cliffs beyond. Senmut gave to Hatshepsut's temple an even more open feeling by creating on each of the three terraces long façades of pillars and columns into which were integrated sculptural accents in a uniquely effective fashion. One other structure at Karnak, even in its melancholy ruin, still produces a similar effect of the blending of statues and architectural mass. This results from the way in which colossal seated figures are proportioned to Pylon VIII, built by Hatshepsut on the southern axis of the temple [223].[7] Certainly this is not the case with the Osiride statues of Tuthmosis I placed close together along the walls of his hall with the papyrus columns and against the back of his second pylon (now Pylon V). Even if some or all of these were an afterthought, brought by Tuthmosis III from a colonnade which is thought to have been built all round the Middle Kingdom temple by his grandfather Tuthmosis I, they were still part of a rather tightly conceived programme.[8]

Tuthmosis III at Karnak overloaded a scheme which in Hatshepsut's time may have produced a somewhat happier impression. Her quartzite chamber for the sacred bark was torn out from the place which is now occupied by that of Philip Arrhidaeus, and Tuthmosis III walled up the two obelisks that she had introduced into her father's hall. It is perhaps not unfair to think that this Tuthmosid temple is more interesting for its historical connexions than it is architecturally. With the older buildings engulfed behind the huge Ramesside hypostyle hall [224] it is not easy to judge, as

225. Deir el Bahari, temple of Hatshepsut. Dynasty XVIII

one looks towards the front of the temple past a corner of the still-standing obelisk of Hatshepsut. The southern of the two obelisks of Tuthmosis I remains erect in front of his ruined pylon which formed the old front of the temple, while his broken Osiride statues line the wall in niches on each side of the doorway. Tuthmosis III tells us that when he was a young prince the image of Amon, carried in a procession through this hall of the papyrus columns, sought him out and recognized him as heir to the throne. One suspects that this was arranged by the boy's father, Tuthmosis II, who was attempting to ensure the succession of this son by a minor queen. He must already have realized the domineering qualities of Hatshepsut, who was his half-sister as well as his wife. Hatshepsut, after her husband's death, laid all possible stress upon her rights as the heiress of her father Tuthmosis I. She at first respected the outward forms of a regency over the young Tuthmosis III, following in the tradition of other able women such as Teti-sheri, Ah-hotep, and her own mother Ahmes, who had apparently dealt with affairs during the minority or absence at war of the men of the family. However, the future great conqueror was relegated to the background for over twenty years. Hatshepsut soon styled herself king and ruled the country with the help of a powerful coterie of which the most important member was her architect Senmut.

To the west of the hall of the papyrus columns, Tuthmosis III made a number of alterations when he came to power, probably inserting a bark chamber of his own in place of that of Hatshepsut and inscribing the walls of the structure which

preceded it with the annals of his Asiatic campaigns. Beyond, east of the old sanctuary of the Middle Kingdom, he erected other buildings. Chief of these is the well-preserved festival hall for his Heb-Sed in which the columns of the central aisle are in the form of tent-poles. These are enormously enlarged examples of the same kind of canopy-poles which had surrounded the bed of Queen Hetep-heres in Dynasty IV. This was an extraordinary transformation of a light tent structure of ancient times into an eternal monument.

These Tuthmosid buildings could never have produced the same sense of a unified plan as does the temple of Deir el Bahari. They had incorporated the Middle Kingdom temple into the main structure with its west front in Pylon IV. On a different north-south axis were added Pylons VII and VIII, apparently as an approach to a temple of Amenhotep I which is presumed to have stood at right angles to the east-west axis of the old temple, west and a little south of its entrance. These buildings evolved according to a principle of additive growth which is so characteristic of the great Egyptian sanctuaries. Karnak, being the best preserved of these, provides the most striking example of such structural accumulation over the centuries [223].

The temple of Queen Hatshepsut at Deir el Bahari was primarily a funerary temple for herself and her father Tuthmosis I, but it was also a sanctuary of Amon, and included shrines of Hathor and Anubis.[9] Although Tuthmosis III erased the name of Hatshepsut and removed her statues, he was particularly concerned with maintaining

226 and 227. Hatshepsut. Upper part and head of Osiride limestone statues from Deir el Bahari. Dynasty XVIII. *Cairo Museum*

his grandfather's connexion with the temple and amplifying the association with his father, Tuthmosis II, who had been given little attention in his wife's scheme. The shrine of Hathor long remained a popular cult place of the Theban necropolis, and the temple as a whole continues to preserve an extraordinary measure of its original aspect. Akhenaten obliterated the names and figures of Amon, which were replaced in Ramesside times, and only a few minor alterations were made to the central Amon chapel under the Ptolemies.

Approaching from the valley up a processional way lined with sandstone sphinxes, the visitor would have been conscious from far away of the great painted limestone Osiride statues of the queen fronting the colonnade of the upper terrace [225-7]. They stood against square pillars, being carved from built-up masonry courses forming an integral part of the architecture. A few have been re-erected from the fragments found with the other broken statues and sphinxes of the queen. The outwardly simple treatment of the two lower colonnades forms an effective base for this line of statues above. The rhythmical repetition of light and shadow is broken only by the broad central ramps which give access to the two terraces. The lowest colonnade was given weight at each end by a large Osiride statue. The glare from the intense sunlight striking the amphitheatre of cliffs behind must always have tended to nullify the surface decoration and to emphasize the simple shapes. The colonnades offered their shade, while the darkness of the inner rooms of the shrines intensified in characteristic Egyptian fashion the solemn feeling of awe as one approached the deity.

One of the great charms of this building is that it combines a broad feeling of openness of space with a nicety of architectural detail which only gradually becomes apparent as one

penetrates into the individual parts. Scarcely visible from outside are the lines of channelled columns behind the piers of the lowest colonnade and the statues of the upper terrace. The minor accent of these columns in the porch of the Anubis shrine and their continuation along the retaining wall on the north side of the second court cannot be appreciated until this level is reached. Similarly, the Hathor columns of the flanking chapel on the south are suggested on the façade only by Hathor heads on pilasters projecting slightly from the two central pillars. Between these two chapels the colonnades with the great series of reliefs of the queen's divine birth and the expedition to Punt employ only rows of square pillars and omit the inner line of polygonal columns. This variation between pillar and column is one of the reasons for Senmut's success in employing the polygonal channelled column which had long been one of the happiest of Egyptian inventions. It is used again round the peristyle court of the upper terrace, concealed behind the façade until the gateway at the top of the ramp is reached. The columns in the porch of the Anubis shrine are particularly well preserved [232], and between them, as in the colonnades, there was always a glimpse of the wide view of the Theban valley towards the east.

Perhaps the most impressive way to approach Deir el Bahari is by the precipitous path that winds over the mountain from the Valley of the Kings, which was first used as a royal burial-place by Hatshepsut's father, Tuthmosis I. Here the plan of the whole temple spreads out far below one's feet [228], and its position in relation to the old Mentuhotep temple is easier to visualize. It also becomes clear how the Dynasty XVIII temple backs up against the great wall of rock that separates this offering place from the tombs of the Tuthmosid family. It was placed in a more direct relationship

228. Deir el Bahari, Dynasty XI and Dynasty XVIII temples

to the burial-chambers of Hatshepsut and her father than one would realize from making the long circuit around the northern extent of the Theban necropolis to the entrance of the Valley of the Kings and then winding back westwards through this defile to the first tombs that were cut behind Deir el Bahari. The constant search for greater secrecy and protection for the body of the dead ruler had led away from the ancient system by which the offering temple was placed at the foot of the pyramid. The funerary temples of the New Kingdom kings lie in a long line at the foot of the Western Theban mountain, with considerable distances separating them from the actual tombs. Their function, nevertheless, remained the same as it had in the Old and Middle kingdoms.

In the centre of the upper terrace the peristyle court can be recognized [228], although its colonnades have virtually disappeared. A Ptolemaic construction now fronts the entrance to the partly rock-cut central sanctuary, where the bark of Amon was intended to rest when brought for the Festival of the Valley. It was looked down upon by four Osiride statues of the queen placed in the corners of the room, and other similar statues were placed in recesses alternating with niches along the sanctuary façade. Adjoining the court, to the south, was the chapel for the funerary cult of Tuthmosis I, and beyond this the larger offering place of the queen with its wall

reliefs modelled after the designs of such an Old kingdom chapel as that in the temple of Pepy II at South Saqqara. Directly below us [228], at the foot of the cliff, lies a second northern court with a stepped solar altar devoted to the worship of Amon in his form of the sun god Ra. When the picture was taken, no attempt had yet been made to restore the pillars and Osiride statues along the front of the upper terrace and, viewed from this great height, there is little sign of them or the polygonal columns which ran behind, although the back wall with its entrance gate to the peristyle court is clear.

Modern roofs cover the colonnades of the first (middle) terrace which contain on the nearer, north, side of the ramp the scenes of the queen's divine birth as daughter of Amon. On the south side is displayed her expedition to Punt, while under the modern roof of the southern lowest colonnade, beyond the ramp, are the reliefs showing the transport by river boat from Aswan of the queen's Karnak obelisks. The line of columns which runs at right angles to the Anubis shrine follows the retaining wall on the north side of the second broad court, while on the opposite side, in the direction of the Eleventh-Dynasty temple, can be seen the roofless outer hall of the Hathor shrine.

Missing from this scene are not only the Osiride statues, but the red granite sphinxes which crossed the second court between the two ramps. Huge kneeling granite figures of the queen faced each other on the axis of the upper peristyle court leading to the sanctuary of Amon, and smaller figures were apparently placed between the columns. These, with other statues of the queen, have been ingeniously reconstructed from the pieces found thrown down into the quarry to the north-east of the lower court and into the depressions on each side of the avenue of sandstone sphinxes when Tuthmosis III ordered them to be destroyed. As they can now be seen in the Metropolitan Museum and in Cairo as a result of the patience and ingenuity of their discoverer, Herbert Winlock, they provide clear evidence for the use of sculpture throughout a New Kingdom temple.[10]

The freshness and vitality of a new period are less immediately evident in the statues of hard stone than in the painted limestone Osiride figures [226, 227], which recall the few pieces of sculpture in this material recovered from the Middle Kingdom [176]. Reminiscent of these is also the frankly unrealistic use of blue eyebrows and beards against the clear red or yellow of the skin. We are clearly in the presence of a god, not a mortal, the blue suggesting lapis lazuli, a precious material associated with deities. The bright pure colour on the crisply cut limestone surfaces is found again in the wall reliefs and paintings, where the clarity of outline, as in the fluting of the columns, produces a vivid impression. Although the same forms are worked with prodigious skill in the hard-stone statues, the darker colour of the granite inevitably produces a heavier effect. Something of the vivacity is missing, and a certain monotony of features was inescapable in such a large number of repeated forms. In the case of the twenty-two red granite sphinxes only certain details were picked out in paint. There were some twenty-eight free-standing figures of the queen in hard stone and over a hundred painted sandstone sphinxes, in addition to the forty or so limestone Osiride statues.

The facial type established by Hatshepsut is found in her large white limestone seated figure [229]. She is as usual portrayed as a king wearing only the short skirt, royal headcloth, and broad collar. However, the face in this case is that of a woman, rounding to a small, narrow chin. An appealing hint of softness was even more apparent in its fragmentary state before the restoration of the whole figure was undertaken [230]. Not a little of this effect is due to the material in which it is carved. On the whole there is a close resemblance to the head of the well-known standing figure of Tuthmosis III, a figure in hard greenish stone now at Cairo [231]. The great conqueror has a more pronounced curve to his nose, and a comparison of the two heads emphasizes the feminine qualities in Hatshepsut's face. Portrayed in a style which was apparently based on a general family likeness, these two figures stand out from the other sculpture of the period as masterpieces. In their taut slenderness and sense of controlled vitality they truly suggest these remarkable people without making one feel that they are actual portraits. The type continues with minor variations which sometimes give an entirely different appearance to two representations of the same king, as in some of the heads of both Tuthmosis III and Amenhotep II.[11] The extensive artistic activity of the long reign of Amenhotep III produced not only a facial type characteristic of that king but a new stylistic development. This

229 and 230. Hatshepsut. Seated limestone statue (partly restored) from Deir el Bahari, with detail of head. Dynasty XVIII. *New York, Metropolitan Museum of Art*

231. Tuthmosis III. Head of standing statue. Dynasty XVIII. *Cairo Museum*

was to be followed by the remarkable series of experiments at Amarna. However, in the first half of the Eighteenth Dynasty the royal sculpture achieved little of that individuality in portraiture to be found in the best works of Dynasty IV, nor did it suggest anything of that intuitive glimpse of man's inner spirit which briefly appears in a few fine works of the Middle Kingdom.

Large areas of Hatshepsut's beautiful low reliefs are well preserved throughout the Deir el Bahari temple. The effect is particularly pleasing in the Anubis chapel, where the painted surfaces have been protected by the roof of the porch [232]. The excellent lighting, softened a little by the intervening columns, is a welcome contrast to the gloom of the Theban tombs, where so much fine work must be peered at in semi-obscurity. The long familiar array of food offerings is set with elegant precision before the seated jackal-headed god of the dead [233]. However, a scarcely noticeable anticipation of the fondness for curved lines which was to dominate in the latter half of the dynasty is to be detected in the drawing of the gazelle's horn, the tendrils of a bunch of grapes, or the way in which the stem of a lotus bud is wound round a tall vase. Among the scenes which represent the chief events of Hatshepsut's reign, that showing the reception of her envoy to Punt illustrates delightfully the growing interest in a wider world. The less-damaged lower part of the south wall of the Punt colonnade [234–6] adjoins the pictures on the west wall depicting the Egyptian ships arriving at this far-off place, and again departing with their load of incense trees and other products of the god's land which were to be dedicated to

Amon. We are shown a village scattered among trees which probably lay on the Somali coast of Africa somewhere near the Bab-el-Mandeb straits at the lower end of the Red Sea. On the map the distance from Egypt looks so great that we can share the astonishment expressed in the words of welcome inscribed over the little group which comes out to greet Hatshepsut's messenger and his armed guard.[12]

Now missing from behind the chief of Punt is a block which once showed his wife, their two sons, and a daughter who was already beginning to acquire the ample proportions of her mother. There still remains the saddled donkey which is labelled as being the beast which carried the chief's wife.[13] This is a small piece of testimony as to the accuracy of other details concerning this far-off land. It must have seemed remarkable to the Egyptians, who are not pictured as riding animals until the introduction of the horse, and then only rarely,[14] since it was used chiefly to draw a chariot. Probably they were as amused as we are by the thought of the burden the enormous woman would make. Fortunately a second portrait of her has survived on a block in the Cairo Museum [234], which has been replaced in the register above by a cast [236]. Her marvellous fat evidently impressed the expedition, and a later visitor to the temple made a sketch of this figure on a flake of limestone.[15] The African admiration for feminine bulk appears again in late times in the representations of the

232 and 233 (*right*). Deir el Bahari, portico of Anubis sanctuary, with detail of offerings before the jackal-headed god of the dead. Dynasty XVIII

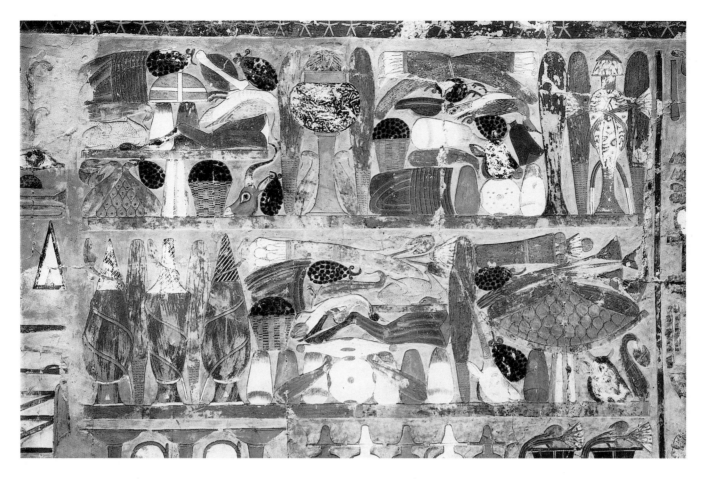

Meroitic queens [419]. It was certainly the antithesis of the Eighteenth-Dynasty ideal of the trim, slender figure. The picturing of this uncouth chieftainess of a far-off land was a skilful tribute to the civilized Queen Hatshepsut.

On this wall the old system of horizontal registers is strictly maintained, and the groups of figures confront one another statically. Below the Egyptians have spread out a small pile of weapons, strings of beads, and other trinkets which they have brought to trade. Not much is shown, since the fiction is maintained that these were simply gifts and that the country's produce which is being carried away and loaded into the ships on the adjoining wall was being exacted as tribute. Actually it must have been a transaction carried out by barter and one which had been going on since the Old Kingdom, when voyages to Punt are frequently mentioned. What is new is that it should be pictured in even this much detail.

In the second register the queen's messenger receives a later visit from the chief of Punt and his wife before his tent, where there is now a great pile of myrrh and trays of gold rings. Men and loaded donkeys bring more of the incense, while cattle are driven out of the village. One animal lowers its head to munch at a tuft of grass. These two registers are bounded above and below by wide bands of water with swimming fish, as if to emphasize their importance as well as to indicate the location on the coast. Above, the houses of the village appear again in several registers on the left side of the wall, while on the right men carry myrrh trees towards the ships. The continuity of the registers is sadly disjointed by many gaps, but enough remains to show that the artist is continuing to develop the use of scenic props which had

appeared more frequently in the Middle Kingdom than in earlier times. He still makes no serious attempt to associate the different registers spatially with one another, but produces nonetheless an impression of a settlement scattered through the trees near water. There is also a convincing sense of local details carefully observed on the spot. The conical mat huts are set on a platform on piles and approached by ladders. Birds flutter among the palms and incense trees or alight on the eggs in their nests. A white dog sits in front of a hut. Perhaps not all the animals were to be found in Punt, but they are of a kind known to belong to the far south. A giraffe, panthers, long-horned cattle, and monkeys appear, and a monster evidently intended by the horn on its nose to be a rhinoceros[16] is confronted under a tree by a mother ape carrying her young on her back.

The aromatic gum is being obtained by cutting at the branches of the myrrh trees with axes of a shape like those carried by the armed guard of the queen's messenger and that among the gifts presented to the chief of Punt [236]. We know this type of Dynasty XVIII axe from plain practical examples and the parade weapon of Ahmose [217]. Other decorated axe-heads were made with a design left in openwork when the blade was cast. A well-preserved axe in Berlin has a lion seizing an antelope,[17] while one which came from the Eighteenth-Dynasty occupation of the Semna fort has the animals arranged in better proportion to one another within the frame of the blade [237]. This use of openwork patterns in metalwork is also found in a few small bronze jar-stands. One is probably of the second half of Dynasty XVIII [238], since the artificial tree placed between the two animals is of a type

which begins to appear on the funerary equipment of Amenhotep II.[18] The new form of axe-blade which appears also in the painting of the Deir el Ballas palace [278A] replaced the old semicircular one used in the Old and Middle Kingdoms. It was an indigenous Egyptian weapon, unlike the Asiatic scimitar which we saw at Byblos during Dynasty XII and which came into use in Egypt as a result of her foreign wars.

Hatshepsut's expedition observed in Punt that there were a few black-skinned people[19] among the predominantly red-skinned inhabitants for whom the Egyptians seem to have entertained a sympathetic feeling of kinship. In fact the chieftain of Punt [234] is differentiated from his visitors only by certain details of his costume and by a long narrow beard such as gods wore in Egypt in ancient times. His followers also have such beards, but their hair falls to the shoulders and sometimes ends in curls. These are not so long as the tresses which the people of the Aegean are shown wearing in

234–6. Deir el Bahari, Punt colonnade, fat queen, village, and reception of Egyptians at Punt. Dynasty XVIII

237. Lion seizing antelope. Bronze axehead from Semna. Dynasty XVIII. *Khartum Museum*

238. Tree between animals. Bronze stand. Dynasty XVIII. *Chicago Natural History Museum*

Tuthmosid times. In the tomb of the vizier of Tuthmosis III, Rekhmira, which gives us one of the most reliable reports on the appearance of foreigners,[20] red-skinned men with shorter hair appear among the other long-haired, bearded people of Punt who carry a myrrh tree. These have been thought to represent the same mixture of elements from Arabia and Africa which is suggested by Hatshepsut's reliefs. Although they bring similar offerings, their features and dress are distinguished from those of the inhabitants of the Sudan [239], who are pictured in a separate register presenting a giraffe and followed by the same long-horned cattle which appear under the incense trees on our wall at Deir el Bahari. In other scenes of foreign tribute the southern animals represented at Deir el Bahari and in the tomb of Rekhmira are shown with the tribute of Kush.[21] With such products as gold, ebony logs, ostrich feathers, and skins, they probably reached Egypt much more frequently through the southern Nile Valley than by way of the east coast of Africa.

Unfortunately the new tendency to give visual form to a heightened awareness of what lay beyond Egypt's borders was not further developed until Ramesside times. Until then there was seldom an attempt to indicate the setting even as

239. Thebes, tomb of Rekhmira (No. 100), Nubian and Syrian tribute. Dynasty XVIII

240 and 241. Thebes, tomb of Menkheperra-seneb (No. 86), Keftiu and Syrian tribute and foreigners bringing tribute. Dynasty XVIII

fully as was done at Deir el Bahari. In the Theban tombs there is an occasional glimpse of a Syrian building.[22] Traders from Syria are shown in a rare instance disembarking their wares at an Egyptian quay.[23] What appears to be a parallel to this shows people of Punt manning primitive, round sailing-rafts which are juxtaposed to a scene of the delivery of their produce to Egyptians on the shore.[24] Can they actually have travelled by such clumsy craft all the way to Qoseir on the Red Sea? This was the traditional starting point for voyages to Punt, lying at the end of the desert road from Coptos. As in so many cases with Egyptian representation, we can only wish that the statement had not been so laconic. In another case, when Tuthmosis III had the flora and fauna of Syria represented on the walls of a room behind his festival hall at Karnak, the craftsmen have been suspected of inventing specimens by giving an exotic touch to things well known at home.[25] Often the artist must have been working from second-hand knowledge or from what he could observe of foreigners at Thebes and of examples of their crafts. However, while the newness still exerted fascination, in the reigns of Hatshepsut and Tuthmosis III, there are freshly made studies of the men from foreign lands and typical products from abroad.

Because the Egyptian's pictorial record was unique among his contemporaries, it is now infinitely precious, but his remarkable powers of observation have paradoxically laid him open to criticism for his carelessness. Obviously he was not impelled by a scientific interest in the modern sense and was capable of all sorts of inconsistencies. Hence there is a danger in drawing too exacting conclusions from his work. However, these pictures are, all the same, astonishingly accurate where they can be compared with the actual remains of civilized peoples such as those of the Aegean and Syria. There has been a warmly contested argument as to whether the men of Keftiu and those of the Isles in the midst of the Great Sea,

represented in certain tombs of the early Eighteenth Dynasty, are the same people or whether the former came from Cilicia or northern Syria and only the latter were native to Crete. More recently it has been suggested that many of the objects which they bring are Mycenaean rather than Minoan.[26] In attempting to establish their source in Crete, mainland Greece, or the Levant it is not surprising that features common to all three have not always been stressed. It would perhaps be well to remember, though, that the Egyptian representations show dress which is similar to that of both Crete and western Asia[27] and different from the long garment with sleeves or the plain short skirt of the frequently pictured inhabitants of Palestine and Syria [239, 240]. Thus we find a wide metal belt, with or without a spiral design, a short skirt with patterned bands or all-over ornament, and sometimes with pendant tassels, leg gaiters over boots with turned-up toes, and hair worn in long separate locks hanging below the shoulders.[28] That the Egyptian mixed the Aegeans pictorially with people of western Asia, in whose company he saw them [240], is not surprising when we remember the lively trade which had long been carried on in the Syrian ports, with its resulting counter-influences. However, he seems to have captured an essential quality in these people which belongs to the Minoan civilization of Crete. It seems to be these Minoans of whom the artist was thinking when he made the records that appear in the tomb of Senmut [242] under Hatshepsut and in those of Rekhmira, Useramon, and Menkheperra-seneb [240, 241] in the reign of Tuthmosis III.[29]

The newly discovered achievements of Mycenaean Greece and the expansion of her trade with the Orient at the expense of Crete, which is certainly evident in the second half of Dynasty XVIII, should not overshadow in our minds the impression which the Minoan spirit was making upon Egypt in Tuthmosid times. In spite of objections which have been made, one is inclined to accept the theory that Keftiu and the

equivalent Asiatic words Kaptara and Kaphtor meant Crete, but this need not exclude some long-continued relationship between the people of that island and the Levant coast. Traces of such a connexion have already been claimed at Alalakh,[30] in the Antioch plain. It is now clear that there was an important Mycenaean element at the port of Ugarit (Ras Shamra) in the later New Kingdom, and it is not too much to expect, in view of the great advances in our knowledge of the eastern Mediterranean in recent years, that further excavation may elucidate the nature of earlier contacts with Crete by the discovery of written record.

Such fascinating problems must not be allowed to carry us too far away from Thebes and Egypt's internal development. The reliefs in Hatshepsut's temple and the foreigners in the tombs of the period make it clear, however, that one cannot

242. Thebes, tomb of Senmut (No. 71), Cretans. Dynasty XVIII

overlook the increasing complexities of Egypt's empire and her wide foreign trade. The conquests of Tuthmosis I had followed up the beginning made by Ahmose and carried Egyptian arms to the banks of the Euphrates and far southward to the Fourth Cataract in the Sudan. There was a lull during the reign of Hatshepsut, the only tangible sign of her foreign interests being the peaceful trading venture to Punt and battles in Nubia and Asia. Tuthmosis III included these years in his own reign, dating his accession from the regency set up in his youth by Hatshepsut at the death of his father, Tuthmosis II. Thus it was not until his twenty-second regnal year that he was able to set out on the long series of well-planned campaigns which completed the subjugation of Palestine and Syria as far as the Euphrates. In the Sudan the southern city of Napata was to become a centre of Egyptian culture, with the temple of Amon at nearby Gebel Barkal rivalling in sanctity the god's great shrine at Theban Karnak.

The fine workmanship of the Hatshepsut reliefs is found again in a certain number of private tombs of the early Eighteenth Dynasty. These were cut in the sounder rock formation at the foot of the Qurneh hill and at Dra abu'l Nega, between Deir el Bahari and the entrance to the Valley of the Kings. This had been the old royal cemetery of the end of the First Intermediate Period and was used again in Dynasty XVII. The poor stone of the upper slopes of the Qurneh hill south of Deir el Bahari was unsuitable for the carving of reliefs. Inene had laid out a tomb there (No. 81) with pillared portico and deep inner offering chamber decorated with paintings, perhaps at about the time that he was supervising the preparation of the tomb of Tuthmosis I. He died soon after the succession of Tuthmosis III, but not until he was able to observe in his biographical inscription that it was Hatshepsut who was ruling the country after the death of her husband, Tuthmosis II. Inene's example was followed by Senmut (No. 71) and three viziers of Tuthmosis III, Ahmose (No. 83), his son Useramon (Nos. 61, 131), and the latter's nephew Rekhmira (No. 100), the fashion thus being set for painted chapels.[31] The upper Qurneh slopes continued to be used until the reign of Amenhotep III, when more space and the sounder rock at a lower level were needed to lay out the elaborate chapels with columned halls that were favoured by the great men of this time in imitation of the temple plan of the period. This also brought about a renewal of relief decoration. In general, though, the friable rock of this site made painting on prepared plaster surfaces more practicable than relief decoration. The result was the remarkable development of painting in Dynasty XVIII. For the first time it was really freed to become an art of its own, and not used simply as a cheaper substitute for the more permanent painted relief.

The Tuthmosid private tombs have either suffered serious damage or else have survived in a battered and grimy condition after having served as dwelling-places for the inhabitants of the villages of Qurneh and Dra abu'l Nega. Their distinctive beauty can only be captured fully where the fresh colouring has been protected on a portion of a wall or on a fragment buried in the debris. As in the Hatshepsut temple, the effect is gained by clarity of outline and the juxtaposition of clean bright colours. The cutting of the reliefs, as in Dynasty V, leaves a good deal of uneven background surface with deeper carving in proximity to the figures [244]. How different must

243. Thebes, Tomb of Duwaerneheh (No. 125), dog under master's chair. Dynasty XVIII

the twisting-back of their heads are repeated in Rekhmira's painting (No. 100) and become even more contorted in the contemporary hunting scene of Puyemra, No. 39, where the relief is finer than in No. 53. Here apparently is one instance where the Minoan sense of freedom of motion has had an effect upon the major arts in Egypt.[32] It is to be found also in the panther which turns back its head to a raised hind leg in the Hatshepsut reliefs.[33] That these new experiments in the representation of moving animals are of Aegean inspiration has been doubted.[34] However, we have seen the spirit evinced already in the figures on the dagger of Ahmose [216]. In that case one can hardly question that the stimulus is from the Aegean, where such a feeling for movement is so basically involved in representation. It might be well to remember in this connexion the twisted pose of the little silver lion which was brought into Egypt in the Twelfth Dynasty from some Asiatic source. It is a simple precursor of the more complicated intertwined composition of a lion attacking a bull on a red jasper weight of the Amarna Period.[35] Since the latter might be assumed to represent a mixture of Aegean and Mesopotamian elements, cannot the same be said for the earlier piece?[36]

have been the impression produced by their painted surfaces when new can be seen by comparing the detail [243] of the appealing black puppy called 'Ebony' which sits under his master's chair in the tomb of Duwaerneheh (No. 125) with the hunting scene in that of Amenemhet (No. 53), where most of the paint has disappeared [244, 245]. Recent attention has been centred on the unusual animation of the game being hunted by Amenemhet. The wild leaping of the animals and

244 and 245. Thebes, tomb of Amenemhet (No. 53), hunting scene, with detail. Dynasty XVIII

246. Thebes, tomb of Senmut (No. 71), hall. Dynasty XVIII

Whatever we think the source may be for the active poses of these animals, the fact cannot be overlooked that they are arranged very stiffly in the scenes of the early Eighteenth Dynasty and that there was a purely Egyptian development towards a more smoothly organized composition. Just as the rather tightly drawn spirals on the ceiling of the tomb of Senmut [246] develop into the more flowing lines of the better integrated and richer interweaving patterns of the reign of Amenhotep III [285], so the use of curved lines increases in the drawing of animals and other figures. This stylistic change, which in painting is accompanied by more impressionistic brushwork and a certain sketchiness of handling, actually produces a more naturalistic sense of movement towards the end of the dynasty [283].[37] Even in the period we are discussing a change can be seen taking place. The same pose is attempted for the hound [244, 247], but Inene's artist

247. Thebes, tomb of Inene (No. 81), hunting scene (detail). Dynasty XVIII

has supported the wobbly front legs of his clumsily drawn dog on a little hillock, as if he did not quite dare to represent the forward spring of Amenemhet's splendid animal. However, in the latter tomb (No. 53), no account has been

248. Thebes, tomb of Kenamon (No. 93), hunting scene (detail). Dynasty XVIII

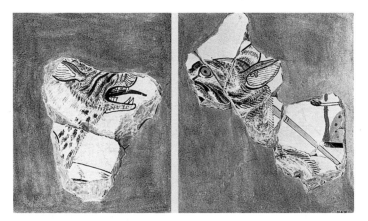

249. Thebes, tomb of Intef (No. 155), hyena heads. Dynasty XVIII

taken of the Middle Kingdom attempt at Meir [189, 190] to imitate the rolling ground of the desert by diagonally curving lines. The draughtsman has gone back to the old system of horizontal registers with a few hillocks indicated above each flat base-line. It was not until the reign of Amenhotep II that an especially gifted painter had the idea of setting his animals against irregular blank areas of background surrounded by winding strips of desert gravel and occasionally enlivened by a small bush (Kenamon, No. 93 [247]). Variations of this manner of suggesting the terrain were to be used infrequently for other landscape elements in the Eighteenth Dynasty and were developed further in the Ramesside Period.

The detail of the hunting scene in the tomb of Inene (No. 81) [247] might easily be mistaken for a provincial work of the Middle Kingdom. It repeats the old motif of the hyena at bay trying to pull an arrow from its muzzle,[38] used again in the tomb of Intef the Herald (No. 155) [249]. Here, as in the pose of the hunting dog, can be seen another advance that was made in the course of some fifty years. The skilful brushwork of the beast's fur in the second example has been developed from the fussy, hard detail meticulously employed by Inene's painter. He could do better than he has in this hunting scene on the back of one of the portico pillars. On the west wall there is a pair of butting rams with a certain naive charm in their determined stance and the way in which each lock of fleece is outlined to form an intricate pattern of fine red lines. A pinkish cast has been given to the cream-coloured wool and a warm tone to the grey of the horns. Unfortunately, except for parts of the scene of foreign tribute and a picture of Inene's house and garden, the paintings are so badly pitted and scratched that it is scarcely possible to reproduce photographically such details as the counting of the herds or the activities of the marshes. The general light tonality and clarity of the colouring links these paintings with other better-painted tombs of the reigns of Hatshepsut and Tuthmosis III.[39] The background is a very light bluish-grey, against which the warm pale tones are used with canary yellow, clear blues, greens, and light reds, and accents of darker red and black. The scheme recalls the Bersheh paintings of Dynasty XII. It was supplemented by a richer palette in the reign of Amenhotep II, as the surfaces were more and more broken up by brush-strokes of different pigments which let the body colour show through.

The firm outlines and deft brush-strokes of the two hyena heads [249] appear again in a fragment from the tomb of Intef

[250] showing a fat elderly man. Age is indicated by facial lines that remind us of the portrait of Senmut [220] and by a red-brown bald spot above the shock of hair. Fine red strokes indicate the hair on face and body much as the minute flecks of the brush ranging from grey to black suggest the fur of the animals. The old man's skin is a light pink, the colour ordinarily associated with desert ground, as in the little green-

250. Thebes, tomb of Intef (No. 155), old man. Dynasty XVIII

spotted hillock behind the hyena, but also used for the animal's eye and the stripes on its ears.[40] He may be holding the pole of a chariot in a craftwork scene, but is represented in the same fashion as a figure who may be the owner of the tomb. Therefore it is perhaps an Egyptian who is represented, and not one of the light-skinned Syrians who appear in the lower register of the tribute scene of Rekhmira [239] and with the red-skinned Aegeans and Asiatics in the mixed group of foreigners of the tomb of Menkheperra-seneb (No. 86) [240, 241]. The scene in Tomb 86 is one of those cases where we should like to be able to depend upon the painter's identification of racial types but suspect that he copied at least some of his figures from the tomb of Rekhmira. He was certainly not clear as to the appearance of a Hittite, although he may have known that Tuthmosis III in his last two campaigns had received gifts from the chief of Great Kheta (or Hatti) as well as a silver vessel in Keftiu work from a place called Tinay.[41] The few early representations of Hittites[42] make them look like Syrians. The men with long locks, wearing figured kilts and bearing Aegean objects [240] like those in the tombs of Rekhmira and Senmut [242], are preceded by three chieftains. One is prostrate before the king, the second kneeling, and the third holding forward a child. They are all in Syrian costume and bearded like the Prince of Kadesh who holds up a two-handled vase below them. They are labelled respectively the Great Ones of Keftiu, Kheta, and Tunip.

The repertoire of scenes in Rekhmira's tomb (No. 100) provided a rich source for the painters in the Theban necropolis. The great size and impeccable workmanship of this tomb form a culminating point of the classic style in the second half of the reign of Tuthmosis III. The typical simple plan of cross hall and deep inner offering-corridor is here carried to monumental proportions. The outer hall is plain without the line of pillars sometimes to be found in tombs of this time, while the inner hall is of such great height that it is difficult to see the figures in the upper registers without scaffolding. In fact, in spite of many subtle variations in the composition of the scenes in each register, the vast number of figures tends to become monotonous, and much of the fine detail can never have been visible. The often-cited example of the serving girl viewed from the back [251] splendidly illustrates the quality of line maintained throughout, and is moreover a daring experiment. It was an experiment not carried through logically from our point of view, since the far foot crosses over the one nearest to the observer. It remains, however, one of the most successful of those recurring flashes of observation in which a draughtsman set down a figure as he saw it, and not according to a preconceived idea of how it should be.

Now that the dirt has been cleared from the walls of this great tomb it is more immediately apparent how the light, clear colouring is in perfect accord with other works of its time. The grime somehow falsely implied the richer colour scheme of the following reign and, in the pervading gloom of both tombs, suggested closer affinities with the paintings of Kenamon (No. 93) [248] than is actually the case. However, it should not be forgotten that Burton's photographs [239, 251] and the excellent drawings and painted copies of Mr and Mrs Davies have long conveyed a very real sense of the original appearance of the tomb.[43]

251. Thebes, tomb of Rekhmira (No. 100), serving girl. Dynasty XVIII

The agents of Tuthmosis III who wrecked the tomb (No. 71) which Senmut had excavated on the upper terrace of the Qurneh hill left enough of one corner of the hall to give us a vivid glimpse of the decorative scheme planned by Hatshepsut's favourite [246]. It has a kind of severe elegance fit to stand beside the Deir el Bahari temple. The band of hieroglyphic inscription, the Hathor frieze, and the ceiling patterns, which have survived above the precious fragment of wall with the Cretan envoys [242], sum up the style of the period within a small area, where it can be easily grasped. The spare, slender shapes are outlined with exquisite precision, while the colour is lent an even fresher gaiety by the ruin crowding in upon it. The kilts of the Cretans and the designs on the vessels which they carry are recorded in carefully observed detail. Blue wigs frame the yellow faces of the Hathor heads with their cow's ears [252]. They are conceived as though they were column capitals with a red impost block on top of the head. The eyebrows are blue, and there are touches of red, blue, and green on the necklaces and in the border above.

Perhaps the most interesting feature of this corner of Senmut's hall [246] is the way in which architectural details simulated in paint suggest the derivation of the forms and at the same time give us one of our best notions of how the interior of a house or palace might have appeared in the early Eighteenth Dynasty. Again, as in the Middle Kingdom, the ceiling is painted as though it were covered by two hangings stretched on each side of a central beam and in a framework of

252. Thebes, tomb of Senmut (No. 71), Hathor frieze. Dynasty XVIII

timbers supported on the Hathor frieze above the decorated walls. This has already lost much of its structural significance and must long have been copied in paint, but the roofing of the palace of Amenhotep III and the Amarna houses later in the Dynasty [291] show that there is a reflection here of a system of decoration in domestic architecture. In contrast to these later buildings there is here the same restraint we have been observing in the reliefs, paintings, and temple architecture. Although the entirely different purpose to be served by tomb architecture makes dangerous a general comparison between the plan and elevation of a chapel and that of a house, individual elements of house architecture are certainly imitated in the Theban tombs.

One of the simulated textiles has a design of interlocking spirals, while the other alternates rosettes and meanders set in squares.[44] Intricate as are these patterns, they maintain the same neat precision as the figures and hieroglyphs. While they have overcome the stiffness which still shows in the new patterns of Inene (No. 81), they have not yet developed the flowing, looser character of the elaborate designs of the reign of Amenhotep III. Although the quadruple spiral had already appeared on scarabs of the Middle Kingdom, and there was

253. Thebes, tomb of Amenemheb (No. 85), Amenemheb and the hyena. Dynasty XVIII

an anticipation of other elements on small objects and in the tomb decoration of Dynasty XII [206], a fresh stimulus from the Aegean must be sought here.[45]

A somewhat later tomb again gives us an impression of how a domestic interior of the simpler early style may have looked [253]. Geometric patterns are used between the beams of the ceiling, and the rectilinear scheme is carried down on to the face of the pillars by the straight stems of the papyrus. The tall plants, with an open flower flanked by two buds, made an excellent decoration for a pilaster and one which may well have been used frequently in house architecture. The vertical lines are varied by winding another plant round the stem, much as the lotus flowers are twined round the tall vases at Deir el Bahari [233]. The tomb (No. 85) belonged to a military man named Amenemheb who lived on into the reign of Amenhotep II but had, like Intef the Herald, followed Tuthmosis III on at least one campaign in Syria. He tells us how he killed the mare of the prince of Kadesh during the siege of that town, and cut off the trunk ('hand') of the largest of 120 elephants during a hunt at Niy. The king has himself left an account of this hunt both on his Erment stela, where he incidentally mentions a rhinoceros taken in the Sudan, and in his Gebel Barkal inscription. The event evidently occurred on the return from the Mitanni campaign of the year 33.[46] One cannot help thinking of these exploits of Amenemheb in Syria when confronted by the curious scene on the back of the architrave over the pillars [253] as one faces the entrance of the tomb. Amenemheb, stick in hand, faces a huge and angry female hyena. Around them are scattered highly imaginative desert plants like those on fragments which accompany the hyena heads [249] from Intef's hunting scene. They are also reminiscent of some of the Syrian flowers pictured by Tuthmosis III at Karnak. The scene may use a familiar animal of the Egyptian desert to stand for dangerous beasts in general, perhaps with some reference to Amenemheb's experiences in Syria.[47]

CHAPTER 14

The Height of the Eighteenth Dynasty: Amenhotep II–Amenhotep III 1450–1372 B.C.

In statuary, architecture, and the minor arts the first reigns of Dynasty XVIII illustrate both a development from and a harking back to the forms of the Middle Kingdom. These features are seen in the obvious parallel between the terraced structure of Queen Hatshepsut at Deir el Bahari and its Dynasty XI antecedent just to its south, the cloaked statues of Hatshepsut's officials and their Middle Kingdom prototypes, and even in the scenes from the tomb of Inene (No. 81). A freedom to experiment is evidenced after the reign of Tuthmosis III, and it is particularly observable in the work of the tomb painters, for they frequently led the way to change. The episode with the hyena in the tomb of Amenemheb (No. 85) [253] shows a carelessness of execution which is immediately apparent when compared to Intef's paintings [249, 250]. This sketchy treatment was to appear more and more in the tombs of the period between the end of the reign of Tuthmosis III and that of Tuthmosis IV. The painters were developing an impressionistic use of brushwork which is seen at its best in the fish being harpooned by Horemheb in Tomb 78 [254] and the birds on the clump of papyrus behind his light craft.[1] Side by side with this looser technique, the old orderly tradition of carefully drawn detail was to be continued, but combined with an ever-increasing interest in richer texture. Not only were more colours used in different combinations, but they are affected by the breaking up of the surface with fine strokes of the brush to suggest such things as fur and feathers. Thus the newly developed technique of brushwork could be used broadly with wide, swift strokes [254, 283], or meticulously applied with a multitude of fine lines and stippling [255, 307]. We have seen the Egyptian attempting this before, in both the Old and Middle Kingdoms, but he was now learning more about how colour could be manipulated with the brush. Working independently of the carved outlines and modelling of relief sculpture, the painter still placed his chief reliance upon line and was, in fact, making significant new use of curving lines. But there is occasionally a remarkable effort to suggest a tenuous substance, such as the flames and smoke of the furnace in the craftwork scene in the late Eighteenth Dynasty tomb No. 181.[2] A rare Ramesside example seems to carry such an experiment even farther. Pale streamers of blue apparently attempt to imitate the shimmering space through which the winged figure moves [376].

Certainly there was a fairly frequent use of a kind of shading with pigments, as on the darkened ends of the wing-tips and grey upper surface of the body of the ostrich [248]. In other cases there is no darkening, but only the use of a more intense hue which produces deeper accents on the same ground colour. This frequently is very successful in suggesting texture [284],[3] and in the stippling of the bodies of the birds on a ceiling from the Palace of Amenhotep III [286] produces something of a feeling of a rounded form. We shall see that in Ramesside times there was an occasional attempt to indicate form in this fashion [361]. These exploratory beginnings were never consistently developed, but they are unique in early painting, and should be remembered as anticipating a line of investigation to be carried out logically by the Greeks in much later times.[4]

The ostriches [248] form part of the extraordinary hunting scene in the tomb of Kenamon (No. 93). In discussing the 'landscape' of the Hatshepsut Punt reliefs we have referred to the unusual way in which irregular strips of desert gravel surround the animals here, in place of the usual horizontal registers. Along the right border a wider speckled area is provided for the animals diving into and emerging from their holes. It is as though the usual horizontal line of hillocks [245] had been tipped up along the side and then extended across the top of the scene. A wild calf curls up naturalistically in one of the new twisted poses, while below (not visible in the illustration) there is a wild ass giving birth to her young. The artist has differentiated marvellously between the frizzy hair of the baby and the smooth coat of the mother. Outside the illustration on the left the frequently reproduced figure of a magnificent ibex confronts the arrows of the hunter.

This splendid tomb[5] is the finest work of the reign of Amenhotep II. The yellow background used throughout is unusual, but seems a consistent part of the attempt to gain richer colour effects. There was also an exceptional use of a resinous varnish over the paintings to heighten their colour. This has darkened with age, but fortunately has peeled off in many places, so that one can see the original colouring. The new opulence which resulted from the foreign tribute exacted by Tuthmosis III and his energetic son, Amenhotep II, appears here not only in the size of the tomb, which is more elaborately laid out than that of the vizier Rekhmira, but also in the various products of the craftsmen which are shown as presented to the king on New Year's day. These resemble the rich funerary furniture which has been recovered in fragmentary condition from the tombs of Amenhotep II and Tuthmosis IV[6] and which we shall see preserved in marvellous condition from the burials of the parents of Queen Tiy and of Tut-ankh-amon. The ostentatious display which finds its culmination in the buildings of Amenhotep III and at Amarna is well reflected by a wall in the tomb of Onen, the brother of Queen Tiy (No. 120), in the reign of Amenhotep III.[7] As in the paintings of Kenamon, the traditional careful execution is maintained, but with a new sumptuousness of texture and detail. Amenhotep III and Tiy are enthroned under a canopy with a row of foreign peoples ornamenting the side of the platform [255]. The scene can be better understood by referring to the tomb of Ramose [256], where the upper part of similar figures has survived.[8] Carved arm-rests from a wooden chair like that in which Amenhotep sits were recovered from the tomb of Tuthmosis IV and are now in Boston and New York.[9] The queen rests her foot on a cushion similar to those in the Oxford painting from Tell el Amarna of Akhenaten's family [314], but Tiy sits upright among the luxurious fittings of her throne, while Nofretete and the

254. Thebes, tomb of Horemheb (No. 78), fish. Dynasty XVIII

256. Thebes, tomb of Ramose (No. 55), Amenhotep IV enthroned. Dynasty XVIII

255. Thebes, tomb of Onen (No. 120), Amenhotep III and Tiy enthroned. Dynasty XVIII

princesses lounge in easy positions on the cushions at the feet of the king. Nothing could be more indicative of the change that was soon to take place in the representation of the human figure. The openwork design between the legs of the king's chair, with its heavy rosettes, is an elaboration of the old joining of the plants of the two lands, and, with the intricate decoration of the columns of the throne kiosk and the huge artificially contrived bouquet placed before the king, anticipates the overloaded ornament which we shall find in the objects from the tomb of Tut-ankh-amon. In many ways this painting closely resembles the decoration of the palace of Amenhotep III, and with its bright colouring suggests the appearance of one of the apartments of that building.

The first prisoner under the footstool of the queen is one of the most discussed of the representations of the Keftiu.[10] Even more interesting than this detailed but puzzling picture of a foreigner is the lively action taking place between the black-and-white legs of the throne. A pet cat has seized a goose, while over them leaps an excited monkey. The sense of movement and the characteristics of the different animals are captured with remarkable sympathy. They arrest attention even after one has just examined a masterpiece of animal-painting, in the tomb of Kenamon. Here there is a certain sly humour at work which shows how easy it was for the draughtsmen of later times to slip over into caricature of humans in animal guise [378, 381, 382]. It made Norman de Garis Davies think of the fat goose of Amon seized by the queen's cat as a hint of the way in which the enormous wealth of the god's temples was about to be swallowed up by the state in the new changes instigated by Tiy's son, Akhenaten. Davies hastened to add that the artist would not in all probability have consciously dared to portray such an idea. It must be admitted that it would be particularly unsuitable in the tomb of the queen's brother, who was an important figure in the hierarchy of the Amon priesthood.

Much space was devoted in the tombs of this period to representations of the king and to the royal favour by which the owner had made his way in life. There is also a strong indication of how much of the wealth that had been piling up as the result of foreign conquest was being devoted to Amon with the resulting power of his priesthood. In most cases where the products of workshops are shown, these are intended for presentation to the temple, although the New Year's gifts in Kenamon's scene were destined for the palace. Kenamon was one of a number of great men who owed their position to the fact that they had grown up as companions of Amenhotep II. This king has left us some account of his venturesome youth in which he excelled in hunting, rowing, and horsemanship. His great strength with the bow was also admired. He not only emulated the campaigns in Syria of his father, Tuthmosis III, but also the habit of keeping records of them. He was the last of the energetic pharaohs of the Eighteenth Dynasty whose military leadership ensured the maintenance of the Empire abroad. Something personal in his decided nature comes through to us even in his official boasting, with a hint of cruelty in the brutal execution of the Syrian princes, six of whose bodies were suspended from the walls of Thebes and the seventh at Napata in the Sudan. There has survived a copy of a private letter which he wrote to his viceroy of Nubia, Wesersatet, which is couched in a colloquial

style. It refers to a campaign in Syria and the women taken as booty and was evidently written on the spur of the moment in the midst of a feast following the celebration of the king's accession day when he thought of the absence of his old companion.[11] The dancers and musicians of the kind of pleasure palace in which Amenhotep II was celebrating the feast of his coronation are shown us by Kenamon, who was in charge of such an establishment.[12] The luxurious refinement of this scene is in striking contrast to the roughness of the king's words and actions. The manner of representation is here typical also of our difficulties in extricating fact from symbol, for Kenamon, in order to portray his early relations with the king, has at a later date had him portrayed as a small but full-grown figure seated on the lap of his nurse, the mother of Kenamon, in the kiosk around which the entertainment is proceeding.

The successor of Amenhotep II, Tuthmosis IV, is less clear to us as a personality. We glimpse him as a youth hunting lions in the Giza desert. As his father had done when he was living as a prince in Memphis, Tuthmosis was in the habit of going out in his chariot to engage in sport near the pyramids. One day, when the young prince had fallen asleep in the shadow of the Sphinx during the noon heat, the sun god spoke to him, assured him of his succession to the throne, and asked that the sand be cleared away from his image.[13] This picturesque account of repairs to the Sphinx is one of the signs of an increased interest in the Heliopolitan sun cult, since Chephren's old monument was now thought to represent Ra-Horakhte (Ra-Horus of the Horizon). The presence of the princes in Memphis emphasizes the importance assumed by the old capital as an administrative centre. Little is known of other events in the reign of Tuthmosis IV except for his marriage with the daughter of the king of Mitanni.

Tuthmosis I and Tuthmosis III had crossed the Euphrates to attack the land over which the king was to rule and which the Egyptians called Nahrin. Under a new dynasty of rulers it had assumed a dominant role at the expense of the kingdom of Assyria on the east, while on the west it impinged upon the Egyptian sphere of influence in the northern part of Syria. For some time the rise of Hittite power had been checked by internal troubles. It did not become threatening until late in the reign of Amenhotep III. This son of Tuthmosis IV contracted further foreign marriages, maintaining friendly relations with Mitanni and Kassite Babylonia. He corresponded with the kings of Assyria and Cyprus, and had even established contact with the ruler of Arzawa in south-western Asia Minor which bordered on the Hittite homeland, seeking marriage with the daughter of this powerful neighbour of the king of Hatti.[14] Remote though this country may seem from Egypt, it must be remembered that a courier service had also been established between Thebes and Boghazköy, the capital of Hatti on the central Anatolian plateau. We learn from a letter addressed by the Hittite king, Subbiluliumas, to Akhenaten that he had been in correspondence with Amenhotep III.[15] Thus for a period of some fifty years, until Subbiluliumas destroyed Mitanni, a cosmopolitan atmosphere of diplomatic activity replaced that of the earlier military campaigns. Messengers moved back and forth between Egypt and these far-off lands, while the ladies given in marriage travelled to the Nile Valley with large retinues. Gold was what was desired abroad when dowries were discussed and presents exchanged, but in the correspondence are mentioned articles of furniture and dress, statues, and other precious objects. The culmination of Egypt's power and wealth was enjoyed in the reign of Amenhotep III, but before its end stirrings can be sensed among the city-states of Palestine and Syria, as the struggle between the Hittites and Mitanni began.

Something of this atmosphere is reflected in the Theban tombs. The presentation of tribute before the enthroned king gave frequent opportunity for the rendering of foreign objects. We also see much of the workshops in Egypt itself. Here a new elaboration of ornament appears in the articles being manufactured and set out for inspection among the New Year's gifts. It becomes clear that it cannot be easy to distinguish between an imported piece, one which had been made abroad under Egyptian influence, or one made at home from raw materials collected as tribute or received as presents from the rulers of foreign powers.

In the craftwork scenes, as well as those representing agricultural labours and other activities which fell under the supervision of the tomb owner, there were opportunities for inserting a multitude of details of daily life.[16] It is in this intimate field of tomb-painting that the artist of the Eighteenth Dynasty seems to have found his most congenial employment. His inventiveness was spurred to new creation which was more in keeping with his delight in nature and in the life about him than were the efforts of the builder and the sculptor to satisfy the demands of the time for ostentation on a colossal scale. There is here a more substantial expression of the charm and vivacity which, in the minor arts, appear in small frivolous objects made to be enjoyed as ornaments rather than practical utensils. Naturally, one of the principal concerns of the tomb owner was the portrayal of himself and his family in connexion with the food offerings for their maintenance in after life and the picturing of the funeral ceremonies. In the Eighteenth Dynasty these funeral scenes were generally confined to the long inner corridor, with the outer room of the chapel reserved for representations of the owner's life on earth.

The way in which even these funerary scenes are presented seems much less impersonalized than do the illustrations for religious texts in the tombs of the kings. It is as though huge papyrus rolls were spread out on the walls of the royal burial apartments of Dynasty XVIII. Indeed, this is a transference to the walls of a guide to the underworld, the book of Am-duat – What is in the Netherworld – with its cursive hieroglyphic writing and the correspondingly abbreviated lines of the figure drawing.[17] Instead of inspiring the draughtsmen to creations which might frighten us, the terrible demons and monsters of this gloomy underworld have been reduced to orderly, rather dry abstractions. There are only brief references to the royal owner of the tomb. On a pillar in the burial hall of Tuthmosis III, the name of his mother is indeed placed over the woman who stands behind him in a divine bark, while three wives and a daughter follow him in the row of tersely expressed figures below [257]. On the right the king is suckled by a goddess in the form of a sycamore tree drawn in red line with green strokes for the

257. Thebes, tomb of Tuthmosis III, king and family. Dynasty XVIII

leaves.[18] The goddess is called Isis, with perhaps an allusion to his actual mother, who was named after her. The simplified linear style goes back at least to the end of the Middle Kingdom, as in the little pictures added to the text known as the Dramatic Papyrus.[19] It was used in the burial-chambers of Tuthmosis I, Amenhotep II, and Amenhotep III, as well as in the tomb of Tuthmosis III, although paintings of the normal kind are to be found illustrating the texts of the Book of the Dead in the papyri of private persons in Dynasty XVIII. So remote from reality are these guides to the underworld that it is hard to remember, while examining the neat imitations of papyrus rolls spread out over the walls of the burial-hall of Amenhotep II, that we are standing near the stone sarcophagus which contained the body of the man who wrote the letter to Wesersatet and enjoyed himself in the pleasure kiosk shown in the tomb of Kenamon. The concentrated vitality of the simpler linear style is transformed into formal rigidity at the end of the Eighteenth Dynasty, when the more familiar painted reliefs are used in decorating the corridors and chambers of the royal tombs. Typical is a detail [341] from a new addition to the literature concerned with the Netherworld, The Book of Gates, in the Theban tomb of Horemheb.

It is pleasant to turn to the harvest scene in the tomb of Menena (No. 69),[20] where the girls fighting or the one who pulls a thorn from her companion's foot are examples of the observations of unchanging human nature which abound in the Theban private tombs [258]. So is the man asleep under the tree. He is repeated in relief in the tomb of Khaemhet (No. 57), where the hot sun over another grain-field being

258. Thebes, tomb of Menena (No. 69), harvest scene. Dynasty XVIII

259. Thebes, tomb of Khaemhet (No. 57), chariot in harvest scene. Dynasty XVIII

harvested has also made drowsy the wonderfully relaxed charioteer [259]. The walls of Khaemhet's chapel show, too, the most sophisticated development of the use of curved line and elaborate detail [260]. It is hard to believe that the youths with long carefully dressed hair and fine thin garments are in charge of cattle, but they hold up papyrus rolls containing the accounts of the herds.[21] The first work executed in the tomb of the vizier Ramose (No. 55) again represents this very refined use of low relief in the reign of Amenhotep III. It should be noted how the outlines of the body appear through the thin shirt of the man with the bouquet of papyrus who follows Ramose on the east wall of the pillared hall south of the entrance [263]. The paintings on the south wall have the same technical dexterity, while the wonderful draughts-manship is carried on in the work in the new style of Amenhotep IV on the back wall [261, 262] which we shall have to consider later.[22] A glance [263, 264] will show what a striking resemblance there is between the head carved in relief in the tomb of Ramose and that broken from a pair statue of a great personage and his wife.[23] It is seldom that one can illustrate so well the close approximation in style between sculpture in the round and a relief, although we have noticed another instance in the Giza reserve heads of Dynasty IV and the reliefs of Khufukhaf [105–8]. Here again both sculpture and relief are carved in the same material, limestone, and the resemblance is enhanced by the dark touches of paint applied to the eyes on the light-coloured stone. The reliefs had not yet been painted in the uncompleted tomb of Ramose, and only the eyes were drawn in black. On the other hand, the sculptor of the statue of the general Nakht-min[24] and his wife [264, 265] apparently intended only to emphasize certain features

260. Thebes, tomb of Khaemhet (No. 57), bowing men. Dynasty XVIII

by black accents, since he had painted the lips red. This was seldom, if ever, done when an ordinary red or yellow body-colour was used, but can be seen again in the head of Queen Nofretete [293], where the skin is a light flesh colour. The elaborate wigs, the curving fan held by the man, and the way

in which the modelling of the woman's body is seen through the soft folds of her thin flowing robe, betray the same delicate touch that was applied to the reliefs.

The fine workmanship of the tombs of Khaemhet, Ramose, and Surer is to be found in the reliefs of the princesses [266]

261 and 262 (*above, right*). Thebes, tomb of Ramose (No. 55), Amenhotep IV and queen at window of appearances, Ramose receives courtiers. Dynasty XVIII

263. Thebes, tomb of Ramose (No. 55), head of a man. Dynasty XVIII

264 and 265. Nakht-min and his wife from Thebes. Dynasty XVIII. *Cairo Museum*

266. Thebes, tomb of Kheruef (No. 192), princesses. Dynasty XVIII

on the back wall of the large unfinished court of Kheruef (No. 192). The tall, slender girls wear over a short wig the elaborate side-lock which is familiar to us from the many pictures of the small daughters of Akhenaten. On top of that rests a cylindrical headdress, of a kind represented with more detail in the paintings of the ladies of Menena's family,[25] and perhaps also forming a support for the flower garlands [290]. Such 'Children of the King' once appeared behind two named daughters of Amenhotep III and Tiy in the scenes showing the Sed Festival of the thirtieth year in the king's great temple of Soleb in the Sudan,[26] and are also to be found on a block from the Aten shrine of Amenhotep IV at Karnak. Here they form part of two elaborate representations of the Heb-Sed which flank the entrance to an inner hall. The inscriptions refer to the celebrations of the festival in both the years 30 and 36. The reliefs were sheltered by a colonnade of channelled columns, but the courtyard seems to have been left incomplete, with only its eastern entrance decorated under Amenhotep IV.[27]

The plan of the tomb of Khaemhet (No. 57), where reference is made to the festival of the year 30, is relatively simple. It is also smaller than the other two great tombs of the end of the reign. Those of Ramose (No. 55) and Surer (No. 48),[28] in their size and use of columned halls, reflect the great building schemes which had been undertaken by Amenhotep III with the help of Amenhotep son of Hapu.

The name of the later deified wise man, the son of Hapu also called Huy,[29] is associated with the funerary temple of Amenhotep III and the temple of Soleb rather than with the Luxor temple,[30] but he would appear to have been the guiding spirit behind the architectural projects of this reign. It was evidently in his middle years that he was appointed to the post of Scribe of Recruits early in the reign of Amenhotep III. He claims to have reached the age of eighty in the inscription on the lap of the remarkable statue which portrays him as an old man [267].[31] The conscription of men entailed duties in connexion not only with military personnel but with the labourers required for quarrying, transport, and building operations. Thus Amenhotep became Overseer of All the King's Works. He was in charge of the quarries at Gebel Ahmar, a little north of Cairo, from which came the quartzite much favoured for statues during the reign of Amenhotep III. We shall see that the chief sculptor Men had to do with the work in these quarries when we come do consider the similar position occupied by his son Bak under Akhenaten. Men is shown worshipping a statue of Amenhotep III in a rock inscription at Aswan, and it has been thought that he may have been the sculptor of the Colossi of Memnon.[32] The stone for these enormous seated figures, which Amenhotep was charged with erecting in front of the king's mortuary temple, came from Gebel Ahmar. It has been plausibly argued that this was at the time of the first Sed Festival in the year 30

267. Amenhotep son of Hapu. Dynasty XVIII. *Cairo Museum*

which is mentioned on one of a series of statues representing Amenhotep as a young scribe.[33] The king ordered these statues to be set up at Karnak. They must have been in a forecourt of the temple, and perhaps in front of the recently completed Third Pylon, which then formed the western front of the temple. They emphasize the great man's position as Royal Scribe, although listing the other important offices which he held towards the end of his career. It was as a wise scribe that he was revered in later times, and these statues were intended to serve as an intermediary on behalf of worshippers who did not have direct access to the image of Amon with their petitions. It is obvious that the term architect is not wide enough to cover the activities of such a man. At Soleb he is shown taking part in the ceremonies of the first Heb-Sed, and he was permitted – an unheard-of honour – to construct a funerary temple for himself behind that of the king.

In the Luxor temple we find preserved a nearly complete building which had been planned as a compact, regularly disposed structure on a long axis. Here for the first time is

established a plan [268] which is virtually that familiar to us from such later buildings as the mortuary temple of Ramesses III at Medinet Habu, the Khons Temple at Karnak, and the temple of Edfu. In all these buildings there is a progression from an open colonnaded court through halls, diminishing in size, to the sanctuary. There is also a series of rooms symmetrically disposed around the core of the inner temple. However, it has been pointed out that the Luxor temple is peculiar in having two sanctuaries of Amon and that the subsidiary rooms were intended to serve the cult of the god's statue which stood in the second sanctuary against the back wall of the building. Communication with this more intimate part of the temple was by a single doorway in the eastern wall of the first sanctuary which was intended for the bark of Amon.[34] The room for the seated image of Amon was preceded by a columned hall and lay behind the chamber for the sacred bark which was brought here from Karnak on the feast of Opet. Originally the bark rested on a base between four columns, but at the beginning of the Ptolemaic Period these columns were replaced by a granite chamber for the bark and a doorway opened into the hall behind.

Store-chambers run along the side walls of the inner temple and must have served in connexion with the ceremonies of feeding and clothing the statue. The northern of the two rooms with three columns, east of the antechamber to the sanctuary of the bark, was decorated with a series of reliefs recounting the divine birth of Amenhotep III,[35] much as Hatshepsut had shown herself to be the daughter of Amon at Deir el Bahari. There are two side entrances opening into the halls preceding the sanctuary of the bark to facilitate movement, after the procession had borne the bark to its resting-place down the central aisle. The largest of these halls opens directly on to the court, employing the same papyrus-bundle columns, with bud capitals, which continue round the court [269]. The effective balance between the broad open spaces and the architectural mass of the huge columns, with their wonderful play of light and shade, makes this perhaps the most beautiful employment of the plant column anywhere in Egypt. The architects of the funerary temples on the western bank had been experimenting with the use of colonnaded courts since the time of Hatshepsut. Their ruined state makes it difficult to trace any development. It is at least clear that a richer effect is produced at Luxor than in the temple of Tuthmosis IV by reducing the lines of columns round the court to two, and retaining the depth of four only in the hypostyle hall at the back.

Amenhotep III added in front of the gateway to the court a long entrance hall or processional way with seven pairs of enormous columns with open papyrus (campaniform) capitals. The front walls forming its gate were placed slightly askew, so that the court and pylon later added by Ramesses II are not aligned with the axis of the older temple. The side walls of this long entrance hall were decorated by Tut-ankh-amon with lively scenes representing the feast of Opet and Amon's progress on the Nile from Karnak to Luxor.[36] These reliefs were later usurped by Horemheb. A shorter entrance hall of this kind, or porch, with only two pairs of columns, stood in front of the pylon before the temple of Soleb. This magnificent structure seems, like the mortuary temple of the king at Western Thebes, to have been built later in the reign

268 and 269. Luxor temple, plan and court. Dynasty XVIII

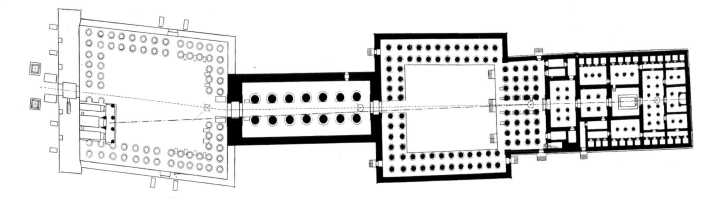

and probably in connexion with the Sed festival of the thirtieth year, since scenes of this ceremony are represented on its walls. As preserved, it is about 400 feet long (122 m) in comparison to a length of some 623 feet (190 m) for the Luxor temple, but it is incomplete, since little or nothing is preserved of the sanctuary at the back. It lay on the west bank of the river north of the Third Cataract. The plans of Cailliaud and Lepsius do not agree as to the badly preserved succession of courts and columned halls, but in one of these palm columns were used instead of the more usual papyrus-bundle columns.[37] As in the mortuary temple, a considerable quantity of sculpture survived, which had mostly lined the way leading up to the temple. Part of this, including ram-headed sphinxes, one of the falcon-gods, the uraeus serpent, Serqet,

and the famous granite lions in the British Museum, was carried away by the Kushite kings to decorate the temple of Amon at Gebel Barkal.[38] The Prudhoe lions are a large-scale example of the unusual pose with head turned towards the observer and crossed paws which is to be found on the lid of a vessel in the tomb of Tut-ankh-amon (who completed one of the Soleb lions) and in a Ramesside painting [343, 344].

We now see the Luxor temple with the addition of a columned forecourt, erected by Ramesses II, and a front pylon on which is carved one of the famous representations of his battle of Kadesh. Other scenes of his Syrian wars are continued along the outer western wall of the temple. In front of the pylon stands one of the obelisks of Ramesses II [354]. Its companion is now in the Place de la Concorde in Paris.

270. Amenhotep III. Head from Thebes. Dynasty XVIII. *London, British Museum*

Only the Colossi of Memnon still look out over the Theban Plain to mark the site of the mortuary temple of Amenhotep III. These two great seated figures were at least 64 feet high (19.5 m), and their mere size is an indication of the vanished grandeur of this great building. Something of the structure could still be seen in the first half of the nineteenth century, and its ruins were worked over for the sculpture which is now in the British Museum and various other collections in Europe.[39] The map printed by Sir John Gardiner Wilkinson in 1835 as a *Topographical Survey of Thebes* shows the position of the columns of a large and smaller hypostyle hall in the mound of debris known as the Kom el Heitan, which lies on the western edge of the cultivation, about half way between the Ramesseum and Medinet Habu. Other stones could still be seen between the mound and the Colossi. There was evidently a long avenue of statues here, but it is now impossible to guess what other structures stood in this intervening space of over 1,000 feet (305 m). There was little left which would appear to repay systematic excavation when Sir Flinders Petrie published his *Six Theban Temples* in 1896, but the site continued to produce an occasional piece of sculpture or an inscription. That this temple formed a culminating point in the taste for ostentatious building which had been growing in Dynasty XVIII is made evident by the seated limestone group, 23 feet high (7 m), of Amenhotep III, Tiy, and three daughters in the Cairo Museum. This has been reconstructed from pieces found by Daressy in the neighbourhood of Medinet Habu and must have ornamented the approach to the temple, on the south side, where a road led to the palace of Amenhotep III.[40]

Some of the sculpture from the mortuary temple, like the seated figure in the British Museum[41] or others which seem to have been identical to the lioness-headed Sekhmet statues

with which the king filled his Temple of Mut at Karnak,[42] represent a perfectly conventional development of the style of the earlier part of the Dynasty. There is a reminiscence of the rather heavy features of some of the faces of Amenhotep II. The emphasis is on bulk and solidity, which replace the wiry strength of Tuthmosid times, and there is little suggestion of the delicacy of the younger heads of Amenhotep son of Hapu or the attempt at individualization in his portrait as an old man [267]. However, there are other heads, the most striking of which are those in the British Museum [270] and in Boston,[43] where a markedly new stylization of the facial planes is immediately apparent. They are cut in brownish mottled quartzite (often called hard sandstone) and probably come from the mortuary temple, although the Boston piece (20½ inches high, 51.2 cm) is from a smaller statue than the other (46 inches high, 116.8 cm). The rather sharp joining of the facial planes with their pronounced curves, the exotic touch lent by the long, narrow eyes and full lips, drawn up at the corners of the mouth, begin to suggest something of that quality which startles us so in the early colossi of Amenhotep IV [294, 295].

Two headless standing black granite figures, a little over life size, that certainly came from the mortuary temple, and a small statuette, also headless, present the king in a new fashion. Here it is a question of the soft, fat form under a long robe with sleeves and the slackness of the pose with the hands folded in front of the body.[44] There is the same suggestion of relaxed indolence as appears on the Amarna stela, where Amenhotep is shown seated at a table of food with his arm thrown around the shoulders of Queen Tiy [317]. Although this relief is often described as representing the king as a sick, tired old man, there is little or no indication of age in the face. The king simply seems fatter and more listless than in his beautiful little ebony figure in the Brooklyn Museum [271]. The inscription on the base of this statuette calls the king 'Lord of Festivals in the House of Rejoicing',[45] which would seem to indicate that at least his second Heb-Sed of the thirty-fourth year had been celebrated in the festival hall of his palace in Western Thebes which bore this name. He was thus an elderly man nearing the end of his reign. In looking at this wonderfully fashioned small piece we are reminded of the youthful figures of Amenhotep son of Hapu, who had reached old age when they were made. The delicate modelling of the small wood carving, which is a little under 11 inches (27.9 cm) in height, hints at the corpulence of the stone figures without stressing it. The statuette may be compared with another small wooden figure, in the Brooklyn Museum, of the singer Mi [272]. The artist has paid special attention to the head with its elaborate wig, and has tapered the limbs under the clinging dress of light material. The dark wood was set off with the gold of the earrings, bracelet, and collar, the last now missing completely.

The plump, rounded face of the king presents a decided contrast to the large heads, although something like their sharply joined planes is to be found in a slightly larger ebony head in the Berlin collection which has been attributed to Queen Tiy [273]. Like a number of other small precious objects of the late Eighteenth Dynasty, this apparently comes from a royal residence in the north at Gurob, near the entrance to the Fayum.[46] The eyes and eyebrows were inlaid, as in her husband's statuette, where they were of opaque

271. Amenhotep III. Ebony statuette from Thebes. Dynasty XVIII. *Brooklyn Museum*

272. The singer Mi. Wooden statuette. Dynasty XVIII. *Brooklyn Museum*

glass. Like his gilded skirt and the details of the Blue Crown, precious materials have been used here for accessories. The earring is of gold and lapis lazuli, and the headcloth has been altered by a covering of plaster and linen in which were closely set small blue beads. This luxurious combination of expensive materials is in keeping with the gorgeous decoration of the furniture and small ornamental objects of the period. However, small as is the scale of these wooden carvings [e.g. 274], we seem to have in them, as in the aged face of Amenhotep son of Hapu [267], an attempt at individuality in portraiture of a kind which we found in the Old and Middle Kingdoms, but which has so far not appeared in Dynasty XVIII. While the deep furrows from the nose to the corners of the full lips and the sharp indentation from the

brow to the heavy-lidded, narrow eyes are employed by the sculptors at Amarna, they are combined in the structure of Tiy's face to produce the impression of an individual which is at the same time in keeping with other representations of the Queen.[47]

The face of the Brooklyn statuette of the king suggests the actual features which formed a basis for the facial type of the large sculpture and reliefs. It bears a considerable resemblance to a life-size plaster head [321, 322] from the workshop of the sculptor Tuthmosis at Tell el Amarna which has been identified as Amenhotep III.[48] In spite of the problems presented by the group of sculptor's models with which this was found, one tends to believe that this face is a likeness of that king. As in the case of several other pieces in this group,

273. Tiy. Ebony head from Gurob. Dynasty XVIII. *Berlin Museum*

274. Officer. Wooden statue. Dynasty XVIII. *Cairo Museum*

it is thought to have been cast from a mould taken from a statue, but certainly no statues have survived from the end of the Eighteenth Dynasty which present the lifelike qualities of the plaster casts from Amarna [321–4]. It has been argued from close examination of the pieces in Berlin that heads modelled in clay formed the basis for the casts, although some of them certainly look like death-masks, and it was once maintained that they could have been made from impressions taken from the face of a living or dead person.[49] Assuming that this particular head is cast from a clay model, it might

have served as a guide for the making of the statues of Amenhotep III which are represented in the twelfth year of Akhenaten's reign standing between the columns of a court in a building called the Sunshade of Tiy,[50] and apparently erected in honour of the visit to Amarna of the mother of Akhenaten. It does not appear to represent the king in his last years[51] and may have been kept for some time, thus bringing up the question of whether such models were already used for sculpture under Amenhotep III.

CHAPTER 15

The Palace of Amenhotep III and New Kingdom Domestic Architecture

We have seen that it was impossible to gain a clear idea of the domestic architecture of the Old Kingdom from the few preserved ground-plans of buildings, which were generally concerned with the administration of the cemeteries, and from the highly schematized pictures on the walls of tombs. The material was more abundant for the Middle Kingdom, with the very instructive town-site of Kahun, which served the Pyramid of Sesostris II at Lahun in Dynasty XII, supplemented by the material from the cataract forts. Models of buildings are very helpful, as is the fact that the Middle Kingdom artist began to make a more varied use of architectural details to accompany the groups of figures in his wall-scenes. This gradual expansion of scenic accessories gathered momentum in the New Kingdom, when we find remarkable attempts to portray architecture and its physical setting. However difficult this may be for the modern mind to understand, as in the case of the many representations of the royal palace and temples at Tell el Amarna which have proved so puzzling when compared feature by feature with the actual excavated remains of these buildings, nonetheless it is an immense stride forward in the recording attempts of an extraordinarily observant people and provides us with an incomparably richer picture of the way in which they lived.

For the first time in Dynasty XVIII we can examine the actual structures in which the royal family lived. At Thebes we can look into the handsomely decorated bed-chamber of Amenhotep III, or see how at Amarna in Middle Egypt the official residence of Akhenaten was laid out in relation to a city. At the little known site of Deir el Ballas, on the edge of the western desert, across the river from the important town of Coptos, some 30 miles north of Thebes and hardly 10 miles from Denderah, there were two palaces of a type otherwise unknown [275, 276]. Both have preserved the foundations for a high central structure, accompanied by columned courts on a lower level. The effect produced is that of a tower or keep. The North Palace lies on a low mound inside a rectangular walled enclosure about 500 feet (152 m) wide and probably twice that long. The southern building occupies an area 327 feet by 144 feet (99 × 43 m) on the top of a high projection of the desert hills. No enclosure wall was found, but the sturdy foundations give even more the impression of a fortified building. A well-preserved stairway [277] leading to the upper level has no exact parallel in Egypt, although it is reminiscent of the stairs giving access to the higher level of the chief building in the Middle Kingdom town of Kahun and the stairway in the Kerma palace. In the area between the two Ballas palaces, which are about half a mile apart, lay a small village with winding streets and a number of outlying groups of houses, one of which was immediately west of the North Palace. These outlying houses were evidently of the New Kingdom, but the village was earlier, since into the rooms of the houses and against their outside walls had been dug the graves of a cemetery of the first half of Dynasty XVIII. The burials were accompanied by scarabs of kings and other well-known persons from the reign of Ahmose to at least that of Tuthmosis III.[1] A jar-sealing of King Ahmose was found in the North Palace, and it is hard to escape the impression that here was a settlement which had a particularly important period of occupancy in the early part of Dynasty XVIII and diminished in importance about the time of Amenhotep III.

The records of the excavations at Deir el Ballas leave many questions unanswered. However, the massive structure of the southern palace is strikingly impressive [275]. Its broad staircase, flanked by a smaller secondary one, rises from the lower level of the eastern portion of the building which at first glance would appear to be a large, almost square court. However, this was a hall with the roof supported by closely placed columns, presumably of wood, on round stone bases. These are better preserved on the western side, but others were still in position farther east, and these rested on a mud floor apparently laid over a series of brick foundation compartments inside a thick retaining wall and resembling the system of foundation compartments which supported the upper storey of the building. It will be seen from the section of the structure that the outer wall was denuded to floor level, so that nothing can be determined concerning the entrances to this hall. The upper portion of the building may have formed a platform on which were erected several smaller buildings, although it is more probable that there was a series of rooms inside a thick outer wall, perhaps in several storeys. It will be observed that the secondary northern staircase does not reach as high as the broad main one, but it may have turned in a smaller stair-well to reach the same level. The unique nature of a broad flight of steps used monumentally should be emphasized. Egyptian staircases are purely utilitarian and generally narrow, fitted into the plan without apparently any thought as to the effect they might produce. Something of this character is retained here, since the stair-well is approached at a right angle up a few steps set in a rather narrow doorway, while the secondary narrow flight of stairs again spoils the impressiveness of the broad flight which must have been hidden when the outer wall was preserved.

The denudation of the outer slopes of the low mound on which the northern palace stood prevented the recovery of the whole of the plan and left only the base of the walls of some of the outer rooms, so that the position of doorways was not determined [276]. However, there is again the use of large halls with their roofs supported by many columns on stone bases, grouped round a roughly square central block of unconnected long compartments. The walls were preserved to a considerable height, and traces of wooden roofing and some elements from an upper storey were recovered. The evidence was complicated by the existence of badly preserved Roman remains in the top level. The excavator's impression was that this was a tower-like structure which rose above the surrounding halls, but that the compartments were not filled as foundations, since they were roofed with wood and might have been some kind of magazines or cellars. If this were the

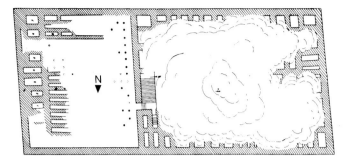

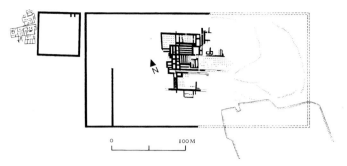

275. (left). Deir el Ballas, South Palace. Dynasty XVIII. Plan and section

276. (above). Deir el Ballas, North Palace. Dynasty XVIII. Plan

277. (below). Deir el Ballas, South Palace, stairway. Dynasty XVIII

case, it is difficult to see how they could have been entered. The southern entrance system is fairly clear, but since it lies rather far from the wall of the outer enclosure, in which no gates were preserved, its connexion with this is obscure. In the paved north-south corridor, which seems to introduce this southern entrance, were recovered the rather miserable vestiges of a wall-painting which nonetheless invokes something of the warlike spirit of the early Eighteenth Dynasty. Only two fragments with the head of a male figure and a pair of battle-axes were sketched in the records, but they suggest a representation of the palace guard and seem a most suitable decoration for such a building [278A]. They can at least be added to the meagre evidence for the decoration of Egyptian secular buildings, as can a fragment of a seated goddess, evidently facing a similar figure, from a private house west of the palace [278B]. It is unfortunate that the denuded condition of these New Kingdom houses at Deir el Ballas makes

their plans so difficult to understand as they were recorded. They are larger and more elaborately laid out than the very simple houses of the earlier village which must have been inhabited by people like those who dwelt in the workmen's quarter of Kahun. The New Kingdom houses have an

278. Deir el Ballas, paintings. (A) North Palace; (B) private house. Dynasty XVIII

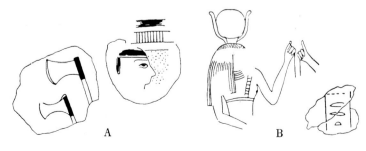

A   B

irregular disposition of the rooms which has little resemblance to the compact tripartite arrangement of the Amarna house.

These buildings at Deir el Ballas are most intriguing, and it is not easy to suggest their purpose. One could surmise that the southern building on the hill may have already been established in the Middle Kingdom to dominate the road on the Denderah side of the river in the important Denderah-Coptos district. The walled residence round which grew up a small town might have been an expansion of this smaller installation, but the present remains on both sites suggest a simultaneous occupation in the early New Kingdom and seem, on the evidence of the meagre facts at present available, to form a part of the Theban expansion accompanying the successful war against the Hyksos. Possibly this could be connected with the building activities of Ahmose and Amenhotep I, again scantily preserved, farther north at Abydos.

It is an entirely different matter when we turn to the fascinating examples of Eighteenth-Dynasty domestic architecture displayed in the Palace of Amenhotep III at Thebes and at Tell el Amarna, the new capital city founded by his son Amenhotep IV (Akhenaten). It is true that we are again faced with the problem of denudation leaving no more than ground-plans to be studied, but long-extended, painstaking excavation has recovered innumerable precious vestiges of structural details and decoration. The hazards of incompletely published records have to be faced. The occasional heavy rains in Upper Egypt have long since worn away the low brick walls to dim outlines of structures that now resemble what appeared on the nineteenth-century plans of Wilkinson and Lepsius more than they do the buildings as they looked when freshly excavated. Today the rare visitor to Amarna is generally disappointed by what little can be seen. Even the practised eye finds it hard to understand the vestiges of buildings or to overlook the senseless hacking out of pieces from the tomb walls, where time has also caused much of the plaster coating and patching to fall away and nearly all the colour to disappear. There still remains the rather wild beauty of the desolate, sandy plain with its encircling cliffs and the narrow fringe of green cultivated land along the river.

Even fewer visitors at Thebes stray south of the tourist-frequented temple of Ramesses III at Medinet Habu to look at the site of the Palace of Amenhotep III. If they do, they will probably be attracted there not by the dim outlines of the palace buildings, but by the huge mounds thrown up from a lake nearly two miles long. Fortunately, as at Amarna, the plans, drawings, and other records, as well as the actual elements of decoration and objects recovered in excavation, give us an adequate impression of these buildings. Moreover, by an accident of preservation it was possible to photograph fallen ceiling paintings in conjunction with existing remains of certain of the rooms to give a more immediate impression of the nature of the structure and its decoration than seems to have been possible at Amarna, where so much has to be conveyed by restored drawings. Much work, unhappily, was done at both sites before it had become the general rule to make a thorough photographic record.[2] Daressy's brief description of the portion of the main Palace of the King which he somewhat sketchily investigated is not easy to

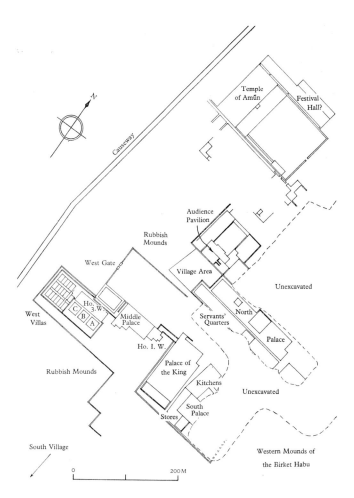

279. Malkata, Palace of Amenhotep III. Dynasty XVIII. General plan

correlate with the descriptions and illustrations given by Tytus, or with the more complete records made later.

The site is called Malkata, and the whole group consisted of a number of large, rambling buildings facing on huge courts or parade-grounds and strung out for a distance of nearly half a mile on the west side of the lake now called Birket Habu [279].[3] It lay about a mile south-west of the funerary temple of Amenhotep III and must have been connected with it by a roadway and probably other structures. All that now remains is a causeway bounding the palace on the west over which runs the modern track to Erment. There was an entrance from this causeway through a gateway on the west into the big court which was adjoined by the principal apartments of the palace as well as various administrative buildings [279]. The eastern part of the enclosure, between the Palace of the King, which formed the chief structure in the centre of the southern side, and the great mounds thrown up in the construction of the lake, has been badly weathered away and is now encroached upon by cultivation. Little can therefore be determined about this frontage on the lake or its entrances. One wonders how the builders can have dealt with these unsightly embankments of earth that even now stand up to a considerable height like small hills.

Many jar-labels show that the structure referred to as the Palace of the King [280] must have been built as early as the eighth year of the reign of Amenhotep III. At the northern end of the site was a chapel of Amon and the late buildings

280. Malkata, Palace of the King and South Palace. Dynasty XVIII. Plan

accompanying it. There was a huge audience pavilion near the centre of the site. South of this and arranged round the great court lay the blocks of buildings forming four loosely connected palaces: the North Palace, the South Palace, the Palace of the King, and the Middle Palace. Adjoining the last and the west gate, in the south-west corner of the enclosure, a series of houses was grouped round a larger dwelling. These apparently accommodated the vizier and served as residences and offices for other high officials. Incongruously a 'village area' of small habitations for palace workmen lies in the middle of the area, between parade-ground or great court and audience pavilion and adjoining the west end of the North Palace. Another such village lay beyond the rubbish mounds by the southern enclosure wall.

It has been suggested that the South Palace (10) (lower left corner [280]) may have belonged to Queen Tiy. It has been only partially excavated, due to the encroaching cultivation on the east, but repeats on a minor scale the pillared hall with throne dais and surrounding living quarters of the harem of the king's palace. Somewhat similar apartments were found in the central part of the long, narrow North Palace. The southern strip of this building consists of a long series of servants' quarters bounded on all sides by a corridor. One would expect this to be connected with the Palace of the King by a wing running across the east side of the great court to form a façade facing the west gate. Nothing is preserved here, and instead of a monumental entrance to the audience-rooms of that palace, the main access is by a wide corridor running eastwards from the Middle Palace [279, 280].

One looks in vain for an organized plan of the whole of this vast, rambling pile. Anyone familiar with the old Ottoman palace on Sarai Point in Istanbul is reminded of its succession of high-walled courts, the labyrinthine tangle of the harem apartments, and the various kiosks set somewhat haphazardly in gardens. There was a very limited use of stone for column bases, door-sills, and the flooring of baths. The construction was in mud brick with wooden columns and roofing beams. In

this use of wood and brick, Amenhotep III was evidently following an established tradition in domestic architecture. The lavish use of stone by his son in the state apartments of the Amarna palace seems to have been an innovation. Possibly Akhenaten may have attempted to strengthen his newly taken political and religious position by an exceptional effort to surround his person with splendour. The Central Palace at Amarna is laid out along more monumental lines, with a striking succession of state apartments on a strictly symmetrical scheme [311]. The North Palace at Amarna [305] also shows this application of formal regularity on a large scale. Even more clearly than the main palace in the town, it gives the impression of having been built all at once according to a preconceived plan. We should expect this to produce a balanced regularity of features in domestic architecture, as it had in temples and tombs, and we have seen that this was so in the Middle Kingdom houses of Kahun which were all laid out as part of one project. The same is true at Amarna, where the use of one group of contractors was responsible for a marked similarity in the plans of the houses. In the palace of Amenhotep III, certain basic features are repeated from one building to another, but no fixed scheme had been evolved for the grouping of the various units that grew up somewhat haphazardly over a period of years. The separate elements provide us with the first recognizable examples which we have of the living quarters and state apartments of the New Kingdom. They are found again at Amarna, at Gurob, and in the small palaces attached to the funerary temples of Dynasties XIX and XX as well as in the palace of Merenptah at Memphis.[4]

The actual living quarters were better preserved in the Malkata Palace than at Amarna, except in the separate buildings called the Royal Estate there. Even in the harem quarters at Amarna one fails to find the rooms in which the ladies of the household are shown lounging in the tomb pictures [313] which so much resemble the suites of rooms arranged around the columned hall (4) in the Malkata harem [280]. The house in the Royal Estate at Amarna is scarcely more than a very large edition of one of the private houses, and it is easy to imagine the king sharing it with his wife and daughters in much the same informal fashion in which they are shown in the numerous pictures of their family life. This close personal relationship reflects the mutual esteem and companionship which Akhenaten's parents, Amenhotep III and Tiy, seem to have shared. On the other hand, it is clear from the Amarna letters that both these kings contracted political marriages with ladies from abroad. These women, and most certainly others, must have been housed in considerable state in one of the Malkata buildings and at Amarna either in the harem of the official palace or in some portion of the building which has not been discovered. At Thebes the most important of these ladies perhaps occupied the suites of rooms around the long, columned hall in the Palace of the King [280]. This portion of the structure is connected with the more public parts of the building only by a single entrance. It contained at the back the private apartments of the king. Perhaps Queen Tiy was housed in the only less sumptuous suite of rooms nearby in the early South Palace.

The Amarna letters give two intriguing references to the women of this household. In one case Amenhotep III silences a complaint of the Kassite king of Babylon by pointing out[5] that when the Babylonian princess appeared, lined up with Amenhotep's other wives, the messengers which Kadashman Enlil had sent to see how his sister was faring did not know her well enough to recognize her. Again Tushratta of Mitanni,[6] writing to Akhenaten, recounts how pleased Amenhotep III was with his marriage to the Mitannian princess Tadukhepa. The messengers from her father were caused to enter the building which led to Tadukhepa, where they left presents and were rewarded in turn by gold which Amenhotep had given the princess to distribute. One would like to think of this as taking place in one of the several audience halls which approach the private quarters on the plan [281]. In view of the size of the Malkata group it is rather unlikely that Amenhotep III had another such residence at Thebes, although there must have been older palaces there belonging to his predecessors.

There were two of these large audience halls (1, 2) and a small one (3) at the north end of the Palace of the King (upper right corner of plan [280]). Each had a throne dais. The largest hall (1) was entered by a wide corridor that led in from the west and formed the main entrance to the palace. Another corridor runs straight south past the second audience hall (2) to the columned antechamber of the great hall (4) of the harem. A side passage along one end of the eastern suite of harem apartments led to a short flight of steps which descended to a lower corridor. This bounded the king's palace on the east and gave access to the block of kitchens (9) and the South Palace (10). East of the second audience hall, and entered through a large room and an antechamber, was a small room (3) with four columns and a base for a throne which was evidently used for more private receptions. This room, like the second audience hall (2) and the harem quarters, had preserved a large part of its rich decoration. The gaily decorated brick dais had painted figures of bound captives on the floor and on the treads of the steps[7] and was surmounted by a wooden canopy. The gorgeous effect of these canopied thrones can easily be imagined from the tomb-paintings of the period [255, 256]. A child's chair which the princess Sitamon probably used in one of the rooms of the Malkata palace is a small replica of the kind of elaborately decorated arm-chair which served as a throne [281].

The plastered walls, ceilings, and floors of these palace rooms were painted. The floors were decorated with a large composition better known from one of the columned halls of the harem of the Central Palace at Amarna.[8] Such floor-paintings were found at Malkata in the small audience chamber (3) and in the columned hall of the harem (4).[9] The main elements of the composition were a central rectangle laid out to represent a pool and a wide border with growing plants and water-birds flying above them. At Amarna figures of running and leaping calves were interspersed between these thickets of greenery, and there was a more formal outer border with rather stiff bouquets of flowers set between stands supporting bowls heaped up with offerings. The central area of the pond was covered with rippled black lines, indicating water in which were pond-lilies, fish, and swimming ducks. The painted surface of the pond was broken at intervals by the circular bases of the stone columns, while at Amarna a strip down the centre of the room (the main way

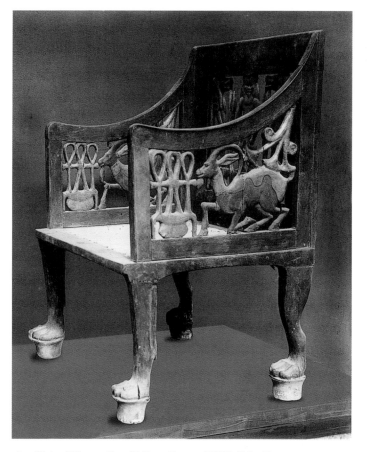

281. Chair of Sitamon from Malkata. Dynasty XVIII. *Cairo Museum*

through the room from the garden court to the next columned hall) had figures of bound captives like those on the steps of throne platforms.

The various elements of this design could be combined in different ways and parts used independently, as was done with sections of the border patterns in the oddly arranged floor-spaces between the rectangular water-basins in the Maru Aten precinct at Amarna.[10] Such small panels with calves leaping among papyrus plants or stands supporting bowls of food were used on the walls of the mud supports for shelves in the storerooms of the women's apartments at Malkata [282, 283] and on the wall-spaces between the cubicles in the colonnade round the garden court in the north harem of the Central Palace at Amarna. Similar motifs drawing upon plant, animal, and insect life were employed on a smaller scale on the charming glazed tiles used in wall decoration at Amarna. They are evidently a development of this freely rendered naturalistic-decorative painting that seems to have been invented for floors and carried over to minor wall-spaces. The omission of human figures helps to explain an otherwise seemingly isolated masterpiece, the wall frieze of the 'green room' of the garden court of the North Palace at Amarna which makes the same use of birds and plants [284].

Other decorative elements, such as dadoes, door-frames, and the floral borders at the top of walls, seem more formal, as do in general the elaborate combinations of geometric plant and bird-forms of the ceilings. In these ceiling designs the curved line predominates in spirals [285] and interweaving

282. Malkata Palace, north-west harem suite, looking south-west. Dynasty XVIII

patterns, and the naturalistic element has penetrated to provide us with one of the Egyptian painter's most ambitious attempts at a kind of illusionistic effect in the bodies of flying pigeons in the ceiling of one of the harem rooms [286]. The dadoes of many of the rooms have a false-door panelling such as we saw in the Twelfth-Dynasty chapel of Ukhhotep III at Meir [191]. An otherwise unknown design with a white band undulating against a darker ground appears often at the base of the walls, as in the antechamber of the small audience hall and the king's bedroom (8) [287, 288]. In the first case a strip of the commonly used flower rosettes separates it from a frieze of dancing Bes figures such as are known from Ramesside wall-paintings in the Deir el Medineh village[11] [289 A, C, and D], on a painted Dynasty XVIII jar from this village [289B],[12] and on furniture from the tomb of the parents of Queen Tiy.[13] Paired naked figures of this popular household god also form a frieze on the west wall of the king's bedroom, where they are placed above a series of large amuletic signs for 'life' (*Ankh*) and 'protection' (*Sa*) set between false-door panels[14] [288]. Bes often holds this *Sa*-sign and is frequently accompanied by another protecting spirit of the house, the hippopotamus goddess Thueris, who

283. Malkata Palace, south-west suite, looking north, painted support for shelf. Dynasty XVIII

284. Amarna, North Palace, birds in papyrus thicket. Dynasty XVIII

285. Malkata Palace, ceiling of king's robing room. Dynasty XVIII

presided over childbirth. They appear together on the back of the chair of the Princess Sitamon [281]. Bes was a genial bearded creature partly human in form, but with the tail, mane, and ears of a lion. He is often shown dancing and playing a tambourine, and he watched over toilet articles and dress. His own costume has foreign touches. Sometimes he wears a panther-skin skirt, but more often a Syrian kilt.[15]

There is very little evidence for the scenes on the upper part of the walls, but on the west wall of the second audience hall (2) a large figure of a court lady with an elaborate head-dress of flowers stood above the red, blue, and white panelling of the dado. Only part of her head [290] and knee were preserved, and part of the floral frieze which ran round the top of the wall.[16] In this same hall, on the wall behind the throne platform, there was a painting of wild animals in the desert which Daressy describes rather incomprehensibly as having a black-and-white bull running across mountains indicated by blue, yellow, and red undulating bands scattered with red rosettes on the blue ground and blue rosettes on the red. The ceiling was painted with flying vultures, as in the

286. Malkata Palace, north-west harem suite, ceiling of robing room. Dynasty XVIII

badly destroyed first audience hall (1), the hall of the harem (4), and the king's bedroom [291E].

The private apartments of the king consisted of a long, columned hall (4) with a throne room (5), at the back of which opened a bath (6) and an antechamber (7) to the king's bedroom (8) [280]. On each side of the hall there were four suites of rooms for the chief ladies of the harem. The floor of the hall was painted to represent a pool in the marshes, and the ceiling had a design of flying vultures. Pieces of a wooden lotus flower and two buds were found which were probably part of one of the capitals of the wooden columns. Tytus describes a painting of the king seated on his throne, on the sides of which captives were represented. This was evidently on one of the flanking south walls of the hall which gave a private character to the throne room but at the same time allowed people assembled in the hall to view the king through the wide door in the centre. So enthroned he would have been framed by paintings of himself seated in state such as we know from private tombs of the period, where they flank the entrance to the inner hall [255, 256]. Thus even in the most intimate part of the palace the decoration still maintained in a formal manner the magnificence of the king's presence.

The excavator's description of the fragments of this painting touches upon an interesting stylistic point. According to him the execution of the drawing was so free from restraint as to appear almost caricature. Tytus was familiar with the floor-paintings of the Maru Aten precinct at Amarna and describes their style over-emphatically as 'the outcome of

licence run riot'. He observed that the floor-paintings which he found were executed in the more careful manner of those in the central palace at Amarna. However, Petrie noticed a shift from careful to sketchy work in the two halves of the best-preserved of these palace floors. The same difference appears in the floor of the small audience room at Malkata, where the central rectangle shows careful, detailed drawing, like that of the pigeons [286] or the frieze of the 'green room' at Amarna [284], while the borders are treated sketchily like the plants and animals [282, 283], and those of the Maru Aten floors. In fact, both at Thebes and at Amarna, the same group of painters seems to have employed both methods of brush-work in treating these naturalistic representations of plants and animals on floors, ceilings, and minor wall-spaces. Akhenaten must have carried some of these men on to Amarna with him. The same skill in imitating the texture of surfaces displayed in the papyrus thicket with its birds in the 'green room' is to be found in the Oxford painting of the princesses [314]. Here, however, it is the new approach to the representation of the human figure which first strikes the eye as so very different from that found in the finest work of the private tombs of the reign of Amenhotep III [255] or the fragmentary court lady in the Malkata palace [290]. Except for the description quoted above, there is no evidence that this new freedom in the treatment of the human figure had entered into painting in the time of Akhenaten's father. It is possible, of course, that the south wall of the harem hall might have been redecorated after the death of Amenhotep III, but in the absence of actual samples of the painting further speculation seems useless.

South of the throne room are three long chambers forming the personal quarters of the king. The largest of these (6) was a bath with a stone slab in the corner. The richly decorated room on the right was the royal bedchamber (8). It was approached through a robing-room with equally handsome paintings. Petrie recognized long ago that the presence of the raised platform in a recess indicated a bedroom. It was found first in the large houses at Kahun of the Twelfth Dynasty and appears in most of the houses at Amarna. Perhaps a kind of wind-chute was raised over an opening in the roof above the recess to catch the breeze in hot weather.[17] The bed placed on the platform of this recess must have been of wood with carved legs and a footboard, like those found in the tomb of Tut-ankh-amon or in that of the parents of Queen Tiy.

The ceiling of the chamber, which, not including the recess, was about 25 feet long by 15 feet wide (7.6 × 4.5 m), was covered with a painting consisting of a row of vultures inside a border of rosettes and a band of chequer pattern [291E]. As the roof collapsed, the painted plaster turned in its fall so that a good deal of the design was found lying face up. With the portion adhering to the west wall of the amulet frieze and wavy-lined pattern of the dado under the dancing Bes figures, the room produced a remarkably vivid impression when first found [287]. The name and titles of Amenhotep III were inscribed in bands of hieroglyphs between the outstretched wings of the great birds. The vulture, like the falcon Horus and the cobra goddess Buto, was especially associated with royalty, being the ancient goddess Nekhbet of the Upper Egyptian sanctuary of El Kab.

Again in the antechamber, or robing-room, there had fallen

287 and 288. Malkata Palace, bedroom of Amenhotep III, (*above*) looking north-west, (*below*) dado. Dynasty XVIII

face upwards a considerable portion of a magnificent ceiling with bulls' heads set in the interstices of an interlocking spiral design [285].[18] This ceiling belongs to a group of Egyptian spiral compositions which resemble those in the palaces of Knossos in Crete and on the mainland of Mycenaean Greece at Tiryns, Mycenae, and Orchomenos. These Aegean examples do not, however, contain bulls' heads.[19] They show a broadly flowing sweep of interweaving spirals complicated by rich plant forms apparently originally derived from Egypt. The marvellously integrated Egyptian designs of Dynasty XVIII have thrown off the stiff, tight quality which they had in the early part of the Dynasty [246]. Bulls' heads are rather infrequently used in these designs. They appear first in the reign of Tuthmosis IV in a poorly integrated pattern between two rows of running spirals. This came from the collapsed barrel vault of what seems to have been the chapel of a private house behind the mortuary temple of Tuthmosis IV.[20] This pattern was repeated again in the Deir el Medineh tomb of Khai-inheret (No. 359)[21] which has preserved one of the rich collections of such designs in Dynasty XX, another being in the tomb of Imiseba (No. 65).

Contemporaneous with the richly developed designs of the palace of Amenhotep III is one where scarabs take the place of the bulls' heads.[22] This sumptuous piece of decoration is like another with bulls' heads, grasshoppers, and volutes in the

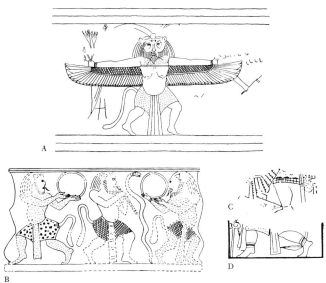

289. Deir el Medineh, Bes figures. Dynasty XVIII

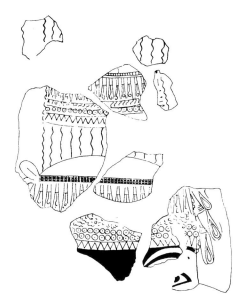

290. Malkata Palace, second audience hall, head of a court lady. Dynasty XVIII

tomb of Neferhotep of the reign of Horemheb.[23] Under Ramesses IX, the bull's head appears once more in one of the series of elaborate panels in the tomb of Imiseba.[24]

We have seen that the bull's head was used as a motif on the Ahmose dagger at the beginning of Dynasty XVIII [215], and it appears with a rosette between the horns on the cup carried by the Cretan envoy in the tomb of Senmut of the reign of Hatshepsut [242]. Actual Aegean examples occur on the magnificent metal vessels of the first half of the fourteenth century B.C. from Dendra in the Argolid and Enkomi in Cyprus.[25] In the Mitanni palace at Nuzi in northern Mesopotamia there are similar bulls' heads in a frieze which employs Egyptian Hathor heads, voluted plants, and grotesque male masks.[26]

To return to the disposition of the harem quarters in the palace of Amenhotep III, four suites of rooms were arranged on each side of the columned hall (4) and the throne-room (5) to make a compact symmetrical plan [280]. This contrasts with the somewhat irregular placing of the state apartments which we have examined to the north of this block. The suites are identical, except that the two on the north are more spacious than the other six [282, a view looking south-west across the north-western group of rooms]. In the foreground is one of the painted brick supports for shelves which ran along the sides of the storage-room. It shows a bull calf and a clump of papyrus. Papyrus flowers are painted on the end of the support. Another of these paintings with a leaping calf was preserved on the support adjoining the door to the robing-room in the southernmost suite [283]. The end in this case had a stand with food.[27] One of the decayed wooden shelves had a cavetto cornice modelled in mud plaster along the edge, and broken pottery was found underneath.[28] Heavier articles could be pushed under the shelves and linen and clothing placed on top. The other suites had similar storage-rooms except that the smaller apartments lacked the row of light columns which supported the roof in the northern suites. The main sitting-room had a brick dais for a chair set against the wall [282]. It was entered from the columned hall through a room which had a raised platform of stone with a small drain for water to run off into a stone receptacle set in the floor.

This was perhaps a place for the storage of water-jars rather than a bath. There were two rooms behind the living-room, the smaller one serving as a bedroom and the other as a dressing-room, since it usually communicates with the long corridor for the storage of clothes and household articles. In the two northern apartments it served as an antechamber to a bedroom. Ceiling paintings were found in these robing-rooms in the western suites, the most interesting being the one with flying pigeons from the northern apartment on this side [286]. Attention has already been called to the way in which a sense of roundness has been given to the bodies by the stippling of the upper parts.[29] The ceilings of the other robing-rooms were somewhat less carefully executed. That in the next suite had a pattern of flying ducks, like those which join on to the top of the fragment with the pigeons,[30] while the one further to the south simulated a trellis with grapes.

The central hall of the South Palace (10) had a ceiling-painting with an interlocking spiral design, as well as another

291. Details of roofs and ceilings. (A) and (B) Amarna, workmen's village; (C), (D), and (E) Malkata Palace. Dynasty XVIII

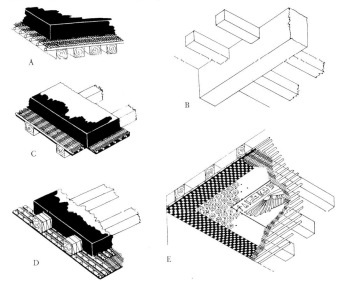

with a trefoil pattern combined with rosettes. Other similar designs are described by Daressy and illustrated by Tytus, but their positions cannot be identified. There was a ceiling from another of the Malkata buildings which had flying ducks and nests with young birds and eggs.[31] All these combinations of complicated ornament are known, with other variations, in Theban tomb-painting and some fragments of similar designs were recovered at Amarna. The grape arbour pattern was used in one of the halls of the Heb-Sed building of Semenkhkara and in the North Palace as well as in a number of the little garden shrines of private houses. Flying ducks were found on a ceiling in the Royal Estate and in an unusual pavilion adjoining a house in the south-east quarter.[32]

The ceiling-paintings should be considered in relation to the structure of the roofing as observed by Tytus and supplemented by architectural details at Amarna. The simplest method of roofing was found well preserved in the small rooms of the workmen's village at Amarna. There the rough timbers of the rafters were set close together and covered by a cross layer of small poles and twigs. Over this was placed matting on which rested a thick layer of mud [291A]. Essentially the same method of roofing short spans in corridors and minor rooms was used in the palace of Amenhotep III, except that the underside of the matting was plastered so that it and the rafters could be painted. In more important rooms the rafters were concealed to provide a large expanse of flat ceiling for paintings. Light poles were lashed under the rafters and mats tied to the poles. This gave support for the mud filling of the roof, and a layer of plaster on the underside of the matting provided a smooth surface for the paintings [291D].[33]

Illustration 291E is a suggested reconstruction for a corner of the ceiling painting in the king's bedroom, with its chequer and rosette borders and the vultures with outspread wings separated by bands of inscription giving the titles and name of Amenhotep III. The big rafters in this room had a span of some 17 feet (5 m) and were evidently completely concealed, as were those hidden behind the spiral ceiling with the bulls' heads in the adjoining robing-room [285]. In the columned hall of the harem, where Tytus recorded these roofing details, it seems that there must have been exposed architraves resting on the lotus-flower capitals of the wooden columns and supporting the concealed roofing-timbers. These architraves probably ran the length of the room. A width of some 16 feet (4.8 m) was estimated for the wing-spread of the vultures painted on the ceiling! There was also part of a rosette border so that the design must have resembled that in the king's bedchamber or in such examples as those in the passages of the tombs of Ramesses VI and Siptah.[34] Such an uninterrupted line of vultures down the ceiling of the central aisle seems to rule out cross-architraves.

The painted ceilings in the Theban rock-cut tombs reflect what must have been a more commonly used system of exposed architraves and roofing-timbers such as we find in the Amarna house [291B]. At Amarna the rafters were covered with plaster and painted red, while the ceiling compartments in between were generally given a flat colour. The main architraves which rested on the four columns of the central hall of such a house were decorated with a block pattern. A few geometric patterns were recovered which seem to have come from the intervening ceiling-spaces.[35] It is probable that, had more of the larger houses been better preserved, these ceiling-paintings would have been found to occur more frequently, since the Theban tombs indicate that they were common in the Eighteenth Dynasty. The cross-rafters left only small strips of flat ceiling for decoration, but the construction was cheaper than that employed in the Palace of Amenhotep III.

CHAPTER 16

The Change to Amarna

Cultural changes seldom lend themselves well to neat chronological arrangement, but the reign of Amenhotep IV (Akhenaten) presents an aggravating problem for anyone attempting to understand the course of his religious revolution with the accompanying effect which this had on the arts. There has been a growing tendency to accept the theory that the young king acted as co-regent with his father during the crucial years in which a profound change occurred. It is possible to trace earlier manifestations of this change and to see how in many details, long-established practice continued under the new regime. The general impression is, nonetheless, one of an abrupt break with tradition. It is not surprising, then, that there was first a tendency to stress the revolutionary character of Akhenaten's reform and then, in reaction, to place a contrary emphasis upon the survival of old details in the new forms. However, until fairly recently, it was at least accepted that some sort of break occurred after a short period of experimentation at Thebes following upon the death of Amenhotep III. This was in the days when three tombs at Thebes, a few blocks from a shrine of the Aten at Karnak, and a very limited number of monuments elsewhere, provided decidedly meagre hints in the face of the overwhelming body of material from the capital which Akhenaten was known to have founded at Tell el Amarna at some time between the 4th and 6th year of his reign. Only a few keen observers stressed the significance of the Amenhotep IV blocks which were first noted by Lepsius and Prisse d'Avennes in the last century and since 1902 had been turning up in the reconstruction work at Karnak.[1] These have now reached an embarrassing number of thousands, while hundreds of similar blocks have been found at other sites.[2] We have seen that a great deal of material has now become available from the palace of Amenhotep III at Thebes, but it has also increased from further excavation at Amarna, as well as from other sources such as the tomb of Tut-ankh-amon. It is obvious that, since the publication of this vast accumulation of material is far from complete, any attempt to interpret it is a somewhat perilous enterprise.

A broader view can be gained than there was some fifty years ago in that rich period of Amarna studies which followed the pre-war German excavations and the post-war recognition of the importance of the extraordinary contents of the workshop of the master sculptor Tuthmosis at Amarna. It must be admitted that this view is still not as clear as one could wish, even though a great deal can be seen through the romantic haze that has always tended to grow particularly dense about the central figure of Akhenaten himself. To no other time in Egyptian history has reconstruction been so lavishly applied by ingenious minds. As in the case of the events themselves, the monuments have taken on almost too concrete a form for the extremely fragmentary elements which compose them. Yet the parts of this whole exist in superabundant quantity. An effort to apply a practical, common-sense approach to this material is apt to founder, because there is an extravagant element here which defies cool analysis.

There is no doubt that the change came at Thebes. Suddenly there is a transformation in the way that the human figure is shown both in statuary and reliefs.[3] It is given new forms, new attitudes, and a different setting. We have seen in discussing the painting of the second half of the Eighteenth Dynasty and the domestic architecture as evinced by the Palace of Amenhotep III, that the techniques, the rendering of plant and animal life, the details of house architecture and decoration, in fact all the minor elements for luxurious living provided by the craftsman, had already been developed. They were to continue much the same. However, neither the persistence of this superficially gay and charming show of wealth and sophistication, nor the maintenance of a basically Egyptian instinct for naturalism, should blind us to a strikingly different attitude towards the representation of human beings which reflects ideas expressed in the writing of the time. It is here that the evidence from a few Theban tombs and the early reliefs from the Aten shrine at Karnak have their importance, because they betray tentative steps in the evolution of a new style. The transformation comes with remarkable swiftness, reminding us in a way of the sudden rise of a new culture in Dynasty I or the appearance of stone architecture in Dynasty III. However, in this later period appears a strange anomaly, if we accept a co-regency covering the four important years before Akhenaten left Thebes for Amarna. Instead of Imhotep serving King Zoser in evolving the new wonders of the Step Pyramid group, the dominant figure at this time of transition in Dynasty XVIII is Amenhotep son of Hapu, who must have held tenaciously to the ideas behind the magnificent building schemes which he had controlled as Overseer of All Works for the old regime under Amenhotep III. Active in connexion with the first Heb-Sed of Amenhotep III, the son of Hapu, who was also called Huy, founded his funerary temple in the year 31. He was the only private person to whom a site was granted in the long line of royal temples that ran along the edge of the cultivation below the Theban necropolis. He was among the donors of offerings to the second Sed festival in the year 34[4] and the reverence for his wisdom which endured into late times seems to imply that his counsels were heeded in the last years of Amenhotep III. It is hard to believe that, while his influence prevailed, much progress could have been made in altering the old style.

It is certainly to Amenhotep IV that we must attribute the stimulus of new ideas. He must have had help in training his artists along the new lines. There are some hints that he drew upon the old traditional workshops, as indeed he must have done. Carved on the rocks at Aswan is a representation of the chief sculptor Bak, who under the new king was following the same profession as had his father Men under Amenhotep III. They were in turn charged with the work in the quarry at Gebel Ahmar near Cairo from which had come the quartzite for the Colossi of Memnon. The inscription tells us that Bak was the assistant whom his majesty, himself, had taught.[5] He is represented with his wife in a naos-stela in Berlin which already shows some of the characteristics of the new, extreme Amarna style, particularly in emphasis on his corpulence [292].

Parennefer, in his tomb at Thebes (No. 188), calls himself Overseer of All the Works in the Mansion of Aten (Hat Aten) which must be the new shrine that was being built at Karnak, mentioned by this name in two other tombs at Thebes.[6] It is possible that Parennefer's name has been scratched out of an important rock carving recording the first occasion on which the sandstone quarries at Gebel Silsileh were worked in this reign to provide a great Ben-ben stone for the Aten in Ipet-

292. The sculptor Bak and his wife. Quartzite stela. Dynasty XVIII. *Berlin, Ägyptisches Museum*

isut (Karnak).[7] Finally, another name 'The Aten is found in the House of Aten' (Gem-pa-Aten-em-per-Aten) occurs in the tomb of the vizier Ramose and frequently on the blocks from Karnak and the Luxor temple precinct. We shall see that these names were later applied to parts of the great temple at Amarna and to the smaller temple (Hat Aten) there. It is most probable that the different names, and Parennefer's work, were connected with a large structure outside the eastern enclosure wall of the temple of Amon at Karnak which had a court lined with remarkable colossal statues of Amenhotep IV [294, 295]. This building was decorated with reliefs which were re-used in later constructions at Karnak.[8]

In the tomb of Huya at Amarna, we find Iuwty, the chief sculptor of the queen mother, Tiy, shown painting a statue of her daughter, Beket-aten, presumably during their visit to Amarna in the year 12.[9] We know only the name and nothing of the origins of another sculptor, Tuthmosis, but need have no doubt of the skill from the wonderful pieces of unfinished sculpture found in his workshop, of which the painted Berlin bust of Queen Nofretete is the most famous [293].[10]

Men of ability, then, fell in with the ideas of Amenhotep IV, and after a few tentative efforts developed a new style with remarkable speed. Norman de Garis Davies has shown how these experiments can be traced in three Theban tombs.[11] It is less easy to demonstrate such a transitional stage in the royal reliefs. The evidence is of an equivocal nature and has provoked much argument. Let us examine first briefly the material in the Theban necropolis. There, the royal scribe Kheruef, who was also steward of the household of Queen Tiy, decorated the main part of his tomb (No. 192) in the finest manner of the reign of Amenhotep III. The scenes on the two back walls of a great pillared court (apparently not completed) are devoted to the representation of a Heb-Sed festival. Reference has already been made to the representation of the princesses [266] which forms a part of the left-hand wall. The inscriptions mention the festivals celebrated in the 30th and 37th years of the reign of Amenhotep III. However, the sunk reliefs of the architrave and jambs of the outer entrance to the court show Amenhotep IV and his mother wor-shipping the gods of the Heliopolitan cycle. This would appear to be the latest work done in the tomb. There is no change in style, the usual funerary deities Osiris and Anubis are still mentioned, and the sun god still appears in the falcon-headed form of Rahorakhte (Ra-Horus of the Horizon). It is significant that Kheruef fell into disfavour and his name was erased in what had been planned as one of the most magnificent private monuments of the old regime.

Parennefer went a step further in his Theban tomb. The subject-matter and inscriptions reflect an early stage in the development of the Aten cult, but these begin to suggest the new forms. Unfortunately the whole is in a very poor state of preservation, but Queen Nofretete was apparently represented for the first time, sitting beside her husband in the old manner under a canopy. The roof has been opened up to allow the rays of the sun-disk to reach down to the royal pair. There is also a tentative use of sunk relief combined with raised reliefs in plaster and some work executed in paint alone, as though the craftsmen were trying out different

techniques as well as new methods of drawing. Parennefer, of the three men we are considering, was the only one who went on to Amarna and executed a new rock-cut tomb there.

The third example presents the change in dramatic fashion as well as in workmanship of superlative quality. This is the tomb of one of the highest officials of the old regime, the vizier Ramose (No. 55). It had been planned with a series of rock-cut columned halls, like those of Amenemhet called Surer (No. 48) and Kheruef (No. 192). As in these and the more modestly planned chapel of Khaemhet (No. 57), the accomplished decoration supplements the architectural scheme to form a culminating example of the taste of the later years of the reign of Amenhotep III. The back wall is divided into two parts, as usual, by the entrance to the inner hall. The decoration is not entirely completed, but on the left of the doorway Amenhotep IV is shown enthroned with Maat, the goddess of Truth, receiving the vizier [256]. There is nothing to distinguish this scene from older representations of a royal appearance. It continues the style of the reliefs on the entrance wall of this same room. The absence of their almost too refined subtleties of surface modelling is perhaps the result of haste. It is more probable that the work was abandoned before the final touches could be given.

If we turn to the flanking wall on the right [261], we might think ourselves at Amarna except that the strata of fine limestone at the foot of the Qurna hill provided a better surface for carving than the craftsman would find at Amarna, where he had to resort to the layers of plaster and patching with which he was already experimenting in the tomb of Parennefer. The king is now accompanied by Nofretete, whereas on Kheruef's entrance he was shown with his mother and here on the neighbouring wall with Maat. Instead of being seated as in Parennefer's tomb, the partially erased figures of the royal pair lean out from a cushioned balcony, the so-called 'Window of Appearances', now fully developed.[12] They are under a broken cornice through which the rays of the sun reach down human hands to offer them symbols of life. The figures are now drawn with that peculiar emphasis upon the irregularities of bodily proportion which carry to the point of caricature what were apparently actual physical characteristics of the king. That predilection for curved lines, which we have watched growing in the second half of the Eighteenth Dynasty, is here given added emphasis in the bowing backs of attendants, the rounded protuberance of the heads, and in the fall of garments. The little columns are beribboned, anticipating a feminine tendency to attach flying streamers and garlands to elements of architecture as well as to elaborate dresses.

The king, who is still called Amenhotep, is again honouring Ramose. Possibly this is one of the last signs of his favour, since Ramose disappears with this scene unfinished, and we find the next vizier, Nakht, building a fine house in the early southern quarter of the new capital after the court has moved to Amarna. Beyond Ramose, in our scene, other persons, including a group of foreigners, are waiting to be received by the king. They are outlined in a preliminary drawing which is one of the most beautiful pieces of draughtsmanship preserved from ancient times. One need only compare the bowing Ramose [262] with any of the earlier figures from this tomb [263], or better with the bowing attendant in the Khaemhet reliefs [260], to realize how much has been altered in the method of representing the human figure. This is not so much a step towards the more accurate imitation of nature as it is a shift of emphasis in stylization. It is an abrupt shift without parallel in Egyptian art and the shock comes still more acutely in the colossal statues of Amenhotep IV from the Karnak Aten Temple [294, 295].[13] The suavity of the line tempers the blow in this drawing, much as the softer modelling and a moderation of the extreme proportions dispel some of the strangeness in the finest of the later sculpture at Amarna. However, whether in an extreme or tempered form, a new twist is given to long-fostered naturalistic tendencies in representation. There is an attempt to express a view of humanity and its frailties which man had been groping to realize since the more austere thought of the Middle Kingdom. Now, as in the Hymn to the Aten, we find a heightened awareness of mankind in general as well as a new sense of life, movement, and that seldom-to-be-expected element, timeliness. Thus in the Amarna tombs the lively dance of some boys expresses their spontaneous joy at the gifts heaped upon Ay by the king. A cold morning is suggested by the brazier of coals when Mahu learns from runners of the whereabouts of a pair of malefactors [296], or again when he reports to the vizier on the provision stores.[14] Something of this interest in actuality seems to be responsible for the remarkable studies of people of the court found in the workshop of Tuthmosis [321-4].

The constantly reiterated word *maat*, which is translated 'truth' or 'right', cannot be connected, however, with the naturalistic side of Amarna art. The use of the word suggests nothing like the more recent conception of a 'search for truth' in the imitation of nature. Apparently it continued to express under Akhenaten, as of old, a sense of fundamental balance and order. The king now assumes an all-important position in the dispensing of *maat* to the people.[15] In all relations with the new god, approach must be made through the personal intercession of Akhenaten. The suppression of the state god Amon, in whom had been incorporated all the qualities of the ancient sun god Ra, brought with it a denial of the other great gods. In the earliest monuments Amon's name remains, although his position diminishes, while the gods of the Heliopolitan cycle retain their place as Ra-Horakhte assumes prominence. The fierce persecution of Amon, with the widespread erasure of his name, seems to have begun in the year 6 with the transfer of the capital to Amarna. A letter was addressed to the king in the 5th year still using his name Amenhotep,[16] but in his boundary stelae at Amarna he changes this to Akhenaten. In a few exceptional cases, as in the tomb of Ramose and on some of the Karnak blocks, the name of Amenhotep in the early inscriptions was allowed to stand. Even more remarkable is the one use of Amenhotep in his father's name on the gold-covered shrine that Akhenaten prepared for his mother, Queen Tiy, which somehow was included with the burial furniture of Semenkhkara.[17]

293. Nofretete. Painted limestone bust. Dynasty XVIII. *Berlin, Ägyptisches Museum*

294 and 295. Amenhotep IV. Colossal statue and head from Karnak. Dynasty XVIII. *Cairo Museum*

Otherwise the hated name of the god Amon was erased in the cartouches of Amenhotep III, who was referred to by his other name Neb-maat-ra during the reign of his son.

The name of the Aten was carefully constructed to convey the new teaching. It was placed in two cartouches like the names of the king and accompanied by a titulary resembling the royal one. The aspect of the god as a universal ruler and his intimate connexion with the throne of Egypt were thus emphasized. At first, Aten was combined with Ra in his form of Horakhte (Horus-of-the-Horizon) and with the god Shu. About the 9th year of the reign, however, Horakhte and Shu were eliminated from this didactic name. In this later, simplified, form only Ra is retained with Aten who becomes 'Ra the Father', the creator of all things.[18]

The disappearance of the old gods and their priesthoods was accompanied by the loss of many of the outward symbols of funerary beliefs. Pictorially, the sun disk of the Aten with its rays provided a meagre substitute, and the old representations were largely replaced by the great set pieces of the royal family which we know from the tombs at Amarna. These were worked out in their essentials at Thebes, as in the scene which we have been considering in the tomb of Ramose. Here can be sensed the highly personal element which pervades Akhenaten's new doctrine. The exclusion of the usual scenes of the life of the owner, except when he is concerned with the

king, produces a visual impression contrasting with that in the Hymn to the Aten. There is here the less pleasant suggestion that the blessings of the Aten are concentrated upon the king with only a vague extension to the rest of humankind.[19]

What at first glance appears to be the whole repertoire of the new style bursts upon us with overwhelming profusion in the thousands of small sandstone blocks that were re-used at Karnak, chiefly in the Second, Ninth, and Tenth Pylons of Horemheb and in the foundations of the great Hypostyle

296. Amarna, tomb of Mahu, Mahu receives runners. Dynasty XVIII

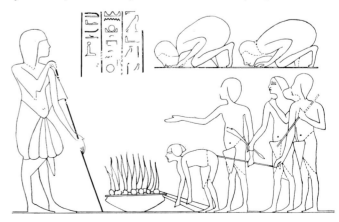

Hall completed by Ramesses II. With them were a few reliefs of Akhenaten's successors, Tut-ankh-amon and Ay, and even one of Horemheb himself. Each little piece[20] bears a tantalizing portion of a scene or inscription. These either remind us of subjects well known from the Amarna reliefs or suggest some unexpected element as yet incomprehensible. They give the impression of belonging to the first nine years of the reign, since they employ the early name of the Aten, while the king is still called Amenhotep IV which has later been altered to Akhenaten.[21] They also show many signs of belonging to a similar stage in the development of the Aten cult as did the tombs of Parennefer and Ramose, and a more advanced one than that of Kheruef. Much discussion has been aroused by a group of larger blocks with raised relief in the old style of Amenhotep III which come from the Ninth and Tenth Pylons. They show figures of Amenhotep IV offering to the Aten in the early falcon-headed human form of Ra-Horakhte. The cartouches have obviously been altered, and, as in those on the outer face of the pylon of the Nubian Temple of Amenhotep III at Soleb, it is most probable that the name of the son has been cut over that of his father. When the best known of these blocks was cleaned and examined in Berlin, it was believed that the figure of the god had also been altered, while the names of the Aten replaced an earlier inscription.[22] The other blocks which lie outside the Tenth Pylon have not been studied under such ideal conditions, and few photographs of them are available. It seems that their obvious alterations were undertaken for the same purpose.[23] The craftsmen of Amenhotep IV, then, seem to have altered reliefs in a building of his father, employing the old style of these reliefs and introducing early features of the Aten cult such as we have found in the Theban tombs. These large blocks were re-used by Horemheb along with the characteristically small blocks in the later style of the Aten Temple. Whether they all came originally from the same building must remain speculation, as it has since at least the days of Maspero, until more is known about the contents of the Ninth and Tenth Pylons.[24]

Certainly the site from which a large proportion of the Karnak reliefs of Amenhotep IV must have come was an important temple of the Aten which lay outside the eastern enclosure wall of the Amon precinct and a little north of the gateway in its east-west axis. All that has so far been excavated is part of a great court with at least twenty-four bases for huge statues of Amenhotep IV standing against walls of which only the foundation trenches remain. There is little indication of where there may have been entrances nor how far to the north and east the walls extended. Two of the statues exhibited in the Cairo Museum are nearly complete, suggesting a height of about 13 feet (3.9 m) for the whole standing figure. The material is sandstone, but the elbow of a red granite statue was found near what may have been the middle of the southern side of the court, and we are reminded that the big statues placed round the great court of the Amarna palace were made of both quartzite and red granite.

These figures of Amenhotep IV are startling as the first uncompromising portrayal of the king in the new style in sculpture in the round. They are executed with the finest technical skill, with no fumbling on the part of the sculptor in carrying out his purpose. It is not surprising that the term 'expressionism' has been applied to them [294, 295]. In form they are reminiscent of the Osiride statues in mummy form, of which perhaps the most striking Eighteenth-Dynasty examples are those of Queen Hatshepsut set along the temple terraces at Deir el Bahari [226, 227]; Amenhotep IV is not shown, however, in the wrappings of the dead god, but in festal royal regalia with plaques bearing the cartouches of the Aten. The face is elongated with eyes slanting upwards, full lips, and pendulous jaw. The body has that soft, slack, big-hipped form which was suggested already in some of the statues of his father. One Cairo figure gives the impression of being naked, but perhaps we are to understand this as a drastic simplification of the thin robe worn by Amenhotep III in two remarkable statues already mentioned from his mortuary temple, where the slumped fat forms and unusual dress lend an uncomfortable informality to the royal figure.[25] The delicacy of the carving in the little wooden statuette of Amenhotep III [271] glosses over the accentuation of certain features of the body as does the less extreme approach of the sculptors to much of the later work at Amarna. We have seen that there were hints of a new stylization of the facial planes in such heads of Amenhotep III as those to be seen in the British Museum [270] and in Boston.

These colossi of Amenhotep IV have a compelling force, a life of their own which is original and not wholly to be explained by seeking out sources upon which stylistic development could have been based. In this odd abstraction of the human figure there is also an uneasy mingling of conflicting elements. Particularly in the face it is as though each part had been thought out separately and rather broadly and then the transitions bridged by subtle gradations of modelling. This mixture of harshness and softness, of naturalistic impulses adjusting themselves to a new stylization, is equally apparent in the relief sculpture. Whether or not we consider the experiment successful, we cannot deny the daring and vitality of these early works.[26] Before the problem was wholly resolved, even under Akhenaten at Amarna, the tendency was to slip back into the old smooth elegance of line and form. The reaction which followed at the end of the Dynasty brought with it an over-refinement of technical skill.

The walls of the court of this Aten Temple have been removed, leaving only their foundation trenches, as was done in the case of the stonework of the palace and temples at Amarna. It seems at present likely that a large part of the small blocks with reliefs from the Theban District were extracted from this building. One is inclined to believe that those found in the Luxor Temple and at Medamud came from Karnak rather than from buildings at those sites.[27] The possibility that some of the reliefs might be part of the stonework removed from the Amarna buildings by Horemheb's contractors[28] should now be rejected. On the other hand, it is more likely that the large number of blocks (in this case limestone and not sandstone) at Hermopolis and a few other reliefs found at such places as Assiut and Abydos were from Amarna.[29] That there was a Temple of the Aten at Memphis, evinced by blocks found there, seems to be indicated by the funerary stela of a man at Saqqara who served in such a temple presumably in the neighbourhood.[30] One would particularly expect buildings to have been erected in Memphis during the reign of Akhenaten, because the influence of the Amarna style remained strong there in the early days of the Amon restoration. It is well to remember, too, that work was undertaken for Akhenaten in Nubia at the temple of Sesebi,[31] as well as at Soleb, where we have seen that it took the form of altering the pylon reliefs of his father. Although Kawa was called Gematen (the Aten is found), no traces have been found there antedating the reign of Tut-ankh-amon.[32]

The Karnak reliefs and those from the other sites are remarkably like the work at Amarna, using the same variety of methods in dealing with sunk relief. The majority of the Hermopolis blocks belong to a late date in the reign, and there is a strong probability that they were brought there from buildings at Amarna. While the Karnak reliefs frequently suggest subject-matter depicted in the tomb scenes at Amarna, they do not contain details which would have to be drawn from the new town. Much of the picturesque 'land-scape' might equally well apply to the environs of the Karnak temple or to activities within its precinct. It will of course be realized that this bears the fascinating implication that a new representational world, as we have known it from the Amarna tombs, was actually invented at Thebes. There are here parts of the familiar family group now including Meritaten, who was perhaps not yet born and certainly not represented when Ramose was decorating his tomb. There is also the royal progress by chariot which was to form such an animated part of the Amarna scene, as the king moved rapidly from palace to temple or on inspections in the neighbourhood of the town. Some of the blocks show Akhenaten, Nofretete, and Meritaten on a very large scale which suggests the decoration of a pylon. An ornamental swag of ducks such as hang down from garlands in the new capital and a large figure of an attendant with a brace of waterfowl seem a suitable accompaniment to one of the family scenes, but the plumed heads of a pair of chariot horses and the nose and ear of a red face with a yellow hand raised beside it inevitably make one speculate as to whether this temple of the Aten may not have had a pylon with the king dominating over foreigners. Innumerable prostrate foreigners appear on a smaller scale, while elsewhere they are shown as part of the old heraldic device bound to the plants of Upper and Lower Egypt.

There are other hints of older practice in the curious figures resembling inhabitants of the underworld in the royal tombs which accompany what must be a portrayal of the celebration of the Sed festival. A jackal-headed figure on one knee in the gesture of jubilation is certainly one of the 'Souls of Pe'. A companion falcon-headed 'soul of Nekhen' is described in the tomb of Parennefer, where there also appeared apes praising the sun and a figure like the prostrate king with apes surmounting an altar balustrade on one of the Karnak blocks. We are reminded that Legrain long ago found statues of these spirits of the ancient sanctuaries, probably dragged from this very temple and buried with the great mass of discarded statues from the Karnak temple.[33] There are now many blocks which belong to this Sed festival group, which was once represented only by a piece now in the Fitz-william Museum in Cambridge from the Gayer Anderson Collection.[34]

Interesting as are these hints of a stage in the Aten cult which still retained some considerable portion of old practices and suggest features to be found in the tombs of Kheruef,

Parennefer, and Ramose, it is the new elements which give the fascinating flavour to these tantalizing portions of a gigantic picture puzzle. The wonderfully modelled animals being brought for sacrifice, the attendants with sunshades and various articles of food and equipment can be paralleled at Amarna, and we have already seen the fan-bearing ladies-in-waiting in Ramose's tomb. The Syrian musicians [297] have associations with the palace at Amarna. There are also dancers in violent motion [297] which need only to be compared with those in Kheruef's tomb to make one realize what a rude contrast their angular attitudes make with the smoothly flowing line of the old style. The new spirit presents its most attractive aspect in the treatment of minor scenes of people going about their tasks in the buildings and gardens, or the activities of animals in the open country [298]. To this last group of scenes belong the bull and hyena running among free-growing plants which so much resemble a relief in Oxford[35] from the Amarna palace and the animals outside the wall of the temple shown in the Royal Tomb there [299].

The craftsmen who cut the Karnak blocks were experimenting with sunk relief much as the men in the Theban tomb of Parennefer had tried both raised relief cut in a thick plaster coating and sunk relief in the poor rock surface. In the tombs at Amarna the varying quality of limestone necessitated some re-working in plaster in the deep cuttings. In general the dressed rock wall was evened up by a coating of plaster into which the scenes were carved. This prevalent use of sunk relief, where all the figures were set back from the surface of the wall, was cheaper in labour than the Old Kingdom method of trying to cut away the background of raised reliefs in a plaster-covered coarse limestone wall. However, when the plaster falls away in the course of time the sunk relief leaves even dimmer traces of the original work than had the old method. There remain only the outlines and a rough suggestion of the modelling, where the chisel had cut into the rock below. This, even more than the wilful damage

297. Women dancers, harem ladies and Syrian musicians. Reliefs from Karnak Aten shrine. Dynasty XVIII. *Luxor Museum*

298. Desert scene with antelopes. Relief from Hermopolis. Dynasty XVIII. *Brooklyn Museum*

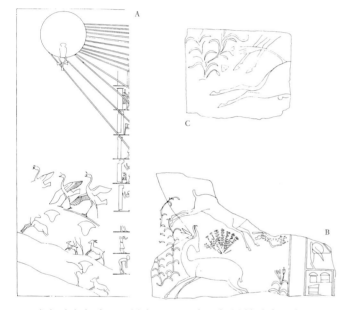

299. Animals in landscape. (A) Amarna royal tomb; (B) block from Amarna palace; (C) block from Karnak Aten shrine. Dynasty XVIII

300. Queen. Sunk sandstone relief. Dynasty XVIII. *Cleveland Museum*

they have suffered, makes the Amarna tombs difficult to examine and to photograph. The impression one receives of haste and uneven workmanship is partly false, but not entirely so. The same disturbing sense of unevenness is felt in the Karnak sandstone blocks [300]. While this partly contributes to their liveliness, there is a suggestion that the problems of representation and technique have not yet been solved. The point of accomplishment which the Amarna craftsmen could reach is attested by the Memphite tomb of Horemheb, where the fine Tura limestone was used for both sunk and raised relief [330–4]. This comes at the very end of the period, perhaps in the reign of Tut-ankh-amon, before Horemheb became king and before there was a return to something like the smooth style of the reign of Amenhotep III. These superbly worked Memphite reliefs present a coherent unity into which have been absorbed the innovations made in the earlier years.

In the early Aten Temple we not only find the boldly modelled larger surfaces of the royal figures, but on a smaller

301. Prostrate attendants. Relief from Karnak Aten shrine. Dynasty XVIII

scale the same treatment applied to such groups of figures as the prostrate attendants [301]. Simpler in treatment are the women dancers [297], still conceived along broad lines but omitting the plastic modelling. Quite different is a sort of miniature style in which the incised lines give more the impression of engraving than of sunk relief. These range from quite small figures to somewhat larger ones, as in the group of harem ladies and Syrian musicians [297]. Not only does the style of carving vary from scene to scene, but there is no longer the maintenance of two relatively flat surfaces for the background and the figures, as in the low raised reliefs of the early Eighteenth Dynasty [244] or even the sophisticated later treatment of the Ramose tomb [263], where subtle surface modelling produces very slight differences in level. In earlier sunk relief the planes were treated simply and kept flat, even when the cutting was deep. This sunk relief had been used too, in general, on the outside of buildings, partly perhaps

302. Akhenaten, Nofretete, and family. Stela from Amarna. Dynasty XVIII. *Cairo Museum*

with the idea that the carving was protected by being set back from the surface of the wall. The effect was gained through the shadow cast in strong light by the sharp edge of the main outlines. In these new sunk reliefs a richer play of light and shadow results from more plastic modelling of a kind which might have been fashioned in soft clay.

An altarpiece in Cairo from an Amarna house has been selected for illustration [302] because it allows us to study the new treatment in detail. Akhenaten is shown handing an ear ornament to his daughter, while Nofretete looks after the smaller children. It will be noticed that the lightly engraved inscriptions and pendants of the ear ornament for which the child reaches, as juxtaposed to the plastic modelling of the figures, again shows a careless indifference to the old consistent unity of surfaces. Apparent here in a small area, it forms a parallel to the variations in carving between the different groups of Karnak blocks. The variation in depth of the planes is as characteristic as is the expressiveness of the use of line. Both are as striking as the new proportions of the figures, exemplified here particularly by the fantastically long skull of the princess in the centre of the block and the nervous drawing of the long, bony fingers stretched out for the earring. The transparent folds of the queen's dress are at a lower level than her arms. The fleshy parts of her arms, and the legs of the baby which she is holding, swell both in modelled projection and in their sweeping outlines. They are accentuated by the narrowness of wrist and ankle. Another important feature of the Cairo stela is brought out even more clearly in a well-known relief stela of the Amarna royal family now in Berlin [303]. Characteristic of both reliefs is a special unity of composition achieved, as has been argued, by the almost concentric arrangement of the figures and objects in the composition. A focal point to this compositional device is provided in the Cairo relief by the small earring and in the Berlin relief by the gesturing finger of the little princess resting on Nofretete's knees. The composition is evidently designed to stress the domestic intimacy of the royal family, and reflects the thematic interest in the informal moment selected for representation.[36]

It should be emphasized that, however daring these innovations of the Amarna sculptor appear in contrast with what had gone before, they stop at a point where the projection of surfaces is still very slight in comparison with the really high reliefs developed in other parts of the world. The modelling conforms perfectly to its outlines, producing none of that unpleasant feeling which we shall find in the Late Period after Nectanebo I, when a kind of soft solidity in the modelled

303. Akhenaten, Nofretete, and
three daughters. Stela from Amarna.
Dynasty XVIII. *Berlin, Ägyptisches
Museum*

forms is uncomfortably contained by traditional outlines that seem to have grown hard by long usage. Thus at the most revolutionary point in the early part of the reign of Akhenaten the instinct to formalize kept naturalistic impulses within bounds which are basically Egyptian. As the freshness of the new ideas wore off, the new style was somewhat tempered. Then, when bitter reaction set in at the end of the Dynasty, it was submerged by the old. The process begins within the reign of Akhenaten himself in almost imperceptible steps, and continues until traces of the Amarna manner become hard to detect in the Ramesside Period. A return to traditional methods was possible because the innovators of the Amarna period had left intact the foundations of Egyptian art.

Before turning to the site of Amarna itself, this would seem to be a suitable point to look briefly again at the question of the co-regency between Amenhotep IV and his father.[37] The rapid evolution of a new style could conceivably have occurred during the co-existence of an old and a new regime, but the political and religious ferment of which it was a part certainly brought about clashes by the fourth year of the reign which caused the removal of the capital from Thebes to the new site at Amarna. It has been assumed that the old, sick Amenhotep III remained in retirement, surrounded by a small coterie of followers, for some nine to twelve years after appointing his son co-regent. It must be admitted that the whole course of the revolution is easier to conceive if Amenhotep IV were in complete power upon his father's death at the beginning of a new reign or after a short co-regency.

The view that Amenhotep III was still alive in the twelfth year, when Akhenaten held a great reception of foreign tribute at Amarna during a visit of the queen mother Tiy, is highly doubtful. The whole character of the famous Amarna letters, the correspondence addressed from abroad to Amenhotep III and Akhenaten and collected in the archives at Amarna, seems to speak against this. It is now clear that Amenhotep III did not die until late in his 38th year, which would have been the 8th or 9th year of Akhenaten, if he had been made co-regent on the occasion of the Heb-Sed of his father's 30th year. It has been argued that the court returned to Thebes from Amarna for the funeral and was in residence there when a letter from Tushratta, the king of Mitanni, was received in 'the Southern City' at 'the Castle of "Rejoicer-on-the-Horizon"', apparently the name given by Akhenaten to his father's old palace of Malkata. The date at the beginning of the notation made by a scribe on the cuneiform tablet is incomplete, reading '[Year] 2, first month of winter, day . . .'. It has been thought that this should be restored to 'Year 12' but this is not certain.[38] The date has been connected with the pictures of Tiy's visit to Amarna and representations of Amenhotep III[39] which appear along with the tribute scene in the tomb of Huya at Amarna. It seems to have been overlooked that the occasion of the bringing of tribute is dated in the second month of winter, while Tushratta's letter referring to the death of the old king was received in Thebes in the first winter month. It seems that Amenhotep III was already dead, even if Tushratta's letter is accepted as of the year 12. One possibility does have to be considered here, due to the awkward New Kingdom system in which regnal years do not correspond with civil years. We do not know the date of Akhenaten's accession, but if it had fallen between the unknown day in the first month of winter and the eighth day of the second month of the civil calendar, then the tablet date would follow the other in the regnal year.[40] Since it has also been suggested that Amenhotep III may have died in the year 8 or 9, involving too long a period for the funeral ceremonies to have lasted until the year 12, it will be seen that much here rests on supposition and that the year 2 for the date of the letter should be given serious consideration. The reference to Amenhotep III in the tomb of Huya may well be commemorative in nature. Other objects found at Amarna with the name of Amenhotep III coupled with the later name of the Aten might also have been made during the visit of Queen Tiy in memory of her husband.[41]

That the letter from Tushratta really could have been received in year 2, while Amenhotep IV still resided at Malkata before the move to Amarna, and that the young king acceded to the throne upon the death of his father at the end of the latter's 38th year, or after a short co-regency beginning in the 36th or 37th year, seems to be backed by the other Amarna foreign correspondence.[42] Tushratta continues a complaint about statues promised as part of his daughter's dowry by Amenhotep III in writing to both Tiy and Akhenaten. He asks Tiy to tell her son about the friendly relations which he had entertained with her husband. Perhaps in our after-knowledge we should not stress the irony of the Mitanni king's statement that his grief at the news of the father's death was quieted by the realization that all would continue the same under the son's new rule. But this, coupled with letters of congratulation on Akhenaten's accession from the heads of other foreign states, does not sound as though it came at the end of a long co-regency during which there had been a political upheaval and the transfer of the capital to Amarna some years before.

CHAPTER 17

The Amarna Period 1372–1350 B.C.

THE CITY OF TELL EL AMARNA

We must now turn to an examination of the new city, called Akhetaten (The Horizon of Aten), which was at least sufficiently habitable for the court to move there some time between the 5th and 6th year of Akhenaten's reign [309].[1] The site chosen was on the east side of the river on sandy desert ground lying a little higher than the cultivation which hugs the river-bank in a narrow strip. The eastern cliffs here open out to form a semicircular plain seven miles long and two to three miles deep. The place has been given the name of Tell el Amarna, apparently from a modern misunderstanding of the village names of El Till and Beni Amran. It lies about half way between Cairo and Luxor, in the region of the ancient town of Hermopolis, but several miles to the south of it on the other side of the river. The region to the north of Amarna, and roughly opposite Hermopolis, contained the Old Kingdom cemetery of Sheikh Said, as well as the better-known Middle Kingdom rock tombs of El Bersheh, which belonged to the Nomarchs of Hermopolis. In late times Hadrian founded nearby the town of Antinoupolis in memory of his favourite Antinous, while some miles farther south, opposite Amarna on the western desert edge, there was to grow up the extraordinary Graeco-Roman cemetery of Hermopolis at Tuneh el Gebel. Actually Hermopolis itself lay too far to the north to impinge upon the boundaries which Akhenaten established by a series of stelae which were cut in the desert cliffs on both sides of the river.

The travertine quarries in the eastern hills had been worked as early as the reign of Cheops in Dynasty IV, but, in spite of attempts to identify earlier traces of habitation at Amarna, there seems no doubt that Akhenaten was founding his capital where there had never before been a city, on new ground as he claimed on his boundary stelae. At least three of these fourteen stelae contained a first version of a proclamation concerning the founding of the city. A dating in the year 4 for two of these (Stelae K and X) is now questioned, but their broken text refers to something which happened in the year 4, and this is thought to reflect events in Thebes which brought about the removal of the capital to Amarna.[2] The other stelae contain a second version of the proclamation dated to the year 6, while a later edition of the year 8 was appended to two of them (Stelae A and B on the western bank) during a further inspection of the boundaries. The first proclamation contains a statement that, if the king, queen, or the princess Meritaten should die in any town of the north, south, west, or east, their bodies should be brought back to Akhetaten for burial. This statement suggests that the king's oath should not be interpreted too rigidly to mean that he would never quit the boundaries of Akhetaten. Certainly he meant, when he stated that he would not pass beyond the limits of his boundary stones, that he would not extend his capital beyond a certain determined area. He intended that this was to remain the capital, and that it was not to be

transferred to some other part of the country.[3] It is plain that Akhenaten's movements cannot be determined from the evidence available at present, but it has an important bearing upon the administration of the country and the question of whether the king constructed buildings in other parts of the country after the court moved to Amarna.

We have seen that no children appear with the royal pair in the Theban tombs, although at least two are shown in the reliefs at Karnak. The early stelae mention only one daughter, the princess Meritaten, but the second group consisted of statue groups of the king, queen, and two princesses, carved from the rock but standing free of the large inscriptions on the face of the cliff. The second proclamation on these stelae specifically mentions the princesses Meritaten and Meketaten, while the figure of the third child, Ankhesenpaaten, was cut on the side of the support for the tablet held by the king and queen, as part of the additions made in the year 8. The little girls eventually reached the number of six, the birth of each child being apparently followed soon afterwards by her appearance on one of the monuments. They are all shown in the reconstruction of the delightful painting from the king's apartments in the Royal Estate [314]. The best-preserved fragment in the Ashmolean Museum in Oxford shows us the masterly skill of the painter in handling line and pigment as well as his ability to suggest the soft, undeveloped bodies of children. Earlier artists had usually been content to repeat the mature forms of older people on a small scale, without much interest in the child itself. Now, with the stress placed upon the private life of the king, these intimate pictures of family life required the sculptor and painter to face this new problem in the innumerable representations of the little girls. The name of the fourth daughter appears only in the tombs of Huya and Mery-ra II, inscribed no earlier than the year 12, and in the Royal Tomb, while the fifth and sixth girls are known only from the tomb of Mery-ra II, unless one of them is the baby carried by a nurse at the funeral of Meketaten shown in the Royal Tomb.[4] The three younger children vanish from history, except for this slight trace, but more is known of the not very happy fate of the three older girls. Meritaten was married to Akhenaten's co-regent and successor, Semenkhkara, and disappears with him with the collapse of the Atenist revolution. Meketaten died before her father and was evidently buried in the Royal Tomb at Amarna. Ankhesenpaaten appears again with her name changed to Ankhesenamon as the wife of the youthful Tut-ankh-amon. From the state archives of the Hittite capital at Boghazköy comes the surprising information that as a young widow she sought the son of King Subbiluliumas as a husband.[5]

The boundary stelae evidently delimited the rich farmlands on the wide plain west of the river, as well as the more restricted area of the city for which this cultivated land was intended to provide food supplies. The whole was fixed as a region approximately seven miles square, north–south and east–west, by enumerating in the second proclamation the distances between the six stelae on which this edict was inscribed. The plans sketched out in these proclamations were carried out to a considerable extent, albeit somewhat hastily, but Akhenaten's new city did not endure long. After the king's death in the 17th year of his reign,[6] it can hardly have been more than a year before his successor Semenkhkara died while attempting to effect a reconciliation with the Amon priesthood. The boy Tut-ankh-amon, who was only nine years old at the time of his accession, soon moved permanently to Thebes, and Amarna was effectively dismantled by its departing inhabitants. A few years later, at the end of the dynasty, Horemheb seems to have begun the demolition of the public buildings, particularly the temples of the Aten and the palace, all usable stone and wood being removed for buildings elsewhere.

Tell el Amarna requires a detailed examination. It has been in large part excavated and may prove to be the only Egyptian city available for study, owing to the fact that it lay away from the cultivated land and, being abandoned, was never built over. As it stands, it was not a typical urban community.[7] There was room for expansion on a new site, especially where there was no question of being cramped by the tilled fields which were so valuable to the nation's economy in a narrow river valley. The congestion of the older towns is absent, and there is little of that tendency for buildings to grow vertically on narrow streets which must have been characteristic of such cities as Memphis and Thebes. We can derive some notion of these town houses of the big cities, which had several storeys and granaries and store-rooms on the roof, from Theban tomb-paintings and relief blocks, house models, and the later Coptic dwellings preserved in the enclosure of the Medinet Habu temple.[8] On the other hand, at Amarna, habitation could not extend too far laterally into the desert plain. It was restricted to the long strip of lower ground near the river bank, where wells could be sunk to subsoil water or where the distance was not too great to fetch water from the river. As the new town grew, it was beginning to assume a crowded character. Small houses were being fitted in between the large estates of the wealthy citizens who had chosen the best sites and laid them out in the manner of the Egyptian country house with large gardens and outbuildings set within enclosure walls which bounded considerable areas [304]. It has been pointed out that bad slum areas were growing on the

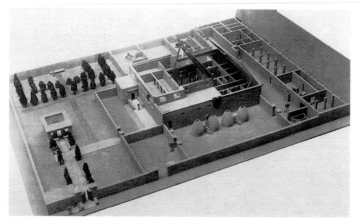

304. Model of a house at Tell el Amarna. *Chicago, Oriental Institute*

southern edge of the North Suburb. The western end of the part of this suburb which lay south of a dry river-course or wady consisted of more compactly arranged houses which seem to have belonged to people of the merchant class who may have settled here to be close to the quays along the river.

The city was not walled, being bounded by the river on one side and the semicircle of cliffs on the other. There was a military barracks, however, on the eastern edge of the central official quarter, with stables and offices which probably served as police headquarters, the activities of which are shown in the tomb of its chief Mahu. The tracks used in patrolling the eastern perimeter of the district have been found on the rough desert slopes. There must have been guard-houses here as are shown in the scene where Mahu accompanies the king on an inspection of the measures taken to protect the city.[9] At both the north and south ends of the site, the cliffs close in to the edge of the river, leaving only narrow entrances to the Amarna plain. The district could also be entered from several of the desert valleys, but the principal access to the town by land must have been the road along the river. Although it becomes a mere rocky track as it rounds the headland of Sheikh Said north of the plain, this way has continued to be used to the present day.[10] Much of the traffic must have been by ship to the city quays. However, the river road had probably been in use long before the founding of Akhetaten and became the principal thoroughfare of the new town. Called at the time the Sikket el-Sultan, it has been dubbed by the excavators the Royal Road.

On the north, where the narrow space between cliffs and river began to open out, the road passed through a suburb which was one of the latest construction jobs undertaken in Akhenaten's reign. A large north-south brick wall contained a monumental gateway which opened into a building scantily indicated by a few vestiges of walls running under the cultivation on the river side of the road. It is thought to be a palace round which this northernmost quarter was in the process of growing up. The material is not yet fully published,[11] but the gateway has been ingeniously restored. The wide entrance was flanked by stone-lined false-doors, and fragments of statues of the royal family formed part of its decoration. Rooms above it were entered by staircases from a passage in the thickness of the wall, and pieces of wall-painting indicate that these state apartments were decorated with a scene showing a royal progress with the king, his daughter Meritaten, and her husband Semenkhkara in chariots. Bits of stone jars from the building inside the gate on the west bore the names of Akhenaten and Nofretete. This slender evidence does not exactly confirm the suggestion that Nofretete retired to this building after being supplanted in favour by her daughter Meritaten. This idea of Nofretete's disgrace is largely based on the somewhat inconsistent erasure of her cartouches, and the replacing of her name and figure by those of Meritaten, in the precinct of Maru Aten on the south of the town, which might be susceptible of some other explanation.[12]

There seems to have been little construction between this northernmost area and the North Suburb but for one notable exception: the North Palace [305]. This series of buildings

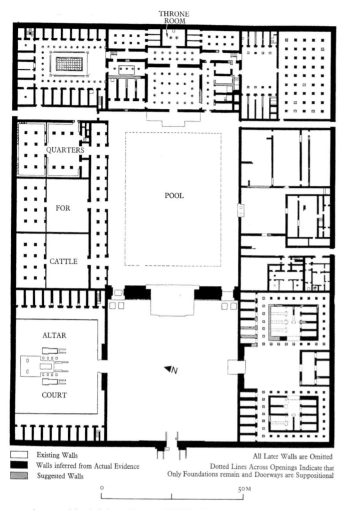

was regularly planned on a west-east axis inside a rectangular enclosing wall and faced the river with its back to the Royal Road. The state apartments contained no identifiable living quarters. There was a large court with altars for the worship of the Aten, while the plan allows a disproportionate amount of space for stalls with stone managers having remarkable carvings of the animals kept here. A garden court [306], opening from the halls north of the throne room, was surrounded by cubicles, as in the similar columned court of the northern harem of the palace in the main city. The little rooms opening from this were decorated with wonderful paintings of birds [307], the finest of these being the frieze with the papyrus thicket teeming with bird life in the so-called 'green room' [284]. The decorated walls were cut into by little niches which suggested to the excavators that the whole was an aviary.[13]

South of the North Palace the road then crossed the North Suburb and entered the central part of the town [308], with the main official palace lying along the river on the west side. This was connected by a bridge over the road with an extensive private establishment of the king, the Royal Estate. The Great Temple of the Aten lay to the north of the Royal Estate, while the Small Temple flanked it on the south. Behind these on the east were various administration buildings and, still farther to the east, the police barracks. South of the palace, the road continued through the old southern residential quarter of the town towards the southern edge of the plain. Here in open country it passed the precinct of Maru Aten, two adjoining enclosures with pavilions and small shrines set in gardens laid out with ponds.

On the plan [309] it will be seen that two other principal streets intersected the town on somewhat meandering north-

THRONE
ROOM

QUARTERS

POOL

FOR

CATTLE

ALTAR

COURT

◀N

☐ Existing Walls
■ Walls inferred from Actual Evidence
▨ Suggested Walls

All Later Walls are Omitted
Dotted Lines Across Openings Indicate that
Only Foundations remain and Doorways are Suppositional

0   50 M

305. Amarna, North Palace. Dynasty XVIII. Plan

306. Amarna, North Palace, garden
court, looking north. Dynasty XVIII

307. Goose. Painting from the North Palace at Amarna. Dynasty XVIII.
Oxford, Ashmolean Museum

south lines through the two main residential quarters which lay north and south of the central block of official buildings. These residential quarters were again broken up by cross streets and also by several dry watercourses which must have filled during the very infrequent rainstorms. These have changed their outlines during the centuries, cutting away once-habitable portions of ground, but must always have prevented buildings from being erected at certain points in their course. Not all the area of the residential quarters has been excavated, but the plan [309] indicates roughly their extent as shown by the decayed brick and surface debris.

The tombs of Akhenaten's courtiers were prepared in two groups, one of which was north of the valley which led back in the eastern hills some eight miles to the Royal Tomb. The other group was cut in the lower-lying projections of ground south of the entrance to this valley. Midway between the two groups of tombs, and hidden in a fold of the rolling terrain, was a walled village for the men engaged in cutting the rock tombs. Inside the gate was a larger house for the foreman. We have here again one of those projects on a unified plan with a repetition of the individual structures such as in the Middle Kingdom town of Kahun and the artisans' village at Deir el Medineh. Nearby were several

308. Amarna, official central quarter. Dynasty XVIII. Plan

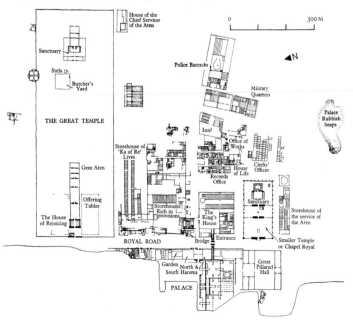

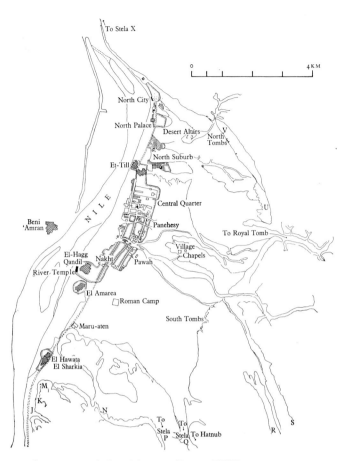

309. Amarna, general plan of the town. Dynasty XVIII

brick chapels. Architrave fragments mentioning the god Amon suggest that some of these belong to the end of the period, when attempts were being made to reconcile the Theban priesthood. Somewhat to the north of these was an enclosed area with three platforms approached by ramps which have been called the desert altars. Their structure suggests the pavilion in which the king received foreign tribute. This has been identified as the building which is placed astride the north wall of the Great Temple, but none of these buildings exactly resembles the tomb pictures. The open desert would have made an excellent setting for such a display of pomp as we see in the tombs of Huya and Mery-ra II.[14]

The first part of the town to be laid out after the central official quarter seems to have been the southern residential district which contained the residences of the vizier Nakht, the general Ramose, and the priests Pawah and Panehesy. Two of these properties on the easternmost street were occupied by sculptors. One was on the north side of the wady and belonged to Tuthmosis, while the other lay on the southern edge of this large dry watercourse. Yet a third sculptor's workshop, attached to the palace, seems to be indicated by the large number of granite shawabtis and the plaster model head of Akhenaten found in a mass of debris opposite the gates of the great Aten Temple. There was a glass manufactory at the northern edge of the south residential quarter, quantities of broken glass being found in the waste-heaps which lay south of the police barracks. Throughout the city, the rubbish from houses was either dumped in open spaces or placed in prepared holes in the ground. There was little in the way of sanitation, the water from a bath simply running off into a receptacle in the floor, which had to be emptied, or else through a short channel under the wall, where it was allowed to sink into the ground. Periodically the waste-heaps were burned or levelled off to make the foundations for new construction, as can be seen particularly well in the north-east portion of the North Suburb. This was in process of development when the town was abandoned. New houses were left in various stages of construction from the first laying out of an enclosure wall to near completion with the walls up and a stone lintel laid out ready to be set in place.

Many of the features of the Amarna palaces and houses have been discussed in connexion with the Palace of Amenhotep III, where the structure [282, 283, 285–7] provides us with one of the most illuminating examples of New Kingdom domestic architecture. However, new elements appear at Amarna in the main town palace, the North Palace, and the curious precinct of Maru Aten south of the town. They are reflected in less sumptuous fashion in the houses and in the rock-cut tombs. The radical departure from the old forms would be more evident if the stonework from the two temples, like that of the palace, had not been completely carried away, leaving only impressions of the first course of the wall masonry or traces of guiding-lines on the plaster-flooded areas of the shallow foundation trenches. Much reliance has to be placed on the tomb pictures of the temples.[15] Although the relative simplicity of these buildings enabled the ancient artist to represent them in a manner more comprehensible to us than was the case with the more complicated palace, the pictures still leave much to be desired. In comparison with the Theban temples the chief difference lies in the open character of the Amarna structure. There is not, as in the Luxor Temple, that progression from an open court through halls to a dark, mysterious sanctuary hidden from all but the qualified priesthood. Instead there is a series of spacious unroofed areas leading to the altar of the god which is itself open to the sky, all being accessible to the rays of the Aten. The first essay at this scheme seems to have been the sanctuary of the Great Temple (Per Aten) approached by a long avenue of sphinxes and trees. A temporary brick chapel was almost immediately replaced by a larger one of stone. To this a portico gave access through a curious bent entrance of small screen walls which opened into a colonnaded enclosure. East of this lay a smaller rectangular enclosure containing the large altar. Outside the portico on the west stood a large round-topped stela with a statue of the king beside it. This stela is thought to be the Amarna version of the Ben-ben which had been the central element in the old temple of Ra at Heliopolis, and the sanctuary as a whole is probably referred to as the Mansion of the Ben-ben. Little is left of the temple at Heliopolis, but the squat masonry obelisk on a high platform which is preserved in the Sun Temple of Neuser-ra at Abu Gurob is an Old Kingdom reflection of this Ben-ben. The small temple, the Hat Aten, south of the Royal Estate [308], repeats the scheme of the sanctuary. Access to it is through two open enclosures by gate pylons, and the whole was surrounded with a wall having a regular series of projecting buttresses [310].

The early sanctuary of the Per Aten may have been largely

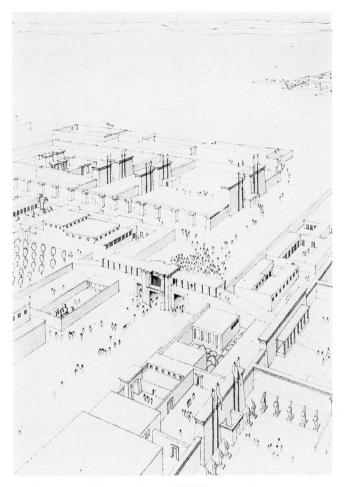

310. Amarna, central quarter. Dynasty XVIII. Reconstruction

supplanted later in the reign, when the western end of the sphinx avenue was covered by a long structure (the Gem-Aten) which again more or less repeats the sanctuaries of the two earlier temples at its east end and is preceded by three courts containing closely packed rows of altars. The whole building was entered by a columned pavilion with open central passage (the Per-Hai) which was set a little back from the gateway giving access from the Royal Road. The tomb pictures show that the spaces between the columns of these temples were filled with statues, of which badly smashed fragments were recovered in the excavations. The walls were decorated with reliefs of which very little remained after the virtually complete removal of the stonework.[16] A curious features of the later addition to the Great Temple is the huge foundations for an enormous number of altars in the space outside the north and south walls of the western portion of the Gem-Aten and Per-Hai.

The gateway to the great temple may have faced an open space across the Royal Road and north of the east wing of the main palace. The main entrance to the palace lay here, and one is tempted to postulate some formal treatment of the access from the river to these two important buildings, in view of the obvious care with which the various official buildings are laid out in this part of the town. All this area is under cultivation, and nothing has been found except for the debris from a sculptor's workshop described by Petrie. The excavators have suggested that another huge wing on the

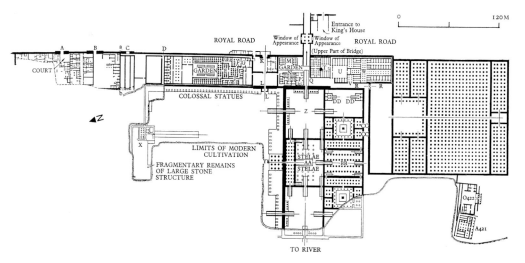

river side of the palace balanced the structures containing the north and south harems and store chambers which lie along the west side of the Royal Road. This river façade of the palace is totally lost under the cultivation, but is possibly represented, with its approach from the water, in the delightful drawing in the tomb of May.[17] The two very marked axes of the official apartments of the palace suggest that there was probably a minor approach which ran from a river entrance eastwards through the central halls, south of the broad court, to the bridge which connected with the Royal Estate, while more solemn state progresses could be made from the now destroyed northern entrance debouching on the north side of the court through what was probably a great gate flanked by columned pavilions.[18] The southern halls were entered by an impressive but smaller columned portico.[19] It is most probable that there was a principal royal landing-place which served both the northern entrance to the palace and the principal western gateway to the great temple of the Aten.

Much of the character of this great group of official buildings in the central city can be grasped from the plan [308], the restored plan of the palace [311], and the ingenious perspective reconstruction [310] of the eastern part of the palace, the Royal Road with its bridge crossing to the Royal Estate and the smaller temple of the Aten. One is looking south-east towards a corner of the southern section of the town and across the plain to the circle of desert hills [310]. In the immediate foreground is the south-east corner of the broad court with the roofs of the northern harem buildings to the left of the entrance to the court from the Royal Road. The trees in the garden of the smaller south harem can be seen over its walls and the portico from which the ramp to the bridge led from the central halls. To the right of the ramp are the palace store-rooms. In the lower right corner can be seen one of the balustraded ramps that appear on the plan [311] leading up and down from the raised entrances of the central halls and forming one of the unusual features of this building. The central portico on the south side of the broad court, with its huge palm columns sparkling in the sun with bits of glazed inlays and gilding, falls just outside the picture to the right. This was all that was completed of a pretentiously planned colonnade on this side, large statues of the king and queen being substituted for the columns as on the harem side of the

court. It should be noted that instead of the standing statues of the king in Osiride form, restored here, the very fragmentary pieces recovered showed that there were seated statues along the side wings and standing figures on the south façade. These were about twice life size, and those of the king were made of either granite or quartzite, while the queen's figures were all made of quartzite. As in the case of the buildings on the north side of the court, the walls were also decorated with sunk reliefs. Very few of these had not been carried away in the very thorough demolition of the building, but they resemble those found at Karnak, particularly one with lively figures of running gazelles [299B].

Across the Royal Road the flat-roofed structures of the king's house, with its tree-filled court and terraced garden on two levels adjoining the road, probably produce somewhat the same impression as would have the residence of Akhenaten's father at Thebes. Beyond lie the succession of courtyards of the smaller Aten temple, with their gate pylons and porticoed sanctuary at the back. A feature of this building, clear here and on the general plan, is the buttressing of the enclosure wall. Little can be said about the details of the administrative buildings to the west [308] except that the southernmost structure in the line of offices behind the Royal Estate was the 'House of the Correspondence of the Pharaoh', in which were found the famous clay tablets containing in cuneiform writing the 'Amarna letters'. The military and police barracks can be easily distinguished on the eastern edge of the official quarter (at the top of the plan) by the huge oval depression in the ground round its well.

Even more than in the open character of the Amarna temples and the thoroughly Egyptian attempt to impress by the grandiose quality of the regularly laid out state apartments of the palace, it is in the structural details that the Amarna architects show their originality. While these are in the main variations on long-tried basic elements of Egyptian design, nevertheless some of them are strikingly fresh. The plant ornament of the columns anticipates features generally considered a late development in Egyptian architecture. Other elements either disappear or are altered almost beyond recognition. Ubiquitous is the use of a broken architrave, invented in pictorial representation to afford space for the rays of the Aten over the royal pair [261]. This may have been suggested by the cornices of the pylons which flanked

313. Amarna, tomb of Tutu, harem of the palace. Dynasty XVIII

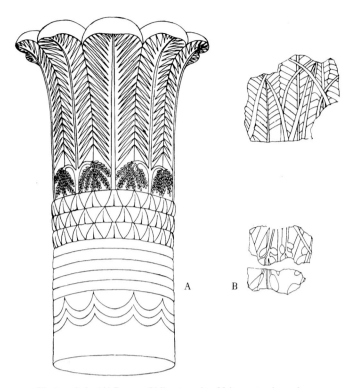

312. Plant capitals. (A) Roman, Philae, temple of Isis, west colonnade; (B) Amarna Palace

the unroofed gate of a temple [354]. It appears in the 'window of appearances' (restored over the main gateway of the bridge [310]) and in the openings of small shrines and screen walls.

The Amarna architect shows a special preference for the palm column, which has not been too frequently preserved in stone from other periods, although in use since the Old Kingdom and frequently represented in pictures of buildings. It was evidently common in wooden architecture. Like the other plant forms it acquires a squat, heavy form when employed in stone. This is particularly clear in the few columns left standing in the Nubian temple of Sesebi erected by Akhenaten.[20] At Amarna the form can only be restored from fragments, as in the huge inlaid capitals from the southern portico of the broad court,[21] or those in the River Temple and the entrance hall to the precinct of Maru Aten.[22] One capital, found by Petrie among the debris of the portico of the broad court, adds freely-drawn bunches of dates to the palm form in a startling anticipation of Roman work at Philae [312].

Perhaps the other traditional form of support, with a shaft of bound plant stalks topped by clusters of lotus or papyrus buds, or open papyrus flowers, was less clumsy and bulbous when constructed of stone than it was when cut from the rock in tombs. However, it is shown with a characteristically swelling profile in the representations of buildings in reliefs. Actual examples recovered from buildings in the town were again in very fragmentary condition. They present an extraordinary variety of treatment. The papyrus-bundle column is found with bands of inscription and a wider band near the top of the shaft with hanging swags of ducks. A light wooden version of this column with single open flower capital and pendant streamers appears in Tutu's picture of the harem

[313]. In stone it was used with a capital of clustered open flowers in the colonnade round the garden court in the north harem and in rock-cut examples in the tomb of Tutu, where the buds of the capitals are covered with a mass of lightly engraved and painted detail which anticipates the heavily overloaded formal patterning of such Ramesside examples as the supports for the great Hypostyle Hall at Karnak.[23]

Somewhat similar columns, grander in scale, formed the northern portico of the first hall opening south of the broad court, but here apparently the shafts were covered with closer reed-like stems and the capitals formed of freely treated foliage carving. Again, in the little temple which adjoins the island kiosk at Maru Aten, pendant ducks and plaques of the royal family were applied near the top of reeded shafts that evidently were thought of as the stems of lotuses, since here and there a drooping flower head is carved in relief against the lightly ribbed surface of the shaft. The capitals in this case were formed of lotus flowers and leaves.[24] They were of alabaster inlaid with blue paste like the lower drums of the sandstone shafts. There was evidently a very similar use of reed-like stems and lotus capitals, inlaid with coloured faience, in the eastern columned hall of the northern harem which adjoined the Royal Road.[25] However, the most charming and original treatment of freely growing forms is in the convolvulus vines covering the shafts of the kiosk-like structures in the court by the magazines at the east end of the southern halls and south of the court with the ramp leading to the bridge. These fragments do not seem to have been studied since their first publication.[26] The pieces from the shaft are described as having irregular surfaces as though imitating the trunk of a tree.

These richly varied columns must be imagined against a background of painted stone reliefs in the central halls of the main palace, where there was also a good deal of wall encrustation of coloured glazed tiles. The carved ramp balustrades and low screen walls were of alabaster, hard limestone, and granite. There were also statues of various materials. The plastered brick walls and the floors of the harem apartments were covered with paintings, as in the Palace of Amenhotep III. The outer faces of the brick screen walls and piers surrounding the garden court of the north harem have a badly preserved continuous scene[27] with men and cattle along a winding canal on which are boats, evidently resembling the strip of pastoral activities that runs around the lower part of the walls in the tomb of Huya.[28] With the figures of bowing negroes on an outer wall of the king's house this is

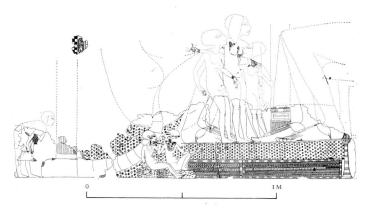

314. Daughters of Akhenaten. Reconstruction of painting from the Royal Estate, Amarna. Dynasty XVIII

a rare example of painting on the exterior of a building. The continuity of the scene is also unusual but is found again on the walls of the columned hall south of the garden court in the north harem which also contained one of the best preserved of the painted pavements.[29] Above a dado of red, blue, and white false-door panelling was a narrow strip which continued from one wall to the next showing servants cleaning and preparing the hall for a meal.[30] The finest of these continuous friezes is of course that masterpiece of plant and bird life in the 'green

room' of the Northern Palace [284] which covers three walls of the small room.[31] This would dispel any doubt as to the extraordinary skill of these painters, as would the marvellous goose [307] from another cubicle of the garden court of the North Palace[32] or the delightful little princesses in Oxford from a wall in Akhenaten's private apartments in the Royal Estate [314]. A sculptor's study preserved in the Cairo Museum [315] perhaps served as preparation for a scene which, when completed, would have closely resembled the Ashmolean painting. The artist first drew on the limestone fragment with a swift, sure black line, and then followed the indications of his sketch with his tools to model the figure in three dimensions. Equally fine figure subjects are testified by the fragments of wall-paintings from the bridge leading to this estate and the apartments over the gate in the ill-preserved palace in the northernmost quarter.[33]

The same charming use of line and colour, made more brilliant by the glaze, appears in the faience tiles which were found particularly in the houses of the northern suburb, in the buildings of the island group in the Maru Aten precinct, and in the festival hall of Semenkhkara. In the latter case they covered the lower part of the west wall and appear to have formed a dado round the hall. They consist of fairly regularly spaced white daisies with yellow centres moulded separately

315. Princess. Drawing on limestone from the North Palace at Amarna. Dynasty XVIII. *Cairo Museum*

and set into rectangular small plaques coloured a bluish green and with the leaves and stems of the flowers drawn on in a darker colour. A fluttering bird, a thistle, and little overlapping blue and yellow ovals that look like the pebbles in Aegean landscapes but may be stylized flowers indicate that this was not a formal decorative pattern and that the design may have been continued by other fragments which have various kinds of freely growing plants, birds, and animals on them. These delicate designs are on so small a scale that they seem more suitable to an intimate chamber than to the vast area with its forest of square pillars in which some of them were found. They must have presented, at any rate, a sparkling surface in the dim light which the windows near the top allowed to filter between these pillars. As in the adjoining hall on the north, the flat ceiling was probably covered with a painted trellis of blue grapes on yellow ground.

Petrie thought that other tiles with fish and water birds were used on the floor, since they so much resemble the designs of painted pavements. Others have rounded tops as though they projected above the straight line of a dado. One of these in the Brooklyn Museum [350] has a subtle blending of autumnal yellows, browns, and greens, as well as a fascinating mixture of plant forms that merge into one another as in so many of the small carvings in wood and ivory.[34]

The private house at Amarna, roughly square in plan, was primarily a one-storeyed affair, although the central hall rose higher than the surrounding rooms.[35] The staircase, ordinarily reached from this hall, led to the roof. In several instances, however, extra column bases fallen from above indicate that there was a columned loggia over the reception-hall which usually lay on the north side of the house. This reception-hall adjoined the main entrance, which was approached by a few steps or a ramp, since the larger houses were set on a low platform. It must be remembered that the buildings at Amarna have been badly denuded by weathering and that any idea of their elevation must be gained from their ground-plans, from stone elements such as door casings or column bases, and whatever vestiges of painted plaster could be recovered. Columns were of wood and like the other woodwork have disappeared. The larger houses suffered the most complete dismantling and later plundering. It was usually the more modest, middle-class dwellings, particularly those which were harder to reach along the eastern edge of the town, in which the painted decoration and structural details were best preserved. The wealthier inhabitants, uncertain of future political changes, when they departed at first bricked up the doorways to their houses and left a caretaker behind. Later, convinced that the change was permanent, they sent back for usable materials such as wooden columns and roofing timbers. Many of the poorer inhabitants remained for some time gradually settling into the better quarters and repairing them with materials from their own homes.

Sometimes, as in the house of the vizier Nakht [316],[36] there was a second columned room, beside the central hall. The plan of this house shows well the common tripartite arrangement. Here there is a projecting vestibule, then the reception-hall flanked by smaller rooms. The central division of the house has the large hall, with a second reception room on the west, and an eastern unit with the staircase, two small store-rooms and a corridor connecting with the back of

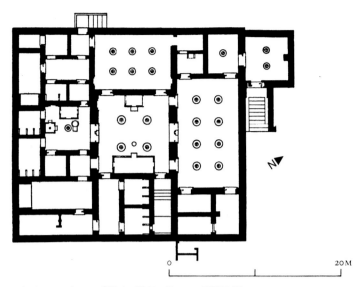

316. Amarna, house of Vizier Nakht. Dynasty XVIII. Plan

the house. The southern section, which contains the private quarters, is unusually commodious, with a smaller sitting-room in the middle which repeats the features of the central hall and has a bedroom suite on each side, the master's apartments having a separate entrance. The intention was evidently to enclose the chief living-room with outer rooms, both to retain heat in winter and to ward off the hot sun from its walls in summer. Windows placed near the ceiling, above the roofs of the outer rooms, would let in air and all the necessary light in a country where this can be so blindingly bright. In Nakht's house there was certainly an upper room, probably a sort of loggia open to the north, over the northern reception-room. It was evidently built against the higher walls of the hall. It has often been assumed that the reception-hall had big windows to form a kind of porch on the entrance side of the house, but the walls were never found high enough to preserve the base of such windows. In one house were recovered dummy mud grilles fallen from the upper part of the wall. They seem to have alternated with actual window openings which had the vertical bars modelled in mud around reeds. From this and certain details of the painted frieze, it was concluded that large windows did not exist in these houses.[37] Indeed in many cases the opening would have been obscured by outbuildings or granaries. Nevertheless, it is difficult to be sure here: the hall is oriented to receive the cool breezes, or so it has been argued, and the loggia presumed to have been placed over this hall was probably well-ventilated.

The central hall was evidently used as the principal living-room, for dining and for entertaining guests. It was provided with a brazier for heating set in the middle of the room between the four columns which supported the roof. A low raised platform, probably covered with cushions or rugs, formed a divan against the principal wall which was decorated by an elaborate representation of a false-door. Opposite the divan was a similar raised platform for water jars. People could wash here before meals and also in connexion with worship at the household shrines which have been recovered in several of the houses. These were placed sometimes in the central hall, and once in a little room

317. Amenhotep III and Tiy. Stela from Amarna. Dynasty XVIII. *London, British Museum*

opening off it beside the divan, which corresponded to the corridor in the house of Nakht. This shrine consisted of a mud-brick, railed platform approached by a short flight of steps with a balustrade. On this was set a small stone stela like that in Cairo [302] which pictured the king, queen, and their children, the king offering an earring to the larger princess standing in the centre.[38] Holes in the stone indicated that it was provided with wooden doors like a medieval altarpiece. A similar stela was found in the private residence of the chief servitor of the Aten, Panehesy [317]. It shows the fat Amenhotep III slumped in an easy Amarna attitude before a table of food and with one arm round the back of his wife's chair. The official residence of Panehesy,[39] beside the southern enclosure wall of the Great Temple of Aten, had one of the more elaborate shrines set up in the central hall. It was a stepped altar with figures of the royal family worshipping the sun disk on the frame of the opening into the stone screen wall. This had the usual broken cornice which we saw first in the 'window of appearances' in the tomb of Ramose [261]. The wall round the altar platform may have enclosed one of the statuettes of members of the royal family which have been recovered from private houses or their garden shrines. The larger estates sometimes had one of these

shrines in the form of a garden kiosk, a small edition of the building constructed of more precious materials on the island in the Maru Aten precinct. This was a little platform approached by steps, with light columns connected by screen walls and supporting a flat roof. The ceiling was painted to imitate a vine trellis. One of these garden shrines is described as containing paintings of the royal family worshipping the Aten.[40]

In discussing the roofing structure of the palace of Amenhotep III, it was pointed out that in the Amarna houses the ceiling-spaces were generally broken up by the exposed roofing-timbers. The more expensive method of covering these over to provide large flat expanses for painting is seldom attested by portions of ceiling-paintings even from the palaces at Amarna, and only once in a pavilion adjoining a private house, where there was a large fragment of a design with flying ducks.[41] In general the walls and plastered timbers of the roof were covered by flat washes of colour, although the main architrave was usually decorated with a block pattern like that framing window-grilles, and a few fragments of formal geometric patterns evidently came from narrow spaces in the ceiling between the rafters. It is likely that, had the larger houses been better preserved, there might have been more paintings resembling those in the palaces, including figure subjects. The German expedition found a painting of a clump of papyrus on plaster set in a square wooden frame. This formed part of the revetment of a bedroom wall, as it had fallen over on to the floor of the adjoining bathroom. It is like the plants from pavement borders and small decorative wall panels in the palaces and reminds one of the flowers set around the court in the picture of the palace harem [313].[42]

Otherwise the only painted decoration preserved in the hall and reception-room consisted of the painted frieze at the top of the wall. Here looped flower-garlands were enlivened by the pendant figures of ducks which were a favourite device in Amarna decoration. They contribute a complicated outline to the old horizontal floral frieze. The garlands are derived from those actually worn at feasts and are to be seen on the mummy cases of the New Kingdom. A shrine-shaped pectoral hanging from the middle of the garland on one of the Amarna fragments stresses the close connexion between this seemingly fresh Amarna invention and the commonest pattern of the funerary craftsman.[43]

It will be seen from the plan [316] that Nakht's house had two bedrooms with a raised platform in an alcove for the bed, such as appeared in the Middle Kingdom houses at Kahun and in the magnificently decorated chamber of Amenhotep III. A bath adjoined, and store-rooms with shelves like those in the Malkata harem open off the private sitting-room. The second large bedroom fills the space ordinarily occupied by a group of small rooms. The wife seems usually to have shared her husband's rooms, and there are in none of these houses the separate women's quarters which appear in the big Kahun houses of the Twelfth Dynasty. The bath consisted of a stone slab with a low coping, occasionally walled off from the room by a stone screen. The walls behind it were either faced with stone or plastered. The water drained off into a receptacle in the floor or occasionally through an outlet under the wall. There was generally a walled-off space for a simple earth closet with brick supports for a seat and a removable vessel.[44]

There were no rooms inside the house which can be identified as kitchens. Some cooking could have been done on the roof, but it must generally have been undertaken in the outbuildings near the granaries and storehouses. The servants' quarters were also outside. Access to the house could sometimes be gained by a secondary entrance through the reception-hall. Some smaller houses had the kitchen built against the house with direct access to it. The extensive grounds were surrounded by a brick wall with a rather small gateway, but one wide enough for a chariot of the period to pass. Gardens were restricted in extent owing to limitations on the amount of water available, and the fact that Nile mud had to be brought for flower beds and to fill the pits in which trees were planted. The pond so frequently depicted in Egyptian tomb-paintings was too expensive for most private people to contrive, where the water level lay some 26 feet (7.9 m) below the surface. What at first appeared to be ponds turned out, when excavated, to be the broken ground around the wells which occur only on the larger properties and had to serve the smaller houses of the neighbourhood, unless water was carried from the river. A circular brick stair descended to

a platform part-way down to the water level. Here a man stood filling containers with the water which was lifted in a bucket on a rope by a weighted wooden arm erected at the well's mouth, an arrangement like the modern *shaduf* [369, 370]. In this Theban painting from a Ramesside tomb the men are fetching their water from a pond by means of two of these simple machines.

In addition to the storehouses and garden, the grounds of these town houses resembled the self-contained country estate in having offices, workshops, and stables. It has been pointed out that the latter need not have been extensive, since only a few head of cattle for slaughter and a few cows for milking need be brought over at one time from the farms on the west bank of the river. There was evidence for leather-working, weaving, and dyeing, as well as the making of pottery and faience. On the property of the master sculptor Tuthmosis many precious examples of sculptor's studies, plaster casts, and unfinished masterpieces were recovered from the outbuildings of a house like those described above. A less extensive group of fine pieces was recovered from a similar workshop further down the same easternmost street of the southern quarter on the northern edge of the big wady.[45] Less wealthy and influential citizens had to be content with more cramped quarters. Particularly along the edges of the wady in the North Suburb, the houses, although still comfortably arranged inside, were built much more closely together. The reconstruction [318] shows how the south side of this depression looked with steps leading up from the dry watercourse to a crowded block of buildings between the Royal Road and the next thoroughfare to the west of it. This region gave indications of having been inhabited by the merchant class who may have settled there to be near the main city quays north of the palace and the Great Temple of the Aten. Parts of this North Suburb were densely packed with miserable hovels by the time the town was abandoned. If Amarna had continued to grow in population, it would soon have resembled the crowded quarters of Thebes and Memphis.

318. Amarna, North Suburb, houses on the edge of the wady. Dynasty XVIII. Reconstruction

319. Nofretete. Standing statuette from Amarna. Dynasty XVIII. *Berlin Museum*

which the craftsmen went about achieving their finished statues.[46] There were plaster casts in the form of masks [321–4], parts intended for composite figures made up of different kinds of stone, and other work in various stages of completion. The standing figure of Queen Nofretete [319] is a nearly finished statuette, but it has as yet been given only a few touches of colour, red on the lips, black on the eyes, and a yellow band over the forehead at the base of the crown. The slumped pose of the figure is realistically portrayed, as is the long, thin neck which is thrust a little forward as though straining to support the head. The queen's tired-looking face, with its lines beside the mouth, is less haggard than in many of the reliefs, but has here none of the radiant, confident beauty expressed in the famous bust from the same workshop [293]. It is perhaps not quite fair to compare the head of a figure little more than a foot high with the life-size masterpiece, but the range covered by the sculptors of the time can be grasped if we realize that this statuette is characteristic of work which falls between the extremes of the large statues of the king [294, 295] and the head of Nofretete [293]. The fully painted bust, by employing a very light red for the skin and the deeper tone of the lips, produces a more natural effect than could be achieved by the conventional yellow of Nofret's statue in the Old Kingdom [80]. One of the inlaid eyes is missing and is thought never to have been inserted, reminding us, as do the cut-off shoulders which leave the broad collar incomplete, that this was evidently intended, like most of the other pieces in the workshop, as a model to be followed by other craftsmen. Nofretete's characteristic tall crown is painted blue. The headband on which it fits is yellow to imitate gold as in the case of the uraeus. Fastened round the crown is a yellow band with streamers, also of gold with red, blue, and green inlays.[47] The same colours are used for the elements of the necklace. The fresh preservation of this colour gives us a perfect example of the New Kingdom Egyptian's conception of life conveyed in a statue, just as the statues of Rahotep and Nofret [80] present with equal vividness the ideal of earlier times. Nofretete also appears in a relief block in the Brooklyn Museum which represents her kissing one of her small children [320]. Although the block has been mutilated, it is still possible to discern the nature of

320. Nofretete and her daughter. Hermopolis relief from Amarna. Dynasty XVIII. *Brooklyn Museum*

SCULPTURE AT AMARNA

Much of the sculpture in the round which has been recovered from the ruins of the city of Akhenaten does not show the strongly exaggerated qualities of his Karnak colossi [294, 295] or of so many of the reliefs. One senses a tendency to soften the harsher aspects of the early treatment of the human figure as time went on. The contents of the workshop of the sculptor Tuthmosis, abandoned there when the town was deserted, give us an unexpected glimpse of the way in

 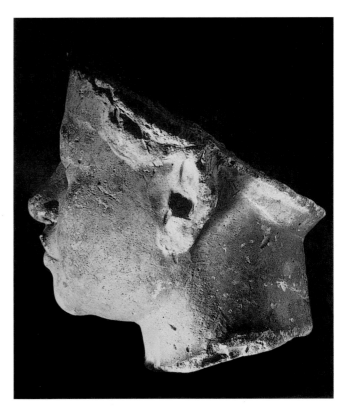

321 and 322. Amenhotep III(?). Plaster head from Amarna, front and side views. Dynasty XVIII. *Berlin Museum*

the original sculpture. The artist employed a bold outlining which provided him with a deep enough area to model naturalistically. The bone structure of both faces has been carefully observed. Nofretete here appears as a youthfully elegant queen, with a long slender neck and elaborately set hair. The contrast between this representation of sophisticated elegance and the humble tenderness of the action has been exploited to produce an impression of naturalness and grace. The living ray of the sun-disk extends the sign of life to bless the couple and their action.

The bust by the sculptor Tuthmosis[48] is only one of a number of superb heads of the royal family where individual peculiarities have been gracefully refined rather than stressed. The gold mask of Tut-ankh-amon [325] and his Turin statue usurped by Horemheb [327] are excellent examples of this stylization of the appearance of members of a family who seem to have borne a resemblance to one another but are also difficult to distinguish individually because of the persistence of a type created to portray the king and queen. Nofretete's bust represents also a continuation of the taste and consummate craftsmanship of the reign of Amenhotep III in its delicate modelling and subtle interpenetrating curves. The tendons of the throat as well as the natural colouring of the skin reveal that the artist was studying the human form with renewed interest before making his abstractions. If we turn to the plaster casts found in his studio [321–4], this becomes even more startlingly apparent.[49] Whether we view them as taken from heads modelled in clay or as somehow fashioned from impressions of the face of a living or dead person, they are extraordinary documents of the actual appearance of members of the court at Amarna. Except in the

case of the Giza reserve heads, we have at no other time in Egypt such a vivid impression of being in the presence of a whole group of the contemporaries of a ruler. It goes without saying that the severely simplified limestone heads of the Fourth Dynasty do not present anything comparable to their lifelike detail.

In the Old Kingdom the linen-wrapped body was sometimes covered with plaster and the face modelled to approximate the features of the dead person [104].[50] These are of course not death-masks in the usual sense of the word. Such a mask does actually exist in the form of a plaster mould taken from the face of a dead person. It was found in the funerary temple of the Sixth-Dynasty King Tety and is thought to be contemporary.[51] There is a considerable difference between the appearance of a cast taken from this mould and the Amarna masks [321–4]. For one thing the eyes are closed in the early example. If the others were death-masks, one would have to assume considerable reworking, but they are said to show no marks of tooling after they were cast. This would necessitate alterations made to the mould itself, or an intermediary head cast from the mould and re-cut in the hard plaster before the present impression was made. There are many details however which look as though they had been modelled in clay, and there appear to be no signs of cutting in a substance such as hardened plaster or stone. In fact one of the chief differences between these faces and those of the statues of the period, apart from the stylization of the finished pieces, is that between the technique of stone carving and work in a material used when soft. This is one reason why it is hard to believe that the head attributed to Amenhotep III [321, 322] was cast from a stone statue. While one still has

323. Old man. Plaster mask from Amarna. Dynasty XVIII. *Berlin Museum*

324. Old woman. Plaster mask from Amarna. Dynasty XVIII. *Berlin Museum*

reservations about some of the masks,[52] the suggestion that they were casts taken to give more permanent form to exceptionally realistic sculptor's studies in clay deserves serious consideration. The head attributed to Amenhotep III [321, 322] is not, like others [323, 324], simply a mask of the face, flattened at the back, but is treated as a head in the round and, as can be detected in other cases, cast from a mould that

consisted of several parts. The wrinkles round the eyes and on the forehead of the old woman [324] and on the brow of the extraordinary old man [323] are unprecedented in earlier sculpture. In the last case one would like to think that we have the face of the courtier Ay, who later became pharaoh. Unfortunately, there is no certain means of identifying these people who had accompanied Akhenaten to Amarna.

CHAPTER 18

The Post-Amarna Period 1350–1314 B.C.

Some of the most accomplished works of the Amarna period were produced in that time of transition after Akhenaten's death when first the young Semenkhkara and then the boy Tut-ankh-amon, under the tutelage of Ay, attempted to come to terms with the opposition to the cult of the Aten and allowed the priesthood of Amon to be re-established at Thebes. Many objects from the tomb of Tut-ankh-amon are important documents of the first tentative steps of the restoration, while the tomb equipment as a whole illustrates to an unparalleled degree the luxurious appointments of the royal household in the second half of the Eighteenth Dynasty. The statues of Tut-ankh-amon, like the gold mask from his mummy [325] or the small head in the Metropolitan Museum [326], continue a softened version of the facial type of Akhenaten. This appears strikingly in the profile of the king's head in the Turin statuette usurped by Horemheb [327]. It is significant of the change which is taking place that Tut-ankh-amon stands beside a seated figure of the god Amon.

The large grey granite statue of Horemheb in the pose of a scribe [328] is related stylistically to those of Amenhotep son of Hapu, but it clearly illustrates how the traditions of the reign of Amenhotep III have been modified by the experiments which came in between. The earlier statues seem more severe by contrast, although Horemheb has the same plump, well-fed body and wears a long wig similar to that of the aged wise man [267]. The erect position of the body has now relaxed into easy curves, the delicate contours of the face have acquired a contemplative expression, and the sleeves of the thin pleated garment flare out decoratively. This is indeed a strange way in which to represent the strong man who was supporting the throne in Memphis during the brief reigns of Tut-ankh-amon and Ay and was soon to become pharaoh. It is no wonder that the sculptors of Ramesside times returned to the more virile forms of earlier times, although traces of the Amarna facial type lingered on in some of the royal statues as late as the reign of Ramesses III.

Horemheb was commander-in-chief of the army when he had this statue set up in the Temple of Ptah at Memphis, as Amenhotep son of Hapu had placed the figures of himself in an outer part of the Karnak temple. Like Amenhotep he had been Scribe of Recruits, and it is as a Royal Scribe and not a military man that he was portrayed by one of the finest sculptors of the end of the dynasty. He was equally fortunate in his choice of the craftsmen who decorated the tomb which he erected at Saqqara, probably in the reign of Tut-ankh-amon [329]. The work is in both raised and sunk relief and of exceptional quality, employing the fine limestone quarried in the neighbourhood of Tura on the east bank of the river across from Memphis. The blocks from the tomb are far from complete and are scattered in various museums, but it is clear that much space was devoted to Horemheb's concern with foreign affairs.[1] Some control seems to have been maintained over the restless inhabitants of Egypt's neglected Asiatic empire in spite of the confused conditions in the north vividly

pictured in the Amarna letters and a contemptuous statement made by Tut-ankh-amon in his Karnak stela. He was concerned chiefly with the condition of the temples which had to be restored after Akhenaten's persecution. However, in speaking of the sad state of the country at the time of his accession he says that 'If an [army? was] sent to Djahy[2] to widen the frontiers of Egypt, it met with no success at all'.[3] Nevertheless we find Horemheb in one tomb scene honoured by the king in the presence of long lines of shackled Asiatics. On another wall he converses through an interpreter with a group of prostrate foreign chiefs and issues instructions to Egyptian officials who may be envoys to the lands from which the foreign notables have come begging for Egypt's protection. This is in keeping with the correspondence of Akhenaten's time which shows that, while the small city-states were constantly attacking one another, each claiming to be loyal to Pharaoh and protesting the disloyalty of their neighbours, Egyptian representatives and some troops were still maintained abroad.[4] Some of the northern states in Syria had long been intriguing with the Hittites. In fact the forces of the Hittite king Subbiluliumas had pushed southwards past Kadesh, which guarded access to the north Syrian plain at the upper end of the broad valley between the mountain ranges of Lebanon and Anti-Lebanon. One of these expeditions was at the end of the successful campaign against Tushratta of Mitanni. However, when his raiding parties appeared again in this valley, which they called the land of Amka, Subbiluliumas still considered it Egyptian territory and was himself occupied much farther north once again subduing the town of Carchemish on the great bend of the Euphrates. This is clear from the records of his reign compiled by his son Mursilis, where it is stated that it was at the time when messengers came to Subbiluliumas from the widow of Pharaoh with the proposal that he send one of his sons to be her husband.[5] Ugarit at the northern end of the Syrian coast was still within the sphere of Egyptian influence throughout this period. Protected behind the barrier of Mount Cassius (Gebel Akra), this important city-state continued friendly relations with Egypt and managed to maintain herself against the encroachment of the Hittites, even after their menace had become more formidable in the reigns of Sety I and Ramesses II.[6] The part that may have been played by Aegean sea-power in the developing contest between Hatti and Egypt is yet to be determined, but Mycenaeans formed an important part of the community at Ugarit at the end of the fourteenth century B.C. There is a growing conviction that these Achaeans are to be identified with the people of Ahhiyawa who are first mentioned in connexion with Milliwanda, a town on the coast of Asia Minor thought to be Miletus, in the time of the Hittite king Mursilis who was a contemporary of Horemheb.[7]

It is a pity that the scenes in Horemheb's tomb are not better preserved, for their animated depiction of ethnic types and employment of pictorial devices which had been

326. Tut-ankh-amon. Head of statue. Dynasty XVIII. *New York, Metropolitan Museum of Art*

327. Statue group of Tut-ankh-amon usurped by Horemheb, detail of heads. Dynasty XVIII. *Turin, Museo Egizio*

328. Horemheb as a scribe, from Memphis. Head of granite statue. Dynasty XVIII. *New York, Metropolitan Museum of Art*

325. Tut-ankh-amon. Gold mask from Thebes. Dynasty XVIII. *Cairo Museum*

developed at Amarna might have given us something more of an illustration of conditions described in the Amarna letters. One regrets particularly that so much is missing of a camp scene which appears on blocks in Bologna and a fitting piece in Berlin.[8] In the detail of one of the Bologna blocks [330] the men straining to carry a heavy timber are urged on by an overseer whose gesture is as expressive as are the attitudes of his labourers. No finer or more characteristic group has survived from the Amarna period. The craftsmen in cutting the fine low reliefs have changed the position of the head of the second figure so that the discarded outline of a face appears above. One can be less certain about the alteration to the leg and hip of the first figure, which now gives it the appearance of an experimental back view. This skilfully composed group of figures follows a boy riding a spirited horse, which has frequently been reproduced owing to the rarity of the subject. The Egyptians, like the other peoples of western Asia of this time, were accustomed to using the horse for drawing a chariot, although an occasional rider does appear among the chariotry in the battle-scenes of Sety I and Ramesses II.[9] A pair of such chariots stands ready with their drivers in the upper part of the scene. Like the running man on the left, they have been placed on an undulating line which suggests uneven terrain. We have found this in an early hunting

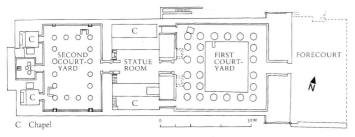

329. Saqqara, tomb of Horemheb. Dynasty XVIII. Plan

scene [190], but here it is part of an increased interest in more naturalistic backgrounds, lively action, and expressive gesture. Two relief blocks discovered during recent investigation at the tomb are also fine examples of this style. One shows a group of squatting Nubians [331] who chat among themselves, while guarded by the imperial soldiers. From the south wall of the second court comes another fine relief, the paint of which is still extremely well preserved, representing Asiatic prisoners [332]. The artist has made a special effort to distinguish the varying ages of his subjects. In the centre of the block, the youths gaze about them curiously, obviously enchanted and fascinated by the new sights, while the older men are fearful and distraught. Despite the freshness of these scenes, there are other examples of work from this tomb itself

which suggest a movement away from the naturalistic and expressive achievements of the mature Amarna style. One block, for example, shows an Egyptian soldier striking a Nubian captive [333]. The nature of the action the artist intended to represent is obvious, but the expressions of the participants are blank and their postures, although lively, are somewhat awkward. A similar blankness of expression may be seen on a wonderfully carved block depicting Egyptian courtiers with curiously billowing skirts [334]. The sculptor has laboured over the intricately dressed hair and pleated clothing of his subjects, but the faces of the courtiers are all alike, similarly devoid of life and sentience. It seems that novel subjects, such as the Nubian and Asiatic prisoners, could still intrigue and inspire, but more familiar material received a finicky and sterile treatment.

This is again apparent in the hunting scene painted in a miniature technique on the lid of the chest from the tomb of Tut-ankh-amon [335]. As in the case of the lion hunt on the other half of the lid and the battle-scenes on the sides of the chest, the desert is impressionistically indicated by a pink wash sprinkled with darker dots and small plants, or an occasional wavy band of pink with darker accents. There is a wonderfully free sense of movement and a seldom equalled suggestion of texture in the deft brushwork.[10] The confused tangle of the bodies of the fallen blacks and Syrians in the

330. Overseer and labourers. Relief from the tomb of Horemheb at Saqqara. Dynasty XVIII. *Bologna, Museo Civico*

331. Saqqara, tomb of Horemheb, Nubian captives. Dynasty XVIII

two battle-scenes seems less successful than the animals, although they certainly produce the required impression of disaster to the enemy. The colour makes it possible, however, to distinguish the different parts of these complicated compositions which were to be so much used for the huge Ramesside battle-scenes. The paint has disappeared from most of these, and it is evident that the relief sculptor had now come to depend upon the painter to make clear the meaning of the intricately overlapping parts. It is curious that these little

panels of the young king, who can himself have taken no part in such battles, should give us our best impression of the finished appearance of one of these large wall-scenes.[11]

A remarkable fragment of relief in Brooklyn showing an old man standing with outstretched arms before the royal kiosk [336] represents another aspect of the art of Amarna, although it is most probably from one of the Saqqara tombs built by other officials at about the same time as that of Horemheb.[12] The exaggerated details of the man's anatomy

332. Saqqara, tomb of Horemheb, Egyptian officers with Asiatic captives. Dynasty XVIII

333. Saqqara, tomb of Horemheb, Egyptian officer striking a captive. Dynasty XVIII

334. Saqqara, tomb of Horemheb, Egyptian courtiers. Dynasty XVIII

335. Hunting scene on the painted chest of Tut-ankh-amon from Thebes (detail). Dynasty XVIII. *Cairo Museum*

336. Old man. Relief from Saqqara. Dynasty XVIII. *Brooklyn Museum*

betray the same interest as inspired the making of the plaster masks which we have been examining at Amarna. Even more extraordinary than the wrinkles on the forehead and the lines on the open hand is the plastic treatment of the flabby face, the accentuated collar-bones, and the tendons of the wrist. The deep furrows of the cheeks and the whole character of the face resemble the way in which foreigners, particularly Hittites, are sometimes treated in the temple reliefs from now on.[13]

The more charming, light side of these versatile artists is to be seen in the coloured ivory carving of Tut-ankh-amon and his queen on the lid of another chest from his tomb [337]. They seem touchingly young and innocently remote from the grim realities of the political situation which was shaping itself about them. They are surrounded by a garden, delightfully suggested by the little panels of flowers which frame the central scene, and are themselves in the midst of tall elaborately fashioned bouquets in front of a garlanded couch like the cushions on which Nofretete sits in the painting [314]. The same lively spirit of the painted hunting scene is to be found in the animals in the ivory panels on the sides and end of the inlaid chest. The hound and hunting leopard attacking their prey are again in the midst of a luxuriant floral setting, which seems to have been adapted from the more formal plants along the base of the paintings of the North Palace at Amarna [284]. Their movement continues a method of representation which had been tried out in the early New Kingdom [245], and is found again in the magnificent carving of Ramesses III hunting wild bulls at Medinet Habu some two hundred years later [367]. Such animal subjects are frequently to be found on the small toilet objects of the latter half of the Eighteenth Dynasty.[14]

The sketchier treatment which we have seen developing in the paintings after the reign of Amenhotep II, and which is apparent in so much of the hasty workmanship at Amarna, can be seen in its most attractive form in the Theban tomb of Huy, Tut-ankh-amon's viceroy of Ethiopia (Kush).[15] It shows the tribute of Syria, but the better-preserved flanking wall is probably a more honest record of the regular income accruing to Egypt from the Sudan, which had remained faithful to its overlord during these troubled times. The Kushite princess under a sunshade in her chariot drawn by oxen [338] lends a touch of authenticity to the scene. We should like to know more about her visit to Egypt, and whether the artist was indulging in a little contemptuous

337. Tut-ankh-amon and his queen. Lid of inlaid chest of Tut-ankh-amon from Thebes. Dynasty XVIII. *Cairo Museum*

humour by substituting cattle for horses, or whether this was customary in her land. These paintings are on the verge of slipping over into the careless execution of so much Ramesside painting.

The over-large heads of some of the figures in Huy's tomb are continued from Amarna in the paintings hastily executed

338. Thebes, tomb of Huy (No. 40), Kushite princess and her retinue. Dynasty XVIII

339. Thebes, tomb of Tut-ankh-amon, wall painting. Dynasty XVIII

at Ay's command in which he is shown officiating at the funeral of his young predecessor in Tut-ankh-amon's burial chamber. The new pharaoh, although the return to orthodoxy is now virtually completed, still has the figure and long skull of Akhenaten. He stands on the right [339] of a scene representing the translation of Tut-ankh-amon's spirit into the other world of the gods. Dressed in the leopard skin of the Sem Priest, Ay undertakes the ceremony of the opening of the mouth before a figure of Tut-ankh-amon as Osiris. Behind him, on the adjoining wall, priests drag the coffin on the sledge. Such an unusual subject in a king's tomb is evidently connected with the portrayal of the burial of the Princess Meketaten in the Royal Tomb at Amarna. There is little in addition to the large figures just described except for

a group of divinities including the apes which welcome the Sun Bark, from the first division of the Book of What is in the Netherworld. It should be remembered, however, that portions of this, as well as chapters from the Book of the Dead, are inscribed on the four gold-covered shrines which enclose the king's sarcophagus.[16]

The Sun Boat and apes appear again in Ay's own tomb.[17] This lies near that of Amenhotep III in a side ravine which branches off from the Valley of the Kings. It is thought to have been commenced for Tut-ankh-amon. The paintings are in a very bad state of preservation, but enough remains to make it clear that they are close in style to those of Tut-ankh-amon. There is the same unconventionality of subject-matter, particularly in the fowling scene, where Ay and his queen

340. Thebes, tomb of Ay, Ay and his queen boating. Dynasty XVIII

341. Thebes, unfinished reliefs in the tomb of Horemheb. Dynasty XVIII

enjoy an outing in the papyrus swamps much as any noble might be shown in one of the Qurneh chapels [340]. In the decorations of the tomb which Horemheb prepared for himself at Thebes after his accession to the throne there is a complete return to traditional methods and subject-matter. Even here, however, as in Ramesside paintings, some of the figures are disproportionately short for the large heads. The scenes of the underworld are treated again in the burial hall, but in a new series called The Book of Gates. One wall [341] is in several stages of completion, with the original black drawing lines above, some outlines partially cut away, and much of the fine relief finished except for the application of the paint.[18]

The bewildering quantity and richness of the contents of the small tomb of Tut-ankh-amon make one realize what must have disappeared through the plundering of the great burial-places of more important pharaohs of the New Kingdom. A mass of broken equipment, including fine pieces of figured textiles and glass vessels, was indeed recovered from the tombs of Amenhotep II and Tuthmosis IV.[19] Complete pieces of beautifully designed furniture survived in the intact tomb of Yuya and Tuyu, the parents of Queen Tiy,[20] but there was nothing like the profusion and variety of articles which were so closely packed into the four chambers of Tut-ankh-amon that it is difficult to believe that the tomb could have contained them all now that they are spread out in the Cairo Museum.[21] Something of the task involved in removing these objects can be grasped from a glimpse into the 'Treasury' [342] which opens off the burial hall and contained the canopic chest encased in a shrine under a canopy set on a sledge. The shrine, overlaid with gold, is a smaller version of those which surrounded the quartzite sarcophagus. The

wooden figure of Anubis crouched alertly on a portable chest-shrine inside the door has that eerie quality of life in another world which the funerary craftsmen knew so well how to impart to their images. This is partly achieved by exaggerating characteristic features, as in the sweeping curve of the gilded ears of this guardian god of the dead or the long slender copper horns of the gold-covered cow's head which stands on the floor in front of the canopic shrine.

Beyond are stacked chests, dismantled chariot parts, and a model boat. One of the four mourning goddesses which guard the shrine stands with her back to us and arms outstretched. These graceful figures turn their heads in a manner not at all in conformity with the usual frontal pose of statues.[22] A similar turning of the head is given to an alabaster lion which forms the lid of a jar [343]. He lies serenely with his tongue hanging out and one paw crossed over the other, just inside the opened door of the outermost gold-covered shrine which contained the king's sarcophagus. The jar is among the poles which supported a pall covering the second shrine. Pieces of the darkened linen hang down with gold rosettes still attached to them. The little lion has already been mentioned as repeating the pose of the large granite animals set up in the temple of Amenhotep III at Soleb. A daring draughtsman successfully imitated it in the wall painting of a Ramesside prince in Dynasty XX [344].[23]

The lion lid is an amusing *tour de force*, but the alabaster monstrosity which stands behind it is characteristic of far too many of the pretentious set-pieces which strain hard for effect with their heavily overloaded ornament. The tall-necked vase which forms its central element is a variation of an Eighteenth-Dynasty form which can be very beautiful, when its graceful lines are left unadorned in pottery or

342 and 343. Thebes, tomb of Tut-ankh-amon, 'treasury' and objects inside outer sarcophagus shrine. Dynasty XVIII

metal.[24] It was to continue in favour in later times. Here the shape is obscured by the heavy plants of the North and South which Nile gods tie around it. Other alabaster vessels, which one might describe as being in the 'Syrian taste', stand beside an inlaid arm-chair under one of the funerary couches in the antechamber. One, with a fluted body and volutes on the stem, is very like the metal vessels pictured among Asiatic tribute, which one might have thought a fantasy of the painter if it were not for these actual examples. There can be no doubt that the importation of these hybrid forms and the demand for novelty and the display of wealth has had a disastrous effect upon design. The ceremonial chair [345, 346] is another instance. It combines the backrest of an ordinary chair with a curved seat imitating leopard skin and supported by legs ending in duck's heads derived from a folding camp-stool of a kind which also occurs in the tomb. One can only marvel at, without admiring, the skill, ingenuity, and variety of the precious materials expended here. The rather sombre magnificence of the intricately inlaid rectilinear panels of ivory and ebony on the back anticipates strangely the work of

Arab craftsmen in Islamic times in spite of the hieroglyphic inscriptions, protective vulture, and uraeus frieze above. The cartouches of the Aten still remain under the sun disk in the middle of the uraeus cornice,[25] while the king's name is partly given as Tut-ankh-aten and partly as Tut-ankh-amon in the inscriptions. Glass, faience, and coloured stone are used for

345 and 346 (*right, bottom*). Inlaid chair of Tut-ankh-amon from Thebes, with detail. Dynasty XVIII. *Cairo Museum*

344. Thebes, tomb of Khaemwaset, lion with crossed paws. Dynasty XX

347. Thebes, tomb of Tut-ankh-amon, second state chariot (detail). Dynasty XVIII

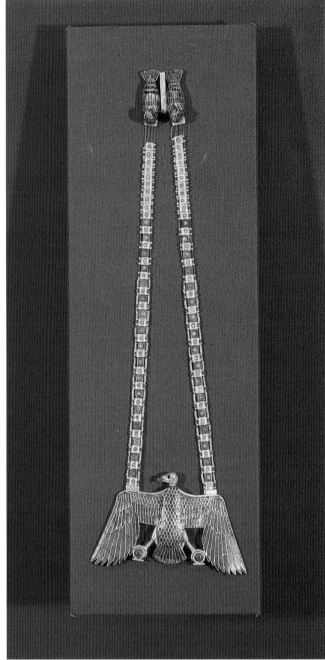

348. Necklace with vulture pendant of Tut-ankh-amon from Thebes. Dynasty XVIII. *Cairo Museum*

the inlays set in sheet gold, and the whole piece is as richly encrusted as is the more frequently reproduced throne which has on its back panel the queen standing before the seated king under the rays of the Aten disk.[26]

If the general character of some of the large pieces strikes us as florid and heavy, one cannot help being delighted by much of the detail. There is the superb serpent inlay [347], which has come loose to lie beside an encrusted disk with a sacred eye which forms a protective emblem inside the body of the second state chariot.[27] The golden surfaces of this chariot are patterned with running spirals and rosettes between bands of coloured inlays. Among much jewellery which is coarse in feeling, the vulture pendant [348] shows

349. Painted pottery plate from Malkata Palace. Dynasty XVIII. *New York, Metropolitan Museum of Art*

350. Glazed tile from Amarna. Dynasty XVIII. *Brooklyn Museum*

that it was still possible to recapture the firm delicate touch of the Middle Kingdom gold-worker. The counterpoise is formed by a pair of small ducks.[28]

The enrichment of the decorative arts had grown, throughout the Eighteenth Dynasty, being enormously stimulated by the flow of foreign tribute into the country and the diplomatic exchanges of the second half of the Eighteenth Dynasty. The elaborate vase forms and the patterns such as those on the chariot [347] go back at least to the reign of Amenhotep II. Similar shapes are pictured in metal vessels in the craftwork and tribute scenes. The regular production of glass was a development of the New Kingdom, and a high degree of technical excellence was achieved in the brilliantly coloured vessels of the time of Amenhotep II.[29] One vase is an opaque purple blue with the fluted panels outlined in yellow. The crosses are yellow, and the rosettes were made separately and fused into the body. Their petals are tomato red, light blue, and purple blue on white.[30] The variegated patterns of such royal vases find a parallel in Mesopotamia in the glass recovered from the Mitannian palace and temple at Nuzi and the Kassite palace of Dur Kurigalzu in the south.[31] Both Assyria and Babylonia were famous for their glazed wares in later times. Multi-coloured vessels, possibly of glazed ware or even glass, were presented to Tuthmosis III by the prince of Assyria.[32] It was at about this time that painted pottery with elaborate light on dark patterns began to appear in the region of the Mitanni sphere of influence.[33] In Egypt, where painted pottery had scarcely been known since the Predynastic Period, the Eighteenth-Dynasty craftsmen made use of several colours for such attractive designs as those in the plate from the Palace of Amenhotep III [349]. Both in connexion with this palace and at Amarna there have been found extensive remains of the manufacture of glass and associated glazed products such as the tiles [350] which have been discussed earlier.

There can be no doubt that the exchange of decorative motifs in the minor arts which we have seen going on since the Middle Kingdom became even more widespread in this period of closer contact. The mingling of influences is particularly clear in Syrian metalwork and ivory carving.[34] The ivory panels from a bed found at Ugarit strikingly illustrate how strong a basic Egyptian influence remained at the end of the Eighteenth Dynasty. The subject-matter is local, but the drawing conventions are those of Egypt. It is interesting to see the contrast in these panels between the careful workmanship and a certain clumsiness of conception. Certainly, various elements of dress and decoration are drawn from a number of different sources.[35] The annals of Tuthmosis III list among tribute or booty taken in the Asiatic campaigns[36] such things as a great ewer in work of Khor, vessels of Djahy (Palestine), and a vase of Keftiu (Cretan) work. A silver statue and tables, chairs, and footstools of ivory, ebony, and carob wood are also mentioned. In the Amarna letters[37] we find Amenhotep III and his son sending presents of rich furniture, such as the ten ebony chairs inlaid with ivory and lapis lazuli dispatched to the king of Arzawa or the gold-decorated beds, chairs, footstools, and a headrest sent to Babylonia, when Pharaoh heard that its king was building a new house. By no means all the objects can be identified which are listed tantalizingly among the dowries of foreign princesses arriving in Egypt or the presents exchanged, but textiles and articles of clothing are mentioned. There is no doubt that there was strong emphasis upon the intrinsic value of the materials from which the articles were made. Tushratta of Mitanni demanded that the statues sent to him be of solid gold and makes an interesting reference to his messengers having seen such statues cast. The Hittite king also wanted gold statues, one standing and one seated, as well as silver statues of women. Figures of ivory are also mentioned. Presumably these were relatively small pieces of sculpture which were sent abroad. In return an image of a foreign deity must have travelled to Egypt, for Tushratta writes to Amenhotep III that Ishtar of Nineveh has declared that she will go to Egypt and return, as she had in the time of his father, and that he has sent her.[38] We do not know what the King of Babylon meant when he asked to have his animals fashioned as though they were alive, although it is easier to visualize the coloured ivory trees and plants which he requested.[39]

We have looked at some of the furniture of the period, but there were innumerable small objects which were fashioned as delightful trifles. They might well have been included among the gifts sent abroad, since they were both precious and easily portable. One of the handsomest of these is a toilet spoon or ointment container of coloured ivory in the form of a pomegranate spray; in characteristically playful fashion other flowers are fastened to the branch.[40] A little ivory grasshopper is another of these charming toys, delicately fashioned to amuse an idle court lady.[41] Two pairs of movable wings form a cover for an eye-paint receptacle inside the ivory body.

351. Ivory ointment box in the shape of a swimming duck. Dynasty XVIII. *Baltimore, Walters Art Gallery*

The engraved wings of an ivory duck are used in somewhat the same fashion. They open on pivots to give access to an ointment container inside the body of the swimming bird [351].

CHAPTER 19

The Ramesside Period: Dynasties XIX–XX 1314–1085 B.C.

Politically, Dynasty XIX began with the accession of Horemheb about the middle of the fourteenth century B.C., when the strong reaction set in which obliterated the memory of the successors of Amenhotep III. On the other hand, we have seen that the work executed for Horemheb before he became king is so closely linked with Amarna that it has been necessary to discuss the monuments of his time in connexion with the style of the late Eighteenth Dynasty. Nor was he related to the new family of soldiers who came into power with Ramesses I, showing special partiality to the city of Avaris in the eastern Delta which was probably their place of origin. Ramesses I, who reigned briefly as an elderly man, was the Paramesses who had served as vizier under Horemheb, and, like his father and the son who succeeded him as Sety I, held the military title of Chief of Archers.[1] Horemheb's reorganization of the country had been facilitated by a relaxation of pressure from the Hittites after the death of Subbiluliumas. They had maintained themselves in the plains of northern Syria centring on Aleppo, but were chiefly occupied with the Kaska in the north and the Arzawa lands in the west of Anatolia. The Assyrians under Assur-Uballit had occupied the Mitanni country beyond the Euphrates.

An aggressive policy was adopted by Sety I, immediately upon his accession, which recovered a large measure of Egypt's dominance in Palestine and Syria. He first clashed directly with the Hittites at Kadesh on the Orontes [352], which in the next reign was to be the scene of the much vaunted exploit of Ramesses II. This famous battle of Kadesh[2] really resulted in a draw which was finally recognized by both parties some fifteen years later in a treaty between Hatti and Egypt. This pact of alliance with Hattusilis III, certainly inspired in part by fear of the growing power of Assyria, was further sealed by the marriage of a Hittite princess to Ramesses II. It resulted in fifty years of peace for the Levant from about 1280 to 1230 B.C., when Merenptah met the first impact of the great mass movement of peoples which eventually overwhelmed Hatti around 1200. Ramesses III, the last great ruler of Dynasty XX, beat off attacks on Egypt from both land and sea similar to but even more formidable than those which had struck his predecessor Merenptah.

Combined with the migrating mass which moved by land from the Balkans and Black Sea region down across Asia Minor, past Carchemish and through the Levant, were northerners who came by ship. These were the Peoples of the Sea whom Ramesses III speaks of as making a conspiracy in their islands. An Indo-European element among the Libyans who attacked Egypt in the time of Sety I seems to have anticipated the larger numbers of newcomers who were mixed with the Libyan tribes which attempted to push into the Delta in the time of Merenptah and Ramesses III. Some of the sea peoples had served as allies of the Hittites at Kadesh and as mercenary troops in Egypt during the Ramesside Period. Driven off from Egypt by Ramesses III, the Philistines (Pelesti) settled along the coast of Palestine, while

others such as the Sherden and Turshu moved into western Mediterranean lands, probably to find homes much later in Sardinia and Etruria. What part exactly the Achaeans played in all this is still not entirely clear, but Cyprus was one of the islands engulfed in the movement, and we find the Hittites having difficulties with the Ahhiyawa at the end of their rule. If the Akaywash or Ekwesh of the time of Merenptah are these Achaeans, they are no longer listed among the peoples of the sea by Ramesses III.[3]

Internally Egypt remained stable on the basis of Horemheb's reforms, although weakened by the struggle for the throne among the successors of Merenptah which was drawn out over a period of twenty-five years. Sety-nekht brought a new family to power in Dynasty XX and made possible the strong administration of Ramesses III which was able to meet the dangerous shock of foreign invasion. However, towards the end of this reign very real signs of political corruption and economic instability began to appear. Conditions deteriorated under the later Ramessides into an unmistakable decline which was accompanied by a disastrous loss of prestige abroad.

The dozen years of the reign of Sety I and the very long rule of Ramesses II, which stretched well over half a century, constituted a period of lavish building on a grandiose scale. The great columned hall between the Second and Third Pylons at Karnak [359] is a joint work of these two reigns and remains the most breathtaking of these achievements, but huge works were undertaken up and down the Nile Valley from the Delta to Nubia. The collapsed and shattered stonework of Ramesses II in the temple of Tanis suggests that, if it were standing, it would seriously rival his work at Thebes. The site is still bewilderingly impressive, overlaid with the fallen additions of the Twenty-first and Twenty-second Dynasties. It is as though one were looking at Karnak levelled to the ground.[4]

The larger of the two temples cut out of the rock by Ramesses II at Abu Simbel, on the east bank of the Nile some forty miles north of the Second Cataract, is celebrated for the four seated figures of the king on its façade. They are over 65

352. Karnak, Hypostyle Hall (exterior), Sety I attacks Kadesh. Dynasty XIX

353. Abu Simbel, temple of Ramesses II. Dynasty XIX

feet high, that is larger than the Colossi of Memnon [353].[5] In spite of the tremendous impression produced, a certain emptiness of conception is evident here which pervades the work of Ramesses II. Too much reliance is placed on mere size and there is a decided coarsening in workmanship. In the sunk relief decoration of the interior, considerable ingenuity is expended upon the topographical details of the battle of Kadesh, with a rare emphasis upon factual record.[6] Nonetheless one misses a vital force which had prevailed in the time of the king's father, Sety I. The traditions of the Egyptian craftsmen were to prove so deeply rooted that in the future they would be susceptible to new stimulus and impressive revival, while capable of the ordinary maintenance of extraordinarily high quality. Nevertheless, the vast schemes of Ramesses II overtaxed the means at hand and contributed to a further impoverishment of the Egyptian spirit. This is evident in the widespread re-use of earlier materials. Kings had always usurped the monuments of their predecessors, but not to the degree practised by Ramesses II.

The outward show and colossal scale certainly command respect. The impressive nature of the pylon which Ramesses II added in front of the Luxor temple is well conveyed by a photograph taken early in the last century [354]. The debris which had accumulated for centuries had not yet been cleared from the front of the temple, and a man walks at a level which nearly reaches the shoulders of the two huge statues which flank the gate. One of the two obelisks still towers above the pylon, although its mate has been in the Place de la Concorde

in Paris since early in the nineteenth century. On the left (east) tower of the pylon Ramesses II charges in his chariot towards the town of Kadesh ringed in by the river Orontes, while on the western tower are spread out the scenes of the Hittite attack on the Egyptian camp before the town. The sunk reliefs of these great scenes are scarcely visible in the photograph, and are exceedingly difficult to study even on the spot, due to the height at which they are placed, the loss of colour, and the now prominent outlines of the masonry blocks which confuse the eye.[7]

A simpler version of the battle superimposed over an earlier essay at the composition is found on the back (west face) of the south tower of the first pylon of the funerary temple of Ramesses II in Western Thebes, known as the Ramesseum. It is flanked by a representation of the camp before Kadesh on the north tower.[8] The battle scene, which forms a separate half of the whole story, is essentially a representation of the counter-attack by which Ramesses freed himself from the trap laid by the Hittite king. Although the essential incidents, which begin with the camp scene, are shown and are supplemented by the written account, the extreme plight of the Egyptians and the doubtful outcome of the contest are overshadowed by the dominating figure of Ramesses and the emphasis upon his superhuman prowess. Muwatallis had let it be thought that he was far to the north in the region of Aleppo, while withdrawing his Hittite forces to the other side of Kadesh. He allowed the Egyptian king to set up his camp with only the one division which had pushed ahead of the rest

355. Thebes, Ramesseum, second court. Dynasty XIX

356. Thebes, Ramesseum. Dynasty XIX. Plan

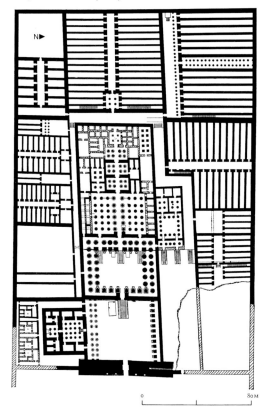

0   80M

354. Luxor temple, pylon of Ramesses II. Dynasty XIX

of the army. The Hittite chariotry then attacked simultaneously the camp and the second division of the Egyptian army,
while it was crossing the Orontes. Ramesses II fought his way
out of the camp with his own personal guards and, while the
Hittites were plundering the camp, managed to rally parts of
his scattered divisions and continue his attack until reinforce-
ments arrived. At the end of the day Muwatallis withdrew his
forces into the town, but the Egyptians themselves were also
forced to retire without laying siege to Kadesh.

The King's counter-attack on the Hittites is similarly
repeated on the west face of the partially preserved north
tower of the second pylon behind the pillars with the Osiride
statues which face the second court [355].[9] Presumably the
Egyptian camp appeared again on the destroyed southern
tower, repeating the scheme of the first pylon. This badly
damaged funerary temple of Ramesses II is now one of the
most picturesque of the monuments of Thebes.[10] Brick store-
rooms surround it at the back, some of which have preserved
their long barrel vaults. Most of the Hypostyle Hall still
stands, as do the Osiride figures of the northern half of the
second court, while the shattered seated granite figure of the
king which once stood by the gate of the second pylon [355]
has long been famous. The main axis of the temple is slightly
askew, probably due to the fact that a small temple of Sety I
had been at least begun on the north and was left in position
to be rebuilt against the north wall of the Hypostyle Hall. The
restored plan [356], taken with the much better preserved
mortuary temple at Medinet Habu [357] constructed in
Dynasty XX by Ramesses III along the lines of that of his
admired predecessor,[11] gives a clear idea of the ambitious
nature of such an establishment in the later New Kingdom.

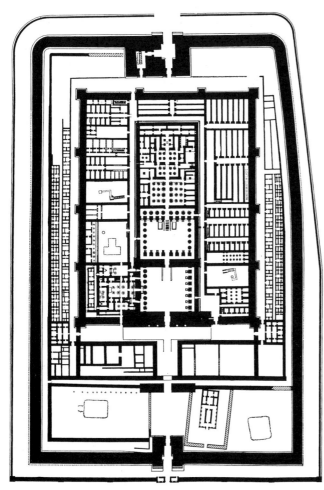

357. Medinet Habu, temple of Ramesses III. Dynasty XX. Plan

The whole covered an area of some 870 feet by 580 feet (265 × 177 m), which is larger than the inner enclosure at Medinet Habu, to which it corresponds, but smaller than the finally completed precinct at Medinet Habu (1030 feet by 688 feet, 314 × 210 m). The temples themselves are about the same size, the Ramesseum being a few feet longer than Medinet Habu.

The first court in both temples had statues of the king against the pillars of the north side of the court. Destroyed nearly to ground level at the Ramesseum, the original appearance of the court can be better understood at Medinet Habu [358], where the ramp leading up to the higher level of the second court is preserved in front of the gateway. A colonnade along the south face of the court in both temples formed a portico in front of a window of appearances which opened from a small palace, with columned hall, audience hall, and subsidiary apartments, built against this south wall. At Medinet Habu the two halls were covered with brick barrel vaults. The whole structure was considerably altered when it was rebuilt by Ramesses III later in his reign.[12] The second court of both temples had a columned terrace on the west, reached by three low flights of stairs at the Ramesseum and by only one in the centre at Medinet Habu. In front of the columns were square pillars with Osiride figures of the king. These were repeated across the east wall and are well preserved at the Ramesseum, on the northern half of the court, where they form one of the most impressive features of the building. There is a pair of the double line of papyrus-bud columns which originally ran along the north and south sides of the court [355]. At Medinet Habu these were reduced to a single line of columns, as was the colonnade fronting the palace in the first court.

358. Medinet Habu, temple of Ramesses III, first court. Dynasty XX

The Hypostyle Hall was entered from the columned porch of the second court and was followed by smaller halls leading to a sanctuary for the divine bark. This inner part of the temple was surrounded by other chambers for the cult. The Hypostyle Hall is better preserved in the Ramesseum than at Medinet Habu and forms a smaller version of the great Karnak hall, with a central aisle flanked by open papyrus columns, rising above side aisles formed of single-bud papyrus columns. In addition to the palace, magazines, and slaughter-courts contained within the inner enclosure at Medinet Habu, which correspond to the groups of buildings as preserved at the Ramesseum, Ramesses III added an outer enclosure which included the Eighteenth-Dynasty temple on the east and contained rows of houses for the priests who administered the temple along the north and south sides of the inner enclosure. The very thick wall was entered on west and east by elaborate fortified stone gates with apartments in the upper storeys. The whole was surrounded by a lower subsidiary wall, and a landing-stage was prepared at the end of a canal which gave access to the temple on the east. The apartments in the two upper storeys were decorated with reliefs showing the king entertained by the ladies of his household.[13]

The great hall at Karnak, which was begun by Sety I and completed by Ramesses II, is 338 feet (103 m) wide and 170 feet (52 m) deep. It consists of sixty-one single papyrus-bud columns on each side of two lines of taller columns with open papyrus capitals which form three central aisles 79 feet high (24 m). These twelve campaniform columns with an enclosing wall, which was torn down to give place to the first line of lower columns on each side, were already in position when Sety began his work, and it has been argued that they were erected by Amenhotep III in the style of his Luxor colonnade, which they strongly resemble. In this case they would have been in position before Horemheb began the Second Pylon. The foundations of these columns contain none of the blocks from the Aten shrine which were used under the other columns in the north and south sides of the hall.[14] The vast scale of this hall, with its fine play of light and shade [359], is best seen as one looks between the huge central columns towards the north half of the structure. Above the cornice of the first line of bud columns can be seen one of the pillars which supported the roof of the higher central aisles. These pillars were separated by stone grilles which let in the light, which must have been more subdued than it is now with much of the roofing gone. One feels here a certain heaviness in the simple shape of the columns and the coarseness of the sunk-relief decoration with which every inch of the surfaces is covered. A sense of constrained space is produced by this forest of supports. This remains so in spite of the wide spaces of the three aisles on the west-east axis and a somewhat narrower cross aisle that runs from the doorway in the north wall to that in the centre of the south side of the hall [223].

It must be admitted that the craftsmen of Sety I had not themselves been entirely successful in recapturing the fresher spirit of the earlier New Kingdom. The wall decorations on the inner walls of the north half of the Hypostyle Hall at Karnak[15] and those in the fine temple which accompanied his cenotaph at Abydos[16] are the last of the great series of large-scale works in traditional raised relief. This was already in the

process of being replaced by sunk relief, as in the battle scenes on the outer face of the north wall of the Hypostyle Hall. Raised relief of such fine quality was to be found again in some tombs of the Saite Period and in a few smaller works of later times, but the revival of raised relief in Ptolemaic-Roman times was to produce results of an entirely different nature. Sety's sculptors were returning to the style of the reign of Amenhotep III, following a tendency which had commenced under Tut-ankh-amon and Horemheb.[17] Beautiful though these reliefs are, as in the case of the two goddesses standing before Osiris on the north wall of the inner Hypostyle Hall at Abydos [360], they have lost something of the spontaneous vitality so richly expressed in the best of their graceful models. Somewhat too coldly perfect in their overall effect, they lack in detail a little of the technical dexterity to be found at the height of the Eighteenth Dynasty.

Low relief of this classic quality continues in the seemingly interminable wall expanses of the Ramesside royal tombs, as in that of Sety I himself.[18] The style is reflected in the paintings of Queen Nofretari, the wife of Ramesses II, in her burial-place in the Valley of the Queens.[19] Here [361] some new experiments at shading with pigments have been attempted in darkening the folds of the sleeves, accenting the corners of lips and nostrils with black, and indicating lines on the throat in red. A patch of deeper red on the cheek, chin, and nose is matched by a wash of red along one side of the arm and hand. The lips are also a deeper red than the very light colour of the skin, as we have seen in certain Dynasty XVIII sculpture such as the Nofretete bust [293]. Other inconsistently applied attempts to indicate a kind of shading by deepened colour appear infrequently in the paintings of the later New Kingdom.[20] In spite of these experiments of the painter, there is remarkably little to distinguish these decorations of Nofretari from the painted low reliefs of the royal tombs. One has to look twice to distinguish whether Nofretari's work is in paint alone, just as in the Ramesside royal tombs one is conscious more of the outlines and the rather heavy colouring than of the surfaces which are raised slightly from the background. It appears that the painter, having to a certain extent won his freedom in Dynasty XVIII and having introduced certain painter-like qualities into some of the great temple reliefs of the Ramesside Period, is now resuming his traditionally anonymous partnership with the relief sculptor. Certainly fine painting is about to be submerged by more and more slovenly craftsmanship in the private tombs, and will virtually disappear at Thebes with Dynasty XX, although there are some hints that a fine tradition was kept alive in the illustration of papyrus rolls [381, 382, 387].

The New Kingdom elegance of form which is maintained in the Abydos reliefs of Sety I enters also into some of the statues. Of these, the large seated black granite figure of Ramesses II in Turin is undoubtedly the outstanding example [362].[21] It is a little over six feet high. One feels that in the head there has been a return for inspiration to the time of Tuthmosis III. There is more emphasis upon the accessories, however, in the details of the Blue Crown and necklace, the heavy crook of royal authority and, above all, in the finely pleated garment, one sleeve of which flares decoratively on the right arm. The treatment of this costume is developed from such works as the statue of Horemheb as a seated scribe

360. Abydos, temple of Sety I, inner Hypostyle Hall, two goddesses on the north wall. Dynasty XIX

[328], or even the gold-covered wooden goddesses who stand around the canopic shrine of Tut-ankh-amon [342]. Although this presents a considerable departure from the severe outlines of the first half of the Eighteenth Dynasty, the statue as a whole recaptures impressively the virile qualities of

361. Valley of the Queens, painting of Nofretari in her tomb. Dynasty XIX

359. Karnak, Hypostyle Hall. Dynasty XIX

362. Ramesses II. Upper part of seated granite statue. Dynasty XIX. *Turin, Museo Egizio*

the time before Amarna. However skilfully this statue, like the reliefs and paintings we have been examining, retains the quality of a fine tradition, there is nothing here like the inventiveness to which the battle-scenes of the reign of Sety I inspired the craftsmen. In these a definitely new contribution was made.

On the vast outer face of the north wall of the new Hypostyle Hall which he was constructing at Karnak, Sety I wished to have his Syrian campaigns commemorated.[22] Out of the formula of the king towering in his chariot above the tangled mass of the enemy fallen under the rearing horses of his chariot the artists developed a remarkable kind of composition. They drew upon earlier, more timid attempts to identify a locality, as in the Hatshepsut Punt scenes [235], and used methods of suggesting landscape which had been worked out already in the reliefs of the Aten shrine at Karnak [299]. Something more specific was now attempted in the way of historical record, and a sense of dramatic conflict was achieved in a more topical narrative style than had hitherto been contemplated by an Egyptian artist. This is immediately apparent in one of the most successful of these scenes, the attack on Kadesh [352]. The part of the wall with the figure of the king has disappeared, but the horses drawing his chariot indicate how this group was balanced by a fortified town on a hill, with the intervening space filled by the overwhelmed

363 and 364. Karnak, Hypostyle Hall (exterior), the Palestinian wars of Sety I. Dynasty XIX

enemy and a fleeing chariot. The landscape is economically reduced to a few trees and bushes set along irregularly curving lines beneath the crenellated walls of the fortress manned by an agitated garrison. The pressing immediacy of the attack is further heightened by the little figure of a herdsman driving his cattle off to the right. A somewhat similar scene shows the archer-king, mounted in his battle-chariot, overcoming singlehanded the defenders of a fort named Pakana'an [363]. In the register above, he has dismounted from his chariot to receive the homage of Lebanese chieftains,

illustrated in the detail shown here [364]. Behind the chieftains is a scene of tree-felling: two Syrians chop at the base of the tall, slender cedar and two others brace with ropes against the fall of the tree.

These scenes were provided with a considerable variety of detail, as in the Nubian village deftly conjured up by a few women, children, goats, and a tree towards which a wounded black is being carried [365] in the temple of Ramesses II at Derr, in the bend of the river south of the First Cataract, towards Abu Simbel.[23] They tend to become more stere-

365. Derr, temple of Ramesses II, the king attacks a Nubian village. Dynasty XX

367. Medinet Habu, First Pylon, Ramesses III hunting wild bulls. Dynasty XX

otyped as one progresses into the reign of Ramesses II, with increasingly lifeless copying. However, their most elaborate development came in the several attempts to portray that king's battle at Kadesh which seems to have culminated in the composite picture of all the incidents in the story of that day on the wall at Abu Simbel. If something is lost of the dramatic tension so vigorously portrayed by the craftsmen of Sety I, there is at Abu Simbel a unique attempt to place the different parts of a complicated narrative in factual relationship to one another. Ramesses III produced a less coherent record of his battle against the Sea Peoples and their land forces.[24] The mêlée of hundreds of figures in the sea and land battles on the north wall at Medinet Habu produces chiefly an impression of confused overlapping shapes. The bullock-carts and accoutrements of the foreigners, their ships with high sterns and bird-headed prows[25] contribute the chief points of interest. All these enormous Ramesside compositions are difficult to study, even when they are fairly well preserved, because of the great height at which they are often placed on the walls and the loss of their colour.[26] How much the painting could clarify the confusing outlines of overlapping figures can be seen in a well-preserved block in New York [366] from an unidentified wall re-used in a late Ramesside temple at the mouth of the Asasif near the foot of the Deir el Bahari causeway.[27] It shows a portion of the group of Syrians shot down by the arrows of the king who are lying prostrate under the horses of his chariot.

A secondary result of the influence of painting is to be seen in the way in which the magnificent bulls are partially concealed behind the rushes in the hunting-scene on the back of

366. Fallen Asiatics. Ramesside relief from Deir el Bahari. Dynasty XIX–XX. *New York, Metropolitan Museum of Art*

the projecting part of the south wing of the First Pylon at Medinet Habu [367]. Again the topographical creation of a setting is achieved by carrying down from the main scene the wavy edge of the water to the feet of the archers in the subsidiary register below, who head the row of men attending the king. This rising line approximates the mass of the hill on which the town stands in the battle-scene of Sety I [352]. The transition between the upper and lower divisions of the scene is made both by the reeds which spring from the edge of the water and by the raised bows of the men who direct their arrows towards the bull which has collapsed in the thicket above them. There is here well exemplified, too, a greater plastic quality in the modelling of the sunk relief surfaces which had been especially developed by the sculptors of the reign of Ramesses III. The tendency towards deeper cutting and more boldly swelling surfaces had appeared in the fine sunk reliefs of Sety I and Ramesses II in their temples at Abydos.[28]

We have seen how this had developed in Akhenaten's time. It now reaches its most accomplished and boldest treatment in the finest of the work at Medinet Habu. The old naturalistic impulse, heightened at Amarna, comes out with new force in the obvious concentration of interest in the animals. Even in the more perfunctorily executed chariot group [367] there is an element which can be traced back to the intimate groups of the royal family at Amarna, but which had taken a new turn under Sety I. Ramesses III is no longer aloof from his surroundings, but throws one leg over the front of the chariot in the excitement of the chase. In one of his Karnak reliefs, Sety I had descended from his chariot to engage in hand-to-hand combat with a Libyan[29] who, owing to the exigencies of the composition, had made almost as large as the king himself. So was his compatriot in the adjoining fight, where the king assumes the same stance in his chariot as does Ramesses III at Medinet Habu. Although the king is shown thoroughly in command of the situation, with the enemy limply collapsing or throwing up his arms in a gesture of despair, nonetheless this new conception of the king's status in itself implies a certain vulnerability which underlies the

368. Karnak, the high priest Amenhotep before a statue of Ramesses IX. Dynasty XX

of the now somewhat simplified sunk reliefs were to endure as a characteristic style for a long time, appearing in Dynasty XXV in the Gebel Barkal reliefs of Piankhy, and in the beautiful drawings of a papyrus in the first reign of Dynasty XXVI [387]. A few years after Amenhotep was thus shown before the statue of the king, the high priest Herihor appears along with Ramesses XI as though sharing responsibility for the construction of the Khons Temple at Karnak. He ended by seizing the throne as the first king of Dynasty XXI, although he had to share his rule with Smendes at Tanis in the north.

Although the painting in the Ramesside private tombs was definitely on the decline, they contain many interesting features and a number of minor masterpieces. The chapel of the sculptor Ipy (No. 217) at Deir el Medineh is one of these. It is dated to the reign of Ramesses II by the king's cartouche on a shrine on a boat in the register beneath the little temple [369]. We have had occasion to mention this picture of a peripteral building in connexion with similar structures of Tuthmosid times and the destroyed temple of Amenhotep III at Elephantine. The garden is being irrigated by men raising water from a pool by means of a bucket hanging from the end of a weighted pole (*shaduf*). This lively interlude appears beneath the routine portrayal of the coffin in its shrine, being dragged in the funeral procession. An unpublished photograph taken by the Italian expedition early in this century shows the wall before it suffered later irretrievable damage [369].[31] With it is reproduced the drawing made by N. de G. Davies [370] when only fragments remained. It shows more clearly the dog behind the gardener and is a fine example of that remarkable interpreter's feeling for the character of Egyptian painting. He correctly restored vertical lines for the door-posts instead of the splayed shape given to them in an earlier copy.[32] In the delightful picturing of daily life in this tomb there has survived into early Ramesside times a good deal of the Amarna spirit. The animated toiling figures [371] are treated with a sympathetic humour, as they dry their fish which have been caught in a drag-net between two boats, or trample out the grapes at the vintage. Above, women squat under a booth on the shore beside a grain-ship and barter their produce with the sailors. Behind them several boys herd their goats [372]. One, accompanied by his dog, carries his

high-sounding claims of the historical records of Ramesses II and Ramesses III. It was not to be such a long step to the portrayal of the powerful high priest of Amon, Amenhotep, on the same scale as the king before a statue of Ramesses IX in a manner formerly reserved for great ministers of state [368]. This relief appears on the outer (east) face of the eastern wall connecting Pylons VII and VIII at Karnak.[30] The high priest has the characteristic Ramesside head with protruding skull which appears also in the little figures arranging his dress. This feature and the suave, rather mannered outline

369 and 370. Thebes, tomb of Ipy (No. 217), garden shrine, with detail. Dynasty XIX

371. Thebes, tomb of Ipy (No. 217), fishing and agricultural scene. Dynasty XIX

belongings on a sort of yoke over his shoulders. Another plays the flute, while a third cuts off branches which are too high for the animals to nibble. There is the same impromptu capturing of a pastoral incident as in the Nubian village in the Derr relief [365].

A link between Amarna and the Ramesside interest in genre scenes and topographical detail survives in the paintings of the tomb of Neferhotep (No. 49) of the reign of Ay. The extraordinary representations of the gardens of the temple of Amon at Karnak and of the dispensing of favours in the palace have now grown dim and blackened from misuse.[33] The Amarna 'Window of Appearances' continues here, as it does in Ipy's chapel and elsewhere in the Theban necropolis.[34] We have seen its actual use in the façade of the palace

372. Thebes, tomb of Ipy (No. 217), agricultural scene. Dynasty XIX

373–5. Thebes, tomb of Sennedjem (No. 1), interior, cat and serpent on door jamb, and goddess of the horizon with sun-disk on entrance ceiling. Dynasty XIX

which opened on the first court of the mortuary temples of Ramesses II and III. The love of plant forms and foliage still adds a lighter touch in the old naturalistic-decorative manner here and there in the private tombs amid the growing absorption with the symbolic representation of the underworld. Thus on the end wall of the burial-chamber of Sennedjem (No. 1) at the end of Dynasty XIX [373] a row of fruit trees and palms surmounts a flower-border which might have

graced one of the pavements at Amarna. They accompany the tilling of the fields of Yaru by the owner and his wife in an enlargement of one of the map-like vignettes from the papyrus rolls of the Book of the Dead.[35] Remarkable effects are produced in the treatment of bouquets and garlands or in a composition showing the tree goddess dispensing cool refreshment.[36] There are continued, too, the rich floral friezes and complicated ceiling patterns which have been mentioned already in discussing the elaboration of these designs in the second half of Dynasty XVIII.

The yellow ochre background and the juxtaposition of blue and green in the foliage are characteristic of the new Ramesside colour scheme, but produce a happier effect in the tomb of Ipy (No. 217)[37] than in the later tombs. In general, there is an increasing use of thick black outlines and harsh flat colours against the dull yellow ground. These bold, sometimes very roughly executed paintings, are now to be found mostly in the dark vaulted brick burial-chambers of the cemetery of the artisans' village at Deir el Medineh. Their subject-matter tends to reflect that of the royal tombs somewhat in the same way that the texts and vignettes of the wooden coffins of Middle Kingdom date made available to non-royal persons the spells of the Pyramid Texts which in the Old Kingdom had been intended solely for the protection of the king in the afterworld. The chapel above was usually not very large and was surmounted by a small brick pyramid.[38] Some large Ramesside rock-cut chapels in the old style were, however, still employed in other parts of the Theban necropolis, as well as being used at Deir el Medineh itself.

The burial-chamber of Sennedjem (No. 1) at Deir el Medineh presents a well-preserved cycle of typical paintings in workmanship which is well above the average [373]. It was entered from a shaft in the courtyard in front of the pyramids of the owner and his son.[39] Above the text on the side of the entrance doorway, the sun god Ra in the form of a cat raises a knife to cut off the head of the serpent Apophis, one of the formidable enemies which nightly obstructs the passage of the Sun Bark through the underworld [374]. This broadly conceived symbol of the soul's triumphant progress through obstacles to the fields of Yaru, where a pleasant country life awaits it, receives a naturalistic treatment in the swift, sure strokes with which the cat and the persea tree are sketched in. There is certainly here an extension of the impressionistic manner which the artists of the second half of Dynasty XVIII had sometimes adopted [254, 283]. Even more striking is the diagrammatic rendering which accompanies the owner's prayer on the ceiling of the doorway [375]. The arms of the goddess Nut stretch out from the hieroglyph of the mountain and grasp the sun-disk. Although the prayer is directed to Ra, who shines on his eastern horizon, this particular way of showing the goddess is frequently connected with the Western Mountain, and she is perhaps here receiving the sun into the dark underworld. In other words, we have an abstraction of a sunset rather than a sunrise, with all the implications of the journey of the deceased, like the sun, through the night of the underworld.[40]

A somewhat different evocation of a supernatural being appears in the rock-cut chapel of Nakhtamon (No. 341) behind the Ramesseum, not far from that of the Eighteenth-Dynasty vizier Ramose (No. 55).[41] Above a representation of

376. Thebes, tomb of Nakhtamon (No. 341), winged spirit over Anubis with scales. Dynasty XIX

a Ramesside funeral the dead man and his wife are being led by Horus to the scales, where the heart of the deceased is being weighed against an image of the Goddess of Truth [376]. Anubis kneels, steadying the plummet. Into this conventional judgement scene descends a male spirit. A sense of movement is conveyed by the taut stretching of the widely extended limbs and the four sweeping wings. Even more remarkable are the pale blue streamers that ray out from the body as though to suggest the shimmering atmosphere through which the figure rushes. Nothing quite like this had been attempted before by the painter, although we have seen him trying to portray glowing coals and smoke. In an inscription which was set on the staircase leading out at the back of the Abydos temple of Sety I in the direction of the cenotaph, a beautiful hieroglyph [377] of a similar winged being completes a word which means 'to spread out over' in the sense of the king protecting his people.[42]

Dating to the Ramesside period are small sketches and trial studies on flakes of limestone or other material commonly

377. Abydos, temple of Sety I, hieroglyph of winged figure. Dynasty XX

378. Cat, mouse, and captive. Ostracon. Dynasty XIX. *University of Chicago, Oriental Institute*

379. Baker tending an oven. Ostracon. Dynasty XIX. *Leipzig University, Egyptian Museum*

380. Acrobat-dancer. Ostracon. Dynasty XIX. *Turin, Museo Egizio*

referred to as *ostraca figurés*. In the main these are humorous drawings, as in the fragment showing a captive before a cat and mouse [378], or drawings of small and humble subjects, as in the famous piece in Leipzig showing a baker tending an oven [379], or the Turin dancer [380]. However, a number of royal portraits are known and are presumably studies for or copies from finished official monuments. Several hundred of these *ostraca figurés* have been found and published, many from the site of Deir el Medineh, and they present a rather different picture of the interests of Egyptian draughtsmen from that presented by the tomb-paintings. Illustrated papyri should also be cited at this point. The two-foot-long fragment illustrated here in part [381] represents four cats tending a mouse-queen and her baby. It is not definitely known whether certain scenes on the *ostraca* illustrate popular stories and fables, but it seems likely that this was the case with regard to the scraps of illustrated papyrus [382]. That a vigorous tradition in sketching and free-hand drawing under-lies much of the large-scale, mature, or official art of this period is an important lesson to be learned here.

In 1906 a hoard of silver and gold vessels was found acci-dentally during the removal of earth from the mounds around the temple of the ancient city of Bubastis near modern Zagazig in the Delta. With them was a gold cup inscribed with the name of Queen Tausert, the wife of Sety II who followed Merenptah on the throne towards the end of Dynasty XIX. A second group of precious objects was soon located nearby, including a pair of magnificent bracelets of Ramesses II.[43] The finest piece is a silver jug in Cairo with a gold handle in the form of a goat [383]. A more simply fash-ioned gold animal-handle in Berlin may possibly have belonged to an incomplete silver jug in Cairo, while a third silver vessel in New York has a plain handle joined to the rim by the head of a lion. These three jugs were inscribed with the name of a man who was a Royal Messenger to all Countries, and a panel on the front of each of the two Cairo jugs shows him worshipping a foreign goddess, possibly in one case Anat and in the other Astarte, both of whom were known in New Kingdom Egypt. Instead of the shallow flutings on the New York jug, the body of the two otherwise similar Cairo vessels has vertical lines of overlapping scales with the surface round them beaten out to leave them in relief. These occur again on a gold vase at Berlin, while elliptical protuberances appear similarly on a gold vessel in Cairo. In this case the handle is in the form of a ring fastened on the rim by a figure of a calf with its head turned like the lion on the lid of Tut-ankh-amon's ointment jar [343].

The upper of the two engraved bands round the neck of the Cairo jug with the finely modelled goat-handle [383] has griffins and animals attacking their prey, separated by valuted plants. Below, little figures are engaged in trapping birds and other activities of the marshes. Similar engraved scenes appear on the necks of the other two silver jugs and are worked in repoussé on two bowls in Cairo and New York. The gold vessels are more simply decorated with incised garlands of fruit and flowers. There were also some plain vessels and silver strainers. The outer band of the Cairo bowl has animals and voluted plants similar to those on the neck of the jug [383]. The inner zone on the other hand, with swim-ming girls, a boat, fish, and water-birds, is like the somewhat

381. Cats serving a mouse-queen. Papyrus painting. Dynasty XX (?). *Cairo Museum*

less elaborately ornamented dish from the tomb of King Psusennes at Tanis about a hundred years later in date.

These vessels, as was originally recognized, form a uniform group of the late Nineteenth Dynasty. Although it has been argued that they are of Syrian workmanship,[44] they seem rather to be the products of an Egyptian workshop, in Bubastis itself or in the cosmopolitan atmosphere of one of the other large cities of Lower Egypt, where there must have been many foreigners residing as mercenaries, merchants, and possibly craftsmen. Vessels of precious metals have rarely survived, owing to their intrinsic value, and these form an important bridge between the few earlier examples and the remarkable treasure found at Tanis in the tomb of King Psusennes of Dynasty XXI. They have none of the fanciful quality of the Syrian vases pictured in the last of the paintings of such produce from abroad in the tomb of Imiseba in the reign of Ramesses IX.[45] Nor is there the out-and-out foreign character of the Egyptianizing ivory carvings found abroad such as those from Megiddo and Tell Fara in Palestine of the Ramesside Period.[46] The plants and fighting animals on the jug [383] and the outer band of the Cairo silver[47] plate are obviously derived from designs like those on the ivory reliefs of the chest or the embroidered panels of the tunic of Tut-ankh-amon.[48] Although these are related to the similar designs on one of the two gold bowls from Ugarit (Ras Shamra) which belong to the Amarna-Mitanni Period, the latter show marked deviations from the Egyptian examples.[49] In general the Ras Shamra bowls differ, too, from the few decorated metal vessels known from Egypt in the Eighteenth Dynasty. One of these is a gold bowl with embossed papyrus and fish which, with a similar incomplete silver vessel, belonged to a general of Tuthmosis III.[50] The beautiful bronze bowl from the tomb of Hatiay at Thebes of the early part of the reign of Akhenaten also seems thoroughly Egyptian. The

383. Silver jug with gold handle from Bubastis. Dynasty XIX. *Cairo Museum*

papyrus thicket with animals and birds on its interior is closer to the naturalistic spirit of the paintings of the North Palace at Amarna [284] than it is to the more decorative manner of the ivory panels of Tut-ankh-amon [337].[51] One other fine vessel is known in precious metal, the silver vase in the form of a pomegranate with incised floral garlands from the tomb of Tut-ankh-amon.[52] Plain bronze vessels of various shapes are also known, such as the fine group from the Theban Dynasty XVIII tomb of Kha.[53] This includes a tall-necked carafe which anticipates the shape of a fine gold vessel from Tanis.

The decoration of the Bubastis vessels is derived from the repertoire which had been formed in the second half of the Eighteenth Dynasty and which had acquired a certain international flavour. Since various motifs from this repertoire continued to be used abroad with a considerable amount of free adaptation, it is not surprising that resemblances occur and that a Syrian origin has been suggested for the Tell Basta treasure. We have seen that fluted metal vessels came into

382. Comic papyrus. Dynasty XX–XXI. *London, British Museum*

Egypt as early as the Middle Kingdom with the Tod treasure, and that they are frequently pictured among the Syrian vases in the Eighteenth-Dynasty tomb paintings which resemble the alabaster examples from the tomb of Tut-ankh-amon [343]. Such Ramesside designs as those on the Bubastis vessels were to be a source of inspiration for the Egyptianizing elements in the Phoenician metal bowls[54] and for the relief decorations on faience objects, particularly the lotus cups and bowls which begin to appear in Dynasty XXII and extended at least into the Kushite Period.[55]

PART FIVE

The Later Periods

CHAPTER 20

The Period of Decline: Dynasties XXI–XXII 1085–730 B.C.

The weakening of the royal authority in the latter part of Dynasty XX brought with it a slackening of the large-scale building activities which had been characteristic of Ramesside times. The temple of Khons at Karnak was indeed completed in Dynasty XXI, and the first king of Dynasty XXII, Sheshonq I (950–929 B.C.), constructed the court in front of the Second Pylon of the Temple of Amon. This impressive work included colonnades along the north and south sides and the Bubastite Portal which entered along the southern way of access to the temple between the Second Pylon and the temple of Ramesses III. It was carried out late in the reign, in the king's 21st year, and a triumphal relief on the south face of the wall adjoining the portal on the east commemorated Sheshonq's campaign in Palestine, which occurred in the fifth year of Rehoboam the successor of Solomon.[1] The great First Pylon, never completely finished, was apparently not a part of this project. It may have taken the place of an eastern colonnade with a gateway in its centre on the east-west axis of the temple, where a processional way of sphinxes had been laid out by Ramesses II westwards from the Second Pylon to the temple landing-stage. It has been plausibly argued that the First Pylon was not actually constructed until the Ptolemaic Period [223].[2]

Little else of architectural importance is known for a period of some three hundred and fifty years, until a new stimulus came from the south with the invasion of the Kushite king Piankhy, about 730 B.C. Even then, in Dynasty XXV, royal construction was largely concentrated in the Sudan at the temples of Gebel Barkal, Sanam, and Kawa, and in the pyramid fields of El Kurru and Nuri. The badly ruined condition of the great Delta cities makes it difficult to judge of the additions made to them after Ramesside times. However, the restricted size and poorer workmanship of the tombs of the royal family, which were built inside the enclosure of the temple of Tanis in Dynasties XXI and XXII, betray a considerable impoverishment in comparison to the monuments of their predecessors at Thebes. The fragmentary remains of the other constructions of this time in the Tanis temple[3] show a widespread re-use of earlier materials, as does the equally ruined work of Osorkon II (870–747 B.C.) at Bubastis.[4] There, however, most of the blocks have survived from a large granite gateway between the first and second courts of the temple. These blocks have been fitted together to form one of the most complete versions of the Heb-Sed ceremonies, celebrated in the case of this king in his 22nd year.[5]

A glimpse of the political situation in the first quarter of the eleventh century at the beginning of Dynasty XXI can be gained from the account of Wenamon's mission to Byblos to fetch cedarwood for the bark of Amon.[6] He was sent by Herihor, the high priest of Amon, who was about to assume the crown at Thebes. However, approval of the project and passage to Syria had to be sought from Smendes (Nesu-ba-neb-ded) and his wife Tanetamon who were in control in the north at Tanis. After Herihor's short reign, Smendes was recognized as king throughout Egypt, as was his successor Psusennes I (Pasebkhanu). Thus the Tanite royal house of Dynasty XXI was founded, although the high priests of Amon who succeeded Herihor at Thebes maintained a considerable measure of independence and on occasion assumed royal titles. They are generally termed priest kings, but their line did not originate from among the clergy of Amon. Herihor's rise seems rather to have resulted from an attempt to absorb the power of the Amon priesthood as represented by the influential Amenhotep [368] and to utilize its revenues from taxation which had been diverted from the state to the temple. Herihor had been a military man who assumed the position of high priest as he did that of commander-in-chief and viceroy of Kush. He in turn appointed his son to these key positions.

The administration of the Sudan had been maintained throughout the Ramesside Period and seems to have continued into Dynasty XXII, although the title of viceroy of Kush disappears at the beginning of Dynasty XXI, the son of Herihor being the last man to hold it. The control of the resources of Kush, particularly the gold, was vital at this time. The economic inflation of Late Ramesside times, evinced by the alarming rise in grain prices, had been in no small part due to the cutting off of Egypt's source of silver through the collapse of the Hittite Empire under pressure from the Sea Peoples. It was the period also when bronze was being replaced by iron, a metal which Egypt could only obtain from abroad. Strikes of the unpaid workmen working on the Theban necropolis had begun even under Ramesses III, while the records of investigations into fraudulent dealing in grain and the even more shocking robberies in the royal tombs betray the prevailing corruption and political instability.[7] It is clear how dependent Egypt had become upon her foreign relations. From the Wenamon account it appears that, while these economic adjustments were being made, Tanis was still keeping up a lively sea trade with Syria even though Egyptian prestige was low. It is significant, too, of the generally amicable relations between the two parts of the country, in a period when the rule was frequently divided between the Delta and Thebes, that it was Smendes who forwarded payment for the timber and arranged for its shipment when Wenamon finally succeeded in obtaining it from the prince of Byblos, Zakar-baal. The rude treatment which Wenamon received in the ports of Palestine and Syria or from the inhabitants of Cyprus, when he was cast up on the shore there after a storm, was an unpleasant indication of the changed times, as were the hostile ships of the Theker who had settled with the Philistines along the Palestine coast. On the other hand, the recollection of Egypt's former power is still explicit in Zakar-baal's vehement insistence that he was not a servant of the ruler of Egypt, or his remarkable statement that Amon had founded all lands, but Egypt first of all, and that it was from there that skill and learning had come to the place where he was (that is to Byblos).

It was not until about 900 B.C. that Assyria recovered from a period of depression and began to move westward. For a century before this, Aramaean tribesmen had been pushing out of the desert into northern Syria, where they occupied several of the city-states which had grown up in place of the former vassals of the now vanished Hittite Empire. In Palestine the consolidation of the kingdom of Israel by David in the first half of the tenth century led to the destruction of Philistine power along the coast. This probably contributed to the prosperity of Phoenician Tyre and Sidon. Towards the end of the Twenty-first Dynasty, at about the middle of the tenth century B.C., one of the Tanite kings seems to have interfered in Palestine. We are told in the Bible that he took Gezer and gave it as a dowry to his daughter who was married to Solomon.[8] Sheshonq's campaign in Palestine, about 930 B.C., after the death of Solomon, brought about a renewal of Egyptian prestige which was to have serious consequences in the future; for it was not backed by sufficient strength when that was needed against Assyria.

Sheshonq I came from a family of Libyan extraction that had grown powerful in Heracleopolis. He made Bubastis the royal residence of Dynasty XXII. Several of the kings were, however, buried beside their predecessors of the previous dynasty inside the enclosure of the temple of Tanis. A unified country was maintained for the first half of the two hundred years in which the dynasty endured (950–730 B.C.) by appointing a member of the royal family as high priest of Amon at Thebes. However, in the reign of Takelot II (847–823 B.C.) civil war broke out in Thebes and spread to the rest of the country. Not long afterwards a rival Dynasty XXIII was set up which ran parallel to that of Bubastis for some eighty years until the Kushite invasion from the Sudan. At the end of this time a number of other rulers had established themselves so that the country, particularly in the Delta, was reminiscent of the small provincial segments into which it had fallen in the First and Second Intermediate Periods. The Assyrians had continued steadily to encroach upon Syria and Palestine after the defeat of a coalition at Karkar by Shalmaneser III in 853. The danger must have been evident, and Tef-nekht of Sais succeeded in bringing the petty rulers of the Delta into some sort of union about 730 B.C. under the brief Dynasty XXIV, which consisted only of that Saite king and his son Bakenrenef, who was known to the Greeks as Bocchoris. The success of this union, which was spreading into Upper Egypt, aroused the Kushite king Piankhy into invading Egypt. This successor of Kashta, the origins of whose Egyptianized family have been much discussed, had been quietly gaining strength at Napata in the Sudan while conditions in Egypt itself worsened.

The surprising wealth of objects made from precious materials which survived plundering in the tomb of Psusennes I at Tanis maintain the high level of craftsmanship of the New Kingdom.[9] The gold mask [384] comes from the rich burial of General Wenw-djebaw-n-djedet, one of two companions-at-arms of Psusennes who were laid to rest in the side chambers of the king's tomb. Its peculiar cast of features, partly due to the angle of the projecting ears and partly to the bold modelling of the straight nose and sensuous lips, is more distinctive than the king's own gold mask.[10] The latter is conventionally reminiscent of the New Kingdom, as is the gilded wood mask of King Amenemipet of Dynasty XXI and the better modelled gold mask of the otherwise unknown Dynasty XXII king Heqa-kheperra-Sheshonq.[11]

The burials of both these kings were later inserted in the Psusennes tomb. Sheshonq's falcon-headed outer coffin was of silver. A finely worked pectoral of this king [385] shows two winged goddesses protecting the sun's disk in a bark. Inside the disk the Goddess of Truth praises Amon-Ra-Horakhte. The inlays, which are partly lapis lazuli, are predominantly blue against their gold setting, with a touch of red in the disks on the heads of the goddesses and the flower of the voluted plant of the south which forms the frame on the left and matches the papyrus on the right. The general character of the design and the rather heavily rounded projection of the gold parts suggest the style of the Egyptianizing Phoenician ivories which began to appear contemporaneously in the ninth century[12] and for which such jewellery may have served as a model. Another remarkable object which has a related group of decorative patterns in a similar style is the huge tinted-leather funerary canopy of Isit-m-kheb from the Deir el Bahari cache[13] where in Dynasty XXI the bodies of many of the New Kingdom pharaohs were collected for re-burial with members of the families of the priest kings of Thebes. A silver bowl with girls swimming among fish and water-plants is part of a remarkable group of vessels of gold and silver which belonged to Wenw-djebaw-n-djedet. It has been mentioned as continuing the type of the Ramesside bowl from the Bubastis treasure. These vessels from the tomb of Psusennes would seem to have provided a source of inspiration for the Phoenician metal bowls just as other designs influenced the ivories. The Tanis objects provide ample material to suggest the source of a new stimulus upon work in Palestine and Syria in the second half of the tenth century and in the ninth, when contacts are known to have been close. One of the most beautiful vessels which formed part of Psusennes's own equipment is at the same time the simplest. It is a tall-necked gold vase with a papyrus design around the flaring mouth and the king's cartouches incised on the shoulder.

The most original contribution to the sculpture of the period of Dynasties XXI–XXII was in a form connected with the fine metalwork from Tanis. Bronze statues began to be inlaid with complicated patterns of more precious metal. The largest of these ($27\frac{1}{8}$ inches high, 69 cm) probably belongs to the end of the period or a little later. It is the statuette of the lady Takushit in the Athens Museum [386], said to have been found at Bubastis. It has been assigned to the Kushite period, around 700 B.C.[14] The sturdy body and full face framed with heavy curls have an earthy, peasant quality which appears in other sculpture of Dynasty XXV. The body and arms are covered with processions of gods and sacred emblems inlaid with silver as though to represent a figured robe. This is the most elaborate use of such inlaid patterns which has been preserved, and since the technique is known from other pieces to have been highly developed in Dynasty XXII it is not impossible that the Takushit statuette may belong to Bubastite times, as Maspero originally suggested.[15] The slender, more graceful figure of Queen Karomama, the wife of Takelot II, in the Louvre, presents a different aspect.[16] The treatment of face and body, as well as the flaring pleated

385. Pectoral from Tanis. Dynasty XXII. *Cairo Museum*

386. Takushit. Inlaid bronze statuette from Bubastis. Dynasty XXII–XXV. *Athens Museum*

sleeves of her dress, are more in the Ramesside tradition. The designs of the broad collar were inlaid with gold, silver, and electrum. Most of the precious metal has been lost from the feathers of the wings which are folded about the lower part of the body, and only traces remain of the gold leaf which once covered the face and arms. Much simpler than the tapestry of figures which covers the dress of Takushit are the few sacred emblems inlaid in gold on the torso of a smaller standing bronze figure of Osorkon I which was found in the Delta near Tell el Yahudiyeh.[17] Such inlaying of bronzes with precious materials was to continue in late times in Egypt, but is preserved only in minor objects which are hardly comparable to these three fine pieces. Composite use of metals in sculpture is perhaps reflected in the large Kushite royal statues, where roughened surfaces were left for the gilding of bracelets, anklets, and necklaces.

The disillusionment of the times between the last Ramesside kings and the coming of the Ethiopians from Kush is bitingly illustrated by the satirical drawings which appear in the papyri. These take the form of mocking at the foibles of human beings by putting them into the guise of animals. They are closely related to the sketches on flakes of limestone which have been recovered in such quantity from the artisans' village at Deir el Medineh in Dynasties XIX–XX,[18] and the satirical papyri are perhaps to be dated to the latter part of this period rather than to Tanite and Bubastite times. However, the fine quality of their drawing is also comparable to such funerary papyri as that of the princess Maat-ka-ra of Dynasty XXI,[19] and we shall see that paintings in this New Kingdom style continued down into the early Saite Period [387].

There had always been a tendency to portray animals with a somewhat humorous touch, just as the artist had sometimes exaggerated the fatness or leanness of his peasant types or the grotesqueness of foreigners. A playful element certainly

384. Gold mask from Tanis. Dynasty XXI. *Cairo Museum*

appeared here and there throughout Egyptian art, and it was emphasized at Amarna and in a few tomb-paintings of the early Ramesside Period [371, 372]. The real satire of these new representations is in a much more developed vein and seems to follow naturally upon the social disintegration of the latter part of Dynasty XX. There is something of the same reversal of the values of normal life as had appeared in the literature inspired by the disruption of society at the end of the Old Kingdom in such works as the Lamentations of Ipuwer.[20] The surviving manuscript of this early text is a copy that was made in the Nineteenth or Twentieth Dynasties, so that it must have been familiar at this time as a literary work. The idea of the cats attending a mouse dressed as a great lady [381] is in somewhat the same spirit as the sayings of Ipuwer concerning the owners of robes who are now in rags, while the one who never wove for himself has fine linen, or the woman who once looked at her face in the water, but now has a mirror. The chief difference is that in the more sophisticated late times a means has been found to point the irony of the thought and to express it pictorially. In the portion of this Cairo papyrus[21] [381], a cat with a side-lock fastened on with a pin is dressing the hair of a seated mouse in a fashionable

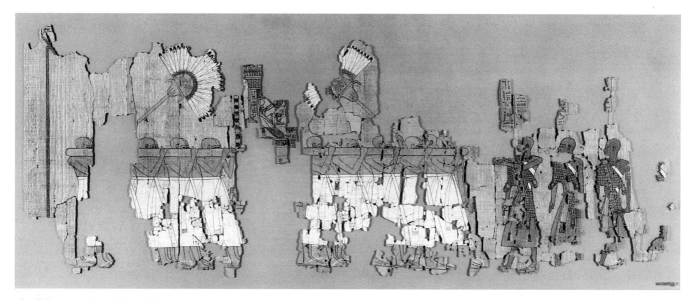

387. Priests carrying a shrine of Amon. Fragment of a Saite papyrus. Dynasty
XXVI. *Brooklyn Museum*

thin robe who raises a wine-glass to her lips. A cat nurse
follows with a baby mouse. The fan or sunshade carried by a
third cat is painted blue. The smooth coats of the mice are
coloured grey, and fine brushstrokes indicate the fur on the
yellowish buff bodies of the cats. The wig of the lady mouse
is black, and her dress and the underparts of the cats are
painted white. There are also touches of red. It is clear, then,
that this is treated as painting and is not just a drawing in line.
Similar but apparently less fine work appears in the extraordinary papyrus in Turin,[22] and somewhat rougher drawing
and washes of colour are to be found on a third example in the
British Museum [382].

Among the many amusing animal groups of the Turin
papyrus is a parody of one of the Ramesside battle-scenes
with a mouse king in a chariot attacking a fortress manned by
cats. The vigorous drawings of the British Museum papyrus

[382] again show a mouse attended by cats, wolves herding
goats (compare the Ramesside painting in the tomb of Ipy
[372]), and a cat tending geese. A lion plays at draughts with
a gazelle, while a bird beside a basket of fruit under a tree is
probably part of a scene similar to that in the Turin papyrus,
where a black bird climbs a ladder to reach a hippopotamus in
a fig tree.

No texts have survived for which these animal groups
might have served as illustration. Only a few scraps of writing
appear above some of the figures, and there are a few short
labels in the erotic portion of the Turin papyrus, which is
separated from the animals by a vertical line.[23] Whether
columns of text preceded or followed the drawings can
apparently not be determined from what has been preserved
of the satirical papyri. Such texts do occur in a recently
identified papyrus of non-funerary character. Part of the

388. Women mourners. Coffin painting from Thebes (detail). Dynasty XXII.
Berlin Museum

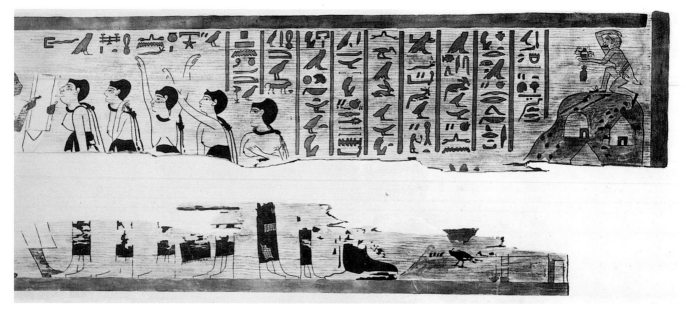

painting which illustrates them shows priests carrying a shrine of Amon [387]. This accompanies an account of an oracle which occurred at Karnak in the 14th year of Psamtik I at the beginning of the Saite Period. Listed among the witnesses to this event are a number of men who were known to have been prominent at Thebes in the last days of Kushite rule, including Mentuemhat, the governor at the time of the Assyrian invasion.[24] The name of the Kushite king Taharqa appears beside the shrine. Thus there is now evidence that a fine tradition in painting continued at least into the second half of the seventh century. Quite as remarkable as the beauty of the drawing is the persistence of the Ramesside style here, particularly in the long shaven skulls of the priests, which are unlike the round-headed type introduced in Kushite reliefs and statues. However, a procession of priests carrying a sacred barque was carved in sunk relief in a strikingly similar style nearly a hundred years earlier on a wall of the first court of the temple of Amon at Gebel Barkal in the Sudan, just after Piankhy had conquered Egypt.[25] This is clear if one compares the man holding out an incense burner before the first bearer of one of the bark poles with the figures in the Brooklyn papyrus [387].

The virtual disappearance of wall-paintings in the Theban tombs certainly speaks for a decline in monumental painting, but a few examples of fine workmanship have survived which help to bridge the gap between Ramesside times and the Brooklyn papyrus of the beginning of the Saite Period. A group of tombs of Dynasty XXII behind the Ramesseum at Thebes produced some fragmentary wall-paintings of fine quality which have certain points in common with both the Piankhy relief and the Brooklyn papyrus.[26] There was an even more remarkable series of paintings on a wooden coffin[27] from one of these tombs. The lector priest with a feather in his headband who leads the funeral procession to the left of the wailing women is remarkably like one of the figures on a fragment of the Brooklyn papyrus. Even more interesting than this further example of the continuation of the Ramesside style are the freely drawn poses of the women mourners [388]. They stand in front of the necropolis hillside on top of which is an impressive figure of a kneeling bald-headed man. The attempt to represent the tombs naturalistically on the rocky slope is paralleled by a remarkable cemetery landscape on the lower part of a fine painted stela in Cairo.[28]

CHAPTER 21

The Kushite and Saite Revival and the End of Dynastic Egypt 730–332 B.C.

At Gebel Barkal, the Holy Mountain of Napata, the Kushite capital in the Sudan, King Piankhy repaired the New Kingdom temple of Amon (B 500) and enlarged it with a big columned hall. To this a colonnaded forecourt and front pylon were added after the conquest of Egypt about 730 B.C.[1] One looks down from the great rock mass of the Gebel Barkal upon the impressive remains of this building with the partly reconstructed New Kingdom rooms in the foreground [389]. Beyond the three chambers of the sanctuary is a room which was rebuilt by Taharqa for his inscribed grey granite altar [392] which was perhaps a support for the bark of Amon. This can still be seen in place, as can a broader black granite platform, possibly the base for a shrine, which Piankhy had placed in a side room that he constructed earlier on the right. On the other side of the hall, with two rows of columns which had formed the front part of the New Kingdom temple, lies Piankhy's large columned hall, the badly preserved second pylon, and the first court which appears encumbered with mud-brick huts built there after the temple had fallen into disuse. At this stage of the excavations, the ram-sphinxes of Amenhotep III, brought from Soleb, had not yet been cleared in front of the first pylon. Others stood in front of the second pylon with various pieces of sculpture brought here by Piankhy, who apparently had no craftsmen who could make large statues, although they were able to carve the excellent reliefs on the walls of this forecourt [391]. Here he set up his triumphal stela and that of Tuthmosis III, which was brought from another New Kingdom temple at this site. Other stelae were added later. Neither of Piankhy's immediate successors, Shabako or Shebitku, has left any monuments at Gebel Barkal, although their rich burial equipment was found at El Kurru, and some construction has survived from the reign of Shabako at Thebes. However, Taharqa (690–664 B.C.) set up the first and finest [395, 396] of a series of ten large statues in this court. Tanwetamani, the last Kushite ruler of Egypt, added two more of these, and the others were made by kings of the Second Napatan Kingdom over a period of nearly a hundred years until the time of Aspelta in the first half of the sixth century B.C.

The granite stela of Piankhy in the Cairo Museum which records his conquest of Egypt was found in the first court of the Amon temple by an Egyptian officer in 1862.[2] The right side of the scene at the top shows the submission of the various rulers of Egypt [390]. King Namlot of Hermopolis is leading a horse, while, below, other princes prostrate themselves before Piankhy. The Kushite conqueror tells us in the text of his anger at finding that the horses in Namlot's stables had been starved during the siege of Hermopolis. Piankhy carried his love of horses to the point of burying his favourite animals with all their trappings beside his tomb at El Kurru. It is not surprising, then, that one of the truly individual contributions of Kushite art should be the procession of men leading horses which was carved on the left (west) side wall of the court as one entered through the first pylon [391].

The animals have the same long-legged rangy form as does the smaller horse of Namlot on the granite stela. The men are portrayed with the round heads that now begin to appear in Kushite reliefs and statues, and the style of the sunk relief has a different character from the more smoothly treated Ramesside manner of the priest censing the bark on the opposite wall. There is here a strain of brutal realism which is to be found in other reliefs and in the statues. The procession of horses evidently followed a group of princes making obeisance, as on the stela. The back of the bowing prince of Mendes was all that survived, with part of his titles. A loose block from the upper part of the wall bore the name of the ruler of Heracleopolis.

A new emphasis upon anatomical detail, stylized in a peculiar way which is suggestive of the treatment of muscles in contemporary Assyrian reliefs, is found already in the arms and legs of the figure of Piankhy's successor, Shabako, who performs a purification rite before the god on the side of a granite naos from Esna in Cairo.[3] It is particularly evident in the torso and leg-muscles of the figures of Taharqa holding up the star-studded emblem of the heavens on the side of his grey granite altar in Temple B 500 at Gebel Barkal [392]. The finest modelling of this sort, with very slight gradations of surface in the sunk relief, is to be seen in the better-designed groups of figures on the similar altar of Atlanersa from Temple B 700, in Boston [393]. Here, a dozen or so years after the Kushites had been expelled from Egypt by the Assyrians, Atlanersa, who now ruled only the Sudan, still chose to employ the old symbolism of a United Egypt which went back to the time of the joining of the two lands at the beginning of the First Dynasty. With both hands the king supports the sky-sign while standing on a platform formed by the emblem of union. The falcon-headed Horus and the ibis Thoth, representing respectively northern and southern Egypt, draw taut the stems of the papyrus and the southern plant to bind the two halves of the country together. Nothing could illustrate more clearly the continued acceptance of Egyptian thought at Napata or the availability to Atlanersa of a particularly fine craftsman, who must have been an Egyptian like his predecessors who had executed the best of the earlier Kushite reliefs and statues. The muscles of the king's arms and legs, as well as those of the torsos and legs of the gods, have received pronounced attention. The modelling of the knees shows a similar stylization of bone and muscles to that employed on the large royal statues, as in that of Taharqa [395]. While, as has been remarked, there is a certain resemblance to the modelling of muscles in Assyrian reliefs, it is hardly possible that an Egyptian sculptor could have examined the decoration of the royal palaces in Assyria itself. It is more probable that a similar interest in portraying muscular strength arose simultaneously in two vigorous peoples.

Somewhat more crudely executed sunk reliefs, in the style of Piankhy's triumphal scene at Gebel Barkal, are to be found

389. Gebel Barkal, temple of Amon. Dynasty XXV

391. Gebel Barkal, temple of Amon, Piankhy (Piye) relief of men leading horses. Dynasty XXV

at Sanam across the river in a temple erected by Taharqa.[4] The men riding donkeys as well as driving chariots and six-wheeled carts must have formed part of an unusual scene which one could wish to be more fully preserved. Taharqa's temple at Sanam and another which he constructed at Kawa[5] were somewhat simpler versions of Piankhy's structure at Gebel Barkal, but the Kawa temple was much finer in detail. Taharqa had brought here exceptionally able sculptors who must have belonged to the workshops which produced the remarkable reliefs in the Theban tombs of officials of the reign of Taharqa and the beginning of Dynasty XXVI. They

decorated the walls of the Hypostyle Hall with bold raised reliefs which are comparable to those in the tombs of Mentuemhat and Pabasa [394] except that the subtleties of modelling which could be achieved in the Theban limestone were not possible in the sandstone used here.[6] However, although only the lower parts of elaborate garments like those of Pabasa [394] are preserved on the Taharqa reliefs, there must have been something similar to the modelling of the shoulder and arm under the projecting parts of a thin pleated linen robe or shawl; for this was copied much later in the Meroitic reliefs of Temple B at Kawa.[7] The raised relief of the shrine at the back of the temple[8] shows the less distinguished, simpler, broad style of the Kushite reliefs in sandstone at Thebes, as in the Medinet Habu chapel of Kashta's daughter, Amenirdis.[9] This lady, whose fine alabaster statuette in the Cairo Museum was found by Mariette at Karnak,[10] was the sister of Shabako. She was established by Piankhy at Thebes as Divine Consort of Amon, through adoption by her predecessor Shepenwepet I, the daughter of Osorkon III. This practice was continued,

390. Submission of Egyptian rulers. Piankhy (Piye) stela (top) from the temple of Amon at Gebel Barkal. Dynasty XXV. *Cairo Museum*

392. Gebel Barkal, temple of Amon, altar of Taharqa. Dynasty XXV

393. Altar of Atlanersa, 653–643 B.C., from Temple B700 at Gebel Barkal.
Boston, Museum of Fine Arts

and Psamtik I, the first king of Dynasty XXVI, sent his daughter, Nitocris, from Sais to Thebes to be adopted by Piankhy's daughter, Shepenwepet II,[11] after the Assyrians had left Egypt and order had been restored. The establishment of this female line of Votaresses and Divine Consorts of Amon had finally eliminated the temporal power of the High Priest of Amon, who no longer assumes any political role. Mentuemhat, the powerful official of Taharqa, who survived the Assyrian attack as governor of Thebes and Upper Egypt, was only Fourth Priest of Amon.

On the back of the pylon of Taharqa's temple at Kawa, under a colonnade of palm columns reminiscent of the Fifth-Dynasty funerary temple of Sahura at Abusir, are carved sunk reliefs which reproduce the Old Kingdom version of the king as a sphinx trampling on his enemies, as it is found in the temples of Sahura, Ne-user-ra, and Pepy II. They even show the family of the conquered Libyan chieftain with the same names of the wife and two sons which in Dynasty VI were copied from Sahura's representation by Pepy II.[12] The reliefs in the tiled chamber under the Step Pyramid of Zoser were copied in Saite times, since they are covered with a network of squared lines which make use of the later canon of proportions introduced at about this time.[13] The study of these reliefs may even have been undertaken in connexion with the carving of the Heb-Sed scenes on a gateway found at Memphis in the palace of Apries, the fourth king of Dynasty XXVI. These draw upon earlier sources to such an extent that they were long ascribed to the Twelfth Dynasty and even to the time of Zoser himself, when his Step Pyramid sculpture first became known.[14] At Thebes in tomb 36, Iby, the steward of Nitocris, seems to have copied some of the scenes in an Old Kingdom tomb of a namesake of his.[15] The use of Old Kingdom royal models at Kawa is the most striking and one of the earliest of these examples of the archaizing spirit of late times. This diligent search for ancient models in literature and art was responsible for the revival of the use of the Pyramid Texts and caused Shabako to transfer to a granite stela an old text known as the Memphite Theology which deals with the creation of all things by the god Ptah.[16]

Taharqa undertook the building of monuments at Thebes, the best known of which has long been the single column which remained standing of the five pairs with open papyrus capitals that lined the central axis of the First Court at Karnak [223]. He erected similar colonnades or kiosks at the eastern

394. Thebes, tomb of Pabasa (No. 279), Pabasa and attendant. Dynasty XXVI

approach to the temple and in front of the Monthu Temple on the north, as well as one which served as an approach to the Pylon of Ramesses II at the Luxor Temple.[17] His huge black granite statue from Gebel Barkal, which is a little over 12 feet high (3.6 m) [395, 396], and the remarkable Cairo head [397, 398] from a slightly smaller figure[18] are the most impressive pieces of royal sculpture to survive from Dynasty XXV. The heads are similar, but that of the Barkal statue seems more smoothly and conventionally worked, lacking the forceful modelling of the Cairo piece and suggesting less the attempt at portraiture which one feels in the latter. The profile view of the Cairo Taharqa shows well the characteristic round Kushite skull. The hair is treated as though it were a padded covering to protect the head under the peculiar cap-like base of the crown which supported the tall plumes that are preserved on the Barkal statue. The discovery of the bases of three other large statues of Taharqa is a sharp reminder of the quick reversals of fortune which occurred in this period of the collapse of empires, for they were found in a gateway at Nineveh, probably carried off by Esarhaddon when he drove Taharqa out of Memphis in 671 B.C.[19] It was on his way back from this campaign that the Assyrian king set up a stela at Sinjirli in northern Syria, on which a Kushite with the uraeus on his forehead is portrayed kneeling before him. Perhaps this was Ushanahuru, the heir apparent, rather than Taharqa himself; for this prince and the queen are mentioned in the text as having been captured with the palace treasure at Memphis. On his rock-carving at the Dog River near Beyrut, Esarhaddon adds the interesting information that goldsmiths and cabinet-makers were among the persons and booty which he seized, although no mention is made of statues being carried away.[20] Taharqa had retired into the south, but returned soon after the departure of Esarhaddon. He was

defeated again in the Delta by the army which Ashurbanipal sent to Egypt in 667 B.C. Taharqa's successor, Tanwetamani, provoked Ashurbanipal's forces into invading Upper Egypt with the ensuing sack of Thebes in 663. This brought Kushite rule over Egypt to an end. It was not long before the Assyrian Empire in its turn suffered sudden collapse. Taharqa's statues were almost completely destroyed by the fire which raged through Nineveh when it fell in 612 B.C. to the combined forces of the Babylonians and the Medes.

We have come close to the time of the first contact of the Ionian Greeks with Egypt. The rise of Sais was evidently in great part due to the shift in foreign trade away from Tanis to the western Canopic branch of the Nile. Naucratis, which lay on the river a little north of Sais, was apparently not founded until towards the end of the seventh century B.C. Under the later Saite kings all Greek shipping was confined to this port, which was given special privileges as a foreign settlement. However, even as early as the time of Tef-nekht, the first seafaring Ionian traders may already have entered the river here in competition with the Phoenician merchants who had long been doing a profitable business with Tanis. The successor of Tef-nekht, Bakenrenef, was known to the Greeks as Bocchoris. They told stories of him as a law-giver who was captured and burned alive by the Ethiopian Shabako. In fact Sais regained its independence under Piankhy's loose control of the Delta and seems to have continued prosperous, ruled by these two kings of Dynasty XXIV, until Shabako finally seized the city about 715 B.C. Nevertheless, the Assyrians found a prince named Necho ruling this part of the Delta and left him as their representative in Sais. His son, Psamtik I, succeeded in regaining Egypt's independence when Ashurbanipal was faced with civil war in Babylonia and the pressure of a new movement of peoples along his northern borders.

395 and 396. Taharqa. Granite statue, with detail of head, from Gebel Barkal. Dynasty XXV. *Khartum Museum*

Considering the legends concerning Bocchoris it is odd that a vase [399] bearing his name should have been found in an Etruscan tomb at Tarquinia.[21] Its decoration has much in common with the beautiful but fragmentary ivories discovered in Shabako's tomb at El Kurru[22] [400]. Both make use of the papyrus plant and palms with hanging bunches of fruit. In the case of the Tarquinia vase the papyrus provides an appropriate setting of the Delta swamps for the goddess Neith of Sais and the other gods in whose company the king is shown in the upper register. The palm trees with monkeys had been a favourite decorative motif in the minor arts of the New Kingdom, but here they also suggest a suitable locale for the bound prisoners. It is ironic, in view of Shabako's subsequent triumph over Bocchoris, that these should be

Kushites, but the craftsman was following an age-old tradition of representing these as a subject people. On the Kurru ivories the men who lead the ostrich or bring offerings of other birds and animals are thoroughly Egyptian. In fact these processions of figures are derived, like others in the so-called neo-Memphite reliefs, from Old Kingdom tombs, with the addition of certain picturesque details drawn from New Kingdom sources. Perhaps the most interesting stylistic feature of the vase is the modelling of the muscles, which is like that which we have seen in Kushite reliefs but which does not appear in the more delicate carving of the ivories.[23] This tall jar with a shoulder (about 8 inches high, 20 cm) is the largest of the faience vessels with raised relief decoration to which reference has been made, and which with the Shabako

397 and 398. Taharqa. Front and side views of head. Dynasty XXV. *Cairo Museum*

and Shebitku ivories provide another series of Egyptian designs which could have been drawn upon by the makers of the Phoenician metal bowls, ivories, and other small decorated objects which had such a widely extended range in the Mediterranean and western Asia.

In the working of metals a high standard of skill continued to be maintained. The material has largely been recovered from the Sudan, where the Napatan kings and their successors at Meroë continued to control the output of the gold-mines. The shape and the workmanship of the gold vase of Aspelta (563–568 B.C.) is so thoroughly in the classic Egyptian tradition [401] that one would not have been surprised to find it among the handsome objects in the tomb of Psusennes nearly 500 years earlier. A gilded silver mirror-handle from the tomb of Shabako at El Kurru employs again the palm column, but makes a most unusual use of the figures of goddesses encircling the shaft [402].[24] It seems probable that some earlier object of this sort provided the model for the ninth-century Phoenician ivory fan-handle found in the Assyrian palace of Nimrud.[25] One of the most attractive examples of gold working of this period is the handle of a dish [403] which makes effective use of the voluted plant form. Here, as in the Eighteenth Dynasty,[26] the base of the palmette is clearly derived from the papyrus. This gold handle is not from the Sudan, but was found at Daphnae (Tell Defenneh), the fortress on the eastern edge of the Delta where Psamtik I had established his Ionian and Carian mercenaries as frontier guards. The fort was probably destroyed during the invasion of Cambyses,[27] although Herodotus tells us that Amasis withdrew the foreign garrison to Memphis.

These designs on minor objects stress how firmly Egypt continued to hold to her old traditions in a changing world.

399. Bocchoris with gods and goddesses. Design on a vase from Tarquinia

400. Ostrich. Ivory carving of Shabako from El Kurru. Dynasty XXV

401. Gold vase of Aspelta, 593–568 B.C. *Boston, Museum of Fine Arts*

It is extraordinary how little the monuments reflect the turbulence of the times, except perhaps in some instance like the erasure of the names of Kushite rulers by Psamtik II (594–588 B.C.), when he broke off the peaceful relations with the south that had continued through the first two reigns of Dynasty XXVI and undertook a campaign into Kush. Certainly Egypt enjoyed a considerable degree of internal stability and prosperity under the Saite kings in spite of the small measure of success achieved in attempting to regain a strong position in the Levant. A series of military reversals followed the invasion of Palestine by Necho (609–594 B.C.) after the fall of Nineveh in 612 B.C. Apries (588–568 B.C.) was able to do nothing to prevent the taking of Jerusalem by the Babylonians. Nor did Lydia derive much benefit from its alliance with Egypt. During the early part of his long reign (568–526 B.C.), Amasis was able to control Cyprus briefly by means of his fleet, but in spite of his friendship with Polycrates of Samos and with Croesus he could give no real help to Lydia against the swift rise of Persian power. When Babylon fell to Cyrus in 539 B.C., Amasis must have felt that he could expect the next blow. Actually it was shortly after his death that Psamtik III was overwhelmed by Cambyses in 525 B.C.

The brief Assyrian occupation had left little or no mark upon Egyptian art, although the same cannot be said for the much longer Persian domination which lasted, with only a short interlude of independence, down to the conquest by Alexander in 332 B.C. It is perhaps not surprising that the Greeks who were actively present in the country as merchants and soldier adventurers should have produced little effect

402. Goddesses and palm column. Gilded silver mirror-handle of Shabako from El Kurru. Dynasty XXV. *Boston, Museum of Fine Arts*

403. Gold handle of dish from Daphnae. Dynasty XXVI. *Boston, Museum of Fine Arts*

upon an old civilization. To begin with, in Saite times there was probably more to be learned from Egypt than they could contribute themselves. It is nonetheless astonishing how little Egyptian culture was visibly affected by contact with the Greeks over some four hundred years from the time when Tef-nekht was driven into the Delta swamps by Piankhy to that of the founding of Alexandria.

Egypt was to prove extraordinarily resistant to Hellenic conceptions of art, even under the Ptolemies. The outward appearance of Archaic Greek work of the sixth century had perhaps not developed sufficiently for its new spirit to be evident to the Egyptian who was not responsive and in fact never proved capable of assimilating forms which were opposed to his own. Some of this work must have been accessible, even outside the settlement at Naucratis which had its own architecture and sculpture, as did Greek colonies elsewhere in the Mediterranean which maintained their specifically Hellenic character. At least one Archaic statue has been found at Memphis, which resembles the maidens of the Acropolis, but is of coarser local workmanship. It has been attributed to the last quarter of the sixth century at the end of the Saite period.[28] However, as we shall see, it was only the sense of depth and volume conveyed by the fully developed Greek art of the fifth and fourth centuries B.C. that finally had an effect upon Egyptian sculpture, although this was to be sporadic and largely superficial.

The revival of Egyptian art soon before Dynasty XXV was, then, part of a resurgence of the Egyptian spirit which, without any real modification from abroad, was stimulated by the vigorous Kushite rulers who had close religious ties with Thebes and a long tradition of Egyptian civilization. We have seen, in examining the royal work in the Sudan, that an attempt to reduplicate Old Kingdom models went side by side with a continuance of the Ramesside style and a new hard realism. The last seems to have been a concession to the taste of the Kushite conqueror on the part of the Egyptian artist whose fundamentally naturalistic instincts would have responded readily enough. There has been a tendency to overstress the copying of the forms of the pyramid age in Saite times, although it has long been pointed out that the artists drew upon the Middle and New Kingdoms as well. These various factors resulted in a perplexing diversity of forms which continued along parallel lines down into Ptolemaic times both in statues and reliefs. The portrait sculpture of the beginning of the Saite Period at Thebes achieved a masterly integration of the component parts. We have seen such a portrait already in Dynasty XXV in the Cairo head of Taharqa [397, 398]. Only a few of these extraordinary pieces have survived in the midst of a far greater body of less distinguished works. However, enough minor examples exist to show an interest in such realistic portraiture which continued to make itself felt over a long period of time both in sculpture in the round and in relief.[29] We shall see that only one statue out of a group may have such a portrait head, while the rest are conventionally lacking in individuality. This combined with the fact that there are still only a limited number of examples for which the date is firmly fixed makes it impossible yet to trace the steps in the manifestation of this tendency of late times towards individualistic representation.

In the north, where the court now resided at Sais, in the other great cities of the Delta, and at Memphis, the complexity of forms remains too great for one to be able to speak of a prevailing style, unless it be in the royal statues which aimed at the ancient ideal of the timeless aspect of royalty without recapturing its essential quality. It was only at Thebes that a really unified style, which we have recognized already in the reliefs of Taharqa's temple at Kawa, was maintained in a series of tombs down to the end of Dynasty XXVI. At a time when Thebes must have been impoverished by the depredations of the Assyrians and when its former political supremacy was centred in the Delta, we nevertheless find the most pretentious tombs which were ever constructed at the old southern capital. We cannot be sure whether Mentuemhat or Petamenopet, like the somewhat earlier Harwa and Akhamenru, constructed their monuments in the last days, when they enjoyed the favour of Taharqa and Tanwetamani, or during the period of reconstruction which Mentuemhat undertook while he was virtually ruler of Upper Egypt after the withdrawal of Ashurbanipal's troops. Certainly the expensive constructions of the series of stewards of the households of Nitocris and her successor Ankhnes-nefer-ib-ra were due to the pomp with which the Saite kings surrounded these ladies. Their long incumbency of the office of Divine Consort of Amon covered the whole of Dynasty XXVI and formed a kind of regency by which a peaceful control of the south was maintained. Nitocris had been sent to Thebes by Psamtik I evidently with the intention of curbing such power as had been displayed by Mentuemhat.

At about the beginning of the reign of Psamtik I, the decoration of the tomb of Mentuemhat (No. 34) presents an amazing freshness of conception and execution which makes one forget the eclectic elements which are present. Inevitably one is reminded of a similar quality which had appeared in the Theban limestone reliefs of Dynasty XI. As at Kawa and in the other Theban tombs, the work is in raised as well as sunk relief. Since the time of Sety I at Abydos, no craftsman had attempted work of such quality in raised relief. We have seen that the sandstone used at Thebes and at Kawa by the Kushite kings for their raised reliefs was not suitable for attaining such fine detail, but the style, nevertheless, appears first at Kawa in the time of Taharqa.

The huge brick pylon of Mentuemhat's tomb in Western Thebes is still an impressive landmark as one approaches the Deir el Bahari temple across the flat ground of the Asasif. With its arched gate it is the best preserved of the entrances to the big brick enclosures which formed the superstructures of a remarkable group of tombs of officials. The earliest of these (No. 37) belonged to Harwa, who was steward of Shabako's sister the Divine Consort of Amon, Amenirdis,[30] and to Akhamenru whose rock-cut chambers have been identified as opening out of the court of Harwa.[31] Akhamenru served Shepenwepet, the successor of Amenirdis. The statues of these men, found mostly at Karnak, are more important than the little that has so far been recovered of the decoration of their tombs. An even more valuable series of statues of Mentuemhat and Petamenopet has also survived, but the tomb of the latter (No. 33) was the largest and most impressive of the whole series. Partly excavated lengths of its vast

404. Mourning men. Relief from the tomb of Nesi-pa-ka-shuty at Thebes. Dynasty XXVI. *Brooklyn Museum*

brick enclosing wall show a series of recessed panels, as though the builder were turning back for inspiration to the archaic enclosures at Abydos, or the First-Dynasty tombs at Saqqara and Nagadah. The vaulted entrance hall, which led from the court to a labyrinth of rock-chambers covered with funerary texts, is decorated with offering scenes in raised relief resembling those at Deir el Bahari in which Hatshepsut's craftsmen had themselves drawn upon Old Kingdom royal models. The ceiling of this hall is painted with the last of the series of patterns, including the figure-8 plant spiral, which first appeared in Dynasty XII at Assiut, Qaw el Kebir, and Meir [205].[32]

In addition to the reliefs in the tombs of Petamenopet and Mentuemhat, other important series have survived nearly complete in the tombs of Iby (No. 36) and Pabasa (No. 279) which belong to the latter part of the reign of Psamtik I. The vizier Nesi-pa-ka-shuty remodelled one of the old Dynasty XI tombs of the courtiers of Mentuhotep and decorated it with a funeral scene which draws on New Kingdom sources [404], while the boldly carved rows of offering bearers might

at first sight be mistaken for work of the early part of Dynasty IV.[33] There is at present a gap between these reliefs and the end of the Dynasty which is represented by one large figure of the owner in sunk relief on the stairway of the tomb of Sheshonq (No. 27). This man served the last of the Votaresses of Amon, Ankhnes-nefer-ib-ra, and appears on a wall at Karnak with this lady and Psamtik III in the year in which the Persians invaded Egypt.[34] The area occupied by the whole group of tombs in the Asasif has only been partially excavated, and the protruding portions of brick walls and half-filled sunken courts amidst the deeply accumulated debris make it difficult to judge of their original appearance in relationship to one another. The underground chambers are at a considerable depth[35] and sometimes in two tiers, as in the tombs of Petamenopet (33) and Mentuemhat (34), where the burial apartments are at a lower level than the rock-cut rooms and court of the chapel. They are reached by a long open staircase which, in the case of Mentuemhat and Pabasa, extended beyond the enclosure wall on the north and was entered through a small pylon at right angles to the larger

405. Philae, west colonnade,
capitals. Ptolemaic

one which gave access to the brick enclosure wall. A feature of most of these tombs, which is best preserved in those of Mentuemhat and Pabasa, was a court at the level of the underground rooms but open to the sky. Its walls were lined with brickwork above the rock level to hold back the rubble, and the top of these brick walls evidently formed a parapet round the large opening in the floor of the brick enclosure.

The open court of the tomb of Mentuemhat has been cleared.[36] It was entered through two partially excavated halls with channelled columns that connect it with the open stairway. At the west end of the court a columned portico leads to the entrance of the burial apartments, which are on a lower level. The walls of this portico are decorated with a partly destroyed series of raised reliefs. The eastern wall of the court has rock-cut statues in elaborately framed niches, and a series of side chapels decorated with sunk reliefs open from the north and south walls. On the north wall is preserved a series of magnificent panels with bound papyrus plants placed between the doorways of the chapels. This old motif, which goes back to the First-Dynasty use of the heraldic plant of the North, is here carved in a fashion which gives us a first taste of the wonderful sculptural treatment of plant forms which was to be best exemplified in late architecture by the composite capitals [405]. Their first developed use was in the addition which Nectanebo II made in Dynasty XXX to the temple of Darius I in the Khargeh Oasis. However, fragments of capitals with the plant forms carved in low

406. Woman nursing a child. Saite relief from Thebes. Dynasty XXVI. *Brooklyn Museum*

relief have been found in the Saite tombs constructed in the Weserkaf temple at Saqqara. These suggest that the development may have begun somewhat earlier.[37] We have seen that the idea had been anticipated at Amarna [312].

Fine fragments of relief from the tomb of Mentuemhat have for some time existed in European and American collections, but their source was not recognized until excavations revealed the character of this tomb's decoration. It had been known only through drawings of one of the chapels and a stone in Florence which bears the owner's titles and name in connexion with a very small portion of a swamp scene.[38] This last piece was part of a series of scenes from daily life, now in scattered fragments, which in all probability decorated the south wall of the portico embrasure, adjoining the superimposed groups of Mentuemhat and his wife at their funerary meal on the back wall and facing the partially preserved funeral scenes on the opposite north wall. One of the most attractive details of this series is that in Brooklyn of a woman nursing her child under a fruit tree, while in the register above, a girl pulls a thorn from the foot of her companion [406]. Only the lower part of these figures is preserved, but they repeat a well-known group in the Eighteenth-Dynasty tomb of Menena [258], where the woman under the tree also appears as a minor figure in the harvesting scene. There is no question in this case that the Saite artist has copied figures which are known only in one New Kingdom tomb. He has executed them in a style, however, which is reminiscent of the nearby Mentuhotep temple of Dynasty XI. In the same limestone of the floor of the Asasif the sculptor has achieved a crisp freshness of cutting as well as a harmony of style which would be considered distinguished during any of the best periods of Egyptian art.

The more forceful side of the Kushite-Theban school appears in a handsome relief in Kansas City which certainly belongs with this group of Theban tombs and probably represents Mentuemhat himself [407].[39] The chief figure wears an elaborate costume, as at Kawa, in the tomb of Pabasa [394], and in others of this group, including sandals with flaring straps and one of those thin skirts through which the modelling of the body shows. The chief interest lies, however, in the brutally realistic treatment of the head. Its characteristic shape and the indication of flesh and muscle are to be found in those statues of late times which portray an ageing man in contrast to the smoothly treated forms of youth which are so much more frequently shown.[40] The head of the attendant who stands before Pabasa in the relief on the wall of the ante-chamber to his Theban tomb [394] has the shape and a similar roundness of modelling which is characteristic of these reliefs, but, like the head of the seated owner, is more conventionalized. We have already remarked upon the bold modelling of the forms under the thin garments. The elaborate wig of Pabasa and the serrated edge of his pleated cloak present the more mannered elements in these reliefs. Other signs of the times are the lotus in the mouth of the gazelle, the flowers instead of food over the peculiar rectangular offering table, and the jars under the table and chair.

The groups of statues dedicated at Karnak by Harwa, Akhamenru, Petamenopet, and Mentuemhat each included at least one which represented the owner as an older man in a fashion reminiscent of the head of the figure on the Kansas City relief. One of Harwa's figures, an unusual squatting type with one knee raised and the other leg drawn back along the ground, as in a few Old Kingdom statues,

407. Mentuemhat (?). Saite relief.
Dynasty XXVI. *Kansas City,
William Rockhill Nelson Gallery of
Art*

emphasizes the flabby forms of a corpulent body. The face is fat with sagging features, softly worked as though in clay, although the material used is hard stone.[41] This particularly plastic treatment anticipates a later series of heads with ageing features whose date has been much contested.[42] The Petamenopet group, which includes a handsome late reflection of the scribe type of the Old Kingdom, has another of the realistic heads on one of the popular cubical squatting figures which draw up both knees in front of them. However, the masterpieces of early Saite times are the standing statue which Mentuemhat dedicated at Karnak and the even more remarkable head and shoulders of a figure from the Mut Temple which probably also belonged to him. The nearly life-size standing figure of Mentuemhat in Cairo wears a short kilt derived from the Old Kingdom but a wig which continues

a form of the Eighteenth Dynasty [408]. The torso shows a kind of modelling of the abdomen which had been used in royal statues of Dynasty XII and in the fragmentary torso from Qaw el Kebir [178].[43] It is to be found in at least one of the Gebel Barkal statues[44] and would seem to correspond to the interest in muscular structure shown in the Kushite reliefs.

It is in the forceful portraiture of the head, however, that this statue makes its impression [408]. The broad mouth, deep lines at the corners of the nostrils, and the conventional treatment of the eyebrows in slight relief are repeated in the life-size head and shoulders broken from another statue [409] and found in the Temple of Mut with a headless squatting figure of Mentuemhat. The nose is broken off so that one cannot compare it with the prominent coarse one of the

408. Mentuemhat. Dynasty XXV. *Cairo Museum*

409. Mentuemhat. Head and shoulders of a statue from Karnak. Dynasty XXV. *Cairo Museum*

standing Karnak figure, but it has the same broad base of the nostrils. The name is lost from the inscription on the back pillar. The titles, however, are those held by Mentuemhat. The scooped-out depressions under the eyes resemble those of Taharqa [397], but the strange projecting hair around the bald forehead is not duplicated anywhere else. By extending the fold of the eyelid above an incised line at the outer corner of the eye and by suggesting the sagging facial muscles, the sculptor has changed the hard ruthless face of the Karnak head into the crafty features of an older man. In both these heads one feels oneself in the presence of a man without illusions who could prove capable of surviving, as did Mentuemhat, the difficult conditions created by the Assyrian occupation of Thebes. There is no longer in these features the calm confidence of the Old Kingdom, or that troubled awareness of the responsibilities of a ruler which appeared in Dynasty XII. The artist, still approaching his work with the same basic naturalistic instincts that produced all Egyptian portraiture, shows us a man who plainly lived in the declining years of a long civilization.[45]

The few statues of Saite rulers which have been identified show that the court in the north turned away from this realistic style for royal portraiture.[46] In them the tension resulting from the attempt to combine various conflicting formal elements defeats the intention of recreating the old ideal of the timeless aspect of kingship. In spite of the sophisticated mastery of the hardest materials, which is one of the outstanding features of late sculpture, they betray a certain emptiness of spirit. This is to be found, too, in the majority of the private statues with their highly polished surfaces and set smiles and in the innumerable figures of deities in bronze and hard stone.[47] An even more mannered style made its appearance in that period of some sixty years of independence from Persian rule (Dynasties XXVIII–XXX) which began with the revolt of Amyrtaios under Darius II at the end of the fifth century B.C. and lasted until the brief reoccupation of the country by the Persians in 341 B.C. It is Nectanebo I (378–360 B.C.) and Nectanebo II (359–341 B.C.) of Dynasty XXX who have left the chief monuments of this new style, which formed a basis for the early Ptolemaic work that was executed after the conquest of Alexander in 332 B.C.

Strange portraits of three kings, Psamtik I and II and Nectanebo I, are to be found in royal reliefs, and these seem to show that the taste for representing individual characteristics had not disappeared in the time between early Dynasty XXVI and the Ptolemaic Period. They appear on basalt slabs, 4 feet high (1.2 m), which seem to have formed a balustrade for a single monument. It is not easy to visualize the original appearance of this monument or to explain how a large part of it came to be left uninscribed for over 200 years until Nectanebo took up the work again. The same scheme of decoration appears on the two sets of slabs which are carved on both sides. On one side, closely spaced kneeling figures of the king make offering to various deities, with a vulture frieze above. On the other side of the slab a single figure of the king is set against a blank background, and there is a uraeus cornice.[48] If a deity appeared it must have been carved on an adjoining block. There is too profound a difference in style between the two sets of slabs for those inscribed with the

410. Nectanebo I. Relief from Alexandria. Dynasty XXX. *London, British Museum*

411. Psamtik I. Dynasty XXVI. *London, British Museum*

name of Psamtik to have been executed by the later king as a pious tribute to the family which founded Dynasty XXVI. On the Nectanebo slab in the British Museum [410], found in Alexandria (No. 926), the modelling of the body, as well as the hieroglyphs, produce an uneasy sense of volume within the traditional outlines which seems to betray a new consciousness of Greek works.[49] The softness of the forms, which had perhaps appeared a little earlier in some of the neo-Memphite reliefs,[50] is here somewhat paradoxically frozen into cold mannerism. That this is not entirely due to the hard material used but was characteristic of the period can be seen from the similar hieroglyphs cut in raised relief in limestone on some fragments of royal inscriptions of Dynasty XXX.[51]

On the other hand, in the carving of the Psamtik I slab [411] the figures and the inscriptions maintain a relatively flat plane in harmony with their outlines and the background, as had all earlier Egyptian relief whether sunk or raised. Hitherto, when we have called attention to relatively high relief or to surface modelling, it has never produced a sense of conflict between the sculptured surfaces and their background, even in work of the Amarna Period or in Ramesside times. This conflict seems to be the result of attempting to combine two opposed points of view towards representation, that of the old world of the Orient and the newer Hellenic one. The better preserved head of Psamtik [411] seems to be a northern development of the type originating in Kushite reliefs and small bronzes. It exaggerates the height of the

round skull, which is made more strange by the way in which the uraeus is placed on the cap. A few lines accentuate the fleshy nostrils and tip of the prominent nose and suggest full cheeks and throat around the mouth and small chin. It is a ruthless portrayal of ugliness matched in a different way by the more pronounced modelling of the Nectanebo head [410], where jutting chin and nose seem to close like pincers around the small mouth.

The sparing use of line and slight gradations of modelling of the Psamtik head are to be found again on a small scale in two heads with ageing features in reliefs which can be assigned plausibly to the latter half of the Saite Period. One belongs to the owner, praying before the Memphite triad of gods on a small lintel in sunk relief in Boston, while the other is a minor figure of a scribe leading a procession of offering bearers before a seated figure of Henat in a very low raised relief in Berlin.[52] The Henat carving is of the type of the so-called neo-Memphite reliefs, and the genealogical material from other monuments of this man has been used to provide a fixed point for the employment of such reliefs in the reign of Amasis, about 535 B.C. The subtle use of line in the drawing of the figures is paralleled on the Boston block and in the sunk relief kneeling figure of Harbes on the wall of the chapel which he added early in the Saite Period to the Isis Temple at Giza which had been constructed in Dynasty XXI round the old chapel of the third pyramid of one of Cheops' queens, Henutsen.[53]

The supple outlines of the figures in these Memphite

412. Musicians and dancers. Detail
of Zanofer relief. Early fourth
century B.C. *Alexandria Museum*

reliefs, combined with details derived from Kushite work executed by Theban sculptors, has been noted in work in the north for which a Saite date had been suggested.[54] Unfortunately, as in the case of the statues, we cannot be sure without more dated monuments how long the elements of the older style lingered on. Traces of the costume and type of figure favoured by the Kushite-Theban school still survived in the carefully executed sunk reliefs of the temple which Darius I built in the Oasis of Khargeh,[55] although the work in raised relief is not comparable in quality to that of the Saite Theban tombs. A cruder reflection of the figure style of the Brooklyn papyrus [387] appears in the interesting series of paintings of the Dynasty XXVI tombs in the Bahrieh Oasis.[56] It is not yet possible to gain a clear impression of the use of colour in these gradually accumulating examples of late painting, but the pink flesh of a woman in one of the Bahrieh tombs and the combination of pink and blue in the Darius relief of Horus spearing Apophis[57] begin to suggest the new tonality of the painted reliefs of Petosiris which anticipate what we think of as a characteristic Alexandrian colour scheme.

With the Zanofer reliefs and a similar group closely connected with them we certainly reach the most developed neo-Memphite style. A detail of the finest piece of Zanofer in Alexandria[58] is illustrated [412]. These stones are like small architrave blocks with a roll moulding and cornice above the relief. The Alexandria piece, for example, is a little under 4 feet (1.2 m) long and about 1 foot (0.3 m) high. It has been suggested that they were placed round the top of a block of masonry which contained the sarcophagus, a construction combining tomb and chapel suitable for the Delta, where the inundation would make difficult the construction of underground chambers. Such a new type of construction has been found, but without the decorated friezes.[59] Some of the stones came, however, from some older type of chapel construction, and the Alexandria relief of Zanofer clearly formed the lintel over the door of a small niche or shrine. There was a border

round the opening and two columns of inscription on each side. It is probable that a panel in Berlin fits below the inscription on the right to frame one side of this opening. The standing figure on this relief is dressed like Zanofer and has a head like the old harper in the group with the musicians and dancers [412].[60]

While the rows of offering bearers on many of these reliefs bear superficial resemblance to their Old Kingdom models, most of the details are derived ultimately from the picturesque repertoire of the New Kingdom. The woman playing a drum, with her long-fringed scarf and bizarre head-dress, like her companions [412], is more directly related to some rare fragments from Theban temple reliefs of Dynasty XXV. These show women musicians and dancers against a background of a papyrus thicket which also contained animals parodying the acts of human beings, as in the papyri and ostraca of the end of the Ramesside Period.[61] In the Zanofer relief all that remains of this background is a series of artificially contrived bouquets with birds perched on top. The figures have the same heavy build that had appeared at Thebes in Dynasty XXV or perhaps even earlier in the Delta with the bronze statue of Takushit [386]. In spite of the very low surfaces, there is a soft plastic quality in the modelling and more than a hint of the awareness of Greek forms. One can actually look into the opening of the sleeves of the second woman, although this bit of foreshortening is carried out almost entirely in line and appears as a purely isolated feature.[62] There is none of the exaggerated mixing of Greek and Egyptian elements or the rather cramped modelling that was soon to appear in the tomb of Petosiris.

The Alexandria carving of Zanofer stands out as a masterly piece of work and one of the last harmonious examples of the old tradition of fine low relief. One would like to think that it was executed at a time when a new style was setting in, before it had hardened into the mannerisms of the royal work of Dynasty XXX. However, the Cairo relief of the same man

413. Green stone head of an old man. Early fourth century B.C. *Boston, Museum of Fine Arts*

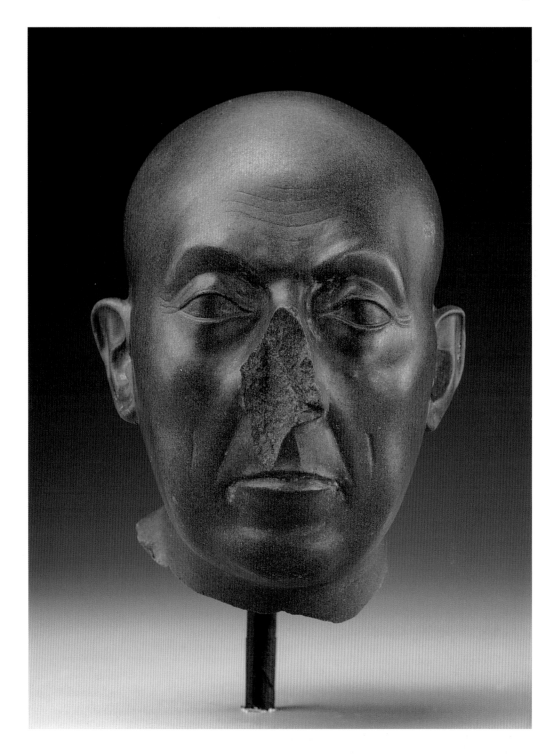

and some of the other closely connected reliefs do begin to show some traces of this, especially in a kind of puffy modelling of the faces. These are on a very small scale, and the nose, mouth, and chin are treated as separate raised blobs in front of the fat cheeks.[63] There is also a playful artificiality in the treatment of the plants and animals and in the accessories of the offering bearers which takes on a fantastic quality in the similar processions of figures in the tomb of Petosiris. It is a first expression of a spirit which was to be one of the characteristics of Alexandrian art, and it may be necessary to date these reliefs to the middle, not the beginning, of the fourth century B.C.

The head of the old harper seems to form a guide as to the relative position among late portrait sculpture of the remarkable little green stone head in Boston [413] which has been dated from Saite times to well down in the Ptolemaic period. Wrinkles are indicated on the forehead and at the corners of the eye, and there is a plastic treatment of the arched brows and eyelids. The configuration of the head in profile is much like that of the Zanofer harper, a type which goes back to reliefs of early Dynasty XXVI [407]. The Boston head is reminiscent of a better-known head of green stone in Berlin which is twice as large.[64] The longer one examines these pieces the more the feeling grows that the Berlin head has

414. Priest of Amon. Archaistic diorite statue. Dynasty XXX. *Brooklyn Museum*

erous shifts in the loyalties of mercenary troops, the Greeks usually joined forces with the Egyptians in their struggle for independence. Athens and Sparta were in particularly close contact with Egypt in the period following the revolt of Inaros under Artaxerxes I at about the middle of the fifth century B.C. Shortly afterwards the Ionian historian Herodotus visited Egypt, where he examined the skulls still lying on the battle-field of Papremis in the Delta, where the forces of Inaros had routed the Persians and driven them back to Memphis. It is his description of the country which forms the background for the monuments we have been examining. A different and more lively colouring is given to our impressions of the Saite rulers and the men of the first Persian domination by the Greek interest in individuality which pervades this account. The historian's observation of the manners and customs of the people is supplemented by tales which Herodotus heard from his guides. In contrast to the old records, we find his inquiring mind seeking rational explanations for the origin of things and the behaviour of man.

In the last quarter of the fourth century, not long after Alexander's expedition to Egypt in 332 B.C., an extraordinary funeral monument was erected in the cemetery of Hermopolis, the capital of the old Hare Nome.[65] Petosiris, the high priest of Thoth, constructed this on the edge of the western desert opposite the Middle Kingdom rock-cut tombs in the eastern cliffs. It was in the form of a small temple with a porch supported by columns with composite plant capitals such as had been developed in Dynasty XXX.[66] The low screen walls connecting these columns, as well as the walls of the porch and the chapel behind, have a well preserved series of painted reliefs.[67] The mortuary texts are illustrated in a conventional manner, but an unmistakable mixture of Greek and Egyptian methods of representation appears in the long rows of offering-bearers and the scenes of daily life. The men harvesting grain [415] look more Greek than Egyptian with their light skin and blue and buff tunics. Wrinkles on the face and the muscles of the limbs are rather roughly indicated by red lines painted on the lighter flesh colour. The man behind the pile of sheaves is shown front-view, while the little boy is more convincingly worked out in a three-quarter view. The sculptor has tried to give volume to the garments, but since he retains many of his old conventions, the draping of the tunic is bunchy. While gaining some effect of depth, he has lost the old sureness of outline. The hieroglyphs have become simi-

advanced further in the direction of a new plastic treatment. The Boston portrait is severely conceived within the framework of the old traditional style, maintaining its harmony as does the Alexandria Zanofer relief. Both are outstanding works in which the old spirit still strongly asserts itself. The Brooklyn statue of a priest of Amon [414], dated to Dynasty XXX, also reaches back to work of the Twenty-sixth Dynasty and thus in turn to Old Kingdom sculpture. The extremely high polish of the hard black diorite is characteristic of the sculpture of this period. The Macedonian occupation must have seemed, at least to the upper-class Egyptian, a deliverance from Persian rule. Although the Egyptian fleet had been employed by Xerxes at Salamis and there had been treach-

415. Hermopolis, tomb of Petosiris, agricultural scene. *c.* 325 B.C.

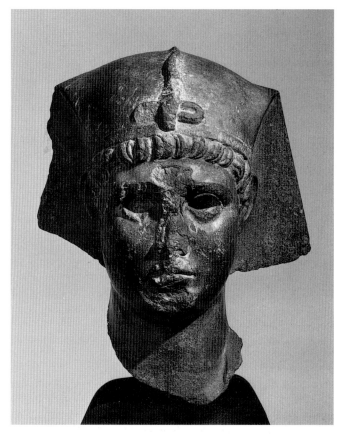

416. Hellenistic king. Head of statue. Ptolemaic-Roman. *Yale University, Peabody Museum*

continue much the same today in the fields that spread out to the east of the columned porch of Petosiris. The Hellenic approach to representation was too diametrically opposed to the old point of view for any fusion to be successful. An illustration demonstrates this more forcefully than any description of the historical situation. An early Ptolemaic head in the Yale University Art Gallery [416] presents Hellenistic features forced into a rigidly frontal position. The Egyptian headdress grafted on to the imperial portrait does not disguise the Greek curls escaping underneath. The Egyptian held tenaciously to his ways for a few centuries more, but in the different atmosphere of the Ptolemaic Period the vital forces originated in the Hellenistic world and that of Rome and not from the declining civilization of Egypt. A native contribution still was to be made to portrait sculpture, and the same naturalistic impulses may have contributed something to the painted Fayum panels and the heads on linen mummy shrouds.

These are, however, in the direct tradition of Greek painting, and one of their values lies in that they may provide a hint of the appearance of lost Hellenistic originals, while they form a welcome addition to the body of Roman portrait painting to which they are closely allied. Great buildings were erected in the pharaonic style by the Ptolemies and the Romans, but most of Egypt became a provincial backwater, while Alexandria assumed a position of cultural significance in the Mediterranean world.[73] The Alexandrian artists, in general, made little more than a playful use of misunderstood Egyptian motifs, much as such Egyptian elements entered

417. Philae, temple of Isis, Second Pylon. Ptolemaic

larly awkward and cramped. The colour scheme has changed completely and is much more like that which we know from Hellenic works of the fourth century. It perhaps had a brighter, harder tonality originally. It is not easy to determine the original colour of the background, which is now a pale greenish hue that lends a pastel effect to the faded blues and browns set against it. However, the light colouring of the men's skin must have given a new aspect to the whole, which we have seen anticipated in the Saite paintings in Bahrieh Oasis.[68] In the craftwork scenes metalworkers are fashioning various examples of the animal rhyton[69] such as had been developed in Achaemenid Persia[70] but which had also found favour in the Greek workshops.

Behind the tomb of Petosiris there grew up in the third century A.D.[71] a remarkable cemetery of house tombs for the wealthy members of the Greek community of Hermopolis. These were mainly Hellenic in architecture and decoration but with an adaptation to Egyptian funerary practices. Among paintings which were purely Greek in tradition were mixed others in the old pharaonic style. These are hardly more than a travesty of earlier Egyptian art, like the crude figures of gods and religious symbols which appear on the mummy cloths of the first to fourth centuries A.D. along with Graeco-Roman painted portraits.[72] In fact a crucial stage was reached in the tomb of Petosiris, where a group of able craftsmen made a serious attempt to grapple with a new point of view and failed. It is significant that they should have done so in the old medium of painted relief, while reproducing for the dead man the familiar agricultural pursuits which

418. Naga, Lion Temple and Kiosk B. First century B.C.

419. Naga, Lion Temple, pylon, Meroitic queen. First century B.C.

into the fashionable decorative scheme of Imperial Rome or as they were revived in Napoleonic France.

Of the imposing monuments of the Ptolemaic-Roman Period, none have captured the attention more than the buildings of the Isis Temple which once rose picturesquely above the palm trees on the little island of Philae at the First Cataract. The worship of the old gods still continued there until the pagan temples were finally closed by Justinian in A.D. 543. Many of us have seen no more than the top of a pylon rising out of the expanse of water which covers them during the greater part of the year behind the Aswan Dam. An old photograph shows the flooded court [417] in front of the Second Pylon of the Isis Temple. The buildings were mostly completed in the third century B.C. under Ptolemy II and III, but work on the relief decoration continued for a long time, to the end of the Ptolemaic Period and under Roman rule. The Hathor head above the composite plant capital of the colonnade of the Birth House on the left continues a type which had been used in the porch of Nectanebo I. Fine examples of these boldly sculptured plant forms are used also in the west colonnade which was completed in the first century A.D. (see above, illustrations 312 and 405) and connects the Nectanebo porch with the First Pylon of the Isis Temple. Their varied combinations, as in the temples of Edfu, Kom Ombo, and Esna, formed one of the freshest and most attractive late contributions.

It was not only in Egypt that the old forms continued to survive side by side with the new. Far to the south in the Sudan a clumsy, provincial-looking kiosk in Roman style still stands at Naga in front of the Egyptian temple which the Meroitic King Natakamani erected there. This was shortly after Petronius in the reign of Augustus in 23 B.C. led

420. Meroë, royal cemetery. Third century B.C.–fourth century A.D.

an invading force as far as the old Kushite capital of Napata. The seat of government had been transferred from Napata southwards to Meroë at the end of the sixth century, and the new capital is mentioned by Herodotus in the middle of the fifth century B.C. The attention of the Ethiopian kings had turned to the development of the southern part of their country, and cultural links with Egypt were growing weaker and weaker, stimulated chiefly by contacts with merchants and the occasional importation of craftsmen, or a scribe, or perhaps the visit of a few priests. Something of the old spirit still remained, as in the figure of the fat queen of Natakamani

who dominates a group of prisoners on the right half of the pylon of the Lion Temple at Naga [418, 419]. In view of her arresting bulk it is not surprising that stories of such royal ladies were carried back to Rome by the soldiers of Petronius. In the royal cemetery of Meroë, the kings still continued to build pyramids [420] until some time in the fourth century A.D. The traditional forms had proved exceptionally durable. They persisted a little longer, penetrating even into the iconographic system of Coptic art.[74] However, Christianity proved even more powerful than the Hellenistic spirit in altering the old civilization.

Abbreviations

ÄAbh	*Ägyptologische Abhandlungen*
ÄAT	*Ägypten und Altes Testament*
AJA	*American Journal of Archaeology*
AJSL	*American Journal of Semitic Languages and Literatures*
Annales	*Annales du Service des Antiquités de l' Égypte*
AV	*Archäologische Veröffentlichungen DAIAK*
BÄBA	*Beiträge zur Ägyptischen Bauforschung und Alter-tumskunde*
BASOR	*Bulletin of the American Schools of Oriental Research*
BES	*Bulletin of the Egyptological Seminar*
BIFAO	*Bulletin de l'Institut français d'archéologie orientale du Caire*
BiOr	*Bibliotheca Orientalis*
BMFA	*Museum of Fine Arts Bulletin/Boston Museum Bulletin*
BMA	*Brooklyn Museum Annual*
BMMA	*Bulletin of the Metropolitan Museum of Art*
Breasted, *Ancient Records*	J. H. Breasted, *Ancient Records of Egypt*, 5 vols. (Chicago, 1906–7)
BSFE	*Bulletin de la Société française d'Égyptologie*
Bull. Inst. Égypte	*Bulletin de l'Institut d'Égypte*
CdE	*Chronique d'Égypte*
CNI	Carsten Niebuhr Institut
CRIPL	*Cahiers de Recherches de l'Institut de Papyrologie et d'Égyptologie de Lille*
DAIAK	*Deutsches Archäologishces Institut, Abteilung Kairo*
DE	*Discussions in Egyptology*
Emery, *Great Tombs*	W. B. Emery, *Great Tombs of the First Dynasty*, 3 vols. (Cairo, 1949, and London, 1954, 1958)
Frankfort, *Ancient Orient*	Henri Frankfort, *The Art and Architecture of the Ancient Orient*, 4th (integrated) edition (Harmondsworth, 1970)
GM	*Göttinger Miszellen: Beiträge zur ägyptologischen Diskussion*
HÄB	*Hildesheimer Ägyptologische Beiträge*
HÄS	*Hamburger Agyptologische Studien*
Helck and Otto, *Lexikon*	Wolfgang Helck and E. Otto, eds., *Lexikon der Ägyptologie*, 7 vols. Wiesbaden (1972–1992)
IFAOC, B d'É	*Institut français d'archéologie orientale du Caire, Bibliothèque d'Étude*
JAOS	*Journal of the American Oriental Society*
JARCE	*Journal of the American Research Center in Egypt*
JEA	*Journal of Egyptian Archaeology*
JNES	*Journal of Near Eastern Studies*
JSSEA	*Journal of the Society for the Study of Egyptian Antiquities*
MÄS	*Münchner Ägyptologische Studien*
MÄU	*Münchner Ägyptologische Untersuchungen*
MDAIK	*Mitteilungen der Deutschen Archäologischen Instituts Abteilung Kairo*
Mitt. Deutsch. Orient-Gesell.	*Mitteilungen der Deutschen Orient-Gesellschaft*
MjbK	*Münchner Jahrbuch der bildenden Kunst*
MMJ	*Metropolitan Museum Journal*
MMS	*Metropolitan Museum Studies*
Mon. Piot	*Foundation Eugène Piot, Monuments et Mémoires*
NARCE	*Newsletter, American Research Center in Egypt*
OLA	*Orientalia Louvaniensa Analecta*
OLZ	*Orientalistische Literaturzeitung*
Porter-Moss, *Bibliography*	B. Porter and R. L. B. Moss, *Topographical Bibliography of Ancient Egyptian Hieroglyphic Texts, Reliefs, and Paintings* (see Bibliography)
RdE	*Revue d'Égyptologie*
Reisner, *Tomb Development*	G. A. Reisner, *The Development of the Egyptian Tomb* (Cambridge, Mass., 1936)
Ricke, *Bemerkungen*	Herbert Ricke, *Bemerkungen zur ägyptischen Baukunst des alten Reichs*, 2 vols. (Zürich, 1944, and Cairo, 1950)
SAGA	*Studien zur Archäologie und Geschichte Altägyptens*
SAK	*Studien zur altägyptischen Kultur*
Smith, *Interconnections*	William Stevenson Smith, *Interconnections in the Ancient Near East* (New Haven, 1965)
Smith, *Sculpture and Painting*	William Stevenson Smith, *A History of Egyptian Sculpture and Painting in the Old Kingdom*, 2nd ed. (Boston, 1949)
Vandersleyen, *PKG*	Claude Vandersleyen, ed., *Das alte Ägypten* (*Propyläen Kunstgeschichte*, 15) (Berlin, 1975)
Vandier, *Manuel*	J. Vandier, *Manuel d'archéologie égyptienne*, 6 vols. (Paris, 1952–78)
Wreszinski, *Atlas*	W. Wreszinski, *Atlas zur altägyptischen Kulturgeschichte*, 3 vols. (Leipzig, 1923, 1935, 1936)
WZKM	*Wiener Zeitschrift Für die Kunde des Morgenlandes*
ZÄS	*Zeitschrift für Ägyptische Sprache und Altertumskunde*

Notes

CHAPTER 1

1. At this point the reader should be referred to the most important theoretical considerations of Egyptian art. These issues will concern us further only indirectly. See Heinrich Schäfer, *Principles of Egyptian Art*, 4th ed., ed. Emma Brunner-Traut, trans. with additions J. R. Baines (Oxford, 1974); Emma Brunner-Traut, 'Aspektive', in W. Helck and E. Otto, eds., *Lexikon der Ägyptologie*, 1 (Wiesbaden, 1973), 474–88, and 'Epilogue: aspective', in Schäfer, *op. cit.*, 421–46; Henrietta A. Groenewegen-Frankfort, *Arrest and Movement: Space and Time in the Representational Art of the Ancient Near East* (London, 1951), 15–141; Erik Iversen, *Canon and Proportions in Egyptian Art*, 2nd ed. with Yoshiaki Shibata (Warminster, 1975); Rudolf Arnheim, *Art and Visual Perception* (Berkeley, 1974), 112–16; Maurice Pirenne, *Optics, Painting, and Photography* (Cambridge, 1970), 175–80; Robert L. Scranton, *Aesthetic Aspects of Ancient Art* (Chicago, 1966); William Kelly Simpson, 'Aspects of Egyptian Art: function and aesthetic', in Denise Schmandt-Besserat, ed., *Immortal Egypt* (Malibu, 1978), 19–25; Herbert Senk, 'Gestalt und Geschichte der altägyptischen Kunst', *OLZ*, 54 (1959), 117–31; an important review article of W. Wolf, *Die Kunst Ägyptens* (Stuttgart, 1957), and 'Ägyptische Kunstgeschichte: zur Problematik ihrer Erforschung', *OLZ*, 58 (1963), 5–13: E. H. Gombrich, *Art and Illusion* (London, 1960), 120–5; Jan Assmann, 'Preservation and Presentation of Self in Ancient Egyptian Portraiture,' in Peter Der Manuelian, *Studies in Honor of William Kelly Simpson* (Boston, 1996), 55–81; Lise Manniche, *L'art égyptien*. Translated from an unpublished English text by T. Préaud (Paris, 1994); Gay Robins, *The Art of Ancient Egypt* (London, 1997).

2. As the Greeks themselves noted: Plato, *Laws*, II, 656–7, and Isocrates, *Busiris*, 16–17. See Whitney M. Davis, 'Plato on Egyptian Art', *JEA*, 65 (1979), 121–7.

3. H. Frankfort, *The Art and Architecture of the Ancient Orient*, 4th (integrated) edition (Pelican History of Art, Harmondsworth, 1970), illustrations 88 and 89.

4. *Ibid.*, illustration 142.

5. Sir Arthur Evans, *The Palace of Minos*, 1 (London, 1921), 529, figure 385.

6. Frankfort, *Ancient Orient*, illustrations 152 and 153.

7. Recent studies of climatic change in ancient times point up the close relation between the stability of the environment and that of the social and ideological order. Barbara Bell, 'The First Dark Age in Egypt', *AJA*, 75 (1971), 1–26, brings the relevant Egyptian texts and modern scientific analyses into apt juxtaposition. Consult also Karl W. Butzer, *Early Hydraulic Civilization in Egypt* (Chicago, 1976), 'Perspectives on Irrigation Civilization in Pharaonic Egypt', in Denise Schmandt-Besserat, ed., *Immortal Egypt*, 13–18; Wolfgang Schenkel, *Die Bewässerungsrevolution im alten Ägypten* (Mainz, 1978), for further study of the foundations of the Egyptian economic and political system; and Erika Endesfelder, 'Zur Frage der Bewässerung im pharaonischen Ägypten', *ZÄS*, 106 (1979), 37–51.

8. The relationship between Egyptian art and hieroglyphic writing is explored in Henry G. Fischer, 'L'orientation des textes', in *Textes et languages de l'Égypte pharaonique*, 1 (Cairo, 1973), 21–3, and *The Orientation of Hieroglyphs*, part 1, *Reversals* (New York, 1977). A statue even served as the hieroglyphic 'determinative' for the inscribed name of the subject: see remarks by and further references in Henry G. Fischer, 'Redundant Determinatives in the Old Kingdom', *MMJ*, 8 (1973), 7–25, and Richard Fazzini, *Images for Eternity: Egyptian art from Berkeley and Brooklyn* (Brooklyn, 1975), xxiii. On the use of narrative, see G. A. Gaballa, *Narrative in Egyptian Art* (Mainz, 1976); Helene J. Kantor, 'Narrative in Egyptian Art', *AJA*, 61 (1957), 44–54.

9. Cyril Aldred, 'Some Royal Portraits of the Middle Kingdom in Ancient Egypt', *MMJ*, 3 (1970), 27–50.

10. The Greek form Tuthmosis has been used here instead of the Egyptian Djehuty-mes (Thoth is born), although a private name which also includes that of the god whom the Greeks called Thoth will be found as Djehuty-hetep (Thoth is gracious). On the other hand, the same initial sound of the word is represented by another letter in the names of the kings Zer and Zoser. The writer is only too conscious of these inconsistencies, but has tried to present frequently used forms of names which can be easily recognized. Again the classical royal names Menes, Cheops, Chephren, and Mycerinus have been employed. The absence of vowels and the lack of general agreement as to usage in a language where the vocalization is uncertain have made uniformity impossible. The reader is referred to the admirable discussion of the transcription of Egyptian proper names in Sir Alan Gardiner's *Egyptian Grammar*, 3rd ed. (London, 1950), 434.

11. See H. Frankfort, *Kingship and the Gods* (Chicago, 1948); *Ancient Egyptian Religion* (New York, 1948); J. Vandier, *La religion égyptienne*, 2nd ed. (Paris, 1949). Among many recent publications and discussions of Egyptian religious literature, see R. O. Faulkner, *The Ancient Egyptian Pyramid Texts*, 2 vols. (Oxford, 1969), and *The Ancient Egyptian Coffin Texts*, 3 vols. (Warminster, 1973, 1977, 1978); Erik Hornung, *Ägyptische Unterweltsbücher* (Zürich and Munich, 1972); Thomas G. Allen, *The Book of the Dead* (Chicago, 1974); and S. Morenz, *Egyptian Religion*, trans. Ann E. Keep (London, 1973); Stephen Quirke, *Ancient Egyptian Religion* (London, 1992). James P. Allen, *Genesis in Egypt: The Philosophy of Ancient Egyptian Creation Accounts*, Yale Egyptological Studies 2 (New Haven, 1988).

CHAPTER 2

1. O. H. Myers, 'Abka Re-excavated', *Kush*, 6 (1958), 131–41, and 'Abka Again', *Kush*, 8 (1960), 174–81, obtained radiocarbon dates for several archaeological layers which can be associated with drawings.

2. Among many publications, see R. Engelmayer, *Die Felsgravierung im Distrikt Sayala-Nubien*, 1: *Die Schiffsdarstellungen* (Österreichische Akad. der Wiss., Phil.-Hist. Kl., Denkschriften, 90) (Vienna, 1965); Walter F. E. Resch, *Die Felsbilder Nubiens* (Graz, 1967); M. Almagro Basch and M. Almagro Gorbea, *Estudios de arte rupestre nubio*, 1 (*Memorias de la Misión arqueológica española en Egipto*, 10) (Madrid, 1968); Pontus Hellström, with the collaboration of H. Langballe, *The Rock Drawings* (*Scandinavian Joint Expedition to Sudanese Nubia*, 1) (Odense, 1970); Pavel Červíček, *Felsbilder des Nord-Etbai, Oberägyptens, und Unternubiens: Ergebnisse der VIII. D.I.A.F.E. nach Ägypten 1926* (Wiesbaden, 1974). For chronology, see W. M. Davis, 'Toward a Dating of Nile Valley Prehistoric Rock-Drawings', *Journal of the Society for the Study of Egyptian Antiquities*, 8 (1977), 25–34; 'Dating Prehistoric Upper Egyptian and Nubian Rock-Drawings', *Current Anthropology*, 19 (1978), 216–17; 'Sources for the Study of Rock Art in the Nile Valley', *GM*, 32 (1979), 59–74.

3. For the culture-history of the prehistoric period in Egypt, see Bruce G. Trigger, 'The Rise of Civilization in Egypt', *The Cambridge African History*, 1 (1982), 478–547, and *Beyond History: the methods of prehistory* (New York, 1968); Elise J. Baumgartel, *The Cultures of Prehistoric Egypt*, rev. ed., 1 (Oxford, 1955), and II (Oxford, 1960); William C. Hayes, *Most Ancient Egypt* (Chicago, 1965); Karl W. Butzer, *Die Naturlandschaft Ägyptens während der Vorgeschichte und der Dynastischen Zeit* (Abh. der Akad. der Wiss. und der Lit. (Mainz), Math.-Naturw. Kl., 1) (Wiesbaden, 1959), and *Early Hydraulic Civilization in Egypt* (Chicago, 1976); Wolfgang Schenkel, *Die Bewässerungsrevolution im alten Ägypten*. The chief documents of Predynastic art are collected with bibliographies in R. T. Ridley, *The Unification of Egypt: a study of the major knife-handles, palettes, and maceheads* (Deception Bay, Australia, 1973); a complete survey is provided by Henri Asselberghs, *Chaos en Beheersing: Documenten uit Aeneolithisch Egypte* (*Documenta et Monumenta Orientis Antiqui*, 8) (Leiden, 1961). See also selected illustrations with commentaries by Helene J. Kantor, 'Ägypten', in M. J. Mellink and Jan Filip, eds., 'Frühe Stufen der Kunst' (*Propyläen Kunstgeschichte*, 13) (Berlin, 1974), 227–56, and Barry J. Kemp, 'Architektur der Frühzeit', in Vanderslueyen, *PKG*, 99–112.

4. Helene J. Kantor, 'The Final Phase of Predynastic Culture: Gerzean or Semainian(?)', *JNES*, 3 (1944), 110. The problem was avoided by the terms Nagadah I and II, derived from the site where the succession of the material was first recognized, and applied to Amratian and Gerzean. Further on Predynastic chronology, see Werner Kaiser, 'Stand und Probleme der ägyptischen Vorgeschichtsforschung', *ZÄS*, 81 (1956), 87–109, and 'Zur inneren Chronologie der Naqadakultur', *Archaeologia Geographica*, 6 (1957), 69–77; A. J. Arkell and Peter J. Ucko, 'Review of Predynastic Development in the Nile Valley', *Current Anthropology*, 6 (1965), 145–66; H. J. Kantor. 'Egypt' in R.W. Ehrich (ed.), *Chronologies in Old World Archaeology*, 3rd ed. (Chicago, 1992), vol. I, 3–21, vol. II, 2–45 (with charts). W. C. Hayes, *Most Ancient Egypt* (Chicago, 1965), and 'The Chronology of Egypt to the End of the Twentieth Dynasty', in I. E. S. Edwards, C. J. Gadd, and N. G. L. Hammond, eds., *The Cambridge Ancient History*, 3rd ed., I, part 1 (Cambridge, 1970), 174–6; Elise J. Baumgartel, 'Predynastic Egypt', in *ibid.*, 463–97.

5. W. C. Hayes, *The Scepter of Egypt*, 1 (New York, 1953), 27.

6. B. V. Bothmer, *BMFA*, 46 (1948), 64.

7. G. A. Reisner, *The Development of the Egyptian Tomb* (Cambridge, Mass., 1936), 378, figure 188, and Richard Fazzini, *Images for Eternity: Egyptian Art in Berkeley and Brooklyn* (Brooklyn, 1975), 14, no. 10.

8. W. S. Smith, *A History of Egyptian Sculpture and Painting in the Old Kingdom*, 2nd ed. (Boston, 1949), 7; Günter Dreyer, 'Die Datierung der Min-Statuen aus Koptos,' in Stadelmann, Rainer and Sourouzian, Hourig, *Kunst des Alten Reiches: Symposium im Deutschen Archäologischen Institut Kairo am 29. und 30. Oktober 1991.* (DAIAK Sonderschrift 28), Mainz am Rhein, 1995, 49–56. Bruce Williams, 'Narmer and the Coptos Colossi,' *JARCE* 25, 35–59, 1988. See also n. 26.

9. George Steindorff, *Catalogue of the Egyptian Sculpture in the Walters Art Gallery* (Baltimore, 1946), 19, plate I.

10. W. M. F. Petrie, ed. M. A. Murray and H. F. Petrie, *Ceremonial Slate Palettes* (*Publications of the British School of Egyptian Archaeology*, 66A) (London, 1953).

11. For example, the small seated figure of a dwarf or a child, Zaki Saad, *Royal Excavations at Helwan*, Supplement 14, *Annales* (1951), plate 43. For this early material in general, see J. Vandier, *Manuel d'archéologie égyptienne*, I (Paris, 1952), 527, 533, 957; Smith, *op. cit.*, I, 110; Jean Capart, *Primitive Art in Egypt* (London, 1905).

12. Kantor, 'The Final Phase of Predynastic Culture', 111, Brunton, in *Studies Presented to F. Ll. Griffith* (London, 1932), 272; Michael A. Hoffman, 'A Rectangular Amratian House from Hierakonpolis', *JNES*, 39 (1980), 119–37; 'City of the Hawk – Seat of Egypt's Ancient Civilization', *Expedition*, 18 (1976), 32–41; Walter Fairservis, 'Preliminary Report on the First Two Seasons at Hierakonpolis', *JARCE*, 9 (1972), 7–68; Michael A. Hoffman, *Egypt before the Pharaohs* (New York, 1979).

13. W. M. F. Petrie, *Abydos I* (London, 1903), plate 50(23).

14. J. E. Quibell and F. W. Green, *Hierakonpolis II* (London, 1902), 21, plates 75–9. Published photographs and drawings of the wall-painting should be carefully compared with the description by Barry J. Kemp, 'Photographs of the Decorated Tomb at Hierakonpolis', *JEA*, 59 (1973), 36–43. The objects from the Decorated Tomb are definitely typical of the Late Gerzean period: H. C. Case and J. C. Payne, 'Tomb 100: the Decorated Tomb at Hierakonpolis', *JEA*, 48 (1962), 5–18, and J. C. Payne, 'Tomb 100: the Decorated Tomb at Hierakonpolis Confirmed', *JEA*, 59 (1973), 31–5. Possibly the tomb was part of an Early Dynastic or Protodynastic royal cemetery, as suggested by Werner Kaiser, 'Zur vorgeschichtlichen Bedeutung von Hierakonpolis', *MDAIK*, 16 (1958), 189–91.

15. Capart, *op. cit.*, figures 171–2; Asselberghs, *Chaos en Beheersing*, plates 70–71; also Petrie, *Ceremonial Slate Palettes*, plate F (15–16). Cf. Capart, *op. cit.*, figures 169–85 for the group of palettes, and 186–9 for the two Hierakonpolis mace-heads; also Quibell, *Hierakonpolis I* (London, 1900), plate 16a, and Barbara Adams, *Ancient Hierakonpolis* (Warminster, 1976), 3–4, no. 2, for a third mace-head.

16. An important work in this regard is the so-called 'Lion-hunt palette' (Asselberghs, *Chaos en Beheersing*, plates 65–7). Here some figures are arranged in a scattered fashion, while others are more strictly arranged in lines, although no base- or register-lines appear (note the appearance of a short base-line on the Decorated Tomb painting). See W. M. Davis, 'The Origins of Register Composition in Predynastic Egyptian Art', *JAOS*, 96 (1976), 404–18.

17. Erik Iversen, *Canon and Proportions in Egyptian Art*, 2nd ed., 60–6, and Klaus-Heinrich Meyer, 'Kanon, Komposition, und "Metrik" der Narmerpalette', *SAK*, I (1974), 274–65, have demonstrated, it would seem successfully, that the canon of proportions as it appears in later 'classic' Egyptian art appears fully developed on the Narmer palette.

18. See references in Notes 3 and 10 above; Orly Goldwasser, 'The Narmer Palette and the "Triumph of Metaphor",' *Lingua Aegyptia* 2 (1992), 67–97. With extensive bibliography, Alan R. Schulman, 'Narmer and the Unification: a Revisionist View,' *Bulletin of the Egyptological Seminar* 11, 1991–1992, 79–105. Regards the scenes of the Narmer palette as the traditional re-enactment of the conquest scene, an event which may have taken place well prior to Narmer. With abundant illustrations of related material, Bruce G. Trigger, 'The Narmer Palette in Cross-Cultural Perspective', in M. Görg and E. Pusch (eds.), *Festschrift Elmar Edel* (Bamberg), 409–41.

19. Capart, *op. cit.*, figure 176 and figure 182, which is the other face of our illustration II.

20. E. Ayrton, C. Currelly, A. Weigall, *Abydos III* (London, 1904), plates VI, VII.

21. Reisner, *Tomb Development*, 271, figure 166.

22. See particularly H. Frankfort, *AJSL*, 58 (1941), 329, where Mesopotamian influence upon Egyptian brick architecture is strongly argued. An important point to note is that the niched façade appears in Egypt not only in funerary architecture but also in secular building, as for instance on a structure which has been interpreted as a palace: see Kent R. Weeks, 'Preliminary Report on the First Two Seasons at Hierakonpolis, part 2, The Early Dynastic Palace', *JARCE*, 9 (1971–2), 32–3. There are some who dispute the parallels with protoliterate

Mesopotamia in this respect: see especially Herbert Ricke, *Bemerkungen zur ägyptischen Baukunst des Alten Reichs*, I (Zürich, 1944), 46 and II (Cairo, 1950), 20, note 27; W. Helck, *Die Beziehungen Ägyptens zu Vorderasien im 3. und 2. Jahrtausend v. Chr.* (*Ägyptologische Abhandlungen*, 5), 2nd ed. (Wiesbaden, 1971), 6–9. Helene J. Kantor, in *Chronologies in Old World Archaeology* (Chicago, 1965), 13–15, E. J. Baumgartel, *op. cit.* (Note 3), II, 139, and W. A. Ward, 'Relations between Egypt and Mesopotamia from Prehistoric Times to the End of the Middle Kingdom', *Journal of the Economic and Social History of the Orient*, 4 (1964), 19–27, stress common conception and analogies in design. Ward concludes strongly with Frankfort that the niched façade is a Mesopotamian feature and not an indigenous Egyptian development.

23. Although no very satisfactory explanation has yet been given why mats lashed to wooden frames should be associated with the recessed elements of an Egyptian brick wall, the painted imitation of such matwork on the narrow surfaces of the brick niches is apparently as early as the first use of the brick construction. Frankfort doubted this before the discovery at Saqqara of painted designs of Dynasty I which are like those of the better preserved example in the Dynasty III tomb of Hesy-ra; W. B. Emery, *Great Tombs of the First Dynasty*, III (London, 1958), plates 6–8. Similar mat patterns covered the flat wall of a chapel in a small tomb subsidiary to those of Dynasty I; W. B. Emery, *Great Tombs of the First Dynasty*, I (Cairo, 1949), plate 50.

24. The elements of a building shown on a frequently reproduced Mesopotamian seal (Frankfort, *Ancient Orient*, illustration 27) are combined in a manner unlike that of the examples of Egyptian panelling to which they have been compared (see, for example, Emery, *Annales*, 45 (1947), 147). The seal does not represent as clearly a niched construction in brick as does the 'Palace-façade' of the frame containing the Horus name (*serekh*) of the Egyptian king which has the same form as the panelling on the brick tombs of Dynasty I. The paired plants on the seal suggest tied papyrus flowers. Since the papyrus is accepted as typical of Egypt, this has forced an explanation that the Egyptian adopted a Mesopotamian plant form which he altered into the papyrus in his design. That the resemblance is fortuitous would seem more likely. The value of the seal as evidence has been questioned by Herbert Ricke, who doubts the transmission of architectural forms from Mesopotamia to Egypt (*Bemerkungen*, II, 20, note 27).

25. Frankfort, *Ancient Orient*, illustrations 24–9.

26. There is a considerable literature on this important subject. See particularly Henri Frankfort, *Studies in Early Pottery of the Near East*, I (London, 1924), 93–142, and *The Birth of Civilization in the Ancient Near East* (New York, 1953), appendix; H. J. Kantor, 'The Early Relations of Egypt with Asia', *JNES*, I (1942), 174–213, and 'Further Evidence for Early Mesopotamian Relations with Egypt', *JNES*, 11 (1952), 239–50; A. Scharff, 'Neues zur Frage der ältesten ägyptisch-babylonischen Kulturbeziehungen', *ZÄS*, 71 (1935), 89–106; E. J. Baumgartel, 'The Three Colossi from Koptos and their Mesopotamian Counterparts', *Annales*, 48 (1948), 533–53; Pierre Gilbert, 'Synchronismes artistiques entre Égypte et Mésopotamie', *Chronique d'Égypte*, 26 (1951), 225–36, William A. Ward, 'Egypt and the East Mediterranean from Predynastic Times to the End of the Old Kingdom', *Journal of the Economic and Social History of the Orient*, 6 (1963), esp. 2–19; R. M. Boehmer, 'Das Rollsiegel im prädynastichen Ägypten', *Archäologischer Anzeiger* (1974), Heft 4, 495–514. Recent studies have stressed the likelihood that the Western Asiatic influences stem from Elam (Iran) instead of Sumer (Mesopotamia). See R. M. Boehmer, 'Orientalische Einflüsse auf verzierten Messergriffen aus dem prädynastischen Ägypten', *Archäologische Mitteilungen aus Iran*, 7 (1974), 15–40. The influences may have been stimulated by trade in copper and lapis lazuli. H. S. Smith, 'The Making of Egypt: A review of the influence of Susa and Sumer on Upper Egypt and Lower Nubia in the 4th millennium B.C.,' in Friedman, R. and Adams, B. (eds.), *The Followers of Horus: Studies dedicated to Michael Allen Hoffman* (Egyptian Studies Association No. 2, Oxbow Monograph 20) (Oxford, 1992), 235–46. Note should also be made of the finds from the Nubian A-Group cemetery at Qustul (late Predynastic and Dynasty I): Bruce Williams, 'A Lost Kingdom in Nubia at the Dawn of History', *The Oriental Institute News and Notes*, no. 37 (November 1977), 1–4.

27. For the pottery parallels with Palestine, see Helene J. Kantor in R. W. Ehrich, ed., *Chronologies in Old World Archaeology*, 15–16; Ruth Amiran, 'The Egyptian Alabaster Vessels from Ai', *Israel Exploration Journal*, 20 (1970), 170–9, and 'An Egyptian First Dynasty Jar', *Israel Museum News*, 4 (1970), 89–94. The discovery at Tell Gath of a pottery relief incision of the serekh of King Narmer has prompted considerable discussion. See S. Yeivin, 'Early Contacts between Canaan and Egypt', *Israel Exploration Journal*, 10 (1960), 193–203, 'Further Evidence of Narmer at Gat', *Oriens Antiquus*, 2 (1963), 205–13, and 'The Ceremonial Slate-palette of King Narmer', in *Studies in Egyptology and Linguistics in Honour of H. J. Polotsky* (Jerusalem, 1964), 22–4. William A. Ward, 'The Supposed Asiatic Campaigns of Narmer', *Mélanges de l'université Saint-Joseph, Beyrouth*, 45 (1969), 203–21, and Ruth Amiran, 'An Egyptian Jar Fragment with the Name of Narmer from Arad', *Israel Exploration Journal*, 24 (1974), 4–12, advance persuasive arguments against viewing these artifacts as evidence for an Egyptian domination of Canaan at this time.

28. W. S. Smith in G. A. Reisner, *A History of the Giza Necropolis*, II (Cambridge, 1955), 64, 73–7. A Protodynastic Syro-Palestinian flask has been found in a Second-Dynasty tomb at Helwan (Z. Saad, *Ceiling Stelae in Second Dynasty Tombs from the Excavations at Helwan* (Cairo, 1957), Supplement to *Annales*, 21, plate 34[3]).

CHAPTER 3

1. The dates used throughout this volume follow the chronological table in my *Ancient Egypt as Represented in the Museum of Fine Arts* (Boston, 1960). In the introduction to that table, p. 193, and more fully in *JNES*, 11 (1952), 113–23, an explanation has been offered for the dating used for the early period to the end of the Old Kingdom. I have suggested that if any lowering of the date 3200 B.C. for the beginning of Dynasty I is felt necessary for the purposes of relative chronology, attention should be turned to the seemingly excessive length of the first two dynasties rather than to shortening the First Intermediate Period. Perhaps the compiler of the Turin papyrus may have included in his figure of 955 years from the reign of Menes to that of Aba in Dynasty VIII part of the time before Menes. The name of Menes is apparently associated with that of the Horus Aha on the wooden plaque from the great panelled mastaba of his queen Neith-hetep at Nagadah; see W. B. Emery, *Ḥor-Aha* (Cairo, 1939), 4–7. Vandier, *Manuel*, I, 828, recapitulates the arguments favouring an identification of Menes with Narmer, who certainly seems to have been the predecessor of Aha. Later tradition probably attributed to Menes the achievements of these first two rulers of Dynasty I as well as some of the actions of their predecessors. The chronology and dates used in the first edition of this book have been retained, although there have been many studies in the interval. These generally favour a reduction for the beginning of Dynasty 1, Dynasty 18, and Dynasty 19. For a recent interpretation of the totals for the early dynastic period and the Old Kingdom in the Turin Royal Canon, see Barta, in *MDAIK*, 35 (1979), 11–14.

2. Karl W. Butzer, *Early Hydraulic Civilization in Egypt*, and 'Perspectives on Irrigation Civilization in Pharaonic Egypt', in Denise Schmandt-Besserat, ed., *Immortal Egypt* (Malibu, 1978), 13–18; Wolfgang Schenkel, *Die Bewässerungsrevolution im alten Ägypten*; Barry J. Kemp, 'The Early Development of Towns in Egypt', *Antiquity*, 51 (1977), 185–200; Werner Kaiser, 'Einige Bemerkungen zur ägyptischen Frühzeits, III: Die Reichseinigung', *ZÄS*, 91 (1964), 86–125. There is a considerable and important literature on the origin and early development of writing in Egypt: Siegfried Schott, *Hieroglyphen: Untersuchung zum Ursprung der Schrift* (Akad. der Wiss. und der Lit., Abh. der Geistes und Soz. Kl., 24) (Mainz-Wiesbaden, 1950); Peter Kaplony, *Die Inschriften der ägyptischen Frühzeit*, 3 vols. (Wiesbaden, 1963), *Kleine Beiträge zu den Inschriften der ägyptischen Frühzeit* (Ägyptologische Abhandlungen, 15) (Wiesbaden, 1966), and 'Die Principien der Hieroglyphenschrift', in *Textes et langages de l'Égypte pharaonique*, I (Cairo, 1973), 3–14; Wolfhart Westendorf, 'Die Anfänge der altägyptischen Hieroglyphen', in *Frühe Schriftzeugnisse der Menschheit* (Göttingen, 1969), 56–87; Henry G. Fischer, 'Hieroglyphen', in Helck and Otto, *Lexikon*, II, 1189–99; Also H. G. Fischer, 'The Origin of Egyptian Hieroglyphs,' in Wayne Senner (ed.), *The Origins of Writing* (Norman, 1990), 59–76; John Ray, 'The Emergence of Writing in Egypt', *World Archaeology* 17 (1986), 307–16; Kathryn A. Bard, 'Origins of Egyptian Writing,' in Friedman and Adams (eds.), *The Followers of Horus* (Oxford, 1992), 297–306; W. V. Davies, *Egyptian Hieroglyphs* (Berkeley and London, 1987).

3. Zaki Saad, *Royal Excavations at Helwan, Supplement to Annales*, 3 (1947), 161; *idem*, 14 (1951).

4. J. E. Quibell, *Archaic Mastabas* (Excavations at Saqqara, VI) (Cairo, 1923), 5, plates v–viii.

5. W. B. Emery, *The Tomb of Hemaka* (Cairo, 1938), 6, plate 5; Reisner, *Tomb Development*, 122, where he calls attention to the early use here of the hardened copper chisel in dressing limestone. The use of worked stone is found at Saqqara for a door-frame, Emery, *Great Tombs*, III, plates 54–7; Vandersleyen, *PKG*, plate 5a, and a portcullis, Emery, *Great Tombs*, I, plate 44, both in the reign of Den, and for the roofing of the passage in a smaller tomb in the last reign of Dynasty I, *Great Tombs*, plate 49. In Emery's tomb of Queen Her-neith, an architrave block sculptured with a row of recumbent lions supported the stone roofing in the substructure. The theft of stone may be responsible for the loss of other features such as this which would never have been thought to exist a few years ago; Emery, *Great Tombs*, III, plate 96b.

6. Emery, *Great Tombs*, I, 101, plate 40, A and B.

7. A large door-jamb from the Hierakonpolis temple is in Cairo. Smaller fragments of granite raised reliefs were found at Hierakonpolis and across the river at El Kab; J. E. Quibell and F. W. Green, *Hierakonpolis I* (London, 1900), plate 2; R. Engelbach, 'A Foundation Scene of the Second Dynasty', *JEA*, 20 (1934), plate 24; Ambrose Lansing, 'The Museum's Excavations at Hierakonpolis', *BMMA*, part 2 (November 1935), 44, figure II; Smith, *Sculpture and Painting*, 131.

8. See Vandier, *Manuel*, I, 724, for this and other round-topped royal stelae of Dynasty I. A list of the Abydene royal stelae is provided by H. G. Fischer, in *Artibus Asiae*, 24 (1961), 53–4.

9. Barry J. Kemp, 'Abydos and the Royal Tombs of the First Dynasty', *JEA*, 52 (1966), 13–33, and 'The Egyptian First Dynasty Royal Cemetery', *Antiquity*, 41 (1967), 22–32.

10. Possibly the first three, if both Ra-neb and Hetep-sekhemuwy were buried in the underground galleries in which their sealings were found; but compare Henry G. Fischer, 'An Egyptian Royal Stela of the Second Dynasty', *Artibus Asiae*, 24 (1961), 46–8, and figures 8–9, where the tombs are ascribed to Nynetjer and Ra-neb or Hetep-sekhemuwy. A second series of galleries contained the name of the third king, Nynetjer: J.-Ph. Lauer, *Bull. Inst. Égypte*, 36 (1953–4), 363, figure 4. Emery, *Archaic Egypt* (Harmondsworth, 1961), 94, feels that Tomb 2302 at Saqqara should be identified with the tomb of Nynetjer (Quibell, *Archaic Mastabas*, 29–30, plates 17 [1, 2], 30, 31 [1, 3]), although stone jar fragments recovered there provide the name of Ruaben (see references in B. Porter and R. Moss, *Topographical Bibliography*, III, *Memphis*, 2nd ed. with J. Málek, part 2, fasc. 1, *Saqqara to Dahshur* (Oxford, 1978), 437).

11. See Ricke, *Bemerkungen*, I, 56, for the 'forts' at Abydos and Hierakonpolis; he rejects, however, any possible connection with the later valley temple. See D. B. O'Connor, 'New Funerary Enclosures (*Talbezirke*) of the Early Dynastic Period at Abydos', *JARCE* 26, 1989, 51–86.

12. A small niched shrine with a niched wall around it, not unlike the buildings of the two Second-Dynasty enclosures, was found inside the Zer rectangle of graves. Reisner suggested that the graves surrounded panelled dummy mastabas (*Tomb Development*, 10, 246). Petrie first thought of buildings like the later Valley Temple; *Tombs of the Courtiers* (London, 1925), I, plates i and xv–xix; for the Dynasty II enclosures, see Ayrton, Currelly, Weigall, *Abydos III*, 2, plates v–viii.

13. Hermann Kees, *Der Götterglaube im alten Ägypten* (Leipzig, 1941), 329. The shrine at Abydos once thought to be the Dynasty I–II temple of Khentiamentiu is now regarded as of later Old Kingdom date; cf. Barry J. Kemp, 'The Osiris Temple at Abydos. A postscript to *MDAIK* 23 (1968) 138–55', *GM*, 8 (1973), 23–5. The royal tomb area of Umm el Gaab is now being excavated again. For the last report with references to earlier reports, see Günter Dreyer et al., 'Umm el-Qaab,' *MDAIK* 54, 1998, 3–15. See also Aidan Dodson, 'The So-Called "Tomb of Osiris" at Abydos,' *KMT* 8, no. 4 (Winter 1997–98), 37–47.

14. Emery, *Great Tombs*, II, 1, and III, 3, after setting forth the various difficulties in the way of seeing Saqqara as a royal cemetery, concluded that the balance of evidence definitely favours the view that the Dynasty I kings were buried there. He was followed in this by J.-Ph. Lauer, *BIFAO*, 55 (1955), 153–71, who in addition proposed (p. 170, note 1) that the monuments of Peribsen and Khasekhemuwy at Abydos are cenotaphs like those of Dynasty I, and that their tombs should be looked for at Saqqara. The Fourth-Dynasty tomb of Shery, overseer of the priests of Peribsen, would suggest a tomb at Saqqara for Peribsen at least. The main opponent of Emery's contention was Kees: 'Zur Problematik des archäischen Friedhofes bei Sakkara', *OLZ*, 52 (1957), 12–20, and 'Neues vom archäischen Friedhof von Sakkara', *OLZ*, 54 (1959), 565–70. See also remarks by W. C. Hayes, *The Scepter of Egypt*, I (New York, 1953), 52–5; Alan Gardiner, *Egypt of the Pharaohs* (Oxford, 1961), 410–14; I. E. S. Edwards, C. J. Gadd, and N. G. L. Hammond, eds., *The Cambridge Ancient History*, I, part 2 (Cambridge, 1971), 17–22. Kemp's conclusions are worth quoting: 'Whatever the true explanation of the factors at work, there is no doubt that the royal funerary monuments of the First Dynasty at Abydos were constructed on a rather larger scale than is usually assumed when making comparisons of size and complexity between the royal tombs at Abydos and those claimed as royal at Saqqara. From the point of view of sheer size, the monuments at Abydos seem quite appropriate for actual royal burial places, and with their large open courtyards containing small buildings seem a much more obvious prototype [for] the Step Pyramid complex.' Cf. Barry J. Kemp, 'Abydos and the Royal Tombs of the First Dynasty', *JEA*, 52 (1966), 13–22; 'The Egyptian First Dynasty Royal Cemetery', *Antiquity*, 41 (1967), 22–32. Some possible confirmation of Kemp's views is to be found in the most recent interpretation of the Step Pyramid complex: Hartwig Altenmüller, 'Bemerkungen zur frühen und späten Bauphase des Djoserbezirkes in Saqqara', *MDAIK*, 28 (1972), 1–12; Werner Kaiser, 'Zu den königlichen Talbezirken der 1. und 2. Dynastie in Abydos und zur Baugeschichte des Djoser-grabmals', *MDAIK*, 25 (1969), 1–21; Wolfgang Helck, 'Zu den "Talbezirken" in Abydos', *MDAIK*, 28 (1972), 95–9. However, the most recent thorough consideration of the problem returns to the Lauer and Emery hypothesis that the real burials were at Saqqara and the burials at Abydos merely cenotaphs (dummy burials), with the 'forts' at Abydos the setting for the Sed Festival arrangements. See Jürgen Brinks, *Die Entwicklung der königlichen Grabanlagen des Alten Reiches* (Hildesheimer Ägyptologische Beiträge, 10) (Hildesheim, 1979).

15. W. M. F. Petrie, *A History of Egypt*, I (London, 1923), 4–6; *The Royal*

Tombs of the Earliest Dynasties, II (London, 1901): *Abydos I* (London, 1902), 4; W. G. Waddell, *Manetho* (Cambridge, London, 1948), 5, 27–35.

16. W. B. Emery, *Archaic Egypt* (Harmondsworth, 1961), 54–6; J.-Ph. Lauer, 'Évolution de la tombe royale égyptienne jusqu'à la Pyramide à Degrés', *MDAIK*, 15 (1957), 154–7, and plate 19(2).

17. See Lauer, *BIFAO*, 55 (1955), 156; Emery, *Archaic Egypt*, 1 ff.; the tomb of Her-neith published as No. 3507 in Emery, *Great Tombs*, III, 73–9. Emery, *ibid.*, 4, among others, has suggested that Semerkhet was a usurper.

18. Smith, *Antiquity*, 25 (1951), 40. The tomb of the official Hemaka at Saqqara, No. 3035, has been reassigned by Emery to Den himself (Emery, *Great Tombs*, III, 3, and *Archaic Egypt*, 75–6); the newly investigated Tomb 3506 is associated with the various officials.

19. A roughly shaped stela of a man named Merka [21] was found in the corridor of a great panelled tomb of the time of Qay-a, but may have marked the subsidiary grave in this corridor (Emery, *Great Tombs*, III, 5, 30–1, plates 23(b), 39). See Kemp, *Antiquity*, 41 (1967), 22–32.

20. Ricke, *Bemerkungen*, II, 19.

21. Ricke, *Bemerkungen*, I, passim.

22. See the interesting discussion of Junker in *Giza XII* (Vienna, 1955), 28–31.

23. This does not mean that we must adopt the extreme view that the Delta was so uninhabitable in Predynastic times as to prevent cultural development; E. J. Baumgartel, *The Cultures of Prehistoric Egypt* (London, 1947), 3. Compare H. Frankfort, *Kingship and the Gods* (Chicago, 1948), 15–23, for his belief that Menes was not confronted by a united Delta and that the conception of the dual monarchy 'expressed in political form the deeply rooted Egyptian tendency to understand the world in dualistic terms as a series of pairs of contrasts balanced in unchanging equilibrium'. Frankfort's contention has been 'resolutely combated' by Alan Gardiner, *Egypt of the Pharaohs*, 423.

24. *Tomb Development*, 320 ff. Reisner pointed out that brick packing over the roofing and solid filling of the mastaba would have contained a concealed corbel vault which would lessen considerably the weight on the wooden logs. He thought (pp. 63, 125, 128, 335) that a corbel-vaulted roofing, like that in the Dynasty II stairway tombs at Naga-ed-Dêr, was used in the chambers on each side of the stairway in the tomb of Qay-a at the end of Dynasty I and for the roofing of the chambers of Peribsen and Khasekhemuwy late in Dynasty II. Emery (*Tomb of Hemaka*, 7) noted that the roofing of the deep rock-cut pit of Tomb 3035 must have supported great weight, in considering whether the rectangular stones found there were part of the architraves. It is now clear that the tomb of Herneith of the time of Den had a second chamber above the burial apartment with a second roofing structure at ground level; Emery, *Great Tombs*, III, 75–7. The southern part of the lower chamber was roofed with stones laid on an architrave carved with a row of recumbent lions in relief: Emery, *Great Tombs*, III, plate 96(b).

25. Lauer, *BIFAO*, 55 (1955), 159, plate iv, has heightened the structure suggested by Ricke, *Bemerkungen*, II, 14, figures 1 and 2, and given it a slightly curving top in conformity with the shape of the South Tomb in the Dynasty III Zoser complex at Saqqara, which he thinks reflects this Upper Egyptian type of tomb. Junker, *Giza XII*, 31, points out that the top should be covered with brickwork since the wind would attack the sand or gravel filling of any grave mound.

26. Emery, *Great Tombs*, I, 82, plates 21–35.

27. Lauer, *op. cit.* (Note 25), 160.

28. See Junker, *op. cit.*, 6–12; P. Haider, 'Gefolgschaftbestattungen in universalhistorischer Sicht', *Innsbrücker Beiträge zur Kulturwissenschaft*, 18 (1974), 89–120.

29. Emery, *Great Tombs*, III, 73–97.

30. Emery, *The Tomb of Hemaka*, 28, plates i and xii. On another one of these discs of uncertain use there is the representation of herons or cranes in a clap-net trap, a theme which is well attested with other fowl in royal and private reliefs from the reign of Sneferu at the beginning of Dynasty IV onwards. This disk has been discussed in detail by H. Altenmüller, 'Bemerkungen zur Kreiselscheibe Nr. 310 aus dem Grab des Hemaka in Saqqara', *GM*, 9 (1974), 13–18. Although there is no indication that the motives on the disks derive from as yet unattested Dynasty I reliefs or paintings, perhaps we should assume the possibility of the use of paintings with such themes in the domestic architecture of the first two dynasties.

31. Smith, *Sculpture and Painting*, 11–12.

32. Apparently discovered in the tomb of Semerkhet; E. Amélineau, *Les nouvelles fouilles d'Abydos, 1895–96* (Paris, 1899), 128, 306, plate xxxi; Petrie, *Royal Tombs*, I (1901), plate xxxvii, 76; II (1901), plate xliii, 22.

33. A. Lucas, *Ancient Egyptian Materials and Industries*, 4th ed. by J. R. Harris (London, 1962), 155–6; C. Kiefer and A. Allibert, 'Pharaonic Blue Ceramics: The Process of Self-glazing', *Archaeology*, 24 (1971), 107–17; H. C. Wulff, H. S. Wulff, and L. Koch, 'Egyptian Faience: A Possible Survival in Iran', *Archaeology*, 21 (1968), 98–107; and especially Elizabeth Riefstahl, *Ancient Egyptian Glass and Glazes in the Brooklyn Museum* (1968).

34. W. B. Emery, *Hor-Aha* (Cairo, 1939), 17; *Great Tombs*, II, 11, plate xiii.

35. Petrie, *Royal Tombs*, II (1901), 16, plate 1.

36. G. A. Reisner, *The Early Dynastic Cemeteries of Naga-ed-Dêr*, I (Leipzig, 1908), 30, plates 6–9.

37. Smith, *Sculpture and Painting*, 9; Emery, *Great Tombs*, III, plate 27.

38. Smith, *Sculpture and Painting*, 8, plate 1; also note 1 for the Cairo statuette, No. 71586.

39. *Ibid.*, 9, plate 2.

40. Professor Emery has kindly allowed me to illustrate this relief and that of our illustration 32. Cf. Walter B. Emery, *A Funerary Repast in an Egyptian Tomb of the Archaic Period* (Leiden, 1962), plate 3a.

41. Smith, *Sculpture and Painting*, 256.

42. Emery, *Great Tombs*, III, plates 6–8; I, plate 50; II, 9; see also 146, 147, where green like that splashed on the east façade of the main tomb was found with the red, black, and yellow pigments of the paint-pots in a subsidiary burial.

43. Zaki Saad, *Royal Excavations at Helwan*, plates lxxix–lxxxii; Leclant, in *Orientalia*, 22 (1953), 96, 97, figures 34 and 35; see Junker, *Giza XII*, 52. The use of these slab stelae on the ceiling of the underground burial chambers at Helwan is now thought to have been extremely unlikely: see G. Haeny, 'Zu den Platten mit Opfertischszene aus Heluan und Giseh', in *Festschrift Ricke* (*Beiträge zur ägyptischen Bauforschung und Altertumskunde*, 12) (Wiesbaden, 1971), 143–64.

44. Smith, *Sculpture and Painting*, 115–16, figure 32.

45. Two fragmentary reliefs, one in Turin and one in Cairo, are apparently from the early temple of Hathor at Gebelein. They should probably be dated to Dynasty II, and perhaps both belong to the same scene of a foundation ceremony; Smith, *Sculpture and Painting*, 137, plate 30d. See, however, a different interpretation of the Turin block, Silvio Curto, *Aegyptus*, 33 (1953), 105–24, and cf. Ernesto Scamuzzi, *Egyptian Art in the Museum of Turin* (New York, 1965), plate 8.

46. Quibell, *Hierakonpolis I*, plates xxxix–xli; Smith, *Sculpture and Painting*, 13, 133, and 'Two Archaic Egyptian Statues', *BMFA*, 65 (1967), 70–84.

CHAPTER 4

1. For the basic work on the Step Pyramid and selected studies of particular interest, see: C. M. Firth and J. E. Quibell, with plans by J.-Ph. Lauer, *The Step Pyramid . . .*, I–II (Cairo, 1935–6); J.-Ph. Lauer, *Fouilles à Saqqarah. La pyramide à degrés. L'architecture*, tome 1–3 (Cairo, 1936–9); P. Lacau and J.-Ph. Lauer, *Fouilles à Saqqarah. La pyramide à degrés*, tome 4: *Inscriptions gravées sur les vases*, 2 fascs. (Cairo, 1959–61); tome 5: *Inscriptions à l'encre sur les vases* (Cairo, 1965); J.-Ph. Lauer, *Histoire monumentale des pyramides d'Égypte*, tome 1. *Les pyramides à degrés (IIIe Dynastie)* (IFAO, Bibl. d'Étude, 39) (Cairo, 1962); Ricke, *Bemerkungen*, 1 (Cairo and Zürich, 1944); Werner Kaiser, 'Zu den königlichen Talbezirken der 1. und 2. Dynastie in Abydos und zur Baugeschichte des Djoser-Grabmals', *MDAIK*, 25 (1969), 1–22; Hartwig Altenmüller, 'Bemerkungen zur frühen und späten Bauphase des Djoserbezirkes in Saqqara', *MDAIK*, 28 (1972), 1–12; J.-Ph. Lauer, 'Remarques sur les stèles fausses-portes de l'Horus Neteri-Khet (Zoser) à Saqqarah', *Monuments et Mémoires Académie des Inscriptions et Belles Lettres. Monuments Piot*, 49 (1957); 1–15; Dietrich Wildung, 'Two Representations of Gods from the Early Old Kingdom', *Miscellanea Wilbouriana*, 1 (Brooklyn, 1972), 145–60. F. D. Friedman, 'The Underground Relief Panels of King Djoser at the Step Pyramid Complex,' *JARCE* 32 (1995), 1–42. *Ibid.*, 'Notions of Cosmos in the Step Pyramid Complex,' in P. D. Manuelian, (ed.), *Studies in Honor of William Kelly Simpson*, Boston, 1996, 337–51. W. Kaiser, 'Die unterirdischen Anlage der Djoserpyramide und ihrer entwicklungsgeschichtlichen Einordnung,' in I. Gamer-Wallert and W. Helck (eds.), *Gegengabe: Festschrift für Emma Brunner-Traut*, Tübingen (1992), 167–90; *Ibid.*, 'Zu die Granitkammern und ihren Vorgängerbauten unter der Stufenpyramide und im Südgrab von Djoser,' *MDAIK* 53 (1997), 195–207 (indicates that the granite chambers beneath the pyramid and south building were not part of the original scheme but were added at the same time the superstructure was converted from a square mastaba to a step pyramid.) J.-Ph. Lauer, 'Sur l'emploi et le rôle de la couleur aux monuments du complexe funéraire de roi Djoser,' *RdE* 44 (1993) 75–80. Missing plate provided in *RdE* 45, (1994); *Ibid.*, 'Sur certaines modifications et extensions apportées au complexe funéraire de Djoser au cours de son règne,' in John Baines et al. (eds.), *Pyramid Studies and other Essays presented to I.E.S. Edwards*. London, 1988, 12–22. *Ibid.*, 'Remarques concernant l'inscription gravé sur le socle de statue de l'Horus Neteri-Khet (roi Djoser),' in P. D. Manuelian (ed.), *Studies in Honor of William Kelly Simpson*, Boston, 1996, 493–8.

2. Firth and Quibell, *op. cit.*, II, plates 59 and 95.

3. In *Révue Archéologique*, 47 (1956), 17, Lauer favours the idea that Sa-nekht was a brother of Zoser who preceded him with a shorter reign and

began the mastaba under the later Step Pyramid. Sa-nekht was certainly closely connected with Zoser, who in early times is given only his Horus name, Neterkhet. It is less probable that Sa-nekht is the same as Neb-ka who precedes Zoser in the Turin Papyrus and the Abydos King List, for Neb-ka follows Zoser in the Westcar Papyrus and is perhaps the Neb-ka-ra who precedes the last king of the Dynasty, Huni, in the Saqqara King List. In spite of Lauer's feeling that the unfinished pyramid at Zawiyet el Aryan is later than Dynasty III, the quarry-marks there may well be read Neb-ka, while the oval granite sarcophagus sunk in the granite flooring of the great pit would seem to accord better with the next to last reign of Dynasty III, as would the mention of the priesthood of a temple of Neb-ka held by a man named Akhet-aa. Compare *AJA*, 46 (1942), 518, where I was still under the impression that Sethe had read correctly the name of Neb-ka in a cartouche on a sealing with the name of Sa-nekht from the large brick mastaba at Beit Khallaf which adjoins another containing the name of Zoser. The use of a cartouche around a royal name is not known this early, and the reading doubtful. One might tentatively suggest the following order for the kings of Dynasty III: Neterkhet (Zoser), Sekhem-khet, Sa-nekht, Kha-ba, Neb-ka, Huni. Further chronological discussion in W. Stevenson Smith, 'The Old Kingdom in Egypt', in I. E. S. Edwards, C. J. Gadd, and N. G. L. Hammond, eds., *The Cambridge Ancient History*, 3rd ed., I, part 2 (Cambridge, 1971), 461–5.

4. For the pyramid at Zawiyet el Aryan, see J.-Ph. Lauer, *Observations sur les pyramides* (IFAO, *Bibl. d'Étude*, 30) (Cairo, 1960), figure 17 and plate 10 (top); V. Maragioglio and C. A. Rinaldi, *L'architettura delle piramide Menfite*, II (Turin, 1963), 41–9; and references in Note 9, below.

5. A reference to Imhotep has also been discovered on an unfinished block from the uncompleted Step Pyramid of Sekhemkhet: Dietrich Wildung, *Imhotep und Amenhotep: Gottwerdung im alten Ägypten* (*Münchner Ägyptologische Studien*, 36) (Munich-Berlin, 1977), 12. For the statue-base with Imhotep's name and titles, see H. Junker, *Giza XII* (Vienna, 1955), 101 and figure 7; J.-Ph. Lauer, *Les pyramides de Sakkareh* (Cairo, 1972), 3, figure 55; Wildung, *op. cit.*, 1–2.

6. Zakaria Ghoneim, *Horus Sekhem-khet: The Unfinished Step Pyramid at Saqqara*, I (Cairo, 1957); Maragioglio and Rinaldi, *op. cit.*, 11–39; Lauer, *Histoire monumentale des pyramides d'Égypte*, I, 179–206; *idem*, 'Recherche et découverte du tombeau sud de l'Horus Sekhem-khet dans son complex funéraire à Saqqarah', *Revue d'Égyptologie*, 20 (1968), 97–107; review of Ghoneim, *op. cit.*, in *BIFAO*, 59 (1960), 315–20. With the Sinai relief it is interesting to compare a second Sinai monument of Sekhemkhet, discovered and published by Raphael Giveon, 'A Second Relief of Sekhemkhet in Sinai', *BASOR*, 216 (Dec. 1974), 17–20.

7. See Lauer, *Revue archéologique*, 47 (1956), 19; *Bull. Inst. Égypte*, 36 (1953–4), 357. Reisner, *Tomb Development*, 134, assigned the layer pyramid of Zawiyet el Aryan to Dynasty II, but his original attribution to King Kha-ba of Dynasty III on the basis of the royal name found on stone bowels in a tomb in the neighbouring cemetery has for some time appeared to be the correct one. See A. J. Arkell, in *JEA*, 42 (1956), 116; Dows Dunham, *Zawiyet el-Aryan: the Cemeteries Adjacent to the Layer Pyramid* (Boston, 1978), 34.

8. See the air view which Zakaria Ghoneim reproduces in figure 1 of his report on the excavation of the Sekhem-khet monument and Lauer, *Bull. Inst. Égypte*, 36 (1953–4), 559. This photograph also suggests that perhaps another enclosure lay north of that of Sekhem-khet.

9. Barsanti in *Annales*, 7 (1906), 260, 8 (1907), 201, 12 (1912), 57; Vandier, *Manuel*, I, 942; J.-Ph. Lauer, *Le problème des pyramides d'Égypte* (Paris, 1948), 76–7; Jaroslav Černý, 'The Name of the King of the Unfinished Pyramid at Zawiyet el-Aryân', *MDAIK*, 16 (1958), 25–9. J.-Ph. Lauer, 'Sur l'âge et l'attribution possible de l'excavation monumentale de Zaouiêt el-Aryân', *Revue d'Égyptologie*, 14 (1962), 21–36, and V. Maragioglio and C. A. Rinaldi, *L'architettura delle piramide Menfite*, VI (Rapallo, 1967), 22, would place the structure in the second half of the Fourth Dynasty. Klaus Baer reads the name as Wehemka, placing the pyramid and its builder near the end of Dynasty IV between Mycerinus and Shepseskaf.

10. This has been interpreted by Ricke as a reproduction of the royal palace, *Bemerkungen*, I, 101. His explanation of these buildings differs from that of Lauer, *La pyramide à degrés*, I–III (Cairo, 1936–9), which has been followed generally here; see also Vandier, *Manuel*, I, 867–941.

11 Firth and Quibell, *op. cit.*, I, frontispiece in colour; II, plates 48–54 for the South Tomb; plates 13–17 for the tile-lined gallery under the pyramid. See Note 1 above.

12. This view has been contested by Ricke, who would see instead a protective binding around the ends of brick walls imitated here; compare Lauer's reply to this, *Supplement to Annales* 9, 1948, 30 ff.

13. See Lauer, *op. cit.*, (Note 12), 41 for criticism of Ricke's reconstruction of a wooden prototype for these capitals, *Bemerkungen*, I, 82, figure 20, plate 2; compare also Alexander Badawy, *A History of Egyptian Architecture*, I (Giza, 1954), 84, 85, figure 61. Lauer, *La pyramide à degrés*, I, 161–2, notes the resemblance to the columns of a similar edifice with Hathor capitals pictured at Deir el

Bahari but would not reconstruct the same here, as did L. Borchardt, *Ägyptische Tempel mit Umgang* (Cairo, 1938), 27, figure 8.

14. See Ricke's fine drawing, *Bemerkungen*, I, plate 4, for the form of the original structure [42B].

15. For the reliefs of King Zoser from Room III, see Cecil M. Firth, *The Step Pyramid*, II (Cairo, 1935), plates 15–17, and J.-Ph. Lauer, 'Remarques sur les stèles fausses-portes de l'Horus Neteri-khet (Zoser) à Saqqarah', *Mon. Piot*, 49 (1957), 1–15; for reliefs from Room II of the South Tomb, see Firth, *Step Pyramid*, II, plates 40–1, 44, with remarks by Gardiner, *JEA*, 30 (1944), 32. See now F. D. Friedman, 'The Underground Relief Panels of King Djoser at the Step Pyramid Complex,' *JARCE* 32 (1995), 1–42.

16. Smith, *Sculpture and Painting*, plate 30c, and A. H. Gardiner and T. E. Peet, *The Inscriptions of Sinai*, 2nd ed. with J. Černý (London, 1952), plate 4(3).

17. Smith, *op. cit.*, plate 31. J.-Ph. Lauer, 'Remarques concernant l'inscription gravé sur le socle de statue de l'Horus Neteri-Khet (roi Djoser),' in P. D. Manuelian (ed.), *Studies in Honor of William Kelly Simpson*, Boston, 1996, 493–8.

18. Smith, *op. cit.*, figure 48.

19. Smith, *op. cit.*, plate 44; Reisner, *Giza Necropolis*, II, 6, figure 9; Dunham and Simpson, *Giza Mastabas*, I, figure 7; Simpson, *Giza Mastabas*, III, figures 13, 26.

20. Smith, *op. cit.*, 134, figure 50.

21. J. E. Quibell, *Excavations at Saqqara, The Tomb of Hesy* (Cairo, 1913). There are many reproductions of these reliefs, but note especially that of E. L. B. Terrace and H. G. Fischer, *Treasures of Egyptian Art from the Cairo Museum* (London, 1970), 33–6; the stela removed by Quibell is discussed by Fischer, *MMJ*, 5 (1972), 17–19.

22. For this and the following chapels, see Smith, *op. cit.*, 148 ff.; also plate 34; a plan of the chapel in Helen Jacquet-Gordon, *Les noms des domaines funéraires sous l'ancien empire égyptien* (IFAO, *Bibl. d'Étude*, 34) (Cairo, 1962), figure 117.

23. Smith, *op. cit.*, plate 35; *AJA*, 46 (1942), 518.

24. Reisner, *Tomb Development*, 203, 267–9, figures 158–63.

25. See Smith, *op. cit.*, 15, plates 3–4; Vandier, *Manuel*, I, 978–86.

26. R. Weill, *La IIe et la IIIe dynastie* (Paris, 1908), 180–4; J. Garstang, *Mahasna and Bêt Khallâf* (London, 1903), plate xxvi. For the reading of the name as simply Ankh, see Keimer, *Annales*, 31 (1931), 178. The owner of the statues Leiden D.93 and Louvre A.39 is to be distinguished from another man named Ankh with an archaic statuette, Leiden D.94.

27. M. Eaton-Krauss and C. E. Loeben, 'Some Remarks on the Louvre Statues of Sepa (A 36 and 37) Nesames (A 38),' in E. Goring, N. Reeves, and J. Ruffle (eds.), *Chief of Seers: Egyptian Studies in Memory of Cyril Aldred* (London and New York, 1997), 83–7; Henry G. Fischer, 'An Elusive Shape within the Fisted Hands of Egyptian Statues', *MMJ*, 10 (1975), 9–21, who interprets the shape as a piece of cloth.

CHAPTER 5

1. Smith in Reisner, *Giza Necropolis*, II, 1; *JNES*, 11 (1952), 124; where the dates given in these quarry-marks are discussed. For the decree of Pepy I, see Borchardt, *ZÄS*, 42 (1905), 1.

2. Ahmed Fakhry, *The Bent Pyramid of Dahshur* (Cairo, 1954) (extracts from *Annales*, 51 (1951), 510–21; 52 (1954), 563–623). See Note 4 below.

3. Ahmed Fakhry, *The Monuments of Sneferu at Dahshur*, II, part 2 (Cairo, 1961), plates 33–4, 36–7. For reconstruction, Ricke in Fakhry, *The Bent Pyramid of Dahshur*, figure 5.

4. For the temples of Sneferu at Dahshur, see Ahmed Fakhry, *The Monuments of Sneferu at Dahshur*, I, *The Bent Pyramid* (Cairo, 1959); II, *The Valley Temple*, part 1, *The Temple Reliefs* (Cairo, 1961), part 2, *The Finds* (Cairo, 1961).

5. J. de Morgan, *Carte de la nécropole memphite* (Cairo, 1897), plate 1.

6. Alan Rowe, in *The Museum Journal* (University of Pennsylvania), 22 (1931), 5–36, plate viii. A recent theory proposes that the Medum pyramid partially collapsed owing to a structural fault. See K. Mendelssohn, 'A Building Disaster at the Meidum Pyramid', *JEA*, 59 (1973), 60–71. There is some controversy about the exact nature of this structural flaw (Davey, *JEA*, 62 (1976), 178–9) and about the date of the supposed collapse (Edwards, *JEA*, 60 (1974), 251–2).

7. For the disposition of these interior rooms and passages see the drawing, Fakhry, *Bent Pyramid at Dahshur* (1954), plate 4, following p. 601 (our illustration 70).

8. Rowe, *op. cit.*, plates xi, xxvi–xxxvi.

9. For these tombs see W. M. F. Petrie, *Medum* (London, 1892).

10. Smith, *Sculpture and Painting*, plates 33, 34.

11. *JEA*, 23 (1937), 17–26.

12. For the seasons relief-cycle from the sun temple of Ne-user-ra, see S. Wenig, *Die Jahreszeitenreliefs aus dem Sonnenheiligtum des Königs Ne-User-Re*

(Berlin, 1966); E. Edel and S. Wenig, *Die Jahreszeitenreliefs aus dem Sonnenheiligtum des Königs Ne-User-Re* (*Staatliche Museen zu Berlin, Mitteilungen aus der ägyptischen Sammlung*, 7) (Berlin, 1974). A reconstruction of the cycle is offered by Smith, *Interconnections*, 141–7, 152–3, and figures 178(a, b), 183(b). See Chapter 6, n. 22.

13. Quibell, *Tomb of Hesy*, 10, plate vii.

14. See the valuable discussion by Junker, in *Giza* XII, 61. He calls attention to the personal character of the scenes in Nefermaat's tomb where the sons display their abilities before their parents. An element of sport is involved in the bird-trapping scene as much as any idea of obtaining food. To this the flower-crowns lend a festive note, as they do to the men sowing and ploughing who also may represent Atet's sons.

15. See the coloured reproduction, Nina M. Davies, *Ancient Egyptian Paintings* (Chicago, 1936), plate i.

16. See the report by Daninos-Bey to Maspero of the work undertaken in 1871 at Medum, with its amusing reference to the fact that Mariette was too occupied with the preparations for the opera Aida to be present at the first excavations; *Recueil de travaux*, 8 (1886), 69.

17. Smith, *Sculpture and Painting*, 27, plate 6a.

18. References in Note 3 above; one was life-size and the other a little larger.

19. J. D. Cooney, *The Brooklyn Museum Bulletin*, 9 (1948), 1–12; Richard Fazzini, *Images for Eternity*, 26, no. 15.

20. Reisner and Smith, *Giza Necropolis*, II. Mark Lehner, *The Pyramid Tomb of Hetepheres and the Satellite Pyramid of Khufu*. (SDAIK 19) (Cairo, 1985).

21. This was Haroeris, Horus the Elder, whose home was in this Second Nome of the Delta; see Sethe, *Urgeschichte und älteste Religion der Ägypter* (Leipzig, 1930), 39, note 3; also Junker, *Giza II* (Vienna, 1934), 51, 191. I overlooked this possible connection in studying these designs and the similar ones on the Dynasty V inlaid vases of King Neferirkara; *Giza Necropolis*, II, 31, 39. The two eyes of this sky god were the sun and the moon, and the loss of the eye, through the waning of the moon, and its recovery forms an important theme in religious literature. Hence the amuletic protection of the parts of the Horus eye. Zaki Saad has found a 'Min' emblem at Helwan of the First Dynasty with a pair of eyes on the central portion which would seem again to represent the Horus of Letopolis.

22. A similar design appears on an alabaster vase lid; Loat, *JEA*, 9 (1923), 161, plate xxix. For three head-bands found at Giza with disks of a different design, see Dunham, *BMFA*, 44 (1946), 23. The sail of the state ship of Sahura has similar patterns, one of which includes feathers with the plant forms; L. Borchardt, *Das Grabdenkmal des Königs S'ahure*, II (Leipzig, 1913), plate 9.

23. G. A. Reisner, *Giza Necropolis*, I (Cambridge, 1942), 46, figure 8. See also the socket emplacements, probably for wooden columns, in the exterior chapel of Kawab (G 7120): William K. Simpson, *The Mastabas of Kawab, Khafkhufu I and II, Giza Mastabas*, vol. 3 (Boston, 1978), 1, and figures 2, 4.

24. See Chassinat, in *Mon. Piot*, 25 (1921–2), 55, where it is suggested that the granite columns re-used in the nearby convent of Nahiya may have come from the Abu Roash temple.

25. Even here we must remember that there were inscriptions flanking the doors to the two deep niches which formed the entrances in the granite-cased façade. They may have been surmounted by the hollow cornice so much used in later architecture. Granite blocks from such a cornice were found in the debris and one had part of a Horus falcon which may have belonged above the king's name in one of the façade inscriptions. It makes little difference for the date when such a cornice was introduced, whether these blocks, which do not seem to have been studied, came from the Valley Temple or the granite casing of the building which adjoins it on the north. This was intended to serve the Great Sphinx which Chephren's sculptors cut in the image of the king from a great piece of rock left by the quarrymen; Selim Hassan, *The Great Sphinx and its Secrets* (Cairo, 1953), plate xvi; H. Ricke, 'Der Harmachistempel des Chefren in Giseh', and S. Schott, 'Ägyptische Quellen zum Plan des Sphinxtempels', in *Beiträge zur Ägyptischen Bauforschung und Altertumskunde*, 10 (Wiesbaden, 1970). A cavetto cornice appears above the shrines in the little temple at Kasr el Sagha on the edge of the Fayum, which is one of the few buildings that possibly could be assigned to Dynasty IV outside Giza; *MDAIK*, 5 (1934), 1; *Chronique d'Égypte*, 20 (1945), 83; Junker, *Giza VI* (1943), 11, figure 2; Dieter and Dorothea Arnold, *Der Tempel Qasr el-Sagha* (Cairo, Mainz, 1979), where a date in the Middle Kingdom, probably the reign of Sesostris II, is argued.

26. For a block of priests' houses and the workmen's barracks at Giza, see Alexander Badawy, *A History of Egyptian Architecture*, I, 54–5 and *passim* for his valuable illustrations of other examples of Old Kingdom architecture. Few important changes seem to have occurred in the Old Kingdom level of the Abydos temple of Khentiamentiu, where the ivory statuette of Cheops [82] was found. It is difficult to be certain what additions were made to the archaic temple at Hierakonpolis, where the copper statues of Pepy I and his son [143, 144] were dedicated. One other temple is known, constructed by Pepy I at Bubastis in the Delta; *Chronique d'Égypte*, 20 (1945), 83; Labib Habachi, *Tell Basta*, Supplément aux *Annales*, 22 (Cairo, 1957).

27. See I. E. S. Edwards, *The Pyramids of Egypt*, rev. ed. (London, 1961); L. Grinsell, *Egyptian Pyramids* (Gloucester, 1947), for details of construction in Old Kingdom pyramids.

28. Lauer, *Annales*, 46 (1947), 245; 49 (1949), 111; Ricke, *Bemerkungen*, II, figure 13, pp. 43–4.

29. For the fragments from the temple, found by Selim Hassan, and this chapel, see Reisner, *Giza Necropolis*, II, 4, figures 5, 6, 7.

30. See Smith, *Sculpture and Painting*, 157–61, and Hans Goedicke, *Re-used Blocks from the Pyramid of Amenemhet I at Lisht* (New York, 1971), for these and other low reliefs.

31. The function of the various parts of these buildings has been studied by Herbert Ricke, who with Siegfried Schott has attempted to trace in the Pyramid Texts the ritual performed here; *Beiträge zur Ägyptischen Bauforschung und Altertumskunde*, 5, *Bemerkungen*, II. Formidable difficulties are involved in the interpretation of these spells, which first appear in the burial chamber of King Unas at the end of Dynasty V to aid the king in the transition between his earthly functions and the position which he was to assume amongst the gods after death. Arnold has now reaffirmed that the function of the pyramid temple, on the basis of its architecture, wall reliefs, statuary, and relevant inscriptions, is the promotion of the corporeal afterlife of the dead king through the funerary cult, his continued victories over his enemies in the hereafter, the continuance of his kingship, and his deification, all achieved through the building and decoration programme of the pyramid complex. Cf. Dieter Arnold, 'Rituale und Pyramidentempel', *MDAIK*, 33 (1977), 1–14; he thereby rejects the pyramid-as-ritual function advocated by Ricke and Schott. A close analysis of the various elements of the pyramid complex and their development with regard to the function of the several parts has been contributed by Jürgen Brinks, *Die Entwicklung der königlichen Grabanlagen des Alten Reiches* (Hildesheim, 1979).

32. Ricke, *Bemerkungen*, II, 50–4, 116, where he points out that the relief with an Asiatic prisoner found in the clearance of the Chephren temples comes from here rather than from the causeway, where no decoration was observed on the walls near the foot. I had thought that weathering of the walls made this uncertain, but Hölscher's earlier examination should be respected. Such representations are associated in the Fifth Dynasty both with the sacrifice of prisoners and the presentation of booty in the pyramid temple and the king as a sphinx or griffin trampling upon his foreign foes in the causeway reliefs. It seems that Cheops introduced the roofing of the causeway to protect the 'carvings of animals' mentioned by Herodotus; Edwards, *op. cit.*, 102, 112; Smith, *Sculpture and Painting*, 158.

33. For the Cheops boat, see A. Abubakr and A. Youssef, 'The Funerary Boat of Khufu', in *Aufsätze zum 70. Geburtstag von Herbert Ricke* (*Beiträge zur ägyptischen Bauforschung und Altertumskunde*, 12) (Wiesbaden, 1971), 1–16; Z. Nour, Z. Iskander, S. Osman, and A. Youssef, *The Cheops Boat*, part 1 (Cairo, 1960); Nancy Jenkins, *The Boat beneath the Pyramid: King Cheops' Royal Ship* (New York, 1980).

34. Selim Hassan, *Excavations at Giza*, IV (Cairo, 1943), 90, figure 47.

35. See the Reqaqnah and Beit Khallaf tombs, J. Garstang, *The Tombs of the Third Egyptian Dynasty* (London, 1904).

36. See Alexander Badawy's discussion of the use of brick vaults at Giza in Abdel-Moneim Abu-Bakr, *Excavations at Giza, 1949–50* (Cairo, 1953), 129–43.

37. For the family history of Dynasty IV, see Reisner, *Giza Necropolis*, II, 5, and W. Stevenson Smith, 'The Old Kingdom in Egypt', in I. E. S. Edwards, C. J. Gadd, and N. G. L. Hammond, eds., *The Cambridge Ancient History*, 3rd ed., I, part 2 (Cambridge, 1971), 160–79.

38. Dows Dunham and William K. Simpson, *The Mastabas of Queen Mersyankh III, Giza Mastabas*, vol. 1 (Boston, 1974).

39. Smith, *Sculpture and Painting*, plate 48.

40. Smith, *Sculpture and Painting*, 23; *ibid.*, 25, plates 6–9 for the series of reserve heads; also Reisner, *Giza Necropolis*, I, plates 22, 34, 52–6; Claude Vandersleyen, 'Ersatzkopf', in Helck and Otto, *Lexikon*, II, 11–14; Allyn L. Kelley, 'Reserve Heads: a review of the evidence for their placement and function in the Old Kingdom', *Newsletter of the Society for the Study of Egyptian Antiquities* 5, no. 1 (1974), 6–12; P. Lacovara, 'The Riddle of the Reserve Heads,' *KMT: A Modern Journal of Ancient Egypt* 8, no. 4, Winter 1997–1998, 28–36; Roland Tefnin 'Les têtes magiques de Gizeh', *BSFE* 120 (1991), 25–37. *Ibid.*, *Art et Magie au temps des Pyramides: L'énigme des têtes dites 'de renplacement,'* Monumenta Aegyptiaca V (Brussels, 1991).

41. Another example appears in the reliefs of the treasurer Nofer which resemble the profile of his reserve head; Smith, *Sculpture and Painting*, plate 48; *AJA*, 45 (1941), 514–28.

42. Smith, *Sculpture and Painting*, plates 43, 44; *BMFA*, 32 (1934), 2; Simpson, *The Mastabas of Kawab and Khafkhufu I and II*.

43. Smith, *Sculpture and Painting*, 159; Junker, *Giza I* (Vienna, 1929), coloured plate and *passim*; Reisner, *Giza Necropolis*, I, plates 17–20, 39, 57.

44. Smith, *Sculpture and Painting*, coloured plate A; *idem*, 'The Stela of Prince Wepemnofret', *Archaeology*, 16 (1963), 2–13, and colour plate on cover; Fazzini, *Images for Eternity*, 28–9, 34.

45. Andrey Bolshakov, 'What did the Bust of Ankh-haf Originally Look Like?', *Journal of the Museum of Fine Arts, Boston*, 3 (1991), 5–14.

46. The statue had been broken up in another part of the temple. See Reisner, *Mycerinus* (Cambridge, Mass., 1931), 22; Smith, *Sculpture and Painting*, 35, plate 13; the Cairo head is 11¼ inches high (29 cm), while that of the Boston figure which stood nearly 8 feet high (2.35 m.) is 14¼ inches (37 cm). For the triads of King Mycerinus, see E. L. B. Terrace, 'A Fragmentary Triad of King Mycerinus', *BMFA*, 59 (1961), 40–9, and Wendy Wood, 'A Reconstruction of the Triads of King Mycerinus', *JEA*, 60 (1974), 82–93.

47. Smith, *Sculpture and Painting*, 167, figures 62, 63, 65, 66; the huntsman in figure 65 probably came from the chapel of G 7420 and not from that of Min-khaf (G 7430) as stated there and in *AJA*, 46 (1942), 520–30, where the Hemiunu fragments are also illustrated.

48. Reisner, *BMFA*, 25 (1927), 64–79; Smith, *Sculpture and Painting*, 169, figure 64, plates 44, 49; Dows Dunham and William K. Simpson, *The Mastaba of Queen Mersyankh III* (Boston, 1974).

CHAPTER 6

1. B. Grdseloff, *Annales*, 42 (1943), 64. For other interpretations of the difficult evidence for these family relationships, see Selim Hassan, *Excavations at Giza*, III (Cairo, 1943), 3; Borchardt, *Annales*, 38 (1938), 209; Junker, *MDAIK*, 3 (1932), 139. That there was a second Queen Khent-kaw-s married to Neferirkara is confirmed by an unpublished block found at Saqqara, where she stands behind the king with a Prince Ranofer. This queen is represented by a pyramid complex at Abusir: M. Verner, 'Excavations at Abusir, Season of 1978, Preliminary Report', *ZÄS*, 105 (1978), 155–9.

2. William Kelly Simpson, et al., *The Literature of Ancient Egypt*, 3rd revised printing (New Haven, 1977), 15–30. R. B. Parkinson, *The Tale of Sinuhe and other Ancient Egyptian Poems 1940–1640 BC* (Oxford, 1997), 102–27. This story of King Cheops and the Magicians is not only one of the most attractive which has come down from antiquity but contains valuable material for the history of Dynasties III–V. On the story and the beginning of Dynasty V, see H. Altenmüller, in *Chronique d'Égypte*, 45 (1970), 211–31.

3. H. Ricke, et al., *Das Sonnentempel des Königs Userkaf*, I, *Der Bau*, II, *Die Funde* (*Beiträge zur ägyptischen Bauforschung und Altertumskunde*, 7–8) (Wiesbaden, 1965, 1969).

4. Smith, *Sculpture and Painting*, 46, and Vandier, *Manuel*, III, 29–30.

5. Reisner, *Mycerinus*, chapter VII; Terrace, *BMFA*, 59 (1961), 40–9; Wood, *JEA*, 60 (1974), 82–93.

6. W. C. Hayes, *The Scepter of Egypt*, I (New York, 1953), 70.

7. In addition to the heads of lions and prisoners of Dynasties V and VI listed in my *Sculpture and Painting*, 54, 55, there are some puzzling figures of recumbent calves, a seated lion, and a sphinx(?), as yet unpublished, from the pyramid temple of Zedkara (Isesy); quoted in preface, cf. preface to second edition (1949), i.

8. Reisner, *op. cit.*, plate 64.

9. Schäfer, *OLZ*, 29 (1926), 723.

10. Ricke, *Bemerkungen*, II, 101–2.

11. H. Schäfer, *Ein Bruchstück altägyptischer Annalen* (Berlin, 1902), 39.

12. Smith, *op. cit.*, plate 18b, d; 45 ff. for the sculpture of Dynasty V.

13. See the map of the Saqqara cemetery, Reisner, *Tomb Development*; A. J. Spenser, 'Researches on the Topography of North Saqqara', *Orientalia*, 43 (1974), 1–11, with folding map.

14. Smith, *op. cit.*, plate 18e.

15. Smith, *op. cit.*, 31; William K. Simpson, *The Mastabas of Kawab, Khafkhufu I and II* (Boston, 1978), 7–8.

16. Found in the excavations of Dr Abdel-Moneim Abu-Bakr, who has kindly permitted its reproduction; cf. *AJA*, 56 (1952), 40, plate 3.

17. Lauer, *Annales*, 53 (1956), 119, and V. Maragioglio and C. Rinaldi, *L'architettura delle piramide Menfite*, part 7 (Rapallo, 1970), plate 1.

18. Ricke, *Bemerkungen*, II, 69, figure 27. The unusual placement of the pyramid has been thought to reflect an intended relationship to the axis of the sun altar of the adjacent Step Pyramid of Zoser. See Altenmüller, *MDAIK*, 28 (1972), 9–12; Brinks, *Die Entwicklung der königlichen Grabanlagen*, 133–5.

19. Smith, *op. cit.*, 122, figure 39.

20. Since describing these unpublished fragments in my *Sculpture and Painting*, 178, I have been able to study them again in the store-rooms at Saqqara in 1946 and 1951 and to make drawings, two of which are reproduced for the first time here. Through Lauer's painstaking examination of the architectural remains, more pieces have been added to the original group excavated by Firth in 1928 (*Annales*, 29 (1929), 64; 53 (1956), 119).

21. Chapel of Akhet-hetep: C. Boreux, *Antiquités égyptiennes, guide-catalogue sommaire*, Musée national du Louvre, I (Paris, 1932), 220; Leiden chapel of Akhet-hetep-her: Wreszinski, *Atlas*, I, plate 108, and Herta T. Mohr,

The Mastaba of Hetep-her-akhti: Study on an Egyptian tomb chapel in the Museum of Antiquities, Leiden (Leiden, 1943).

22. For the seasons relief-cycle at the sun-temple of Ne-user-ra, see E. Edel, 'Zu den Inschriften auf den Jahreszeitenreliefs der "Weltkammer" aus dem Sonnenheiligtum der Niuserre, I–II', *Nachrichten der Akad. der Wiss. in Göttingen, Phil.-Hist. Kl.*, Jahrgang 1961, Nr. 8, Jahrgang 1963, Nrs. 4–5 (Göttingen, 1961, 1963); E. Edel and S. Wenig, *Die Jahreszeitenreliefs aus dem Sonnenheiligtum des Königs Ne-user-re* (*Staatliche Museen zu Berlin, Mitt. aus der ägyptischen Sammlung*, 8) (Berlin, 1974); the relief-cycle of the king's jubilee is studied by Werner Kaiser, 'Die kleine Hebseddarstellung in Sonnenheiligtum des Neuserre', in *Festschrift Ricke: Aufsätze zum 70. Geburtstag von Herbert Ricke* (*Beiträge zur ägyptischen Bauforschung und Altertumskunde*, 12) (Wiesbaden, 1972), 87–105. For the king's statues, see comments by and references in B. V. Bothmer, 'The Karnak Statue of Ny-user-ra', *MDAIK*, 30 (1974), 165–70. See references also in Chapter 5, Note 12, above.

23. For references to the material at Abusir and Abu Gurob, see Porter–Moss, *Bibliography*, III, part 1, 314–50; also Ricke, *Bemerkungen*, II, passim, and Alexander Badawy, *A History of Egyptian Architecture*, I, 105–43. M. Verner, *Forgotten Pharaohs, Lost Pyramids: Abusir.* (Prague, 1994). An abundantly illustrated account of the important new excavations at Abusir, with the discovery of statuary, significant architecture, and a hitherto unknown pyramid, as well as private tombs, including the huge mastaba of Ptahshepses. *Ibid.*, 'Les sculptures de Renceref découvertes à Abousir,' *BIFAO*, 85 (1985), 267–80. Publication of extremely fine small statues of the king from his pyramid complex. *Ibid.*, 'Les statuettes en bois d'Abousir,' *RdE*, 36 (1985), 145–52. A group of a small wooden statuettes of prisoners.

24. Kaiser, in *Festschrift Ricke* (see above, Note 22).

25. Conveniently illustrated, as are a number of other large Egyptian wall compositions, by H. A. Groenewegen-Frankfort, *Arrest and Movement* (London, 1951), figure 4.

26. For the Asiatic booty scene, see Wreszinski, *Atlas*, III, plate 121; for the Libyans with Seshat writing, see Oric Bates, *The Eastern Libyans* (London, 1914), plate 7. See Chapter 7, Note 2.

27. Breasted, *Ancient Records*, I, 142; extensive portions of Weni's autobiography are translated and discussed by Sir Alan Gardiner, *Egypt of the Pharaohs* (Oxford, 1961), 94–8. See also H. Goedicke, 'The Alleged Military Campaign in S. Palestine in the Reign of Pepi I (VIth Dynasty)', *Rivista degli Studi Orientali*, 38 (1963), 187–97; Alan R. Schulman, 'Beyond the Fringe: Sources for Old Kingdom Foreign Affairs', *The SSEA Journal* (Toronto), 9, no. 2 (March 1979), 79–104.

28. Breasted, *Ancient Records*, I, 161; among a number of works on this problem, the reader should consult *ibid.*, II, 246–68; W. Stevenson Smith, 'The Land of Punt', *JARCE*, I (1962), 59–61; D. M. Dixon, 'The Transplanting of Punt Incense Trees in Egypt', *JEA*, 55 (1969), 55–65; Rolf Herzog, *Punt* (*DAIK Abh., Äg. Reihe*, 6) (Glückstadt, 1968); K. A. Kitchen, 'Punt and how to get there', *Orientalia*, 40 (1971), 184–207; A. A. Saleh, 'Some Problems relating to the Pwenet Reliefs at Deir el-Bahari', *JEA*, 58 (1972), 140–58.

29. Smith, *Sculpture and Painting*, 182, 207, figures 85, 86.

30. *Archiv für ägyptische Archäologie*, I (Vienna, 1938), 175–83; A. Labrousse, J.-Ph. Lauer, and J. Leclant, *Le temple haut du complexe funéraire du roi Ounas* (*Mission archéologique de Saqqarah II, IFAO Bibl. d'Études*, 73) (Cairo, 1977); Selim Hassan, *Annales*, 38 (1938), 519; publication of the Seasons cycle from the Unas causeway in Selim Hassan, 'The Causeway of *Wnis* at Saqqara', *ZÄS*, 80 (1955), 136–9, with a reconstruction by Smith, *Interconnections*, 145, and figure 179.

31. Drioton, *Bull. Inst. Égypte*, 25 (1942–3), 45; for another block, see Vandier, *Bulletin, Musées de France*, 15 (1950), 29, figure 4. The famine reliefs are discussed by S. Schott, 'Aufnahmen vom Hungersnotrelief aus dem Aufweg der Unaspyramide', *Revue d'Égyptologie*, 17 (1965), 7–13, and Donald B. Redford, *A Study of the Biblical Story of Joseph* (Leiden, 1970), 91–9. Z. Hawass and M. Verner, 'Newly discovered blocks from the causeway of Sahure,' *MDAIK*, 52 (1996), 177–86. Among the most significant blocks is a representation of men dragging a pyramidion as well as a block of bedouin in a 'famine' scene, the latter indicating a prototype for the famous scenes at the causeway of Unas at the end of the dynasty, which have now lost their claim to priority and originality. A possible explanation of the scene may be a visit by Egyptians to the deserts to search for stone for a pyramidion and the discovery of emaciated bedouin during their mission.

32. Georg Steindorff, *Das Grab des Ti* (*Veröffentlichungen der Ernst von Sieglin Expedition*, II) (Leipzig, 1913); Lucienne Épron, François Daumas, and Henri Wild, *Le tombeau de Ti* (*Mémoires de l'Institut français d'archéologie orientale du Caire*, 65, fasc. 1–3) (Cairo, 1939, 1953, 1966).

33. Compare the beautiful photographs of Hassia in André Lhote, *La peinture égyptienne* (Paris, 1954), plates 60, 61.

34. N. de G. Davies, *The Mastaba of Ptahhetep and Akhethetep at Saqqareh*, I (London, 1900), particularly plates xxvii, xxviii.

35. Smith, *Sculpture and Painting*, plate 56a, cf. p. 208, where it has not been

made sufficiently clear that this style began in the last years of Dynasty V. See also W. Barta, 'Bemerkungen zur Darstellung der Jahreszeiten im Grabe des Mrr-wj-k³.j', *ZÄS*, 97 (1971), 1–7. Excellently illustrated in Prentice Duell *et al.*, *The Mastaba of Mereruka*, 2 vols. (Chicago, 1938).

36. These are partly in Cairo and partly in the Metropolitan Museum in New York; Firth, *Annales*, 26 (1926), 101, plates iv, v; Hayes, *The Scepter of Egypt*, I, figures 64, 65.

37. Smith, *Sculpture and Painting*, plate 23; for other wooden statues and statuettes of the later Old Kingdom cf. pp. 59–61.

38. Hellmuth Müller, *MDAIK*, 7 (1937), 104, plate 19. Cherpion, N., 'De quand date la tombe du nain Seneb', *BIFAO*, 84, 1984, 35–54. Although generally dated to Dynasty 5 or 6, author proposes a date in Dynasty 4, specifically the reign of Dedefre.

39. H. Junker, *Giza V* (Vienna, 1941); for other statuettes of dwarfs, Smith, *op. cit.*, 57.

40. Estimated at one hundred in the case of the favoured official of Neferirkara, Ra-wer, and thirty to fifty for Ba-ba-f (formerly read Khnum-ba-f), a descendant of the old royal family: Smith, *Sculpture and Painting*, 46, 50.

41. See the discussions of the group by John D. Cooney, *Bulletin of the Brooklyn Museum*, 15 (1953), 1–25; B. V. Bothmer, *BMFA*, 46 (1948), 30 ff.; Peter Kaplony, *Studien zum Grab des Methethi* (*Monographien der Abegg-Stiftung Bern*, 8) (Bern, 1976).

42. Compare the Dynasty V statues of Pen-meru and the Dynasty VI Nekhebu statuettes from Giza in Boston: Smith, *Sculpture and Painting*, plates 21c, d, 26 a–c. E. R. Russman, 'A Second Style in Egyptian Art in the Old Kingdom,' *MDAIK*, 51 (1995), 269–79. Consideration of a different style of statuary well represented in Dynasty 6 with exaggeration of some features and suppression of others, the features including overlarge heads with long, narrow bodies pinched at the waist.

CHAPTER 7

1. J.-Ph. Lauer and Jean Leclant, *Le temple haut du complexe funéraire du roi Téti* (Mission archéologique de Saqqareh, 1, IFAO, Bibl. d'Étude, 51) (Cairo, 1972), and for a statue possibly to be assigned to Tety, discussed and illustrated by Vandier, *Manuel*, III, 33–4, plate 7(5); Smith, *Sculpture and Painting*, 82. G. Jéquier, *Le monument funéraire de Pépi II*, I–III (Cairo, 1938–40). For the material from the reign of Pepy I, cf. Jean Leclant, 'Recherches à la pyramide de Pépi Ier à Saqqarah (1972–1976)', *BSFE*, 77–8 (1977), 26–38, and J.-Ph. Lauer and Jean Leclant, 'Découverte de statues de prisonniers au temple de la pyramide de Pépi I', *Revue d'Égyptologie*, 21 (1969), 55–62; *Recherches dans la pyramide et au temple haut du pharaon Pépi Ier, à Saqqarah* (Scholae Adriani de Buck Memoriae Dictae, 6) (Leiden, 1979).

2. Jéquier, *op. cit.*, I–III. For the scene of the Libyan booty, copied later in Dynasty XXV, see M. F. Laming Macadam, *The Temples of Kawa*, II, *History and Archaeology of the Site*, text (London, 1955), 63–7, plates 9, 49, with references to the Sahura, Ne-user-ra, and Pepy II examples. Discussed also by Anthony J. Spalinger, 'Some Notes on the Libyans of the Old Kingdom and Later Historical Reflexes', *The SSEA Journal* [Toronto], 9, no. 3 (June 1979), 125–60.

3. Jéquier, *op. cit.*, III, plate 32.

4. Jéquier, *op. cit.*, II, plate 41.

5. Cyril Aldred, *Old Kingdom Art in Ancient Egypt* (London, 1949), plates 60–3; John D. Cooney, *Egyptian Art in the Brooklyn Museum Collection* (Brooklyn, 1952), plates 19–21. The kneeling statue with jars is represented earlier as a statue type by a fragment in Hildesheim assigned to the reign of Chephren by Eva Martin Pardey, *Plastik des Alten Reich*, Teil 1 (Pelizacus-Museum Hildesheim, *Corpus Antiquatatum Aegyptiacarum*, Lieferung 1) (Mainz, 1977), 70–3. Later examples of the type are listed by Erika Schott, 'Eine Antef-Statuette', *Festschrift Elmar Edel* (Bamberg, 1979), 390–6.

6. Jéquier, *Annales*, 27 (1927), 60, plate v.

7. Sethe, *JEA*, 1 (1914), 233; Petrie found some very small Early Dynastic copper figurines in the Abydos temple: *Abydos II*, plate v.

8. This was the final opinion of A. Lucas, *Ancient Egyptian Materials and Industries*, 4th ed. by J. R. Harris (London, 1961), 214–15. Various opinions have been expressed and it has never been definitely established whether certain parts may not have been cast.

9. J. E. Quibell, *Hierakonpolis I* (London, 1900), plates xliv, xlvi, *II* (London, 1902), plates l–lvi.

10. Quibell, *op. cit.*, I, plates xli–xliii, II, 44, plate xlvii; Ursula Rössler-Köhler, 'Zur Datierung des Falkenbildes von Hierakonpolis (CGC 14717)', *MDAIK*, 34 (1978), 117–25 (on reattribution to Dynasty XVIII).

11. For the biographical inscriptions of the Sixth Dynasty, see Breasted, *Ancient Records*, I, 131 ff.; J. A. Wilson in James B. Pritchard, ed., *Ancient Near Eastern Texts relating to the Old Testament*, 3rd ed. with suppl. (Princeton, 1969),

227–8; Alessandro Roccati, *La Littérature historique sous l'Ancien Empire Égyptien*, Paris, 1982; Alan H. Gardiner, *Egypt of the Pharaohs* (Oxford, 1961), 94–9; Gerald E. Kadish, 'Old Kingdom Activities in Nubia: Some Reconsiderations', *JEA*, 52 (1966), 23–33. For Punt and Byblos, see Newberry, *JEA*, 24 (1938), 182–4, and many other studies. For a general discussion, see Alan R. Schulman, 'Beyond the Fringe: Sources for Old Kingdom Foreign Affairs', *The SSEA Journal*, 9, no. 2 (1979), 79–104.

12. *Ancient Egypt as represented in the Museum of Fine Arts*, 6th rev. ed. (Boston, 1960), 64–9; Dunham, *JEA*, 24 (1938), 2; Reisner and Smith, *Giza Necropolis*, 11, 55, 56; Breasted, *Ancient Records*, 1, 121.

13. Naguib Kanawati, *The Egyptian Administration in the Old Kingdom: Evidence on its economic decline* (Warminster, 1977). Kanawati believes that the relative prosperity of the officials in the provinces follows that of the higher officials at the court, and that the idea of a decentralization towards the provinces now seems to be untenable. Recent studies have also laid stress upon the famines at the end of the Old Kingdom as the primary cause for its decline; see Barbara Bell, 'The Dark Ages in Ancient History. I. The First Dark Age in Egypt', *AJA*, 75 (1971), 1–26. Contrary opinions have been expressed by J. Vercoutter, 'Égyptologie et climatologie. Les crues du Nil à Semneh', *Études sur l'Égypte et le Soudan anciens* (*Cahier de Recherches de l'Institut de Papyrologie et d'Égyptologie de Lille*, 4 (1976), 139–72).

14. Translation by R. O. Faulkner, in William K. Simpson, ed., *The Literature of Ancient Egypt*, 214.

15. Reisner and Smith, *Giza Necropolis*, II, 64, 73–6.

16. Egyptian stone vessels with the names of Chephren and Pepy (I?) were found at the site of Ebla in Syria, south of Aleppo; Paolo Matthiae, 'Tell Mardikh: Ancient Ebla', *AJA*, 82 (1978), 540–3.

17. For instance, Jean Vercoutter, *Égyptiens et Préhellènes* (Paris, 1954), particularly 61–72.

CHAPTER 8

1. Hayes, *JEA*, 32 (1946), 3; Hans Goedicke, *Königliche Dokumente aus dem Alten Reich* (Wiesbaden, 1967).

2. William K. Simpson, 'Two Egyptian Bas Reliefs of the late Old Kingdom', *North Carolina Museum of Art Bulletin*, 11, no. 3 (December, 1972), 3–13.

3. Hermann Junker, *Giza IV* (Vienna and Leipzig, 1940); J. Capart, *Une chambre funéraire de la sixième dynastie* (Brussels, 1906); W. K. Simpson, *The Mastabas of Qar and Idu*, 12, note 30.

4. Smith, *Sculpture and Painting*, chapter XII; Mohamed Saleh, *Three Old Kingdom Tombs at Thebes* (Cairo, Mainz, 1977).

5. A. M. Blackman, *The Rock Tombs of Meir*, V (London, 1953).

6. *Ibid.*, IV (London, 1924).

7. Henry G. Fischer, *Dendera in the Third Millennium B.C., down to the Theban Domination of Upper Egypt* (Locust Valley, New York, 1968), 93–175.

8. Caroline N. Peck, *Some Decorated Tombs of the First Intermediate Period at Naga ed-Der* (University Microfilms, Ann Arbor, 1958).

9. H. E. Winlock, *Excavations at Deir el Bahri* (New York, 1942), 204.

10. H. Ranke, 'The Egyptian Collections of the University Museum', *University Museum Bulletin*, 15, nos. 2–3 (Philadelphia, 1950), 31, figure 18.

11. J. Vandier, *Mo'alla* (Cairo, 1950); see particularly 34 ff. for the date; 45, 101 for that of the Gebelein chapel of Ity; also 265 ff. for the badly preserved but important paintings of the small tomb of Sebek-hotep at Mialla.

12. The paintings are in Turin; Giulio Farina, *La pittura egiziana* (Milan, 1929), plates xviii–xxi; illustrations in Anna Maria Donadoni Roveri (ed.). *Civilta' Degli Egizi: La Vita Quotidiana*. Turin, 1987. *Le Credenze Religiose*. Turin 1988. *Le Arti della Celebrazione*. Turin, 1989. See also Enrichetta Leospo, 'La necropoli dalla fine dell Antico Regno al Medio Regno: La tomba dipinta di Iti,' in Anna Maria Donadoni Roveri et la., *Gebelein: Il villagio e la necropoli*, Turin, 1994, 45–53.

13. Excavated by Labib Habachi.

14. H. G. Fischer, 'The Nubian Mercenaries of Gebelein during the First Intermediate Period', *Kush*, 9 (1961), 44–80. Fischer shows that these Nubians are frequently represented on their own stelae at this time [147]. They lived in and were buried near the Egyptian community which they served. See addendum in *Kush*, 10 (1962), 333–4.

15. Vandier, *op. cit.*, 110, plate xxxviii.

16. Smith, *Sculpture and Painting*, 101; H. E. Winlock, *Models of Daily Life in Ancient Egypt* (Cambridge, Mass., 1955). But see the recent revision of the date to Dynasty 12, reign of Sesostris I: D. Arnold, 'Amenemhat I and the Early Twelfth Dynasty at Thebes.' *Metropolitan Museum Journal*, 26 (1991), 5–48.

17. The mummy lying on top of the coffin appears under a shelter on an unpublished wall of the Dynasty XI tomb of Djar at Thebes which resembles so much in subject matter and style the Gebelein and Mialla chapels. The mummy

on a bier or the dead man on a bed was a favoured subject (like that of the woman having her hair dressed) for painted coffins as well as stelae and wall decorations in the region south of Thebes: Smith, *Sculpture and Painting*, 229, Vandier, *op. cit.*, 282.

18. Winlock, *Excavations at Deir el Baḥri*, 204.

19. Vandier, *op. cit.*, 90, 111.

20. For the scanty remains of the well executed paintings of Tef-ib and the neatly cut sunk reliefs of Khety II, which include three rows of soldiers (Wreszinski, *Atlas*, II, plate 15), see Smith, *Sculpture and Painting*, 231; F. Ll. Griffith, *The Inscriptions of Siut and Der Rifeh* (London, 1889); also F. Ll. Griffith and P. E. Newberry, *El Bersheh II* (London, 1895), plates xii–xvii for the chapel of Aha-nekht (no. 5).

21. Quibell, *Excavations at Saqqara (1905–1906)* (Cairo, 1907), plates xiii, xv, pp. 20–3.

22. *BMFA*, 3 (1905), 13.

CHAPTER 9

1. Recent investigation favours the idea that the two kings formerly called Mentuhotep II and III were the same man who assumed a different titulary after the conquest of Heracleopolis. It is also thought that his supposed predecessor, Mentuhotep I, may represent an earlier version of his name; E. Drioton and J. Vandier, *L'Égypte*, Collection 'Clio', 4th ed. (Paris, 1962), 276; see also J. J. Clère's study of Middle Kingdom history, *Cahiers d'histoire mondiale*, 1 (Paris, 1954), 643 ff., and W. C. Hayes in I. E. S. Edwards, C. J. Gadd, and N. G. L. Hammond, eds., *The Cambridge Ancient History*, 3rd ed., I, part 2 (Cambridge, 1971), 476–85.

2. See H. E. Winlock, *Excavations at Deir el Bahri: The rise and fall of the Middle Kingdom at Thebes*; Vandier, *Manuel*, II, 154 ff.; E. Baldwin Smith, *Egyptian Architecture* (New York, 1938), 100; Dieter Arnold, *Der Tempel des Königs Mentuhotep von Deir el-Bahari*, I, *Architektur und Deutung*, and II, *Die Wandreliefs des Sanktuares* (Cairo-Mainz, 1974), and 'Deir el-Bahari, II', in Helck and Otto, *Lexikon*, I, 1011–17.

3. Winlock, *op. cit.*, 11 ff., plates 3, 33; D. Arnold, *Gräber des alten und mittleren Reiches in el-Tarif* (*AV*, 17) (Cairo-Mainz, 1976).

4. W. M. F. Petrie, *Gizeh and Rifeh* (London, 1907), plates i, xv, xxii.

5. E. Naville and H. R. Hall, *The XIth Dynasty Temple at Deir el-Bahari*, III (London, 1913), plate xiv, 2; cf. plates xii, xiii; *ibid.*, I (1907), plates xiii–xviii; II (1910), plates v, vi, ix–xx for other reliefs from the temple. In addition to the references which I have given for these reliefs in my *Sculpture and Painting*, 235, see Cyril Aldred, *Middle Kingdom Art in Ancient Egypt* (London, 1950), plates 14, 15.

6. Daressy, *Annales*, 17 (1917), 226; Labib Habachi, 'King Nebhepetre Mentuhotep: his monuments, place in history, deification, and unusual representations in the form of gods', *MDAIK*, 19 (1963), 16–52; Vandersleyen, *PKG*, figure 267; David B. O'Connor, 'The Dendereh Chapel of Nebhepetre Mentuhotep,' in *Studies in Honour of Harry Smith* (forthcoming).

7. F. W. von Bissing, *Denkmäler ägyptischer Sculptur* (Munich, 1914), plates 33ᵃ, 77.

8. Winlock, *BMMA*, section II (December, 1924), 13, figure 10.

9. W. C. Hayes, *The Scepter of Egypt*, I (New York, 1953), 163, figures 100, 101.

10. Porter-Moss, *Bibliography*, I, part 1, 391–3; Elizabeth Riefstahl, 'Two Hairdressers of the Eleventh Dynasty', *JNES*, 15 (1956), 10–17; Winlock, *op. cit.* (Note 2), 101–4; William K. Simpson, 'The Middle Kingdom in Egypt: Some Recent Acquisitions', *BMFA*, 72 (1974), 100–16, with bibliography, p. 115, note 13.

11. Naville and Hall, *op. cit.*, I, plates xix–xx; Winlock (Note 2), plate 8; Aldred, *op. cit.*, plates 8, 9.

12. Naville and Hall, *op. cit.*, I, plates xxii–xxiii; III, plates ii, iii.

13. See particularly the two pieces, Aldred, *op. cit.*, plates 14, 15.

14. N. de G. Davies, *Five Theban Tombs* (London, 1913), plates xxix–xxxviii; Hayes, *op. cit.*, I, 163, figure 99.

15. Winlock, *op. cit.* (Note 2), 32; Smith, *Sculpture and Painting*, 356. An important and interesting discussion of Eleventh-Dynasty relief art may be found in Henry G. Fischer, 'An Example of Memphite Influence in a Theban Stela of the Eleventh Dynasty', *Artibus Asiae*, 22 (1959), 240–52. Fischer also studies a puzzling stela in the Theban style, with references to relevant other monuments of this dynasty, in 'An Eleventh Dynasty Couple holding the Sign of Life', *ZÄS*, 100 (1973), 16–28. For the text of the sculptor Iritsen, see Winfried Barta, *Die Selbstzeugnis eines ägyptischen Künstlers (Stele Louvre C 14)* (*Münchner Ägyptologische Studien*, 22) (Berlin/Munich, 1970); A. Badawy, 'The Stela of Irtysen', *Chronique d'Égypte*, 36 (1961), 269–76.

16. F. Bisson de la Roque, *Tod* (*Fouilles de l'Institut français du Caire*, XVII) (Cairo, 1937), 79, plates xx–xxviii.

17. Aldred, *op. cit.*, plates 16–18; Richard Fazzini, *Images for Eternity*, Cat. 35, pp. 49, 135; cf. Vandersleyen, *PKG*, plate 268b (from Elephantine).

18. Winlock, *The Rise and Fall*, 52, plates 7, 33.

19. A selection is illustrated in colour in Vandersleyen, *PKG*, plate xxvi.

20. H. E. Winlock, *Models of Daily Life in Ancient Egypt* (Cambridge, Mass., 1955); D. Arnold, 'Amenemhat I and the Early Twelfth Dynasty at Thebes'. *Metropolitan Museum Journal*, 26 (1991), 5–48.

21. For a façade of a tomb at Deir Rifeh near Assiut also copying wooden construction, see Montet, *Kemi*, 6 (1936), plate vi, opp. p. 136.

22. The sheathing has been omitted in painting the cattle pavilion but appears in the house models, where the porch has an outer row of lotus columns and an inner row of papyrus; Winlock, *op. cit.* (Note 20), plates 11, 56.

CHAPTER 10

1. Vandier, *Manuel*, II, 619–40, and A. Badawy, *A History of Egyptian Architecture*, II, *The First Intermediate Period, the Middle Kingdom, and the Second Intermediate Period* (Berkeley and Los Angeles, 1966), 48–49.

2. E. Naville, *Bubastis* (London, 1891), 10 ff.; Porter-Moss. *Bibliography*, IV, 29; for part of one papyrus-bundle column and one of the large Hathor capitals in the Boston Museum of Fine Arts, see Smith, *Ancient Egypt* (1960), 79–81; Badawy, *op. cit.*, 88–9, plate 13. On these Middle Kingdom temple elements, see Labib Habachi, *Tell Basta* (*Supplément aux Annales*, 22) (Cairo, 1957); D. Arnold, 'Hypostyle Halls of the Old and Middle Kingdom?,' in Peter Der Manuelian, *Studies in Honor of William Kelly Simpson* (Boston, 1996), 39–54.

3. As in the New Kingdom temple at Sinai; Petrie, *Researches in Sinai* (London, 1906), plates 101–4.

4. Chevrier, *Annales*, 34 (1934), 174; 38 (1938), 567; P. Lacau and H. Chevrier, *Une chapelle de Sésostris Ier à Karnak*, 2 vols. (Cairo, 1956, 1969); Vandersleyen, *PKG*, plate 270a; C. Strauss-Seeber, 'Zu Bildprogramm und Funktion der Weissen Kapelle in Karnak,' in R. Gundlach and M. Rochholz (eds.), *Ägyptische Tempel – Struktur, Funktion und Programm* (HÄB 37), 1994, 287–318.

5. Vandier, *Manuel*, II, 619, figure 326; A. Vogliano, *Secundo rapporto . . . Madīnet Māḍi* (Milan, 1937).

6. Vandier, *Manuel*, II, 193, figure 135; Edwards, *The Pyramids of Egypt*, 188; Alan B. Lloyd, 'The Egyptian Labyrinth', *JEA*, 56 (1970), 81–100; K. Michalowski, 'The Labyrinth Enigma: Archaeological Suggestions', *JEA*, 54 (1958), 219–22; Dieter Arnold, 'Das Labyrinth und seine Vorbilder', *MDAIK*, 35 (1979), 1–9.

7. Ricke, *Bemerkungen*, II, 50; Hans Goedicke, *Reused Blocks from the Pyramid of Amenemhet I at Lisht* (New York, 1971), 23–4.

8. See Vandier, *Manuel*, II, 167 ff. A meticulous re-excavation of the site of the Amenemhet III pyramid at Dahshur has been undertaken by the German Archaeological Institute in Cairo. For the first reports, see Dieter Arnold and Rainer Stadelmann, 'Dahschur: Erster Grabungsbericht', *MDAIK*, 31 (1975), 169–74; 'Dahschur: Zweite Grabungsbericht', *MDAIK*, 33 (1977), 15–20. D. Arnold, *Der Pyramidenbezirk des Königs Amenemhet III in Dahschur*. Band I: *Die Pyramide* (*AV* 53), Mainz, 1987.

9. W. M. F. Petrie, *Illahun, Kahun and Gurob* (London, 1891), 5, plates xiv, xvi; a portion of the plan connecting the workmen's dwellings with the scanty remains of the valley temple of Sesostris II is to be found in Petrie, *Kahun, Gurob and Hawara* (London, 1890), plate xv; for a sketch plan of the site with the pyramid, see Porter-Moss, *Bibliography*, IV, 108. For the houses at el Lahun, see Badawy, *op. cit.* (Note 1), 22–7.

10. See Petrie, *Illahun, Kahun and Gurob*, plate vi, for these fragments of columns.

11. A. J. Arkell, *A History of the Sudan* (London, 1955), 55 ff.; Reisner, *BMFA*, 27 (1929), 64; Vandier, *Manuel*, II, 995–1004; Somers Clarke, *JEA*, 3 (1916), 155. The two fortresses at Semna and those at Uronarti, Shalfak, and Mirgissa were cleared by the Harvard–Boston Museum of Fine Arts Expedition. The Nubian salvage campaign initiated in 1957 to record and in part remove the monuments in the path of the lake created by the building of the High Dam at Aswan resulted in the intensive examination and excavation of many of the Middle Kingdom fortresses and fortress-town sites. At the same time final reports on earlier excavated sites appeared. An extensive bibliography cannot be provided here, but references to some of the work are appropriate: Dows Dunham and Jozef M. A. Janssen, *Semna Kumma* (*Second Cataract Forts*, I) (Boston, 1960); Dunham, *Uronarti Shalfak Mirgissa* (*Second Cataract Forts*, II) (Boston, 1967). Reports on Buhen: Walter B. Emery in *Kush*, 7 (1959), 7–14; 8 (1960), 7–10; 9 (1961), 81–6; 10 (1962), 106–8; 11 (1963), 116–20; 12 (1964), 43–6; *JEA*, 44 (1958), vii–viii; 45 (1959), 1–2; 47 (1961), 1–3; 48 (1962), 1–3; 49 (1963), 2–3. On Mirgissa, see Wheeler in *Kush*, 9 (1961), 87–179, and Vercoutter in *Kush*, 12 (1964), 57–62; 13 (1965), 62–73; *BSFE*, 37–8 (1963), 23–30; 40 (1964), 4–12; 43 (1965), 7–13; 49 (1967), 5–11; 52 (1968), 7–14; *Revue d'Égyptologie*, 15 (1963),

69–75; 16 (1964), 179–91. On Askut, see Badawy in *Kush*, 12 (1964), 47–53; *Archaeology*, 18 (1965), 124–31; *JARCE*, 5 (1966), 23–7. For a general discussion, see A. W. Lawrence, 'Ancient Egyptian Fortifications', *JEA*, 51 (1965), 69–94; William Y. Adams, *Nubia: Corridor to Africa* (London, 1977), 175–92; Badawy, *History of Egyptian Architecture*, II, 198–234. For final reports, see Jean Vercoutter and others, *Mirgissa I* and *II* (Paris, 1970, 1975). W. B. Emery, H. S. Smith, and Anne Millard, *The Fortress of Buhen*, part 1, *The Archaeological Report* (London, 1979); part 2, *The Inscriptions* (London, 1976). Suart Tyson Smith, *Askut in Nubia: the Economics and Ideology of Egyptian Imperialism in the Second Millenium B.C.*, London, 1995.

12. P. E. Newberry, *Beni Hasan II* (London, 1893), plate xv.

13. Petrie, *Koptos* (London, 1896), plate ix; Cyril Aldred, *Middle Kingdon Art in Ancient Egypt*, plate 22; Vandersleyen, *PKG*, plate 271.

14. H. G. Evers, *Staat aus dem Stein* (Munich, 1929), plates 26–30. The fine plates and text of these two volumes are indispensable for their thorough treatment of Middle Kingdom sculpture in the round.

15. W. C. Hayes, *BMMA*, 5 (second series) (1946), 119; see also the comments of Winifred Needler, 'Four Relief-sculptures from the Pyramid of Sesostris I at Lisht', *Annual of the Art and Archaeology Division, Royal Ontario Museum* (Toronto, 1961), 15–26, and Cyril Aldred, 'Some Royal Portraits of the Middle Kingdom in Ancient Egypt', *MMJ*, 3 (1970), 27–50. It has been suggested that the pair of wooden statues from the pyramid site of Sesostris I at Lisht are not contemporary with this king, since they were found as a deposit in a chamber in the enclosure wall of the mastaba of Imhotep at the site and not in the king's own enclosure. Hence they may have been made after the king's death. Alternatively, they could have been made for his own funerary equipment and subsequently placed in Imhotep's deposit.

16. Vandier, *Manuel*, II, 194; J. von Beckerath, 'Hor', in Helck and Otto, *Lexikon*, II, 1274; Bruce Williams, in *Serapis*, 3 (1975–6), 41–57.

17. Henri Frankfort, *Kingship and the Gods* (Chicago, 1948), 61 ff.

18. G. A. Reisner, *Excavations at Kerma, I–III, IV–V* (*Harvard African Studies*, V, VI) (Cambridge, Mass., 1923). Reisner and Smith both regarded the tumulus burial at Kerma as that of Hepzefa and considered Kerma as a trading colony administered by Hepzefa as governor. This seemed a logical explanation of the finding of these statues at so remote a place, and it was further assumed that Hepzefa had been buried in local fashion with his retainers ritually slain to accompany him. The view has been challenged by Hintze and others, for it now appears that the series of tumulus burials represents a cemetery of local rulers who had obtained the statues by trade or through plunder, perhaps from Assiut itself or from a temple complex such as that of Heka-ib at Aswan. See Fritz Hintze, 'Das Kerma-Problem', *ZÄS*, 91 (1964), 82–5; Bruce G. Trigger, 'Kerma: the Rise of an African Civilization', *The International Journal of African Historical Studies*, 9 (1976), 1–21; W. Y. Adams, *Nubia: Corridor to Africa*, 195–216; Brigitte Gratien, *Les cultures Kerma* (Lille, 1978). Kerma is now thought to represent the independent Nubian kingdom of Yam, and the series of tumulus tombs to belong to the height of its power in the Second Intermediate Period.

19. Dr Ernesto Scamuzzi has kindly permitted the reproduction of a photograph of the newly joined pieces; for upper fragment, see Evers, *op. cit.*, plate 21. For an example of the block statues, see B. V. Bothmer, 'Block Statues of the Egyptian Middle Kingdom, II: The Sculpture of Teta's Son', *BMA*, 2 (1960–2), 18–35. On the concept of the early block statues, see Arne Eggebrecht, 'Zur Bedeutung des Würfelhockers', *Festgabe für Dr Walter Will* (Köln, Berlin, Bonn, München, 1966). 143–63. Eggebrecht believes that they represent the deceased in the process of resurrection from the earth.

20. N. de G. Davies and Alan Gardiner, *The Tomb of Antefoker* (London, 1920), plates xxxviii, xxxix.

21. Steindorff, in Hans Steckeweh, *Die Fürstengräber von Qâw* (Leipzig, 1936), 8; for the sculpture see plates 10, 15. The order of the tombs has now been reversed by Berlev, *CdE*, 69 (1994), 292.

22. R. O. Faulkner, in W. K. Simpson, ed., *The Literature of Ancient Egypt*, 3rd revised printing (New Haven, 1977), 193–7. R. B. Parkinson, *The Tale of Sinuhe and Other Egyptian Poems 1940–1640 BC* (Oxford, 1997), 203–11.

23. H. W. Müller, *Die Felsengräber der Fürsten von Elephantine* (Glückstadt–Hamburg–New York, 1940).

24. Labib Habachi has kindly permitted the reproduction of one of these remarkable pieces. L. Habachi (with contributions by Haeny, G. and Junge, F.). *The Sanctuary of Heqaib. Elephantine IV*. (AV 33), 2 vols Cairo, 1985. D. Franke, *Das Heiligtum des Heqaib auf Elephantine: Geschichte eines Provinzheiligtums im Mittleren Reich*. SAGA 9, Heidelberg, 1994.

25. Petrie, *Antaeopolis* (London, 1930); for these tombs see also Steckeweh, *Die Fürstengräber von Qâw*.

26. The orchard scene was noted by Montet, *Kêmi*, I (1928), 67, and I possess a tracing which I made of this part of the north wall in 1951. Unfortunately this important and interesting tomb (the largest rock-cut tomb of the Middle Kingdom) is in extremely poor condition, and has been only partially published.

George A. Reisner's original report ('The Tomb of Hepzefa, Nomarch of Siut', *JEA*, 5 (1918), 79–98) must be supplemented by W. S. Smith, 'A Painting in the Assiut Tomb of Hepzefa', *MDAIK*, 15 (1957), 221–4, and *Interconnections*, 135–7, and figure 167. Still more recently the possibility of Minoan influence on, or the adoption of Minoan motifs in, the ceiling decoration of this tomb has been argued; see Maria C. Shaw, 'Ceiling Patterns from the Tomb of Hepzefa', *AJA*, 74 (1970), 25–30.

27. A. M. Blackman, *The Rock Tombs of Meir*, I–III (London, 1914–15).

28. *Ibid.*, VI (London, 1953). On plate xviii the stippled bands are omitted from the cloak; cf. *op. cit.*, III, plate xxxv.

29. Dunham and Smith in *Studi in Memoria di Ippolito Rosellini*, I (Pisa, 1949), 263; E. L. B. Terrace, *Egyptian Painting of the Middle Kingdon: The tomb of Djehuty-nekht* (New York, 1968); 'The Entourage of an Egyptian Governor', *BMFA*, 66 (1968), 5–27. A. M. Roth, and C. Roehrig, 'The Bersha Procession: A New Reconstruction,' *Journal of the Museum of Fine Arts, Boston* (1989), 31–40.

30. F. Ll. Griffith and P. E. Newberry, *El Bersheh*, II (London, 1895), plates i–ix.

31. Griffith and Newberry, *op. cit.*, I; W. S. Smith, 'Paintings of the Middle Kingdom at Bersheh', *AJA*, 55 (1951), 321.

32. Davies and Gardiner, *op. cit.* (Note 20).

33. P. E. Newberry, F. Ll. Griffith, et al., *Beni Hasan I–IV* (London, 1891–1910). A. G. Shedid, *Die Felsgräber von Beni Hassan in Mittelägypten*. Mainz, Zaberns Bildbände zur Archäologie 16, 1994. Particularly valuable for the colour photographs of the recently cleaned wall surfaces.

34. The style of the paintings can best be appreciated from the copies made by Mr and Mrs Norman de Garis Davies; *BMMA*, section II (April 1933), 23–9; Nina M. Davies, *Ancient Egyptian Paintings*, I, plates vii–xi, see also *JEA*, 35 (1949), 13.

35. For a coloured detail of the tree on the left, see Nina M. Davies, *Ancient Egyptian Paintings*, I, plate ix.

36. Newberry and Griffith, *Beni Hasan I*, plate xxxi.

37. A picture of an Old Kingdom man riding in a litter carried by two donkeys has been destroyed by weathering on the wall of a Giza tomb; Selim Hassan, *Excavations at Giza*, V (Cairo, 1944), 245, figure 104. In the tomb of the 'Two Brothers' of Dynasty V date at Saqqara the owners are each shown borne on a litter carried by pair of donkeys: Ahmed M. Moussa and Hartwig Altenmüller, *Das Grab des Nianchchnum und Chnumhotep* (Mainz am Rhein, 1977), 114–15, plates 42–3.

38. J. Černý, A. H. Gardiner, T. E. Peet, *The Inscriptions of Sinai*, I (London, 1952), plates xxxvii, xxxix, lxxxv; II (1955), 114, 118, 206; see also the man riding a donkey on the Byblos dagger sheath, Frankfort, *Ancient Orient*, illustration 281. The subject of horses and riding is taken up extensively by Alan R. Schulman, 'Chariots, Chariotry, and the Hyksos' *The SSEA Journal*, 10 (1980), 105–53. Charles Bonnet and Dominique Valbelle, *Le Sanctuaire d'Hathor . . . Sinai* (Paris, 1996).

CHAPTER 11

1. J. de Morgan, *Fouilles à Dahchour*, I, II (Vienna, 1895, 1903); Guy Brunton, *Lahun*, I, *The Treasure* (London, 1920); Émile Vernier, *Catalogue général du Musée du Caire, Bijoux et orfèvreries* (Cairo, 1927), plates i, ii, vii, viii, xxxviii, lxvi–lxxxi; Cyril Aldred, *Jewels of the Pharaohs* (London, 1971); Alix Wilkinson, *Ancient Egyptian Jewellery* (London, 1971). Adela Oppenheim, 'The Jewellery of Queen Weret.' *Egyptian Archaeology*, 9, 1996, 26.

2. H. E. Winlock, *The Treasure of El-Lahun* (New York, 1934).

3. Arthur Mace and Herbert Winlock, *The Tomb of Senebtisi at Lisht* (New York, 1916), plate xxi; W. C. Hayes, *The Scepter of Egypt*, I (New York, 1953), 230, figure 146; Bruce Williams, 'The Date of Senebtisi at Lisht and the Chronology of the Major Groups and Deposits of the Middle Kingdom', *Serapis*, 3 (1975–6), 41–57. For the Khnumet circlet in colour, see Aldred, *op. cit.*, plate 28. Bruce Williams has shown (*op. cit.*) that Senebtisi lived in Dynasty XIII and not earlier, as thought by Winlock and Mace.

4. The design on one pectoral (sun's disk with uraei and Lower Egyptian crowns above) can be seen in the coloured drawing, P. E. Newberry, *El Bersheh*, I (London, 1895), frontispiece.

5. A daughter of Sesostris II who lived into the reign of Amenemhat III but was buried near her father's pyramid at Lahun.

6. Vernier, *op. cit.*, plates xxxviii, lxvii; Winlock, *op. cit.*, plates ii–iv. For the Khnumet circlet with lyre-shaped elements in colour, see Aldred, *op. cit.*, plate 27. A side view of the Sat-hathor-yunet crown is illustrated in colour by Aldred, *op. cit.*, plate 39, with the wig ornaments restored.

7. Cf. Smith in Reisner, *Giza Necropolis*, II, 31.

8. For this figure-8 pattern see Helene J. Kantor, *The Aegean and the Orient in the Second Millennium B.C.* (Bloomington, 1947), 43.

9. The real fastenings on the back of similar clasps are shown in Winlock, *op. cit.*, plate xiii, p. 54; for girdles, *ibid.*, 37–41, figure 4; see also Hayes, *The Scepter of Egypt*, I, 231, figure 147.

10. Cf. Lucas and Brunton in *Annales*, 36 (1936), 197–200, where similar miniature paintings are mentioned on objects in the tomb of Tut-ankh-amon (throne, an earring, and a gold heart scarab with a *bennu*-bird). These are said to be covered with a thin sheet of glass. The tiny portrait of the king on the earring is shown in Penelope Fox, *Tutankhamen's Treasure* (Oxford, 1951), plate 49a, where the covering is called translucent quartz. The Dahshur plaque is shown in a coloured drawing in *JEA*, 6 (1920), plate xvi, and in colour in Aldred, *op. cit.*, plate 29. The substance of the background on which the painting was done is still uncertain, but the technique is apparently different from that of the bull-baiting scene painted on the back of a sheet of crystal in Crete (Sir Arthur Evans, *Palace of Minos*, III (London, 1930), 108).

11. Brunton, *op. cit.* (Note 1), plates i, vi, xi; Winlock, *op. cit.*, plate vii; Aldred, *op. cit.*, plates 37, 38 (colour).

12. de Morgan, *Fouilles à Dahchour*, I, plates xix, xx, xxi; Aldred, *op. cit.*, plates 41, 42 (colour); Wilkinson, *op. cit.*, plate 11 (colour).

13. P. E. Newberry and F. Ll. Griffith, *Beni Hasan*, II (London, 1893), plate xvi; N. de G. Davies, *BMMA*, section 11 (April 1933), 28, figure 5.

14. Pierre Montet, *Byblos et l'Égypte* (Paris, 1928). Several of the objects are illustrated in Smith, *Interconnections*, figures 26 (chest), 28 (pectoral), and 29 (small bronze sphinx).

15. Comparison with the inlaid jewellery from the graves of non-royal persons in Egypt which lack some of the finesse of the pieces belonging to the princesses brings out even more the strangeness of the Byblos workmanship. See the jewel of Sesostris II with an early use of the winged scarab and the pectoral in the Manchester Museum, R. Engelbach, *Riqqeh and Memphis*, VI (London, 1915), plate i; *JEA*, I (1914), plate vi, p. 44; Aldred, *op. cit.*, plates 79–81. A similar silver pectoral of Sesostris II and a silver hornet worked out in the round on a clasp were found in the grave of a woman at Harageh; Engelbach, *Harageh* (London, 1923), plate xv, p. 15.

16. T. Eric Peet, *The Stela of Sebek-khu* (Manchester, 1914); Wilson in Pritchard, *Ancient Near Eastern Texts relating to the Old Testament*, 3rd ed. with suppl. (Princeton, 1969), 230.

17. John A. Wilson, *Culture of Ancient Egypt* (Chicago, 1956), 134, where he seems to have returned to a belief in influence based on cultural supremacy and trade in contrast to views expressed in his publication of the Djehuty-hetep statuette in *AJSL*, 58 (1941), 225–36. There he reviewed Egypt's contacts with Palestine and Syria with an inclination to accept a considerable measure of political domination. This dominance supported by military force is assumed by W. F. Albright, *The Archaeology of Palestine* (Harmondsworth, 1949), 85, and Sir Leonard Woolley, *A Forgotten Kingdom* (Harmondsworth, 1953), 61, although William A. Ward has argued differently in a more recent survey (*Orientalia*, 30 (1961), 22–45, 129–55). See also James M. Weinstein, 'Egyptian Relations with Palestine in the Middle Kingdom', *BASOR*, 217 (February 1975), 1–16.

18. Ukh-hotep II (B 4): A. M. Blackman, *The Rock Tombs of Meir*, III (London, 1915), 11–13, plates iii, v. Cf. Blackman's views on the Bersheh inscription, *JEA*, 2 (1915), 13.

19. Khnumet-nefer-hedjet, which is inscribed on her statue base, is ordinarily a title of royal ladies, not a name, and is frequently used without the name (Brunton, in *Annales*, 49 (1949), 99 ff.). However, in the case of this particular princess, it is possible that it is her full name which was shortened to Khnumet on most of the objects in her tomb (Winlock, *op. cit.* (Note 2), 4, note 6). Cf. O. Perdu, 'Khenemet-nefer-hedjet: une princesse et deux rois du moyen empire', *Revue d'Égyptologie*, 29 (1977), 66–85. For the statues from Ugarit, see Claude F. A. Schaeffer, *Ugaritica*, I (Paris, 1939), 20, plate iii; *Syria*, 13 (1932), plate xiv; 15 (1934), 131 ff.; from Qatna: *Syria*, 9 (1928), plate xii, pp. 10, 11, 16–17.

20. Porter-Moss, *Bibliography*, VII, 374 (Gezer), 392 (Qatna), 393 (Ugarit), 405 (Knossos), 398 (Adana), 399 (Kurigin Kale); Smith, *Interconnections*, 14–15, figures 23–5. The presence of these Egyptian statues in western Asia has been explained by W. Helck as the product of trade or booty during the later Hyksos dominion ('Ägyptische Statuen im Ausland: Ein chronologisches Problem', *Ugaritische Forschungen*, 8 (1976), 113–15. See also the comments of James Weinstein, 'A Statuette of the Princess Sobeknefru at Tell Gezer', *BASOR*, 213 (1974), 49–57.

21. Helene J. Kantor, *op. cit.* (Note 8), and in R. W. Ehrich, ed., *Chronologies in Old World Archaeology* (Chicago, 1965), 1–46. For the Aegean chronology, see V. Hankey and P. Warren, 'The Absolute Chronology of the Aegean Late Bronze Age', *Bull. Inst. of Classical Studies*, 21 (1974), 142–52. The Aegean–Egyptian connexion has been the subject of several important studies; see especially Jean Vercoutter, *Essai sur les relations entre égyptiens et préhellènes* (Paris, 1954) and *L'égypte et le monde égéen pré-hellénique* (Paris, 1956); Fritz Schachermeyr, *Ägäis und Orient* (*Akad. der Wiss. und der Lit.*, Phil.-Hist. Kl. Denkschriften, 93) (Vienna, 1966); Frankfort, *Ancient Orient*, 243–8; Wolfgang Helck, *Die Beziehungen*

Ägyptens und Vorderasiens zur Ägäis bis ins 7. Jahrhundert v. Chr. (*Erträge der Forschung*, Bd 120) (Darmstadt, 1979); Manfred Bietak (ed.), *An International Symposium at the Metropolitan Museum: Trade, Power and Cultural Exchange: Hyksos Egypt and the Eastern Mediterranean World 1800–1500 B.C.* Vienna, 1995. Several essays, including studies of the Minoan wall paintings from Avaris and the parallels from Knossos and elsewhere.

22. F. Bisson de la Roque, *Cairo, Catalogue général, Trésor de Tod* (1950); *Le trésor de Tod* (*Documents de fouilles de l'Institut français*, XI) (Cairo, 1953).

23. Schaeffer, *Ugaritica*, I, 56; M. Dunand, *Fouilles de Byblos*, I (Paris, 1939), 191 (no. 2986), 193, figure 178, plate clxxvii. It would require too much space to detail here all of the problems connected with the Egyptian presence in the east Mediterranean at this time. Ward has argued that there is little evidence for Egyptian military control over Palestine, although certainly some aspects of the Egyptian presence in Palestine and Syria may be a political response to the Hurrian influx (W. A. Ward, 'Egypt and the East Mediterranean in the Early Second Millennium B.C.', *Orientalia*, 30 (1961), 22–45, 129–55). Particularly important for the art historian are the discoveries of Montet and Dunand at Byblos. The most comprehensive recent treatment of this material, apart from Dunand's monumental *Fouilles de Byblos*, II, 3 vols. (Paris, 1959), is provided by Olga Tufnell and William A. Ward, 'Relations between Byblos, Egypt and Mesopotamia at the End of the Third Millennium B.C.: a study of the Montet Jar', *Syria*, 43 (1966), 165–241, although Edith Porada, 'Les cylindres de la jarre Montet', *ibid.*, 243 ff., has questioned certain crucial datings. Ward has reaffirmed his dating of the Montet jar in 'Scarabs from the Montet Jar: A Late Eleventh Dynasty Collection from Byblos', *Berytus*, 26 (1978), 37–53. See O. Tufnell and W. A. Ward, *Studies on Scarab Seals*, vol. I (Ward): *Pre-Twelfth Dynasty Scarab-Amulets* (Warminster, 1978); vol. II (Tufnell): *Scarab-Seals and their Contribution to History in the Early Second Millennium B.C.* (Warminster, 1979). Apart from the closed deposit containing the so-called 'Montet jar' the tombs of several princes of Byblos, contemporary with the later years of the Twelfth Dynasty, must also be considered. The most important of these tombs can be securely dated to the reigns of Amenemhat III and IV; see Donald P. Hansen, 'Some Remarks on the Chronology and Style of Objects from Byblos', *AJA*, 73 (1969), 281–4. Much of this material is surveyed in Smith, *Interconnections*, to which may be added further comments in *idem*, 'Influence of the Middle Kingdom of Egypt in Western Asia, especially in Byblos', *AJA*, 73 (1969), 277–81. Daphna Ben-Tor, 'The Absolute Date of the Montet Jar Scarabs,' in Leonard H. Lesko, *Ancient Egyptian and Mediterranean Studies in Memory of William A. Ward* (Providence, 1998), 1–17.

24. Sidney Smith, *AJA*, 49 (1945), 1 ff., and Helene Kantor in *Chronologies in Old World Archaeology*, 19–22. Miss Kantor has made a telling comparison between certain of the Tod silver vessels, and the fluted decoration imitated from such metal forms in Middle Minoan IIa pottery (Evans, *Palace of Minos*, I, 241, figure 181, plate ii, b, *Suppl.* plate iii, b; IV, 132, figure 100).

25. Engelbach, *Harageh*, 2, 9–17, plates x, xiv, xv; *Riqqeh and Memphis*, VI (London, 1915), 12, plate i; compare a simple pectoral said to be from Dahshur, Burlington Fine Arts Club, *Ancient Egyptian Art* (London, 1922), plate, I, p. 20. These objects and many others are discussed and illustrated in Aldred, *op. cit.*, and Wilkinson, *op. cit.*

26. Schaeffer, *Ugaritica*, I, 56, figures 43, 44; Helmuth Th. Bossert, *Altsyrien* (Tübingen, 1951), no. 727 on p. 217. A later version of this palmette design appears on a ceiling pattern in the Theban tomb (No. 48) of Surer in the reign of Amenhotep III (coloured copy in the Metropolitan Museum, no. 30.4.27), on a textile from the tomb of Tut-ankh-amon, and on a ceiling of a window niche in the eastern gate at Medinet Habu in the reign of Ramesses III; Uvo Hölscher, *The Mortuary Temple of Ramses III*, II (Chicago, 1951), plate 24c. For a somewhat similar contemporary example from Crete on a Middle Minoan IIa cup, see Evans, *Palace of Minos*, IV, 132, figure 100.

27. The thick heavy black ware of this sherd was thought to be of neither Cretan nor Egyptian fabric, and possibly Anatolian; E. J. Forsdyke, *Catalogue of Greek and Etruscan Vases in the British Museum*, I, *Prehistoric Aegean Pottery* (London, 1925), 94, No. A 567, figure 115.

28. The colour was mistakenly changed to yellow and green in the later editions of his book: Sir Gardiner Wilkinson, *The Manners and Customs of the Ancient Egyptians* (Boston, 1883), I, plate viii, opp. p. 362.

29. Ukh-hotep II (B 4); Blackman, *op. cit.* (Note 18), plates ix, xxviii. The design is placed sideways and not vertically [206C]; for Qâw see Sir Flinders Petrie, *Antaeopolis* (London, 1930), plate i; H. Steckeweh, *Die Fürstengräber von Qâw* (Leipzig, 1936), plates 9, 12.

30. Prisse d'Avennes, *Histoire de l'art égyptien*, I (Paris, 1878–9), plate 34, I. G. A. Wainwright has discussed these figure-8 spirals to establish his contention that Keftiu was not Crete but western Cilicia; *Anatolian Studies*, 4 (1954), 33, cf. W. Lamb, *ibid.*, 21 for similar early spirals from eastern Anatolia and Azerbaijan.

31. Griffith and Newberry, *El Bersheh*, I, II, figure 1; G. A. Reisner, *Harvard African Studies*, V, *Kerma I–III* (Cambridge, Mass.), 1923), plate 17, 3. The Kerma culture is discussed by David O'Connor, 'Nubia before the New

Kingdom', in *Africa in Antiquity: The Arts of Ancient Nubia and the Sudan*, I, *The Essays* (Brooklyn, 1978), 47–61; objects are illustrated and discussed in Steffen Wenig, *Africa in Antiquity: The Arts of Ancient Nubia and the Sudan*, II, *The Catalogue* (Brooklyn, 1978), 30–41, 145–61, cat. nos. 44–69. For the glazed wares, see Robert S. Bianchi, 'Faience at Kerma', *The SSEA Journal*, 10 (1980), 155–60.

32. Compare L. Borchardt, *Das Grabdenkmal des Königs S'aḥu-re'*, II (Leipzig, 1913), plate 9, with Steckeweh, *op. cit.*, plate 12c. In the Sahura example it cannot be certain that the individual elements are taken from the lotus flower, and indeed in some of the rosettes conventional feather elements have been inserted; the Qâw rosette is composed of several open lotus flowers somewhat as in the head band worn by a lady in the reliefs at that site, or even from Bersheh [197].

33. Reisner, *Kerma IV–V*, 49–55, 134–75. See Note 3 above.

34. E. Naville, *The XIth Dynasty Temple at Deir el Bahari*, III (London, 1913), plates xxvi, xxvii; W. M. F. Petrie, *Researches in Sinai* (London, 1906), plates 147–58.

35. Petrie, *Antaeopolis*, plate xxi, 5, 6; grave 7163; Brunton, *Qau and Badari*, III, 9.

36. Reisner only mentions and illustrates the jar, *Kerma I–III*, 30–3, figure 9, which he thought was Meroitic. He was particularly concerned with the fragments of stone vases with the names of Pepy I, Neferkara, Amenemhat I, and Sesostris I found near by. There was also one sherd with polychrome decoration, like the painted vessels in the great tumulus, and a small portion of a vessel of almost certainly Aegean fabric with simple dark bands on light ware. More of the polychrome sherds were found in the addition to the 'fort' on the east. They are in the Boston Museum of Fine Arts.

37. *BMMA*, section II (December 1923), 31, figure 25; Hayes, *The Scepter of Egypt*, I, 58, figure 28; G. Vittmann, 'Zur Plastik des mittleren Reiches: Sebekemsaf und Jui', *GM*, 10 (1974), 41–4 (dates Yuy in Dynasty XIII).

38. Evans, *Palace of Minos*, IV, 112, figure 77. Compare also the designs in *Palace of Minos*, I, 246, figure 186.

39. H. J. Kantor, *op. cit.* (Note 24), 23. Janine Bourriau, 'The Dolphin Vase from Lisht,' in P. D. Manuelian (ed.), *Studies in Honor of William Kelly Simpson* (Boston, 1996), 101–16.

40. Petrie, *Kahun, Gurob and Hawara*, 25, plate xxvii.

41. Montet, *Byblos et l'Égypte*, plate cxlviii, cf. plates cxlvi and cxlv for a vase in the form of a fish; l'Émir Maurice Chehab in *Mélanges syriens offerts à Monsieur René Dussaud*, II (Paris, 1939), 803 ff.

42. In the far north there are some infrequent examples of similar decoration on a dark incised ware which extends into New Kingdom times. At Alalakh (Tell el Atchana in the Antioch plain) was found a vase somewhat similar in form and decoration (H. Th. Bossert, *Altanatolien*, 153, no. 660). See also *ibid.*, 147, nos. 626, 629 for sherds from Boğazköy, and Hetty Goldman, *AJA*, 44 (1940), 77–9, figure 39, for a small flask from Tarsus and reference to similarly decorated incised ware from Tell Judeideh in the neighbourhood of Alalakh.

43. Reisner, *Kerma IV–V*, 320 ff.; Smith, *Ancient Egypt* (Boston, 1960), 98, figure 61; Wenig, *op. cit.* (Note 31), figure 15, cat. nos. 61–2.

44. C. M. Firth, *The Archaeological Survey of Nubia, Report for 1909–1910* (Cairo, 1915), plates 39, 40; Wenig, *op. cit.*, cat. nos. 27–40, 42.

45. Reisner, *Kerma I–III*, plate 9, *IV–V*, 473, figure 340; Wenig, *op. cit.*, figure 17. Two painted vessels came from the burial chamber of the great tumulus (K III C), those with plant and figure decoration from subsidiary burials in the compartments near by, as did others with geometric patterns. Three more were found in tumuli K IV, K VIII, and K XIV, while a few unpublished sherds were found in the annex to the 'fort' and in room H east of it.

46. Reisner, *Kerma I–III*, plate 19; O'Connor, *op. cit.* (Note 31), figure 37.

47. Reisner, *Kerma I–III*, 136.

48. See Smith, *Ancient Egypt*, 100, figure 63, and Wenig, *op. cit.*, figure 13, for the restoration of one of these beds in the Boston Museum of Fine Arts.

49. Reisner, *Kerma IV–V*, 13–14; for the ivory and mica inlays, 265–81; Wenig, *op. cit.*, cat. nos. 45–57.

50. There is a hint in these designs covering the top of the head on leather (?) caps of the unique metal piece supporting the chains of rosettes in a headdress of the time of Tuthmosis III: H. E. Winlock, *The Treasure of Three Egyptian Princesses* (New York, 1948), plates iii, iv.

51. Reisner, *Kerma I–III*, 343, plate 26.

CHAPTER 12

1. T. Säve-Söderbergh, *Ägypten und Nubien* (Lund, 1941); more recently and conclusively on the Kerma issue, see Fritz Hintze, 'Das Kerma-Problem', *ZÄS*, 91 (1964), 79–86, and B. G. Trigger, 'Kerma: The Rise of an African Civilization', *International Journal of African Historical Studies*, 9 (1976), 1–21. See Note

18 to Chapter 10 and Note 31 to Chapter 11. Hintze concluded that Kerma was not an Egyptian trade factory of the Middle Kingdom but the centre of an indigenous Nubian culture and the residence of its ruler, the Egyptian objects found there being acquired through trade with the Hyksos and through the plunder of the Egyptian forts to the north at the Second Cataract. Trigger supports this view, and regards the 'Hepzefa' tumulus (K III) as the latest and largest in the development. For the extent of the Kerma area, see B. Gratien, 'Les nécropoles Kerma de l'île de Saï III', *Études sur l'Égypte et le Soudain anciens* (*Cahier de Recherches de l'Institut de Papyrologie et d'Égyptologie de Lille*, 3) (1975), 43–66. Charles Bonnet, *Kerma: Territoire et Métropole* (Cairo, 1986).

2. Pieces of one painted coffin are, however, illustrated in Reisner, *Kerma I–III*, plate 26.

3. Reisner, *Kerma I–III*, 38–9; *Kerma IV–V*, 76.

4. Smith, *Ancient Egypt as Represented in the Museum of Fine Arts*, 6th ed. (Boston, 1960), 94, figure 57.

000. 5. Compare the heads of Sobkemsaf of Dynasty XVII, Sekhem-ra-khutawy, the founder of Dynasty XIII, and Sesostris III, at Medamud: Rémy Cottevieille-Giraudet, *Fouilles de l'Institut français du Caire*, IX (1893), plates xliv, xlv, xlvi.

6. H. G. Evers, *Staat aus dem Stein*, I (Munich, 1929), plates 143–8.

7. W. C. Hayes, *The Scepter of Egypt*, I (New York, 1953), 341 ff.; *JEA*, 33 (1947), 3–11.

8. J. J. Tylor, *The Tomb of Sebeknekht* (London, 1896); W. Wreszinski, *Bericht über die photographische Expedition von Kairo bis Wadi Halfa* (Halle, 1927), plates 34–7, 42–3; Hayes in *JEA*, 33 (1947), 3.

9. Robert M. Engberg, *The Hyksos Reconsidered* (Chicago, 1939); Albright, *The Archaeology of Palestine*, 85 ff.; T. Säve-Söderbergh, 'The Hyksos Rule in Egypt', *JEA*, 37 (1951), 53 ff.; John van Seters, *The Hyksos* (New Haven, 1966). K. S. B. Ryholt, *The Political Situation in Egypt during the Second Intermediate Period c.1800–1550 B.C.* Carsten Niebuhr Institute Publications 20 (Copenhagen, 1997). See Note 12 below.

10. Frankfort, *Ancient Orient*, 124, 246, 247. Spirals, sphinxes, and a tree with papyrus flowers occur at Mari, where the 'guardian of the heavens' is an example of the light on dark technique in painting, as are the plants on a red ground at Alalakh; *Syria*, 18 (1937), 325–54, plates xxxix, xxxviii, 2, figure 14; Woolley, *A Forgotten Kingdom*, plate 6. Max Mallowan has speculated on a source common to the Mari paintings and those on Middle Kingdom ceilings in Egypt as influencing the light on dark designs of pottery common to the Mitanni sphere of influence after 1500 B.C.: *Mélanges syriens offerts à Monsieur René Dussaud*, II, 887 ff. Sir Leonard Woolley kindly allowed me to examine photographs of the fragmentary Alalakh paintings described in *Antiquaries Journal*, 28 (1948), 14. For all of this material see Smith, *Interconnections*, 96–106.

11. Georges Dossin in *Syria*, 20 (1939), 110–11; Schaeffer, *Ugaritica I*, 16.

12. Manfred Bietak, 'Vorläufiger Bericht über die erste und zweite Kampagne der Österreichischen Ausgrabungen auf Tell Ed-Deb'a im Ostdelta Ägyptens' (1966, 1967), *MDAIK*, 23 (1968), 79–114; 'Vorläufiger Bericht über die dritte Kampagne', *MDAIK*, 26 (1970), 15–42. Cf. also R. S. Merrillees, 'El-Lisht and Tell el-Yahudiya Ware . . .', *Levant*, 10 (1978), 75–98; 'Die Hauptstadt der Hyksos und die Ramsesstadt', *Antike Welt*, 6 (1975), 28–43; Bietak, *Tell el-Dab'a II. Der Fundort im Rahmen einer archäologisch-geographischen Untersuchung über das ägyptische Ostdelta* (Vienna, 1975). M. Bietak (ed.). *An International Symposium at the Metropolitan Museum: Trade, Power and Cultural Exchange: Hyksos Egypt and the Eastern Mediterranean World 1800–1500 B.C.* (Vienna, 1995). Several essays, including studies of the Minoan wall paintings from Avaris and the parallels from Knossos and elsewhere. The individual articles are not listed in this bibliography. Idem, *Avaris: The Capital of the Hyksos. Recent Excavations at Tell el-Dab'a*. London, 1996. Idem, 'Dab'a, Tell el–', in E. Myers (ed.), *The Oxford Encyclopedia of Archaeology in the Near East*. Vol. II, 99–101 (New York, 1997).

13. Evans, *The Palace of Minos*, I, 419, figure 304b; Porter–Moss, *Bibliography*, VII, 396; *Guide to the Egyptian Collections*, British Museum (1930), 333, figure 179. The stratification and bearing of the Egyptian objects discovered on Crete has now been challenged with reason by several scholars who regard the objects as much later imports. See, in particular, Leon Pomerance, 'The Possible Role of Tomb Robbers and Viziers of the 18th Dynasty in Confusing Minoan Chronology', *Antichità Cretesii: Festschrift Prof. Doro Levi* (1971), 21–9.

14. On the second stela at Karnak, see L. Habachi, *The Second Stela of Kamose* (*DAIK, Abhandlungen, Archäologische Reihe*, 8) (Glückstadt, 1972); H. S. Smith and A. Smith, 'A Reconsideration of the Kamose Texts', *ZÄS*, 103 (1976), 48–76.

15. H. E. Winlock, *The Rise and Fall of the Middle Kingdom at Thebes* (New York, 1947), 145.

16. Manfred Bietak and Eugen Strouhal, 'Die Todesumstände des Pharaohs Seqenenre (17. Dynastie)', *Ann. Naturhist. Mus. Wien*, 78 (1974), 29–52.

17. For these texts, see Wilson in Pritchard, ed., *Ancient Eastern Texts relating to the Old Testament*, 3rd ed. with supp. (Princeton 1969), 230–4.

18. Tylor, *The Tomb of Sebeknekht*, plate ii; N. de G. Davies, *JEA*, 12 (1926), III; Émile Vernier, *Catalogue général du Musée du Caire, Bijoux et orfèvreries* (Cairo, 1927), plate xlix.

19. An El Kab example has been attributed to the reign of Amenhotep I (J. J. Tylor, *The Tomb of Renni* (London, 1900), plate ii), but the rather roughly executed reliefs in this tomb resemble work of the time of Hatshepsut and Tuthmosis III. Mme Desroches-Noblecourt has called attention to a scarab of Tuthmosis I showing that king in a chariot, *Revue d'Égyptologie*, 7 (1950), 43 ff.; A. R. Schulman, 'Egyptian Representations of Horsemen and Riding in the New Kingdom', *JNES*, 16 (1957), 253–71, presents these and other examples. See also Chapter 10, Note 38.

20. Vernier, *Bijoux et orfèvreries*, plates iii, ix–xi, xxxix, xlii–xlvi, xlix–lii; Aldred, *Jewels of the Pharaohs*, plates 49–58 (both *op. cit.*, Chapter 11, Note 1).

21. The cat spacers of Queen Sebekemsaf (Burlington Fine Arts Club, *Ancient Egyptian Art* (1922), plate 1, p. 18, and Wilkinson, *Ancient Egyptian Jewellery*, plate XXVIIB) were given a more sophisticated twist in the reign of Tuthmosis III; Winlock, *The Treasure of Three Egyptian Princesses*, plate xvi, and Aldred, *Jewels of the Pharaohs*, plate 84. The bodies of the animals curve round with one front paw crossed over the other, and the heads are turned. They are reminiscent of the Asiatic silver lion from Tod and set a precedent for the Soleb lions of Amenhotep III in the British Museum or the jar lid of Tut-ankh-amon [344, lower right corner]. Compare the straight frontal pose of the little Lahun gold lions (H. E. Winlock, *The Treasure of El-Lahun* (New York, 1934), plate xii) and the curving movement of the silver lion (F. Bisson de la Roque, *Le trésor de Tod*, (Cairo, 1953), plate iv). For the Kamose lions, see Winlock in *JEA*, 10 (1924), plate 17.

22. Sir Arthur Evans (*Palace of Minos*, I, 715) believed that the workmanship of this dagger was Minoan, although he did not go so far as to claim that the dagger was therefore worked in the Aegean itself. His view was disputed by Kantor, 'Aegean and the Orient in the Second Millennium B.C.', *AJA*, 51 (1947), 64, note 38. The king wears an early example of the battle helmet, the Blue Crown. His vanquished opponent has a close-fitting protective cap and not the long hair of the Libyans who ordinarily wear such a short skirt and crossed bands on the chest. The absence of a hair lock has puzzled the craftsman into placing the king's clenched hand on the man's head, and he has not known how to treat the dagger and the right elbow of the foreigner. The slight digression from the traditional model may indicate, as has been suggested, that he is trying to show one of the Hyksos, as on an earlier crude precursor of the Ahmose dagger. This belonged to a follower of the Hyksos king Nebkhepesh-ra Apophis and was found in a grave at Saqqara: Daressy, *Annales*, 7 (1906), 115 ff. The gold-covered handle has hunted game leaping with a new freedom as well as the new palmette form more elegantly treated on the Ahmose dagger. It seems more likely that it was made in Lower Egypt under the Hyksos than in Syria itself; cf. Frankfort, *Ancient Orient*, 245–6.

23. Frankfort, *Ancient Orient*, 264, and in the *Annual of the British School at Athens*, 37 (1940), 106 ff.; Evans, *Palace of Minos*, III, 41, figure 25; *Syria*, 18 (1937), 325 ff.

24. Lucas, *Ancient Egyptian Materials and Industries*, 4th ed. by J. R. Harris, 249–51.

25. Evans, *Palace of Minos*, III, 113 ff.; Georg Karo, *Die Schachtgräber von Mykenai* (Munich, 1930–3), plates xciii, xciv.

26. At Edinburgh and in the Louvre: Aldred, *New Kingdom Art in Egypt* (London, 1951), plates 1, 2; Winlock, *JEA*, 10 (1924), plates xii, xviii–xx.

27. Aldred, *op. cit.*, plate 11, in the Turin Museum.

CHAPTER 13

1. For the debt of Hatshepsut to Mentuhotep, see Bengt J. Peterson, 'Hatshepsut and Nebhepetre Mentuhotep', *Chronique d'Égypte*, 42 (1967), 266–8; also A. Dodson, *JEA*, 75 (1989), 224–6; V. A. Donohue, *DE*, 29 (1994), 37–44.

2. E. Ayrton, A. Weigall, C. Currelly, *Abydos III* (London, 1904), plates xxxvi, liii, lxi; Vandier, *Manuel*, II, figures 149, 152, 154. See S. Harvey in new bibliography.

3. E. Naville, *The Temple of Deir el Bahari*, V (London, 1906), plates cxlix, cl, p. 11, and Alexandre Varille, *Inscriptions concernant l'architecte Amenhotep, fils de Hapou* (IFAO, Bibl. d'Étude, 44) (Cairo, 1968).

4. For Inene and Hapu-seneb, see Breasted, *Ancient Records*, II, 40, 160, and H. Kees, *Das Priestertum im ägyptischen Staat vom neuen Reich bis zur Spätzeit* (Leiden, 1953), 11–12. See the interesting suggestions in regard to Senmut's contribution made by Fr. W. von Bissing, 'Baumeister und Bauten aus dem Beginn des Neuen Reichs', *Studi in Memoria di Ippolito Rosellini*, I (Pisa, 1949), 120–234; Alan R. Schulman, 'Some Remarks on the Alleged "Fall" of Senmut', *JARCE*, 8 (1969–70), 37–42; Barbara Switalski-Lesko, 'The Senmut Problem', *JARCE*, 6 (1967), 113–17. In addition to the above cited study by Schulman,

several important discussions have been devoted to the statuary of Senmut: B. V. Bothmer, 'Private Sculpture of Dynasty XVIII in Brooklyn', *BMA*, 8 (1966–7), 66–7, and 'More Statues of Senenmut', *ibid.*, 11, part 2 (1969–70), 124–43; M. Marciniak, 'Une nouvelle statue de Senenmout récemment découverte à Deir el-Bahari', *BIFAO*, 63 (1965), 201–7; H. Jacquet-Gordon, 'Concerning a Statue of Senenmut', *ibid.*, 71 (1972), 139–50; J. Berlandini-Grenier, 'Senenmout, stoliste royal, sur une statue cube avec Neferourê', *ibid.*, 76 (1976), 111–32. On the origin of the courtyard tomb of Senmut as the burial place of the statue for the proposed Sed Festival of Hatshepsut, see Wolfgang Helck, 'Zum thebanischen Grab Nr 353', *GM*, 24 (1977), 35–40; Peter F. Dorman, *The Tombs of Senenmut: The Architecture and Decoration of Tombs 71 and 353*. (MMA Egyptian Expedition 24), New York, 1991.

5. For the history and chronology of the period, see Donald B. Redford, *History and Chronology of the Eighteenth Dynasty of Egypt* (Toronto, 1967), 57–87.

6. For these buildings see Vandier, *Manuel*, II, 620, 745 ff., 793 ff.; L. Borchardt, *Ägyptische Tempel mit Umgang* (*Beiträge zur ägyptischen Bauforschung und Altertumskunde*, 2) (Cairo, 1938).

7. von Bissing has called attention to this, *op. cit.*, 156, 224, suggesting that Hatshepsut erected the six statues, of which only the central one of the three in front of the west half of the pylon is fairly well preserved. Tuthmosis III re-dedicated this statue of Amenhotep I, while, according to this suggestion, he would have replaced the name of Hatshepsut by his own on the westernmost statue, leaving the name of his father Tuthmosis II on the two flanking the gate of the pylon. Whether or not this was the case, or the original conception that of Senmut, it seems probable that the whole forms part of one plan. The alternative would be that the statue of Amenhotep I was carved in his own reign to form part of the approach to a temple which he seems to have constructed north of Pylon VII (dismantled during the erection of Pylon III by Amenhotep III). Mariette thought that this colossal figure had been transferred here from a position in front of the old Middle Kingdom temple.

8. For an admirable presentation of the development of the Karnak temple in the early Eighteenth Dynasty, see Vandier, *Manuel*, II, 862. L. Borchardt's fundamental study is to be found in K. Sethe (ed.), *Zur Baugeschichte des Amonstempels von Karnak* (*Untersuchungen*, V) (Leipzig, 1905), 3 ff. The standard presentation of the site is now Paul Barguet, *Le temple d'Amon-Rê à Karnak* (Cairo, 1962). Although sections of the temple are illustrated or discussed in many publications and specialized monographs, the reader is referred to the following for a general over-view: Georges Legrain, *Les temples de Karnak* (Brussels, 1929); Kazimierz Michalowski, *Karnak* (New York, Washington, London, 1970). References to specific parts, reliefs, and statuary, etc., will be found in Porter-Moss, *Bibliography*, II (2nd ed., 1972). For the 'red chapel', see Pierre Lacau and Henri Chevrier, *Une chapelle d'Hatshepsout à Karnak*, 2 vols. (Cairo, 1977, 1979).

9. For the history of the temple and its decoration, see H. E. Winlock, *Excavations at Deir el Bahri* (New York, 1942); E. Naville, *The Temple of Deir el-Bahri*, I–VI (London, 1894–1908); Marcelle Werbrouck, *Le temple d'Hatshepsout à Deir el Bahari* (Brussels, 1949). For the Polish excavations at the mortuary temple of Hatshepsut, consult L. Dabrowski, 'The Main Hypostyle Hall of the Temple of Hatshepsut at Deir el-Bahari', *JEA*, 56 (1970), 101–4; J. Lipinska, 'Studies on Reconstruction of the Hatshepsut Temple at Deir el-Bahari: a collection of the temple fragments in the Egyptian Museum, Berlin', in *Festschrift zum 150 jährigen Bestehen des Berliner Ägyptisches Museum* (*Mitt. aus der ägyptischen Sammlung*, 8) (Berlin, 1974), 163–71. An account of the Deir el-Bahari temples, with further references, is provided by Dieter Arnold, 'Deir el-Bahari', in Helck and Otto, *Lexikon*, I, 1006–26, to which must be added J. Lipínska, *Deir el-Bahari II: The Temple of Tuthmosis III, Architecture* (Warsaw, 1977), with a thoughtful review by P. Gilbert, *Chronique d'Égypte*, 52 (1977), 252–9. W. C. Hayes, 'A Selection of Tuthmoside Ostraca from Deir el-Bahri', *JEA*, 46 (1960), 29–52, offers an important discussion of certain associated chapels and kiosks, for which also see J. Lipińska, 'Names and History of the Sanctuaries built by Tuthmosis III at Deir el-Bahri', *JEA*, 53 (1967), 25–33. Recent exploration and architectural analysis of the jubilee temple of Tuthmosis III at Karnak is the subject of Jean Lauffray, 'Le secteur nord-est du temple jubilaire de Thoutmosis III à Karnak: état des lieux et commentaire architectural', *Kêmi*, 19 (1969), 179–218.

10. An excellent account of the Hatshepsut statuary series may be found in W. C. Hayes, *The Scepter of Egypt*, II (New York, 1959), 89–101.

11. Recent study of the variations in detail is beginning to make possible a closer dating of uninscribed pieces; cf. H. W. Müller in *Münchner Jahrbuch der bildenden Kunst*, 3–4 (1952–3), 67; B. V. Bothmer, *BMFA*, 52 (1954), 11, for the identification of two pieces of Amenhotep II. What different aspects one of these traditional heads can present is well illustrated by the photographs of the fine piece attributed to Tuthmosis III in the British Museum; H. R. Hall, *JEA*, 13 (1927), 133. Compare plates xxvii, xxviii with plate xxx where the profile seems closer to the Cairo standing figure, or the front view, plate xxix, which recalls the facial type of Hatshepsut.

12. On Punt and the Punt reliefs, see Rolf Herzog, *Punt* (*DAIK Abh. Äg. Reihe*, 6) (Gluckstadt, 1968); K. A. Kitchen, 'Punt and how to get there', *Orientalia*, 40 (1971), 184–207; W. S. Smith, 'The Land of Punt', *JARCE*, 1 (1962), 59 60; Abdel-Aziz Saleh, 'Some Problems relating to the Pwenet Reliefs at Deir el Bahari', *JEA*, 58 (1972), 140–58; Emma Brunner-Traut, 'Noch einmal die Fürstin von Punt, ihre Rasse, Krankheit und ihre Bedeutung für die Lokalizierung von Punt', *Festschrift zum 150 jährigen Bestehen des Berliner Ägyptischen Museums* (Berlin, 1974), 71–85; Nina M. Davies, 'A Fragment of a Punt Scene', *JEA*, 47 (1961), 19–23; E. Danelius and H. Steinitz, 'The Fishes and Other Aquatic Animals on the Punt-reliefs at Deir el-Bahri', *JEA*, 53 (1967), 15–24; D. M. Dixon, 'The Transplantation of Punt Incense Trees in Egypt', *JEA*, 55 (1969), 55–65; F. Nigel Hepper, 'Arabian and African Frankincense Trees', *JEA*, 55 (1969), 66–72; idem, 'An Ancient Expedition to Transplant Living Trees: Exotic Gardening by an Egyptian Queen', *Journal of the Royal Horticultural Society*, 92, part 10 (1967), 435–8; B. Couroyer, 'Pount et la terre du Dieu', *Revue Biblique*, 80 (1973), 53–74; Abdel Moneim A. H. Sayed, 'Discovery of the Site of the 12th Dynasty Port at Wadi Gawasis on the Red Sea Shore', *Revue d'Égyptologie*, 29 (1977), 138–78; 'The Recently discovered Port on the Red Sea Shore', *JEA*, 64 (1978), 69–75.

13. A. Mariette, *Deir-el-Bahari* (Leipzig, 1877), plate v, shows this group as it was found; repeated in L. Klebs, *Die Reliefs und Malereien des Neuen Reiches* (Heidelberg, 1934), figure 125, p. 199. Both this block and the other in Cairo with the figure of the fat lady are omitted from the drawings of the whole wall in Naville, *The Temple of Deir el-Bahari*, III, plates lxix–lxxi. The loose blocks shown here, and others found later, have now been built into the wall: Nicholas B. Millet, 'A Fragment of the Hatshepsut Punt Relief', *JARCE*, 1 (1962), 55–7, with W. Stevenson Smith, 'The Land of Punt', *JARCE*, 1 (1962), 59–60 (reconstruction also published in Smith, *Interconnections*, figure 173).

14. Another rider appears on an Eighteenth-Dynasty battle-axe in the British Museum, no. 5419a; W. M. F. Petrie, *Tools and Weapons* (London, 1917), plate ii; *Archaeologia*, 53 (1892), 84, plate iii. Alan R. Schulman, 'Egyptian Representations of Horsemen and Riding in the New Kingdom', *JNES*, 16 (1957), 264–5, provides a list of several such riding scenes, one at least probably older than the one cited here.

15. Cf. N. de G. Davies, *BMMA*, section II (December 1930), figure 1, p. 30. The piece is from Deir el-Medineh and now in Berlin: Emma Brunner-Traut, *Die altägyptischen Scherbenbilder (Bildostraka) der Deutschen Museen und Sammlungen* (Wiesbaden, 1956), no. 76, William H. Peck, *Egyptian Drawings* (New York and London, 1978), 115, no 46; Heinrich Schafer, *Jahrbuch der königliche preussischen Kunstsammlungen*, 37 (1916), figure 17, pp. 34, 45, observed that such drawings are sketches from finished monuments, whereas preliminary studies would have been more carefully prepared on papyrus. Schafer's view is otherwise refuted by several figured ostraca which preserve guidelines and are therefore clearly preparatory studies. Certain ostraca may be brought into connection with scenes on temple walls, in royal or private tombs, or on stelae. Others seem possibly to illustrate literary texts. Still others may be votive offerings or copies from finished works.

16. This rarely represented beast is found at Erment in the next reign; Sir Robert Mond and Oliver H. Myers, *The Temples of Armant* (London, 1940), plates xciii, ciii; cf. also L. Keimer, 'Note sur les rhinocéros de l'Égypte ancienne', *Annales*, 48 (1948), 47.

17. Berlin no. 22450; W. Wolf, *ZÄS*, 61 (1926), 98–104, plate viii, with references to other Eighteenth-Dynasty examples such as those in Turin and the British Museum.

18. Chicago Natural History Museum no. 30177–1: G. Steindorff, *ZÄS*, 73 (1937), 122, plate xxi; two others from Aniba: Steindorff, *Aniba II* (Gluckstadt, 1937), 147, plates 96, 97; and a simpler one from an Eighteenth-Dynasty tomb in Turin: E. Schiaparelli, *La tomba intatta dell'architetto Cha* (Turin, 1927), 143.

19. Naville, *Deir el-Bahari III*, plate lxxi (coloured).

20. N. de G. Davies, *Paintings from the Tomb of Rekh-mi-rē' at Thebes* (New York, 1934), plate i; *The Tomb of Rekh-mi-rē' at Thebes*, II (New York, 1943), plate xvii.

21. For example, Tomb No. 84 (Amunezeh): *JEA*, 28 (1942), plate v, p. 50; 27 (1941), plate xiii, p. 96 for the Syrians.

22. Tomb No. 42 (Amenmose): Wreszinski, *Atlas*, I, plate 168; Davies, *The Tombs of Menkheperrasonb, Amenmose and Another* (Theban Tombs Series, v) (London, 1933), plate xxxvi.

23. Tomb No. 162: N. de G. Davies and R. O. Faulkner, *JEA*, 33 (1947), plate viii, p. 40.

24. Tomb No. 143: N. de G. Davies, *BMMA*, section II (November 1935), 46, figures 2, 3. Without the rafts, a similar scene is in Tomb 89 (Amenmose): *JEA*, 26 (1940), plate xxv, p. 131.

25. Wreszinski, *Atlas*, II, plates 26–33. For a lively discussion of this whole problem of the dependability of the Egyptian record, see Davies in *BMMA*, section II (November 1929), 35; *ibid* (December 1930), 29. Nathalie Beaux, *Le*

Cabinet de curiosités de Thoutmosis III. Plantes et animaux du <Jardin botanique> de Karnak. (OLA 36), Leuven, 1990.

26. There is a considerable literature on this subject. Important earlier studies include Sir Arthur Evans, *The Palace of Minos*, II (London, 1928), 534–6, 736 ff., Davies, *The tomb of Rekh-mi-rē' at Thebes*, I, 22 ff., Helene J Kantor, 'The Aegean and the Orient in the Second Millennium B.C.', *AJA*, 51 (1947), 1–103; Arne Furumark, 'The Settlement at Ialysos and Aegean History', *Opuscula Archaeologica*, 6 (1950), 215 ff.; G. A. Wainwright, 'Asiatic Keftiu', *AJA*, 56 (1952), 196. See more recently Jean Vercoutter, *L'Égypte et le monde égéen préhellénique*, and *Essai sur les relations entre Égyptiens et Préhellènes* (Paris, 1954); Smith, *Interconnections*; Fritz Schachermeyr, *Ägäis und Orient* (*Akad. der Wiss und der Lit., Phil.-Hist. Kl. Denkschriften*, 93) (Vienna, 1966); R. S. Merrillees, 'Aegean Bronze Age Relations with Egypt', *AJA*, 76 (1972), 281–94; W. Helck, 'Ägäis und Ägypten', in Helck and Otto, *Lexikon*, I, 70–5; and Helck, *op. cit.* (Chapter 11, Note 21).

27. As has been pointed out by Marian Walker, 'The Painted Pottery of the Near East', *Transactions of the American Philosophical Society*, 38, part 2 (1948), 221. P. Montet, *Les reliques de l'art syrien dans l'Égypte du nouvel empire* (Paris, 1937), covers this material in close detail.

28. Compare the dress of the figure on the Boğazköy gate, the Ras Shamra stela and small bronzes (Frankfort, *Ancient Orient*, illustrations 255, 257–9, 294) with Aegean examples (Evans, *Palace of Minos*, II, plate xii, 704 ff., I, 691, figure 513; III, 418, figure 282) and the representations in the tomb of Rekhmira. The tassels on the kilt of the first figure in Rekhmira's procession, as well as in the Aegean examples, appear on one of the ivory panels from Ras Shamra (Schaeffer in *Syria*, 31 (1954), plate 10, p. 57) dated to the end of Dynasty XVIII and are characteristic of the Philistines in Ramesside times (H. H. Nelson, *Medinet Habu I* (Chicago, 1930), plate 44). Boots with turned-up toes and worn with gaiters (contrary to Vercoutter, *Essai*, figure 27, p. 120) occur in Rekhmira, at Knossos (*Palace of Minos*, III, plate xxi, figure 144, p. 214), and in Anatolia on decorated pottery shoes strikingly like Rekhmira (H. Bossert, *Altanatolien* (Berlin, 1942), plate 80, no. 400; O. R. Gurney, *The Hittites* (Harmondsworth, 1952), plate 24). A similar footwear is widespread in modern times. Davies mentions the use of decorated gaiters in Macedonia, and one thinks of the gaily patterned woollen socks worn in North Syria with leather slippers with turned-up toes. H. H. von der Osten illustrates a striking survival in south-eastern Turkey of tunic, belt, round cap, gaiters, and shoes in *Oriental Institute Communications*, no. 8 (Chicago, 1930), figure 91, pp. 87–90.

29. Nina M. Davies, *Ancient Egyptian Paintings* (Chicago, 1936), plates xiv (Senmut), xxi–xxiii (Menkheperra-seneb) in colour; N. de G. Davies, *BMMA*, section II (March 1926), 41 (Useramon); *Paintings from the Tomb of Rekh-mi-rē' at Thebes*, plates ii–v (colour), *the Tomb of Rekh-mi-rē' at Thebes*, II, plates xviii–xx; *The Tombs of Menkheperrasonb, Amenmose and Another*, plates iv, v. Cretans and their products appear in several other tombs: Nos. 39, 85, 119, 155, and possibly 120.

30. Woolley, *A Forgotten Kingdom*.

31. For the private tombs of Thebes, see Porter-Moss, *Bibliography*, I, part 1. The stylistic development has been studied by Max Wegner, *MDAIK*, 4 (1933), 38–164. The style and affinities of early-Eighteenth-Dynasty sculpture have recently been treated by Roland Tefnin, 'contribution à l'iconographie d'Aménophis I', *Annuaire de l'Institut de philologie et d'histoire orientales et slaves*, 20 (1968–72), 433–7; James F. Romano, 'Observations on Early Eighteenth Dynasty Royal Sculpture', *JARCE*, 13 (1976), 97–111; Hellmut Brunner, 'Eine Statuette Amenophis I', *ZÄS*, 83 (1958), 82–9. Tefnin, R. *La Peinture Égyptienne Ancienne: Un Monde de Signes à Préserver*. Monumenta Aegyptiaca VII, Série Imago no. 1, Brussels, 1997. Essays from a colloquium in 1994 with contributions on specific tombs and a series of articles on conservation problems and computer programs.

32. Helene J. Kantor, *The Aegean and the Orient in the Second Millennium B.C.* (Bloomington, 1947), 62, plates xiii, xvi–xix.

33. Naville, *The Temple of Deir el-Bahari*, III, plate lxx.

34. Particularly by Furumark, *Opuscula Archaeologica*, 6 (1950), 215 ff.

35. Compare Bisson de la Roque, *Le trésor de Tôd*, plate iv, with Frankfort, *Ancient Orient*, illustration 321, p. 272.

36. Compare *Interconnections*, 155–6. There are several points which might militate against accepting strong Aegean influence on Egyptian art of this period. Furumark, 'Settlement at Ialysos' (Note 26 above), 218–19, has attempted to show that Aegean artifacts which are supposed to have influenced Egyptian craftsmen are historically not anterior to the Egyptian examples at all. A redating of the so-called Lasithi dagger (Charlotte R. Long, 'The Lasithi Dagger', *AJA*, 82 (1978), 35–46) tends to support this view. It should also be stressed that Egyptian Middle Kingdom works present rudimentary examples of the 'free motion' style and 'flying gallop' motif as found in New Kingdom art, where the style is possibly to be attributed to Aegean influence (these historical parallels cited by William F. Edgerton, *JAOS*, 56 (1936), 178–89, and Smith,

Interconnections, 155–6, to which add an important fragment from the tomb of Kheti, in W. C. Hayes, *The Scepter of Egypt*, I (New York, 1953), 164, figure 100). That the free motion style was an indigenous tradition, or an indigenous evolution, is perhaps also indicated by several trial studies in which Egyptian artists evidently experimented with the techniques, although such studies are not necessarily to be dated to the early Eighteenth Dynasty. Since virtually all Eighteenth-Dynasty Theban wall-paintings of the hunt – not simply those in the tomb of Puyemra – appear more or less in a style of free motion, perhaps Aegean influence on developed wall art was slight. Certainly, however, the dagger of King Ahmose from the very beginning of the dynasty shows strong Aegean influence, especially in its association with an axe-blade bearing a 'Cretan griffin' (see remarks by Henri Frankfort, 'The Cretan Griffin', *Papers of the British School at Athens*, 36 (1936), 114 ff., and compare W. Needler, 'A Dagger of Ahmose I', *Archaeology*, 15 (1962), 172–5).

37. W. S. Smith, 'An Eighteenth Dynasty Toilet Box', *BMFA*, 50 (1952), 74.

38. Smith, *Sculpture and Painting*, figure 70, p. 181. Eberhard Dziobek, *Das Grab des Ineni Theben Nr. 81*. (AV 68), Mainz am Rhein, 1992.

39. Little of the colouring or details is conveyed by the schematic coloured plates in H. Boussac, *Le tombeau d'Anna* (*Mémoires, Mission archéologique française*, XVIII) (Paris, 1896). An excellent idea of the colour scheme of the period can be gained from Nina M. Davies, *Ancient Egyptian Paintings*, plate xiv (Tomb No. 71), xv (No. 179), xvi (No. 100), xvii–xx (No. 82), and A. Mekhitarian, *Egyptian Painting* (Geneva, 1954), 40, 41 (Tomb No. 82).

40. For the context of these fragments, see Davies, *BMMA*, section II (March 1932), 51 ff.

41. Breasted, *Ancient Records*, II, 213, 217.

42. See for example the robed figure in Tomb 91, Wreszinski, *Atlas*, I, plate 290. See John Darnell, 'Supposed Depictions of Hittites in the Amarna Period,' *SAK*, 18, 1991, 132–40.

43. N. de G. Davies, *Paintings from the Tomb of Rekh-mi-rēʿ at Thebes*; *The Tomb of Rekh-mi-rēʿ at Thebes*, I, II; Nina M. Davies, *Ancient Egyptian Paintings*, plate xiv.

44. These designs have been schematized with disconcerting differences of detail in G. Jéquier, *Décoration égyptienne* (Paris, 1920), plates xxi, xxv, and Prisse d'Avennes, *Histoire de l'art égyptien*, I, plate 29, nos. 1, 2.

45. The Aegean origin of certain unusual designs in other tombs of the early Eighteenth Dynasty is argued by Helene J. Kantor, *op. cit.* (Note 32), 25, for quadruple spirals; 29, plate vi, C, E, meander; 56, plates I K, X, J for diagonal running spirals and interlocking cross in Tomb 82; 59, plate xi, B, C, D for contiguous S-spirals with palmette in Tombs 67, 162, 251. See also Fritz Schachermeyr, *Ägäis und Orient*, 40–3.

46. In his valuable discussion of the topography and peoples of northern Syria in *Ancient Egyptian Onomastica*, I (Oxford, 1947), Sir Alan Gardiner (pp. 158 ff.) translates the Amenemheb passage (cf. Breasted, *Ancient Records*, II, 233) and considers the records of Tuthmosis III and other much discussed evidence. He concludes that Niy, which is also mentioned in a badly destroyed inscription concerning an elephant hunt of Tuthmosis I at Deir el Bahari, was not in Nahrin (Mitanni) or on the Euphrates but within range of the Orontes and possibly on the lake of Apamea. He inclines to the opinion that Amenemheb's biography refers only to the Mitanni campaign of the Year 33.

47. Nina M. Davies, *JEA*, 26 (1940), plate xvi, p. 82.

CHAPTER 14

1. The boating scene appears in Wreszinski, *Atlas*, I, plate 70, and the register below in plates 249–50. Compare André Lhote, *Les chefs-d'œuvre de la peinture égyptienne* (Paris, 1954), plate 58, for a fine photograph of the fish and papyrus clump beside them; see Nina M. Davies, *Ancient Egyptian Paintings* (Chicago, 1936), plates xxxviii–xli for large coloured details of other parts of the tomb. Artur and Annalies Brack, *Das Grab des Haremhab. Theben Nr. 78* (AV 35). Mainz, 1980. Dated to Thutmose IV. Artur and Annalies Brack, *Das Grab des Tjanuni – Theben Nr. 74*. (AV 19), Mainz, 1977.

2. N. de G. Davies, *The Tomb of Two Sculptors at Thebes* (New York, 1925), coloured plate xiii.

3. See the wonderful treatment of the cat and birds in the fragment from a swamp scene in the British Museum, Nina M. Davies, *op. cit.*, plates lxv, lxvi.

4. H. Schäfer, *Principles of Egyptian Art*, trans. with additions J. R. Baines (Oxford, 1974), 72–3; Smith, *Sculpture and Painting*, 263.

5. N. de G. Davies, *The Tomb of Ken-amūn at Thebes*, 2 vols. (New York, 1930); Nina M. Davies, *op. cit.*, plates xxix–xxxiii.

6. For objects from the tombs of Tuthmosis III, Amenhotep II, and a contemporary of the latter, Maherpa, see M. G. Daressy, *Fouilles de la Vallée des Rois*,

Catalogue général (Cairo, 1902); for Tuthmosis IV, Theodore M. Davis, *The Tomb of Thoutmosis IV* (London, 1904).

7. Davies, *BMMA*, section II (November 1929), 35; Porter-Moss, *Bibliography*, I, part 1, 234, no. 122.

8. Here in the tomb of Ramose (No. 55) Amenhotep IV is accompanied by a goddess. Other versions of a state appearance in the time of his father are to be found in paint in Tomb 226 (Davies, *Theban Tombs Series*, V, plates xli, xlii), and in relief in those of Khaemhet (No. 57, Wreszinski, *Atlas*, I, plates 88b, 203), Surer (No. 48, *MDAIK*, 4 (1933), plate xix), and Kheruef (No. 192, *Annales*, 42 (1943), 94, 449 ff.). The Epigraphic Survey of the Oriental Institute, University of Chicago, *The Tomb of Kheruef: Theban Tomb 192*, OIP 102, Chicago, 1980. The fragments of the scene from Tomb 226 have been assembled in the Luxor Museum and are illustrated in colour in *Catalogue: The Luxor Museum of Ancient Egyptian Art* (Cairo, 1979), no. 101, pp. 78–9, plate vii; for the tomb, see also Habachi, in *Festschrift . . . Schott* (1968), 61–70.

9. Davis, *The Tomb of Thoutmosis IV*, plates vi, vii.

10. Wainwright, *Anatolian Studies*, 4 (1954), 33, cites the costume of this man as evidence for the Asiatic origin of the people of Keftiu. Facial type and boots suggest a Hittite, but there is no reliable representation of these people as early as Amenhotep III. A similar prisoner in a Karnak relief of Horemheb (Wreszinski, *Atlas*, II, plate 62) is called one of the 'vile chiefs of the Haunebut', but Vercoutter (*BIFAO*, 48 (1948), 168) argues that these are not the Aegean islands but the shores of the eastern Mediterranean. Compare the head of an old man with long curls on the Leiden relief from the Memphite tomb of Horemheb (H. Ranke, *The Art of Ancient Egypt* (Vienna, 1936), plate 229), or the cap, hair, and costume of one of the Medinet Habu tiles (*ibid.*, plate 267, second from left above). Consult E. Vermeule, *Greece in the Bronze Age*, 5th printing (Chicago, 1972), 148–51.

11. Semna stela in Boston, no. 25.632: Dows Dunham and J. M. A. Janssen, *Second Cataract Forts*, I (Boston, 1960), plate 82, with translation by W. Helck in *JNES*, 14 (1955), 22–31. William K. Simpson, 'Usersatet,' in W. Helck and W. Westendorf, *Lexikon der Ägyptologie*, 6, 1985, cols. 901–3; Edward F. Wente, *Letters from Ancient Egypt*, Atlanta, 1990, 27–8.

12. Davies, *The Tomb of Ken-amūn at Thebes*, I, plates ix, x, II, plates ixA, xA.

13. For the stelae set up by Amenhotep II, Tuthmosis IV, and others at the Sphinx, see Selim Hassan, *The Great Sphinx and its Secrets* (Cairo, 1953).

14. Formerly thought to lie in Cilicia, Arzawa is now believed to be farther west. Pamphylia has been suggested, but more recently evidence has been produced that it may have lain in the upper Meander valley. The problem is closely associated with the identification of the Ahhiyawa as Achaeans and the Mycenaean settlements at Miletus, in the islands of Calymnos, Cos, Rhodes, and Cyprus, Mycenaean trade with Cilicia, and a Mycenaean colony at Ugarit on the north Syrian coast; see O. R. Gurney, *The Hittites*; Seton Lloyd in *Anatolian Studies*, 5 (1955), 81–3; C. F. A. Schaeffer, *Enkomi-Alasia* (Paris, 1952), 350. G. A. Wainwright has discussed the location of Arzawa in attempting to identify Keftiu as Karamania, that is, western Cilicia, *Anatolian Studies*, 4 (1954), 33. On the subject of these diplomatic marriages see Alan R. Schulman, 'Diplomatic Marriage in the Egyptian New Kingdom', *JNES*, 38 (1979), 177–93.

15. William J. Moran, *The Amarna Letters* (Baltimore, 1992). EA 41 (pp. 114–15). For the Arzawa Letters, see EA 31–2.

16. For the distribution of scenes and the general character of the Theban tombs, see Chapter 1 of N. de G. Davies, *The Tomb of Nakht at Thebes* (New York, 1927), and Sir Alan Gardiner's discussion in Davies and Gardiner, *The Tomb of Amenemhet* (London, 1915), 10 ff.

17. Hermann Grapow, 'Studien zu dem thebanischen Königsgräbern', *ZÄS*, 72 (1936), 12. The Book of Gates is similarly treated in the Theban tomb of King Horemheb: Erik Hornung, *Das Grab des Haremhab im Tal der Könige* (Bern, 1971).

18. Given in colour, Mekhitarian, *Egyptian Painting*, 38.

19. Kurt Sethe, *Dramatische Texte* (*Untersuchungen*, X) (Leipzig, 1928).

20. See Nina M. Davies, *Ancient Egyptian Paintings*, plates l–lv, and Mekhitarian, *Egyptian Painting*, 76–94, for fine coloured plates of details of this tomb, which is probably of the reign of Tuthmosis IV.

21. For the whole wall as preserved with the cattle being led, see Wreszinski, *Atlas*, I, plate 206.

22. For the tomb, see N. de G. Davies, *The Tomb of the Vizier Ramose* (London, 1941); for coloured reproductions of the paintings, Nina M. Davies, *Ancient Egyptian Paintings*, plates lxxi–lxxiii.

23. L. Borchardt, *Statuen und Statuetten*, III, *Catalogue général du Musée du Caire* (1930), 87, no. 770; Spiegelberg in *Recueil de travaux*, 28 (1906), 177.

24. For the possible identification of this commander-in-chief of the army as a younger son of Amenhotep III, see H. W. Helck, *Der Einfluss der Militärführer in der 18. ägyptischen Dynastie*, in K. Sethe and H. Kees, *Untersuchungen*, XIV (1939), 31. For the career of Nakht-min and his placement at the end of the Dynasty, see A. R. Schulman, *JARCE*, 4 (1965), 61–6.

25. Nina M. Davies, *Ancient Egyptian Paintings*, plate liii.

26. R. Lepsius, *Denkmäler*, III, plate 86b.

27. For the tomb of Kheruef, see Ahmed Fakhry, 'A Note on the Tomb of Kheruef at Thebes', *Annales*, 42 (1942), 447–509; Labib Habachi, 'Clearance of the Tomb of Kheruef', *Annales*, 55 (1958), 325–38; certain of the scenes form the basis for a study by Edward F. Wente, 'Hathor at the Jubilee', *Studies in Honor of John A. Wilson* (Chicago, 1969), 83–91. The Epigraphic Survey of the Oriental Institute, University of Chicago, *The Tomb of Kheruef: Theban Tomb 192*, OIP 102, Chicago, 1980.

28. For a plan, see N. de G. Davies, *The Tomb of Nakht at Thebes* (New York, 1918), 17, figure 1.

29. In my *Sculpture and Painting*, 355, I called Huy a Ramesside painter, overlooking the identification of later pictures of the revered scribe Amenhotep; see C. Robichon and A. Varille, *Le temple du scribe royal Amenhotep fils de Hapou* (*Fouilles de l'Institut français du Caire*, XI) (1936), 9. On the temple of Amenhotep, son of Hapu, see also recent references in Porter-Moss, *Bibliography*, II, 455–6. The tomb of Amenhotep has recently been discussed; fragments of two granite sarcophagi have long been known (Leclant, *Orientalia*, 39 (1970), 341, and D. Bidoli, 'Zur Lages des Grabes des Amenophis, Sohn des Hapu', *MDAIK*, 26 (1970), 11–14); Bengt Peterson, 'A Sarcophagus Puzzle', *Chronique d'Égypte*, 53 (1978), 222–5.

30. For the building inscriptions of Amenhotep III, the dedication of his funerary temple, and inscriptions of Amenhotep son of Hapu, see Breasted, *Ancient Records*, II, 353–79. The career of the latter has been studied by H. W. Helck, *Untersuchungen*, XIV (1939), 10ff.; Alexandre Varille, *Inscriptions concernant l'architecte Amenhotep, fils de Hapou* (*IFAO, Bibl. d'Étude*, 44) (Cairo, 1968); Dietrich Wildung, *Imhotep und Amenhotep: Gottwerdung im alten Ägypten* (*Münchner Ägyptologische Studien*, 36) (Munich-Berlin, 1977).

31. G. Legrain, *Catalogue général du Musée du Caire, Statues et statuettes de rois et particuliers*, I (Cairo, 1906). no. 42127, p. 78, plate lxxvi; Vandersleyen, *PKG*, plate 189(a, b) (notes by M. Seidel and D. Wildung); see also remarks by E. L. B. Terrace and H. G. Fischer, *Treasures of Egyptian Art from the Cairo Museum* (London, 1970), 117–20.

32. L. Habachi, 'Varia from the Reign of King Akhenaten', *MDAIK*, 20 (1965), 85–92, and figure 11.

33. For the statues of Amenhotep, in addition to Helck, *op. cit.*, see B. V. Bothmer, *BMFA*, 47 (1949), 42. See above, Note 30.

34. P. Lacau, *Mémoires, Académie des inscriptions et belles lettres*, 43, part 2 (Paris, 1951), 77 ff.; summarized and discussed by Vandier, *Manuel*, II, 843 ff.

35. Cf. Vandier, *Manuel*, II, 681, figure 347; Hellmut Brunner, *Die Geburt des Gottkönigs* (*Ägyptologische Abhandlungen* 10) (Wiesbaden, 1964); idem, *Die südliche Räume des Tempels von Luxor* (*DAIK Arch. Veröff.*, 18) (Cairo-Mainz, 1977).

36. W. Wolf, *Das schöne Fest von Opet* (*Ernst von Sieglin Expedition*, V) (Leipzig, 1931); Porter-Moss, *Bibliography*, II, 314–15. The Epigraphic Survey of the Oriental Institute of the University of Chicago, *The Festival Procession of Opet in the Colonnade Hall*. Reliefs and Inscriptions at Luxor Temple, Vol 1, OIP 112, Chicago, n.d.

37. See the plan in F. Cailliaud, *Voyage à Méroé*, II (Paris, 1823), plate xiii, repeated in Vandier, *Manuel*, II, 967, figure 457, as well as the plan and view in Lepsius, *Denkmäler*, I, plates 116, 117; also the description and photographs by J. H. Breasted, *AJSL*, 25 (1908), 83 ff.; Michela Schiff-Giorgini in *Kush*, 6 (1958), 82–98; 7 (1959), 154–70; 9 (1961), 182–97; 10 (1962), 152–69; 12 (1964), 87–95; *Soleb*, I, *1813–1963* (Florence, 1965), and II, *Les nécropoles* (Florence, 1971).

38. E. A. Wallis Budge, *Egyptian Sculptures in the British Museum* (London, 1914), plates xxv, xvii; for other Gebel Barkal pieces, now partly in Boston, see G. A. Reisner, *ZÄS*, 66 (1931), 81, and W. K. Simpson, 'A Horus-of-Nekhen Statue of Amunhotep III from Soleb', *BMFA*, 69 (1971), 152–64; Dows Dunham, *The Barkal Temples* (Boston, 1970).

39. Porter-Moss, *Bibliography*, II, 449–54; E. Edel, *Die Ortsnamenlisten aus dem Totentempel Amenophis III* (*Bonner Biblische Beiträge*, 25) (Bonn, 1966); Herbert Ricke, 'Eine Ausgrabung im Totentempel Amenophis III', in *Göttinger Vorträge von ägyptologischen Kolloquium der Akademie am 25. und 26. August 1964* (*Nachr. der Akad. der Wiss. Gött., Phil.-Hist. Kl.* (Göttingen, 1965), 199–203.

40. G. Jéquier, *L'architecture et la décoration dans l'ancienne Égypte*, I (Paris, 1920), plate 77; G. Maspero, *Guide du visiteur, Musée du Caire* (1915), 170, no. 610; Daressy, *Recueil de travaux*, 24 (1902), 165; Christiane Desroches-Noblecourt, *Tutankhamen* (New York and London, 1963), 102, figure 50.

41. Budge, *op. cit.*, plate xxii.

42. Lythgoe in *BMMA*, part II (October 1919), H. Gauthier, 'Les statues thébaines de la déesse Sakhmet', *Annales*, 19 (1920), 178–207; H. Ranke, 'The Egyptian Collections of the University Museum', *Bulletin of the University Museum, University of Pennsylvania*, 15, nos. 2–3 (1950), 16, figure 3.

43. Budge, *op. cit.*, plate xxi; Vandersleyen, *PKG*, plate 190; Vandier, *Manuel*, III, 319–21; head A 19 in the Louvre, Varille, *BIFAO*, 35 (1935), plate v, p. 161.

44. For the two Cairo statues, see *BIFAO*, 11 (1914), plate v, p. 25; for the statuette in the Metropolitan Museum from the Dattari and Theodore M. Davis collections, *ibid.*, 7 (1910), 169; *BMMA*, section II (March 1931), 4, figure 10; Desroches-Noblecourt, *Tutankhamen*, 122, figure 61; Hayes, *The Scepter of Egypt*, II, figure 142. A novel method of handling the royal garment appears in which deep folds replace the formal pleating of earlier sculpture: C. Barocas, 'Un motivo stilistico della XVIII dinastia', *Oriens Antiquus*, 6 (1967), 9–18.

45. W. C. Hayes in *JNES*, 10 (1951), 178.

46. L. Borchardt, *Der Porträtkopf der Königin Teje* (Leipzig, 1911). For the Sinai head, see Vandersleyen, *PKG*, plate 188(a, b); for the Berlin head, see also Cyril Aldred, *Akhenaten and Nefertiti* (Brooklyn, 1973), plate opp. p. 80, and no. 19. Dietrich Wildung, 'Métamorphoses d'une reine. La Tête berlinoise de la reine Tiyi', *BSFE*, 125, 1992, 15–46. Examination of the changes of the head with the newly reunited plumes on the headdress.

47. So interpreted by Borchardt, *op. cit.*, and Heinrich Schäfer, *Amarna in Religion und Kunst* (Berlin, 1931), plate 8. The difficulty of attributing uninscribed pieces is stressed by the comparison made by Cyril Aldred, *New Kingdom Art in Ancient Egypt* (London, 1951), plates 78–81. Using, as did Borchardt, the Sinai head of Tiy and the relief from the tomb of Userhet (No. 47), he concludes that the Berlin wooden head is not Tiy but her daughter Sitamon. The mummy of Queen Tiy has been identified: James E. Harris, et al., 'Mummy of the "Elder Lady" in the Tomb of Amenhotep II', *Science*, 200 (1978), 1149–51.

48. Borchardt, *Mitt. Deutsch. Orient-Gesell.*, no. 57 (March 1917), 14, 15; Schäfer, *op. cit.*, plate 8, cf. plate 9 for what has been considered a possible death mask of Amenhotep III.

49. See *Chronique d'Égypte*, 18 (1943), 107, for E. Bille-de-Mot's review of Günther Roeder, *Lebensgrosse Tonmodelle aus einer altägyptischen Bildhauerwerkstatt* (*Jahrbuch der Preussischen Kunstsammlungen*, 62) (Berlin, 1942).

50. N. de G. Davies, *The Rock Tombs of El Amarna*, III (London, 1905), plates x, xi.

51. There has been some question of the identification of his mummy, which was that of a man suffering from abscesses of the teeth, but which did not provide sufficient evidence for a precise estimate of the age. The impression is left that he must have been at least fifty but would have appeared prematurely aged; see S. R. K. Glanville in Winifred Brunton, *Great Ones of Egypt* (London, 1929), 116; G. Elliot Smith, *The Royal Mummies, Catalogue général, Musée du Caire* (Cairo, 1912), no. 61074, p. 46; Selma Ikram and Aidan Dodson, *Royal Mummies in the Egyptian Museum*, Cairo, 1997.

CHAPTER 15

1. The scarabs bore the names of Ahmose, Tuthmosis I, a Queen Ahmes, probably his wife, Hatshepsut and her favourite Senmut, born of the Lady Hatnefert, Tuthmosis III, and probably Tuthmosis IV. Painted jars found in the North Palace resemble those of the end of Dynasty XVIII at Thebes and Amarna, but the decoration is fairly simple and could have occurred earlier. Neither palace was very rich in objects. The northern one was re-occupied in Roman times and contained the remains of three badly preserved Christian chapels. Both palaces had column bases cut from Middle Kingdom reliefs and inscriptions, the name of the Dynasty XI king Neb-hepet-ra Mentuhotep occurring at both sites. This long neglected material, the records made by G. A. Reisner, Albert M. Lythgoe, and F. W. Green as part of the first work done in 1900 for the Hearst Expedition of the University of California, is housed in the Boston Museum of Fine Arts. In this connexion, the portion of a lintel of King Sekenenra of Dynasty XVII found in the nearby village of Ballas should have some significance; see Porter-Moss, *Bibliography*, V, 117, where some of the inscriptions from Deir el Ballas are also listed. See now Peter Lacovara, *The New Kingdom Royal City*. New York, 1997; Peter Lacovara (ed.), *Deir el-Ballas: preliminary report on the Deir el-Ballas Expedition, 1980–1986*. Winona Lake, Indiana, 1990.

2. Dr William C. Hayes has generously allowed the use of unpublished records of the excavations of the Metropolitan Museum of Art, without which this description would have been impossible. Mr John D. Cooney and Mrs Elizabeth Riefstahl have also facilitated the examination in the Brooklyn Museum of portions of the wall-paintings found by Tytus, supplementing the better known pieces in Cairo and the Metropolitan Museum excavated in turn by the Service des Antiquités, Tytus and Newberry, and the Metropolitan Museum. Work at the site began with a chance discovery of a floor-painting by Daressy in 1888. The Wilbour Library and the Egyptian Department of the Metropolitan Museum have also made available two of the otherwise virtually unobtainable copies of the privately printed report on the Tytus excavations: Robb de P.

Tytus, *A Preliminary Report on the Pre-excavation of the Palace of Amenhotep III* (The Winthrop Press, New York, 1903). See also: Daressy in *Annales*, 4 (1903), 165; Winlock, Evelyn-White, and Lansing respectively in *BMMA*, 6 (1912), 184; 10 (1915), 253; Special Supplement (March 1918), 8. These references should be consulted in connexion with William C. Hayes's definitive study: *Inscriptions from the Palace of Amenhotep III*, reprinted from *JNES*, 10 (1951). See also A. Badawy, *A History of Egyptian Architecture*, III, *The Empire* (Berkeley and Los Angeles, 1968), 47, 54, figures 26–8, and plate 2.

3. Barry J. Kemp and David O'Connor, 'An Ancient Nile Harbor: University Museum Excavations at the "Birket Habu"', *International Journal of Nautical Archaeology and Underwater Exploration*, 3 (1974). 101–36. Of final reports on the Malkata excavations issued to date, see M. A. Leahy, *The Inscriptions (Malkata IV)* (Warminster, 1978), and Colin Hope, *Jar Sealings and Amphorae of the 18th Dynasty: A Technological Study (Malkata V)* (Warminster, 1978).

4. Vandier, *Manuel*, II, 1006, figure 476; C. Fisher, *The Museum Journal, University of Pennsylvania*, 8 (1917), 221 ff.; H. Ricke, *Der Grundriss des Amarna-Wohnhauses* (Leipzig, 1932); Badawy, *op. cit.*, 54–5, and 82–8 for the Amarna palaces; Barry J. Kemp, 'The Harim-Palace at Medinet el-Ghurab', *ZÄS*, 105 (1978), 122–33. David B. O'Connor, 'Mirror of the Cosmos: the Palace of Merenptah', in R. Freed and E. Bleiberg (eds.), *Fragments of a Shattered Visaage: The Proceedings of the International Symposium on Ramesses the Great*, Memphis, 1993, 167–98; 'Beloved of Ma'at, the Horizon of Re. The Royal Palace of the New Kingdom', in D. B. O'Connor and D. P. Silverman (eds.), *Ancient Egyptian Kingship*, Leiden, 1995, 263–300.

5. William L, Moran, *The Amarna Letters* (Baltimore, 1992), EA 1, 1–5.

6. *Ibid.*, EA 29, 92–9.

7. The larger of two sets of painted black and Syrian captives in Cairo came from the dais in the second audience hall (2), the smaller figures apparently from the little reception room (3); Daressy, *Annales*, 4 (1903), 170, unnumbered plate.

8. W. M. F. Petrie, *Tell el Amarna* (London, 1894), 13–14, plates ii–iv.

9. One is largely dependent upon the descriptions of Daressy and Tytus. No copy was made of the floor in the harem hall, and only details, apparently from the small audience hall, were reproduced by Tytus, *op. cit.*; plate 1: swimming ducks from central panel (more accessible in A. Weigall, *Ancient Egyptian Works of Art* (London, 1924), 171); figure 9: a fish in the Cairo Museum, also from the central panel; figure 8: ducks flying over papyrus from a border painted in a more sketchy impressionistic manner like that of the Maru Aten floor-paintings at Amarna.

10. T. E. Peet, L. Woolley, B. Gunn, *The City of Akhenaten*, I (London, 1923), 118, plates xxxvii–xxxix; F. W. von Bissing, *Der Fussboden aus dem Palaste des Königs Amenophis IV zu el Hawata* (Munich, 1941).

11. These are found, like other paintings in the houses, on the outer walls of an enclosed bed cubicle in the front room; Bernard Bruyère, *Deir el Médineh (Fouilles de l'Institut français du Caire*, XVI) (Cairo, 1939), 54, 64, 255–9, 273, 330, plates ix, x.

12. *Ibid.*, XIV (1937), 111–14, figures 48, 49, plate xv.

13. Theodore M. Davis, *The Tomb of Iouiya and Touiyou* (London, 1907), plate opposite p. 37; figure 2, p. 39; figure 3, p. 40.

14. Reconstructed from sketches by H. E. Winlock and photographs.

15. See the ivory from Megiddo of the Ramesside period, where Bes appears as he does in the Deir el Medineh paintings: Frankfort, *Ancient Orient*, illustration 311.

16. These fragments (Tytus, *op. cit.*, figure 10, plate iv) are now in the Brooklyn Museum.

17. Either this or a vaulting over the recess which would allow for an opening at a higher level than the roof of the main room is suggested by the picture of the royal bedchamber at Amarna in the tomb of Huya: N. de G. Davies, *The Rock Tombs of Amarna*, III (London, 1905), plate xiii. On windows, see Badawy, *op. cit.* (Note 2), 34–5.

18. Portions of this are in the Metropolitan Museum and in Cairo. Another view of part of the ceiling in postion appears in H. Frankfort, *The Mural Painting of El-'Amarneh* (London, 1929), plate xiii.

19. See Sir Arthur Evans, *The Palace of Minos*, IV (London, 1935), 875, figure 864; 876, figure 866; G. Rodenwaldt, *Tiryns*, II (Athens, 1912), plate vii; A. J. B. Wace, 'Excavations at Mycenae', *Annual of the British School at Athens*, 25 (1921–3), plate xxix; Helene J. Kantor, *The Aegean and the Orient in the Second Millennium B.C.* (Bloomington, 1947), plate iiH.

20. Anthes in *MDAIK*, 12 (1943), 15.

21. B. Bruyère, *Deir el Médineh (Fouilles de l'Institut français du Caire*, VIII) (1933), plate iii; cf. plates iv–vi.

22. In the tomb of a Ramose (No. 46) who lived in the reign of Akhenaten and is not to be confused with the vizier of the same name (No. 55); Prisse d'Avennes, *Histoire de l'art égyptien*, I (Paris, 1878–9), plate 30, below; p. 367; J. Capart, *L'art égyptien*, 2nd series, IV (Brussels, 1947), plate 729.

23. Tomb No. 50; Nina M. Davies, *Ancient Egyptian Paintings* (Chicago, 1936), II, plate lxxxiv; Capart, *op. cit.*, plate 729.

24. Tomb No. 65; the Aichése of Prisse d'Avennes, *op. cit.*, plate 33, above.

25. A. W. Persson, *The Royal Tombs at Dendra near Midea* (Lund, 1931), plate xii; C. F. A. Schaeffer, *Enkomi-Alasia*, 379–89.

26. Frankfort, *Ancient Orient*, 251 2, illustration 291; R. F. S. Starr, *Nuzi* (Cambridge, Mass., 1937–9), plates 128, 129.

27. The bull calf and end-panel with papyrus clumps are in the Cairo Museum, the leaping calf in the Metropolitan Museum in New York; see Frankfort, *op. cit.* (Note 18), plate xiii; Hayes, *The Scepter of Egypt*, II, figure 149.

28. Winlock in his notes has called attention to the resemblance to the benches carved in stone in a room adjoining the burial chamber of Sety I, as well as similar stone shelves in the treasury of the Medinet Habu temple and in the tomb of Nofretari, the wife of Ramesses II.

29. The portion illustrated is in the Metropolitan Museum. It differs a little from the circular arrangement of the birds, with butterflies in the intervening spaces, in the piece illustrated by Tytus, *op. cit.*, plate ii (Weigall, *Ancient Egyptian Works of Art*, 171).

30. Tytus, *op. cit.*, plate iii.

31. Partly in Cairo and partly in New York: *BMMA*, 6 (1912), 185, figure 2.

32. Petrie, *Tell el Amarna*, 7; Frankfort, *op. cit.* (Note 18), 2: *JEA*, 10 (1924), 297, plate xxxii; Pendlebury, *City of Akhenaten*, III, 87, 140, plate lv.

33. U. Hölscher (*Das Hohe Tor von Medinet Habu* (Leipzig, 1910), 39, figure 31) suggests a somewhat different method for the roofing and flooring of an upper storey. The poles were pushed through holes bored in the rafters and the matting inserted over and under poles.

34. N. Rambova, *The Tomb of Ramesses VI* (New York, 1954), plate 172; Theodore M. Davis, *The Tomb of Siptah* (London, 1908), plate 4.

35. H. Frankfort and J. D. S. Pendlebury, *The City of Akhenaten*, II (London, 1933), plate lvi.

CHAPTER 16

1. For example, C. Ransom Williams, 'Wall Decoration of the Main Temple of the Sun at El-'Amarneh', *Metropolitan Museum Studies*, 2 (1930), 138–9.

2. Ahmed Fakhry has compiled an important collection of this material while making known the blocks from the precinct of the Luxor temple, in *Annales*, 35 (1935), 35 ff.; see the reports of Donald B. Redford, 'Studies on Akhenaten at Thebes, I: a report on the work of the Akhenaten Temple Project of the University Museum, University of Pennsylvania', *JARCE*, 10 (1973), 77–94; 'Studies on Akhenaten at Thebes, II: a report on the work of the Akhenaten Temple Project of the University Museum, University of Pennsylvania', *JARCE*, 12 (1975), 9–14; 'The Sun-disc in Akhenaten's Program: Its Worship and Antecedents', *JARCE*, 13 (1976), 47–61; and 'Preliminary Report of the First Season of Excavation in East Karnak, 1975–1976', *JARCE*, 14 (1977), 9–32; commencement of full publication in R. W. Smith and Donald B. Redford, *The Akhenaten Temple Project*, I: *Initial Discoveries* (Warminster, 1976), with brief summary in L. Greener, 'Reconstructing the Temple of a Heretic Pharaoh', *Archaeology*, 28 (1975), 16–22. See also Note 24 below.

3. Charles F. Nims, 'The Transition from the Traditional to the New Style of Wall Relief under Amenhotep IV', *JNES*, 32 (1973), 181–7.

4. Hayes, *JNES*, 10 (1951), 100; for the funerary temple, see Robichon and Varille, *Le temple du scribe royal (Fouilles de l'Institut français*, XI) (1936); Alexandre Varille, *Inscriptions concernant l'architecte Amenhotep, fils de Hapou (IFAO, Bibl. d'Étude*, 44) (Cairo, 1968); Dietrich Wildung, *Imhotep und Amenhotep: Gottwerdung im alten Ägypten (Münchner ägyptologische Studien*, 36) (Munich-Berlin, 1977).

5. Breasted, *Ancient Records*, II, 401; Labib Habachi, 'Varia from the Reign of King Akhenaten', *MDAIK*, 20 (1965), 85–92, and plates 27–31. In spite of this clear statement, there seems to be no very strong impression of the new style, although the Aten is called Lord of the House of the Aten in the new town of Akhetaten, and Gunn believed that the inscription must have been cut after the sixth year; *JEA*, 9 (1923), 171. The figures of Bak and his father suggest something of the rather fussy Amarna officials in their voluminous skirts. The figure of Akhenaten has been erased but was perhaps in the form of a statue like that of Amenhotep III to whom the father Men makes offerings on the right. Varille, *Annales*, 34 (1934), 14–16, in discussing the quarry inscription, suggested that this statue might represent one of the colossi which stood in front of the mortuary temple of Amenhotep III.

6. On the coffin of Hatiay, *Annales*, 2 (1901), 2–4; from this tomb came two precious objects: a little wooden kneeling man with a jar on his shoulder (cf. Capart, *L'art égyptien*, 2nd part, IV, *Les arts mineurs*, plate 718) and a bronze bowl with a scene of swamp life. The second tomb is unpublished and belonged to a Ramose (No. 46) who is not the same man as the vizier of that name (see Fairman in *City of Akhenaten*, III, 191). It contained the elaborate spiral ceiling painting

with inset scarabs, mentioned above, Chapter 15, Note 2; Prisse, *Histoire de l'art égyptien*, I, plate 30; Capart, *op. cit.*, plate 729.

7. See Davies's suggestions in *JEA*, 9 (1923), 151; for Silsileh, Legrain in *Annales*, 3 (1902), 263; Breasted, *Ancient Records*, II, 382.

8. For the siting of Gem-aten, see Cyril Aldred, *Akhenaten and Nefertiti* (New York, 1973), 29, with which compare C. Desroches-Noblecourt, 'La statue colossale fragmentaire d'Aménophis IV, offerte par l'Égypte à la France', *Mon. Piot*, 59 (1974), 23–4. See Notes 2 above and 24 below.

9. Davies, *The Rock Tombs of El Amarna*, III, plates xvii, xviii.

10. For the discovery of this workshop with a plan and some of the sculpture, see Borchardt, *Mitt. Deutsch. Orient-Gesell.*, 52 (1913), 29–50; Aldred, *op. cit.*, 43–7, 63. Dorothea Arnold (with contributions by J. P. Allen and L. Green), *The Royal Women of Amarna: Images of Beauty from Ancient Egypt*. New York, 1996, 41–83. Prepared in connection with the exhibition of the same name at the Metropolitan Museum. Particularly valuable are the chapter on the workshop of the sculptor Thutmose and the extensive bibliography.

11. *JEA*, 9 (1923), 132 ff.; *BMMA*, part II (December 1923), 40–53; the Tomb of the Vizier Ramose. For the tomb of Kheruef, see above, Chapter 14, Note 27.

12. Problems associated with this interesting architectural feature and the representations of it in contemporary relief are discussed by R. Stadelmann, 'Tempelpalast und Erscheinungsfenster in der Thebanischen Totentempeln', *MDAIK*, 29 (1973), 227–42, and Barry J. Kemp, 'The Window of Appearance at El-Amarna, and the Basic Structure of this City', *JEA*, 62 (1976), 81–99. Ramesside examples are illustrated in *Medinet Habu*, II, plates 22, 23, and 42, and III, plate 75.

13. It has been suggested that in such works Akhenaten was having himself represented as a primeval god: Wolfhart Westendorf, 'Amenophis IV. in Urgottgestalt', *Pantheon*, 21 (1963), 269–77, and Erik Hornung, 'Gedanken zur Kunst der Amarnazeit', *ZÄS*, 97, (1971), 74–8. The discussion has been continued by Winfried Barta, 'Zur Darstellungsweise der Kolossalstatuen Amenophis' IV. aus Karnak', *ZÄS*, 102 (1975), 91–4, and J. R. Harris, 'Akhenaten or Nefertiti', *Acta Orientalia* (Copenhagen), 38 (1977), 5–10. See Notes 2 and 24.

14. Davies, *The Rock Tombs of El Amarna*, VI, plate xxix (Ay); IV, plates xxiv–xxvi (Mahu), An attendant warms his hands at another brazier in a building which may be the house of Mahu from which he has come to interview the runner.

15. Cf. Rudolph Anthes, 'Die Maat des Echnaton von Amarna', Supplement to *JAOS*, 72 (1952), 1–36. For the status of the king, see John A. Wilson's sensitive remarks in 'Akh-en-aton and Nefert-iti', *JNES*, 32 (1973), 235–41.

16. F. Ll. Griffith, *Hieratic Papyri from Kahun and Gurob* (London, 1898), 91, plate xxxviii.

17. Daressy, in Theodore M. Davis, *The Tomb of Queen Tiy* (1910), 14; cf. also R. Engelbach in *Annales*, 40 (1940), 139. Valley Tomb No. 55 has been discussed by Cyril Aldred, *Akhenaten, Pharaoh of Egypt – A New Study* (London, 1968), 140–62, and very frequently elsewhere.

18. B. Gunn, *JEA*, 9 (1923), 168–76; L. V. Žabkar, 'The Theocracy of Amarna and the Doctrine of the Ba', *JNES*, 13 (1954), 87–101; John Bennett, 'Notes on the "Aten"', *JEA*, 51 (1965), 207–8; S. Tawfik, 'Aton Studies', *MDAIK*, 29 (1973), 77–86, and 32 (1976), 217–26; Donald B. Redford, 'The Sun-disc in Akhenaten's Program: Its Worship and Antecedents, I', *JARCE*, 13 (1976), 47–61.

19. For an illuminating discussion of the problems of representation, see H. A. Groenewegen-Frankfort, *Arrest and Movement* (London, 1951), 96–110. An effort has been made to trace the relation between contemporary religious and social practice and Amarna art by W. M. Davis, 'Two Compositional Tendencies in Amarna Relief', *AJA*, 82 (1978), 387–93. Barry J. Kemp, 'Wall Paintings from the Workmen's Village at El-'Amarna', *JEA*, 65 (1979), 47–53, offers an interesting discussion of paintings concerned with childbirth: here the anthropological significance of the surviving art is a focus of attention. John A. Wilson has examined the development of the thought of the period in *The Burden of Egypt* (Chicago, 1952), chapter ix. These discussions are representative of present-day elaboration of and reaction to the earlier studies of J. H. Breasted, Norman de Garis Davies, and Heinrich Schäfer.

20. They average in size 20 by 9 inches (50 × 22 cm) for the inscribed face. References to selected talatat may be found in Porter-Moss, *Bibliography*, II, 39–40, 190–1. See Notes 2 above and 24 below.

21. One limestone block from the north half of the Second Pylon employs the later name of the Aten and mentions a shrine or temple called the 'Northern Maru of the Aten in the Island of the Aten in Akhetaten' which appears to refer to the new town at Amarna, although the only building of the sort so far known is the 'Maru of Aten' south of that town. Another block from here names the Princess Meketaten, while a third shows two little princesses sitting back to back at tables of food, which would imply two others broken away, four girls in all. These are mentioned by Marianne Doresse in a remarkable early survey of this material, 'Les temples atoniens de la région thébaine', *Orientalia*, 24 (1955),

113–35, and Redford, *JARCE*, 10 (1973), 81. I had noted them in the course of examining these blocks, in 1951. Many more have since been found and the number is now estimated at 40,000. Mme Doresse (p. 28) seems to imply that Akhenaten's name occurs also in original use and not as alteration; see also Redford, *JARCE*, 12 (1975), 10.

22. The evidence for the alteration of the name is accepted by Doresse, *op. cit.*, 128. Schäfer was convinced by Borchardt's evidence that the name of Amenhotep III was replaced by that of his son both at Soleb and on the Berlin block (2072) around which discussion had been centred (his conclusions concerning this block are to be found in *Berliner Museen*, 41 (1920), 159 ff., *Amarna in Religion und Kunst* (Berlin, 1931), plate 4, and in Wolf, *ZÄS*, 59 (1924), 114; see also *Mitt. Deutsch. Orient-Gesell.*, 57 (1917), 20, figure 17; *Berliner Museen*, 40 (1919), 212–29, 284–5, figure 147). A recent re-examination of the relevant blocks, the results of which were published by Charles F. Nims, 'The Transition from the Traditional to the New Style of Wall Relief under Amenhotep IV', *JNES*, 32 (1973), 185, suggests that the earlier investigators were mistaken, and no earlier name was replaced by the praenomen of Amenhotep IV. Fairman seems to have overlooked the photograph of the Soleb cartouches in his figure 147 when he assumed that Amenhotep IV cut these reliefs in the old style. Originally Amenhotep III was apparently shown offering to himself as Lord of Nubia, as again occurs on the gate to the Hypostyle Hall. Breasted assumed in *AJSL*, 25 (1908), 87, that Amenhotep IV cut the reliefs on the pylon left blank by his father. He appears to have been misled by restorations of the name of Amenhotep III at the end of the Dynasty. The Berlin block (2072) is illustrated by Aldred, *op. cit.* (Note 17), plate 45.

23. They show the early didactic name of the Aten written in vertical columns above the figure of Ra-Horakhte as on Berlin 2072, except for one fragment which has the names in cartouches. One block, with a particularly disturbed surface, has a large part of the early titulary of Amenhotep IV.

24. A considerable amount of investigation has been conducted at the Ninth Pylon: R. Saad, 'New Light on Akhenaten's Temple at Thebes', *MDAIK*, 22 (1967), 64–7; Serge Sauneron and R. Saad, 'Le démontage et l'étude du IXe pylône à Karnak', *Kêmi*, 19 (1969), 137–78; Laurent Daniel, 'Reconstitution d'une paroi du temple d'Aton à Karnak', *Kêmi*, 21 (1971), 151–4; Lise Manniche, 'Les scènes de musique sur les talatat du IXe pylône de Karnak', *Kêmi*, 21 (1971), 156–64. The dismantling of the pylon revealed an important offering list of Akhenaten: R. Saad and Lise Manniche, 'A Unique Offering List of Amenophis IV recently found at Karnak', *JEA*, 57 (1970), 70–2, and W. Helck, 'Zur Opferliste Amenophis IV', *JEA*, 59 (1972), 95–9. Colour photographs of a reconstructed wall and various blocks from the site are included in *Catalogue: The Luxor Museum of Ancient Egyptian Art* (Cairo, 1979), 104–12, 116–19, 122–3.

25. Cyril Aldred, *New Kingdom Art in Ancient Egypt* (London, 1951), plates 102–4. For the report on the excavation, see Chevrier in *Annales*, 26 (1926), 121–5; 27 (1927), 143–7. Chevrier recovered nine heads and many parts of bodies. Several partly restored figures have been set up in a special storeroom at Karnak, where unusually fine lighting conditions enable one to appreciate the subtle differences brought out by the play of light and shadow over the seemingly similar faces. (See also Note 13 above.) The face and arm of another of these statues was found much earlier: Legrain, *Catalogue général, Statues et statuettes de rois et particuliers*, I (1925), plate liv, p. 51. Two of the statues have been illustrated and discussed in *Catalogue: The Luxor Museum of Ancient Art*, 113–15, 120–1.

26. It is doubtful that the ten somewhat similar figures found by Legrain in the Karnak 'cachette' represent Amenhotep IV. They are much smaller (about 3 feet high, 0.9 m) and seem to have been placed in front of ram-headed sphinxes. They appear to belong to the post-Amarna period rather than to be examples of an early transitional style. See Legrain, *Statues et statuettes*, I, plate lxv, p. 60, for illustrations of two of them in Cairo, and also *Annales*, 7 (1906), 228–31.

27. Cf. Doresse, *Orientalia*, 24 (1955), 113–35, versus the contrary views expressed by Ahmed Fakhry, *Annales*, 35 (1935), 35 ff., and R. Cottevieille-Giraudet, *Médamoud* (1932) (*Fouilles de l'Institut français du Caire*, XIII) (Cairo, 1936), 1–5. Redford concluded that there were Aten temples at Luxor and Medamud: Ray Winfield Smith and Donald B. Redford, *The Akhenaten Temple Project*, I, *Initial Discoveries* (Warminster, 1976), 48–9.

28. C. R. Williams, *Metropolitan Museum Studies*, 2 (1930), 138–9.

29. For Hermopolis, see Günther Roeder, *Amarna-Reliefs aus Hermopolis* (Hildesheim, 1969); Rainer Hanke, *Amarna-Reliefs aus Hermopolis* (*Hildesheimer Archäologische Beiträge*, 2) (Hildesheim, 1978); John D. Cooney, *Amarna Reliefs from Hermopolis in American Collections* (Brooklyn, 1965); O. Muscarella, ed., *Ancient Art: the Norbert Schimmel Collection* (Mainz, 1973), nos. 241–65; Aldred, *op. cit.* (Note 8), *passim*. For Assiut, see Borchardt, *ZÄS*, 61 (1926), 48, plate 3. The Hermopolis blocks show the later form of the name of the Aten and give special prominence to the third daughter Ankhesenpaaten.

30. Mariette, *Monuments divers* (1889), plate 56b; Lacau, *Catalogue général, Stèles du Nouvelle Empire* (1909), no. 34182, plate lxix. The Memphis blocks

were published by Sir Charles Nicholson, *Aegyptiaca* (1891), 115 ff., plates 1, 2 ('On Some Remains of the Disk Worshippers', reprinted from *Transactions of the Royal Society of Literature*, 9 (1870), 197–214); Beatrix Löhr, 'Aḫanjati in Memphis', *SAK*, 2 (1975), 139–87, plates iii–viii. They were built into a pavement near the colossus of Ramesses II. Not far away, in the excavation of the Palace of Merenptah, was found the yellow quartzite head, sometimes called Semenkhkara or Nofretete (now at Cairo): *The Museum Journal, University of Pennsylvania*, 8 (1917), 228; Drioton, *Le Musée du Caire, 'TEL' Encyclopédie photographique de l'art* (1949), plate 102; Aldred, *op. cit.* (Note 8), 60, figure 37.

31. Breasted, *AJSL*, 25 (1908), 51 ff.; Blackman, *JEA*, 23 (1937), 145 ff.; 24 (1938), 151 ff.

32. M. F. Laming Macadam, *The Temples of Kawa*, II (London, 1955), 12 ff., plates 1a, 40c.

33. For the representations in the tomb of Parennefer, see Davies, *JEA*, 9 (1923), 144–5. In the Karnak 'cachette' Legrain found part of the figure of a standing sandstone ape and a fragment of a black granite 'soul of Pe'; *Annales*, 7 (1906), 228–9. These statues of Amenophis IV evidently followed a practice instituted by his father, as testified by the two statues with that king's name, one of a falcon-headed 'soul of Nekhen' and one of a jackal-headed 'soul of Pe', restored from fragments in the Cairo Museum; Engelbach, *Annales*, 42 (1943), plate ii, pp. 71–3. These were again found by Legrain at Karnak.

34. F. Ll. Griffith, *JEA*, 5 (1918), 61–3; Cyril Aldred, 'The Gayer Anderson Jubilee Block of Amenophis IV', *JEA*, 45 (1959), 104, and 'The Beginning of the el-'Amarna Period', *JEA*, 45 (1959), 19–33; exhibited and published in Aldred, *op. cit.* (Note 8), no. 11 (to Aldred's bibliography add remarks by Henri Frankfort, 'Heresy in a Theocratic State', *Journal of the Warburg and Courtauld Institutes*, 21 (1958), 157–8, and plate 12c). For the scenes at Karnak, see Jocelyn Gohary, 'Jubilee Scenes on Talatat', in R. W. Smith and D. B. Redford, *The Akhenaten Temple Project*, 1: *Initial Discoveries* (Warminster, 1976), 64–7; for such scenes in general, J. J. Clère, 'Nouveaux fragments de scènes du jubilé d'Aménophis IV', *Revue d'Égyptologie*, 20 (1968), 51–4.

35. Ashmolean Museum; Petrie, *Tell el Amarna*, plate ix; cf. two Karnak blocks, Leclant, *Orientalia*, 24 (1955), plate xxiii, and Bouriant, *Mémoires de l'Institut français du Caire*, VIII, plate i.

36. For the Cairo relief, see Aldred, *op. cit.* (Note 8), figure 2; for the Berlin stele, and remarks on the composition of these reliefs, W. M. Davis, 'Two Compositional Tendencies in Amarna Relief', *AJA*, 82 (1978), 387–94, and figure 1.

37. H. W. Fairman has contributed a summary of material bearing upon the co-regency in *City of Akhenaten*, III (London, 1951), 152–60. Two other studies assume the existence of a long co-regency: W. C. Hayes, *Inscriptions from the Palace of Amenhotep III*, reprinted from *JNES*, 10 (1951), and Keith C. Seele, 'King Ay and the Close of the Amarna Age', *JNES*, 14 (1955), 168 ff. Helck and Redford have sparked controversy with extended rebuttals of the co-regency theory. See W. Helck, 'Die Sinai-Inschrift des Amenmose', *Mitteilungen des Instituts für Orientforschung*, 2 (1954), 189–207; D. B. Redford, 'The Alleged Coregency of Amenhotep III and Akhenaten', in *History and Chronology of the Eighteenth Dynasty: Seven Studies* (Toronto, 1967), 88–169. Further comments and references may be found in Edward F. Campbell, *The Chronology of the Amarna Letters* (Baltimore, 1964), 6–31, and Cyril Aldred, 'The Amarna Period and the End of the Eighteenth Dynasty', in I. E. S. Edwards, C. J. Gadd, and N. G. L. Hammond, eds., *The Cambridge Ancient History*, 3rd ed., II, part 2 (Cambridge, 1975), 49. A bibliography on this topic would run to well over a hundred items.

38. Erman proposed the emendation in *ZÄS*, 27 (1889), 63, but was willing to reconsider his opinion when J. A. Knudtzon prepared his translation of the letters and decided to accept 'Year 2' (*Die El-Amarna Tafeln* (Leipzig, 1907), 240–1). The hieratic inscription is shown in a photograph in C. Desroches-Noblecourt, *Tutankhamen: life and death of a pharaoh* (New York, 1963), 111, figure 55. Walter Fritz, 'Bemerkungen zum Datierungsvermerk auf der Amarnatafel Kn 27,' *SAK*, 18, 1991, 207–14; Also William Murnane, *Texts from the Amarna Period*, Atlanta, 1995, 42.

39. On an architrave, a figure of the king seated with Tiy and Princess Baketaten flanks a group of Akhenaten, Nofretete, and four daughters. Amenhotep's name is included with those of Tiy and Akhenaten in an inscription and is attached to statues shown in a building called the Sunshade of Tiy. That he formed part of a living group on the steps of a shrine in that building was suggested to Davies by the odd nature of the representation, but must evidently still be discarded in favour of a statue group, as Davies concluded in *Rock Tombs of El Amarna*, III, 23. Mrs Williams, *Metropolitan Museum Studies*, 3 (1930), 97, suggested they were living figures representing Akhenaten, Nofretete (or Tiy), and Semenkhkara and Meritaten. See C. Aldred, 'Year Twelve at El-'Amarna', *JEA*, 43 (1957), 114–17.

40. Alan H. Gardiner, 'Regnal Years and Civil Years in Pharaonic Egypt', *JEA*, 31 (1945), 23.

41. The names of the two kings on a fragment of the granite coffin of the Princess Maketaten from the Royal Tomb cannot be explained in this way, as Fairman has pointed out (*City of Akhenaten*, III, 155). It might, though, be part of a statement of her relation to her grandfather. The other objects usually cited are the relief of the old king with Tiy [318] from an altar shrine in the private residence of Panehesy (Griffith, *JEA*, 12 (1926), 1–2, and Aldred, *op. cit.* (Note 8), figure 3); the rim fragments of a granite bowl from the area of the desert altars (*City of Akhenaten*, II, 102, 108, plate xlviii, 2); and an offering table broken from the hands of a statue found in the sculptor's workshop north of the palace (*ibid.*, III, 81, 155, plate lxiv).

42. No double datings have been recovered to establish the co-regency. Some weight should be given to a series of documents involving one person and apparently stretching over some 15 years which are dated in the years 27 and 33 of Amenhotep III and years 2, 3, 4 of his son (A. H. Gardiner, 'Four Papyri of the 18th Dynasty from Kahun', *ZÄS*, 43 (1906), 27 ff.). The bearing of these documents in favour of a co-regency is discussed by Aldred, *op. cit* (Note 17), 110–11.

CHAPTER 17

1. The plan of the site (our illustration 308) has been adapted from Paul Thimme, *Tell el Amarna vor der deutschen Ausgrabung im Jahre 1911* (Leipzig, 1917), with additions from Erbkam's map in R. Lepsius, *Denkmäler aus Ägypten und Äthiopien* (Berlin, 1849–59), I, plates 63, 64, and the plans of the Egypt Exploration Society in T. E. Peet and L. Woolley, *The City of Akhenaten*, I (London, 1922); H. Frankfort and J. D. S. Pendlebury, *The City of Akhenaten*, II (London, 1933); J. D. S. Pendlebury and others, *The City of Akhenaten*, III (London, 1951); see also the valuable description and plan, in H. W. Fairman, 'Town Planning in Pharaonic Egypt', *The Town Planning Review*, 20 (1949), 32–51, figure 1; Porter-Moss, *Bibliography*, IV, plan opposite p. 197, pp. 192 ff. Recent analyses of the site include A. Badawy, *History of Egyptian Architecture: The Empire* (Berkeley, 1968), 76–148; Barry J. Kemp, 'Temple and Town in Ancient Egypt', in P. J. Ucko, R. Tringham, and G. W. Dimbleby, eds., *Man, Settlement, and Urbanism* (London, 1972), 657–80; idem, 'The Window of Appearance at El-Amarna, and the Basic Structure of this City', *JEA*, 62 (1976), 81–99; idem, 'The City of El-Amarna as a Source for the Study of Urban Society in Ancient Egypt', *World Archaeology*, 9 (1977), 123–39; 'Preliminary Report on the el-Amarna Survey, 1977', *JEA*, 64 (1978), 22–34. D. Arnold (with contributions by J. P Allen and L. Green), *The Royal Women Amarna: Images of Beauty from Ancient Egypt*. New York, 1996.

2. N. de G. Davies, *The Rock Tombs of El Amarna*, V (London, 1908), 30–1, plate xxx. William J. Murnane and Charles C. Van Siclen, *The Boundary Stelae of Akhenaten*, London and New York, 1993.

3. W. Westendorf, 'Achenatens angebliche Selbstverbannung nach Amarna', *GM*, 20 (1976), 55–7.

4. Bouriant, *Mémoires de l'Institut français*, 8, plates vii, ix. See, however, Keith C. Seele, *JNES*, 14 (1955), 174, who proposes that this may be an otherwise unknown daughter of the princess Meritaten, carried by the princess who was by this time the wife of Semenkhkara. Seele's plausible restoration of the inscription over the child as the name of the mother should be viewed with reserve, partly because of the deplorable condition of the wall and partly because the woman carrying the child is not represented like the other princesses and is set apart from them, really looking like a nurse. Sethe, in 'Beiträge zur Geschichte Amenophis IV', *Nachrichten der königlichen Gesellschaft der Wissenschaften zu Göttingen, Phil.-Hist. Kl.* (1921), 116, assumed, like Davies, *The Rock Tombs of El Amarna*, II, 7, that the name was that of the child, but suggested that there was space for it to be written Nefer-neferu-aten Tasherit, that of the fourth daughter. On the subject of the daughters, see Redford, in Smith and Redford, *The Akhenaten Temple Project*, I, 83–5, 87–94.

5. In spite of the seemingly incontrovertible evidence of a broken inscription from Hermopolis (H. Brunner, *ZÄS*, 74 (1938), 104 ff.), it is very difficult to believe that at an age which at the most could be 13 and is more probably 9, in the last year of Akhenaten's reign, she married her father for state reasons and bore him a child called 'Ankhesenpaaten the Little'. On the other hand, one tends to share Seele's disbelief that she was finally married to King Ay for dynastic reasons after the failure of negotiations with the Hittites (*JNES*, 14 (1955), 180). Redford has advanced the controversial proposition that it was Nofretete, not Ankhesenamon, who wrote to Subbiluliumas: *History and Chronology of the Eighteenth Dynasty* (Toronto, 1967), 159–62. This hypothesis requires that we repudiate the traditional view that Nofretete died in or about year 14 (Aldred, *Akhenaten: Pharaoh of Egypt – a new study* (London, 1968), 242–3). Redford's thesis rests in part on the point that the actual name of the queen involved does not appear in the Hittite records, but only her title 'king's wife' (see Walter Federn, 'Dahamunzu', *Journal of Cuneiform Studies*, 14 (1960), 33). Further

discussion and interpretation is offered by R. Krauss, 'Meritaten as Ruling Queen of Egypt and Successor to her Father Niphururia-Achenaten', *Abstracts of Papers, First International Congress of Egyptology, Cairo* (Munich, 1976), 67–8; *idem, Das Ende der Amarnazeit* (Hildesheim, 1978); see also summary and approval of this hypothesis in Rainer Hanke, *Amarna-Reliefs aus Hermopolis* (Hildesheim, 1978), 199–204. Krauss regards Meritaten as the queen who wrote to the Hittite king.

6. Seele, in *JNES*, 14 (1955), 175, stresses the date on a jar fragment from Amarna which certainly looks like year 21. Gunn doubted this reading (*City of Akhenaten*, I, 165, plate lxiii, graffito no. 169), while Fairman (*City*, II, 104) states that the reading of another date, year 18, is shown to be wrong by a facsimile of the inscription. In *City*, III, 159, plate xcv, no. 279, Fairman reminds us that the date year 1 was added to another jar label, where an earlier year 17 had been partially erased. It seems that weight should be given to the conclusion of the various excavators that the body of evidence points to the year 17 as being the highest of the reign.

7. On the other hand, Kemp considers the planning at Amarna to reflect a mature, developed urbanism which must have been transplanted from a parent site. See Barry J. Kemp, 'The City of el-Amarna as a Source for the Study of Urban Society in Ancient Egypt', *World Archaeology*, 9, no. 2 (1977), 123–9.

8. N. de G. Davies, 'The Town House in Ancient Egypt', *Metropolitan Museum Studies*, 1 (1929), 233–55; C. Desroches-Noblecourt, 'Un modèle de maison citadine du nouvel empire', *Revue d'Égyptologie*, 3 (1938), 17–25; Uvo Hölscher, *Post-Ramesside Remains, Excavations of Medinet Habu*, V (*Oriental Institute Publications*, LXVI) (1954), 45 ff.; Badawy, *op. cit.* (Note 1), 15–21. Pierre Anus, 'Un domaine thébaine d'époque "amarnienne" sur quelques blocs de remploi trouvés à Karnak', *BIFAO*, 69 (1971), 69–88, has produced extremely interesting reconstructions of a variety of city dwellings from the diagrammatic representations of such dwellings found on certain contemporary relief blocks.

9. Davies, *The Rock Tombs of El Amarna*, IV, plates xx–xxii.

10. Pendlebury, *City of Akhenaten*, III, 1, says that the road was still used for the droves of camels brought from the Sudan to Cairo.

11. See the preliminary reports in *JEA*, 12 (1926), 10–12; 17 (1931), 242; 18 (1932), 144–5, and plate 13(3, 5), with plan locating structures in Porter-Moss, *Bibliography*, IV, 200, and photograph in E. Bille-de-Mot, *The Age of Akhenaten* (London, 1966), plate 26. Compare the remarks of Barry J. Kemp, 'The Window of Appearance at El-Amarna, and the Basic Structure of this City', *JEA*, 62 (1976), 92–6.

12. The queen's name was erased on one relief fragment from the great Temple (*City of Akhenaten*, III, 18, no. 68), while the king's name was erased, leaving that of the queen, on the lintel of a house and the faience knob of a box lid in the North Suburb (*City of Akhenaten*, II, 64–5).

13. Davies in Frankfort, *The Mural Painting of el-'Amarneh*, 58–71; *JEA*, 10 (1924), 294–8, 12 (1926), 3–9, 13 (1927), 218.

14. Cf. Fairman in *City of Akhenaten*, III, 208 ff.; for the 'altars', *op. cit.*, II, plates xxvi–xxvii; the 'Hall of Foreign Tribute', *op. cit.*, III, plates x, xxix; and the tomb chapels, *op. cit.*, I, plates xxv–xxvii.

15. Since the names of these buildings are apt to prove puzzling, it might be well to list them according to the identifications of H. W. Fairman in *City of Akhenaten*, III, 189 ff. The smaller temple was called 'The Mansion of the Aten in Akhetaten', often referred to as Hat Aten. This name applied to the whole neighbouring area, east of the road, including the temple buildings to the south and the Royal Estate adjoining the Hat Aten on the north. The great temple was called 'The House of the Aten in Akhetaten' (Peraten-em-Akhetaten), and this of course referred to the sanctuary on the west, when this was the only building on the site. This temple has been the subject of considerable discussion; see particularly A. Badawy, 'The Symbolism of the Temples at "Amarna"', *ZÄS*, 87 (1962), 79–95, and *idem, op. cit.* (Note 1), 203–6; Eric P. Uphill, 'The Per Aten at Amarna', *JNES*, 29 (1970), 151–66; Jan Assmann, 'Palast oder Tempel? Überlegungen zur Architektur und Topographie von "Amarna"', *JNES*, 31 (1972), 143–55; P. Barguet, 'Note sur le grand temple d'Aton à el-Amarna', *Revue d'Égyptologie*, 28 (1976), 148–51. To these were added the building called 'The Aten is found' (Gem-pa-aten), possibly the long series of courts which form the main body of the later building. This name was also given to the early shrine of the Aten at Karnak and to several temples in Nubia. With it is associated the 'Mansion of the Ben-ben' (*Ht-Bnbn*) (which probably designates the sanctuary). Finally there is the 'House of Rejoicing' or Per-Hai, a name derived from that of the Palace of Amenhotep III, which was applied both to the entrance pavilion of the temple and to the palace.

16. The finest piece from the Great Temple is the block with chariots in the Metropolitan Museum. For a valuable study of the wall decorations and statuary, see Caroline Ransom Williams, *Metropolitan Museum Studies*, 2 (1930), 135 ff.; 3 (1930), 81 ff. A reconstruction of the reliefs on one of the altars has been made by Simpson and Cooney, *Bulletin of the Brooklyn Museum*, 12 (1951), 1–13.

17. N. de G. Davies, *The Rock Tombs of El Amarna*, V, plate v.

18. The Weben Aten of the inscriptions, which is only preserved in the foundations of the eastern pavilion, but which is named in the fragments of relief decoration from this area.

19. It is curious that those who planned the late addition of the Heb-sed hall of Semenkhkara did not make a culminating point to this north-south axis. This building can only be reached from the southernmost hall by a long detour along a passage to the west, outside the old south wall enclosing the block of state apartments. The excavators were puzzled by the way in which the north-south axis of the building ends simply in an exit from the last columned hall. This, like many other puzzling features of the building, may be due to the inability of the architects to complete the grandiose scheme within the lifetime of the king.

20. Lepsius, *Denkmäler*, I, plates 118, 119; *AJSL*, 25 (1908), 51 ff.; *JEA*, 23 (1937), plate xv.

21. Petrie, *Tell el Amarna* (London, 1894), plate vi; *City of Akhenaten*, III, plate xxxvii, 5; lxix, 6 (from the eastern court).

22. For this structure, see A. Badawy, 'Maru-aten: Pleasure Resort or Temple?', *JEA*, 42 (1956), 58–64, where it is argued that the building served as a sacred viewing place for statues (and see also *idem, op. cit.* (Note 1), 209–14). Columns in *City of Akhenaten*, I, plates 40, 42. The first of these plates typifies the difficulties presented by Egyptian plant ornament, particularly in its complicated later phases. While so much at Amarna is originally conceived, it is unlikely that this palm column should be restored with papyrus sheathing at the base. No evidence is cited for this (pp. 112, 113). Capitals of the open papyrus form from the island kiosk of Meru Aten (plate xxxi, 3, 4) are called palm.

23. Davies, *The Rock Tombs of El Amarna*, VI, plate xiv; Petrie, *Tell el Amarna*, plate vii.

24. *City of Akhenaten*, I, 121, plate xxxi, 5, 6.

25. Petrie, *op. cit.*, plate vii.

26. Petrie, *op. cit.*, plate viii.

27. *City of Akhenaten*, III, plate xv; Petrie, *op. cit.*, 15.

28. Davies, *The Rock Tombs of el Amarna*, III, plates v, vii, viii.

29. Petrie, *op. cit.*, 13–14, plates ii–iv. This was later almost completely destroyed, and what is now exhibited in the Cairo Museum is largely a copy. For the floor-paintings in the two adjoining halls and those in the south harem, see J. D. S. Pendlebury, *City of Akhenaten*, III, 38–46.

30. Petrie, *op. cit.*, 14, plate v.

31. Frankfort, *The Mural Painting of el-'Amarneh*, plates ii–ix; Nina de Garis Davies, *Ancient Egyptian Paintings*, II, plates lxxv, lxxvi.

32. In the Ashmolean Museum in Oxford (Frankfort, *op. cit.*, plates x, xi).

33. *JEA*, 17 (1931), plates lxxii, lxxviii.

34. The glazed tiles are best illustrated in *City of Akhenaten*, II, plate xxx, III, plates lxii, lxxii, lxxvi; *JEA*, 13 (1927), plate li; J. Vandier, *Musées de France*, 15 (1950), 25 (Louvre E 17359); Burlington Fine Arts Club, *Illustrated Catalogue of Ancient Egyptian Art* (1922), plate xl; Henry Wallis, *Egyptian Ceramic Art* (1900), plate i; C. Aldred, *Akhenaten and Nefertiti* (New York, 1973), 215–16, nos. 158–60.

35. The pertinent material is collected by Peet in *City of Akhenaten*, I, 37–50, where evidence from the preliminary reports of the German excavations is also carefully assessed, and by Frankfort and Pendlebury in *City of Akhenaten*, II. See further also Badawy, *op. cit.* (Note 1), 92–110, and an interesting study by Seton Lloyd, 'Model of a Tell el-Amarna House', *JEA*, 19 (1933), 1–7. Herbert Ricke has contributed a valuable study in *Der Grundriss des Amarna-Wohnhauses* (Leipzig, 1932).

36. See sketch of house as restored by Badawy, *op. cit.* (Note 1), 101, figure 57.

37. Frankfort in *City of Akhenaten*, II, 6–11.

38. L. Borchardt, *Portrats der Königin Nofretete* (Leipzig, 1923), plate i, p. 2; Aldred, *op. cit.* (Note 34), figure 2. Compare the Berlin stele: Vandersleyen, *PKG*, plate 299, with comments by W. M. Davis, 'Two Compositional Tendencies in Amarna Relief', *AJA*, 82 (1978), 388–90, with figure 1.

39. Pendlebury, *City of Akhenaten*, III, plates xi, xxxi; *JEA*, 13 (1927), 211–13.

40. *Mitt. Deutsch. Orient-Gesell.*, 46 (1911), 15; *City of Akhenaten*, I, 48.

41. See *City of Akhenaten*, III, plate lv, 3 for this painting, and plates xxii, lv for the interesting structure from which it came. A court lined on two sides with light columns led to a small columned room with a dais flanked by two engaged papyrus shafts. The wall behind the dais was painted with the panel pattern of false-doors, and the whole suggests a small audience room, as in the palaces, rather than a shrine.

42. Borchardt, *Mitt. Deutsch. Orient-Gesell.*, 52 (1913), 22, figure 6.

43. These friezes have been studied and illustrated in colour by Glanville in Frankfort, *The Mural Paintings of el-'Amarneh*. For the pectoral see Borchardt, *op. cit.*, 18, figure 4. A beautifully painted pigeon, head-down and with what appears to be a papyrus bundle behind, seems to be an unusually rich variant of this design, which usually employs ducks. It is from the room over the palace gate in the northernmost quarter; *JEA*, 17 (1931), plate lxxviii.

44. For the bathrooms see Ricke, *Der Grundriss des Amarna-Wohnhauses*, 35, where two wooden stools from Theban tombs are illustrated. See also Peet in *City of Akhenaten*, II, 46, 47, plate xlii, where a stone seat is pictured; and P. Honigsberg, 'Sanitary Installations in Ancient Egypt', *Journal of the Egyptian Medical Association*, 23 (1940), 199–246.

45. For the wells, gardens, outbuildings, and workshops, see Ricke, *op. cit.*, 44–50; *City of Akhenaten*, I, 11, 48; II, *passim*; for the sculptors' workshops, Borchardt, *Mitt. Deutsch. Orient-Gesell.*, 50 (1912), 29–35; 52 (1913), 28 ff. D. Arnold, *The Royal Women Amarna: Images of Beauty from Ancient Egypt.* New York, 1996.

46. Jean Capart, 'Dans le studio d'un artiste', *Chronique d'Égypte*, 32 (1957), 199–217.

47. J. R. Harris, 'Nefertiti rediviva', *Acta Orientalia*, 35 (1973), 10; Earl L. Ertman, 'The Cap-crown of Nefertiti', *JARCE*, 13 (1976), 63–7.

48. Borchardt, *op. cit.* (Note 38); Rudolf Anthes, *The Head of Queen Nofretete* (Berlin, 1954).

49. L. Borchardt, *Mitt. Deutsch. Orient-Gesell.*, 52 (1913), 28 ff.; H. Schäfer, *Amarna in Religion und Kunst*, plates 8, 9, 13, 38–43; Cyril Aldred, *New Kingdom Art in Ancient Egypt*, plates 118, 123, 124; *idem, Akhenaten and Nefertiti*, 43–7, 179–80, 182.

50. Smith, *Sculpture and Painting*, 24.

51. J. E. Quibell, *Excavations at Saqqara (1907–1908)* (Cairo, 1909), plate lx, p. 112.

52. Schäfer, *op. cit.*, plate 9, for example.

CHAPTER 18

1. Sir Alan Gardiner, 'The Memphite Tomb of the General Horemheb', *JEA*, 39 (1953), 3–12, where the pertinent inscriptions are translated and references given to the various parts of the tomb, with additions to those pieces first identified by Breasted and Capart. Extremely important material is published and discussed in Robert Hari, *Horemheb et la reine Moutnejemet* (Geneva, 1965), 69–135; G. T. Martin, 'The Excavations at the Memphite Tomb of Horemheb: Preliminary Report', *JEA*, 62 (1976), 5–13; 63 (1977), 13–19; 64 (1978); 5–9; 65 (1979), 13–16; 'Le tombeau d'Horemheb à Saqqarah', *Bulletin de la société française d'Égyptologie*, 77–8 (1976–7), 11–25, and 'The Tomb of Horemheb', *Archaeology*, 31 (1978), 14–23; 'A Block from the Memphite Tomb of Horemheb in Chicago', *JNES*, 38 (1979), 33–5; Hans D. Schneider, 'Het memphitische Graf van Horemheb', *Phoenix*, 22 (1976), 3–35. Geoffrey T. Martin, *The Memphite Tomb of Horemheb Commander-in-Chief of Tut'ankhamun*, London, 1989.

2. Palestine, as far north as Lebanon, A. H. Gardiner, *Ancient Egyptian Onomastica*, I, 145.

3. J. Bennett, *JEA*, 25 (1939), 9.

4. See the instructive series of letters selected by Albright in J. B. Pritchard, *Ancient Near Eastern Texts relating to the Old Testament*, 3rd ed. (Princeton, 1969), 483–90, with full references to the whole body of the Amarna correspondence.

5. Götze in Pritchard, *op. cit.*, 319–95; cf. 318 for the earlier Mitanni campaign, and also Gurney, *The Hittites*, 28–32. An excellent summary of the historical situation is provided by K. A. Kitchen, *Suppiluliuma and the Amarna Pharaohs* (Liverpool, 1962), and Edward F. Campbell, *The Chronology of the Amarna Letters* (Baltimore, 1964); for the identification of the Egyptian queen who wrote to the Hittite ruler, see Chapter 17, Note 5 above.

6. See Schaeffer in *Syria*, 31 (1954), 14–67, for the palace archives at Ugarit and the fragments of Egyptian vases with names of Tuthmosis III, Amenhotep III, Akhenaten, Nofretete, Horemheb, and Ramesses II; cf. also C. F. A. Schaeffer, C. Desroches-Noblecourt, and P. Krieger, 'Matériaux pour l'étude des relations entre Ugarit et l'Égypte', in C. F. A. Schaeffer, et al., *Ugaritica III* (*Mission de Ras Shamra*, 8) (Paris, 1956), 164–226.

7. Gurney, *op. cit.*, 46–58; Schaeffer, *Enkomi-Alasia*, 350 ff. equates the Ahhiyawa with the Akaywash or Ekwesh who appear among the sea peoples in the inscriptions of Merenptah in the last quarter of the thirteenth century. See also Smith, *Interconnections*, 31–2, 183.

8. First recognized by Capart, *JEA*, 7 (1921), 31, who thought that the grounds of a palace like that at Amarna were shown here and not a military encampment. See also Smith, *Interconnections*, 168; Silvio Curto, *L'Egitto antico nelle collezioni dell'Italia settentrionale* (Bologna, 1961), plates 30–31; Hari, *Horemheb et la reine Moutnedjemet*, figures 18, 19.

9. Wreszinski, *Atlas*, II, plates 45, 57, 64, 170; Alan R. Schulman, 'Egyptian Representations of Horsemen and Riding in the New Kingdom', *JNES*, 10 (1957), 267–70.

10. Howard Carter and A. C. Mace, *The Tomb of Tut-ankh-amen*, I (London, 1923), plates l–liii; Nina M. Davies, *Ancient Egyptian Paintings*, plates lxxvii, lxxviii, for the lion hunt and Syrian battle in colour; R. Hamann,

Ägyptische Kunst (Berlin, 1944), 248, for a detail of the blacks; N. M. Davies and A. H. Gardiner, *Tutankhamun's Painted Box* (Oxford, 1962).

11. The earliest complete example of such a composition, although without colour, is in the stucco reliefs on the chariot of Tuthmosis IV in Cairo; Theodore M. Davis, *The Tomb of Thoutmosis IV* (London, 1904), 24–33.

12. Elizabeth Riefstahl, *JNES*, 10 (1951), 65. Other especially fine Saqqara reliefs from the end of the Eighteenth Dynasty are that in Berlin, no. 12411, from the tomb of the high priest Ty (A. R. Schulman, 'The Berlin Trauerrelief', *JARCE*, 4 (1965), 55–68), and those from the tomb of Pa-aten-em-heb (P. A. A. Boeser, *Beschreibung der Aegyptischen Sammlung, Leiden*, IV (The Hague, 1911), plates i–xii). Compare the girl seated under her parents' chair (plate iii) with a more clumsily drawn Ramesside painted group in the tomb of Khai-Inheret (No. 359) (A. Lhote, *Les chefs-d'oeuvre de la peinture égyptienne* (Paris, 1954), plate 39). Both are derived from such an Amarna design as the painting of the Oxford princesses [313]. The New Kingdom tombs at Saqqara have recently become the focus for increased attention and study on the part of several scholars, particularly J. Berlandini, E. Graefe, S. Wenig, and Ch. Zivie, all of whom continue to write on the subject in various journals. See J. Berlandini-Grenier, *La nécropole memphite du Nouvel Empire (de l'époque post-amarnienne à la fin du XIXᵉ dynastie)*, Université de Paris-Sorbonne, thèse de 3ᵉ cycle, 1973; J. Berlandini, 'Varia Memphitica I (I)', *BIFAO*, 76 (1976), 301–16; 'Varia Memphitica II (II–III). II. La tombe de Pay, supérieur du harem. III. La tombe du général Kasa', *BIFAO*, 77 (1977), 29–44; E. Graefe, 'Das Grab des Schatzhausvorstehers und Bauleiters Maya in Saqqara', *MDAIK*, 31 (1975), 221–36; Steffen Wenig, 'Das Grab des Prinzen Cha-em-waset, Sohn Ramses II. und Hohenpriester des Ptah von Memphis', *Forschungen und Berichte* (Berlin), 14 (1972), 39–44; 'Das Grab des Soldatenschreibers *Hwj*. Untersuchungen zu den Memphitischen Grabreliefs des Neuen Reiches II', *Festschrift zum 150 jährigen Bestehen des Berliner Ägyptischen Museum* (Berlin, 1974), 239–45.

13. These lines are found on a sandstone hand intended for a composite statue from the workshop of the sculptor Tuthmosis; Borchardt, *Mitt. Deutsch. Orient-Gesell.*, 52 (1913), 40, figure 18. Particularly interesting are the representations of Hittites on the Hypostyle Hall at Karnak and on the first and second pylons of the Ramesseum (references in Porter-Moss, *Bibliography*, II, 56–7, 433–5). John Darnell, 'Supposed Depictions of Hittites in the Amarna Period', *SAK*, 18, 1991, 132–40.

14. W. S. Smith, *BMFA*, 50 (1952), 74, where the effect of Aegean influence is discussed. A generous selection of cosmetic vessels and implements is provided in J. Vandier d'Abbadie, *Catalogue des objets de toilette égyptiens, Musée du Louvre* (Paris, 1972).

15. N. de G. Davies and Alan H. Gardiner, *The Theban Tomb Series*, IV; Nina M. Davies, *Ancient Egyptian Paintings*, plates lxxix–lxxxi.

16. A. Piankoff, *The Shrines of Tut-ankh-amon* (New York, 1955). For the suggestion that Ay usurped another tomb and a funerary temple with colossal statues originally planned by Tut-ankh-amon along the lines of those of Amenhotep III, see Steindorff in *Annales*, 38 (1938), 641, and Aldred, *Akhenaten: Pharaoh of Egypt* (London, 1968), 253.

17. Lepsius, *Denkmäler*, III, plate 113. Further references in Porter-Moss, *Bibliography*, I, part 2, 550–1.

18. Theodore M. Davis, *The Tombs of Harmhabi and Toutânkhamanou* (London, 1912), and Erik Hornung, *Das Grab des Haremhab im Tal der Könige* (Bern, 1971), with important evaluations by J. Zandee, *Bibliotheca Orientalis*, 30 (1973), 232–6, and P. Kaplony, *Orientalia*, 43 (1974), 94–102.

19. G. Daressy, *Fouilles de la Vallée des Rois, Catalogue général, Musée du Caire*; Davis, *The Tomb of Thoutmosis IV*.

20. Theodore M. Davis, *The Tomb of Iouya and Touiyou* (London, 1907).

21. Howard Carter, *The tomb of Tut-ankh-amen*, I–III (London, 1923–33); Penelope Fox, *Tutankhamun's Treasure* (Oxford, 1951); Christiane Desroches-Noblecourt, *Tutankhamen: the life and death of a pharaoh* (New York, 1963); I. E. S. Edwards, *The Treasures of Tutankhamen* (London, 1972); Cyril Aldred, *Tutankhamen's Egypt* (London, 1972); T. Buckley, E. F. Wente, and I. E. S. Edwards, *The Treasures of Tutankhamen* (New York, 1976); Kemal el Mallakh, Arnold C. Brackman, and W. K. Simpson, *The Gold of Tutankhamen* (New York, 1978); R. Pfister, 'Les textiles du tombeau de Toutankhamon', *Revue des Arts Asiatiques*, 11 (1937), 207–18. Nicholas Reeves, *The Complete Tutankhamun: The King, the Tomb, and the Royal Treasure*, London, 1990; Frances Welsh, *Tutankhamun's Egypt*, Buckinghamshire, 1993; Special colour portfolio, cf. George B. Johnson, 'KV 62: Its Architecture and Decoration,' *KMT* 4, No. 4, 1993, 38–47, 88.

22. Carter, *op. cit.*, III, plates vii, viii; Fox, *op. cit.*, plates 42, 43; A. Piankoff, *The Shrines of Tutankhamon* (New York, 1955), 19–20, plate 24; Edwards, in Buckley *et al.*, *op. cit.*, 154–5, no. 43, and plates 24–5.

23. E. Schiaparelli, *Esplorazione della 'Valle delle Regine'* (Turin, 1923), 140, figure 98.

24. E. Schiaparelli, *La tomba intatta dell'architetto Cha* (Turin, 1927), 134,

figure 117; see passim for other metal vessels, painted pottery, and small objects as well as furniture of Dynasty XVIII.

25. Engelbach in *Annales*, 40 (1940), 162.

26. Fox, *op. cit.*, plates 9, 10; colour illustration in K. Lange and Max Hirmer, *Egypt: Architecture, Sculpture, Painting*, 4th ed. (New York, 1968), plate xxxv (cf. plate 194).

27. Carter, *op. cit.*, II, plates xvii, xviii.

28. For the vulture pendant, see Edwards, in Buckley *et al.*, *op. cit.*, 132, no. 23, and plate 13; Cyril Aldred, *Jewels of the Pharaohs* (London, 1971), 225–6, and plate 111.

29. A. Lucas, *Ancient Egyptian Materials and Industries*, 4th ed. by J. R. Harris (London, 1962), 179; Daressy, *Fouilles de la Vallée des Rois*, plates 43–5. See in general John D. Cooney, 'Glass Sculpture in Ancient Egypt', *Journal of Glass Studies*, 2 (1960), 11–44; F. Schuler, 'Ancient Glassmaking Techniques: The Egyptian Core-vessel Process', *Archaeology*, 15 (1962), 32–7.

30. Glass vessel from the tomb of Amenhotep II in the Cairo Museum: W. Stevenson Smith, *The Art and Architecture of Ancient Egypt*, 1st ed. (Harmondsworth, 1958), plate 155 (A). I owe these details to the kindness of John D. Cooney.

31. Richard F. S. Starr, *Nuzi* (Cambridge, Mass., 1939), plates 128–30; Taha Baqir in *Iraq*, 8 (1946), 91, plate xx.

32. Breasted, *Ancient Records*, II, 191; Sidney Smith, *The Early History of Assyria* (London, 1928), 227.

33. Frankfort, *Ancient Orient*, 248–50.

34. *Ibid.*, 260 ff.

35. Schaeffer, *Syria*, 31 (1954), 14–67; Smith, *Interconnections*, 33, and figures 55–7; W. A. Ward, 'La déesse nourricière d'Ugarit', *Syria*, 46 (1969), 225–39. The pattern of the disk on the head of the goddess in Schaeffer, plate viii, is to be found not only on Hittite seal impressions (Bossert, *Altanatolien*, II, nos. 656, 683) but also on a Ramesside glazed tile where it appears between the horns of a bull (W. C. Hayes, *Glazed Tiles from a Palace of Ramesses II at Kantir* (1937), plate xii).

36. Breasted, *Ancient Records*, II, 188, 203, 217; Gardiner, *Ancient Egyptian Onomastica*, I, 182.

37. Particularly letters 5, 10, 11, 14, 22, 24, 26, 27, 31, and 41; William L. Moran, *The Amarna Letters*, 10–11, 19–23, 27–37, 51–61, 63–71, 84–90, 101–3, 114–15.

38. Letter 23: Moran, *op. cit.*, 61–2.

39. Letters 10, 11: Moran, *op. cit.*, 19–23. For much of this material, see also Smith, *Interconnections, passim*.

40. John D. Cooney, *Bulletin of the Brooklyn Museum*, 10 (1958), 1.

41. *Ibid.*; in the Guennol Collection, on loan to the Brooklyn Museum.

CHAPTER 19

1. Two scribe statues of Paramesses follow the tradition of those of Horemheb and Amenhotep son of Hapu. Set up beside two of the latter behind Pylon X at Karnak, they give his parentage and titles under Horemheb: *Annales*, 14 (1914), 29, plates i, ii; Vandersleyen, *PKG*, plate 201b; Porter-Moss, *Bibliography*, II, 188. On the position of Horemheb in relation to the outgoing and incoming dynasties, see S. Sauneron, 'La tradition officielle relative à la XVIIIᵉ dynastie d'après un ostracon de la Vallée des Rois', *Chronique d'Égypte*, 26 (1951), 46–9; Allan K. Phillips, 'Horemheb, Founder of the XIXth Dynasty?', *Orientalia*, 46 (1977), 116–21.

2. J. H. Breasted, *The Battle of Kadesh*, reprinted from the Decennial Publication of the University of Chicago, v (1903); R. O. Faulkner, 'The Battle of Kadesh', *MDAIK*, 16 (1958), 93–111; Sir Alan Gardiner, *The Kadesh Inscriptions of Ramesses II* (Oxford, 1960); Hans Goedicke, 'Considerations on the Battle of Kadesh', *JEA*, 52 (1966), 71–80; Alan R. Schulman, 'The Nʿrn at the Battle of Kadesh', *JARCE*, 1 (1962), 47–53; Jan Assmann, 'Krieg und Frieden im alten Ägypten: Ramses II. und die Schlacht bei Kadesh,' *Mannheimer Forum 83/84* (1984), 175–231; Thomas von der Way, *Die Textüberlieferung Ramses' II. zur Qades-Schlacht: Analyse und Struktur* (HÄB 22), 1984.

3. See above, Chapter 14, Note 14. For a synopsis of the much discussed question of the sea peoples, see N. K. Sandars, *The Sea Peoples: Warriors of the Ancient Mediterranean, 1250–1150 B.C.* (London, 1978).

4. Vandier, *Manuel*, II, 819. It is now recognized, largely on the basis of work by Habachi, that the vast remains of Tanis reflect the moving of many monuments there from Qantir-Avaris at a later date.

5. Vandier, *Manuel*, II, 955; Steindorff in Baedeker, *Egypt* (Leipzig, 1929), 431. The temples of Abu Simbel have become increasingly well known in the course of their salvage, removal, and reconstruction as part of the programme to save the monuments of Nubia. For views, see Vandersleyen, *PKG*, plates 86–8.

6. This aspect of Ramesside art has been the subject of extensive and important comments by H. A. Groenewegen-Frankfort, *Arrest and Movement* (London, 1952), 114–41, and G. A. Gaballa, *Narrative in Egyptian Art* (Mainz, 1976),

94–129; see also K. A. Kitchen, 'Some New Light on the Asiatic Wars of Ramesses II', *JEA*, 50 (1964), 47–70, and G. A. Gaballa, 'Minor War Scenes of Ramesses II at Karnak', *JEA*, 55 (1969), 82–8.

7. Wreszinski, *Atlas*, II (1935), plates 81–9.

8. Wreszinski, *op. cit.*, plates 92–9.

9. Wreszinski, *op. cit.*, plates 100–6; less well-preserved versions of the battle occur on the western face of the outer wall at Luxor (plates 63–4); at Karnak in palimpsest on the outside of the south wall of the Hypostyle Hall (Breasted, *op. cit.*, plate vii, Wreszinski, *Atlas*, II, plate 56a), and on the outer face of the west wall connecting Pylons VIII and IX (plates 68–70); as well as at Abydos on the outer wall of the temple of Ramesses II (plates 16–24). The various elements of the battle and camp scenes are combined in the large composition at Abu Simbel (Wreszinski, *op. cit.*, plates 169–78).

10. Uvo Hölscher, *The Mortuary Temple of Ramesses III*, I (*Oriental Institute Publications*, LIV) (Chicago, 1941), 71, Appendix, *The Ramesseum*.

11. *Ibid.*, 4, 60, chapters I, III.

12. *Ibid.*, 37, chapter II.

13. *Ibid.*, II, *passim* for the two gateways and the coloured faience tiles of prisoners recovered from a stone door-frame in the palace; also *idem, Das hohe Tor von Medinet Habu* (Leipzig, 1910).

14. Vandier, *Manuel*, II. 912.

15. Porter-Moss, *Bibliography*, II, 43–6.

16. *Ibid.*, VI, 1. See Edouard B. Ghazouli, 'The Palace and Magazines attached to the Temple of Sety I at Abydos and the Façade of this Temple', *Annales*, 58 (1964), 99–186.

17. A. M. Calverley, *The Temple of Sethos I at Abydos*, I–IV (London and Chicago, 1933–58); Jean Capart, *Abydos, Le temple de Séti Ier* (Brussels, 1912).

18. Porter-Moss, *Bibliography*, I, part 2, 535–45. Erik Hornung, *The Tomb of Seti 1, Das Grab Sethos' 1*, Zurich. Munich, 1991.

19. E. Schiaperelli, *Esplorazione della 'Valle delle Regine'* (Turin, 1923), 51. For coloured plates, see Nina M. Davies, *Ancient Egyptian Paintings*, plates xci–xciii; H. Goedicke, *Nofretari: Eine Dokumentation der Wandgemälde ihres Grabes* (Graz, 1967). John K. McDonald, *The Tomb of Nefertari: House of Eternity*, Cairo, 1996. An introduction to the tomb based on the work of the Getty Conservation Institute with excellent colour reproductions of the paintings.

20. Smith, *Sculpture and Painting*, 263; cf. also Heinrich Schäfer, *Principles of Egyptian Art*, 4th ed. trans. by J. R. Baines (Oxford, 1974), 71–2.

21. F. W. von Bissing, *Denkmäler ägyptischer Sculptur* (Munich, 1911), plates 48, 49.

22. Porter-Moss, *Bibliography*, II, 53–6.

23. Wreszinski, *Atlas*, II, plate 168a; similar scenes are to be found in another Nubian temple of Ramesses II at Beit el-Wali, plates 165–6, and at Medinet Habu in the time of Ramesses III. Harold H. Nelson, *Medinet Habu*, I, *The Earlier Historical Records of Ramesses III* (Chicago, 1930), plate 9; Herbert Ricke, George R. Hughes, and E. F. Wente, *The Beit el-Wali Temple of Ramesses II* (Chicago, 1967), plates 7–15.

24. Nelson, *op. cit.*, plates 31–44; for the texts: William F. Edgerton and John A. Wilson, *The Historical Records of Ramesses III: The Texts in Medinet Habu, vols. 1 and 2* (Chicago, 1936), 35 ff.

25. Compare the similar prow on a boat shown on a silver bowl from Cyprus in Berlin; P. Montet, *Les reliques de l'art syrien* (Paris, 1937), 153, figure 191; H. Schäfer, *Ägyptische Goldschmiedearbeiten* (Mitt. aus der ägyptischen Sammlung, 1) (Berlin, 1910), plate 15. A prow with a duck's head appears on a small Egyptian pleasure craft in the tomb of Ipy (No. 217); N. de G. Davies, *Two Ramesside Tombs at Thebes* (New York, 1927), plate xxx.

26. They are even more difficult to illustrate except by large plates, but Mrs H. A. Groenewegen-Frankfort contributed a valuable service in making the subject more accessible through the excellent illustrations and stimulating discussion in *Arrest and Movement*, 114–41.

27. *BMMA*, 9 (1914), 21. Now dated in Dynasty 18, Tuthmosis II to Amenhotep II., probably the latter. See Peter Brand, in Nancy Thomas (ed.), *The American Discovery of Ancient Egypt*, Los Angeles, 1995, 170–1.

28. Capart, *op. cit.* (Note 17), plates xlviii, xlix; M. A. Murray, 'The Temple of Ramesses II at Abydos', *Ancient Egypt* (1916), 121–38, figure 3; G. Jéquier, *L'architecture et la décoration dans l'ancienne Égypte, Les temples ramessides et saïtes* (Paris, 1922), plate 27.

29. Groenewegen-Frankfort, *Arrest and Movement*, plate xlv.

30. For a similar flanking group, Gustave Lefebvre, *Les grands prêtres d'Amon Romê-Roÿ et Amenhotep* (Paris, 1929), plate ii, cf. p. 47; see also Lefebvre, *Histoire des grands prêtres d'Amon de Karnak* (Paris, 1929), 185, for Amenhotep. It is actually a statue of Ramesses IX before which the high priest Amenhotep stands, as pointed out by B. Piotrovskij, 'Das Karnak-relief des Hohenpriesters Amenhotep', *Comptes rendus de l'Academie de l'USSR* (1929), 115–19; W. Federn, 'Roi ou statue royale?', *Chronique d'Égypte*, 68 (1959), 214; A. Hermann, *ZÄS*, 90 (1963), 63–6.

31. It is to the kindness of the authorities of the Museo Egizio in Turin that I am indebted for permission to reproduce this valuable old record which justifies

the reconstruction of N. de Garis Davies, *op. cit.* (Note 25), plates xxviii, xxix, p. 51, as against the frequently reproduced copy by Legrain.

32. Legrain drawing, plate i, in Scheil, *Mémoires mission archéologique française*, v (Cairo, 1891), 604–12.

33. N. de G. Davies, *The Tomb of Nefer-hotep at Thebes* (New York, 1933), i, plates ix–xviii, xli–xlix; ii, plates i, iii, vi.

34. Davies, *Two Ramesside Tombs at Thebes*, plate xxvii, p. 47.

35. Coloured detail, A. Mekhitarian, *Egyptian Painting* (Geneva, 1954), 149.

36. Userhet (No. 51) of the time of Sety I; Davies, *Two Ramesside Tombs at Thebes*, plates i, vii; also in colour, Nina M. Davies, *Ancient Egyptian Paintings*, plates lxxxvii–lxxxix; Mekhitarian, *op. cit.*, 136, 137.

37. In addition to the coloured plates in N. de G. Davies, *Two Ramesside Tombs at Thebes*, see Nina M. Davies, *op. cit.*, plates xcvi–xcix; Mekhitarian, *op. cit.*, 146–8.

38. Vandier, *Manuel*, ii, 367, figure 254.

39. B. Bruyère, *Fouilles de Deir el Médineh (1924–5)*, *Fouilles de l'Institut français . . . du Caire*, 3 (1926), 190, figures 126, 127.

40. Other details of the repertoire of these Deir el Medineh tombs can be studied to advantage among the fine photographs of Theban tombs by Hassia which are reproduced in André Lhote, *La peinture égyptienne* (Paris, 1954).

41. N. de G. Davies, *Seven Private Tombs at Kurnah* (London, 1948), plate xxvi, p. 38.

42. A. Mariette, *Abydos*, i (Paris, 1869), plate 52, line 16.

43. Edgar in G. Maspero, *Le Musée égyptien*, ii (Cairo, 1907), 93, plates xliii–xlviii; *Annales*, 25 (1925), 256, plate i, for the cleaning of the designs on the goat-handled jug; Simpson, *BMMA*, 8 (1949), 61; Scharff, *Berliner Museen*, 51 (1930), 114; *Ramsès le grand* (exhibition catalogue, Galeries nationales du Grand Palais) (Paris, 1976), no. 60, pp. 288–93; Vandersleyen, *PKG*, plate 52 (colour); Simpson, 'The Vessels with Engraved Designs and the Repoussé Bowl from the Tell Basta Treasure', *AJA*, 63 (1959), 29–45.

44. Montet, *op. cit.* (Note 25), 138.

45. Wreszinski, *Atlas*, i, plate 224. Attention has been called to the rich ceiling patterns in the new decorations of this tomb which was taken over by Imiseba from an earlier owner.

46. Frankfort, *Ancient Orient*, 269–70; W. M. F. Petrie, *Beth-Pelet*, i (London, 1930), plate lv, p. 19.

47. Maspero, *Le Musée égyptien*, ii, plate xlviii.

48. Crowfoot and Davies, *JEA*, 27 (1941), 113.

49. Frankfort, *Ancient Orient*, 260.

50. C. Boreux, *Antiquités égyptiennes, Guide-catalogue sommaire*, Musée national du Louvre, ii (Paris, 1932), 341, 348; Montet, *op. cit.*, 168–9; É. Vernier, *La bijouterie et la joaillerie égyptiennes* (Cairo, 1907), plate 20. Now regarded as a forgery based on a silver fragment.

51. Daressy, *Annales*, 2 (1901), 11, figure 10; F. W. von Bissing *Metallgefässe*, Catalogue général du Musée du Caire (1901), 60; Montet, *op. cit.*, 149, includes this vessel among the work of Syrian origin.

52. Fox, *Tutankhamun's Treasure*, plate 68; Edwards, *et al.*, *The Treasures of Tutankhamen* (New York, 1976), plate 30 (colour).

53. A cup was inscribed with the name of Amenhotep III: E. Schiaparelli, *La tomba intatta dell'architetto Cha* (Turin, 1927), 84, 134, 135, 143, 172, 173.

54. Frankfort, *Ancient Orient*, 322.

55. Fr. W. von Bissing, 'Die zeitliche Bestimmung der mit Reliefs geschmückten ägyptischen Kelchgefässe', *Nachrichten der königlichen Gesellschaft der Wissenschaften zu Göttingen, Phil.-Hist. Kl.* (1941), ii, 249; G. A. D. Tait, 'The Egyptian Relief Chalice', *JEA*, 49 (1963), 93–139.

CHAPTER 20

1. George R. Hughes and members of the Epigraphic Survey, *The Bubastite Portal* (Oriental Institute Publications, lxxiv) (Chicago, 1954).

2. Uvo Hölscher, 'Der Erste Pylon von Karnak', *MDAIK*, 12 (1943), 139.

3. P. Montet, *Tanis* (Paris, 1942); Henri Stierlin and Christiane Ziegler, *Tanis: Trésors des Pharaons*, Fribourg, 1987; Jean Leclant, Jean Yoyotte, Christiane Ziegler, Pascal Vernus, et al., *Tanis: L'Or des pharaons*. Exhibition Catalogue, Paris and Marseilles, 1987.

4. E. Naville, *Bubastis* (London, 1891).

5. E. Naville, *The Festival Hall of Osorkon II in the Great Temple of Bubastis* (London, 1892); W. Barta, 'Die Sedfest Darstellung Osorkons II. im Tempel von Bubastis', *SAK*, 6 (1978), 25–42; C. Favard-Meeks, *Le temple de Behbeit el-Hagara, essai de reconstitution et d'interprétation*. Hamburg, 1991.

6. E. F. Wente in W. K. Simpson, ed., *The Literature of Ancient Egypt*, 3rd rev. printing (New Haven, 1977), 142–55.

7. J. A. Wilson, *The Burden of Egypt*, 267–88.

8. I Kings ix. 16.

9. P. Montet, *La nécropole royale de Tanis*, ii, *Les constructions et le tombeau de Psousennès* (Paris, 1951).

10. Montet, *op. cit.*, plates civ, cv.

11. *Ibid.*, plates xxii, cxxxi, cxxxii.

12. Frankfort, *Ancient Orient*, 314.

13. G. Maspero, *Les momies royales de Déir El-Bahari* (*Mémoires, Mission archéologique française*, i) (Paris, 1889), 585–7.

14. F. W. von Bissing, *Denkmäler ägyptischer Sculptur* (Munich, 1911), plate 59; Porter-Moss, *Bibliography*, iv, 33; G. Maspero, *The Struggle of Nations* (London, 1910), plate iii.

15. J. Capart, *Documents pour servir à l'étude de l'art égyptien*, ii (Paris, 1931), 77, plate 85.

16. $23\frac{1}{4}$ inches high (59 cm); Capart, *op. cit.*, 76, plates 82–4; E. Chassinat, *Mon. Piot*, 4 (Paris, 1897), 15.

17. *Proceedings of the Society of Biblical Archaeology*, 6 (1884), 205, plate opp. p. 201; B. V. Bothmer and J. Keith, *Brief Guide to the Department of Ancient Art* (Brooklyn, 1970), 58; Vandersleyen, *PKG*, plate 209a.

18. J. Vandier-d'Abbadie, *Ostraca figurés de Deir el-Médineh* (Cairo, 1936–46). References to the extensive literature on figured ostraca may be found in the most recent comprehensive treatment of the subject: Bengt E. J. Peterson, *Zeichnungen aus einer Totenstadt* (Stockholm, 1973), *Medelhavsmuseet Bulletin*, 7–8 (1973). Similar animals appear in Dynasty XXV reliefs in the temple of Medamud; Bisson de la Roque, *Médamoud, Fouilles, Institut français du Caire*, viii, 73, plate 6.

19. Maspero, *op. cit.* (Note 13), plate xxiv; *Art in Egypt* (*Ars Una*) (London, 1921), plate opp. p. 280; G. Farina, *La pittura egiziana* (Milan, 1929), plate cciii.

20. R. O. Faulkner in W. K. Simpson, ed., *The Literature of Ancient Egypt*, 3rd rev. printing (New Haven, 1977), 210–29; R. B. Parkinson, *The Tale of Sinuhe and other Ancient Egyptian Poems 1940–1640 B.C.*, Oxford, 1997, 166–99.

21. Attributed by E. Brugsch to Dynasty XXII (*ZÄS*, 35 (1897), 140), but thought by Černý to be Dynasty XX; M. Gauthier-Laurent, *Mélanges Maspero*, i (*Mémoires, Institut français du Caire*, 66) (Cairo, 1935–8), 684; E. L. B. Terrace and H. G. Fischer, *Treasures of Egyptian Art from the Cairo Museum*, no. 34, pp. 149–52.

22. J. A. Omlin, *Der Papyrus 55001 und seine satirisch-erotischen Zeichnungen und Inschriften* (Turin, 1973); Lothar Störk, 'Erotik', in Helck and Otto, *Lexikon*, ii, 4–11.

23. For the presumed fables which lie behind the animal scenes, see E. Brunner-Traut, *Altägyptische Tiergeschichte und Fabel: Gestalt und Strahlkraft* (Darmstadt, 1968). Also L. Keimer, *Études d'égyptologie*, iii (Cairo, 1941), 4. In the old coloured copies the cheeks of the woman have been painted red as in several Ramesside paintings and the British Museum papyrus of Anhai (E. A. Wallis Budge, *Facsimiles of Papyri of Hunefer, Anhai, Karasher and Netchemet* (London, 1889). See also the interesting discussion of the possible relationship between the Turin papyrus and Alexandrine illustrated books, K. Weitzmann, *Illustrations in Roll and Codex* (Princeton, 1947).

24. Richard A. Parker, *A Saite Oracle Papyrus from Thebes in the Brooklyn Museum* (Providence, 1962).

25. This scene is preserved only in the unpublished photographs from Breasted's survey. It had apparently disappeared by the time Reisner excavated the temple in 1916. Breasted states in *AJSL*, 25 (1908), 34, that the procession was on the east wall of the first court. This would be the right-hand wall as one entered the court proceeding towards the second pylon. Porter-Moss, *Bibliography*, vii, 216, and 12–13 on map, p. 210, places here an important scene with men leading horses which a Reisner photograph shows to be on the opposite (west) wall at about the point where the plan gives 48 on the outer face of the wall. Thus it is improbable that the procession could be at 32–3 in the second court of the Hall of Columns as suggested, *ibid.*, 219. Unfortunately, all these reliefs are now weathered away or buried.

26. H. Ranke, *The Egyptian Collection of the University Museum*, 48 (*University Museum Bulletin*, 15, November 1950, Philadelphia); Quibell, *The Ramesseum* (London, 1896), plates 22–3, p. 11.

27. Berlin 20132; R. Anthes, *MDAIK*, 12 (1943), 37, plate 12; E. Lüddeckens, *ibid.*, 11 (1943), 161, plate 20; M. Werbrouck, *Les pleureuses dans l'Égypte ancienne* (Brussels, 1938), 101, plate xlvi.

28. Maspero, *Art in Egypt*, coloured plate opp. p. 88.

CHAPTER 21

1. Porter-Moss, *Bibliography*, vii (1951), 207–23, with a sketch plan showing the relationship of b 500 to the temples built by Piankhy's successors, including b 300 of Taharqa, with its Hathor columns and inner inscribed rock-cut rooms, and b 700 which contained the granite altar of Atlanersa. For the excavation of the site, see Reisner in *JEA*, 4 (1917), 213–27; 5 (1918), 99–112; 6 (1920), 247–67. The plan of b 500, which had not been completely excavated

when these reports were written, is given in *ZÄS*, 69 (1933), opp. p. 76; see also *idem*, 66 (1931), 80 for a list of inscribed monuments from this temple. See now Dows Dunham, *The Barkal Temples* (Boston, 1970). Temple architecture of the Late Period is the subject of an important study by Barbara Ruszcyc, 'The Egyptian Sacred Architecture of the Late Period: A Study against the Background of the Epoch', *Archeologia* (Warsaw), 24 (1973), 12–49.

2. A. Mariette, *Monuments divers* (1889), plate 1.

3. G. Roeder, *Naos, Catalogue général du Musée du Caire* (Leipzig, 1914), no. 7007, p. 25, plate 7.

4. F. Ll. Griffith, *Liverpool Annals of Archaeology and Anthropology*, 9 (1922), 67 ff.

5. M. F. Laming Macadam, *The Temples of Kawa*, II (Oxford, 1955).

6. *Ibid.*, plates xiii–xiv, liii.

7. *Ibid.*, plate vii.

8. *Ibid.*, plate lvi.

9. Uvo Hölscher, *Excavations at Medinet Habu*, V, *Post Ramessid Remains* (Chicago, 1954), plate 17.

10. F. W. von Bissing, *Denkmäler ägyptischer Sculptur* (Munich, 1911), plate 64.

11. For these ladies and the relationships of the Ethiopian (Kushite) royal family, see M. F. Laming Macadam, *The Temples of Kawa*, I (Oxford, 1949), 119; M. Lichtheim in *JNES*, 7 (1948), 163; Ricardo A. Caminos, 'The Nitocris Adoption Stela', *JEA*, 50 (1964), 71–101; Peter Der Manuelian, *Living in the Past: Studies in Archaism of the Egyptian Twenty-sixth Dynasty* London, 1994, 297–321; Anthony Leahy, 'The Adoption of Ankhnesneferibre at Karnak,' *JEA*, 82, 1996, 145–65.

12. Macadam, *op. cit.*, II, plates ix, xlix, pp. 63 ff. Reproduced also in *Africa in Antiquity, The Arts of Ancient Nubia and the Sudan* (New York, The Brooklyn Museum, 1978), I, figure 58. Discussed in detail in Anthony J. Spalinger, 'Some Notes on the Libyans of the Old Kingdom and Later Historical Reflexes', *The SSEA Journal* (Toronto), 9, no. 3 (1979), 125–60.

13. Twenty-one vertical squares from base of foot to the eye instead of the older system of eighteen squares to the forehead; C. M. Firth and J. E. Quibell, *The Step Pyramid* (Cairo, 1935), plate 15; Erik Iversen, *Canon and Proportions in Egyptian Art*, 2nd ed. (Warminster, 1975).

14. W. M. F. Petrie, *The Palace of Apries* (London, 1909), plates ii–ix; Capart, *Documents*, II, 81, plates 88, 89; Barry J. Kemp, 'The Palace of Apries at Memphis', *MDAIK*, 33 (1977), 101–8; 'A further Note of the Palace of Apries at Memphis', *GM*, 29 (1978), 61.

15. N. de G. Davies, *The Rock Tombs of Deir el Gebrawi*, I (London, 1902), 36, plates 24, 25. It is the figure of the Saite Iby which provides the best evidence for the later system of guiding squares; *JEA*, 4 (1917), 74, plate xviii. It is also argued that these 'copies' rather reflect the use of standard models instead (not an 'archaeological copy'); see W. Schenkel, 'Zur Frage der Vorlagen spätzeitlicher "Kopien",' in J. Assmann, E. Feucht, and R. Grieshammer (eds.), *Fragen an die altägyptische Literatur (Festschrift Otto)* (Wiesbaden, 1977), 417–41; Peter Der Manuelian, *Living in the Past: Studies in Archaism of the Egyptian Twenty-sixth Dynasty*, London, 1994.

16. Wilson in Pritchard, *Ancient Near Eastern Texts relating to the Old Testament*, 3rd ed. (Princeton, 1969), 4–6. The text is now generally recognized as archaizing rather than as a copy of an earlier text; Junge, in *MDAIK*, 29 (1973), 195–204.

17. Leclant, *Orientalia*, 22 (1953), 85, plate vii; *BIFAO*, 53 (1953), 113.

18. The statue is Khartum no. 1841 which is kept at Merawe. The Cairo head was purchased at Luxor and is 13¾ inches high (35 cm) as compared to about 19¼ inches (48 cm) for the same portion of the head of the statue from Gebel Barkal.

19. Dr Naji al Asil, *Sumer*, 10 (1954), 110, 193; W. K. Simpson, *ibid.*, 193–4; V. Vikentiev, 'Quelques considérations à propos des statues de Taharqa trouvées dans les ruines du palais d'Ésarhaddon', *Sumer*, 11 (1955), 111–16.

20. Oppenheim in Pritchard, *Ancient Near Eastern Texts (op. cit.)*, 293. On p. 296, in Ashurbanipal's account of his father's victories, there is mention of fifty-five statues of Egyptian kings on which the Assyrian wrote of his triumph.

21. E. Schiaparelli, *Monumenti Antichi, Reale Accademia del Lincei*, VIII (Milan, 1898), 90, plates ii–iv. An apparently identical, slightly smaller faience vase was found in equivocal circumstances at Lilibeo in Sicily. E. Gabrici, *Notizie degli Scavi di Antichità*, II, *Atti della Reale Accademia d'Italia*, Anno 1941 (Rome, 1942), 284, figure 25a–c.

22. Dows Dunham, *El Kurru, The Royal Cemeteries of Kush*, I (Cambridge, 1950), figure 20g, plate xxxiii; similar ivories were found in the tomb of Shebitku, figure 23e, plate xxxv.

23. The incised figures on a few of the Shabako fragments are closer in style to the Barkal and Sanam sunk relief; Dunham, *op. cit.*, figure 20h, plate xxxiv.

24. *Ibid.*, plate lxii. The scheme is repeated with gods round a papyrus column on a silver mirror from a sixth-century tomb at Nuri; Dunham, *Royal Cemeteries of Kush*, II (Boston, 1954), plate xci.

25. Frankfort, *Ancient Orient*, illustration 369.

26. For example, the ceiling painting attributed to the reign of Tuthmosis III (H. Kantor, *The Aegean and the Orient in the Second Millennium B.C.*, plate xi) or the carving from the tomb of Amenhotep II (Daressy, *Fouilles de la Vallée des Rois*, plate xx).

27. The Greek pottery ends abruptly in the last quarter of the sixth century with the abandonment or destruction of part of the buildings, contrary to the earlier view that the painted vases were not later than the early part of the reign of Amasis; R. M. Cook, *Corpus Vasorum Antiquorum* (British Museum Fasc. 8) (London, 1954), 59; cf. W. M. F. Petrie, *Tanis*, II, *Nebesheh and Defenneh* (London, 1888), 47.

28. Picard in *Annales*, 26 (1926), 113.

29. The dated statues down to the Ptolemaic period are collected by Käthe Bosse, *Die menschliche Figur in der Rundplastik der ägyptischen Spätzeit* (Scharff, *Ägyptologische Forschungen*, 1) (Glückstadt, 1936), and see also the collection of sculpture assembled and discussed in the Brooklyn Museum exhibition catalogue, B. V. Bothmer and others, *Egyptian Sculpture of the Late Period, 700 B.C. to A.D. 100* (Brooklyn, 1960). Among a number of individual studies, see especially Werner Kaiser, 'Ein Statuenkopf der ägyptischen Spätzeit', *Jahrbuch der Berliner Museen*, 8 (1966), 5–33; B. V. Bothmer, 'Apotheosis in Late Egyptian Sculpture', *Kêmi*, 20 (1970), 37–48; Edna R. Russmann, *The Representation of the King in the XXVth Dynasty* (Brussels-Brooklyn, 1974); Claudio Barocas, 'Les statues "réalistes" et l'arrivée des Perses dans l'Égypte saïte', in *Gururājamanjarikā: Studi in onore di Giuseppe Tucci* (Naples, 1974), 113–61; Edna R. Russmann, 'The Statue of Amenemope-em-hat', *MMJ*, 8 (1973), 33–46.

30. For the sequence of these tombs and the statues belonging to their owners, see Miriam Lichtheim, *JNES*, 7 (1948), 163.

31. Leclant, *Orientalia*, 22 (1953), 89. A considerable amount of work has been published on these Theban tombs of the later periods. Among the published results of these excavations and copying projects, one may cite a few: Jan Assmann, *Das Grab des Basa (Nr. 389) in der thebanischen Nekropole, Grabung im Assasif 1963–70*, II (Mainz am Rhein, 1973); *Das Grab der Muterdis, Grabung im Assasif 1963–70*, VI (Mainz am Rhein, 1977); Sergio Donadoni, 'Relazione preliminare sulla II campagna di scavo nella tomba di Šešonq all'Asasif (1971)', *Oriens Antiquus*, 12 (1973), 19–22; Manfred Bietak and Elfriede Reiser-Haslauer, *Das Grab des 'Anch-Hor', Oberschofmeister der Gottesgemahlin Nitokris*, I, parts 1 and 2 (Vienna, 1978). K. Kuhlman and W. Schenkel, *Das Grab des Ibi Theben Nr. 36. Band I: Beschreibung der Unterirdischen Kult und Bestattungsanlage* (AV 15), 2 vols (Text and Plates), Mainz, 1983. The design and conception of the royal tomb is the subject of a special inquiry by R. Stadelmann, 'Das Grab im Tempelhof: der Typus des Königsgrabes in der Spätzeit', *MDAIK*, 27 (1971), 111–23.

32. von Bissing in *ZÄS*, 74 (1938), 2. For the tomb of Petamenopet (No. 33), see the extensive references collected in Porter-Moss, *Bibliography*, I, part 1, 50–6.

33. Herbert Winlock, *Excavations at Deir el Bahri*, 81, plate 91; Fazzini, *Images for Eternity*, Cat. 97a–b, p. 115; Vandersleyen, *PKG*, plate 312.

34. Lichtheim, *op. cit.* (Note 30), 166; for Sheshonq's tomb, see *BMMA*, section II (January 1937), 4, figure 3; S. Donadoni *Annales*, 61 (1973), 11–20; and see Note 31 above.

35. The floor of the court of Pabasa (No. 279) was 46 feet (14 m) below the surface of the ground; see *BMMA*, section II (July 1920), 16 ff., where a plan and section of this tomb are given.

36. The early work of Scheil (*Mém. Miss.*, 5 (Paris, 1894), 613–23) has been extended by Zakaria Ghoneim for the Department of Antiquities: see J. Leclant in *Orientalia*, 19 (1950), 370–2, plates li–lii; 20 (1951), 473, plates lxiii, lxiv; 22 (1953), 88, plates xi, xii; 23 (1954), 66, plate xx; Helene J. Kantor, 'A Fragment of Relief from the Tomb of Mentuemhat at Thebes (No. 34)', *JNES*, 19 (1960), 213–16; Jean Leclant, *Montouemhat, quatrième prophète d'Amon, prince de la ville* (Cairo, 1961), plates 55–65; J. D. Cooney, 'Fragments of a Great Saite Monument', *JARCE*, 3 (1964), 79–87; Barbara S. Lesko, 'Three Reliefs from the Tomb of Mentuemhat', *JARCE*, 9 (1971–2), 85–8; Hans Wolfgang Müller, 'Der "Stadtfürst von Theben" Montemhêt', *MJbK*, 26 (1975), 7–36, with bibliography, and other references in Porter-Moss, *Bibliography*, I, part 1, 56–61. See also Peter Der Manuelian, 'Two Fragments of Relief and a New Model for the Tomb of Montuemhet at Thebes,' *JEA*, 71, 1985, 98–121. E. R. Russmann, 'Relief Decoration in the Tomb of Mentuemhat (TT 34),' *JARCE*, 31, 1994, 1–19. An overall survey of the reliefs of this important tomb with many of the reliefs represented in museums in America and elsewhere, with detailed references. *Idem.*, 'The Motif of the Bound Papyrus Plants and the Decorative Program in Montuemhat's First Court.' *JARCE*, 32, 1995, 117–26. Points out that the bound papyrus plants occur on many coffins, and that this suggests that the large court actually represents a huge coffin with its ceiling the open sky. *Idem.*, 'Mentuemhat's Kushite Wife (Further Remarks on the Decoration of the Tomb of Mentuemhat, 2),' *JARCE*, 34, 1997, 21–40. For the various sculptural portraits and relief representations of Mentuemhat, see J. von Beckerath, *ZÄS*,

87 (1962), 2, n. 2, to which add G. Legrain, *ASAE*, 8 (1907), 122–5, for the statuette in Athens.

37. Lauer in *Annales*, 51 (1951), 471, figure 2, plate xvi.

38. J. D. Cooney, *JNES*, 9 (1950), 193; S. A. Wunderlich, *Bulletin of the Cleveland Museum*, 39 (1952), 44; W. S. Smith, *BMFA*, 47 (1949), 21. Having since examined the Florence block 2604 (Porter-Moss, *Bibliography*, I, part 1, 60), and a Vatican piece attributed to the Old Kingdom (H. Ranke, *The Art of Ancient Egypt* (London, 1936), plate 189), I am convinced from their measurements and style that they adjoined one another and are probably part of the swamp scene to which belong other pieces in the British Museum (also attributed to the Old Kingdom: Keimer, *BIFAO*, 36 (1936), 85), Florence, Cleveland, and Chicago (J. A. Wilson, *The Burden of Egypt*, figure 32a). See Note 36 above for fragments in Munich and other pieces.

39. *The William Rockhill Nelson Collection*, 3rd ed. (Kansas City, 1949), 15.

40. It should be noted that this type of head, which appears in the neo-Memphite reliefs of a time approaching the conquest of Alexander, as well as in later sculpture in the round, is strikingly anticipated in the remarkable figures of Ptahmes of the time of Ramesses II, on the columns in Leiden, probably from a tomb at Saqqara; J. Capart, *Documents*, I (Paris, 1927), plate 62; P. A. A. Boeser, *Beschreibung der ägyptischen Sammlung, Leiden*, IV (1911), plate xxvi.

41. Gunn and Engelbach, *BIFAO*, 30 (1931), 791–815.

42. B. V. Bothmer, *BMFA*, 49 (1951), 69; see Note 29 above.

43. For the Cairo scribe and the group of Petamenopet statues as a whole, see G. Loukianoff, *Annales*, 37 (1937), 219. The Berlin squatting figure has been studied in connexion with other late portrait sculpture by R. Anthes, *ZÄS*, 73 (1937), 25. For the head and shoulders of Mentuemhat, see E. L. B. Terrace and H. G. Fischer, *Treasures of Egyptian Art from the Cairo Museum* (London, 1970), cat. no. 37, pp. 161–4; Vandersleyen, *PKG*, plate 216, for the standing statue.

44. Anlamani, Museum of Fine Arts, Boston, No. 23.732, for which see Vandersleyen, *PKG*, plate 410.

45. For Mentuemhat's statues and those of his family, see K. Bosse, *Die menschliche Figur in der Rundplastik der ägyptischen Spätzeit*.

46. Studied by H. W. Müller in *Studi in Memoria di I. Rosellini*, II (Pisa, 1955), 183–221, and *ZÄS*, 80 (1955), 46; J. Vandier, 'Un tête royale de l'époque saïte', *ZÄS*, 90 (1963), 115–18; see also Note 29 above; Jack A. Josephson, *Egyptian Royal Sculpture of the Late Period 400–246 B.C.* (SDAIK 30), Mainz 1997.

47. The frequently reproduced green stone statue of the hippopotamus goddess Thueris is, however, an outstanding example of the Egyptian genius for treating animal forms. It was made for Pabasa, the owner of Tomb 279, and, together with its shrine, bears the names of Shepenwepet, Nitocris, and Psamtik I; Lichtheim, *op. cit.* (Note 30), 165, note 19; G. Daressy, *Statues de divinités*, Catalogue général (Cairo, 1906), no. 39145.

48. For the Vienna slab of Psamtik II decorated on two faces, see E. von Bergmann, *Recueil de travaux*, 9 (1887), 53, 54. For the slab of Psamtik I and the two of Nectanebo I in the British Museum, see E. A. Wallis Budge, *British Museum, A Guide to the Egyptian Galleries (Sculpture)* (1909), 222 (no. 800), 250 (nos. 926, 927). A slab of Nectanebo I in Bologna has only one face preserved (Curto, *L'Egitto antico*, plate 39). Of the British Museum pieces, two are said to have come from a temple of Atum at Rosetta and one was found in Alexandria. They have generally been called intercolumnar slabs, but the inscription along the top should have continued without breaks between, and they seem small for the screen walls which appear so often in late times as part of colonnades or kiosks.

49. This has been contested, for example, by Georg Steindorff, in studying royal temple reliefs of Dynasty XXX and the Ptolemaic Period from Sebynnytos and Iseion, *Journal of the Walters Art Gallery*, 7–8 (1944–5), 58, and B. V. Bothmer in discussing a relief of Nectanebo II in Boston, *BMFA*, 51 (1953), 6.

50. W. S. Smith, *BMFA*, 47 (1949), 21–9.

51. W. Spiegelberg, *ZÄS*, 65 (1930), 102.

52. Smith, *op. cit.*; R. Anthes, *ZÄS*, 75 (1939), 21, and *Jahrbuch des Deutschen Archäologischen Instituts*, 54 (1939), 375, where a comparison is made between the scribe's head on the Henat relief and sculpture in the round.

53. Selim Hassan, *The Great Sphinx and its Secrets*, plate liii, cf. p. 112. A headless squatting cubical figure of this man gives the name of his mother as in the chapel and has a cartouche of Psamtik I on one arm; Otto Koefoed-Petersen, *Catalogue des statues et statuettes égyptiennes* (Copenhagen, 1950), 57, plate 106. For the Giza reliefs, see reference in Simpson, *The Face of Egypt* (Katonah, 1977), 69, no. 53.

54. As in Mme C. Desroches-Noblecourt's study of the charming vintage scene connected with a singer of the goddess Neith of Sais in the Louvre, *Arts asiatiques*, 1 (1954), 40. This assumes, with Drioton, that the group of neo-Memphite reliefs, like those of Zanofer, are of the end of the Saite Period rather

than later, as I should be inclined to place them. Cf. F. Daumas, in Vandersleyen, *PKG*, 333, plate 314.

55. N. de G. Davies, *The Temple of Hibis in El Khargeh Oasis*, III (New York, 1953), plates 7, 11, 31–3, 35.

56. A Fakhry, *The Egyptian Deserts, Bahria Oasis*, I (Cairo, 1942), particularly plates xiii, xvii.

57. Compare Fakhry, *op. cit.*, plate i, with Davies, *op. cit.*, plate 43.

58. G. Maspero, *Le Musée égyptien*, II (Cairo, 1907), plates xxxix–xli; plate xxxii, centre, for a second block of Zanofer; 74–92, plates xxxii–xlii for other neo-Memphite reliefs in Cairo. E. Drioton, *Le Musée du Caire, Encyclopédie photographique de l'art* (1949), plates 185–91, gives excellent details of some of these. See also *Annales*, 21 (1921), 27, plate ii.

59. At Athribis near Benha; H. Gauthier, *Mon. Piot*, 25 (1921–2), 171; Ch. Kuentz, *ibid.*, 33 (1933), 41, figure 4.

60. The measurements correspond. This Berlin relief no. 15415 is reproduced by A. Scharff, *ZÄS*, 74 (1938), 44, figure 3. The Louvre relief of Psamtikmerneith also has the top of two columns of inscription on the left, suggesting again a lintel piece; G. Bénédite, *Mon. Piot*, 25 (1921–2), 1, plates iv, v.

61. Cl. Robichon, P. Barguet, J. Leclant, *Karnak-Nord*, IV, *Fouilles de l'Institute français du Caire*, 25 (1954), 131, plate cxiv; F. Bisson de la Roque, *Fouilles de Medamoud* (1930), same series, 8 (1931), 73–4, figures 53–5, plate vi.

62. It must be admitted that something very like it had appeared once before in the post-Amarna relief of General Horemheb in Leiden; P. A. A. Boeser, *Beschreibung der ägyptischen Sammlung, Leiden*, IV, plate xxivb.

63. This is to be found not only in the Cairo relief of Zanofer (Drioton, *op. cit.* (Note 58), plate 188) but also in other pieces most nearly related to the Alexandria piece: the Cleveland musicians which evidently adjoin a Berlin relief with an old harper (Scharff, *ZÄS*, 74 (1938), 42, plate iii) and a Baltimore fragment (G. Steindorff, *Catalogue of the Egyptian Sculpture in the Walters Art Gallery* (Baltimore, 1946), no. 273, plate lvi).

64. G. Steindorff, *Die Kunst der Ägypter* (Leipzig, 1928), plate 258. For these heads, see Bothmer and others, *op. cit.* (Note 29), plates 100 (Boston) and 118–19 (Berlin); Vandersleyen, *PKG*, plate 235 (Berlin). The Boston head is $4\frac{1}{8}$ inches high (10 cm), the Berlin head $8\frac{1}{4}$ inches (20 cm).

65. For the date of this tomb, see G. Roeder, *Annales*, 39 (1939), 731.

66. In the porch of Nectanebo I (Nekht-neb-f) at Philae; Ibrahim Noshy, *The Arts in Ptolemaic Egypt* (London, 1937), 77, plate ix, 3; and in the additions made by Nectanebo II (Nekht-hor-heb) to the temple of Darius I; H. E. Winlock, *The Temple of Hibis in El Khargeh Oasis*, I (New York, 1941), 10, 26, plates viii, xix, xlvi, xlvii.

67. Gustave Lefebvre, *Le tombeau de Pétosiris*, I–III (Cairo, 1923–4).

68. See Lefebvre, *op. cit.*, coloured plates xiv, xv, xxi, xlii. One detail in colour, H. Schäfer and W. Andrae, *Die Kunst des alten Orients, Propyläen Kunstgeschichte*, II, plate xxiii (1942 and earlier editions); Vandersleyen, *PKG*, plate xxxix, a, b (also in colour). For a discussion of other obviously Greek elements in these curious painted reliefs, Picard, *BIFAO*, 30 (1931), 201.

69. Lefebvre, *op. cit.*, plates vii, viii.

70. Frankfort, *Ancient Orient*, illustration 444. A silver rhyton in the form of a winged animal was found with a group of metal bowls at Toukh el Qarmous in the Egyptian Delta; Edgar in Maspero, *Musée Egyptien*, II, 57, plates xxv–xxviii.

71. Sami Gabra, *Rapport sur les fouilles d'Hermopolis Ouest (Touna el-Gebel)* (Cairo, 1941).

72. H. Drerup, *Die Datierung der Mumienporträts* (Paderborn, 1933); A. F. Shore, *Portrait Painting from Roman Egypt*, rev. ed. (London, 1972); E. Guimet, *Les portraits d'Antinoë, Musée Guimet, Annales*, 5 (1905); A. Streikov, *Fayum Portraits* (in Russian) (Moscow, 1936); W. S. Smith, *Ancient Egypt as represented in the Museum of Fine Arts*, 3rd ed. (1952), 166, figure 112; G. Grimm, *Die römischen Mumien-masken aus Ägypten* (Wiesbaden, 1974). For a selection of Fayum portraits, see Hilde Zaloscer, *Porträts aus dem Wüstensland* (Vienna and Munich, 1961); David L. Thompson, *The Artists of the Mummy Portraits* (J. Paul Getty Museum, Malibu, 1976). M. L. Bierbrier (ed.), *Portraits and Masks: Burial Customs in Roman Egypt*. London, 1997; S. Walker and M. L. Bierbrier (eds.) *Ancient Faces: Mummy Portraits from Roman Egypt*. London, 1997.

73. P. M. Fraser, *Ptolemaic Alexandria*, 2 vols. (Oxford, 1972). Getty, The J. Paul Getty Museum, *Alexandria and Alexandrianism: Papers Delivered at a Symposium Organized by the J. Paul Getty Museum and the Getty Center for the History of Art and the Humanities and Held at the Museum April 22–5, 1993*. Malibu, 1996. A collection of important studies on Ptolemaic art. Various authors, *La Gloire d'Alexandrie*. Exhibition catalogue, Musée du Petit Palais, 1998.

74. Alexander Badawy, *L'Art copte, Les influences égyptiennes* (Publications de la société d'archéologie copte) (Cairo, 1949); 'Les influences hellénistiques et romaines', *Bull. Inst. Égypte*, 34 (1951–2), 151.

Bibliography

GENERAL WORKS

ALDRED, C. *The Development of Egyptian Art*. London, 1952. Original edition in 3 vols.: *Old Kingdom* (London, 1949); *Middle Kingdom* (London, 1950); *New Kingdom* (London, 1951).

BREASTED, J. H. *Ancient Records of Egypt*. 5 vols. Chicago, 1906–7.

CAPART, J. *L'art égyptien*. 2 vols. Brussels, 1909, 1911. Second part: I, *L'architecture* (1922), II, *La statuaire* (1948), III, *Les arts graphiques* (1942), IV, *Les arts mineurs* (1947).

CAPART, J. *Documents pour servir à l'étude de l'art égyptien*. 2 vols. Paris, 1927, 1931.

CARTER, H., and MACE. A. C. *The Tomb of Tut-ankh-amen*. 3 vols. London, 1923–33.

DRIOTON, É., and VANDIER, J. *Les peuples de l'orient méditerranéen*, II, *L'Égypte*, 4th ed. Paris, 1962.

FRANKFORT, H., FRANKFORT, H. A., WILSON, J. A., and JACOBSEN, T. *Before Philosophy*. Harmondsworth, 1949. Original edition: *The Intellectual Adventure of Ancient Man*. Chicago, 1946.

GARDINER, SIR ALAN. *Egypt of the Pharaohs*. Oxford, 1961.

GROENWEGEN-FRANKFORT, H. A. *Arrest and Movement*. London, 1951.

HAMANN, R. *Ägyptische Kunst*. Berlin, 1944.

HARRIS, J. R., ed., *The Legacy of Egypt*. 2nd ed. Oxford, 1971.

HAYES, W. C. *The Scepter of Egypt*. 2 vols. New York, 1953, 1959.

JAMES, T. G. H. and DAVIES, W. V. *Egyptian Sculpture*. London, 1983.

LANGE, K., and HIRMER, M. *Egypt: Architecture, Sculpture, and Painting in Three Thousand Years*. 4th ed. London, 1968.

LUCAS. A. *Ancient Egyptian Materials and Industries*. 4th ed. by J. R. Harris. London, 1962.

MANNICHE, L. *L'art égyptien*. Translated from a not yet published English text by T. Préaud. Paris, 1994.

PORTER, B., and MOSS, R. *Topographical Bibliography of Ancient Egyptian Hieroglyphic Texts, Reliefs, and Paintings*. 7 vols. Oxford, 1927–51. Greatly amplified 2nd ed. of vols. I, II, and III, parts 1 and 2, fasc. 1. Oxford, 1960, 1964, 1972, 1974, 1978.

PRITCHARD, J. B., ed. *Ancient Near Eastern Texts relating to the Old Testament*. 3rd ed. with suppl. Princeton, 1969.

QUIRKE, S. and SPENCER, A. J. eds. *The British Museum Book of Ancient Egypt*. London, 1992.

RANKE, H. *The Art of Ancient Egypt*. Vienna, 1936.

REDFORD, D. B., ed. *The Oxford Encyclopedia of Ancient Egypt*. New York, 1999 (?).

ROBINS, G. *Proportion and Style in Ancient Egyptian Art*. Austin, 1994. With useful bibliography of the author's other publications on p. 277.

ROBINS, G. *The Art of Ancient Egypt*. London, 1997.

ROSS, E. D., ed. *The Art of Egypt Through the Ages*. New York and London, 1931.

SASSON, J. ed. *Civilizations of the Ancient Near East*. 4 vols. New York, 1995. The essays in this substantial publication cover many aspects of Egyptian art.

SCHÄFER, H., and ANDRAE, W. *Die Kunst des alten Orients*. 3rd ed. Berlin, 1942.

SCHÄFER, H. *Principles of Egyptian Art*, ed. by Emma Brunner-Traut, trans. by J. R. Baines, 4th ed. Oxford, 1974.

SCHULZ, R. and SEIDEL, M. eds. *Egypt: The World of the Pharaohs*. Cologne, 1998.

SILVERMAN, D. P. ed. *Ancient Egypt*. New York, 1997.

SIMPSON, W. K., ed. *The Literature of Ancient Egypt*, 3rd rev. printing. New Haven, 1977.

SMITH, W. S. *Ancient Egypt as Represented in the Museum of Fine Arts*. 4th rev. ed. Boston, 1960.

STEINDORFF, G. *Die Kunst der Ägypter*. Leipzig, 1928.

STEINDORFF, G. and SEELE, K. C. *When Egypt Ruled the East*, 2nd rev. ed. Chicago, 1957.

VANDERSLEYEN, C., ed. *Das alte Ägypten (Propyläen Kunstgeschichte, 15)*. Berlin, 1975.

VANDIER, J. *Manuel d'archéologie égyptienne*. 6 vols. Paris, 1952–78.

WILDUNG, D. *Die Kunst des alten Ägypten*. Freiburg–Basel–Wien, 1988.

WILSON, J. A. *The Culture of Ancient Egypt*. Chicago, 1951.

WOLF, W. *Die Kunst Ägyptens*. Stuttgart, 1957.

ARCHITECTURE

ARNOLD, D. *Building in Egypt: Pharaonic Stone Masonry*. New York, 1991.

ARNOLD, D. *Lexikon der ägyptischen Baukunst*. Zürich, 1994.

ARNOLD, D. *Die Tempel Ägyptens: Götterwohnungen, Kultstätten, Baudenkmäler*. Zürich, 1992.

AUFRÈRE, S., GOLVIN, J. C. and GOYON, J. C., *L'Égypte restituée* 1: *Sites et temples de haute Égypte (1650 av. J. C.-300 ap. J. C.)*. Paris, 1991; 2: *Sites et temples des déserts de la naissance de la civilisation pharaonque à l'époque gréco-romaine*. Paris, 1994; 3: *Sites et temples et pyramides de Moyenne et Basse Égypte de la naissance de la civilisation pharaonque à l'époque gréco-romaine*. Paris, 1997.

BADAWY, A. *A History of Egyptian Architecture*, I. *From the Earliest Times to the End of the Old Kingdom*. Giza, 1954. II. *The First Intermediate Period, the Middle Kingdom, and the Second Intermediate Period*. Berkeley and Los Angeles, 1966. III. *The Empire (the New Kingdom)*. Berkeley and Los Angeles, 1968.

BIETAK, M. ed. *Haus und Palast im alten Ägypten*. Vienna, 1995.

DE CÉNIVAL, J.-L. *Living Architecture: Egyptian*. Fribourg, 1964.

CLARKE, S., and ENGELBACH, R. *Ancient Egyptian Masonry*. London, 1930.

EDWARDS, I. E. S. *The Pyramids of Egypt*. Harmondsworth, 1947. Revised ed. 1961.

GUNDLACH, R. and ROCHHOLZ, M. eds. *Ägyptische Tempel – Struktur, Funktion und Programm* (HÄB 37), 1994.

HELCK, W. ed. *Tempel und Kult*. (ÄAbh, 46), Wiesbaden, 1987.

KURTH, D. 'The present state of research into Graeco-Roman temples' in Quirke, S. ed. *The Temple in Ancient Egypt. New discoveries and recent research*. London, 1997, 152–8.

O'CONNOR, D. B. 'The Social and Economic Organization of Ancient Egyptian Temples' in Sasson, J. ed. *Civilizations of the Ancient Near East*. New York, 1995, Vol. I, 319–30.

QUIRKE, S. ed. *The Temple in Ancient Egypt*. London, 1997.

ROIK, E. *Das altägyptische Wohnhaus und seine Darstellung im Flachbild*. Frankfurt, 1988.

SMITH, E, B. *Egyptian Architecture as Cultural Expression*. New York, 1938.

WILDUNG, D. *Egypt: From Prehistory to the Romans*. Taschen's World Architecture, London, etc., 1997.

SCULPTURE AND PAINTING

ALDRED, C. *Akhenaten and Nefertiti*. Brooklyn, 1973.

ARNOLD, D. (with contributions by ALLEN, J. P. and GREEN, L.) *The Royal Women of Amarna: Images of Beauty from Ancient Egypt*. New York, 1996.

BOTHMER, B. V., ed. *Egyptian Sculpture of the Late Period (700 B.C. to A.D. 100)*. Brooklyn, 1960.

DAVIES, NINA M., and GARDINER, A. H. *Ancient Egyptian Paintings*. 3 vols. Chicago, 1936.

EVERS, H. G. *Staat aus dem Stein*. 2 vols. Munich, 1929.

FARINA, G. *La pittura egiziana*. Milan, 1929.

KOZLOFF, A. P., BRYAN, B. M., with BERMAN, L. M. *Egypt's Dazzling Sun: Amenhotep III and His World*. Cleveland, 1992.

LHOTE, A. *Les chefs-d'œuvre de la peinture égyptienne*. Paris, 1954.

MEKHITARIAN, A. *Egyptian Painting*. Geneva, 1954.

MÜLLER, H. W. *Alt-Ägyptische Malerei*. Berlin, 1959.

MYŚLIWIEC, KAROL. *Le portrait royal dans le bas-relief du nouvel empire*. Warsaw, 1976.

PECK, WILLIAM H., and ROSS, JOHN G. *Egyptian Drawings*. New York and London, 1978.

RUSSMAN, E. *Egyptian Sculpture: Cairo and Luxor*. Austin, 1989.

SMITH, W. S. *A History of Egyptian Sculpture and Painting in the Old Kingdom*. Boston, 1946. 2nd ed. 1949.

TEFNIN, R. ed. *La Peinture Égypteinne Ancienne: Un Monde de Signes à Préserver*. Monumenta Aegyptiaca VII, Série Imago no. 1, Brussels, 1997.

TERRACE, E. L. B., and FISCHER, H. G. *Treasures of Egyptian Art from the Cairo Museum*. London, 1970.

GENERAL STUDIES

ASSMANN, J. *Stein und Zeit: Mensch und Gesellschaft im alten Ägypten*. Munich, 1991.

ASSMANN, J. *Ägypten: Eine Sinngeschichte*. Munich–Vienna, 1996.

ASSMANN, J. 'Preservation and Presentation of Self in Ancient Egyptian Portraiture' in Manuelian, P. *Studies in Honor of William Kelly Simpson*, Boston, 1996, 55–81.

ÅSTRÖM, P., ed. *High, Middle, or Low? Acts of an International Colloquium on Absolute Chronology.* Gothenburg, 1987.

BAINES, J. 'On the Status and Purpose of Ancient Egyptian Art.' *Cambridge Archaeological Journal* 4:1, 1994, 67–94. With extensive up-to-date bibliography.

BAINES, J. 'Contextualizing Egyptian Representations of Society and Ethnicity' in Cooper, Jerold S. and Schwartz, Glenn M. *The Study of the Ancient Near East in the Twenty-First Century: The William Foxwell Albright Centennial Conference.* Winona Lake, Indiana, 1996, 339–84.

BAINES, J. 'Communication and Display: The Integration of Early Egyptian Art and Writing' *Antiquity* 63, 1989, 471–82.

BAINES, J. and MALEK, J. *Atlas of Ancient Egypt.* New York, 1982.

BIANCHI, R. S. 'Ancient Egyptian Reliefs, Statuary, and Monumental Paintings' in Jack Sasson ed. *Civilizations of the Ancient Near East.* New York, 1995. Vol. IV, 2533–54.

BIANCHI, R. S. 'An Elite Image' in Goring, E., Reeves, N., and Ruffle, J. *Chief of Seers: Egyptian Studies in Memory of Cyril Aldred.* London and New York, 1997, 34–48. Detailed discussion of the validity of the concept of 'portraiture' in Ancient Egypt, for which see third entry under Assmann, above.

BOCHI, P. A. 'Images of Time in Ancient Egyptian Art.' *JARCE* 31, 1994, 55–62.

BOMAN, A. H. *The Private Chapel in Ancient Egypt.* New York, 1991.

BOTHMER, B. V. 'On Realism in Egyptian Funerary Sculpture' *Expedition* 24 (Winter, 1982), 27–39.

BRUNNER-TRAUT, E. *Frühformen des Erkennens: Am Beispiel Altägyptens.* Darmstadt, 1990.

Brunner, H. 'Illustrierte Bücher im alten Ägypten' in *Wort und Bild: Symposium des Fachbereichs Altertums- und Kunstwissenschaften zum 500jährigen Jubiläum der Eberhard-Karls-Universität 1977.* Munich, 1979, 181–200.

BRYAN, B. M. 'The Disjunction of Text and Image in Egyptian Art' in Manuelian, P. D. *Studies in Honor of William Kelly Simpson*, Boston, 1996, 161–8.

DAVIS, W. 'Canonical Representation in Egyptian Art' *Res* 4, Autumn, 1982, 20–46.

DAVIS, W. *The Canonical Tradition in Ancient Egyptian Art.* Cambridge, 1989. Review by R. S. Bianchi, *JAOS* 112, 1992, 328–30.

DEPUTTER, T. J. M. and KARLSHAUSEN, C. 'In Search of the Lost Quarries of the Pharaohs' *KMT: A Modern Journal of Ancient Egypt* 8, No. 3, Fall 1997, 54–9.

FINNESTAD, R. B. *Image of the World and Symbol of the Creator: On the Cosmological and Iconological Values of the Temple of Edfu.* (Studies in Oriental Religion 16), Wiesbaden, 1985.

GABALLA, G. A. *Narrative in Egyptian Art.* Mainz, 1976.

Gamer-Wallert, I. 'Bilder Alltags oder mehr? Beischriften als weltvolle Interpretationshilfen altägyptischer Darstellungen' in *Wort und Bild: Symposium des Fachbereichs Altertums- und Kunstwissenschaften zum 500jährigen Jubiläum der Eberhard-Karls-Universität 1977.* Munich, 1979, 169–80.

GORING, E., REEVES, N., and RUFFLE, J. *Chief of Seers: Egyptian Studies in Memory of Cyril Aldred.* London and New York, 1997.

Grimm, A., SCHOSKE, S., and WILDUNG, D. *Pharao: Kunst und Herrschaft im Alten Ägypten.* Munich and Berlin, 1997.

Gugliemi, W. 'Humor im Wort und Bild auf altägyptischen Grabdarstellungen' in *Wort und Bild: Symposium des Fachbereichs Altertums- und Kunstwissenschaften zum 500jährigen Jubiläum der Eberhard-Karls-Universität 1977.* Munich, 1979, 181–200.

HELCK, W. and WESTENDORF, W. eds. *Lexikon der Ägyptologie.* Vols I–VII, Wiesbaden, 1972–92. Entries on many subjects on art and architecture by major scholars. Individual articles are in German, French, or English, and contain excellent footnotes and bibliographies. Individual entries, many of importance, not listed here.

HORNUNG, E. *Idea into Image, Essays on Ancient Egyptian Thought.* New York, 1992.

IVERSEN, E. *Canon and Proportions in Egyptian Art.* Warminster, 1975.

JAMES, T. G. H. and DAVIES, W. V. *Egyptian Sculpture.* London, 1983.

KEMP, B. *Ancient Egypt: Anatomy of a Civilization.* New York, 1991. An outstanding general treatment of all aspects of Ancient Egypt.

KEMP, B. 'Temple and Town in Ancient Egypt' in Ucko, P. J., Trimingham, R., and Dimbleby, G. W. eds. *Man, Settlement and Urbanism*, London, 1972.

KISCHKEWITZ, H. (text) and FORMAN, W. (photographs) *Egyptian Drawings.* London et al., 1972.

KITCHEN, K. A. 'The Chronology of Ancient Egypt' *World Archaeology* 23, 1991, 201–8. Should be read in conjunction with Åström, 1987, above, since Kitchen revised several dates.

LEHNER, M. *The Complete Pyramids.* London, 1997.

MANNICHE, L. *L'art égyptien.* Translated from a not yet published English text by T. Préaud. Paris, 1994.

MÜLLER, M. 'Die ägyptische Kunst aus kunsthistorischer Sicht' in Eaton-Krauss, M. and Graefe, E. eds. *Studien zur ägyptischen Kunstgeschichte* (HÄB 29), Hildesheim, 1990, 39–56.

PECK, W. H. *Egyptian Drawing.* New York, 1978.

POLZ, D. and GUKSCH, H. eds. *Tempel, Grab und Siedlung: Beiträge zur Kulturgeschichte Ägyptens Rainer Stadelmann gewidmet.* Mainz, 1998, forthcoming.

QUIRKE, S. and SPENCER, A. J. eds. *The British Museum Book of Ancient Egypt.* London, 1992.

RANKE, H. 'The Origin of the Egyptian Tomb Statue,' *Harvard Theological Review* 28, 1935, 45–53.

RAUSCHENBACH, B. V. 'Ancient Egyptian Representation of Space and Spatiality' *GM* 155, 1996, 77–86.

REDFORD, D. B. ed. *The Oxford Encyclopedia of Ancient Egypt*, New York, forthcoming.

ROBINS, G. *Proportion and Style in Ancient Egyptian Art.* Austin, 1994. With useful bibliography of the author's other publications on p. 277.

ROBINS, G. 'Some Principles of Compositional Dominance and Gender Hierarchy in Egyptian Art' *JARCE* 31, 1994, 33–40. Mainly in two-dimensional art. The conventions are analysed.

ROBINS, G. *The Art of Ancient Egypt.* London, 1997.

RUSSMANN, E. *Egyptian Sculpture: Cairo and Luxor.* Austin, 1989. Long review: Marc Gabolde. *CdE* 71, 1996, 91–100.

SASSON, J. ed. *Civilizations of the Ancient Near East.* 4 vols. New York, 1995. The essays in this substantial publication cover many aspects of Egyptian art.

SCHENKEL, W. 'Die Farben in ägyptischer Kunst und Sprache,' *ZÄS* 88, 1963, 131–47.

SCHOSKE, S. 'Historisches Bewußtsein in der ägyptischen Kunst,' *MjbK* 38, 1987, 7–26.

SCHULZ, R. and SEIDEL, M. eds. *Egypt: The World of the Pharaohs*, Cologne, 1998.

SILVERMAN, D. P. ed. *Ancient Egypt.* New York, 1997. The chapter on Egyptian Art is by Rita Freed and the chapter on tombs and temples by Peter D. Manuelian.

TEFNIN, R. 'Éléments pour une Sémiologie de l'Image égyptienne.' *CdE* 66, 1991, 60–88.

te VELDE, H. 'Commemoration in Ancient Egypt.' *Visible Religion* 1, 1982, 135–53.

Thomas, N. ed. *The American Discovery of Ancient Egypt: Essays.* Los Angeles, 1996.

VANDERSLEYEN, C. ed. *Propyläen Kunstgeschichte 15, Das Alte Ägypten.*, Berlin, 1975.

VANDERSLEYEN, C. *L'Égypte et la vallée du Nil.* Tome 2: *De la fin de l'Ancien Empire à la fin du Nouvel Empire.* Paris, 1995.

VERCOUTTER, J. *L'Égypte et la vallée du Nil.* Tome 1: *Des origines à la fin de l'Ancien Empire.* Paris, 1992.

VON BECKERATH, J. *Chronologie des pharaonischen Ägypten: Die Zeitbestimmung der ägyptischen Geschichte von der Vorzeit bis zu 332 v. Chr.* (MÄS 46), Mainz, 1997.

WILKINSON, R. H. *Reading Egyptian Art: A Hieroglyphic Guide to Ancient Egyptian Painting and Sculpture.* London, 1992.

WULLEMAN, R., KUNNEN, M., and MEKHITARIAN, A. *Passage to Eternity*, Knokke (Belgium), 1989. Useful for the magnificent colour photographs of the Valley of the Kings, the Valley of the Queens, the tombs of the Nobles, and Deir el Medina at Thebes.

WILDUNG, D. *Die Kunst des alten Ägypten.* Freiburg–Basel–Wien, 1988.

STATUE TYPES

BOTHMER, B. V. 'Block Statues of Dynasty XXV' in *Hommages à Jean Leclant* I. (IFAO, Bd'E 106/2), Cairo 1994, 61–8.

CHAUDEFAUD, C. *Les statues Porte-Enseignes de l'Égypte.* Paris, 1982.

CLÈRE, J. J. *Les chauves d'Hathor.* Orientalia Lovaniensia Analecta 63, Leuven, 1995

SATZINGER, H. 'Der Heilige Stab als Kraftquelle des Königs: Versuch einer Funktionsbestimmung der ägyptischen Stabträger Statuen' *Jahrbuch der Kunsthistorischen Sammlungen in Wien* 77, 1981, 9–43.

SCHULZ, R. *Die Entwicklung und Bedeutung des kuboiden Statuentypus.* Band 1–2. (HÄB 33–4), Hildesheim, 1992. A detailed study of the so-called block statues with catalogue of examples. Reviewed by H. de Meulenaere. *CdE* 71, 1996, 87–91.

SCOTT, G. 'The History and Development of the Ancient Egyptian Scribe Statue'. Dissertation, Yale University, New Haven, 1989.

SEIDEL, M. *Die königlichen Statuengruppen.* Band 1: *Die Denkmäler vom Alten Reich bis zum Ende der 18. Dynastie.* (HÄB 42), Hildesheim, 1996.

SOUROUZIAN, H. 'Inventaire iconographique des statues en manteau jubilaire de l'époque thinite jusqu'à leur disparition sous Amenhotep III' in Berger, C., Clerc, G., and Grimal, N. eds. *Hommages à Jean Leclant* I. (IFAO, Bd'E 106/1), Cairo, 1994, 499–530.

VASSILIKA, E. 'Egyptian Bronze Sculpture Before the Late Period' in Goring, E. et al. eds. *Chief of Seers: Egyptian Studies in Memory of Cyril Aldred*. London and New York, 1997, 291–302.

WILDUNG, D. 'Der König Ägypten als Herr der Welt? Ein seltener ikonographischer Typus der Königsplastik des Neuen Reiches' *Archiv für Orientforschung* 24, 1973, 108–16. On rulers over prostrate captives.

ON THE EGYPTIAN HOUSE, TEMPLE AND TOMB ARCHITECTURE

ARNOLD, D. *Building in Egypt: Pharaonic Stone Masonry*. New York, 1991.

ARNOLD, D. *Wandrelief und Raumfunktion* (MÄS 2), Berlin, 1962.

ARNOLD, D. *Lexikon der ägyptischen Baukunst*. Zürich, 1994.

ARNOLD, D. 'Hypostyle Halls of the Old and Middle Kingdoms?' in Manuelian, P. D. ed. *Studies in Honor of William Kelly Simpson*. Boston, 1996, 39–54.

ARNOLD, D. *Die Tempel Ägyptens: Götterwohnungen, Kultstätten, Baudenkmäler.* Zürich, 1992. In the first part the meaning, development, and types of the temple are discussed with a glossary of terms, and in the second part an illustrated description of 130 temple sites is provided. With illustrations in colour and black and white, maps, indices, etc.

Aufrère, S., Golvin, J. C., and Goyon, J. C. *L'Égypte restituée* 1: *Sites et temples de haute Égypte (1650 av. J.C.-300 ap. J.C.)* Paris, 1991; 2: *Sites et temples des déserts de la naissance de la civilisation pharaonque à l'époque gréco-romaine*. Paris 1994; 3: *Sites et temples et pyramides de Moyenne et Basse Égypte de la naissance de la civilisation pharaonque à l'époque gréco-romaine*. Paris, 1997.

BADAWY, A. *A History of Egyptian Architecture*. Lawrence, Kansas, 1954; *History of Egyptian Architecture: the first intermediate period, the middle kingdom, and the second intermediate period*. Berkeley, 1966; *A History of Egyptian Architecture: The Empire (the New Kingdom), from the Eighteenth Dynasty to the end of the Twentieth Dynasty, 1580–1085 B.C.).* Berkeley, 1968.

BAINES, J. 'Temple Symbolism'. *Royal Anthropological Institute News*, No. 15, 1976, 10–15.

BAINES, J. 'Temples as symbols, guarantors, and participants in Egyptian civilization' in Quirke, S. ed. *The Temple in Ancient Egypt. New discoveries and recent research*. London, 1997, 216–41.

Barre, E. *Choix et rôle de la pierre dans la construction des temples égyptiens*. Paris, 1993.

BIETAK, M. 'Kleine ägyptische Tempel und Wohnhäuser des späten Mittleren Reiches. Zur Genese eines beliebten Raumkonzeptes von Tempeln des Neuen Reiches' in Berger, C., Clerc, G., and Grimal, N. eds. *Hommages à Jean Leclant* I. (IFAO, Bd'E 106/1), Cairo, 1994, 413–36.

BIETAK, M. ed. *Haus und Palast im alten Ägypten*. Vienna, 1995.

BORCHARDT, L. and RICKE, H. *Die Wohnhäuser in Tell el-Amarna*. Berlin, 1980.

BRUNNER, H. *Die südlichen Räumer des Tempels von Luxor*. (AV 18), Mainz, 1977.

de Cénival, J.-L. *Living Architecture: Egyptian*. New York, 1964.

GUNDLACH, R. and ROCHHOLZ, M. eds. *Ägyptische Tempel – Struktur, Funktion und Programm* (HÄB 37), 1994. Several important essays on the Egyptian temple delivered as papers at two symposia on the subject in 1990 and 1992.

Harrell, J. A. 'An Inventory of Ancient Egyptian Quarries' *NARCE* 146, 1989, 1–7.

Harrell, J. A. 'Misuse of the term "Alabaster" in Egyptology' *GM* 119, 1990, 37–42.

HELCK, W. ed. *Tempel und Kult*. (ÄAbh, 46), Wiesbaden, 1987.

Klemm, D. and Klemm, R. 'Calcit-Alabaster oder Travertin? Bemerkungen zu Sinn und Unsinn petrographischer Bezeichnungen in der Ägyptologie' *GM* 122, 1991, 57–70.

Klemm, D. and Klemm, R. *Steine und Steinbrüche im Alten Ägypten*. Berlin and Heidelberg, 1992.

KURTH, D. 'The present state of research into Graeco-Roman temples' in Quirke, S. ed. *The Temple in Ancient Egypt. New discoveries and recent research*. London, 1997, 152–8.

O'CONNOR, D. B. 'The Status of Early Egyptian Temples: An Alternative Theory' in Adams, B. and Friedman, R. eds. *The Followers of Horus: Studies in Memory of Michael Allen Hoffman*. Oxford, 1992, 83–98.

O'CONNOR, D. B. 'The Social and Economic Organization of Ancient Egyptian Temples' in Sasson, J. ed. *Civilizations of the Ancient Near East*. New York, 1995, Vol. I, 319–30.

OSING, J. 'Zur Funktion einiger Räume des Ramesseums' in Manuelian, P. D. ed. *Studies in Honor of William Kelly Simpson*. Boston, 1996, 636–46.

QUIRKE, S. ed. *The Temple in Ancient Egypt. New discoveries and recent research*. London, 1997.

ROIK, E. *Das altägyptische Wohnhaus und seine Darstellung im Flachbild*. Frankfurt, 1988.

WILDUNG, D. *Egypt: From Prehistory to the Romans*. Taschen's World Architecture, London, etc., 1997.

GENERAL EXHIBITION AND MUSEUM CATALOGUES COVERING MORE THAN ONE PERIOD

Note: In many cases essentially the same exhibition travels from one venue to another. Generally the first venue is cited. When an exhibition consists of objects from one museum shown in another, the entry is usually made under the first city where the exhibition is held. For example an exhibition of works from the Louvre in Cleveland is cited under Cleveland, and an exhibition of works from the British Museum in Atlanta is cited under Atlanta. The entries include temporary exhibitions as well as catalogues of permanent collections. If there is an English edition of the catalogue, it is usually the only one cited. When an exhibition catalogue concerns a specific period, dynasty, or reign, it is generally included in the bibliographical material below for the period involved and not under the city. I apologize for omissions. This is not an attempt to record every exhibition, but it is hoped that the catalogues of permanent collections will be especially helpful. As indicated above, the CAA (Corpus Antiquitatum Aegyptiacarum) fascicles have not been included, although they are important for the museums represented: namely Amsterdam: Allard Pierson Museum; Boston: Museum of Fine Arts; Bremen: Übersee-Museum; Cuba: Musée National Havanne, Musée Bacardi Santiago de Cuba; Hanover: Kestner-Museum; Hildesheim: Roemer- und Pelizaeus-Museum; Oslo: Ethnografik Museum; Museen der Rhein-Main-Region; Wien: Kunsthistorisches Museum; museums in the former Czechoslovakia.

AIX-EN-PROVENCE *Collection Égyptienne*. Musée Granet, Aix-en-Provence, 1995.

AMIENS Perdu, O. and Rickal, E. *La Collection Égyptienne du Musée de Picardie*. Réunion des Musées Nationaux, Paris, 1994.

AMSTERDAM *Egypte: Eender en anders*. Amsterdam, 1994.

Scheurleer, R. A. L. *Egypte Geschenk van de Nijl*. Allard Pierson Museum. Amsterdam, 1992.

ANGERS Affholder, B. and Cornic, M. J. *Angers, Musée Pincé: La Collection égyptienne*. Paris, 1990.

ANNECY Ratié, Suzanne. *Musée-château Chambéry musées d'art et d'histoire Aix-les Bains, musée archéologique: Collections égyptiennes*. Paris, 1984.

ANN ARBOR Richards, J. E. and Wilfong, T. G. *Preserving Eternity: Modern Goals, Ancient Intentions: Egyptian Funerary Artifacts in the Kelsey Museum of Archaeology*. University of Michigan, 1995.

Wilfong, T. G. et al. *Women and Gender in Ancient Egypt from Prehistory to Late Antiquity*. Ann Arbor, 1997.

ANTWERP Gubel, E. ed. *Egypte Onomwonden. Egyptische Oudheden van het Museum Vleeshuis*, 1995.

ATHENS Doumas, A. et al. *The World of Egypt in the National Archaeological Museum*.

ATHENS, 1995. Catalogue of the new installation with introductory essays by several authors, with many objects illustrated in colour.

ATLANTA Robins, G. *Reflections of Women in the New Kingdom: Ancient Egyptian Arts from the British Museum*. Atlanta, 1995.

AUTUN *Les Collections égyptiennes dans les musées de Saône et Loire*. Autun/Mâcon, 1988.

AVIGNON *Égypte et Province*. Musée Calvet, Avignon, 1985.

BASEL Page-Gesser, Madeleine and Wiese, André B., *Ägypten. Augenblicke der Ewigkeit: Unbekannte Schätze aus Schweizer Privatbesitz*. Basel, 1997.

BERLIN Fay, B. *Egyptian Museum Berlin*. Berlin, 1985.

Priese, K. H. ed. *Ägyptisches Museum (Museumsinsel, Berlin)*. Mainz, 1991.

Priese, Karl-Heinz et al. *The Masterpieces of the Pergamon and Bode Museum = The Ancient World on Museum Island, Berlin*. Berlin, 1991.

BIRMINGHAM Spanel, D. B. *Through Ancient Eyes: Egyptian Portraiture*. Birmingham, Alabama, 1988.

BOLOGNA Pernigotti, S. *La Statuaria Egiziana nel Museo Civico Archeologico di Bologna*. Bologna, 1980.

Pernigotti, S. and Govi, C. M. *La collezione egiziana Museo Civico Archeologico di Bologna*. Bologna, 1994.

Pernigotti, S. and Govi, C. M. *Una nuova collezione egiptiana al Museo Civico Archeologico di Bologna*. Pisa, 1994.

BORDEAUX Orgogozo, C. et al. *Égypte et Mediterranné: Objets antiques du Musée d'Aquitaine*. Bordeaux, 1992.

BROOKLYN Bianchi, R. S. *Cleopatra's Egypt: Age of the Ptolemies*. Brooklyn, 1988.

BRUSSELS *La peinture égyptienne ancienne: in Monde de signes à préserver, exposition à l'Académie des beaux arts de Bruxelles*. Brussels, 1994.

Limme, L. *Stèles égyptiennes*. Musée de Bruxelles. Brussels, 1979.

Tefnin, R. *Peintures de l'ancienne Égypte*. Exposition à la Bibliothèque de l'Université Libre de Bruxelles. January–February 1997. Brussels, 1997.

CAIRO Sourouzian, H. and Saleh, M. *Official Catalogue: The Egyptian Museum*. Cairo, 1987.

CAMBRIDGE Vassilika, E. (with contributions by Bourriau, J.) *Egyptian Art (Fitzwilliam Museum Handbook)*. Cambridge, 1995.

Bourriau, J. *Pharaohs and Mortals: Egyptian Art in the Middle Kingdom*. Cambridge, 1988. With loans from United Kingdom museums and collections.

CINCINNATI (and BROOKLYN) Capel, A. K. and Markoe, G. E. eds. *Mistress of the House, Mistress of Heaven: Women in Ancient Egypt*. New York, 1996.

CLEVELAND Berman, L. M. and Letellier, B. *Pharaohs: Treasures of Egyptian Art from the Louvre*. Cleveland, 1996.

Friedman, F. D. *Gifts of the Nile: Ancient Egyptian Faience*. Providence, 1998.

COPENHAGEN Jörgensen, M. *Egypt 1: 3000–1550 B.C.* Catalogues (of the collection in the) Ny Carlsberg Glyptotek. Copenhagen, 1996.

DALLAS Silverman, D. P. ed. *Searching for Ancient Egypt: Art, Architecture and Artifacts from the University of Pennsylvania Museum of Archaeology and Anthropology*. Dallas, 1997. The exhibition scheduled to travel to Denver, Seattle, Omaha, Birmingham, and Honolulu.

DIJON *Antiquités égyptiennes. Inventaire des collections du Musée des Beaux-Art de Dijon*. Dijon, 1997.

FLORENCE Guidotti, M. C. *Museo Egizio di Firenze: Vasi dall'epoco protodinastica al Nuovo Regno*. Rome, 1991.

FRANKFURT AM MAIN Liebighaus. Ägyptische Bildwerke. Band I: *Skarabäen, Amulette und Schmuck*; Band II: *Statuetten, Geräte und Gefässe*; Band III: *Skulptur, Malerei, Papyri und Särge*. Melsungen, 1993.

GENEVA Maystre, C. *Egypte antique*. Guides illustrés 9, Ville de Genève, Musée d'Art et d'Histoire, 2nd ed., Geneva, 1969.

GRENOBLE Kueny, G. and Yoyotte J. *Collection égyptienne, Grenoble, musée des Beaux-Arts*. Paris, 1979. An extensive catalogue.

Kuény, G. *L'Égypte ancienne au Musée de Grenoble*. n.d. A short guide with some colour illustrations.

GUÉRET Quemereuc, M. D. *Collections Égyptiennes. Musée de Guéret*. Guéret, 1992.

HAMBURG Altenmüller, H. and Hornbostel, W. eds. *Das Menschenbild im Alten Ägypten*. Hamburg, 1982.

HANNOVER Drenkhahn, R. *Die Ägyptischen Reliefs im Kestner-Museum, Hannover*. Hannover, 1989.

HEIDELBERG Feucht, E. et al. *Vom Nil zum Neckar: Kunstschätze Ägyptens aus pharaonischer und koptischer Zeit an der Universität Heidelberg*. Heidelberg, 1986.

HILDESHEIM Eggebrecht, E. and A. eds. *Ägyptens Aufstieg zur Weltmacht*. (Exhibition Catalogue Pelizaeus Museum), Mainz, 1987.

Eggebrecht, A. *Suche nach Unsterblichkeit: Totenkult und Jenseitsglaube im alten Ägypten*. Mainz, 1990.

Schmitz, B. et al. *Pelizaeus-Museum Hildesheim: Die Ägyptische Sammlung*. Mainz, 1994.

Eggebrecht, A. ed. *Pelizaeus Museum Hildesheim: The Egyptian Collection, Guidebook*. Mainz, 1996.

Germer, R. *Das Geheimnis der Mumien: Ewiges Leben am Nil*. Munich and New York, 1997.

JERUSALEM Ben-Tor, D. *The Immortals of Ancient Egypt: From the Abraham Guterman Collection of Ancient Egyptian Art*. Jerusalem, 1997.

KARLSRUHE Schürmann, W. *Die Reliefs aus dem Grab des Pyramidenvorstehers Iinefret*, Karlsruhe, 1982.

KARTAUSE ITTINGEN Hornung E. and Staehelin, E. et al. *Vom Euphrat zum Nil: Kunst aus dem alten Ägypten und Vorderasien*. Kunstmuseum des Kantons Thurgau, 1985.

LEIPZIG Krauspe, R. *Statuen und Statuetten. Katalog Ägyptischer Sammlungen in Leipzig* Band 1. Mainz, 1997.

LISBON de Araújo, L. M. *Antiguidades Egípcias*. Lisbon, 1993.

Assam, M. H. *Colecçao Calouste Gulbenkian: Arte Egipcia*. Lisbon, 1991.

LIVERPOOL Bienkowski, P. and Tooley, A. M. J. *Gifts of the Nile: Ancient Egyptian Arts and Crafts in Liverpool Museum*. London, 1995.

LONDON Bierbrier, M. L. ed. *Portraits and Masks: Burial Customs in Roman Egypt*. London, 1997.

Davies, W. V. ed. *Egypt and Africa: Nubia from Prehistory to Islam*. London, 1991.

James, T. G. H. *Egyptian Painting*. London, 1985.

James, T. G. H. and Davies, W. V. *Egyptian Sculpture*. London 1983.

Taylor, John H. *Egypt and Nubia*. London, 1991.

Walker, S. and Bierbrier, M. eds. *Ancient Faces: Mummy Portraits from Roman Egypt*. London, 1997.

LOS ANGELES Thomas, N. (with essays by Scott, G. D. III, and Trigger, B. G.) *The American Discovery of Ancient Egypt*. Los Angeles, 1995.

LUXOR Romano, J. F. et al. *The Luxor Museum of Ancient Egyptian Art*. Cairo, 1979.

El-Saghir, M. *Das Statuenversteck im Luxortempel*. Mainz, 1991.

MARSEILLES *L'Égypte Romaine: L'autre Égypte*. Le Musée d'Archéologie Méditerranéene. Marseilles, 1997.

MEMPHIS Freed, R. *Ramesses the Great*. Memphis, 1987.

MILAN *Iside. Il mito il mistero la magia*. Milan, 1997.

Lise, G. *Museo Archeologico: Raccolta Egizia*. Milan, 1979.

MONTREAL *The great pharaoh Ramses II and his time*. Montreal, 1985.

MOSCOW Hodjash, S. and Berlev, O. *The Egyptian Reliefs and Stelae in the Pushkin Museum of Fine Arts, Moscow*. Leningrad, 1982.

MUNICH Schoske, S. *Schönheit Abglanz der Göttlichkeit; Kosmetik im Alten Ägypten*. Staatliche Sammlung Ägyptischer Kunst. Munich, 1990.

Schoske, S. *Egyptian Art in Munich*. Staatliche Sammlung Ägyptischer Kunst. Munich, 1993.

Wildung, D. ed. *Faszination der Antike: The George Ortiz Collection*. Bern, 1996.

Wildung, D. et al. eds. *Sudan: Ancient Kingdoms of the Nile*, Paris–New York, 1997. The exhibition was initially presented in Munich and scheduled to travel after Paris to Amsterdam, Toulouse, and Mannheim. The English version is a translation from the earlier German and French catalogues.

MUNSTER Falk, M. von, *Ägyptisches in Westfälischen Sammlungen*, 1987.

NEW HAVEN Scott, G. D. III. *Ancient Egyptian Art at Yale*. New Haven, 1986.

NEW YORK Arnold, D. et al. *An Egyptian Bestiary*. The Metropolitan Museum, New York, 1995.

Arnold, D. et al. *The Gold of Meroe*. The Metropolitan Museum, New York, 1993.

Arnold, D. et al. *The Royal Women of Amarna: Images of Beauty from Ancient Egypt*. The Metropolitan Museum, New York, 1997.

PARIS Ziegler, C. ed. *Guide du Visiteur Les Antiquités égyptiennes I, II*. Paris, 1997.

Andreu, G., Rutschowscaya, M. H., Ziegler, C. *L'Égypte ancienne au Louvre*. Paris, 1997.

For catalogues of the Louvre, see under appropriate period in bibliography below.

Various authors, *La Gloire d'Alexandrie*. Exhibition catalogue, Musée du Petit Palais, 1998.

PÉRIGUEUX *L'Égypte en Périgord: Dans les pas de J. Clédat*. Louvain, 1991.

PISA Bresciani, E. *La Collezione Schiff Giorgini* (Catalogo della Collectioni egittologiche. Universita di Pisa. Museo di Ateneo 1) Pisa, 1992.

Various, *Le Vie del Vetro egitto e sudan*. Pisa, 1988.

RIO DE JANEIRO Kitchen, K. A. *Catalogue of the Egyptian Collection in the National Museum, Rio de Janeiro*. Rio de Janeiro, 2 vols (Text and Plates) 1990.

ROANNE *Antiquités égyptiennes du Musée J. Déchelette*. Roanne, 1990.

ROME Grenier, J.-C. *Museo Gregoriano Egizio*. Rome, 1993.

Sist, L. *Museo Barracco: Arte egizia*. Rome, 1996.

ROTTERDAM *Goden en farao's 1 mars–29 avril 1979*. Rotterdam, 1979.

ROUEN Aufrere, S. *Collections Égyptiennes: Musée de Rouen*. Rouen, 1987.

Perin, P. *Les collections du Musée des Antiquités de Rouen, 'De l'Égypte ancienne à la Renaissance rouennaise'*. Rouen, 1992.

SAN ANTONIO, TEXAS Scott, G. D. *Dynasties: The Egyptian Royal Image in the New Kingdom*. Varia Aegyptiaca 10, No. 1. San Antonio, 1995.

Scott, G. D. *Fragments from the Ramesside Age*. San Antonio, 1988.

SAN FRANCISCO Fazzini, R. *Images for Eternity: Egyptian Art from Berkeley and Brooklyn*. San Francisco and Brooklyn, 1975.

SAN MARINO Pernigotti, S. *L'Egitto antico a San Marino: La collezione del Museo di Stato*. Republic of San Marino, 1991.

SÈVRES Bulté, J. *Catalogue des collections égyptiennes du Musée National de Céramique à Sèvres*. Paris, 1981.

STRASBOURG Schweitzer, A. and Traunecker, C. *Antiquités égyptiennes de la collection G. Schlumberger*. Strasbourg. Musée archéologique, Paris, 1997.

ST PETERSBURG, FLORIDA Bianchi, R. *Splendors of Ancient Egypt from the Egyptian Museum, Cairo*. London, 1996. An exhibition organized for the Florida International Museum, St Petersburg, which was cancelled.

STUTTGART Geßler-Löhr, B. *Ägyptische Kunst in Liebigshaus*. Frankfurt, 1981.

Gamer-Wallert, I. *Vermerk: Fundort Unbekannt. Ägyptologische Entdeckungen bei Privatsammlern in und um Stuttgart*. Tübingen, 1997.

Schlick-Nolte, B., von Droste zu Hülshoff, V., Bayer-Niemeier, E. et al. *Ägyptischer Bildwerk*. Liebieghaus-Museum Alter Plastik. 3 vols Melsungen, 1990–1993.

TOULOUSE Aufrere, S. *Catalogue de la collection égyptienne de Toulouse. Cahiers du Musée Labit 1*. Toulouse, 1996.

TÜBINGEN *Kunst und Altertum aus den Sammlungen der Universität*, Tübingen 1977.

Brunner-Traut, E. and Brunner, H. *Die Ägyptische Sammlung der Universität Tübingen*. 2 vols. Mainz am Rhein, 1981.

Gamer-Wallert, I. *Von Giza bis Tübingen: Die bewegte Geschichte der Mastaba G 5170*. Tübingen, 1998.

TURIN Roveri, A. M. D. ed. *Civilta' Degli Egizi: La Vita Quotidiana*. Turin, 1987. *Le Credenze Religiose*. Turin 1988. *Le Arti della Celebrazione*. Turin, 1989. An extensive, well illustrated series sponsored by the Istituto Bancario San Paolo.

VIENNA Seipel, W. *Gott-Mensch-Pharao: Viertausend Jahre Menschenbild in der Skulptur des alten Ägyptens*. Vienna, 1992.

Satzinger, H. *Das Kunsthistorische Museum in Wien: Die ägyptisch-orientalische Sammlung*. Mainz, 1994.

WASHINGTON Kendall, T. *Kerma and the Kingdom of Kush 2500–1500 B.C.: The Archaeological Discovery of an Ancient Nubian Empire*. Washington, National Museum of African Art, Smithsonian Institution, 1997.

OTHER *Pharaonendämmerung, Wiedergeburt des Alten Ägypten*. Strasbourg, 1990.

Stadelmann, R. et al. *Ägyptische Pyramiden: Katalog zur Ausstellung*. Aachen, 1994.

ANNIVERSARY AND MEMORIAL VOLUMES

The volumes represented in this section generally include articles related to art and architecture. A few of them, like the first, are mainly essays on art and architecture.

ALDRED, CYRIL Goring, E., Reeves, N., and Ruffle, J. *Chief of Seers: Egyptian Studies in Memory of Cyril Aldred*. London and New York, 1997.

BAER, KLAUS Silverman, D. ed. *For His Ka, Essays Offered in Memory of Klaus Baer*. Oriental Institute, Chicago, 1994.

BARTA, WINFRIED Kessler, D. and Schulz, R. eds. *Gedenkschrift für Winfried Barta*. MAÜ. Frankfurt, Peter Lang, 1995.

von BECKERATH, JÜRGEN Eggebrecht, A., Schmitz, B. eds. *Festschrift zum 70. Geburtstag am 19. Februar 1990, Festschrift Jürgen von Beckerath*. Hildesheim, Gerstenberg verlag, 1990.

BELL, MARTHA RHOADS Phillips, J. et al. eds. *Ancient Egypt, the Aegean, and the Near East: Studies in Honour of Martha Rhoads Bell*. San Antonio, Van Siclen Books, 2 vols. 1998.

BEHRENS, PETER Mendel D. and Claudi, U. eds. *Ägypten im Afro-Orientalischen Kontext Gedenkschrift Peter Behrens*. Köln, Institut für Afrikanistik, 1991.

BOTHMER, BERNARD V. de Meulenaere, H., Limme, L. eds. *Artibus Aegypti. Studia in honorem Bernardi V. Bothmer a collegis amicis discipulis conscripta quae edenda curaverunt H. de Meulenaere et L. Limme*. Brussels, Musées Royaux d'Art et d'Histoire, 1983.

BRESCIANI, EDDA Bondi, S. F. et al. eds. *Studi in onorre di Edda Bresciani*. Pisa, 1985.

BRUNNER, HELMUT *Die Welt des Orients* 14 (1983); 15 (1984).

BRUNNER-TRAUT, EMMA Gamer-Wallert, I. and Helck, W. eds. *Festschrift für Emma Brunner-Traut*. Tübingen, Atempto Verlag, 1992.

CLÈRE, JACQUES JEAN *Mélanges Jacques Jean Clère*. Cahier de Recherches de l'Institut de Papyrologie et d'Egyptologie de Lille. Lille, Université Charles de Gaulle, 1991.

DAUMAS, FRANÇOIS *Hommages à François Daumas*, 2 vols. Institut d'Égyptologie – Université Paul Valéry ed. Montpellier, Université de Montpellier, 1986.

DE MEULENAERE, HERMAN Limme, L. and Strybol, J. eds. *Aegyptus Museis Rediviva: Miscellanea in Honorem Hermanni de Meulenaere*. Brussels, Musées Royaux d'Art et d'Histoire, 1993.

DERCHAIN, PHILIPPE Verhoeven, U. and Graefe, E. eds. *Religion und Philosophie im alten Ägypten: Festgabe für Philippe Derchain zu seinem 65. Geburtstag am 24. Juli 1991*. Leuven, OLA 39, 1991.

DERCHAIN, PHILIPPE Broze, M. and Talon, P. eds. *L'atelier de l'orfèvre. Melanges offerts a Philippe Derchain*. Louvain, 1992.

DUNHAM, DOWS Simpson, W. K. and Davis, W. eds. *Studies in Ancient Egypt, the Aegean, and the Sudan. Essays in Honor of Dows Dunham on the Occasion of his 90th Birthday*. Boston, 1981.

EDEL, ELMAR Görg, M. et al. eds. *Festschrift Elmar Edel, 12 März 1979*. ÄAT 1, Bamberg, 1979.

FAIRMAN, H. W., Ruffle, J., Gaballa, G. A., and Kitchen, K. A. eds. *Glimpses of Ancient Egypt. Studies in Honor of H. W. Fairman*. Orbis Aegyptiorum Speculum. Warminster, 1979.

FECHT, GERHARD Osing, J. and Dreyer, G. *Form und Mass. Beiträge zur Literatur, Sprache, und Kunst des Alten Ägypten. Festschrift für Gerhard Fecht zum 65. Geburtstag*. Ägypten und Altes Testament 12, Wiesbaden, 1987.

GOEDICKE, HANS Bryan, B. M. and Lorton, D. eds. *Essays in Honor of Hans Goedicke*. San Antonio, Texas, Van Siclen Books, 1994.

GRIFFITHS, J. GWYN Lloyd, A. B. ed. *Studies in Pharaonic Religion and Society in Honour of J. Gwyn Griffiths*. London, Egyptian Exploration Society, 1992.

GUNDLACH, ROLF Schade-Busch, M. ed. *Wege öffnen: Festschrift für Rolf Gundlach zum 65. Geburtstag*. ÄAT 35, 1996.

GUTBUB, ADOLPHE *Mélanges Adolphe Gutbub*. Montpellier, 1984.

HABACHI, LABIB *MDAIK* 37, 1981.

HELCK, WOLFGANG Altenmüller, H., Germer, R. eds. *Miscellanea Aegyptologica: Wolfgang Helck zum 75. Geburtstag*. Hamburg, Archäologisches Institut der Universität Hamburg, Hamburg 1989.

HELCK, WOLFGANG *Festschrift Wolfgang Helck SAK* 11, 1984.

HOFFMAN, MICHAEL ALLEN Friedman, R., Adams, B. eds. *The Followers of Horus Studies Dedicated to Michael Allen Hoffman*. Exeter, Egyptian Studies Publication, 1992.

HUGHES, GEORGE R. *Studies in Honor of George R. Hughes*. Studies in Ancient Oriental Civilization 39. Chicago, Oriental Institute, 1977.

IVERSEN, ERIK Osing, J. and Nielsen, E. K. eds. *The Heritage of Ancient Egypt: Studies in Honour of Erik Iversen*. CNI Publication 13. Museum Tusculum Press, Copenhagen, 1992.

KÁKOSY, LÁSZLÓ U. ed. *The Intellectual Heritage of Egypt: Studies Presented to László Kákosy by Friends and Colleagues on his 60th Birthday*. Studia Aegyptiaca 14. Budapest, Université Eötvös Loránd de Budapest, 1992.

KAISER, WERNER *MDAIK* 47, 1991.

KOROSTOVTSEV, MIKHAIL A. *Ancient Egypt and Kush: In Memoriam Mikhail A. Korostovvtsev*. Russian Academy of Sciences, Institute of Oriental Studies, National Orientalists' Association. Moscow, 1993.

KRAUSE, MARTIN Fluck, C. et al. eds. *Divitiae Aegypti: Koptologische und verwandte Studien zu Ehren von Martin Krause*. Wiesbaden, 1995.

LAUER, J.-P. Berger, C., and Mathieu, B. *Études sur l'Ancien Empire et la nécropole de Saqqara dédiées à Jean-Philippe Lauer*. Orientalia Monspeliensia 9, 2 vols. Montpellier, 1997.

LECLANT, JEAN Berger, C., Clerc, G., and Grimal, N. eds. *Hommages à Jean Leclant*. 4 vols. Vol. 1: *Études Pharaoniques*; Vol. 2: *Nubie, Soudan, Étiopie*; Vol. 3: *Études Isiaques*; Vol. 4: *Varia*. Cairo, *IFAOC BdÉ* 106/1–4. 1994.

LICHTHEIM, MIRIAM Israelit-Groll, S. ed. *Studies in Egyptology Presented to Miriam Lichtheim*. 2 vols. Jerusalem, The Magnes Press, The Hebrew University, 1990.

LIPIŃSKA, JAGWIGA *Essays in honour of Prof. Dr. Jadwiga Lipinska*. Warsaw Egyptological Studies I, Warsaw, 1997.

MICHALOWSKI, KAZIMIERZ *Mélanges offerts à Kazimierz Michalowski*. Warsaw, 1966.

MOKHTAR, GAMAL ED DIN *Mélanges Gamal Eddin Mokhtar*. 2 vols. Cairo, *IFAOC BdÉ* XCVII/1–2, 1985.

PARKER, RICHARD A. Lesko, L. H. ed. *Egyptological Studies in Honor of Richard A. Parker. Presented on the Occasion of his 78th Birthday, December 10, 1983*. University Press of New England, Hanover and London, 1986.

POLOTSKY, HANS JACOB Young, D. W. ed. *Studies Presented to Hans Jacob Polotsky*. Pirtle & Polson, East Gloucester, Massachusetts, 1981.

Ray, J. ed. *Lingua Sapientissima: A Seminar in Honour of H. J. Polotsky Organized by the Fitzwilliam Museum, Cambridge, and the Faculty of Oriental Studies in 1984*. Cambridge, 1987.

Rosen, H. B. ed. *Studies in Egyptology and Linguistics in Honour of H. J. Polotsky*. Jerusalem, 1964.

QUAEGEBEUR, JAN Clarysse, W. et al. eds. *Egyptian Religion, The 1st Thousand Years: Studies Dedicated to the Memory of Jan Quaegebeur*. 2 vols. OLA 84–85, Leuven, 1998.

SADEK, ABDEL AZIZ Van Siclen III, C. C. ed. *Iubilate Conlegae: Studies in Memory of Abdel Aziz Sadek*, 2 parts = *Varia Aegyptiaca* 10, nos 2–3, 1998.

SAUNERON, SERGE *Hommages à la Mémoire de Serge Sauneron 1927–1976*: I: *L'Égypte Pharaonique*. Cairo, *IFAOC BdÉ* 81, 1979.

SÄVE-SÖDERBERGH, TORGNY Englund, G., Hamrén, M., Troy, L. eds. *Sundries in Honour of Torgny Säve-Söderbergh*. Uppsala, Acta Universitatis Upsaliensis, 1984.

SCHENKEL, WOLFGANG Gerstenberg, L. and Sternberg-el Hotabi, H. eds. *Per aspera ad astra: Wolfgang Schenkel zum neun und fünfizigsten Geburgstag*. Kassel, 1995.

SCHOTT, SIEGFRIED Helck, W. ed. *Festschrift für Siegfried Schott zu seinem 70. Geburstag am 20. August 1967*. Wiesbaden, O. Harrrassowitz, 1968.

SCHULMAN, ALAN R. *BES* 10, 1992.

SEELE, KEITH *JNES* 32, 1973.

SHORE, A. F. Eyre, C., Leahy, A., Leahy, L. M. eds. *The Unbroken Reed, Studies in the Culture and Heritage of Ancient Egypt*. London, The Egypt Exploration Society, 1994.

SIMPSON, WILLIAM KELLY Manuelian, P. D. ed. *Studies in Honor of William Kelly Simpson*. 2 Vols Boston, Museum of Fine Art, 1996.

STADELMANN, RAINER Polz, D. and Guksch, H. eds. *Studien: Beiträge zur Kulturgeschichte Ägyptens Raiher Stadelmann gewidmet*. Mainz, 1998, forthcoming.

STRICKER, B. H. DuQuesne, T. ed. *Hermes Aegyptiacus, Egyptological Studies for B.H. Stricker, on his 85th birthday*. Oxford, DE Publications, 1995. Rev. summarized by Derchain *BiOr* 54, 1997: 67–8.

TE VELDE, HERMAN van Dijk, J. ed. *Essays on Ancient Egypt in Honour of Herman te Velde*, Gröningen, 1997.

THAUSING, GERTRUD Bietak, M., Holaubek, J., Mukarovsky, H., Satzinger, H. eds. *Festschrift, Gertrude Thausing*. Wien, Institutes für Ägyptologie der Universität Wien, 1994.

THÉODORIDÈS, ARISTIDE Cannuyer, C. and Kruchten, J. M. eds. *Individu, Société et Spiritualité dans L'Égypte Pharaonique et Copte, Mélanges égyptologiques offerts au Professeur Aristide Théodoridès*. Illustra, Izegem, 1993.

VANDERSLEYEN, CLAUDE Obsomer, C. and Oosthoek, A.-L. eds. *Amosiadès: Mélanges offerts au Professeur Claude Vandersleyen par ses anciens étudiants.* Louvain-la-Neuve, 1992.

VERCOUTTER, JEAN Geus, F., Thill, F. eds. *Mélanges Offerts à Jean Vercoutter.* Paris, Éditions Recherche sur les Civilisations, 1985.

VERGOTE, JOSEPH Naster, P., De Meulenaere, H., Quaegebeur, J. eds. *Miscellania in Honorem Josephi Vergote.* Leuven, Orientalia Lovaniensia Periodica, 1976.

van VOSS, M. S. H. G. HEERMA Kamstra, J. H., Milde, H., Wegtendonk, K. eds. *Funerary Symbols and Religion, Essays Dedicated to Professor M.S.H.G. Heerma va Voss.* Kampen, J. H. Kok, 1988.

WARD, WILLIAM A. Lesko, L. H. ed. *Ancient Egyptian and Mediterranean Studies in Memory of William A. Ward.* Providence, 1998.

WENTE, EDWARD F. Teeter, E. and Larson, J. A. eds. *Gold of Praise: Studies Presented in Honor of Edward F. Wente.* Chicago, The Oriental Institute of the University of Chicago, *Studies in Ancient Oriental Civilization* forthcoming.

WESTENDORF, WOLFHART Behlmer, H. ed. *Quaerentes Scientiam, Festgabe für Wolfhart Westendorf zu seinem 70. Geburtstag.* Göttingen, Hubert & Co., 1994.

Junge, F. ed. *Studien zu Sprache und Religion Ägyptens, zu ehren von Wolfhart Westendorf.* (2 Vols) Göttingen, 1984.

WILLIAMS, RONALD JAMES Kadish, G., Freeman, G. eds. *Studies in Philology in Honour of Ronald James Williams: A Festschrift.* SSEA, Toronto, 1982.

James E. Hoch ed. *Papers Presented in Memory of Ronald J. Williams = JSSEA* 24, 1994.

Hoffmeier, J. K. and Meltzer, E. S. eds. Egyptological Miscellanies: A Tribute to Professor Ronald J. Williams, *The Ancient World* Special Volume 6, 1–4, Chicago, 1983.

WILSON, JOHN A. *Studies in Honor of John A. Wilson.* Studies in Ancient Oriental Civilization 35. Oriental Institute, Chicago, 1969.

CHAPTER 2 PREDYNASTIC EGYPT (4000–3200 B.C.)

CIALOWICZ, K. M. *Les têtes de Massues des Périodes Prédynastique et Archaique dans la Vallée du Nil.* Warsaw, 1987.

CIALOWICZ, K. M. 'Le manche de couteau de Gebel el-Arak. Le problème de l'interprétation de l'art prédynastique' in *Essays in honour of Dr. Jadwiga Lipínska*, Warsaw Egyptological Studies I, Warsaw, 1997, 339–52.

DREYER, G. 'Die Datierung der Min-Statuen aus Koptos' in Stadelmann, Rainer and Sourouzian, Hourig, *Kunst des Alten Reiches: Symposium im Deutschen Archäologischen Institut Kairo am 29. und 30. Oktober 1991.* (DAIAK Sonderschrift 28), Mainz am Rhein, 1995, 49–56.

FINKENSTAEDT, E. 'Egyptian Ivory Tusks and Tubes' *ZÄS* 106, 1979, 51–9.

FINKENSTAEDT, E. 'Regional Painting Style in Prehistoric Egypt' *ZÄS* 107, 1980, 116–20.

HENDRICKX, S. *Analytical Bibliography of the Prehistory and the Early Dynastic Period of Egypt and Northern Sudan.* Leuven, 1995.

KAISER, W. 'Stand und Probleme der ägyptischen Vorgeschichte' *ZÄS* 81, 1956, 87–109.

KAISER, W. 'Zur inneren Chronologie der Naqadakultur' *Archaeologia Geographica* 6, 1957, 69–77.

KELLEY, A. J. 'The evidence of Mesopotamian influence in Predynastic Egypt' (*Newsletter of the Society for the Study of Egyptian Antiquity* 4), Toronto, 1974, 2–22.

MIDANT-REYNES, B. *Préhistoire de l'Égypte des premiers hommes aux premiers Pharaons.* Paris, 1992.

NEEDLER, W. *Predynastic and Archaic Egypt in the Brooklyn Museum.* (Wilbour Monographs 9), New York, 1984.

PARIS: *L'Egypte avant les Pyramides 4e millénaire.* Paris, Grand-Palais, 1973.

PITTMAN, H. 'Constructing context: The Gebel el-Arak Knife – Greater Mesopotamian and Egyptian Interaction in the Late Fourth Millennium B. C. E.' in Cooper, J. S. and Schwartz, G. M., *The Study of the Ancient Near East in the Twenty-First Century: The William Foxwell Albright Centennial Conference.* Winona Lake, Indiana, 1996, 9–32.

RICE, M. *Egypt's Making.* London, 1984.

SMITH, H. S. 'The Making of Egypt: A review of the influence of Susa and Sumer on Upper Egypt and Lower Nubia in the 4th millennium B. C.' in Friedman, R. and Adams, B. eds. *The Followers of Horus: Studies dedicated to Michael Allen Hoffman.* (Egyptian Studies Association No. 2, Oxbow Monograph 20). Oxford, 1992, 235–46.

SPENCER, J. ed. *Aspects of Early Egypt.* London, 1996.

VERCOUTTER, J. 'La Predynastie égyptienne. Anciens et nouveaux concepts' in *Mélanges Jacques Jean Clère* (CRIPL 13), Lille, 1991, 137–46.

WEEKS, K. R. *An Historical Bibliography of Egyptian Prehistory.* Indiana, 1985.

WILKINSON, T. A. H. *State Formation in Egypt: Chronology and Society.* Cambridge, 1996.

CHAPTER 3 DYNASTIES I–II (3200–2780 B.C.)

ADAMS, B. and CIALOWICZ, K. *Protodynastic Egypt.* London, 1997.

ALEXANIAN, N. 'Die Reliefdekoration des Chasechemui aus dem sogenannten *Fort* in Hierakonpolis' in Grimal, N. ed. *Les critères de datation stylistiques à l'Ancien Empire.* Cairo, *IFAOC Bd'E 120*, 1998, 1–30.

BOEHMER, R. M., DREYER, G., and KROMER, B. 'Einige frühzeitliche 14C-Datierung aus Abydos und Uruk.' *MDAIK* 49, 1993, 63–8. With tables of recent Carbon 14 dates from Abydos and Mesopotamia.

DAVIS, W. *Masking the Blow: The Scene of Representation in Late Prehistoric Egyptian Art.* 1992. Essentially a 'decoding' of the message of the Narmer palette and its precursors. Reviewed by R. Gillam, *The SSEA Journal* 23, 1993 (published 1996), 77–9.

DOCHNIAK, C. 'An Early First Dynasty Adaptation of the Nar hieroglyph to the Smiting Posture as a Possible Precursor to Hieroglyph A 24' *Varia Aegyptiaca* 7, 1991, 101–7.

DOCHNIAK, C. 'The Libyan Palette Interpreted as Depicting a Combination Pictorial Year-name' *Varia Aegyptiaca* 7, 1991, 108–14.

DODSON, A. 'The So-called tomb of Osiris at Abydos' *KMT: A Modern Journal of Ancient Egypt* 8, No. 4, Winter 1997–1998, 37–47. The history of the tomb of Djer at Abydos as later interpreted as the tomb of Osiris.

DODSON, A. 'The Mysterious Second Dynasty' *KMT: A Modern Journal of Ancient Egypt* 7, No. 2, Summer 1996, 19–31.

DREYER, G. 'Horus Krokodil, ein Gegenkönig der Dynastie 0' in Friedman, R. and Adams, B. eds. *The Followers of Horus.* Oxford, 1992, 259–64.

DREYER, G. 'Recent Discoveries at Abydos Cemetery U' in van den Brink, Edwin C. M. ed. *The Nile Delta in Transition: 4th.-3rd. Millennium B. C.*, Jerusalem, 1992, 293–9.

DREYER, G. 'The Royal Tombs of Abydos' in Kerner, S. ed. *The Near East in Antiquity*, Vol. III, Al Kutba, Goethe Institut, German Protestant Institute for Archaeology, Amman, 1992, 55–67.

DREYER, G. *Der Tempel der Satet: Die Funde der Frühzeit und des Alten Reiches.* Elephantine VIII (AV 39). Mainz, 1986.

DREYER, G. et al. 'Umm el-Qaab' *MDAIK* 54, 1998, 3–15. With citation of the earlier preliminary reports on the new excavations at Abydos.

GOLDWASSER, O. 'The Narmer Palette and the "Triumph of Metaphor"' *Lingua Aegyptia* 2, 1992, 67–9. With extensive bibliography.

HARVEY, S. P. 'A Decorated Protodynastic Cult Stand from Abydos' in Manuelian, P. D. ed. *Studies in Honor of William Kelly Simpson*, Boston, 1996, 361–78.

MARTIN, G. T. 'Covington's Tomb and Related Early Monuments at Giza' in Berger, C. and Mathieu, B. *Études sur l'Ancien Empire et la nécropole de Saqqara dédiées à Jean-Philippe Lauer.* Orientalia Monspeliensia 9, 2 vols Montpellier, 1997, 279–88.

MILLET, N. B. 'The Narmer Macehead and Related Objects' *JARCE* 27, 1990, 53–9.

MORENZ, L. 'Zur Dekoration der frühzeitlichen Tempel am Beispiel zweier Fragmente des archaischen Tempels von Gebelein' in Gundlach, R. and Rochholz, M. eds. *Ägyptische Tempel – Struktur, Funktion und Programm*, Hildesheim (HÄB 37), 1994, 217–38. These fragments dated by W. Stevenson Smith in Dynasty 3 (possibly late Dynasty 2) are provisionally dated by Morenz in Dynasty 1.

O'CONNOR, D. B. 'The Earliest Royal Boat Graves' *Egyptian Archaeology: Bulletin of the Egypt Exploration Society* 6, 1995, 3–7. Discovery of a fleet of at least twelve boats of Dynasties 1 or 2 at Abydos, the hulls averaging between 18 to 21 metres in length.

O'CONNOR, D. B. 'Boat Graves and Pyramid Origins' *Expedition* 33, No. 3, 1991, 5–17.

O'CONNOR, D. B. 'New Funerary Enclosures' (*Talbezirke*) of the Early Dynastic Period at Abydos, *JARCE* 26, 1989, 51–86.

RIDLEY R. T. *The Unification of Egypt.* Deception Bay, 1973.

SCHULMAN, A. R. 'Narmer and the Unification: a Revisionist View' *BES* 11, 1991–1992, 79–105. Regards the scenes of the Narmer pallette as the traditional re-enactment of the conquest scene, an event which may have taken place well prior to Narmer. With abundant illustrations of related material.

SOUROUZIAN, H. 'L'iconographie du roi dans la statuaire des trois premières dynasties' in Stadelmann, R. and Sourouzian, H., *Kunst des Alten Reiches: Symposium im Deutschen Archäologischen Institut Kairo am 29. und 30. Oktober 1991.* (DAIAK Sonderschrift 28), Mainz, 1995, 133–54.

SOUROUZIAN, H. and Stadelmann, R. 'La statue de Ny-ankh-netjer, un nouveau document de la période archaïque à Saqqara' in Berger, C. and Mathieu, B. eds. *Études sur l'Ancien Empire et la nécropole de Saqqara dédiées à Jean-Philippe Lauer.* Orientalia Monspeliensia 9, Montpellier, 1997, 395–404.

SOUROUZIAN, H. 'Concordances et écarts entre statuaire et représentations à deux dimensions des particuliers de l'époque archaïque' in Grimal, N. ed. *Les critères de datation stylistiques à l'Ancien Empire.* Cairo, *IFAOC Bd'E 120* 1998, 305–52.

SPENCER, A. J. *Early Egypt: The Rise of Civilisation in the Nile Valley*. London, 1993. An outstanding account of the subject with utilisation of the recent German excavations at Abydos; many colour plates of sites and objects.

WILLIAMS, B. 'Narmer and the Coptos Colossi' *JARCE* 25, 35–59, 1988.

PART TWO: THE OLD KINGDOM

GENERAL

ALTENMÜLLER, H. 'Der Grabherr des Alten Reiches in seinem Palast des Jenseits. Bemerkungen zur sog. Prunkscheintür des Alten Reiches' in Berger, C. and Mathieu, B. eds. *Études sur l'Ancien Empire et la nécropole de Saqqara dédiées à Jean-Philippe Lauer*. Orientalia Monspeliensia 9, Montpellier, 1997, 11–19.

BAUD, M. 'À propos des critères iconographiques établis par Nadine Cherpion' in Grimal, N. ed. *Les critères de datation stylistiques à l'Ancien Empire*. Cairo, IFAOC Bd'E 120, 1998, 31–98.

ARNOLD, D. *Gräber des Alten und Mittleren Reiches in El-Tarif* (AV 17), Mainz, 1976.

BERGER, C. and MATHIEU, B. eds. *Études sur l'Ancien Empire et la nécropole de Saqqara dédiées à Jean-Philippe Lauer*. Orientalia Monspeliensia 9, Montpellier, 1997.

BOLSHAKOV, A. O. 'Hinting as a Method of Old Kingdom Tomb Decoration' *GM* 139, 1994, 9–33.

BOLSHAKOV, A. O. 'The Scene of the Boatmen Jousting in Old Kingdom Tomb Representations' *BSEG* 17, 1993, 29–39. The meaning of this frequent scene is explained as rival boatmen anxious to outdo each other's team in first bringing offerings to the tomb owner.

CHERPION, N. 'Sentiment Conjugal et Figuration à l'Ancien Empire' in Stadelmann, R. and Sourouzian, H. *Kunst des Alten Reiches: Symposium im Deutschen Archäologischen Institut Kairo am 29. und 30. Oktober 1991*. (DAIAK Sonderschrift 28), Mainz, 1995, 33–47.

CHERPION, N. *Mastabas et Hypogées d'Ancien Empire: Le Problème de la Datation. Connaissance de l'Égypte Ancienne*. Brussels, 1989.

CHERPION, N. 'La statuaire privée d'Ancien Empire: indices de datation' in Grimal, N. ed. *Les critères de datation stylistiques à l'Ancien Empire*. Cairo, IFAOC Bd'E 120, 1998, 97–142.

Cherpion, N. 'Mastabas et conception de l'au delà à l'Ancien Empire' in Naster, P. and Ries, J. eds. *Vie et survie dans les civilisations orientales*. Leuven, 1983, 71–4.

EATON-KRAUSS, M. *The Representations of Statuary in Private Tombs of the Old Kingdom*, (ÄAbh. 39), Wiesbaden, 1984.

EATON-KRAUSS, M. 'Pseudo-Groups' in Stadelmann, R. and Sourouzian, H. *Kunst des Alten Reiches: Symposium im Deutschen Archäologischen Institut Kairo am 29. und 30. Oktober 1991*. (DAIAK Sonderschrift 28), Mainz, 1995, 57–74. See entry under Rzepka below.

EDWARDS, I. E. S. *The Pyramids of Egypt*. New Edition. New York, 1986. This is the most useful edition in terms of format and illustrations.

EGGEBRECHT, A. *Das Alte Reich: Ägypten im Zeitalter der Pyramiden*. Roemer- und Pelizaeus-Museum, Hildesheim, 1986.

FAY, B. 'Royal Women as Represented in Sculpture during the Old Kingdom' in Grimal, N. ed. *Les critères de datation stylistiques à l'Ancien Empire*. Cairo, IFAOC Bd'E 120, 1998, 159–86.

GRIMAL, N. ed. *Les critères de datation stylistiques à l'Ancien Empire*. Cairo, IFAOC Bd'E 120, 1998.

HANDOUSSA, T. 'Fish Offering in the Old Kingdom' *MDAIK* 44, 1988, 105–9.

HARPUR, Y. *Decoration in Egyptian Tombs of the Old Kingdom, Studies in Orientation and Scene Content*. London and New York, 1987. A major, detailed study of the themes and function of the decoration of mastabas and rock tombs.

KAISER, W. 'Zur Entstehung der Mastaba des Alten Reiches' in Heike Guksch and Daniel Polz (eds.) *Stationen: Beiträge zur Kulturgeschichte Ägyptens Festschrift für Rainer Stadelmann zur Vollendung des 65. Lebensjahres*. Mainz, 1998, forthcoming.

KANAWATI, N. and HASSAN, A. *The Teti Pyramid at Saqqara I: The Teti Pyramid at Saqqara*. Warminster, 1996.

KANAWATI, N. and HASDSAN, A. *The Teti Pyramid at Saqqara II: The Tomb of Ankhmahor*. Warminster, 1997.

MANUELIAN, P. D. 'Presenting the Scroll: Papyrus Documents in Tomb Scenes of the Old Kingdom' in Manuelian, P. D. ed. *Studies in Honor of William Kelly Simpson*, Boston, 1996, 561–88.

MARAGIOGLIO, V. and RINALDI, C. *L'Architettura delle Piramidi Memphite*. Parts II–VIII, Turin, 1963–1977. A comprehesive study with detailed plans of the Memphite Pyramids. The first, projected volume, on the Step Pyramid of Djoser, was postponed.

O'CONNOR, D. 'The Interpretation of the Old Kingdom Pyramid Complex' in Heike Guksch and Daniel Polz (eds.) *Stationen: Beiträge zur Kulturgeschichte*

Ägyptens Festschrift für Rainer Stadelmann zur Vollendung des 65. Lebensjahres. Mainz, 1998, forthcoming.

PIACENTINI, P. *Zawiet el-Mayetin nel III Millennio A. C.* Pisa, 1993.

RZEPKA, S. 'The Pseudo-groups of the Old Kingdom – a New Interpretation' *SÄK* 23, 1996, 335–47. See entry under Eaton-Krauss above.

SALEH, M. *Three Old Kingdom Tombs at Thebes* (AV 14), Mainz, 1977.

SILIOTTI, A. (with preface and contributions by Hawass, Z.) *Guide to the Pyramids of Egypt*, Cairo, 1997.

STADELMANN, R. and SOUROUZIAN, H. *Kunst des Alten Reiches: Symposium im Deutschen Archäologischen Institut Kairo am 29. und 30. Oktober 1991*. (DAIAK Sonderschrift 28), Mainz am Rhein, 1995.

STADELMANN, R. *Die ägyptischen Pyramiden: Vom Ziegelbau zum Weltwunder* (2nd ed.), Mainz, 1991.

ZIEGLER, C. *Catalogue des stèles, peintures et reliefs égyptiens de l'Ancien Empire et de la Première Période Intermédiaire*. Musée du Louvre, Département des Antiquités Égyptiennes, Paris, 1990.

ZIEGLER, C. *Les Statues Égyptiennes de l'Ancien Empire*. Musée du Louvre. Paris, 1997.

ZIEGLER, C. 'À propos de quelques ivoires de l'Ancien Empire conservés au musée du Louvre' in Grimal, N. ed. *Les critères de datation stylistiques à l'Ancien Empire*. Cairo, IFAOC Bd'E 120 1998, 407.

CHAPTER 4 DYNASTY III (2780–2680 B.C.)

ALTENMÜLER, H. 'Bemerkungen zur frühen und späten Bauphase des Djoserbezirkes in Sakkara' *MDAIK* 28, 1972, 1–12.

DREYER, G. 'Der erste König der 3. Dynastie' in Heike Guksch and Daniel Polz (eds.) *Stationen: Beiträge zur Kulturgeschichte Ägyptens Festschrift für Rainer Stadelmann zur Vollendung des 65. Lebensjahres*. Mainz, 1998, forthcoming.

EATON-KRAUSS, M. and LOEBEN, C. E. 'Some Remarks on the Louvre Statues of Sepa (A 36 and 37) Nesames (A 38)' in Goring, E., Reeves, N., and Ruffle, J. eds. *Chief of Seers: Egyptian Studies in Memory of Cyril Aldred*. London and New York, 1997, 83–7.

EATON-KRAUSS, M. 'Two Masterpieces of Early Egyptian Statuary' *OMRO* 77, 1997, 7–21.

EATON-KRAUSS, M. 'Non-Royal Pre-Canonical Statuary' in Grimal, N. ed. *Les critères de datation stylistiques à l'Ancien Empire*. Cairo, IFAOC Bd'E 120 1998, 209–28.

FRIEDMAN, F. D. 'The Underground Relief Panels of King Djoser at the Step Pyramid Complex' *JARCE* 32, 1995, 1–42.

FRIEDMAN, F. D. 'Notions of Cosmos in the Step Pyramid Complex' in Manuelian, P. D. ed. *Studies in Honor of William Kelly Simpson*, Boston, 1996, 337–51.

HAWASS, Z. 'A Fragmentary Monument of Djoser from Saqqara' *JEA* 80, 1994, 45–56.

HELCK, W. 'Zum Statuensockel des Djoser' in Gamer-Wallert, I. and Helck, W. eds. *Gegengabe: Festschrift für Emma Brunner-Traut*. Tübingen, 1992, 143–50.

KAISER, W. 'Zu den königlichen Talbezirken der 1. und 2. Dynastie in Abydos und zur Baugeschichte des Djoser-Grabmals' *MDAIK* 25, 1969, 1–22.

KAISER, W. 'Die unterirdischen Anlage der Djoserpyramide und ihrer entwicklungsgeschichtlichen Einordnung' in Gamer-Wallert, I. and Helck, W. eds. *Gegengabe: Festschrift für Emma Brunner-Traut*. Tübingen, 1992, 167–90.

KAISER, W. 'Zu die Granitkammern und ihren Vorgängerbauten unter der Stufenpyramide und im Südgrab von Djoser' *MDAIK* 53, 1997, 195–207. Indicates that the granite chambers beneath the pyramid and south building were not part of the original scheme but were added at the same time the superstructure was converted from a square mastaba to a step pyramid.

LAUER, J.-P. 'Sur l'emploi et le rôle de la couleur aux monuments du complexe funéraire de roi Djoser' *RdE* 44, 1993, 75–80. Missing plate provided in *RdE* 45, 1994.

LAUER, J.-P. 'Sur certaines modifications et extensions apportées au complexe funéraire de Djoser au cours de son règne' in John Baines et al. eds. *Pyramid Studies and other Essays presented to I. E. S. Edwards*. London, 1988, 12–22.

LAUER, J.-P. 'Remarques concernant l'inscription gravé sur le socle de statue de l'Horus Neteri-Khet (roi Djoser)' in Manuelian, P. D. ed. *Studies in Honor of William Kelly Simpson*. Boston, 1996, 493–8.

LEHNER, M. 'Z 500 and The Layer Pyramid of Zawiyet el-Aryan' in Manuelian, P. D. ed. *Studies in Honor of William Kelly Simpson*. Boston, 1996, 507–22.

STADELMANN, R. 'Die vermeintliche Sonnenheiligtum im Norden des Djoserbezirkes' *ASAE* 69, 1983, 373–8.

STADELMANN, R. 'Origins and Development of the Funerary Complex of Djoser' in Manuelian, P. D. ed. *Studies in Honor of William Kelly Simpson*. Boston, 1996, 787–800.

SWELIM, N. *Some Problems on the History of the Third Dynasty.* The Archaeological Society of Alexandria, Archaeological & Historical Studies 7, 1983.

SWELIM, N. 'The Dry Moat of the Netjerykhet Complex' in John Baines et al. eds. *Pyramid Studies and other Essays presented to I. E. S. Edwards.* London, 1988, 5–11.

CHAPTER 5 DYNASTY IV (2680–2565 B.C.)

BAUD, M. 'La tombe de la reine-mère *H'-mrr-nbty Ire*' *BIFAO* 95, 1995, 11–17.

BAUD, M. 'The Tombs of Khamerernebty I and II at Giza' *GM* 164, 1998, 7–14.

BOLSHAKOV, A. 'What did the Bust of Ankh-haf Originally Look Like?' *Journal of the Museum of Fine Arts, Boston* 3, 1991, 5–14.

CALLENDER, V. G. and JÁNOSI, P. 'The Tomb of Queen Khamerernebty II at Giza. A Reassessment' *MDAIK* 53, 1997, 1–22.

CHERPION, N. 'De quand date la tombe du nain Seneb' *BIFAO* 84, 1984, 35–54. Although generally dated to Dynasty 5 or 6, author proposes a date in Dynasty 4, specifically the reign of Dedefre.

CHERPION, N. 'En reconsidérant le grand sphinx du Louvre A 23' *RdE* 42, 1991, 25–41. Author in a detailed study opts for a date as early as Snefru for this famous monument, for which a Dynasty 12 date has also been proposed (see Biri Fay under Dynasty 12).

DOBREV, V. 'Observations sur deux statues de Menkaoure du musée de Boston' *DE* 27, 1993, 9–18.

DOBREV, V. 'À propos d'une statue fragmentaire du roi Menkaoure trouvée à Abou Rawash' in Berger, C. and Mathieu, B. eds. *Études sur l'Ancien Empire et la nécropole de Saqqara dédiées à Jean-Philippe Lauer.* Orientalia Monspeliensia 9, Montpellier, 1997, 155–66.

DORNER, J. 'Neue Messungen an der Roten Pyramide' in Heike Guksch and Daniel Polz (eds.) *Stationen: Beiträge zur Kulturgeschichte Ägyptens Festschrift für Rainer Stadelmann zur Vollendung des 65. Lebensjahres.* Mainz, 1998, forthcoming.

EDEL, E. 'Studien zu den Relieffragmenten aus dem Taltempel des Königs Snofru' in Manuelian, P. D. ed. *Studies in Honor of William Kelly Simpson.* Boston, 1996, 199–208.

EDWARDS, I. E. S. 'The Pyramid of Seila and its Place in the Succession of Snofru's Pyramids' in Goring, E., Reeves, N., and Ruffle, J. eds. *Chief of Seers: Egyptian Studies in Memory of Cyril Aldred.* London and New York, 1997, 88–96.

EL-METWALLY, E. *Entwicklung der Grabdekoration in den Altägyptischen Privatgräbern: Ikonographische Analyse der Totenkultdarstellungen von der Vorgeschichte bis zum Ende der 4. Dynastie.* Göttinger Orientforschungen IV. Reihe: Ägypten, Band 24. Wiesbaden, 1992.

HARPUR, Y. 'The Identity and Positions of Relief Fragments in Museums and Private Collections: The Reliefs of *R'-htp* and *Nfrt* from Meydum' *JEA* 72, 1986, 23–40; and *JEA* 73, 1987, 197–200.

HAWASS, Z. 'The Discovery of the Satellite Pyramid of Khufu (GI-d)' in Manuelian, P. D. ed. *Studies in Honor of William Kelly Simpson.* Boston, 1996, 379–98.

HAWASS, Z. 'The Discovery of the Harbors of Khufu and Khafre at Giza' in Berger, C. and Mathieu, B. eds. *Études sur l'Ancien Empire et la nécropole de Saqqara dédiées à Jean-Philippe Lauer.* Orientalia Monspeliensia 9, Montpellier, 1997, 245–56.

HAWASS, Z. 'Pyramid Construction: New Evidence Discovered in Giza' in Heike Guksch and Daniel Polz (eds.) *Stationen: Beiträge zur Kulturgeschichte Ägyptens Festschrift für Rainer Stadelmann zur Vollendung des 65. Lebensjahres.* Mainz, 1998, forthcoming.

JUNGE, F. 'Hem-iuni, Anch-ha-ef und die sog. Ersatzköpfe' in Stadelmann, R. and Sourouzian, H. *Kunst des Alten Reiches: Symposium im Deutschen Archäologischen Institut Kairo am 29. und 30. Oktober 1991.* (DAIAK Sonderschrift 28) Mainz, 1995, 103–9.

JOHNSON, G. B. 'The Red Pyramid of Sneferu, Inside and Out' *KMT: A Modern Journal of Ancient Egypt* 8, No. 3, Fall 1997, 18–27. An excellent account with photographs and a useful bibliography in the notes.

JOHNSON, G. B. 'The Mysterious Cache-Tomb of Fourth Dynasty Queen Hetepheres' *KMT: A Modern Journal of Ancient Egypt* 6, No. 1, Spring 1995, 34–50.

KELLEY, A. L. 'Reserve Heads: A Review of the Evidence for their Placement and Function in Old Kingdom Tombs' *JSSEA* 5, No. 1, 1974, 6–12.

LACOVARA, P. 'The Riddle of the Reserve Heads' *KMT: A Modern Journal of Ancient Egypt* 8, No. 4, Winter 1997–1998, 28–36.

LEHNER, M. *The Pyramid Tomb of Hetepheres and the Satellite Pyramid of Khufu.* SDAIK, Cairo, 1985.

LEHNER, M. 'Niches, slots, grooves and stains: Internal frame works in the Khufu Pyramids?' in Heike Guksch and Daniel Polz (eds.) *Stationen: Beiträge zur Kulturgeschichte Ägyptens Festschrift für Rainer Stadelmann zur Vollendung des 65. Lebensjahres.* Mainz, 1998, forthcoming.

LESKO, B. S. 'Queen Khamerernebty II and Her Sculpture' in Lesko, L. H. ed. *Ancient Egyptian and Mediterranean Studies in Memory of William A. Ward.* Providence, 1998, 149–62.

MANUELIAN, P. D. 'The Problem of the Giza Slab Stelae' in Heike Guksch and Daniel Polz (eds.) *Stationen: Beiträge zur Kulturgeschichte Ägyptens Festschrift für Rainer Stadelmann zur Vollendung des 65. Lebensjahres.* Mainz, 1998, forthcoming.

MILLET, N. B. 'The Reserve Heads of the Old Kingdom' in Simpson, W. K. and Davis, W. *Studies in Ancient Egypt, the Aegean, and the Sudan: Essays in honor of Dows Dunham on his 90th birthday, June 1, 1980.* Boston, 1981.

RZEPKA, S. 'Hidden Statues and Reliefs in Old Kingdom Tombs: Some Remarks on the tombs of Mersyankh III (G 7520–7540) and Nebemakhet (LG 86)' *GM* 164, 1998, 101–9.

RZEPKA, S. 'Some Remarks on two Mycerinus Group Statues' *GM* 166, 1998, 77–90.

SCHMIDT, H. 'Zur Determination und Ikonographie der Sogenannten Ersatzköpfe' *SÄK* 18, 1991, 331–48. See also entries under Junge, Kelley, Lacovara and Millet (above) and Tefnin and Wildung (below).

SCOTT, G. D. III 'An Old Kingdom Sculpture in the San Antonio Museum of Art' in Manuelian, P. D. ed. *Studies in Honor of William Kelly Simpson.* Boston, 1996, 718–23.

STADELMANN, R. 'Der Strenge Stil der frühen Vierten Dynastie' in Stadelmann, R. and Sourouzian, H. eds. *Kunst des Alten Reiches: Symposium im Deutschen Archäologischen Institut Kairo am 29. und 30. Oktober 1991.* (DAIAK Sonderschrift 28), Mainz, 1995, 155–66.

STADELMANN, R. 'The development of the pyramid temple in the Fourth Dynasty' in Quirke, S. ed. *The Temple in Ancient Egypt. New discoveries and recent research.* London, 1997, 1–16.

STADELMANN, R. 'Formale Kriterien zur Datierung der königlichen Plastik der 4. Dynastie' in Grimal, N. ed. *Les critères de datation stylistiques à l'Ancien Empire.* Cairo, IFAOC Bd'E 120 1998, 353–88.

TEFNIN, R. 'Les têtes magiques de Gizeh' *BSFE* 120, 1991, 25–37.

TEFNIN, R. *Art et Magie au temps des Pyramides: L'énigme des têtes dites 'de renplacement',* Monumenta Aegyptiaca V, Bruxelles 1991.

WILDUNG, D. 'Technologische Bemerkungen zur Kunst des Alten Reiches. Neue Fakten zu den Ersatzköpfen' in Grimal, N. ed. *Les critères de datation stylistiques à l'Ancien Empire.* Cairo, Bd'E 120 1998, 399–406.

CHAPTERS 6 AND 7 DYNASTY V (2565–2420 B.C.) AND DYNASTY VI (2420–2258 B.C.)

ALTENMÜLLER, H. 'Fragen zur Ikonographie des Grabherrn in der 5. Dynastie des Alten Reiches' in Stadelmann, R. and Sourouzian, H. eds. *Kunst des Alten Reiches: Symposium im Deutschen Archäologischen Institut Kairo am 29. und 30. Oktober 1991.* (DAIAK Sonderscrift 28), Mainz, 1995, 19–32.

ALTENMÜLLER, H. *Die Wanddarstellungen im Grab des Mehu in Saqqara* (AV 42), Mainz, 1998. Dated early in the reign of Teti, Dynasty 6.

BEAUX, N. 'Le mastaba de Ti à Saqqara. Architecture de la tombe et orientation des personnages figurés' in Berger, C. and Mathieu, B. eds. *Études sur l'Ancien Empire et la nécropole de Saqqara dédiées à Jean-Philippe Lauer.* Orientalia Monspeliensia 9, Montpellier, 1997, 89–98.

GAMER-WALLERT, I. *Von Giza bis Tübingen: Die bewegte Geschichte der Mastaba G 5170.* Tübingen, 1998.

HAWASS, Z. and VERNER, M. 'Newly discovered blocks from the causeway of Sahure' *MDAIK* 52, 1996, 177–86. Among the most significant blocks is a representation of men dragging a pyramidion as well as a block of bedouin in a 'famine' scene, the latter indicating a prototype for the famous scenes at the causeway of Unas at the end of the dynasty, which have now lost their claim to priority and originality. A possible explanation of the scene may be a visit by Egyptians to the deserts to search for stone for a pyramidion and the discovery of emaciated bedouin during their mission.

KAISER, W. 'Zu den Sonnenheiligtümern der 5. Dynastie' *MDAIK* 14, 1956, 104–16.

KANAWATI, N. and HASSAN, A. *The Tomb of Ankhmahor.* The Teti Cemetery at Saqqara II, The Australian Centre for Egyptology: Reports 9, Warminster, 1997.

LABROUSSE, A. and MOUSSA, A. M. *Le Temple d'accueil du Complexe Funéraire du Roi Ounas* (IFAO BdE 111) Cairo, 1996.

LABROUSSE, A. *L'Architecture des Pyramides à Textes.* Mission Archéologique de Saqqara III. I Saqqara Nord. 2 vols (IFAOC BdE 114, 1, 2). Cairo, 1996.

MINAULT-GOUT, A. *Le mastaba d'Ima-Pépi (Mastaba II).* Balat II, *Fouilles de l'IFAOC* 33, Cairo, 1992.

MUNRO, P. 'Bemerkungen zur Datierung *Mttj's*, zu seinen Statuen Brooklyn 51.1/Kansas City 51–1 und zu verwandten Rundbildern' in *Hommages à Jean Leclant* I, IFAOC Bd'E 106/1, Cairo 1994, 245–77. Dates the tomb and its statues to the First Intermediate Period or early Middle Kingdom.

Moussa, A. M. and Altenmüller, H. *Das Grab des Nianchchnum und Chnumhotep* (AV 21). Mainz, 1977.

O'Connor, D. 'Sexuality, Statuary and the Afterlife; Scenes in the Tomb-chapel of Pepyankh (Heny the Black). An Interpretive Essay' in Manuelian, P. D. ed. *Studies in Honor of William Kelly Simpson*. Boston, 1996, 621–33.

Patocková, B. 'Fragments de statues découvertes dans le mastaba de Ptahchepses à Abousir' in Grimal, N. ed. *Les critères de datation stylistiques à l'Ancien Empire*. Cairo, IFAOC Bd'E 120, 1998, 227–34.

Rochholz, M. 'Sedfest, Sonnenheiligtum und Pyramidenbezirk: Zur Deutung der Grabanlagen der Könige der 5. und 6. Dynastie' in Gundlach, R. and Rochholz, M. eds. *Ägyptische Tempel – Struktur, Funktion und Programm.* HÄB 37, 1994, 255–80.

Romano, J. 'Sixth Dynasty Royal Sculpture' in Grimal, N. ed. *Les critères de datation stylistiques à l'Ancien Empire*. Cairo, IFAOC Bd'E 120, 1998, 235–304.

Russmann, E. R. 'A Second Style in Egyptian Art in the Old Kingdom' *MDAIK* 51, 1995, 269–79. Consideration of a different style of statuary well represented in Dynasty 6 with exaggeration of some features and suppression of others, the features including overlarge heads with long, narrow bodies pinched at the waist.

Vallogia, M. *Le mastaba de Medou-nefer*. Balat I, Cairo, *Fouilles de l'IFAOC* 31, 1986, 1–2.

Verner, M. 'Les sculptures de Reneferef découvertes à Abousir' *BIFAO* 85, 1985, 267–80. Publication of extremely fine small statues of the king from his pyramid complex.

Verner, M. 'Les statuettes en bois d'Abousir' *RdE* 36, 1985, 145–52. A group of small wooden statuettes of prisoners.

Verner, M. *Forgotten Pharaohs, Lost Pyramids: Abusir*. Prague, 1994. An abundantly illustrated account of the important new excavations at Abusir, with the discovery of statuary, significant architecture, and a hitherto unknown pyramid, as well as private tombs, including the huge mastaba of Ptahshepses.

Verner, M. *Abusir. The Mastaba of Ptahshepses, Reliefs* I. Prague. 1977.

Verner, M. and Callender, G. 'Two Old Kingdom Queens named Khentkaus' *KMT: A Modern Journal of Ancient Egypt* 8, No. 3, Fall 1997, 28–35.

Wildung, D. *Ni-user-re: Sonnenkönig-Sonnengott*. Munich, 1984. Publication of a pair of statues of this ruler acquired by the Munich museum.

Winter, E. 'Zur Deutung der Sonnenheiligtümer der 5. Dynastie' *WZKM* 54, 1957, 222–33.

Ziegler, C. *Le mastaba d'Akhethetep. Une chapelle funéraire de l'ancien empire*. Paris, 1993.

PART THREE: THE GROWTH OF THE MIDDLE KINGDOM AND ITS COLLAPSE

GENERAL

Bourriau, J. *Pharaohs and Mortals: Egyptian Art in the Middle Kingdom* (Exhibition Catalogue). Cambridge, 1988.

Delange, E. *Catalogue des statues égyptiennes du Moyen Empire, Musée du Louvre.* Paris, 1987.

Flammini, 'The "*ḥꜣtyw-*" from Byblos in the Early Second Millennium B. C.' *GM* 164, 1998, 41–61.

Robins, G. ed. *Beyond the Pyramids. Egyptian Regional Art from the Museo Egizio, Turin*. Atlanta, 1990.

Tooley, A. M. J. 'Notes on wooden models and the "Gebelein" Style' in Eyre, C. et al. eds. *The Unbroken Reed: Studies in the Culture and Heritage of Ancient Egypt in Honour of A. F. Shore*, London, 1994, 343–53.

Wildung, D. *Sesostris und Amenemhet: Ägypten im Mittleren Reich*. Munich, 1984. Also in a French translation.

CHAPTERS 8 AND 9 THE FIRST INTERMEDIATE PERIOD: DYNASTIES VII–X (2258–2052 B.C.) AND DYNASTY XI (2134–1991 B.C.)

Allen, J. P. 'Some Theban Officials of the Early Middle Kingdom' in Manuelian, P. D. ed. *Studies in Honor of William Kelly Simpson*. Boston, 1996, 1–26.

Arnold, D. *Der Tempel des Königs Mentuhotep von Deir el-Bahari. Band I: Architektur und Bedeutung* (AV 8). Mainz, 1974; Band II: *Die Wandreliefs des Sanktuares* (AV 11). Mainz, 1974; Band III: *Die Königlichen Beigaben* (AV 23). Mainz, 1981. *The Temple of Mentuhotep at Deir el-Bahari*. New York, 1979.

Arnold, D. *Das Grab des Jni-jtj.f: Die Architektur*. Grabung im Asasif 1963–1970 Band I. Mainz, 1971.

Brovarski, E. J. 'A Stele of the First Intermediate Period from Naga-ed-Dêr' *Medelhavsmuseet Bulletin* 18, 1983, 3–11.

Brovarski, E. J. 'Akhmîm in the Old Kingdom and First Intermediate Period' in Paule Posener-Krieger ed. *Mélanges Gamal Eddin Mokhtar* I, Cairo 1985, 117–54.

Brovarski, E. J. 'Abydos in the Old Kingdom and First Intermediate Period, Part 1' in Catharine Berger et al. eds. *Hommages à Jean Leclant* 1, Paris 1994, 99 ff.

Brovarski, E. J. 'Abydos in the Old Kingdom and First Intermediate Period, Part 2' in David Silverman ed. *For His Ka: Essays Offered in Memory of Klaus Baer*. Chicago, 1994, 15–44.

Brovarski, E. J. 'Ahanakht of Bersheh and the Hare Nome in the First Intermediate Period' in Simpson, W. K. and Davis, W. eds. *Studies in honor of Dows Dunham*. Boston, 1981, 14–30.

Brovarski, E. 'A Coffin from Farshût in the Museum of Fine Arts, Boston' in Lesko, L. H. ed. *Ancient Egyptian and Mediterranean Studies in Memory of William A. Ward*. Providence, 1998, 376–9.

Freed, R. E. 'Relief Styles of the Nebhepetre Montuhotep Funerary Temple Complex' in Goring, E., Reeves, N., and Ruffle, J. eds. *Chief of Seers: Egyptian Studies in Memory of Cyril Aldred*. London and New York, 1997, 148–63.

Hölzl, C. 'Studien zur Entwicklung der Felsgräber: Datierung und lokale Entwicklung der Felsgräber des Mittleren Reiches in Mittelägypten'. Ph.D. dissertation, Vienna, 1984.

Jaroš-Deckert, B. *Das Grab Jnj-jtj.f: Die Wandmalereien der XI. Dynastie.* Grabung im Asasif 1963–1970 Band V. Mainz am Rhein, 1984. With important reviews by H. Willems in *BiOr* 46, 1989, 592–601, M. Eaton-Krauss in *JEA* 74, 1988, and R. Freed in *CdE* 63, 1988, 286–9.

Müller-Wollermann, R. 'Krisenfaktoren im ägyptischen Staat des ausgehenden Alten Reich'. Ph.D. dissertation, Tübingen, 1986.

Seidelmeier, S. J. *Gräberfelder aus dem Übergang vom Alten zum Mittleren Reich: Studien zur Archäologie der Ersten Zwischenzeit*, SAGA 1, Heidelberg, 1990.

Spanel, D. B. 'Beni Hasan in the Herakleopolitan Periuod'. Ph.D. dissertation, University of Toronto, 1984.

Spanel, D. B. 'Ancient Egyptian Boat Models of the Herakleopolitan Period and the Eleventh Dynasty' *SAK* 12, 1985, 243–53.

Spanel, D. B. 'The Herakleopolitan Tombs of Kheti I, *Jt(.j)jb(.j)*, and Kheti II at Asyut' *Orientalia* 58, 1989, 301–14.

CHAPTER 10 DYNASTY XII (1991–1786 B.C.)

Arnold, D. 'Two New Mastabas of the Twelfth Dynasty at Dahshur' *Egyptian Archaeology* 9, 1996, 23–5.

Arnold, D. and D. *Der Tempel Qasr el-Sagha* (AV 27). Mainz, 1979.

Arnold, D. *Der Pyramidenbezirk des Königs Amenemhet III in Dahschur*. Band I: *Die Pyramide* (AV 53), Mainz, 1987.

Arnold, D. 'Amenemhat I and the Early Twelfth Dynasty at Thebes' *Metropolitan Museum Journal* 26, 1991, 5–48.

Bourriau, J. 'The Dolphin Vase from Lisht' in Manuelian, P. D. ed. *Studies in Honor of William Kelly Simpson*. Boston, 1996, 101–16.

Bourriau, J. 'An Early Twelfth Dynasty Sculpture' in Goring, E., Reeves, N., and Ruffle, J. *Chief of Seers: Egyptian Studies in Memory of Cyril Aldred*. London and New York, 1997, 49–59.

Delange, E. *Catalogue des statues égyptiennes du Moyen-Empire. 2060–1560 avant J.C. Musée du Louvre*. Paris, 1987.

Fay, B. 'The Louvre Sphinx, A 23' in Stadelmann, R. and Sourouzian, H. eds. *Kunst des Alten Reiches: Symposium im Deutschen Archäologischen Institut Kairo am 29. und 30. Oktober 1991*. (DAIAK Sonderschrift 28), Mainz, 1995, 75–9.

Fay, B. *The Louvre Sphinx and Royal Sculpture from the Reign of Amenemhat II*. Mainz, 1996. Dated by Cherpion in Dynasty IV (see above).

Fay, B. 'The "Abydos Princess"', *MDAIK* 52, 1996, 115–41. An extensive and detailed account of a statue from Petrie's excavations in the ruins of the Osiris Temple (Cairo JdE 36359) identified by the author as a statue of a deity and dated to the reign of Amenemhet III. With many illustrations and parallels cited.

Fay, B. 'Missing Parts' in Goring, E., Reeves, N., and Ruffle, J. *Chief of Seers: Egyptian Studies in Memory of Cyril Aldred*. London and New York, 1997, 97–112. Locates the missing base of the standing statue of Amenemhet III in the Louvre (N 464) in the Egyptian Museum, Cairo, and the lower part of the statue of Sirenput II (British Museum 1010) with its upper part (British Museum 98).

Franke, D. *Personendaten aus dem Mittleren Reich (20.–16. Jahrhundert v. Chr.). Dossiers 1–796*. ÄAbh 41, Wiesbaden, 1984.

Franke, D. *Das Heiligtum des Heqaib auf Elephantine: Geschichte eines Provinzheiligtums im Mittleren Reich*. SAGA 9, Heidelberg, 1994.

Freed, R. E. 'Stela Workshops of Early Dynasty 12' in Manuelian, P. D. ed. *Studies in Honor of William Kelly Simpson*. Boston, 1996, 297–336.

Gabolde, L. 'Les Temples primitifs d'Amon-Re à Karnak, leur emplacements et leurs vestiges; une hypothèse' in Heike Guksch and Daniel Polz (eds.) *Stationen: Beiträge zur Kulturgeschichte Ägyptens Festschrift für Rainer Stadelmann zur Vollendung des 65. Lebensjahres*. Mainz, 1998, forthcoming.

GALÁN, J. M. 'Bullfight Scenes in Ancient Egyptian Tombs' *JEA* 80, 1994, 81–96.

GORESY, A. et al. 'Egyptian Blue–Cuprorivaite, A Window to Ancient Egyptian Technology' *Die Naturwissenschaften*, 70, Jg., 11, 1983.

HABACHI, L. (with contributions by Haeny, G. and Junge, F.) *The Sanctuary of Heqaib. Elephantine IV.* (AV 33), 2 vols Cairo, 1985.

HIRSCH, E. 'Die Kultpolitik Amenemhets I. im Thebanischen Gau' in Gundlach, R. and Rochholz, M. eds. *Ägyptische Tempel – Struktur, Funktion und Programm*, (HÄB 37), 1994, 137–42.

KAMRIN, J. *The Cosmos of Khnumhotep II.* London, 1998.

O'CONNOR, D. B. 'The <Cenotaphs> of the Middle Kingdom at Abydos' in *Mélanges Gamal eddin Mokhtar, IFAOC Bd'E* 97, Cairo, 1985, 161–77.

OPPENHEIM, A. 'The Jewellery of Queen Weret.' *Egyptian Archaeology* 9, 1996, 26.

QUIRKE, S. 'Gods in the temple of the king: Anubis at Lahun' in Quirke, S. ed. *The Temple in Ancient Egypt. New discoveries and recent research.* London, 1997, 24–48. With extensive bibliography on the site.

POLZ, F. 'Die Bildnisse Sesostris' III. und Amenemhets III.: Bemerkungen zur königlichen Rundplastik der späten 12. Dynastie' *MDAIK* 51, 1995, 227–54. An extensive and well illustrated study of the statuary of the two rulers, with special regard to the facial features and the different styles within each ruler (ex. realistic, idealizing, stylized, youthful) and geographical and material considerations.

ROTH, A. M. and ROEHRIG, C. 'The Bersha Procession: A New Reconstruction' *Journal of the Museum of Fine Arts, Boston*, 1989, 31–40.

SCHOSKE, S. 'Historisches Bewusstsein in der ägyptischen Kunst' *MjbK* 38, Munich, 1987, 7–26.

SHEDID, A. G. *Die Felsgräber von Beni Hassan in Mittelägypten.* Mainz, Zaberns Bildbände zur Archäologie 16, 1994. Particularly valuable for the colour photographs of the recently cleaned wall surfaces.

SOUROUZIAN, H. 'Standing Royal Colossi of the Middle Kingdom Reused by Ramesses II' *MDAIK* 44, 1988, 229–54.

SOUROUZIAN, H. 'A Headless Sphinx of Sesostris II from Heliopolis in the Egyptian Museum. Cairo, JE 37796' in Manuelian, P. D. ed. *Studies in Honor of William Kelly Simpson.* Boston, 1996, 744–54.

STRAUSS-SEEBER, C. 'Zu Bildprogramm und Funktion der Weissen Kapelle in Karnak' in Gundlach, R. and Rochholz, M. eds. *Ägyptische Tempel – Struktur, Funktion und Programm* (HÄB 37), 1994, 287–318.

VALBELLE, D. and BONNET, C. *Le sanctuaire d'Hathor, maîtresse de la turquoise: Sérabit el Khadim au Moyen Empire.* Paris, 1996.

WEGNER, J. W. 'The Nature and Chronology of the Senwosret III-Amenemhat III Regnal Succession: Some Considerations based on New Evidence from the Mortuary Temple of Senwosret III at Abydos.' *JNES* 55, 1996, 249–279.

CHAPTER 12 THE SECOND INTERMEDIATE PERIOD: DYNASTIES XIII–XVII (1786–1570 B.C.)

BIETAK, M. ed. *An International Symposium at the Metropolitan Museum: Trade, Power and Cultural Exchange: Hyksos Egypt and the Eastern Mediterranean World 1800–1500 B.C.* Vienna, 1995. Several essays, including studies of the Minoan wall paintings from Avaris and the parallels from Knossos and elsewhere. The individual articles are not listed in this bibliography.

BIETAK, M. *Avaris: The Capital of the Hyksos. Recent Excavations at Tell el-Dab'a.* London, 1996.

BIETAK, M. 'Dab'a, Tell ed-' in Myers, E. ed. *The Oxford Encyclopedia of Archaeology in the Near East.* Vol. II, 99–101. New York, 1997.

DAVIES, W. V. and SCHOFIELD, L. eds. *Egypt, the Aegean and the Levant: Interconnections in the Second Millennium BC.* London, 1995.

FAY, B. 'Amenemhat V – Vienna/Assuan' *MDAIK* 44, 1988, 67–77.

OREN, E. D. ed. *The Hyksos: New Historical and Archaeological Perspectives.* University Museum Monograph 96, Philadelphia, 1997. A series of essays from a symposium, with studies on the Aegean and Middle Bronze relations of the Hyksos.

POLZ, D. 'Theban und Avaris. Zur <Vertreibung> der Hyksos' in Heike Guksch and Daniel Polz (eds.) *Stationen: Beiträge zur Kulturgeschichte Ägyptens Festschrift für Rainer Stadelmann zur Vollendung des 65. Lebensjahres.* Mainz, 1998, forthcoming.

RYHOLT, K. S. B. *The Political Situation in Egypt during the Second Intermediate Period c. 1800–1550 B.C.* Carsten Niebuhr Institute Publications 20, Copenhagen 1997.

SZAFRANSKI, Z. E. 'Observations on the Second Intermediate Period relief' in Schmitz, B. and Eggebrecht, A. *Festschrift Jürgen von Beckerath zum 70. Geburtstagam 19. Februar 1990.* HÄB 30, 1990, 245–51.

PART FOUR: THE NEW KINGDOM

GENERAL

ARNOLD, D. *Wandrelief und Raumfunktion in Ägyptischen Tempeln des Neuen Reiches.* (MÄS 2). Berlin, 1962.

ASSAAD, H. A. 'The House of Thutnefer and Egyptian Architectural Drawings' *The Ancient World, Egyptological Miscellanies.* VI, Nos 1–4, 1983, 3–20.

ASSMANN, J. 'Flachbildkunst des Neuen Reiches' in Vandersleyen, Claude ed. *Propyläen Kunstgeschichte 15, Das Alte Ägypten.* Berlin, 1975, 304–25.

ASSMANN, J. 'Die Gestalte der Zeit in der ägyptischen Kunst' in *500 Jahre Ägypten – Genese und Permanenz pharaonischer Kunst.* Heidelberg, 1983, 11–32.

BAINES, J. 'Temple Symbolism' *Royal Anthropological Institute News*, No. 15, 1976, 10–15.

CHERPION, N. 'Quelques jalons pour une histoire de la peinture thebaine' *BSFE* 110, 1987, 27–47.

CHERPION, N. 'Note sur l'emploi des fonds jaunes dans la peinture thebaine.' *GM* 101, 1988, 19–20.

CHERPION, N. 'Le «cone d'onguent», gage de survie' *BIFAO* 94, 1994, 79–106.

DAVIES, N. *The Town-House in Ancient Egypt. MMS* I, Part 2, 1929.

DZIOBEK, E., SCHNEYER, T., and SEMMELBAUER, N. *Eine ikonographische Datierungsmethode für thebanisiche Wandmalerei der 18. Dynastie.* SAGA 3. Heidelberg, 1992.

ENGELMANN-VON CARNAP, B. 'Zur zeitlichen Einordnung der Dekoration thebanischer Privatgräber der 18. Dynastie anhand der Fisch- und Vogelfangs-Bildes' in Heike Guksch and Daniel Polz (eds.) *Stationen: Beiträge zur Kulturgeschichte Ägyptens Festschrift für Rainer Stadelmann zur Vollendung des 65. Lebensjahres.* Mainz, 1998, forthcoming.

GUKSCH, H. *Königsdienst zur Selbstdarstellung der Beamten in der 18. Dynastie.* SAGA 11, Heidelberg, 1994.

HORNUNG, E. *Das Tal der Könige, die Ruhestätte der Pharaonen.* Zurich–Munich, 1982.

HORNUNG, E. *The Valley of the Kings: Horizon of Eternity.* New York, 1990.

JAMES, T. G. H. *Egyptian Painting and Drawing in the British Museum.* London, 1985.

VON KAMPP, F. *Die thebanische Nekropole zum Wandel des Grabgedankens von der XVIII. bis zur XX. Dynastie.* Mainz, 1996.

MACKAY, E. *The Representation of Shawls with a Rippled Stripe in the Theban Tombs. JEA* 10, 1924, 41–3.

MANNICHE, L. 'Reflections on the banquet scene' in Tefnin, R. ed. *La Peinture Égyptienne Ancienne: Un Monde de Signes à Préserver.* Monumenta Aegyptiaca VII, Série Imago no. 1, Brussels, 1997, 29–36.

O'CONNOR, D. B. 'City and Palace in New Kingdom Egypt' *CRIPL* 11, 1989, 73–87.

RADWAN, A. *Die Darstellung des regierenden Königs und seiner Familienangehörigen in den Privatgräbern der 18. Dynastie.* (MÄS 21), Munich, 1969.

REEVES, N. and WILKINSON, R. H. *The Complete Valley of the Kings: Tombs and Treasures of Egypt's Greatest Pharaohs.* London 1996.

ROBINS, G. 'The "Feminization" of the Male Figure in New Kingdom Two-Dimensional Art' in Goring, E., Reeves, N., and Ruffle, J. *Chief of Seers: Egyptian Studies in Memory of Cyril Aldred.* London and New York, 1997, 251–65.

SEYRIED, K.-J. 'Kammern, Nischen und Passagen in Felsgräben des Neuen Reiches' in Heike Guksch and Daniel Polz (eds.) *Stationen: Beiträge zur Kulturgeschichte Ägyptens Festschrift für Rainer Stadelmann zur Vollendung des 65. Lebensjahres.* Mainz, 1998, forthcoming.

TEFNIN, R. *La Peinture Égyptienne Ancienne: Un Monde de Signes à Préserver.* Monumenta Aegyptiaca VII, Série Imago no. 1, Brussels, 1997. Essays from a colloquium in 1994 with contributions on specific tombs and a series of articles on conservation problems and computer programs.

TEFNIN, R. 'Réflexions liminaires sur la peinture égyptienne, sa nature, son histoire, son déchiffrement et son avenir' in Tefnin, R. ed. *La Peinture Égyptienne Ancienne: Un Monde de Signes à Préserver.* Monumenta Aegyptiaca VII, Série Imago no. 1, Brussels, 1997, 3–9.

WULLEMAN, R., KUNNEN, M., and MEKHITARIAN, A. *Passage to Eternity.* Knokke (Belgium), 1989. On the tombs on the western bank at Thebes, both royal and private, with impressive colour photography.

CHAPTER 13 THE EARLY EIGHTEENTH DYNASTY: AHMOSE-TUTHMOSIS III (1570–1450 B.C.)

BEAUX, N. *Le Cabinet de curiosités de Thoutmosis III. Plantes et animaux du <Jardin botanique> de Karnak.* OLA 36, Leuven, 1990.

BIETAK, M. 'Le début de la XVIIIe dynastie et les Minoans à Avaris' *BSFE* 135, 1996, 5–29. For the subject, see entries above under the Second Intermediate Period.

DAVIES, W. V. *The statuette of Queen Tetisheri: A reconsideration*. British Museum Occasional Paper No. 36. London, 1984. Shows that the British Museum statuette, illustrated as Pl. 85 (B) in the first edition of this work and fig. 218 of the 1981 edition, is possibly a modern forgery based on a statuette in Cairo.

DORMAN, P. F. *The Monuments of Senenmut, Problems in Historical Methodology*. London and New York, 1988.

DORMAN, P. F. *The Tombs of Senenmut: The Architecture and Decoration of Tombs 71 and 353*. New York, 1991.

DZIOBEK, E. *Das Grab des Ineni, Theben Nr. 81*. (AV 68). Mainz, 1992.

DZIOBEK, E. *Die Gräber des Vezirs User-Amun Theben Nr. 61 und 131* (AV 84), Mainz, 1994. Dated to the first half of the reign of Thutmose III.

FAY, B. 'Tuthmoside Studies' *MDAIK* 51, 1995, 11–22. Study of four uninscribed statues (mainly heads) of Thutmose III, as part of an on-going compilation of sculpture representing the king, and one uninscribed head attributed to Amenhotep II. Inscribed statues of the same period are utilized in making the attributions.

GUKSCH, H. *Die Gräber des Nakht-Min und des Men-cheper-Ra-seneb (Theben Nr. 87 und 79)*. (AV 34), Mainz, 1995.

GUKSCH, H. *Das Grab des Benja, gen. Paheqamen Theben Nr. 343* (AV 7), Mainz, 1978.

HARVEY, S. P. 'Monuments of Ahmose at Abydos' *Egyptian Archaeology* 4, 1994, 3–5.

Lacovara, P. *The New Kingdom Royal City*. New York, 1997.

Lacovara, P. ed. *Deir el-Ballas: preliminary report on the Deir el-Ballas Expedition, 1980–1986*. Winona Lake, Indiana, 1990.

LINDBLAD, I. *Royal Sculpture of the Early Eighteenth Dynasty in Egypt*. Stockholm, 1984. (rev. by Romano *BiOr* 42, 1985, 614–19).

MALEK, J. 'The Locusts on the Daggers of Ahmose' in Goring, E., Reeves, N., and Ruffle, J. eds. *Chief of Seers: Egyptian Studies in Memory of Cyril Aldred*. London and New York, 1997, 207–19.

MANUELIAN, P. D. and LOEBEN, C. E. 'From Daughter to Father: The Recarved Egyptian Sarcophagus of Queen Hatshepsut and King Thutmose I' *Journal of the Museum of Fine Arts, Boston* 5, 1993, 24–65.

MANUELIAN, P. D. and LOEBEN, C. E. 'New Light on the Recarved Sarcophagus of Hatshepsut and Thutmose I in the Museum of Fine Arts, Boston' *JEA* 79, 1993, 121–55.

MEYER, C. *Senenmut: Eine prosopographische Untersuchung*, HÄS 2, Hamburg, 1982.

MYSLIWIEC, K. *Eighteenth Dynasty before the Amarna Period*. Iconography of Religions, Section XVI: Egypt, Fascicle 5. Leiden, 1985.

MYSLIWIEC, K. *Le portrait Royal dans le Bas-Relief du nouvel Empire*. Warsaw, 1976.

ROMANO, J. F. 'Observations on Early Eighteenth Dynasty Royal Sculpture' *JARCE* 13, 1976, 97–111.

TEFNIN, R. 'Contribution à l'iconographie d'Aménophis I' *Annuaire de l'Institut de Philologie et d'Histoire Orientales et Slaves* 20, 1968–1972, 433–7.

VANDERSLEYEN, C. 'Le nez de Touthmosis III' in Cannuyer, C. and Kruchten, J.-M. eds. *Individu, Société et Spiritualite dans l'Egypte Pharaonique et Copte: Melanges Theodorides*. Ath-Brussels-Mons, 1993, 257–62.

WACHSMANN, S. *Aegeans in the Theban Tombs*. OLA 20, Leuven, 1987.

CHAPTER 14 THE HEIGHT OF THE EIGHTEENTH DYNASTY:
AMENHOTEP II–AMENHOTEP III (1450–1372 B.C.)

BEINLICH-SEEBER, C. and SHEDID, A. G. *Das Grab des Userhat (TT 56)*. (AV 50). Mainz, 1987. Dated to Amenhotep II.

BICKEL, S. *Tore und andere wiederverwendete Bauteile Amenophis' III*. Untersuchungen im Totentempel des Merenptah in Theben, Band III, BABA 16, Stuttgart, 1997.

BRACK, A. and A. *Das Grab des Haremhab. Theben Nr. 78* (AV 35). Mainz, 1980. Dated to Thutmose IV.

BRACK, A. and A. *Das Grab des Tjanuni – Theben Nr. 74*. (AV 19), Mainz, 1977.

BRYAN, B. M. *The Reign of Thutmose IV*. Baltimore and London, 1991.

BRYAN, B. M. 'Striding Glazed Steatite Figures of Amenhotep III: An Example of the Purposes of Minor Arts' in Goring, E., Reeves, N., and Ruffle, J. *Chief of Seers: Egyptian Studies in Memory of Cyril Aldred*. London and New York, 1997, 60–82.

BRYAN, B. M. 'The statue program for the mortuary temple of Amenhotep III' in Quirke, S. ed. *The Temple in Ancient Egypt. New discoveries and recent research*. London, 1997, 57–81.

BRYAN, B. M. 'Portrait Scupture of Thutmose IV' *JARCE* 24, 1987, 3–20.

DZIOBEK, E. and ABDEL-RAZIK, M. *Das Grab des Sobekhotep. Theben Nr. 63*. (AV 71) Mainz, 1990. Dated to Thutmose IV.

GEßLER-LÖHR, B. 'Zur Datierung einiger königliche Truchsesse unter Amenophis' III' in Schmitz, B. and Eggebrecht, A. *Festschrift Jürgen von Beckerath zum 70. Geburtstag am 19. Februar 1990*. HÄB 30, 1990, 53–73.

HARTWIG, M. 'Style and Social Identification in Theban Tomb Painting during the Reigns of Thutmose IV and Amenhotep III' *JARCE* 36, 1999, forthcoming.

HARTWIG, M. 'Institutional Patronage and Social Commemoration in Elite Theban Tomb Paintings during the Reigns of Thutmose IV (1419–1410 B.C.) and Amenhotep III (1410–1382 B.C.)'. Ph.D. dissertation, Institute of Fine Arts, New York University, forthcoming.

HEGAZY, S. A. and TOSI, M. *A Theban Private Tomb (Tomb No. 295)* (AV 45), Mainz, 1983. Dated to Thutmose IV/Amenhotep III.

KOZLOFF, A. 'A Study of the Painters of the Tomb of Menna, No. 69' Acts. First International Congress of Egyptology in Cairo. Berlin, 1979, 395–402.

KOZLOFF, A. P. 'The Malqata/El-Amarna Blues: Favourite Colours of Kings and Gods' in Goring, E., Reeves, N., and Ruffle, J. eds. *Chief of Seers: Egyptian Studies in Memory of Cyril Aldred*. London and New York, 1997, 178–206.

KOZLOFF, A. P., BRYAN, B. M., with Berman, L. M. *Egypt's Dazzling Sun: Amenhotep III and His World*. Cleveland, 1992.

KOZLOFF, A. P. 'A Masterpiece with Three Lives: The Vatican's Statue of Tuya' in Manuelian, P. D. ed. *Studies in Honor of William Kelly Simpson*. Boston, 1996, 477–85.

LABOURY, D. 'Une relecture de la tombe de Nakht' in Tefnin, R. ed. *La Peinture Égyptienne Ancienne: Un Monde de Signes à Préserver*. Monumenta Aegyptiaca VII, Série Imago no. 1, Brussels, 1997, 49–81.

LETELLIER, B. 'Thoutmosis IV à Karnak: Hommage tardif rendu à un batisseur malchanceux' *BSFE* 122, 1991, 36–52. Discussion of major works which were reused as fill by later kings and only recently in progress of reconstruction.

MINAULT-GOUT, A. 'Une Tête de la reine Tiyi découverte dans l'Ile de Sai, au Soudan' *RdE* 47, 1996, 37–41.

MOSTAFA, M. F. *Das Grab des Neferhotep und des Meh (TT 257)*. Theben 8, Mainz, 1995.

MÜLLER, M. *Die Kunst Amenophis' III. und Echnatons*. Basel, 1988.

O'CONNOR, D. B. and CLINE, E. eds. *Amenhotep III: Perspectives on his Reign*. Ann Arbor, 1998.

PECK, W. H. 'Two Scribes and a King of Dynasty XVIII' in Goring, E., Reeves, N., and Ruffle, J. *Chief of Seers: Egyptian Studies in Memory of Cyril Aldred*. London and New York, 1997, 229–37.

POLZ, D. *Das Grab des Hui und des Kel Theben Nr. 54* (AV 74), Mainz, 1997. Dated by author to the last third of the reign of Amenhotep III, reused and added to in Dynasty 19.

SHEDID, A. G. 'Stil der Grabmalereien in der Zeit Amenophis' II. Untersucht an den Thebanischen Gräbern Nr. 104 und Nr. 80' (AV 66), Cairo, 1988. A thorough presentation of two tombs with detailed analysis of the grid lines, the different artists, work methods and finds, and an exhaustive bibliography.

SOUROUZIAN, H. 'Raccords de statues d'Aménophis III entre Karnak-Nord et le musée d'Alexandrie' *BIFAO* 97, 1997, 239–52.

STRUDWICK, N. et al. *The Tombs of Amenhotep, Khnummose, and Amenmose at Thebes (Nos 294, 253, and 254)*. Oxford, 1996.

VANDERSLEYEN, C. 'Les deux jeunesses d'Amenhotep III' *BSFE* 111, 1988, 9–30. Statuary of Amenhotep III shows a change toward young looking faces later in reign which the author assigns to just before Year 30 at start of coregency with son, to be followed later by portraits indicating age. This second 'childhood' coincides with the coregency.

WILDUNG, D. *Ägyptische Malerei, Das Grab des Nacht*. Munich–Zurich, 1978. A short account with numerous colour photographs of the tomb, dated on stylistic grounds to Thutmose IV.

WILDUNG, D. 'Métamorphoses d'une reine. La Tête berlinoise de la reine Tiyi' *BSFE* 125, 1992, 15–46. Examination of the changes of the head with the newly reunited plumes on the headdress.

CHAPTER 17 THE AMARNA PERIOD (1372–1350 B.C.)

ALDRED, C. *Akhenaten, King of Egypt*. London, 1988.

ARNOLD, Do. (with contributions by Allen, J. P. and Green, L.). *The Royal Women of Amarna: Images of Beauty from Ancient Egypt*. New York, 1996. Prepared in connection with the exhibition of the same name. Particularly valuable are the chapter on the workshop of the sculptor Thutmose and the extensive bibliography. Since the latter contains the literature up to 1995, the reader is referred to it in place of a listing of many of the same items here.

BIANCHI, R. S. 'New Light on the Aton' *GM* 114, 1990, 35–40, fig. 1. Publication of a statue with a New York dealer with sun disk replacing usual head. Author identifies it as a statue of the Aton late in reign of Amenhotep III, the sceptre and phallus sheath providing a rebus.

BURRIDGE, A. L. 'Akhenaten: A New Perspective. Evidence of a Genetic Disorder in the Royal Family of 18th Dynasty Egypt' *JSSEA* 23, 1993 (published 1996), 63–74.

DARNELL, J. C. 'Supposed Depictions of Hittites in the Amarna Period' *SÄK* 18, 1992, 113–40.

KRAUSS, R. 'Akhetaten: A Portrait in Art of an Ancient Egyptian Capital' in Sasson, J. ed. *Civilizations of the Ancient Near East*. New York, 1995, Vol. II, 749–62.

MARTIN, G. T. *A Bibliography of the Amarna Period and its Aftermath*. London, 1991.

ROBINS, G. 'The Representation of Sexual Characteristics in Amarna Art' *JSSEA* 23, 1993 (published 1996), 29–41.

SAMSON, J. with an Introduction by Smith, H. *Amarna: City of Akhenaten and Nefertiti: Nefertiti as Pharaoh*. Warminster, 1978.

CHAPTER 18 THE POST-AMARNA PERIOD (1350–1314 B.C.)

BEINLICH, H. and SALEH, M. *Corpus der Hieroglyphischen Inschriften aus dem Grab des Tutanchamun*. Oxford, 1989.

ČERNÝ, J. *Hieratic Inscriptions from the Tomb of Tutankhamun*. Tutankhamun's Tomb Series 2. Oxford, 1965.

EATON-KRAUSS, M. and GRAEFE, E. *The Small Golden Shrine from the Tomb of Tutankhamun*. Oxford, 1985. See also Kessler, D. 'Zu den Jagdszenen auf dem kleinem goldenen Tutanchamunschrein.' *GM* 90, 1986, 35–43. Kessler regards the scenes as mythologized and liturgical, and not scenes of life with sexual connotations.

EATON KRAUS, M. *The Sarcophagus in the Tomb of Tutankhamun*. Oxford, 1993. A detailed study of the changes in the construction of the sarcophagus and its lid, which was not part of the original plan.

EDWARDS, I. E. S. *Tutankhamun: His Tomb and its Treasures*. New York, 1977.

EL-KHOULI, A. et al. *Stone Vessels, Pottery, and Sealings from the Tomb of Tutankhamun*. Oxford, 1993.

HORNUNG, E. *Das Grab des Haremhab im Tal der Könige*. Bern, 1971.

JONES, D. *Model Boats from the Tomb of Tutankhamun*. Tutankhamun's Tomb Series 9, Oxford, 1990.

LITTAUER, M. A. and CROUWEL, J. H. *Chariots and Related Equipment from the Tomb of Tutankhamun*. Tutankhamun's Tomb Series 8, Oxford, 1985.

LEEK, F. F. *The Human Remains from the Tomb of Tutankhamun*. Tutankhamun's Tomb Series 5, Oxford, 1972.

MANNICHE, L. *Musical Instruments from the Tomb of Tutankhamun*. Tutankhamun's Tomb Series 6, Oxford, 1976.

MARTIN, G. T. *The Memphite Tomb of Horemheb, Commander in Chief of Tut'ankhamun, Vol. I: The Reliefs, Inscriptions, and Commentary*. London, 1989.

McLEOD, W. *Composite Bows from the Tomb of Tutankhamun*. Tutankhamun's Tomb Series 3, Oxford, 1970.

McLEOD, W. *Self Bows and other Archery Tackle from the Tomb of Tutankhamun*. Tutankhamun's Tomb Series 4, Oxford, 1982.

MEKHITARIAN, A. 'La tombe de Nebamon et Ipouky (TT 181)' in Tefnin, R. *La Peinture Égyptienne Ancienne: Un Monde de Signes à Préserver*. Monumenta Aegyptiaca VII, Série Imago no. 1, Brussels, 1997, 21–8.

MURRAY, H. and NUTTALL, M. *A Handlist of Howard Carter's Catalogue of Objects in Tutankhamun's Tomb*. Tutankhamun's Tomb Series 1, Oxford, 1963.

OCKINGA, B. G. *A Tomb from the Reign of Tutankhamun at Akhmim*. Warminster, 1997.

REEVES, N. *The Complete Tutankhamun*. London, 1990.

RUSSMANN, E. R. 'Vulture and Cobra at the King's Brow' in Goring. E. et al. eds. *Chief of Seers: Egyptian Studies in Memory of Cyril Aldred*. London and New York, 1997, 266–84.

STRUDWICK, H. and N. 'The House of Amenmose in Theban Tomb 254' in Tefnin, R. ed. *La Peinture Égyptienne Ancienne: Un Monde de Signes à Préserver*. Monumenta Aegyptiaca VII, Série Imago no. 1, Brussels, 1997, 37–47.

TAIT, W. J. *Game Boxes and Accesories from the Tomb of Tutankhamun*. Tutankhamun's Tomb Series 7, Oxford, 1982.

CHAPTER 19 THE RAMESSIDE PERIOD: DYNASTIES XIX–XX (1314–1085 B.C.)

ASSMANN, J. *Das Grab des Amenemope TT 41*. Theben 3, Mainz, 1991.

DAVID, R. *Religious Ritual at Abydos (ca. 1300 B.C.)*. Warminster, 1973.

DAVID, R. *A Guide to Religious Ritual at Abydos*. Warminster, 1981.

FEUCHT, E. *Das Grab des Nefersecheru (TT 296)*. Theben 2, Mainz, 1985.

FREED, R. E. *Ramesses the Great (Exhibition Catalogue)*. Memphis, 1987.

HARRELL, J. R. and BROWN, V. M. 'The Oldest Surviving Topographical Map from Ancient Egypt (Turin Papyri 1879, 1899, and 1969)' *JARCE* 29, 1992, 81–105.

HAYNES, J. L. 'Redating the Bat Capital in the Museum of Fine Arts, Boston' in Manuelian, P. D. ed. *Studies in Honor of William Kelly Simpson*. Boston, 1996, 399–408.

HOFFMANN, E. *Das Grab des Neferrenpet Gen. Kenro (TT 178)*. Theben 9, Mainz, 1995.

HORNUNG, E. *The Tomb of Pharaoh Seti I, Das Grab Sethos' I*. Zurich–Munich, 1991.

HORNUNG, E. *Zwei Ramessidische Königsgräber: Ramses IV. und Ramses VI.* Theben 11, Mainz, 1990.

McDONALD, J. K. *The Tomb of Nefertari: House of Eternity*. Cairo, 1996. An introduction to the tomb with many colour illustrations based on the work of the Getty Conservation Institute.

MURNANE, W. J. *United with Eternity: A Concise Guide to the Monuments of Medinet Habu*. Chicago/Cairo, 1980.

MURNANE, W. J. *The Road to Kadesh: A Historical Interpretation of the Battle Reliefs of Sety I at Karnak*. SAOC 42, Chicago, 1985.

NEGM, M. *The Tomb of Simut called Kyky: Theban Tomb 409 at Qurnah*. Warminster, 1997.

O'CONNOR, D. B. 'Mirror of the Cosmos: The Palace of Merenptah' in Bleiberg, E. and Freed, R. eds. *Fragments of a Shattered Visage*. Memphis, Monographs of the Institute of Art and Archaeology 1, 1993, 167–98.

OSING, J. *Der Tempel Sethos' I. in Gurna: Die Reliefs und Inschriften*. Band I (AV 20). Mainz, 1977.

EL SAADY, H. *The Tomb of Amenemhab, No. 44 at Qurnah: The Tomb-Chapel of a Priest Carrying the Shrine of Amun*. Warminster, 1996.

SEYFRIED, K.-J. *Das Grab des Amenmose (TT 373)*. Theben 4. Mainz, 1990.

SEYFRIED, K.-J. *Das Grab des Djehutiemhab (TT 194)*. Theben 7, Mainz, 1995.

SEYFRIED, K.-J. *Das Grab des Paenkhemenu (TT 68) und die Anlage TT 227*. Theben 6, Mainz, 1991.

SHARKAWY, A. E. *Der Amun-Tempel von Karnak: Die Funktion der Großen Säulenhalle, erschloßen aus der Analyse der Dekoration ihrer Innenwände*. Berlin, 1997.

SOUROUZIAN, H. 'Statues et représentations de statues royales sous Séthi I' *MDAIK* 49, 1993, 239–57.

SOUROUZIAN, H. *Les Monuments du Roi Merenptah*. Sonderschrift DAIAK 22, Mainz, 1989.

VANDERSLEYEN, C. 'Ramsès II admirait Sésostris Ier' in Goring, E. et al. eds. *Chief of Seers: Egyptian Studies in Memory of Cyril Aldred*. London and New York, 1997, 285–90.

PART FIVE: THE LATER PERIODS

CHAPTER 20 THE PERIOD OF DECLINE DYNASTIES XXI–XXII (1085–730 B.C.)

FAZZINI, R. A. 'Several Objects, and Some Aspects of the Art of the Third Intermediate Period' in Goring, E. et al. eds. *Chief of Seers: Egyptian Studies in Memory of Cyril Aldred*. London and New York, 1997, 113–37.

FAZZINI, R. A. *Aspects of Egyptian Art and Religious Iconography: Late Dynasty XX–Dynasty XXVI*. Forthcoming.

KITCHEN, K. A. *The Third Intermediate Period in Egypt (1100–650 B.C.)*, 2nd ed. with supplement, Warminster, 1986.

MYSLIWIEC, K. *Royal Portraiture of the Dynasties XXI–XXX*. Mainz, 1988.

NIWINSKI, A. *21st Dynasty Coffins from Thebes: Chronological and Typological Studies*. Theben 5, Mainz, 1988.

STIERLIN, H. and ZIEGLER, C. *Tanis: Trésors des Pharaons*. Paris, 1987.

YOYOTTE, J. et al. *Tanis, L'or des pharaons (Exhibition Catalogue)*. Paris/Marseilles, 1987.

THE KUSHITE SAITE REVIVAL AND THE END OF DYNASTIC EGYPT (730–332 B.C.)

ASSMANN, J. *Das Grab der Mutirdis: Grabung im Asasif 1963–1970*. Band VI (AV 13), 1977. Dated in the reign of Psamtik I.

ASSMANN, J. *Das Grab des Basa (Nr. 389). Grabung im Asasif 1963–1970*. Band II (AV 6), Mainz, 1973. Dated in Dynasty 26.

BIETAK, M. and REISER-HASLAUER, E. with plan volume by Eigner, D. *Das Grab des Anch-Hor I, II*. Untersuchungen der Zweigstelle Kairo des Österreichischen Archäologischen Institutes IV, Vienna, 1978; V, 1982; VI n.d.

EIGNER, D. *Die Monumentalen Grabbauten der Spätzeit in der Thabanischen Nekropolen*. Untersuchungen der Zweigstelle Kairo des Österreichischen Archäologischen Institutes VI. Vienna, 1984.

FAZZINI, R. A. *Egypt: Dynasty XXVI–The Macedonian Period*. Iconography of Religions 16/2. Leiden, forthcoming.

GETTY, The J. Paul Getty Museum, *Alexandria and Alexandrianism: Papers Delivered at a Symposium Organized by the J. Paul Getty Muszeum and the Getty Center for the History of Art and the Humanities and Held at the Museum April 22–25, 1993*. Malibu, 1996. A collection of important studies on Ptolemaic art.

JOSEPHSON, J. A. 'A Portrait Head of Psamtik I?' in Manuelian, P. D. ed. *Studies in Honor of William Kelly Simpson*. Boston, 1996, 429–38.

JOSEPHSON, J. A. *Egyptian royal sculpture of the Late Period: 400–246 B.C.* Sonderschrift DAIK 30. Mainz, 1997.

JOSEPHSON, J. A. '*Egyptian Sculpture of the Late Period* Revisited' JARCE 34, 1997, 1–20. A re-assessment of Bothmer's datings.

KENDALL, T. 'Fragments Lost and Found: Two Kushite Objects Augmented' in Manuelian, P. D. ed. *Studies in Honor of William Kelly Simpson*. Boston, 1996, 461–76.

KUHLMANN, K. P. and SCHENKEL, W. *Das Grab des Ibi, Obergutsverwalter der Gottesgemahlin des Amun (Thebanisches Grab Nr. 36).* Band I, 2 vols (Text and Plates), (AV 15), Mainz, 1983.

KURTH, D. 'The present state of research into Graeco-Roman temples' in Quirke, S. ed. *The Temple in Ancient Egypt. New discoveries and recent research.* London, 1997, 152–8.

LEAHY, A. 'Kushite Monuments at Abydos' in Eyre, C. et al. eds. *The Unbroken Reed: Studies in the Culture and Heritage of Ancient Egypt in Honour of A. F. Shore.* London, 1994, 171–92.

LEAHY, A. 'Saite Royal Sculpture: A Review' GM 80, 1984, 59–76.

MANUELIAN, P. D. *Living in the Past, Studies in Archaism of the Egyptian Twenty-Sixth Dynasty.* London–New York, 1994.

MANUELIAN, P. D. 'Two Fragments of Relief and a New Model for the Tomb of Montuemhet at Thebes' JEA 71, 1985, 98–121.

O'CONNOR, D. *Ancient Nubia: Egypt's Rival in Africa.* Philadelphia, 1993.

RUSSMANN, E. R. 'Relief Decoration in the Tomb of Mentuemhat (TT 34)' JARCE 31, 1994, 1–19. An overall survey of the reliefs of this important tomb with many of the reliefs represented in museums in America and elsewhere. With detailed references.

RUSSMANN, E. R. 'The Motif of the Bound Papyrus Plants and the Decorative Program in Montuemhat's First Court' JARCE 32, 1995, 117–26. Points out that the bound papyrus plants occur on many coffins, and that this suggests that the large court actually represents a huge coffin with its ceiling the open sky.

RUSSMANN, E. R. 'Mentuemhat's Kushite Wife (Further Remarks on the Decoration of the Tomb of Mentuemhat, 2)' JARCE 34, 1997, 21–40.

SHINNIE, P. *Meroe: A Civilisation of the Sudan.* London, 1967.

SHUBERT, S. B. 'Realistic Currents in Portrait Sculpture of the Saite and Persian Periods in Egypt' JSSEA 19, 1989, 27–47.

WELSBY, D. A. *The Kingdom of Kush: The Napatan and Meroitic Empires.* London, 1996.

EGYPT AFTER THE PHARAOHS

ASHTON, S.-A. 'Artistic and Ideological Syncretism in Greek and Egyptian-Style Ptolemaic Portrature from Egypt'. Ph.D. dissertation, King's College, University of London, forthcoming.

ASSMANN, J. *Moses the Egyptian: The Memory of Egypt in Western Monotheism.* Cambridge, Mass. and London, 1997.

BAGNALL, R. S. *Egypt in Late Antiquity.* Princeton, 1993.

BOWMAN, A. K. *Egypt after the Pharaohs: 332 B.C.–A.D. 642.* 2nd ed. London, 1996.

CARROTT, R. G. *The Egyptian Revival: Its Sources, Monuments, and Meaning 1808–1858.* Berkeley, Los Angeles, and London, 1978.

CURL, J. S. *Egyptomania, The Egyptian Revival: A Recurrent Theme in the History of Taste.* 2nd ed. Manchester and New York, 1994.

EMPEREUR, J.-Y. *Alexandrie redécouverte.* Paris, 1998.

FAZZINI, R. A. 'L'Égyptomanie dans l'architecture américaine' in *L'Égyptomanie à l'éprueve de l'archéologie: Actes du colloque international organisé au Musée du Louvre par le Sevice Culturel les 8 et 9 avril 1994.* Paris, 1996, 229–78.

FROIDEFOND, C. *Le mirage égyptien dans la littérature grecque d'Homère à Aristote.* Paris, 1971. A detailed discussion of Egypt's powerful influence on Greek culture.

HARRIS, J. R. ed. *The Legacy of Egypt.* 2nd ed. Oxford, 1971.

HUMBERT, J.-M. *L'Egyptomanie dans l'art occidental.* ACR Édition, Paris, 1990.

HUMBERT, J. M. et al. eds. *Egyptomania: L'Égypte dans l'art occidental 1730–1930.* Paris, 1994.

IVERSEN, E. *The Myth of Egypt and its Hieroglyphs in European Tradition.* 2nd ed. Princeton, 1993.

KYRIELIS, H. *Die Bildnisse der Ptolemäer.* Berlin, 1975.

LEWIS, N. *Greeks in Ptolemaic Egypt.* New York, 1986.

Index

Photographic Acknowledgements

In most cases, the illustrations have been made from photographs and transparencies provided by the owners or custodians of the works. All line drawings have been taken from the first edition of the book (1958). Those illustrations for which further credit is due are:

3: Sam Menefee; 20, 22, 31, 32: W. B. Emery; 36, 82: John Ross, Rome; 37, 38, 39, 40, 41, 42 (reconstruction), 43, 44, 45: J.-P. Lauer; 55, 264, 265, 294, 330, 390, 397, 398, 409: H. W. Müller; 58, 117, 157, 205, 353, 354: Werner Forman Archive; 59: University Museum, Philadelphia; 60, 67, 266: Ahmed Fakhry; 61, 63, 64: Herbert Ricke; 66, 134: Cecil M. Firth; 68, 78, 147, 181, 239, 240, 248, 253, 259, 331, 384: William Kelly Simpson; 69, 123, 129, 319: Abdel Slam Mohammed Hussein; 83, 84, 86, 101, 102, 104, 105, 106, 107, 108, 109, 115, 116, 135, 168, 175, 196, 204, 221, 235, 236, 237, 277, 295, 315, 381, 389, 391, 395, 396, 405, 417, 420: Museum of Fine Arts, Boston; 91, 92, 97, 224, 225, 268: © James Morris/Axiom; 112, 143, 165, 166, 219, 274, 360: Marburg; 114: Giraudon; 118: Abdel-Moneim Abu-Bakr; 133: German Archaeological Institute; 149, 153, 172, 220, 228, 231, 232, 233, 242, 243, 244, 245, 246, 247, 248, 251, 252, 254, 255, 257, 258, 260, 261, 262, 263, 281, 335, 338, 339, 341, 342, 343, 345, 347, 362, 367, 371, 372, 374, 375, 386, 394: Harry Burton/Metropolitan Museum of Art, New York; 150: Museum of Fine Arts, Boston (Emily Esther Sears Fund); 158, 325, 348: Scala; 161, 162, 359, 363, 364: Centre Franco-Egyptien; 185, 302: Labib Habachi; 191, 332, 333, 334: Egypt Explorations Society; 192: Egypt Exploration Fund; 203, 258, 373: © Peter Clayton; 215, 216, 218: The Ancient Egypt Picture Library; 226, 227, 249, 250, 282, 283, 285, 286, 287: Metropolitan Museum of Art; 234: Cairo Museum; 273, 293: Margarete Büsing; 337: Harry Burton/Griffith Institute, Ashmolean Museum, Oxford; 340, 368: Epigraphic Survey, Oriental Institute, Luxor; 346: © John P. Stevens/Ancient Art and Architecture Collection; 362: Alinari; 413: Museum of Fine Arts, Boston (H. L. Pierce Fund); Oriental Institute, University of Chicago: 418, 419.